Vietnam

The travel guide

Footprint Handbook

John Colet

Mariners 'took such an Affection to Vietnam that not a man of them would go away; so that the Captain of the Ship was forc'd to drive them aboard with many Blows and Cuts....'

Borri, Christoforo (1633) *Cochin China*, London: Richard Clutterbuck

Vietnam Handbook
Third edition
© Footprint Handbooks Ltd 2002

Published by Footprint Handbooks
6 Riverside Court
Lower Bristol Road
Bath BA2 3DZ. England
T +44 (0)1225 469141
F +44 (0)1225 469461
Email discover@footprintbooks.com
Web www.footprintbooks.com

ISBN 1 903471 31 1
CIP DATA: A catalogue record for this
book is available from the British Library

Distributed in the USA by
Publishers Group West

Credits

Series editors
Patrick Dawson and Rachel Fielding

Editorial
Editor: Claire Boobbyer
Maps: Sarah Sorensen

Production
Page layout: Emma Bryers
Editorial assistance: Stephanie Lambe,
Robert Lunn and Kevin Feeney
Maps: Claire Benison, Robert Lunn,
Leona Bailey
Colour maps: Kevin Feeney
Cover: Camilla Ford
Proof reader: Ian Emery

Design
Mytton Williams

Photography
Front cover: Impact Photo Library
Back cover: Travel Ink
Inside colour section:
getty one Stone: page 2, 8-9, 12-13, 16
Tim Page/Eye Ubiquitous: page 5,
page 6 (centre), page 15 (centre)
Jamie Marshall: page 6 (bottom left),
page 15 (bottom left)
Caroline Penn/Impact: page 6,
(bottom right)
Daniel White/Impact: page 11 (top)
James Davis Travel Photography:
page 11 (centre)
R. Richardson/The Travel Library:
page 11 (bottom left)
Simon Cooper/Impact: page 11
(bottom right), page 15 (top)
Gina Corrigan/Robert Harding: page 15
(bottom right)
PhotoDisc: page 6 (top)

Print
Manufactured in Italy by LEGOPRINT

Contents

1

5 A foot in the door

2

17 Essentials
19 Planning your trip
19 Where to go
20 When to go
21 Tours and tour operators
26 Finding out more
26 Language
27 Disabled travellers
27 Gay and lesbian
    travellers
27 Student travellers
27 Travelling with children
27 Women travellers
28 Working in Vietnam
29 Before you travel
29 Getting in
30 What to take
30 Money
31 Getting there
31 Air
32 Road
32 Sea
32 Train
33 Touching down
33 Airport information
33 Tourist information
33 Local customs and laws
35 Responsible tourism
37 Where to stay
38 Getting around
38 Air
42 Road
46 Train
47 Sea
47 Keeping in touch
47 Communications
49 Media
50 Food and drink
53 Shopping
54 Entertainment and
    nightlife

54 Holidays and festivals
55 Sport and special
    interest travel
56 Health

3

61 Hanoi
64 Ins and outs
64 Getting there
64 Getting around
64 Orientation
64 Tourist information
64 Background
68 Sights
81 Excursions
86 Essentials
86 Sleeping
90 Eating
94 Bars
94 Cafés
94 Entertainment
95 Shopping
96 Tour operators
97 Transport
99 Directory

4

101 The North
104 The Northwest
104 Hanoi to Dien Bien Phu
     and Sapa
111 Dien Bien Phu
121 Sapa
131 The Northeast
136 Cao-Bac-Lang
138 Cao Bang
141 The Northeast Frontier
146 Hanoi to Haiphong, Do
     Son, Cat Ba Island and
     Halong Bay
146 Haiphong
152 Do Son
154 Cat Ba Island
158 Halong Bay

161 Halong City
165 Hanoi to Ninh Binh
166 Ninh Binh and around

5

171 The Central Region
174 Thanh Hoa to Hué
177 Hué
202 Danang
212 Hoi An
221 Quang Ngai to Phan
     Rang via Nha Trang
224 Central Highlands
234 Nha Trang
249 Dalat
259 Dalat to Saigon
260 Vung Tau

6

271 Saigon
274 Ins and outs
274 Getting there
274 Getting around
274 Safety
274 Orientation
274 History
276 Background
278 Sights
278 Central Saigon
284 Cholon
287 Outer Saigon
288 Excursions
288 Cu Chi Tunnels
289 Tay Ninh
290 Nui Ba Den/
     Black Lady Mountain
290 Can Gio
291 Bien Hoa
292 My Tho
292 Essentials
292 Sleeping
297 Eating
302 Bars
304 Entertainment

Left The Cao Dai Temple at Tay Ninh. "The most outrageously vulgar building ever to have been erected with serious intent..." Norman Lewis

304 Shopping
306 Sport
308 Tour operators
309 Transport
312 Directory

7

315 The Mekong Delta and
the South
318 The Mekong Delta
318 Ins and outs
318 Getting around
318 Best time to visit
318 Background
319 My Tho
322 Ben Tre
323 Vinh Long
324 Sa Dec
325 Tra Vinh
326 Can Tho
330 Soc Trang
331 Long Xuyen
333 Cao Lanh
334 Chau Doc
337 From Chau Doc to
Ha Tien
337 Rach Gia
339 Rach Gia to Ha Tien
340 Ha Tien
343 Phu Quoc Island

8

347 Background
349 History
359 The Vietnam Wars
378 Modern Vietnam
378 Politics
386 Economy
395 Culture
403 Art and architecture
409 Crafts
410 Language
411 Literature
414 Drama
415 Religion
420 Land and environment
426 Books

9

431 Footnotes
435 Useful words and phrases
437 Glossary
439 Food glossary
441 Shopping glossary
442 Index
446 Shorts
448 Map index
450 Advert index
457 Colour maps

Inside front cover
Hotel and restaurant price guide
Exchange rates
Useful websites

Inside back cover
Map symbols
Weights and measures

Right Curtain call: women wearing the ao dai dress

A foot in the door

Right *Vietnam's coastline provides miles of palm-fringed beaches*
Below *The elegant Sunbeam Bridge leading to Ngoc Son Pagoda on Hoan Kiem Lake, Hanoi*

Above *Broom flowers: the red, dyed bristles of hand-made brooms drying in the sun*
Right *A cigarette seller peddles her wares on the streets of Vietnam*
Next page *Wandering through the rippling green fields of Son La Province*

Highlights

In modern-day Vietnam one thing in particular stands out. It is, quite simply, the remarkable speed at which the country is developing. Vietnam now hovers in an enigmatic and paradoxical time zone somewhere between the late Industrial Revolution and the Post Industrial Age. High school children in Saigon vie for the trendiest motorbikes while children in the northern highlands are happy with a pair of sandals. Youngsters in the Mekong Delta have email accounts whereas five years ago they didn't have a telephone. And staff in call centres take bets from around the world on English football while their parents harvest rice by hand. Vietnam has experienced war and bloody revolution in the past 100 years. But the revolution it is now going through is peaceful and prosperous and is what makes contemporary Vietnam the absorbing and gripping place that it is.

Hanoi: ancient & modern

With a wonderful natural setting on the Red River, Hanoi is an elegant and refined city of lakes and parks connected by well-ordered, tree-lined streets. Not yet fully a capital city in the modern sense (thankfully), Hanoi is making rapid strides and has acquired, in the space of ten short years, restaurants to quicken the heart of the most demanding of gourmets, hotels to delight the sternest of critics, and shops to cheer the Imelda Marcos in all of us. And herein lies Hanoi's real charm and delight: it manages to combine ancient with modern - *cyclos* with limos, noodle carts with nouvelle cuisine and, most importantly, every gradation in between.

Saigon nightlife

At just 300 years old, Saigon is a relative youngster compared with Hanoi and this seems to show in the boundless energy of the southern city. Having shrugged off wartime and Communist curfews, the Saigonese seem determined that their city should never sleep. Discos, nightclubs, pleasure-domes and dens – it has them all. If you return home bleary-eyed at four o'clock in the morning after slurping that much needed bowl of *pho*, expect to be greeted by fresh, newly-risen joggers out stretching their legs and grannies practising tai chi.

Baskets & beaches

Any country with as queer a shape as Vietnam might be expected to offer some interesting landscapes and scenery. The country has been likened to a bamboo carrying-pole with rice baskets at either end: the Red River Delta in the north and the Mekong Delta in the south. The narrow central provinces provide the slender connection between these two (literal and metaphorical) baskets. And its sinuous coastline threads its way around 3,000 km of rocky headlands and mountainous promontories, through muddy deltas and swamps, across parched salt pans, sandy dunes and sunny beaches. Many also find pleasure drifting among the thousand islets of Halong Bay; others prefer the quiet of Phu Quoc's coves. Nha Trang's golden miles are busy with tourist traffic, but far fewer make it to Ho Coc's pleasantly isolated shores.

Backbone of the country

Around the Red River Delta are ranged the mountains of the north culminating in Fan Si Pan, Vietnam's highest peak. Further south they form a knobbly backbone to the country and a barrier to cultural influences from the Indianised states to the west. Not only have the mountains proved an effective screen to alien cultures, they have also nurtured in their isolated pockets, small, but vibrant ethnic minorities of diverse traditions. The villages and human landscapes of the Tày, Thái, Ba'na and Hmông tribes reflect their differing beliefs, farming methods, history, crops and technologies: the Thai with their assiduously sculpted rice terraces, the vertiginous fields that the Hmong cultivate and the compact, walled villages of the Ba'na.

Historical heritage

Hué: 19th-century empire building Hué was made capital in 1802 and served as the seat of the Nguyen Dynasty until 1945. Its architecture was consciously modelled on that of imperial China; it is grand in conception, massive in scale and far more ambitious than any other group of buildings in Vietnam. The vast imperial palace was largely destroyed in the Tet offensive of 1968 but a number of pavilions and temples survive. Each emperor, and many leading courtiers, built himself a tomb in the surrounding countryside using court geomancers to select the perfect setting – and these came through the conflict largely undamaged. Today, the tombs are either neglected, or sprucely maintained, depending upon the current interpretation of the incumbent's life by Communist Party historians. Some slide into deeper obscurity obliterated by weeds and decay, while the tombs of those who are thought to have displayed revolutionary fervour are 'restored' to their former glory.

Growing old gracefully Hoi An, a charming town just south of Danang, is a wonderfully preserved slice of history. Hoi An's port silted up 200 years ago and little has changed since then. Most of its buildings date from between the 16th to 19th centuries and the town has retained its compact nature and diminutive scale. The people of Hoi An have also maintained a poise, grace and tranquility which makes the town a glorious place to relax and visit temples, clan houses and burghers' homes.

A thousand years of culture Capital for a thousand years, Hanoi has collected the architecture, artefacts and atmosphere that you would expect from such a history. Generations of monarchs, monks, mandarins and merchants have left their mark on Hanoi's citadels, temples, and artisans' quarters. The pressures of being a capital city in a country frantic to become an economic tiger do show, but Hanoi nonetheless remains a fair and refined city with a rich artistic heritage.

The wounds of war Most people are more familiar with Vietnam's modern history than its ancient history. Indeed, the image of Vietnam carried by some newly arrived visitors is shaped solely by 'The Vietnam War'. Thankfully, there are few visible reminders of those terrible times and those there are tend to be visually disappointing. But to anyone with even the skimpiest understanding of the events of 1945-75, the war sites are invested with strong historical symbolism. Cu Chi, outside Saigon, is one of the more visited sites and although much has been reconstructed, visitors familiar with the story of the men and women who lived and fought in the tunnels cannot fail to be moved by the experience.

Ancient Chama ruins In the arts of sculpture and architecture the Vietnamese rarely displayed the virtuosity or creativity of some of their neighbours. It was left, therefore, to the artistically accomplished Cham, occupants of the kingdom of Champa, in what is now central Vietnam, to produce Vietnam's most lovely architecture and her finest sculpture. The Cham derived their inspiration from the ancient Khmer kingdoms and flourished artistically between the seventh and 12th centuries. Hindu and Sivaists, the Cham ornamented their temples with images of Vishnu, Siva and Ganesh. Cham temples take the form of small but beautifully proportioned towers. The finest examples of Cham building are to be seen at My Son (outside Danang) and Nha Trang, with another distinguished collection at Phan Rang. There is also a museum of Cham sculpture in Danang, which shows the sculptor's art at its very finest.

Left Duck trading at Hoi An market
Below Ngo Mon Gate, the citadel at Hué

Above Priests of the Cao Dai religion
Left Po Klong Garai Cham tower, Phan Rang
Next page Hustle and bustle at the floating market,
Can Tho, Mekong Delta

Highland living

The population of Vietnam is estimated at 75 million people. Of these, around 90% are ethnic Vietnamese, or kinh. Chinese form a large segment of the urban population, especially in Saigon's Chinatown, Cholon, and the remaining minorities, often referred to as *montagnards*, tend to live in the highland areas of north and central Vietnam. Separated from the majority by language, custom, religion and habit, the hill tribes are 'Vietnamese' only in the sense that they live in Vietnam. Having said that, things are changing: ethnic minorities of today are just as likely to wear jeans as sarongs; most speak Vietnamese; many minority children are educated in government schools; in some instances minority girls take Vietnamese husbands, a milestone in the process of ethnic assimilation. Historically, the sentiments of the minorities have not been as resolutely pro-Vietnamese as government propaganda would have us believe. The anti-colonial struggle was nobly supported by hill tribes, but competition between *montagnard* and kinh for land and political supremacy is still a problem.

Cultural patchwork The people of the hill tribes take a bit of finding but diversions into the Central Highlands, excursions from Dalat or a trip up to Sapa will reveal a wholly different Vietnam. Their culture is rich and varied; their beliefs and customs are remarkable; their resourcefulness and utilization of marginal land is a marvel and their scenic assemblages of fields, costume, villages and houses represent some of the most breathtakingly beautiful sights in the country.

Black Hmông Visitors to Vietnam are most likely to meet people from the Black Hmông or the Thái tribes. The Black Hmông are concentrated in the northwest of Vietnam at higher elevations, usually over 1,500 m. Living at such altitudes in the forested hills, high above the rivers and alluvial plains, they make their living by shifting cultivation. They clear steep slopes and plant maize, sweet potatoes, dry rice, bananas and traditionally opium, a valuable cash crop. The Hmông are among the more retiring and reticent of the hill tribes. Their houses and fields are often surrounded by barricades of thorn bushes to deter visitors. Ironically, however, most visitors to Vietnam will meet the Hmông traders of Sapa, who are some of the more gregarious of all the minorities. Being from higher altitudes where temperatures are lower, the Hmông typically dress in heavy clothing. Not surprisingly, the dress of the Black Hmông is predominantly black. The younger girls wear an indigo skirt but graduate to a black, above the knee skirt with black leggings at the onset of puberty. The Hmông, like many of the other minorities, are fond of heavy silver jewellery: necklaces, earrings and bracelets.

Thái In sharp contrast to the Hmông, the Thái live on the valley floors where they cultivate rice in paddy fields just like the Vietnamese. Unlike the Vietnamese, however, the Thái have taken the very sensible precaution of building their houses on stilts to keep themselves and their possessions dry during the annual flood. The space beneath the stilt houses is an ideal place for keeping chickens, pigs, bicycles and so on and where the young children often play. Being lowland folk, their lives are inextricably linked with water. The children splash and swim at all times of day but especially in the evening when they drive the buffaloes down for a well-earned wallow. The Thái are excellent weavers and produce hand-loomed fabrics of great intricacy and beauty. Found all over Northwest Vietnam there are thought to be about one million Thái in total but such is their integration into Vietnamese society that it can be difficult to distinguish them from kinh. However, in the remote country and in small villages their traditions, culture and costumes are still clearly distinctive.

Left *Landscape wounds: Chinese war damage at Sapa*
Below *Thái children in traditional dress, wearing the Vietnamese Non Lá, conical hat, Dien Bien Phu*

Above *Flower Hmông children from a village south of Sapa*
Left *Sheltering from the storm. Red Dao children from near Sapa*
Next page *Bicycle madness at the market on the Perfume River, Hué*

Essentials

2

Essentials

19	**Planning your trip**	**33**	**Touching down**
19	Where to go	**33**	Airport information
20	When to go	**33**	Tourist information
21	Tours and tour operators	**33**	Local customs and laws
26	Finding out more	**35**	Responsible tourism
26	Language	**37**	**Where to stay**
27	Disabled travellers	**38**	**Getting around**
27	Gay and lesbian travellers	**38**	Air
27	Student travellers	**42**	Road
27	Travelling with children	**46**	Train
27	Women travellers	**47**	Sea
28	Working in Vietnam	**47**	**Keeping in touch**
29	**Before you travel**	**47**	Communications
29	Getting in	**49**	Media
30	What to take	**50**	**Food and drink**
30	**Money**	**53**	**Shopping**
31	**Getting there**	**54**	Entertainment and nightlife
31	Air	**54**	**Holidays and festivals**
32	Road	**55**	Sport and special interest travel
32	Sea	**56**	**Health**
32	Train		

Planning your trip

Where to go

Vietnam is a long, thin country with a distinctive and curvaceous S-shaped coastline. Having a capital in the north and its largest city in the south makes it easy for the traveller to fly in at one end of the country and depart from the other and see pretty much everything in between.

Particular highlights which any visitor to Vietnam would do well not to miss are: (from north to south) the hill station of **Sapa** for its stunning scenery and hill-tribes (for those who don't mind roughing it, a tour of North West or North East Vietnam should be given careful consideration); **Hanoi**, which itself is historical, beautiful and cultured, lies at the heart of a vast range of architectural and scenic treasures (which can be done on day trips out); time permitting, **Cat Ba Island** and **Halong Bay** should be included for their coastal scenery. Moving south there then follows a yawning gulf of mediocrity, so it is not until **Hué** that the next stop should be made. Hué's palaces and mausoleums deserve two days, but most visitors give them only one (it does rather depend on the weather). The splendid train journey from Hué to Danang should not be missed but Danang itself has little to commend it (apart from the Cham Museum) which is why most travellers head straight for nearby **Hoi An**, an enchanting 17th-century mercantile town. Between here and Saigon the seaside town of **Nha Trang** is the main attraction but the sleepy resort of **Phan Thiet** is a more tranquil alternative. **Saigon**, although a city of six million, is really a small town: no sensible tourist will stray far from the historical core, containing as it does all anyone could possibly need in the way of hedonistic pleasures (and with scarcely any intellectual or cultural distractions), is the most popular destination in the country. The six million are jammed into suburbs, an indescribable density of bodies living out their days in an inferno of noise, stinking canals and motorbikes. The **Mekong Delta** has plenty of attractions, but to see it at its best it is necessary to get into the depths of the country beyond the main towns.

In summary, short trips to Vietnam tend to be dominated by town visits; longer ones **Short visits** give the visitor a chance to see more of the countryside. In an overwhelmingly rural country it is important to see not just the main historical and cultural highlights of the towns but to get out into the countryside and the way of life of the majority of the population. In a visit of less than two weeks it is possible to capture something of the essence of Vietnam. With careful planning a range of sites can be seen that will give the visitor a feel for the diversity of Vietnam.

    Hanoi, Capital of Vietnam. This is an essential stop both because Hanoi itself is teeming with temples and pagodas and ancient streets but also because it sits at the heart of a region similarly well endowed with monuments recording the nation's history. The scenery around Hanoi is some of the most attractive in the land. Excursions to the Perfume Pagoda and the temples and caves at Tam Coc are particularly worthwhile. The overnight train from Hanoi will get visitors to **Sapa**, the most scenic of all Vietnam's hillstations. This is the best chance to meet some of Vietnam's many ethnic minority people and to see Vietnam's most majestic and rugged scenery. From Hanoi fly to Hué. **Hué** is an old capital, home to Vietnam's last imperial dynasty. There are numerous relics, tombs and palaces which are well worth visiting. From Hué visitors ought to make the journey to **Hoi An**, an old mercantile port crammed with history and absolutely full of charm. It also has a pleasant seaside area. Depending on time available, fly from Danang (the nearest airport to Hoi An) either to Nha Trang for a nice beach holiday or straight to Saigon. Unfortunately it is not possible to fly to Dalat from

Danang hence **Dalat** tends to get overlooked. It is not an essential stop but well worth-while to get a flavour of upland Vietnam particularly if not visiting Sapa. **Saigon** is quite unlike the rest of Vietnam and it generates a very special and dynamic atmosphere. It is a restless city full of enterprise and drive. There are some interesting relics and sites from the Vietnam war, such as the Cu Chi Tunnels and the old Presidential Palace. There is also some attractive French architecture (although not as much as in Hanoi). Saigon has restaurants and bars aplenty and it is impossible not to enjoy soaking up the feel of this vibrant city. Depending on how time has been allocated in the earlier places there is probably only time remaining for a day trip to the **Mekong Delta** from Saigon. This is a shame for the best of the delta is **Can Tho** and around and this cannot be done as a day trip and as a one night trip it is a bit of a rush.

Medium term visits   In three to four weeks it is possible to take the short term itinerary at a more leisurely pace and include some other interesting calls. From Hanoi, **Halong Bay** and **Cat Ba** can be visited. These are often done together as a chance to see one of Vietnam's most spectacular natural landscapes and one of Vietnam's most accessible national parks. In a visit of a month it is easily possible to see more of the mountainous northwest than just Sapa. It may even be possible to fit in a circuit of the northwest, going via the delightful small settlements of **Mai Chau** and **Son La** to **Dien Bien Phu**, scene of the French defeat in 1954. From here complete the circuit to Sapa and back to Hanoi. It will give a completely different insight into Vietnam from what most tourists see. It would be worth visting **Danang** to visit the wonderful China Beach (My Khe) and the Cham Museum. From Danang visit **My Son**, capital of the ancient civilization of Champa. There are Cham temples dating back 1,000 years quietly overrun by vegetation. **Nha Trang** is definitely worth a visit as it has a delightful relaxing seaside atmosphere, islands to explore and numerous excellent restaurants. Failing this, a stay in one of the resorts on **Mui Ne beach** near Phan Thiet is highly recommended. Medium stay visitors will have longer to get to know the people of Saigon and equally important will have time to get into the Mekong Delta properly. Go at least as far as **Can Tho** (those going overland to Cambodia will go on to Chau Doc) and get out into the countryside either by motorbike or by boat to understand the truly vast scale of this productive agricultural region. A visit to **Phu Quoc island** should also be possible.

Long term visits   If time really is not a problem and visitors can stay from upwards of one month then a circuit of the northwest and possibly parts of the northeast, such as **Lang Son** and **Cao Bang** are possible to see the country's mountainous areas and montagnard peoples. The Central Highlands would also certainly warrant a visit to see different minority people, their villages and way of life. In addition visitors would have ample time to become associated with the country's national parks apart from Cat Ba – possibly **Cuc Phuong** or **Bac Ma** or even the remote **Con Dao islands**. In addition it will be possible to explore the Mekong Delta and see some of the more remote and more interesting towns and villages.

When to go

Climatically the best time to see Vietnam is around December to March when it should be dry and not too hot. In the south it is warm but not too hot with lovely cool evenings. Admittedly the north and the highlands will be a bit chilly but they should be dry with clear blue skies. The tourist industry high season is normally November to May when hotel prices tend to rise and booking flights can be hard. Travel in the south and Mekong Delta can be difficult at the height of the Monsoon (particularly September, October and November). The central regions and north sometimes suffer typhoons and tropical storms from May to November. Hué is at its wettest wet from September to January.

Despite its historic and cultural resonance, Tet, Vietnamese new year, is not really a good time to visit. This movable feast usually falls between late January and March and with aftershocks lasts for about a fortnight. It is the only holiday most people get in the year. Popular destinations are packed, roads are jammed and for a couple of days almost all hotels and restaurants are shut.

During the school summer holidays some resorts get busy, Cat Ba, Do Son, Phan Thiet and Long Hai, for example: prices rise, there is a severe squeeze on rooms and weekends are worse.

Tours and tour operators

Essentials

T020-8742 8612, wwwimaginative-traveller.com Offer 15 tours of the country varying in length from six to 30 days and varying in content, from trekking in the north, to gourmet trips, to travelling round the country on a 125cc Honda. *Intrepid Travel UK*, PO Box 34429, London W6 0AF, T020-85638244, F020-85639130. Brochure request service: 0870 903 1040. *Regent Holidays*, 15 John St, Bristol BS1 2HR, T0117-9211711, F0117-9254866, www.regent-holidays.co.uk Tailor-made holidays. Recommended. *Silk Steps Ltd*, Tyndale House, 7 High St, Chipping Sodbury, Bristol, BS37 6BA, T01454 888850, F01454 888851, www.silksteps.co.uk Tailor-made tours and group travel arrangements. *Silverbird Travel*, 4 Northfields Prospect, Putney Bridge Rd, London SW18 1PE, T020-88759090, www.silverbird.co.uk Tailor-made tours covering the whole country. *Symbiosis Expedition Planning*, www.symbiosis-travel.com Specialists in tailor-made tours and expeditions. Symbiosis have established themselves as experts in the organization of cycling tours of Vietnam and specialist charity fund-raising challenges. It now operates almost exclusively through the internet, savings in costs being passed on to charities. *Tennyson Travel*, 30-32 Fulham High St, London, SW6 3LQ, T020 7736 4347, F020 7736 5672, tennyson@visitvietnam.co.uk *Travelbag Adventures*, 15 Turk St, Alton, Hampshire, GU34 1AG. T01420 541007, www.travelbag-adventures.com *Visit Vietnam*, 30-32 Fulham High St, London SW6 3LQ, T020-7736 4347, www.visitvietnam.co.uk

France *La Maison de L'Indochine*, 36 Rue des Bourdonnais, 75001 Paris, T01-47236485, www.afatvoyages.fr *Nouvelles Frontières*, T1-42731064. *Vietnamtourism*, 4 Rue Cherubini 75002, Paris, T1-42868637, www.vietnamtourism.com *Voyageurs Au Vietnam*, 55 Rue Sainte-Anne, 75002 Paris, T1-42861688.

Lernidee Reisen, Dudenstr 78, D-10965 Berlin, T4930-7865056. Germany

Adventure Center, 1311 63rd Street, Suite 200, Emeryville, CA, USA, T (800)227 8747, USA
F510 654 4200. Tours from Hanoi to Saigon and from Hanoi to the northern Hilltribe
areas. *Asian Pacific Adventures*, T800-8251680, www.asianpacificadventures.com
Small group and tailor-made tours. *Geographic Explorer*, T800-7778183. Group and
tailor-made tours for the responsible tourist. *Global Spectrum*, 1901 Pennsylvania Av
NW, Suite 204, Washington DC 20006, T202-2932065, F202-2960815, gspectrum@
gspectrum.com This US-based company specialize in tours to Vietnam, many with a
cultural twist and venturing off the usual routes. A professional and informed outfit.
Kim's Travel, 8443 Westminster CA 92682. *Mekong Travel*, 151 First Ave, Suite 172,
New York, T212-5292891, F212-5292891. *Myths & Mountains*, 976 Tee Court, Incline
Village, NV 89451, T(800) 670-Myth/(775) 832 5454, F(775) 832-4454, travel@
mythsandmountains.com *Nine Dragons Travel & Tours*, PO Box 24105, Indianapolis,
IN 46224-0105, T1-317-3290350, toll free within USA T800-9099050,
F1-317-329-0117, www.nine-dragons.com Offices in Saigon, Da Nang and Hanoi
offering guided and individually customized tours. *Quest Nature Tours*,
T800-3871483. *Tour East*, 5120 West Goldleaf Circle, Suite 310, Los Angeles, California,
90056, T213-2906500, F213-2945531. *Viet Tours Holidays*, 8097 Westminster Av, Garden Grove, California, T714-8952588.

Intrepid, 11 Spring St, Fitzroy, Victoria, 3065, T1300 360 667, F03 9419 5878, Australia
www.intrepidtravel.com.au Intrepid is one of the longest established and most
respected operators working in Vietnam. Their tours are imaginative and well led.

Tour East, 99 Walker St, 12th floor, North Sydney, NSW 2060, T2-9569303, F2-9565340.
Intercontinental Travel, 307 Victoria St, Abbotsford, Victoria 30567, T42877849.
Tara International Travel, Level 3, 427 George St, Sydney 2645811.
World Expeditions, Level 5, 71 York St, Sydney, NSW, 2000, T61-292790188,
www.worldexpeditions.com.au Run mountain biking tours from Hanoi to Hué.

Vietnam **Hanoi** *Asiatica Travel*, 1A Trang Tien St, T9331702, F9331704,
www.asiatica-travel.com *Buffalo Tours*, 11 Hang Muoi St, T8280702, F8269370,
info@buffalotours.com Specializes in adventure and trekking tours. *Darling Café*, 33
Hang Quat St, T8269386, F8256562. Low cost tours around Hanoi and the north.
Diethelm Travel, Hanoi Central Office Tower, Suite 301, 44B Ly Thuong Kiet St,
T9344844, F9344850, dtvl@netnam.vn *Exotissimo*, 26 Tran Nhat Duat, T8282150,
F8282146. Specialize in more upmarket tours, good nationwide service. *Handspan*,
see page 96 for details. *Hanoi Tourism*, 18 Ly Thuong Kiet St, T8268752, F8241101.
Local state run tour company and hotel operator. *Queen Café*, 19 and 65 Hang Bac St,
T8260860, F8250000, queenaz@fpt.vn One of the many tourist cafés but above aver-
age service. *Vietnam Tourism*, 30A Ly Thuong Kiet St, T8264154, F8257583. State tour
operator geared more for group than individual travel.

Saigon *Ann Tourist*, Ton That Tung St, T8334356, F8323866. Generally excellent,
knowledgeable guides. *Asian Trails*, Unit 712, 7th floor, Saigon Trade Center, 37 Ton
Duc Thang St, District 1, T9102871, F9102874, www.asiantrails.com *Diethelm*, 1A Me
Linh Square, T8294932, F8294747. A good regional agent which can advise on visas,
international rail connections and flights. *Exotissimo Travel*, 2B Dinh Tien Hoang St,
T8251723, F8251684. Specialize in upmarket tours, a full range of tours and services.
Kim Café, 270 De Tham St, T8369859, F8488369. *Saigontourist*, 49 Le Thanh Ton St,
T8298129, F8224987. Local state tour operator that now operates on a national scale,
chiefly used by group tours. *Sinh Café*, 246-248 De Tham St, T8367338, F8369322. The
other half of the Kim – Sinh rivalry that invented budget travel in Vietnam. *Vidotour*,
145 Nam Ky Khoi Nghia St, Q3, T8291438, F8291435. One of the most highly regarded
organizers of group travel in the country.

Thailand The greatest number of tour companies outside Vietnam are to be found in Bangkok,
the 'gateway' to Vietnam. They are concentrated on Khaosan Road and Soi Ngam
Duphli and, for the more up-market operations, on Sukhumvit and Silom roads. There
are also companies in the vicinity of the Vietnamese embassy.
     Bangkok Airways, 60 Queen Sirikit National Convention Center, New
Ratchadapisek Rd, Klongtoey, Bangkok 10110, T66 (0) 2229 3456, F66 (0) 2229 3450,
reservation@bangkokair.co.th Operates tours in conjuction with several tour opera-
tors. *BP Tour*, 17 Khaosan Rd, T2815062, F2803642. *Diethelm Travel*, Kian Gwan Build-
ing II, 140/1 Witthayu Rd, T2559150, F2560248, dto@dto.co.th *East-West Group*, 135
Soi Sanam Khli, Witthayu Rd, T2530861, F2536178. *Educational Travel Centre*, Royal
Hotel, 2 Rachdamnern Ave, T2240043, F2246930. *Exotissimo*, 21/17 Sukhumvit Soi 4,
T2835240, F2547683 and 755 Silom Rd, T2359196, F2834885. *Marvel Holidays*, 279
Khaosan Rd, T2829339, F2813216. *MK Ways*, 57/11 Witthayu Rd, T2545583,
F2545583/2802920. *Siam Wings Tours*, 173/1-3 Surawong Rd, T2534757, F2636808.
Vista Travel, 244/4 Khaosan Rd, T2800348, F2800348.

Hong Kong *Skylion Ltd*, Suite D, 11 F Trust Tower, 68 Johnston Rd, Wanchai, T8650363, F8651306.
Vietnam Tours, Friendship Travel, Houston Centre, 63 Moody Rd, Kowloon, T3666862.

Singapore *Tour East*, Head Office, 70 Anson Rd, No 12-00, Apex Tower, Singapore 0207,
T2202200, F2258119.

Finding out more

www.vietvet.org The *Vietnam Veterans Webring* offers not just the chance of a virtual visit but also provides details on specialist Veterans' tours to the country including visits to battle sites as well as reports and diaries from recent visitors.
www.bmi.net/vntours/ *Vietnam Tours* – Saigon-based and Vietnam Vet owned and operated – offers customised packages according to which US Army Corps a Vet belonged.
www.netspace.net.au/~mrfelix/bsa/ For potential bicycle tourists – Mr Pumpy offers a blow by blow account of one route through the Mekong Delta and another through Laos to Vietnam. The routes are well explained and the pitfalls are highlighted.
www.pata.org/ The *Pacific Asia Travel Association*, better known simply as PATA, with a useful news section arranged by country, links to airlines and cruise lines, and some information on educational, environmental and other initiatives.

History and culture **www.asiasociety.org** Homepage of the *Asia Society* with papers, reports and speeches as well as nearly 1,000 links to what they consider to be the best educational, political and cultural sites on the web.
www.cpv.org.vn *Communist Party of Vietnam*. Rather like the Party itself it is thorough, it is loyally supported (over two million 'hits') and slow.
www.hmongnet.org Information on Hmong culture, history and language.
www.mofa.gov.vn *Ministry of Foreign Affairs*. Vietnam's interpretation of world events.
UNHCR website has a series of country reports on human rights and other issues **www.unhcr.ch/cgi-bin/texis/vtx/rsd** The **Human Rights Watch** (**www.hrw.org**) World Report 2002 makes for rather grim reading. It catalogues police and military brutality against the ethnic minorities in the Central Highlands and reports on the asylum seekers who fled to Cambodia.
www.vdic.org.vn/ *Vietnam Development Information Centre*. This is a World Bank sponsored site which has a number of informative papers on Vietnamese society and economy for downloading.

Weather and geographical information **www.rainorshine.com/** A simple but effective weather site with five-day forecasts for 800 cities worldwide.

Language

See page 433 for a list of words and phrases

Outside Saigon, Hanoi, Hué, Hoi An, Nha Trang, Dalat and other tourist centres language can be a problem for those who have no knowledge of Vietnamese. Vietnamese is not easy to pick up and pronunciation presents enormous difficulties. The Vietnamese language uses six tones and has 12 vowels and 27 consonants. Like other tonal languages, one word can mean many things depending upon the tone used: 'ma', for example, can mean horse, cheek, ghost, grave and rice seedling. But it is worth making an effort and the Vietnamese are delighted when foreigners try to communicate in their language. Thanks to Alexandre-de-Rhodes, see page 410, Vietnamese is written in a Roman alphabet making life much easier: place and street names are instantly recognizable. Vietnamese–English and English–Vietnamese dictionaries are cheap and widely available in most towns.

English is much the most useful foreign language despite the vast subsidies the French government pours into French language training. Spoken English is taught pretty badly in secondary schools hence any Vietnamese who wants to learn must enrol at a private language centre if they are to make progress in communication, and enrol they do – in their countless thousands. Visitors will not uncommonly find themselves being asked by bashful students to distinguish between the pronunciation of 'thirst' and 'first' or even to elucidate on some obscure point of grammar (probably something to do with gerunds or syntax) with which, unfortunately, the Vietnamese education system is obsessed.

French is still spoken and often very nicely by the more elderly and educated. Nevertheless, in today's global economy it is studied by far fewer students than are the Chinese and Japanese languages.

Disabled travellers

Considering the proportion of the population that are seriously disabled, foreigners might expect better facilities and allowances for the immobile: expect none. Unless users of wheelchairs wish to tussle for road space with unsympathetic truck drivers, a wheelchair is useless: a wheelchair cannot proceed 20 m down a city pavement. But, in general, expect restaurant and hotel staff to be accommodating and helpful.

Gay and lesbian travellers

There are several bars in central Saigon popular with gays. Cruising in dark streets is not advised. The gay lifestyle is nothing like as well developed as in Thailand. As with exotic religions, Vietnamese are more likely to be curious, than intolerant.

Student travellers

There are no specific discounts for student travellers in Vietnam. However, the backpacker trail which most young people follow offers the best prices available.

Travelling with children

The Vietnamese adore white children. Western children get an awful lot of attention, hugs and pats; children of mixed European – Asian parentage get even more. Apart from the susceptibility of young children to the sun and an exotic diet – just take sensible precautions – it is perfectly safe to travel with them in Vietnam. They are often more tolerant of noise and heat and more adaptable to cramped and uncomfortable travelling conditions than their parents, falling asleep as soon as the bus or train starts to move. If you are travelling with a baby just bring lots of *Calpol* and he'll be fine.

Nappies are available in supermarkets in the big towns

In terms of discounts that are available: *Vietnam Airlines* charges children under two years of age just 10% of the adult ticket price; those aged 2-12 must pay 75% of the adult ticket price. Over 12, it is full price. The railways allow children under five to travel free and charge 50% of the adult fare for those aged 5-10. The travelling café open tickets and tours are likewise free for children under two but those aged 2-10 have to pay half the adult price.

Women travellers

Lone women travellers have fewer problems in Vietnam than in many other Asian countries. The most common form of harassment usually consists of comic and harmless displays of macho behaviour with the odd lewd suggestion thrown in for good measure. Expect such comments as 'you are very beautiful' and 'you have a beautiful body', which are intended to be flattering. At night apply common sense and you will find Vietnam is safer than Britain or America.

Embassies overseas

Argentina, Arribenos 1539, CP 1426, Buenos Aires, T00-54-17830438, F00-54-178250078.

Australia, 6 Timbarra Crescent, O'Malley Canberra, Act 2606, T00-61-262866059/262901549, F00-61-262864534.

Austria, Felix Mottl, STR 20 A, 1190 Vienna, T00-43-13104073, F00-43-13104070.

Belgium, 130 Avenue De La Floride, 1180 Bruselles, T00-32-23749133, F00-32-23749376.

Brunei, LOT 13489, Jalan Manggis Dua (off Jalan Muara), Bandar Seri, Begawan, Brunei Darussalam, T00-673-2343168/2343167, F00-673-2343169.

France, 436 Monivong, Phnom Penh, T00-855-23362741, F00-855-23362314.

Campuchia, 436 Monivong, Phnom Penh, T00-855-23362741, F00-855-23362314.

Canada, 226 Maci Aren St, Ottawa, Ontario, Canada, K2P OL6, T00-1-6132360772/6132321957, F00-1-6132362704.

China, Guang Hua Lu, No 32, Beijing 100600, T00-86-1065321155/1065321125, F00-86-1065325720.

Czech Republic, Stepanska 4/534, 120.00 Praha 2, T00-420-24942235, F00-4720-24942132.

}**France**, 62-66 Rue Boileau, 75016 Paris, T00-33-0144146447/0144146400, F00-33-0145243948.

Germany, Konstantin Strasse 37, 53179 Bonn, T00-49-228357021/228957540, F00-49-228351866.

Hungary, 1068 Budapest, Vi Benczur Utca 18, T00-36-13425583/13429922, F00-36-13528798.

India, 17 Kautilya Marg Chanakya, Puri, New Delhi 11002, T00-91-113018059, F00-91-113017714.

Indonesia, 25 JalanTenku Umar, Jakarta, T00-62-213100358, F00-62-21349615.

Italy, Via Clitunno, No 34-00198, Roma, T00-39-68543223/68543235, F00-39-68548501.

Japan, 50-11 Motoyoyogi-Cho Shibuya-Ku, Tokyo 151, T00-81-334663313/334663314, F00-81-334663391/34667652.

Working in Vietnam

Officially anyone working in Vietnam should have a business visa and a work permit. Expats coming to work in Vietnam will, presumably, have all this taken care of by their firm. In practice there does appear to be a relatively relaxed attitude on the part of the authorities to foreigners working in Vietnam for short periods. Those with specific skills, notably computer skills and English language teaching, will not find it hard to get work. In Hanoi and Saigon there are countless hundreds of language schools keen to engage native speakers and the best ones pay quite well – but only to those with relevant qualifications.

Voluntary work is available but best organized in advance through volunteer agencies such as *Voluntary Service Overseas*, www.vso.org.uk and *Australian Volunteers International*, www.osb.org.au There are few NGOs in Vietnam compared with Thailand and Cambodia. In general, however, people with specific skills (speech therapists for instance) or with management expertise and those willing to make a commitment for four months or more will be of greatest use. Charities in Vietnam are stretched responding to well-meaning but impractical offers of help from people who just happen to be passing through. The first port of call for further information should be the *NGO Resource Centre*, La Thanh Hotel, 218 Doi Can, Hanoi, T04-8328570, F04-832 8611, www.ngocentre.netnam.vn

Laos, 85 That Luang Road, Vientiane, T00-856-21413409, F00-856-21413379/21414601.

Libya, Km number 17, Gargaresh Street, Korboss St, PO Box 587, Tripoli, T00-218-21830674/21833704, F00-218-21830994.

Malaysia, No 4 Persiaran Stonor, 50450 Kualar Lumpur, T00-60-32484534, F00-60-3248/3270.

Mexico, 225 Sierra ventana, 225 Lomas De Chapultepee Delegation Miguel Hidalogo, CP 11000, Mexico, T00-52-55401632, F00-52-55401612.

Myanmar, 36 Wingaba Road, Bahan, Township Yangon-Myanmar, T00-95-1-548905/543494, F00-95-7-549302.

Philippines, 554 Victor Cruz Malate, Manila, T00-63-25240364, F00-63-25260472.

Poland, Kazimierzowska 14, 01-589 Warszawa, T00-48-22446021/22443780, F00-48-22446723.

Republic Of Korea, 28-58 Samchong-Dong, Chongno-Ku 110-230, T00-82-27382318/27392065, F00-82-27392604.

Russia, Moscow, Bolshaya Pirogovskaia 13, T00-7-0952470212, F00-7-0952451092.

Singapore, 10 Leedon Park, Singapore 1026, T00-65-4683747/4625938, F00-65-4625936.

Sweden, Orby Slottsvag 26, 125 Alvsio, Stockholm, T00-46-8861218, F00-46-8995713.

Thailand, 83/1 Wireless Road, Lumpini, Pathumwan, Bangkok 10330, T00-66-22515838, F00-66-22517203.

USA, 1233 20th Street, NW Suite 400, Washington DC 20036, T00-1-2028610737, F00-1-2028610917.

United Kingdom, 12-14 Victoria Road, London W8 5RD, T00-44-2079371912, F00-44-2079376108.

Before you travel

Getting in

Valid passports with visas issued by a Vietnamese embassy are required by all visitors, irrespective of citizenship. Time needed to process a visa varies from country to country and according to type of visa required. Tourist visas (US$25) generally take two to three days. Bangkok is regarded as the easiest and quickest place to get a visa. The US$25 fee is quoted from private travel agencies in Vietnam. Visitors may have to pay a small additional fee at the Vietnamese Embassy when they collect their visa. Visas are also available on arrival in Vietnam, US$45, providing authorization has been obtained from a Vietnamese embassy overseas or the immigration police in Vietnam. Most people get this done via a travel café or tour operator and pay around US$5 – or go direct to the immigration police.

Visas **Visas**

Visas are normally valid only for arrival by air, Noi Bai (Hanoi airport) and Tan Son Nhat (Saigon airport). The standard tourist visa is valid for one month for one entry (mot lan) only. You can extend it for one month at travel agents for US$15-30. Business visas are valid for three months (US$20) or six months (US$25) and usually enable multiple entry (nhieu lan). Those wishing to enter or leave Vietnam by land must specify the border crossing when applying. It is possible to alter point of departure at immigration offices in Hanoi and Saigon. Visa regulations are ever changing: usually it is possible to extend visas within Vietnam but not during Party Congresses. Check your visa carefully: Vietnamese embassies are notoriously sloppy in getting the details right, Vietnamese immigration is famously eagle-eyed in picking up its comrades' errors. And very costly it can prove too.

Customs All luggage entering and leaving Vietnam is x-rayed. Gold and currency must be declared on arrival. The purpose of the x-ray is to identify video tapes. Incoming tapes will probably be confiscated and can be collected a few days later after screening by the culture and information department. This gives them time to duplicate Western movies which are then sold on to video rental shops.

Export of wood products or antiques (that is anything that appears to be more than 20 years old) is banned, thus allowing customs to confiscate most anything that tickles their fancy.

Duty-free allowance The allowance is 200 cigarettes, two litres of spirits. Perfume and jewellery for personal use. In practice the officers are pretty lenient.

What to take

See page 57 for a medical checklist Many travellers take too much. T-shirts and shorts etc can be bought cheaply in Vietnam. Good quality underwear and socks cannot, however. While not yet on a par with Bangkok there is far more available now in Vietnam than even a couple of years ago. Bottled water is widely available. There is no need to bring water filters unless trekking in remote areas. Good books are scarce, so bring plenty. Most young people sensibly carry all their worldly goods in rucksacks and are referred to by the Vietnamese as *tay ba lo*, a term which has acquired derogatory overtones. Hotels, even those at the bottom end of the market, usually provide mosquito nets so it should not be necessary to bring your own.

Passport photographs – a stock of at least four; **a small first aid kit**, a **torch** – can be useful for viewing caves, dark pagodas and during power cuts; **penknife**; **photocopies** of passport and visa (and entry permit, issued on arrival); **clothes** – long-sleeved shirts for cool evenings, severely air-conditioned restaurants and to prevent sunburn. Long trousers and socks to keep mosquitoes from biting in the evening. Warm clothing is necessary for upland areas in winter. Women might consider wearing dresses rather than jeans when travelling, for easier access to squat toilets; **shampoo** with screw-on top (the *Body Shop* is about the only supplier of travel proof shampoo and creams); **reading material** – there is little available, and journeys are long; **slide film** available in Saigon and Hanoi but rarely elsewhere; print film is more widely sold. Do not get slides processed in Vietnam – chemicals tend to be stale with disappointing results; **insect repellent**; **strong padlock** for locking bags in hotel rooms and while travelling; **money belt**.

It is not necessary to take: **Maps** Cheap ones are available in Saigon and Hanoi; **Dictionaries** Available cheaply in most towns; **Foreign cigarettes** They can be bought cheaply in Vietnam (smuggled); **Waterproof/umbrella** For wet season: ubiquitous and cheap in Vietnam; **Video tapes** (See Customs, page 30), although mini VCR tapes are fine; **too many clothes** They are cheap in Vietnam.

Money

Currency The unit of currency is the **dong**. Notes in circulation are in denominations of 200, 500, 1,000, 2,000, 5,000, 10,000, 20,000, 50,000 and 100,000 dong (beware, 20,000 and 5,000 dong notes look very similar). The exchange rate at the time of going to press was US$1 = 15,000d; £1 = 21,440d. From 2001 the value of the dong stabilized somewhat, that is in practical terms its rate of devaluation has slowed. www.oanda.com/converter/classic enables you to select a currency and convert it.

Any amount of foreign currency can be taken into or out of Vietnam, although amounts of over US$3,000 must be declared on the customs form. Do not take dong out of the country as it cannot be converted overseas. In fact it is quite difficult to convert dong back into US dollars even inside Vietnam.

Cash Outside Hanoi and Saigon it is best to take US$ cash. Clean (that is unmarked) US$100 bills receive the best rates. Small US$ bills receive slightly lower rates. US$ can be changed in banks, in larger hotels and in gold shops or jewellers. Do not change money in the street or if approached by strangers. Banks in the main centres will also change other major currencies including Sterling, HK$, Thai baht, Swiss francs, Euro, A$, S$, C$, and Yen. If possible, try to pay for everything in dong, not in US$; prices are usually less in dong, and in more remote areas people may be unaware of the latest exchange rate. Also, to ordinary Vietnamese, 15,000d is a lot of money, while US$1 means nothing.

Credit & debit cards Credit cards are increasingly widely accepted. Large hotels, expensive restaurants and medical centres invariably take them, but beware a surcharge of 3% is often added. ATM cash dispensers are available at *ANZ Bank* in Hanoi and Saigon and at *HSBC* in Saigon. Acquiring cash with your debit card is a hassle-free method, just avoid getting caught short once out of the main cities.

Travellers' cheques Best denominated in US$, can only be cashed in banks in the major towns. Commission of 2-4% payable if cashing into dollars but not if converting direct to dong. When cashing travellers' cheques it is necessary to take proof of purchase and passport to the bank.

Cost of living The standard of living for the average Vietnamese person is not very high. A teacher's basic salary is around US$30 per month. In a town, that will not go far towards keeping a family. Some schools and companies pay their staff small bonuses. Virtually all Vietnamese get paid 13 months of the year because of the double monthly salary paid at Tet. Most people look for extra work. English and maths teachers in particular can charge quite stiff fees for private tuition, perhaps US$2-3 per hour and above. Many people have a small stand at home selling drinks or cigarettes. Looking at prices in even very modest restaurants, these salaries would not feed many mouths for many days. Many families are able to make ends meet by shopping cheaply in the market. Rice costs only around US$0.25-35 per kg and vegetables are very cheap; monosodiumglutamate provides flavour.

Cost of travelling At the bottom end, expect to pay around US$5-US$10 per night for accommodation and about the same each day for food. There are comfort and cost levels anywhere from here up to US$200 per night.

Getting there

Air

Vietnam is relatively isolated in comparison with Bangkok, Hong Kong and Singapore. While there are several direct flights daily from Europe none is non-stop and there are, at the time of writing, still no direct flights from the US although with the Bilateral Trade Agreement now ratified it shouldn't be long. Saigon, and to a lesser extent

Airlines flying to Vietnam

Airline	From	To
Aeroflot	Moscow	Hanoi, Saigon
Air France	Paris	Hanoi, Saigon
Asiana	Seoul	Saigon
Hong Kong	Cathay Pacific	Hanoi, Saigon
China Southern	Nanning	Hanoi
China Airlines	Taipei	Saigon
Eva Air	Taipei	Saigon
Japan Airlines	Tokyo/Osaka	Saigon
KLM Royal Dutch Airlines	Amsterdam	Saigon
Korean Air	Seoul	Saigon
Lao Aviation	Vientiane	Hanoi
Lauda Air	Vienna	Saigon
Lufthansa	Frankfurt	Saigon
Malaysian Airlines	Kuala Lumpur	Hanoi, Saigon
Philippine Airlines	Manila	Saigon
Qantas	Sydney/Melbourne	Saigon
Royal Air Cambodge	Phnom Penh	Saigon
Siem Reap Airways	Siem Reap	Saigon
Singapore Airlines	Singapore	Hanoi, Saigon
Thai International	Bangkok, Sydney/Melbourne	Hanoi, Saigon
Vietnam Airlines	Paris, Hong Kong, Singapore, Bangkok	Hanoi, Saigon

Hanoi, is pretty well connected with other Southeast Asian countries which remain the source of most foreign visitors.

The best deals from Europe tend to involve getting to Bangkok as cheaply as possible and flying in from there. From the States the quickest route is via Japan or Taiwan.

From Europe it is 16 hours and around £500 low season and upto £1000 in the high season depending on carrier. From Australia it is 12 hours and Aus$1,785-$1,900 (ie US$890-950).

Road

There is a road crossing at Moc Bai on Highway 1 connecting Phnom Penh in Cambodia with Saigon. The new crossing into Cambodia via Chau Doc is passable either by road or by boat. There is a road crossing open at Lao Bao, north of Hué, which enables travel through to Savannakhet in Laos, and although few foreigners do it there is a road crossing to Laos from Dien Bien Phu.

Sea

There are no normal sea crossings into Vietnam although an increasing number of cruise liners sail into Vietnamese waters. The only other international connection by boat is the Mekong River crossing from Chau Doc to Phnom Penh.

Train

International rail connections with Vietnam only exist with China. There are connections with Peking via Nanning to Hanoi crossing at Lang Son and from Kunming to Hanoi via Lao Cai. The lines are slow and distances are great.

Touching down

Airport information

Both Noi Bai (Hanoi) and Tan Son Nhat (Saigon) airports have a limited range of facilities including duty-free shops (both on arrival and departure). Banks and post offices (both for posting letters and making local and international calls) are there but cannot be relied upon to be open, particularly the banks.

See pages 64 and 274 for further details

Both airports now have some air bridges, although not enough, and so some passengers are driven from the aeroplane to the terminal by bus. There then follows a frantic scramble for the immigration desks and a long queue while passports and visas are scrutinized for possible inconsistencies. Luggage is then collected (do lock suitcases as thefts are not uncommon at this stage) and customs broached. All luggage is x-rayed in a valiant search to protect the Vietnamese from culturally unsuitable items.

You are then free to face the country, although it will appear that a large proportion of the population has come to meet you: many are taxi drivers anxious to grab your bags. Keep calm and maintain a close eye and firm hand on your possessions. It is only at this stage that money can be exchanged. There are two options: either have a few small dollar bills with which to pay for your taxi or change a small amount at the airport currency exchange. The latter is quite a challenge given the mental gymnastics required to keep accounts of a currency which makes one an instant millionaire, especially for a lone traveller with lots of luggage to guard.

In Saigon there is only one way into town: taxi. To anywhere central, the fare should not be more than about US$6 (90,000d), 20 minutes. Insist on the driver using the meter. In Hanoi there is an airport minibus which charges US$2, one hour. The taxi to central Hanoi is US$10, (150,000d), 45 minutes. The Hanoi airport bus delivers passengers to the *Vietnam Airlines* office at 1 Quang Trung Street and departs from there.

On departure: US$12, payable in US dollars or VND.

Airport tax

Tourist information

The national tourist office is *Vietnam National Administration of Tourism* Vietnamtourism , 80 Quan Su Hanoi, T04-9421061, TITC@vietnamtourism.com Their role is to promote Vietnam as a tourist destination rather than to provide tourist information. Visitors to their offices can get some information and maps but are more likely to be offered tours.

Local customs and laws

Vietnam is remarkably relaxed and easy-going with regard to conventions. The people, especially in small towns and rural areas, can be pretty old-fashioned, but it is difficult to cause offence unwittingly. The main complaint Vietnamese have of foreigners is their fondness for dirty and torn clothing. Backpackers, who are the main exponents of grunge, come in for particularly severe criticism and the term *tay ba lo* (literally Western backpacker) is a contemptuous one reflecting the low priority many budget travellers seem to allocate to personal hygiene and the antiquity and inadequacy of their shorts and vests.

Shoes should be removed before entering temples and before going into people's houses. Modesty should be preserved and excessive displays of bare flesh are not considered good form, particularly in temples and private houses. (Not that the Vietnamese are unduly prudish, they just like things to be kept in their proper place.) Shorts are fine for the beach and travellers' cafés but not for smart restaurants.

Essentials

Emergency and essential numbers

Police *T113*	**IDD code for Vietnam** *T84*
Fire *T114*	**Official time** *GMT + 7*
Ambulance *T115*	**Business hours** *0730-1130, 1330-1630*
Directory enquiries *T1080 or T116*	**Weights and measures** *metric*

Kissing and canoodling in public are likely to draw wide attention, not much of it favourable. But walking hand in hand is now accepted as a common if slightly eccentric Western habit. Hand shaking among men is a standard greeting (often with both hands for added cordiality) and although Vietnamese women will consent to the process, it is often clear that they would prefer not to. The head is held by some to be sacred and people would rather you didn't pat them on it, which amazingly some visitors do, but the Vietnamese do not have the hang-ups which the Thais have about someone's feet being higher than their head. In short, the Vietnamese are pragmatic and tolerant and only the most unfeeling behaviour is likely to trouble them.

Dinner table etiquette happily still survives in Vietnam. But being Vietnam it is pretty informal and again only the least sensitive will cause offence. The obvious things like not starting until everyone has been served their rice apply, and not hogging all the prawns. Dishes are set in the middle of the table for all to dip into with their chopsticks. Take one or two pieces only at a time. Spoon soup into your bowl and eat it with your spoon or put your bowl to your lips. The latter method together with shovelling chopsticks is a perfectly acceptable method for getting rice into the mouth. Nose-blowing is considered unhygienic: if you must, turn away from the table. Meals are generally a family occasion and an opportunity for conversation.

Tipping Practice on tipping varies widely. Vietnamese do not normally tip if eating in small family restaurants but may tip extravagantly in expensive bars. Foreigners normally leave the small change and this is perfectly acceptable and appreciated. Big hotels and some restaurants add 5-10% service charge.

Religion The Vietnamese are open to religious experiences of all kinds. Unlike in Islamic countries, it is not possible to cause a religious offence unwittingly in Vietnam. The Vietnamese government is hostile to proselytizing – particularly by Christians. But the Roman Catholic church is more vital than in many European countries and foreigners are perfectly free to attend services. Vietnam is predominantly a Buddhist country. Following Chinese tradition, ancestor worship is widely practiced and animism (the belief in and worship of spirits of inanimate objects such as venerable trees, the land, mountains and so on) is widespread.

Prohibitions Drugs are common and cheap, and the use of hard drugs by Vietnamese is a rapidly growing problem, with a growth of 400% in drug seizures in 2001. Attitudes towards users is incredibly lax. It is not an uncommon sight to see junkies injecting themselves in back alleys. Periodic bouts of remorse and panic follow when bars and nightclubs are closed for a few weeks. Many healthy, young male visitors to Vietnam just keel over and die as a result of drink and drug cocktails. Partly as a result of increasing demand, cremation in Vietnam is now much cheaper than it was; a few years ago foreigners' bodies were sent to Bangkok to be burned. Attitudes to traffickers are harsh, although the death penalty is usually reserved for Vietnamese and other Asians whose governments are less likely to kick up a fuss.

Responsible tourism

Travel to the furthest corners of the globe is now commonplace and mass movement of people for leisure and business is a major source of foreign exchange and economic development in many parts of southeast Asia.

The benefits of international travel are self-evident for both hosts and travellers – employment, increased understanding of different cultures, business and leisure opportunities. At the same time there is clearly a downside to the industry. Where visitor pressure is high or poorly regulated, adverse impacts to society and the natural environment may be occur.

The travel industry is growing rapidly and increasingly the impacts of this supposedly 'smokeless' industry are becoming apparent. These impacts can seem remote and unrelated to an individual trip or holiday.

In an attempt to promote awareness of and credibility for responsible tourism, organizations such as *Green Globe* (T020-77304428, www.greenglobe21.com) and the *Centre for Environmentally Sustainable Tourism* (CERT) (T01268-795772, www.c-e-r-t.org) now offer advice on selecting destinations and sites that aim to achieve certain commitments to conservation and sustainable development. Generally these are larger mainstream destinations and resorts but they are still a useful guide and increasingly aim to provide information on smaller operations.

Of course travel can have beneficial impacts and this is something to which every traveller can contribute – many national parks are part funded by receipts from visitors. Similarly, travellers can promote patronage and protection of important archaeological sites and heritage through their interest and contributions via entrance and performance fees. Since the early 1990s there has been a phenomenal growth in tourism that promotes and supports the conservation of natural environments and is also fair and equitable to local communities. This 'eco-tourism' segment is probably the fastest growing sector of the travel industry. While the authenticity of some eco-tourism operators claims need to be interpreted with care, there is clearly both a huge demand for this type of activity and also significant opportunities to support worthwhile conservation and social development initiatives.

Organizations such as *Conservation International* (T1-202-4295660, www.ecotour.org) the *Eco-Tourism society* (T1-802-4472121, www.ecotourism.org), *Planeta* (www.planeta.com) and *Tourism Concern* (T020-77533330, www.tourismconcern.org.uk) have begun to develop and/or promote eco-tourism projects and destinations and their websites are an excellent source of information and details for sites and initiatives throughout Latin America. Additionally, organizations such as *Earthwatch* (US/Can1-800-7760188, in UK on T01865-311601, www.earthwatch.org) and *Discovery International* (T020-72299881, www.discovery initiatives.com) offer opportunities to participate directly in scientific research and development projects throughout the region. **www.nautilus.org** is the homepage of the *Nautilus Institute* which focuses on issues connected with the environment and sustainability in the Asia-Pacific region.

Safety This is our most strongly worded warning. Bag and jewellery snatching is a common and serious problem. Do not take valuables on to the streets of Saigon. Possessions are safer in all but the most disreputable hotels than on the streets. Do not wear expensive jewellery or watches: they will be stolen. Wallets in back pockets will vanish. Women should never carry handbags. Thieves work in teams in central Saigon often with beggar women carrying babies as a decoy. Beware of people who obstruct your path (pushing a bicycle across the pavement is a common ruse), your pockets are being emptied from behind. The situation in other cities is not so bad, but take care in Nha Trang and Hanoi.

Essentials

Young men on fast motorbikes cruise the central streets of Saigon waiting to pounce on unwary victims. They snatch at bags, necklaces and watches, often causing serious injury and death as people are dragged mercilessly down the street. Despite multiple warnings it is quite extraordinary how casual many tourists are, flashing video cameras and jewellery around. Just imagine that one or two pairs of eyes in central Saigon are constantly sizing you up waiting to pounce. Consulates in Saigon are faced with an endless string of refugees who have lost all their valuables and papers. Such a loss will ruin your holiday but is easy to avoid.

Stick to tried and trusted *cyclo* drivers after dark or, better still, go by taxi which is cheaper in any case. Never go by *cyclo* in a strange part of town after dark.

If you are robbed, report the incident to the police (for your insurance claim). Otherwise the police are of no use whatsoever. They will do little or nothing.

Travel advisories   www.travel.state.gov/travel_warnings.html The **US State Department**'s continually updated travel advisories on its Travel Warnings & Consular Information Sheets page. **www.fco.gov.uk/travel/** The **UK Foreign and Commonwealth Office**'s travel warning section.

Traffic police   Stand on every street corner collecting fines for supposed breaches of traffic law. If you are invited to make a contribution to the police widows and orphans fund, but clearly you have committed no offence, refuse point blank. Feign total ignorance of English. If this does not work and your motorbike keys have been confiscated, try to negotiate the size of your donation downwards.

Unavoidable problems   Almost all visitors to Vietnam have a great time. But it would be misleading to pretend there are no problems. Apart from theft and the dual-pricing system, the two most common complaints are noise and traffic.

Noise   This is a passion of the Vietnamese. Can ever a people have fallen so helpless a victim to aural excitement as the Vietnamese? While the invention of the metal-tipped plough is regarded as 'quite a useful thing', it pales into insignificance in the annals of popular Vietnamese history by comparison with the invention of the amplifier and microphone.

There are three main sources of noise: vehicles, home electronics and people, and all three are to a large extent unavoidable. Road noise comes principally from car and truck horns, a branch of applied technology in which Vietnam can proudly claim world leadership. Boys in Cholon are taught from the age of five how to wire a motorbike horn directly to the ignition, and by the age of 10 they are able to boost the decibel rating of the humblest hooter by several hundred percent. In their teen years they graduate to cars then trucks, while a few of the most gifted finally emerge in noise heaven where they are given bus horns to tinker with. These are the air horns which screech and wail with vicious ferocity, almost without interruption, from early morning to evening on every major road in the country, in the heroic task of sweeping lesser vehicles, people and animals into the ditch.

Television and karaoke fall into the home electronics category. It is possible that owners of such devices genuinely believe they are providing a community service by adjusting the volume setting to levels at which the entire street can listen in. And, in the bad old days, when few people had sets of their own, perhaps that was the case. Unfortunately, now that everyone has their own machine (just a bit bigger than their neighbours') they still all feel the same noble instincts in regard to community broadcasting. The effects on the hapless traveller are not hard to guess. Noise of this sort was used by the Americans to flush General Noriega of Panama out of his den – it is easy to understand why.

For centuries, children have grown up living with the fact that in a family of 16 there is only one way to make your feelings known. And, in the ensuing competition to make oneself heard, presumably a bit of Darwinesque natural selection crept in. The result: poor hearing but vocal powers of which an Italian tenor would be proud. Family banter pertaining to whose turn it is to cook the rice or which TV channel to watch, sound, to the untutored ear, like violent arguments, while mild family disagreements are sometimes mistaken by foreigners for street riots.

All in all therefore, Vietnam is a noisy place. It may sound amusing but it is not. Those staying in budget accommodation, in densely packed poorer quarters, will quickly need to develop noise tolerance. And adjust to the Vietnamese clock.

Traffic is to physical health what noise is to mental health. In short: a threat. It has to be said that the modern Vietnamese are extraordinarily impatient and (as drivers) wholly deficient in manners and courtesy. Haste, to the taxi driver racing to pick up a fare, is a living. It is death and injury to pedestrians and cyclists. The speed with which Vietnam has developed in the last decade means that men, who three years ago were sitting on the back of trundling buffalo carts, are now driving 30-ton trucks down Highway 1. The technology is different but quickly mastered. What has not had time to evolve is the common sense, manners and courtesy that prevent European roads from being bloodbaths.

Traffic
We describe in the box, Crossing the road, page 278 how to cross a city street safely

Interestingly, debates in the Vietnamese press on road carnage concentrate almost exclusively on technical short-comings – old cars, antique trucks, absence of road signs – and neatly sidestep the true cause – absence of respect for other road users. It is hard to avoid the feeling that Vietnamese drivers regard every journey as a race. A race in which there are no winners and no winning post but in which every vehicle in front represents a loss of face and personal injury. 'How *dare* you block my way?' is what the horn says. 'Just who do you think you are using *my* road space?'

Sadly, until the Vietnamese come to a mature understanding of the lethal nature of cars, trucks and buses, children, pedestrians and cyclists will continue to be mown down by the people behind the steering wheels.

Where to stay

There has been a great spate of hotel building and renovation in Vietnam over the past 10 years and as a result hotels to suit most budgets are available widely across the country (see box Hotel Classification, page 38, for details). Many hotels are state-run but competition from private hotels has forced them to provide at least a degree of service and to moderate their prices. In remote places where there is no competition, dour and surly service remain the order of the day. There are a great many family-run mini-hotels and guesthouses and these often provide spic and span accommodation and friendly attention to guests' needs. There are no youth hostels as such, although some budget hotels provide dormitory accommodation, which are pretty similar in style.

Government restrictions mean that homestays or bread and breakfast type accommodation is generally not possible. In a few places, such as the Mekong Delta and around the northwest of Vietnam, some private homes have a licence to accept foreigners, but this tends to be at the discretion of local police so don't count on it. Police and People's Committee regulations in some towns mean that a foreigner travelling with his Vietnamese wife must bring a marriage certificate in order to share a hotel room with her.

Travellers normally get their laundry done in hotels. In cheap hotels it doesn't cost much but one wishes they actually used some soap powder. The cheaper hotels and laundries which exist in the hotel districts charge by weight, about US$1 per kg. The smarter places charge by the item.

Laundries

Essentials

Hotel classification

LL *US$200+* **Luxury**: *only a couple of newly-built hotels in Saigon and Hanoi fall into this category.*

L *US$100-200* **First class plus**: *chiefly to be found in Saigon and Hanoi but resorts, for example in Danang and Nha Trang, come into this category. Mostly newly-built but some historic buildings that have been upgraded, the* Metropole *in Hanoi for example.*

A *US$50-100* **First class**: *the hotels that can be considered first class are increasingly found in towns other than Hanoi and Saigon. Hotels in this category should offer reasonable business services, and a range of recreational facilities, restaurants and bars. 5-10% service and 10% VAT will be added to the bill.*

B *US$25-50* **Tourist class**: *all rooms will have air-conditioning and an attached bathroom with hot water. Other services should include one or more restaurants, a bar, and room service. Breakfast will often be included in the price. A 10% service may be added to the bill. Prices in these hotels and those above are normally fixed in dollars but can be paid in dong or dollars*

C *US$15-25* **Economy**: *rooms should be air-conditioned and have attached bathrooms with hot water and 'western' toilets. A restaurant and room service will probably be available. Prices in these hotels and those below are normally fixed in dong.*

D *US$8-15* **Budget**: *air-conditioning unlikely although they should have an attached bathroom. Toilets should be Western-style. Bed linen will be provided, towels perhaps. There may be a restaurant. No service charge.*

E *US$4-8* **Vietnamese**: *usually fan-cooled rooms, occasionally air-conditioned, maybe with shared bathroom facilities. Bed linen should be provided, towels may not be. These hotels are generally geared to Vietnamese travellers but many can be found in backpacker areas; staff are unlikely to speak much English. No service charge.*

F *less than US$4* **Dormitory** *type accommodation, with shared bathroom facilities, fan-cooled and probably cold water showers.*

Getting around

Air

Vietnam Airlines is the country's domestic carrier. The two main hubs are Hanoi in the north and Saigon (Ho Chi Minh City) in the south. There are air connections to: Hanoi, Haiphong, Na San and Dien Bien in the north; Vinh, Hué, Danang, Play Ku, Qui Nhon, Buon Ma Thuot, Dalat and Nha Trang in the central region; and Saigon, Phu Quoc and Rach Gia in the south. See the map for routes and tables on pages 40 and 43.

Tickets should be booked for all flights as soon as possible after arrival. Flights can subsequently be altered at no cost at *Vietnam Airlines* booking offices in larger towns along the way, seat availability permitting. Following the Phnom Penh Tupolev crash in 1997, the infamous fleet of Soviet aircraft has been replaced by airworthy Airbuses and capitalist Boeings.

Despite the poor safety record of *Vietnam Airlines*, it is far quicker, and a safer way to travel than going by road. And since the old Russian aeroplanes were scrapped there have been no fatal accidents. *Vietnam Airlines* is making a very real effort to compete with its regional neighbours and has made enormous progress in the past 10 years. The dual pricing system means foreigners pay slightly more than Vietnamese passengers but the differential has narrowed dramatically in recent years.

Vietnam Airlines domestic routes

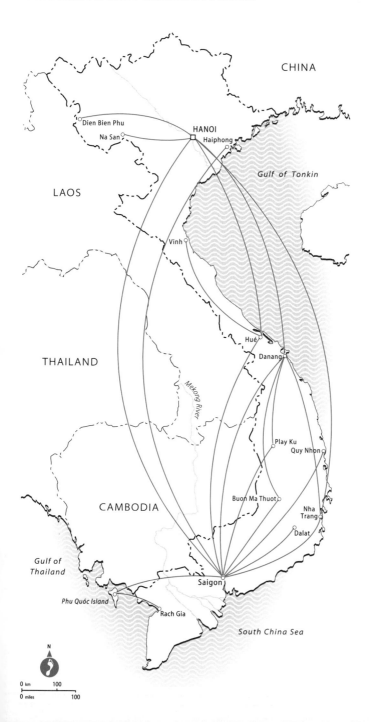

Essentials

Vietnam Airlines Summary Timetable

	Flight No	*Day*	*Depart*	*Arrive*
From Hanoi				
To Danang	VN311	Tue, Fri	0610	0725
	VN311	Mon, Wed, Thu, Sat, Sun	0800	0915
	VN313	Mon, Wed, Sat	1350	1535
	VN313	Tue, Thu, Fri, Sun	1600	1745
	VN317	Mon, Tue, Wed, Sat	1730	1845
To Dien Bien Phu	VN492	Mon, Tue, Thu, Sat	1030	1130
	VN492	Sun	1230	1330
To Saigon	VN741	Daily	0700	0900
	VN211	Thu, Fri, Sat, Sun	0730	0930
	VN219	Mon, Tue, Wed, Thu, Sat, Sun	1130	1330
	VN225	Daily	1430	1630
	VN229	Mon, Tue, Wed, Thu, Fri, Sun	1630	1830
	VN231	Tue, Thu, Sun	1720	1920
	VN235	Mon, Wed, Thu, Sat	1950	2150
	VN781	Mon, Fri	1720	1920
	VN783	Wed, Sat	1720	1920
	VN901	Tue, Fri, Sun	1950	2150
To Hué	VN247	Fri	0630	0740
	VN247	Mon, Tue, Wed, Thu, Sat, Sun	1220	1330
	VN245	Daily	1310	1450
To Nha Trang	VN267	Tue, Thu, Fri, Sun	0640	0830
	VN267	Mon, Wed, Sat	0700	0850
From Saigon				
To Buon Ma Thuot	VN338	Mon, Wed, Fri, Sat	0620	0720
	VN440	Tue, Thu	0700	0800
To Dalat	VN464	Daily	1340	1430
To Danang	VN320	Mon, Tue, Wed, Fri, Sun	0615	0725
	VN320	Thu, Sat	0800	0910
	VN326	Tue	1130	1240
	VN324	Daily	1610	1755
	VN328	Tue, Thu, Sat	1800	1945
To Hanoi	VN900	Tue, Fri, Sun	0700	0900
	VN210	Mon, Wed, Thu, Sat	0700	0900
	VN212	Fri	0730	0930
	VN212	Sun	0730	0930
	VN218	Daily	1130	1330
	VN220	Mon	1200	1400
	VN224	Mon, Tue, Wed, Thu, Sat, Sun	1430	1630
	VN740	Daily	1640	1840
	VN230	Mon, Wed, Fri	1730	1930
	VN780	Tue, Sat	1730	1930
	VN782	Thu, Sun	1730	1930
	VN234	Daily	1930	2130
To Haiphong	VN282	Wed, Fri	1110	1310
To Hué	VN250	Mon, Tue, Wed, Thu, Sat, Sun	0650	0810
	VN254	Daily	0810	1000
	VN250	Fri	1040	1200

	Flight No	Day	Depart	Arrive
From Saigon cont.				
To Nha Trang	VN334	Daily	0620	0730
	VN450	Fri	0800	0910
	VN450	Tue	0800	0900
	VN450	Mon, Wed, Sat	1125	1225
	VN452	Mon, Wed, Sat	1505	1605
	VN452	Tue, Thu, Fri, Sun	1515	1625
To Phu Quoc	VN483	Mon, Tue, Wed, Fri, Sun	0620	0720
	VN481	Thu, Sat	0920	1020
	VN481	Tue, Sun	1020	1120
To Play Ku	VN342	Mon, Wed, Thu, Sat	0625	0740
	VN446	Sun	0635	0750
To Quy Nhon	VN458	Sun	0715	0845
	VN458	Thu, Fri	0800	0900
	VN458	Mon, Wed, Sat	1415	1545
To Rach Gia	VN483	Mon, Tue, Wed, Fri, Sun	0620	0845
From Hué				
To Hanoi	VN244	Daily	1040	1215
	VN246	Fri	1255	1405
	VN246	Mon, Tue, Wed, Thu, Sat, Sun	1430	1540
To Saigon	VN251	Fri	0830	0950
	VN251	Mon, Tue, Wed, Thu, Sat, Sun	0910	1030
	VN255	Daily	1530	1720
From Dalat				
To Saigon	VN465	Daily	1510	1600
From Buon Ma Thuot				
To Danang	VN338	Mon, Wed, Thu, Sat	0800	0910
To Saigon	VN339	Fri	1200	1255
	VN339	Mon, Wed, Sat	1615	1710
	VN441	Tue, Thu	0840	0935
From Danang				
To Buon Me Thuot	VN339	Fri	1010	1120
	VN339	Mon, Wed, Sat	1420	1530
To Hanoi	VN310	Mon, Wed, Thu, Sat, Sun	1010	1120
	VN310	Tue, Fri	0820	0930
	VN312	Daily	0700	0845
	VN316	Mon, Tue, Wed, Sat	1945	2055
	VN316	Thu, Fri, Sun	1955	2110
To Saigon	VN321	Mon, Tue, Wed, Fri, Sun	0815	0925
	VN321	Thu, Sat	1430	1540
	VN325	Mon, Wed, Sat	1615	1805
	VN325	Tue, Thu, Fri		
To Nha Trang	VN335	Daily	1020	1140
To Play Ku	VN343	Mon, Wed, Thu, Sat	1015	1105
To Vinh	VN370	Mon, Wed, Sat	1010	1120

Essentials

	Flight No	Day	Depart	Arrive
From Dien Bien Phu				
To Hanoi	VN493	Mon, Tue, Thu, Sat	1210	1310
	VN493	Sun	1410	1510
From Haiphong				
To Saigon	VN283	Wed, Fri	1410	1610
From Nha Trang				
To Danang	VN334	Daily	0810	0925
To Hanoi	VN266	Tue, Thu, Fri, Sun	0915	1105
	VN266	Mon, Wed, Sat	1645	1835
To Saigon	VN453	Mon, Wed, Sat	0930	1030
	VN451	Tue, Fri	0950	1050
	VN335	Daily	1220	1320
	VN451	Mon, Wed, Sat	1300	1400
	VN453	Tue, Thu, Fri, Sun	1705	1805
From Phu Quoc				
To Saigon	VN480	Thu, Sat	1100	1205
	VN480	Tue, Sun	1200	1305
	VN482	Mon, Tue, Wed, Fri, Sun	1105	1210
From Play Ku				
To Danang	VN342	Mon, Wed, Thu, Sat	0825	0915
To Saigon	VN343	Mon, Wed, Thu, Sat	1150	1300
	VN447	Sun	0830	0940
From Quy Nhon				
To Saigon	VN459	Sun	0925	1050
	VN459	Thu, Fri	0945	1045
	VN459	Mon, Wed, Sat	1625	1750
From Vinh				
To Danang	VN371	Mon, Wed, Sat	1210	1320

Road

Some generalizations you are free to dispute or agree with: distances are great; trains and buses are slow; journeys are uncomfortable; roads are dangerous.

Nevertheless, the majority of travellers go overland. It is perfectly possible to travel the length of the country in this way, although those staying a fortnight or less should consider travelling at least part of the way by air. The Hanoi to Hué sector is the least interesting leg on the north-south Mandarin Route and is best flown. The scenic Hué to Danang sector should not be missed, both road and rail journeys offer fabulous views. Hué to Saigon is full of interest and although some points are far apart, the journey can be done well either by train, public bus or tourist bus (using the open ticket, for example, see page 44).

Bus & tourist minibuses Buses, in general, are slow, old and cramped, but they usually arrive at their destination. The most common roadside enterprises are car (and bicycle) repair outfits. This is indicative of the appalling state of many of the roads and vehicles. It is not uncommon

Domestic Airline fares

Route	Class	One-way (US$)
Hanoi-Danang	B	80
Hanoi-Hué	B	80
Saigon-Hanoi	B	163
Saigon-Haiphong	B	163
Saigon-Danang	B	80
Danang-Buon Ma Thuot	E	37
Danang-Nha Trang	E	37
Danang-Quy Nhon	E	37
Danang-Pleiku	E	37
Danang-Vinh	E	47
Hanoi-Danang	E	67
Hanoi-Hué	E	67
Hanoi-Nha Trang	E	97
Hanoi-Dien Bien Phu	E	43
Hanoi -Danang	E	37
Saigon-Hanoi	E	127
Saigon-Haiphong	E	127
Saigon-Buon Me Thuot	E	43
Saigon-Danang	E	67
Saigon-Dalat	E	30
Saigon-Hué	E	67
Saigon-Nha Trang	E	43
Saigon-Rach Gia	E	47
Saigon-Phu Quoc	E	47
Saigon-Pleiku	E	47
Saigon-Qui Nhon	E	47
Rach Gia-Phu Quoc	E	30

B = business, E = economy

Essentials

to see buses being totally disassembled at the side of the road and it is rare to travel through the country by public transport without experiencing several breakdowns or punctures. Speeds average no more than 35 km per hour; public road transport can be a long and tiresome (sometimes excruciating) business, but it is also fascinating and the best way to meet Vietnamese people. A bewildering array of contraptions pass for buses, from old French jalopies, Chevrolet, Ford and DMC vans, to Soviet buses. Many (and this includes lorries) have ingenious cooling systems in which water is fed into the radiator from barrels strapped to the roof; along the route there are water stations to replenish depleted barrels (look for the sign *nuoc mui* or *do nuoc*).

As American humourist PJ O'Rourke remarked after his visit: "In America they drive on the right side of the road, in England they drive on the left side, and in Vietnam they drive on both sides ... " Roads in Vietnam are notoriously dangerous.

Long-distance buses invariably leave very early in the morning (0400-0500). Buses are the cheapest form of transport, although sometimes foreigners find they are being asked two to three times the correct price. Prices are normally prominently displayed at bus stations. It helps avoid being overcharged if you can find out what the correct fare should be.

Most bus stations are on the outskirts of town; in bigger centres there may be several stations

Less comfortable but quicker are the minibus services (some are air-conditioned) which ply the more popular routes. These are usually grossly overladen and driven by

Essentials

Vietnam Airlines booking offices

Buon Me Thuot	172 Nguyen Tat Thanh Street	T050-956267
Dalat	40 Ho Tung Mau Street	T063-822895
Danang	35 Tran Phu Street	T0511-821130
Dien Bien Phu	Dien Bien Phu Airport	T023-825536
Hanoi	1 Quang Trung Street	T04-8320320
Haiphong	30 Tran Phu Street	T031-921137
Hué	7 Nguyen Tri Phuong Street	T054-824709
Nha Trang	91 Nguyen Thien Thuan Street	T058-825956
Phu Quoc	Phu Quoc Airport	T077-846086
Play Ku	55 Quang Trung Street	T059-823058
Quy Nhon	Nguyen Tat Thanh Street	T056-825313
Rach Gia	180 Nguyen Trung Truc Street	T077-861848
Saigon	116 Nguyen Hue Boulevard	T08-8320320
Son La	Na San Airport	T022-845102
Vinh	78 Nguyen Thi Minh Khai Street	T038-847359

maniacs. Therefore one of the best and most popular ways to travel by road is by travel-ler café minibus. Almost every travellers' café listed in the book will run a minibus ser-vice or act as an agent. There is the popular **Open Ticket**, a flexible, one-way ticket from Saigon to Hanoi or Hanoi to Saigon. The bus runs daily and includes the following stops: Saigon, Mui Ne, Nha Trang, Hué and Hanoi. Confirm at the booking office the day before travel.

Car hire Self-drive car hire is not available. Cars with drivers can be hired for around US$20-50 per day depending on distance travelled and who the car is hired from. It pays to shop around.

Bicycle & motorbike In cities and towns often the best (and cheapest) way to get around is to hire a bicycle or motorbike. Take time to familiarize yourself with road conditions and ride slowly. Most towns are small enough for bicycles to be an attractive option but if taking in a sweep of the surrounding countryside (touring around the Central Highlands, for example) then a motorbike will mean you can see more. Bicycles are pretty hard work in Dalat and Kontum too.

Hotels often have bicycles for hire and there is usually someone willing to lend their machine for a small charge (10,000-15,000d per day). Many travellers' cafés rent out bicycles and motorbikes, the latter for 70,000d-90,000d per day. Some longer stay visi-tors buy bicycles (around US$50) which, if it hasn't been stolen by the time they leave, they sell on or give to Vietnamese friends.

Always park your bicycle or motorbike in a guarded parking place (*gui xe*). Ask for a ticket. The 2,000d this costs is worth every ..., well, every dong even if you are just pop-ping in to the post office to post a letter.

Motorcycle taxi (Honda ôm or xe ôm) *Ôm* means to cuddle. This means of transport is ubiquitous and cheap. You will find them on most street corners, outside hotels or in the street. With their uniform baseball caps and dangling cigarette, *xe ôm* drivers are readily recognizable. In the north and upland areas the Honda is replaced with the Minsk, that Russian workhorse of the hills. A *xe ôm* from the centre of Saigon to the airport would cost around 20,000d (tourists rate). The shortest hop would be at least 5,000d.

Every man and his pig

"Vietnam is great ... except for the transport." This commonly voiced sentiment reflects the views of many visitors to Vietnam. The problem is a reflection of the run-down and underfunded public transport system and the large numbers of people needing to travel. It may be of some consolation to the modern-day traveller to know that discomfort and overcrowding on Vietnam's buses is nothing new, the following account was written in 1928:

"The bus was licensed for six first-class passengers and 16 second. We started with five of the former and 22 of the latter, discarded nobody and picked up every suppliant. Besides the passengers was their luggage, and this did not mean a modest hand-bag apiece. It meant sleeping-mats, boxes, sacks, bales, furniture, crates of merchandise and poultry. In addition we carried a live pig and a bicycle, the latter hung outboard over the side like a life-boat in a steamer's davits. The second-class sufferers sat on each other, on the floor, on the piled-up luggage. The overflow mounted the already overburdened roof. One youth rode all day clinging to the running-boards, another to the step. How the topheavy vehicle contrived to keep its feet when hurtling round corners at top speed was nothing short of miraculous.

We passed out of cultivated country into desolate heaths again and climbing a hill beheld a strange procession racing along the sky-line to cut us off. It consisted of an Annamite and three French priests, skirts and umbrellas tucked up under their arms, mighty beards streaming in the breeze, galloping like colts, whooping like Cherokees. The native convert, being young and slender, reached the road first and executed a sort of war-dance in front of the oncoming bus. It stopped. The three missionaries arrived panting brokenly, sponging their foreheads. One was evidently fresh to the job. He was young, wore a cassock, and his beard was a mere tuft of struggling fluff, but the other two were old stagers, wearing native dress and beards of true tropical exuberance.

The bus by this time contained seven first class passengers and 30 second. It was unthinkable that it would take in any more. But the driver never hesitated. The convert went up to join the throng (and the pig) on the roof. With a modesty commensurate with his beard, the young priest relegated himself to the second-class and the two elders hove their vast carcasses in on top of us. On top of us literally. With a sunny smile, but without any warning or by your leave, the vaster of the pair sank ponderously and devastatingly upon my knees, apparently prepared to stop there all the way to Quang-Tri."

Extract taken from Crosbie Garstin (1928) The voyage from London to Indochina, Heinemann.

Cyclo Tourists, housewives and young school children like them but no one else does. They are, to be blunt, a bloody nuisance. Slow moving, obstructive and driven by elderly gangsters who cannot afford motorbikes, they should be scrapped. *Cyclo* operators, like horse-carriage drivers before them, cling obstinately to their obsolete technology and archaic work practices and, with as much prescience as dinosaurs, add their names to the list of endangered species.

For a start they charge double a *xe ôm*, which, when multiplied by the rich-for-eigner-premium (a touching belief all *cyclo* drivers hold as a sacred creed) makes a slow and hazardous journey by *cyclo* more expensive than a nice air-conditioned taxi ride – especially if there are two or three of you. Hence, while the *xe ôm* drivers are doing brisk business, the local *cyclo* drivers will be snoozing on the street corner dreaming of the crisp dollar bills (*cyclo* drivers always dream in dollars) today will surely bring.

Adding to the *cyclo* drivers' woes is the fact that a number of streets in the centres of Saigon and Hanoi are one-way or out of bounds to *cyclos*, necessitating lengthy

Summary railway timetable

Name of train	S2	S4	S6	S8	S10
From **Saigon** to:	2100	2150	1110	1540	1000
Nha Trang	0410	0647	2000	0047	1850
Danang	1327	1904	0829	1220	0619
Hué	1621	2242	1229	1547	1112
Vinh	2321	0745	2100	0108	2012
Hanoi	0500	1440	0400	0830	0315

Name of train	S1	S3	S5	S7	S9
From **Hanoi** to:	2100	2150	1110	1540	0950
Vinh	0226	0430	1737	2219	1629
Hué	0920	1349	0245	0720	0139
Danang	1208	1726	0607	1044	0508
Nha Trang	2137	0526	1752	2306	1701
Saigon	0500	1440	0400	0830	0300

detours which add to the time and cost. Do not take a *cyclo* after dark unless the driver is well known to you or you know the route.

Not infrequently, though, visitors encounter a *cyclo* driver who regales them with stories of flying Hueys with the Yanks, life in re-education camp and who gives a potted history of all the pagodas he takes them to and then peddles them to a fantastic little diner which does brilliant veggie noodles very cheaply. Taxi drivers never do that. Prices: a *cyclo* from the *New World Hotel* to the Zoo in Saigon, for example would be 10,000d while taking a *cyclo* tour of Cholon could cost a tourist as much as 200,000 d.

Taxi
Official cabs look smart, their drivers are usually uniformed

Taxis ply the streets of Hanoi and Saigon. They are now also to be found in virtually every large town in the country but normally need to be summoned by telephone. They are cheap, around 10,000d per km or less and the drivers generally know their way around and are better English speakers than *cyclo* drivers. But too many are reckless, dangerous and off their heads on drugs, and have an annoying tendency not to carry change. At night use the better known taxi companies rather than the unlicensed cars that often gather around popular nightspots. A number of foreigners have been kidnapped and robbed.

Train

For the sleeper train from Hanoi to Saigon: 566,000d top berth, 732,000d lower berth. A/c sleeper 758,000d

A railway line links Hanoi with Saigon, passing through many of the towns and cities worth visiting, including Hué, Danang and Nha Trang. Other than going by air, the train is the most comfortable way to travel. *But*, this only applies to first class. Fares are cheap: foreigners now pay the same price as locals. The difference in price between first and second class is small and it is worth paying the extra. The express trains plying the Saigon-Hanoi route take between 36 and 46 hours to make the full journey. First class travel is civilized; second class acceptable; for those in other classes it can be a nightmare – the sort of journey to tell one's grandchildren about. The slow local trains are entertaining if you have the time and want to enjoy the local people's company. The kitchen on the Hanoi-Saigon service serves soups and simple, but adequate, rice dishes (it is a good idea to take additional food and drink on long journeys though). First class long-distance tickets include the price of meals. With overnight stays at hotels along the way to see the sights, a rail sight-seeing tour from Hanoi to Saigon, or

S12	S14	S16	S18	LH2	SN2
1230	1700	2000	2220	1320	1840
2110	0157	0542	0806	2246	0515
0926	1441	1743	2017	1053	**
1432	1813	2114	2350	1510	**
2350	0259	0707	0920	**	**
0710	1025	1345	1620	**	**

S11	S13	S15	S17	LH3	SN1
1230	1845	2000	2300	**	**
1902	0112	0342	0557	**	**
0439	1031	1211	1516	0830	**
0752	1420	1552	1927	1158	**
1948	0145	0345	0746	0038	1740
0640	1150	1345	1645	1040	0542

Essentials

vice versa, should take a minimum of 10 days. Sleepers should be booked three days in advance. It is possible to book bicycles onto trains, but this must be done at least two days ahead (example of cost, Nha Trang to Danang US$4). For details of trains from Saigon, see page 310.

Sea

Being rather a wet country, there are rivers just about everywhere. As a means of getting from one place to another, however, boats are rarely an option in Vietnam. In the Mekong Delta it is possible to get from a to b, or at least from Chau Doc to Ha Tien. Also from Rach Gia to the island of Phu Quoc and from Vung Tau to Con Dao. Then there is the hydrofoil from Saigon to Vung Tau and from Haiphong to Cat Ba Island. Otherwise boats are just for fun, taking a look at the country from a perspective slightly different than from the back of a motorbike.

www.lib.utexas.edu Click on the 'map' button. Up-to-date maps of Asia showing Maps
relief, political boundaries and major towns.
www.nationalgeographic.com Click on the 'map' button. National Geographic's cartographic division, which takes maps from their current Atlas of the world.

Keeping in touch

Communications

Vietnam has a long way to go to catch up with neighbouring countries, in terms of Internet
internet communication. All of the first wave of cybercafés were closed down and their *Internet cafés are*
computers confiscated by officials fearful of the effects of a free flow of information on *listed in the Directory*
a closed society. Although emailing is now usually easy enough, access to the internet *throughout the book*
from within Vietnam is restricted as the authorities battle vainly to fire-wall Vietnam-related topics.

Many travellers' cafés in Hanoi, Saigon, Nha Trang and Hoi An provide email access. So too do hotels and guesthouses. Rates for receiving, sending and printing have fallen

Vietnamese addresses

Unlike the systems of some neighbouring countries, addresses in Vietnam do, in general, follow quite a logical pattern. A few points to note:

Odd numbers usually run consecutively on one side of the street, evens on the other. bis after a number, as in 16 bis Hai Ba Trung Street, means there are two houses with the same number and ter after the number means there are three houses with the same number.

Large buildings with a single street number are usually subdivided 21A, 21B, 21C etc; some buildings may be further subdivided 21C1, 21C2, 21C3 and so on.

An oblique (/ – sec or tren in Vietnamese) in a number, as in 23/16 Dinh Tien Hoang Street, means that the address is to be found in a small side street (hem) – in this case running off Dinh Tien Hoang Street by the side of no 23: the house in question will probably be signed 23/16 rather than just 16. Usually, but by no means always, a

hem will be quieter than the main street and it may be worth looking at a guesthouse with an oblique number for that reason (especially in the Pham Ngu Lao area of Saigon).

An address will sometimes contain the letter F followed by a number, as in F6; this is short for phuong (ward, a small administrative area); its inclusion in an address is a reflection of the tidy, bureaucratic nature of the Vietnamese mind not an aid to finding one's destination.

Q in an address stands for quân or district; this points you in the right general direction and will be important in locating your destination as a long street in Hanoi or Saigon may run through several quan. In suburban and rural areas districts are known as huyên, Huyên Nha Be outside Saigon, for instance.

There are no postcodes or zip codes in Vietnam.

---

as competition has spread. Rates are currently around 100-200d per minute in the two main cities but much more in smaller places. The main problems are the slow speed of access and the general unreliability of messages getting in and out.

www.netcafes.com Around 4,200 cybercafés in 148 countries are listed here and it also provides discussion forums for travellers and a language section.

Post   Generally postal services are pretty good. International aerograms take about two weeks in each direction. Every town has a post office, as does every district in every city. And such is the nature of Vietnamese bureaucracy that provincial capitals have two General Post Offices: one for the province and one for the town. Post offices tend to keep long opening hours: 0700-1900 seven days a week, smaller ones closing for lunch.

General Post Offices in the major cities are geared up for sending parcels overseas and usually offer packing services as well for a small additional fee. The cost of sending letters and parcels from Vietnam is given below:

100 g, airmail letter to Australia (US$2.38), UK (US$2.98) and USA (US$4.38). A 1 kg surface parcel to Australia costs US$11.45, to the UK US$14.33, to the USA US$10.75. All prices exclude 10% VAT.

It would be nice to think that in the 21st century foreigners were regarded less suspiciously, but alas no; outgoing packages are opened and the contents checked by the censor before being allowed out. Receiving parcels is also a tedious process. Packages are rarely delivered to your door, but a note is sent to you inviting you to the post office. After a long wait at two or three wrong counters, the checking of your passport and the payment of a fee, the parcel is produced and opened by customs officers. If you are Vietnamese they will pocket what they fancy and you will say thank you. If you are a foreigner they may simply ask you to pay a customs due. All the major international courier companies have offices near the big General Post Offices.

Post offices offer domestic telegram services which can be very useful for getting messages to people who are not on the telephone. There is an express mail service, EMS, which will deliver letters or small packages the length of the country the following day.

Post offices in Saigon, Hanoi, Hué, Hoi An, Nha Trang, Dalat and Danang provide Poste Restante facilities, ask your family and friends to print your surname. For example: Chris ARNOLD, c/o Poste Restante, GPO, Hanoi.

All post offices provide international telephone and fax services. The cost of calls is exorbitant (US$3-4 per minute to Europe or the States) and some post offices and hotels still insist on charging a minimum of three minutes. Hotels then add their own surcharge. To cap it all you start paying for an overseas call from the moment you ring, so whether the called number is unanswered or engaged you will be charged as if the call were made. It is advisable, therefore, to make arrangements to be called from abroad.

Telephone & fax

Long-distance domestic calls are quite pricey but local calls are cheap or even free of charge in some hotels. Most shops or cafés will let you call a local number for 2,000d: look for the blue sign *dien thoai cong cong*, public telephone.

Most mobile phones with global roaming work in Vietnam and coverage is improving. Each town – even a small one – tends to have quite a generous footprint of phone coverage. Calls on global roaming phones from within Vietnam are charged as international, so for people intending to use their mobile phone a lot, it may be cheaper to buy a pay-as-you-go sim card from *Vinaphone* or *Mobiphone* the offices of which duopoly surround every big post office. A fax costs around US$3 to most countries in the world.

Media

One- or two-day-old editions of the *Financial Times*, *International Tribune*, *USA Today*, *Figaro* and some weeklies, such as the *Economist*, *Time* and *Asiaweek* are available in Saigon and Hanoi.

Newspapers

The English language daily *Vietnam News* is widely available and covers Vietnamese and foreign news selectively but not badly. It has especially good sports pages and covers English football thoroughly. The Sunday edition is worth reading for its cultural stories, and is particularly good on the traditions of ethnic minorities. Unlike Western newspapers, Vietnamese papers are less about what has happened (that is, news), and more about what will happen or what should happen: 'Output of fertilizer to grow 200 %' or 'Youth Volunteers to eradicate illiteracy in Central Highlands by 2002', for example. Inside the back page of *Vietnam News* is an excellent 'What's on' which is highly recommended for visitors interested in cultural events or concerts in Hanoi and Saigon.

The *Saigon Times Daily* is more business oriented and a bit dry. There are several weeklies of which the *Vietnam Investment Review* is the best, but somewhat cringeing and not a patch on what it used to be and the monthly *Vietnam Economic Times* which is very thorough and remains forthright in its views. On the web you can find: www.vnagency.com.vn Vietnam's official news agency; www.saigontimesweekly. saigonnet.vn An interesting news summary with full listings of what's on; www.saigontoday.net/index.asp A great round up of local news with fantastic photo galleries of events around town, stretching back for over a year; an amazing resource to get a real feel for Saigon.

There is news in English on the TV once in the evening, but if you have never lived in a Communist country you will not know quite how tedious visits of Party members to tractor factories or presentations of medals to Heroic Mothers, meetings of People's Committee cadres around the table etc etc can be. Makes the test card look exciting. The

Television

Essentials

Distinctive fruits

Custard apple (or sugar apple) Scaly green skin, squeeze the skin to open the fruit and scoop out the flesh with a spoon.

Durian (Durio zibethinus) A large prickly fruit, with yellow flesh, about the size of a football. Infamous for its pungent smell. While it is today regarded by many visitors as simply revolting, early Europeans (16th-18th centuries) raved about it, possibly because it was similar in taste to western delicacies of the period. Borri (1744) thought that "God himself, who had produc'd that fruit". But by 1880 Burbridge was writing: "Its odour – one scarcely feels justified in using the word 'perfume' – is so potent, so vague, but withal so insinuating, that it can scarcely be tolerated inside the house." Banned from public transport in Singapore and hotel rooms throughout the region, and beloved by most Southeast Asians (where prize specimens can cost a week's salary), it has an alluring taste if the odour can be overcome (it has been described as like eating blancmange on the toilet). Some maintain it is an addiction.

Durian-flavoured chewing gum, ice cream and jams are all available.

Jackfruit Similar in appearance to durian but not so spiky. Yellow flesh, tasting slightly like custard.

Mango (Mangifera indica) A rainforest fruit which is now cultivated. Widely available in the West; in Southeast Asia there are hundreds of different varieties with subtle variations in flavour. Delicious eaten with sticky rice and a sweet sauce (in Thailand). The best mangoes in the region are considered to be those from South Thailand.

Mangosteen (Garcinia mangostana) An aubergine-coloured hard shell covers this small fruit which is about the size of a tennis ball. Cut or squeeze the purple shell to reach its sweet white flesh which is prized by many visitors above all others. In 1898, an American resident of Java wrote, erotically and in obvious ecstasy: "The five white segments separate easily, and they melt on the tongue with a touch of tart

---

Vietnamese enjoy Chinese kung fu films which, like all foreign films, are dubbed over with a single monotone voice. Western visitors find these things rather missable. Good hotels will have cable TV which features CNN, Star Sport, BBC World, if you are lucky, and a movie channel. The only chance to watch a film on TV without dubbing in Vietnamese.

Food and drink

See page 438 for a food glossary Food is a major attraction of Vietnam and it is one of the paradoxes of this enigmatic country that so much food should be so readily and deliciously available. Eating out is so cheap that practically every meal eaten by the visitor will be taken in a restaurant or café. Saigon and Hanoi offer a wide range of cuisines besides Vietnamese, so that only Congolese, Icelandic and English tourists will be deprived of home cooking, a fate they are no doubt accustomed to.

What do you get if you cross a corpulent Chinese cook sweating in his string vest and wielding a razor-sharp chopper with a skinny, irate French chef wringing his hands over a deflated soufflé? Answer: Vietnamese cooking. Sprinkle in a good dose of nuoc mam; add lots of green leaves, chillies, innovative flair; leave to mature for several centuries and the result is some of the most exciting, original and tasty food available anywhere between Paris and Peking.

Culinary culs-de-sac Unfortunately, those staying in predominantly tourist hotels may leave the country thinking that Vietnamese cuisine consists of a narrow diet of spring rolls, crab soup, chicken in lemon grass and steamed rice – and that hardy perennial of the backpacker

and a touch of sweet; one moment a memory of the juiciest, most fragrant apple, at another a remembrance of the smoothest cream ice, the most exquisite and delicately flavoured fruit-acid known – all of the delights of nature's laboratory condensed in that ball of neige parfumée." Southeast Asians believe it should be eaten as a chaser to durian.

Papaya (Carica papaya) A New World Fruit that was not introduced into Southeast Asia until the 16th century. Large, round or oval in shape, yellow or green-skinned, with bright-orange flesh and a mass of round, black seeds in the middle. The flesh, in texture and taste, is somewhere between a mango and a melon. Some maintain that it tastes 'soapy'.

Pomelo A large round fruit the size of anything from an ostrich egg to a football, with thick, green skin, thick pith, and flesh not unlike that of the grapefruit, but less acidic.

Rambutan (Nephelium lappaceum) The bright red and hairy rambutan – rambut is the Malay word for 'hair' – with its slightly rubbery but sweet flesh is a close relative of the lychee of southern China and tastes similar. The Thai word for rambutan is ngoh, which is the nickname given by Thais to the fuzzy-haired Negrito aboriginals in the southern jungles.

Salak (Salacca edulis) A small pear-shaped fruit about the size of a large plum with a rough, brown, scaly skin (somewhat like a miniature pangolin) and yellow-white, crisp flesh. It is related to the sago and rattan trees.

Tamarind (Tamarindus indicus) Brown seedpods with dry brittle skins and a brown tart-sweet fruit which grow on a tree introduced into Southeast Asia from India. The name is Arabic for 'Indian date'. The flesh has a high tartaric acid content and is used to flavour curries, jams, jellies and chutneys as well as for cleaning brass and copper. Elephants have a predilection for tamarind balls.

café, the banana pancake. If you want to break out of this dead end cuisine and be a bit more adventurous, then the best plan of attack is to get friendly with a couple of locals – easy enough in Vietnam – and ask them to introduce you to the local fare.

A particular delight that should not be missed is pho. Pho is a bowl of flat, white, noodle soup served with chicken or beef. The soup is made from stock flavoured with star anise, ginger and other spices and herbs but individual recipes often remain a closely guarded secret. Vietnamese usually eat Pho in the morning, often in the evening but rarely at lunchtime, when they require a more filling meal accompanied by rice. On each table of a pho restaurant sits a plate of fresh green leaves: mint, cinnamon basil and the spiky looking ngo gai, together with bean sprouts, chopped red chillies, barbecue sauce and sliced lemons enabling patrons to produce their own variations on a theme. **A national favourite**

Another local speciality which visitors often overlook is com tam or broken rice. Com tam stalls abound on the streets and do brisk trade at breakfast and lunch. They tend to be low cost canteens, but in many cities they have appeal to the wealthier office market and have started to abandon tiny plastic stools in favour of proper tables and chairs and concentrate more on cleanliness and presentation. The steamed broken rice is eaten with fried chicken, fish, pork and vegetables and soup is normally included in the price.

There are many types of roll: the most common are deep-fried spring rolls (confusingly, cha gio in the south and nem ranh in the north) but if these appear on your table too frequently, look for the fresh or do-it-yourself types, such as bi cuon or bo bia. Essentially, these are salads with prawns or grilled meats wrapped in rice paper. Customers **Roll your own**

Essentials

Bird's nest soup

The tiny nests of the brown-rumped swift (Collocalia esculenta), also known as the edible-nest swiftlet or sea swallow, are collected for bird's nest soup, a Chinese delicacy, throughout Southeast Asia. The semi-oval nests are made of silk-like strands of saliva secreted by the birds which, when cooked in broth, softens and becomes a little like noodles. Like so many Chinese delicacies, the nests are believed to have aphrodisiac qualities, and the soup has even been suggested as a cure for AIDS. The red nests are the most highly valued, and the Vietnamese Emperor Minh

Mang (1820-40) is said to have owed his extraordinary vitality to his inordinate consumption of bird's nest soup. This may explain why restaurants serving it are sometimes also associated with a plethora of massage parlours. Collecting the nests is a precarious but profitable business and in some areas mafias of concessionaires vigorously guard and protect their assets. The men who collect the nests on a piecework basis risk serious injury climbing rickety ladders to cave roofs in sometimes almost total darkness, save for a candle strapped to their heads.

who roll their own cigarettes are at a distinct advantage while innocents abroad are liable to produce sagging Camberwell Carrots that collapse in the lap.

Seafood It would be invidious to isolate a particular seafood dish when there are so many to chose from. Prawns are prawns – the bigger and the less adulterated the better. But a marvellous dish that does deserve commendation is crab in tamarind sauce. This glorious fusion of flavours, bitter tamarind, garlic, piquant spring onion and fresh crab is quite delicious. To the Vietnamese, part of the fun of eating crab is the fiddly process of extracting meat from the furthest recesses of its claws and legs. A willingness to crack, crunch, poke and suck is required to do it justice, not a task for the squeamish but great for those who aren't.

Gastronomic priority When it comes to food, Vietnamese do not stand on ceremony and (perhaps rather like the French) regard peripherals such as furniture, service and ambience as mere distractions to the task of ploughing through plates, crocks, casseroles and tureens charged with piping hot meats, vegetables and soups. Do not expect good service, courses to arrive in the right order, or to eat at the same time as your companions, but do expect the freshest and tastiest food you will find anywhere. And as a rule of thumb: if you are not enjoying the food you are eating in the wrong type of place – not in the wrong country.

Markets For day trips, an early morning visit to the markets will produce a picnic fit for a king. Hard-boiled quails' eggs, thinly sliced garlic sausage and salami, pickled vegetables, beef tomatoes, cucumber, pâté, cheese and, of course, warm baguette and fresh fruit. And far from costing a king's ransom it will feed four for around a dollar a head.

Restaurants While it is possible to eat very cheaply in Vietnam (especially outside Hanoi and Saigon) the higher class of restaurant, particularly those serving foreign cuisine, can prove quite expensive, especially with wine. But with judicious shopping around it is not hard to find excellent value for money, particularly in the small, family restaurants. In the listing sections we describe a range of diners which should satisfy every palate and every pocket.

Drink Locally produced fresh **beer** is called bia hoi. It is cold and refreshing, and weak and cheap enough to drink in quite large volumes. It is usually consumed in small pavement cafés where patrons sit on small plastic stools. Most bia hoi cafés serve simple and inexpensive food. Almost all customers are men and they can get a bit jolly. As the beer is fresh it has to be consumed within a short period of brewing hence most towns, even quite small ones, have their own brewery and impart to their beer a local flavour in a way that used to happen in England before the big brewers took over.

Unfortunately bars and restaurants do not sell *bia hoi* as it's too cheap – just 3,000-4,000d per litre. Hence bar customers have a choice of *Tiger*, *Heineken*, *Carlsberg*, *San Miguel*, *333*, *Saigon Beer* or *Huda*. All are brewed in Vietnam but many visitors try to stick to the local beers (*333*, *Saigon* and *Huda*) as they are cheaper and, to many, more distinctively flavoursome than the mass produced international brands. Unfortunately this is not always possible as many bars and restaurants stock only the more expensive beers of the big international brewers which have higher mark ups.

Rice and fruit wines are produced and consumed in large quantities in upland areas, particularly in the north of Vietnam. Rice wines are fairly easily found, however. There are two types of rice wine, *ruou nep* and *ruou de*. *Ruou nep* is a viscous wine made from sticky rice. It is different colours, purple and white due to the different types of rice used to make it. Among the ethnic minorities, who are recognized as masters of rice wine, *ruou nep* is drunk from a ceramic jar through a straw. This communal drinking is an integral part of the way of life of the *montagnards* and no doubt contributes substantially to strengthening the ties of the clan. It is possible to become very drunk drinking *ruou nep* without realizing it. *Ruou de* is a rice spirit and very strong.

There is a fantastic range of different fruit wines but unless you make a real effort it can be quite hard to find them. Wines are made from just about all upland fruits, plum, strawberry, apple and, of course, grapes although grape wine in Vietnam is generally disappointing. The others are fiery and warm, strong and, by the bottle, cheap.

Shopping

Vietnam is not a haven for shoppers in the same way that other countries in the region are. Locally-produced goods are usually rather shoddy, although they can make novel gifts (the overhead lockers on most departing planes are crammed with Vietnamese conical hats). Handicrafts and traditionally-woven fabrics are good buys. Tailors are cheap and can produce skirts, shirts and jackets from patterns and photographs. And ladies, remember the *ao dai* is a most unforgiving garment, exquisite on a slender frame but unsuited to the Western build. Most fabrics tend to be synthetic but in the bigger markets there is now a lot of excellent coarse Vietnamese silk and imported cotton and wool. Antiques and authentic reproductions are available often at reasonable prices. There is a ban on the export of antiques, however, and visitors should get a licence from the customs department, a tedious and time-consuming process.

Lacquerware

Lacquerware is plentiful and cheap. Lacquer pictures are heavy to carry about and should be bought (if at all) near the end of a trip. Small lacquer trinkets, such as boxes and trays, are more portable and make nice presents. Ethnic products, fabrics, wickerware and jewellery is of course best bought (and cheapest) in the uplands but plenty is available in the two main cities. Cham fabrics, for example, are available in Saigon while those of the Thái and Hmông minorities can be widely seen in Hanoi.

Junk

Junk collectors will have a field-day in Saigon and Hanoi – many trinkets were left behind by French, Americans and Russians: old cameras, watches, cigarette lighters (most Zippos are fake), 1960s Coca Cola signs and 1930s Pernod ashtrays.

Manufacturers of outdoor wear, rucksacks, boots and training shoes have located factories in Vietnam. A considerable amount of genuine branded stock finds its way into the shops of Hanoi and Saigon at prices as little as 10% of European shop prices.

Essentials

Entertainment and nightlife

Vietnamese nightlife divides into two categories: Vietnamese and Western. The edges are becoming more diffuse with time, particularly as some Vietnamese incline towards Western tastes. The average tourist will have a good meal and repair to a bar for a drink or two, preferably one with Western sounds. The Vietnamese will go for the meal and then either to a darkened café or nip into the karaoke for an hour or two.

Bars as we know them tend not to exist far from the tourist or ex-pat populations. Cold beer, rock music and pool are easy to find in the main centres but are virtually non-existent elsewhere. Which is not to say the Vietnamese don't know how to enjoy themselves, it is just that they do things differently. A common type of Vietnamese bar is the *bia hoi*. *Bia hoi* is draught beer (fairly weak) but fresh and thirst-quenching. At around 4,000d a litre it is also remarkably good value. *Bia hoi* outlets often sell simple food dishes, *bo luc lac* (diced steak with frites), for example.

Bia ôm is altogether a different kettle of fish. *Bia ôm* bars are girlie bars and another integral part of Vietnamese social fabric. In a Vietnamese *bia ôm,* the girls drink beer with the men. There may be a certain amount of touchy feely but nothing too overt and usually the girls go home to their own beds. It is a form of geisha tea house but without the etiquette and without the tea. In seedier city quarters *bia ôm* bars are brothels.

Holidays and festivals

January **New Year's Day** (1st: public holiday).

February **Tet**, traditional new year (movable, 1st to the 7th day of the new lunar year – late January/March: public holiday). The big celebration of the year, the word Tet is the shortened version of *tet nguyen dan* ('first morning of the new period'). Tet is the time to forgive and forget, and to pay off debts. It is also everyone's birthday – the Vietnamese tend not to celebrate their birthdays, everyone adds one year to their age at Tet. Enormous quantities of food are consumed (this is not the time to worry about money), new clothes are bought, houses painted and repaired, and firecrackers lit to welcome in the new year, at least they were until the government ban imposed in 1995. As a Vietnamese saying has it: 'Hungry all year but Tet three days full.' It is believed that before Tet the spirit of the hearth, Ong Tao, leaves on a journey to visit the palace of the Jade Emperor where he must report on family affairs. To ensure that Ong Tao sets off in good cheer, a ceremony is held before Tet, Le Tao Quan, and during his absence a shrine is constructed (Cay Neu) to keep evil spirits at bay until his return. On the afternoon before Tet, Tat Nien, a sacrifice is offered at the family altar to dead relatives who are invited back to join in the festivities. Great attention is paid to preparations for Tet, because it is believed that the first week of the new year dictates the fortunes for the rest of the year. The first visitor to the house on New Year's morning should be an influential, lucky and happy person, so families take care to arrange a suitable caller.

Founding anniversary of the Communist Party of Vietnam (3rd: public holiday). It is not widely celebrated, but there are lots of conferences for Party members.

March **Hai Ba Trung Day** (movable, 6th day of 2nd lunar month). Celebrates the famous Trung sisters who led a revolt against the Chinese in AD 41 (see page 81).

April **Liberation Day of South Vietnam and Saigon** (30th: public holiday).

Thanh Minh, New Year of the Dead (5th or 6th, 3rd lunar month), or Feast of the Pure Light. People are supposed to walk outdoors to evoke the spirit of the dead and family shrines and tombs are cleaned and decorated.

International Labour Day (1st: public holiday); *Anniversary of the Birth of Ho Chi Minh* (19th: public holiday); *Celebration of the birth, death and enlightenment of the Buddha* (15th day of the 4th lunar month) not a public holiday but one marked by Buddhists. — **May**

Trung Nguyen or Wandering Souls Day (movable, 15th day of the 7th lunar month). One of the most important festivals. During this time, prayers can absolve the sins of the dead who leave hell and return, hungry and naked, to their relatives. The Wandering Souls are those with no homes to go to. There are celebrations in Buddhist temples and homes, food is placed out on tables, and money is burned. — **August**

National Day (2nd: public holiday). — **September**

President Ho's Anniversary (3rd: public holiday).

Tet Trung Thu or Mid Autumn Festival (movable, 15th day of the 8th month). Particularly celebrated by children. Moon cakes are baked, lanterns made and painted, and children parade through towns with music and lanterns.

Confucius' Birthday (movable, 28th day of the 9th month). — **November**

Sport and special interest travel

Trekking is an increasingly popular activity in Vietnam. The main focus for this activity is Sapa, in the north of the country, but some trekking is organized around Dalat. Around Sapa there are walks of varying durations demanding different fitness levels and degrees of stamina. Many of the tour operators in Hanoi, listed on page 96, organize trekking tours. Some of these treks are straight forward and can be done without guides or support (ask your guesthouse for routes), others will require accommodation. Unfortunately there are no accurate maps available for walkers (or any other activity) in Vietnam. One or two agencies and guesthouses in Sapa organize climbing: for the fittest there is Mount Fan Si Pan at 3,143 m. Opportunities for camping in Vietnam are limited mainly because the authorities insist on foreign visitors sleeping in registered accommodation. There are no campsites but visitors bringing their tents may be able to use them around Sapa or on Cat Ba and surrounding islands. Some guesthouses in Mui Ne and other seaside places have tents. — **Trekking, climbing & camping**

Vietnam may not seem like the first choice for a birdwatching holiday (indeed, many visitors comment on the fact that there are so few birds around) but for those birders in the know it has become one of the top birding destinations of the region in recent years. The reason why there is all this birding interest in Vietnam is its endemic species, 10 in total. This is the highest number of endemic bird species of any country in mainland Southeast Asia. Around 850 species have been recorded in Vietnam but in a three-week intensive birding trip it should be possible to tick off around 250-300 species. The places to head for are Cat Tien National Park, the Dalat Plateau, Bach Ma National Park, and Cuc Phuong National Park. Other areas of particular interest to birders are Tram Chim Nature Reserve in the Mekong Delta, the northern hill stations of Tam Dao and Sapa and the Xuan Thuy Nature Reserve in the Red River Delta (for wintering waders). For more information or advice on birding in Vietnam, contact Richard Craik of *Exotissimo Travel* at richard@exotissimo.com — **Birdwatching**

Being flat over great distances cycling is a popular activity. The main problem is the peril on Vietnamese roads due to traffic. It's recommended that any tour is planned off-road or on minor roads, not Highway 1. *Symbiosis*, www.symbiosis-travel.com, has established a particular expertise in the organization of cycling challenges both to Vietnam (from Bangkok) and around Vietnam. Many cyclists prefer to bring their own all-terrain or racing bikes but it's also possible to rent from tour organizers. — **Cycling**

Diving & snorkelling Snorkelling in the seas of Vietnam is a distinctly limited activity. Much of the coast is muddy deltaic swamp. Away from the deltas the water is still quite turbid, reflecting high levels of soil erosion. In those places where snorkelling and diving is reckoned to be good (Nha Trang, page 241, and Phu Quoc, page 344) it is possible for a few months of the year in the dry season only (November-April). Dynamite fishing and anchor damage limit diving in Nha Trang, leaving only Phu Quoc where diving establishments are only just beginning to appear.

Health

The health care in Vietnam is varied: there are some decent private and government clinics and hospitals, but as with all medical care, first impressions count. If a facility is grubby and staff wear grey coats instead of white ones, then be wary of the general standard of medicine and hygiene. If you do get ill, the hospitals and clinics listed under the main centres in this book are the most highly regarded in the country. If they cannot treat you they will know where you should be sent.

Before you go Ideally, you should see your GP or travel clinic at least six weeks before your departure for general advice on travel risks, malaria and vaccinations. Make sure you have travel insurance, get a dental check (especially if you are going to be away for more than a month), know your own blood group and if you suffer a long-term condition such as diabetes or epilepsy make sure someone knows or that you have a Medic Alert bracelet/necklace with this information on it.

Vaccinations for your Vietnam trip

Vaccination	Recommended
Polio	Yes if none in last 10 years
Tetanus	Yes if none in last 10 years (but after five doses you have had enough for life)
Typhoid	Yes if none in last three years
Yellow Fever	The disease does not exist in Vietnam. However, the authorities may wish to see a certificate if you have recently arrived form an endemic area in Africa or South America.
Rabies	Yes if travelling to jungle and/or remote areas
Hepatitis A	Yes - the disease can be caught easily from food/water
Japanese Encephalitis	May be advised for some areas, depending on the duration of the trip and proximity to rice growing and pig-farming areas.
BCG	We are not sure how much protection this vaccination gives the traveller against lung tuberculosis but I would currently advise people to have it in the absence of any better alternative.

Malaria in Vietnam The deadly *P.falciparum* malaria, in a form that is resistant to chloroquine, exists in most of the country, especially high risk are the two southernmost provinces Ca Mau and Bac Lieu, and some highland areas. Despite the fact that the risk may be low and almost non-existent in some areas, the boundaries are not so clear-cut that you should risk exposing yourself to a fatal disease. Areas with low/no risk of deadly *P.falciparum* are truly urban areas, the Red River delta, and the coastal plains north of Nha Trang. The choice of malaria prophylaxis will need to be something other than chloroquine for most people, since there is such a high level of resistance to it. Always check with your doctor or travel clinic for the most up-to-date advice.

Anti-malarials Important to take for the key areas. Specialist advice is required as to which type to take. General principles are that all except Malarone should be continued for four weeks after leaving the malarial area. Malarone needs to be continued for only seven days afterwards (if a tablet is missed or vomited seek specialist advice). The start times for the anti-malarials vary in that if you have never taken Lariam (Mefloquine) before it is advised to start it at least 2-3 weeks before the entry to a malarial zone (this is to help identify serious side-effects early). Chloroquine and Paludrine are often started a week before the trip to establish a pattern but Doxycycline and Malarone can be started only 1-2 days before entry to the malarial area. **NB** It is risky to buy medicinal tablets abroad because the doses may differ and there may be a trade in false drugs.

Mosquito repellents Remember that DEET (Di-ethyltoluamide) is the gold standard. Apply the repellent every 4-6 hours but more often if you are sweating heavily. If a non-DEET product is used, check who tested it. Validated products (tested at the London School of Hygiene and Tropical Medicine) include *Mosiguard*, Non-DEET *Jungle formula* and non-DEET *Autan*. If you want to use citronella remember that it must be applied very frequently (that is hourly) to be effective. If you are a popular target for insect bites or develop lumps quite soon after being bitten, carry an Aspivenin kit. This syringe suction device is available from many chemists and draws out some of the allergic materials and provides quick relief. For anti-malarial tablets, see above.

Sun block The Australians have a great campaign, which has reduced skin cancer. It is called Slip, Slap, Slop. Slip on a shirt, Slap on a hat, Slop on sun screen.

Pain killers Paracetomol or a suitable painkiller can have multiple uses for symptoms but remember that more than eight paractemol a day can lead to liver failure.

Ciproxin A useful antibiotic for some forms of travellers diarrhoea (see below).

Immodium A great standby for those diarrhoeas that occur at awkward times (that is before a long coach/train journey or on a trek). It helps stop the flow of diarrhoea and in my view is of more benefit than harm. (It was believed that letting the bacteria or viruses flow out had to be more beneficial. However, with Immodium they still come out, just in a more solid form.)

Pepto-Bismol Used a lot by Americans for diarrhoea. It certainly relieves symptoms but like Immodium it is not a cure for underlying disease. Be aware that it turns the stool black as well as making it more solid.

MedicAlert These simple bracelets, or an equivalent, should be carried or worn by anyone with a significant medical condition.

For longer trips involving jungle treks, taking a clean needle pack, clean dental pack and water filtration devices are common-sense measures.

Websites **Foreign and Commonwealth Office** (FCO) (UK) www.fco.gov.uk This is a key travel advice site, with useful information on the country, people, climate and lists the UK embassies/consulates. The site also promotes the concept of 'Know Before You Go'. It also encourages the purchase of travel insurance and appropriate travel health advice. It has links to the Department of Health travel advice site, see below.

Department of Health Travel Advice (UK) www.doh.gov.uk/traveladvice This excellent site is also available as a free booklet, the T6, from Post offices. It lists the vaccine advice requirements for each country.

Medic Alert (UK) www.medicalalert.co.uk This is the website of the foundation that produces bracelets and necklaces for those with existing medical problems. Once you have ordered your bracelet/necklace you write your key medical details on paper inside it, so that if you collapse, a medical person can identify you as someone with epilepsy or allergy to peanuts etc.

Blood Care Foundation (UK) www.bloodcare.org.uk The Blood Care Foundation is a charity 'dedicated to the provision of screened blood and resuscitation fluids in countries where these are not readily available.' They will dispatch certified non-infected blood of the right type to your hospital. The blood is flown in from centres around the world.

Items to take with you

Essentials

Further Information

Public Health Laboratory Service (UK) **www.phls.org.uk** This site has up-to-date malaria advice guidelines for travel around the world. It gives specific advice about the right drugs for each location. It also has useful information for those who are pregnant, suffering from epilepsy or planning to travel with children.

Centers for Disease Control and Prevention (USA) **www.cdc.gov** This site from the US Government gives excellent advice on travel health, has useful disease maps and details of disease outbreaks.

World Health Organisation www.who.int The WHO site has links to the WHO Blue Book (it was Yellow up to last year) on travel advice. This lists the diseases in different regions of the world. It describes vaccination schedules and makes clear which countries have Yellow Fever Vaccination certificate requirements and malarial risk.

Tropical Medicine Bureau (Ireland) **www.tmb.ie** This Irish-based site has a good collection of general travel health information and disease risks.

Fit for Travel (UK) **www.fitfortravel.scot.nhs.uk** This site from Scotland provides a quick A-Z of vaccine and travel health advice requirements for each country.

British Travel Health Association (UK) **www.btha.org** This is the official website of an organization of travel health professionals.

NetDoctor (UK) **www.Netdoctor.co.uk** This general health advice site has a useful section on travel and has an 'ask the expert', interactive chat forum.

Travel Screening Services (UK) **www.travelscreening.co.uk** This is the author's website. A private clinic dedicated to integrated travel health. The clinic gives vaccine, travel health advice, email and SMS text vaccine reminders and screens travellers who have returned, for tropical diseases.

Books & leaflets *The Travellers Good Health Guide* by **Dr Ted Lankester** (ISBN 0-85969-827-0.) *Expedition Medicine* (The Royal Geographic Society) **Editors David Warrell and Sarah Anderson** (ISBN 1 86197 040-4.) *International Travel and Health* **World Health Organisation**, Geneva (ISBN 92 4 158026 7.) *The World's Most Dangerous Places* by **Robert Young Pelton, Coskun Aral and Wink Dulles** (ISBN 1-566952-140-9.)

The Travellers Guide to Health (T6) can be obtained by calling the Health Literature Line on 0800 555 777. Advice for travellers on avoiding the risks of HIV and AIDS (*Travel Safe*) available from Department of Health, PO Box 777, London SE1 6XH. *The Blood Care Foundation* order form PO Box 7, Sevenoaks, Kent TN13 2SZ T44-(0)1732-742427.

On the road

The key viral disease is **Dengue fever** (see page 60), which is transmitted by mosquitos that bite during the day. The disease is like a very nasty form of the flu with 2-3 days of illness, followed by a short period of recovery, then a second attack of illness. The south of Vietnam suffered a serious epidemic of Dengue in 1998. Westerners very rarely get the worst haemorrhagic form of the disease. Bacterial diseases include **tuberculosis** (TB) and some causes of the more common traveller's **diarrhoea**.

Diarrhoea & intestinal upset
This is almost inevitable. One study showed that up to 70% of all travellers may suffer during their trip

Symptoms Diarrhoea can refer either to loose stools or an increased frequency; both of these can be a nuisance. It should be short lasting but persistence beyond two weeks, with blood or pain, require specialist medical attention.

Cures Ciproxin (Ciprofloaxcin) is a useful antibiotic for bacterial traveller's diarrhoea. It can be obtained by private prescription in the UK which is expensive, or bought over the counter in Vietnam pharmacies. You need to take one 500 mg tablet when the diarrhoea starts and if you do not feel better in 24 hours, the diarrhoea is likely to have a non-bacterial cause and may be viral (in which case there is little you can do apart from keep yourself rehydrated and wait for it to settle on its own). The key treatment with all diarrhoeas is rehydration. Try to keep hydrated by taking the right mixture of salt, sugar and water.

This is available as Oral Rehydration Salts (ORS) in ready-made sachets or can be made up by adding a teaspoon of sugar and a half teaspoon of salt to a litre of clean water. Drink at least one large cup of this drink for each loose stool. You can also use flat carbonated drinks as an alternative. Immodium and Pepto-Bismol provide symptomatic relief.

Prevention Be careful with water and ice for drinking. Ask yourself where the water came from. If you have any doubts then boil it or filter and treat it. There are many filter/treatment devices on the market. Food can also transmit disease. Be wary of salads (what were they washed in), re-heated foods or food that has been left out in the sun, having been cooked earlier in the day. There is a simple adage that says wash it, peel it, boil it or forget it. Also be wary of unpasteurized dairy products, these can transmit a range of diseases from brucellosis (fevers and constipation), to listeria (meningitis) and tuberculosis of the gut (obstruction, constipation, fevers and weight loss).

Essentials

Symptoms Malaria can cause death within 24 hours and Vietnam can be considered a high-risk country. It can start as something just resembling an attack of flu. You may feel tired, lethargic, headachy; or worse, develop fits, followed by coma and then death. Have a low index of suspicion because it is very easy to write off vague symptoms, which may actually be malaria. All clinics in Vietnam can test for malaria quickly and reliably. If you come down with a fever, get tested as quickly as possible.

Malaria & insect bite prevention

Cures Treatment is with drugs and may be oral or into a vein depending on the seriousness of the infection. Remember ABCD: Awareness (of whether the disease is present in the area you are travelling in), Bite avoidance, Chemoprohylaxis, Diagnosis.

Prevention This is best summarized by the B and C of the ABCD, bite avoidance and chemoprophylaxis. Wear clothes that cover arms and legs and use effective insect repellents. Use a mosquito net dipped in permethrin as both a physical and chemical barrier at night in the same areas. Guard against the contraction of malaria with the correct anti-malarials (see above). The Royal Homeopathic Hospital in the UK does not advocate homeopathic options for malaria prevention or treatment.

Symptoms If you go diving make sure that you are fit to do so. *The British Scuba Association* (BSAC), Telford's Quay, South Pier Road, Ellesmere Port, Cheshire CH65 4FL, United Kingdom, T01513-506200, F506215, www.bsac.com, can put you in touch with doctors who do medical examinations. Protect your feet from cuts, beach dog parasites (larva migrans) and sea urchins. The latter are almost impossible to remove but can be dissolved with lime or vinegar. Keep an eye out for secondary infection.

Underwater health

Cures Antibiotics for secondary infections. Serious diving injuries may need time in a decompression chamber.

Prevention Check that the dive company know what they are doing, have appropriate certification from *BSAC* or *Professional Association of Diving Instructors* (PADI), (Unit 7, St Philips Central, Albert Rd, St Philips, Bristol BS2 0TD, T0117-3007234, www.padi.com), and that the equipment is well-maintained.

Symptoms White Britons are notorious for becoming red in hot countries because they like to stay out longer than everyone else and do not use adequate sun protection. This can lead to sunburn. Aloe vera gel is a good pain reliever. Long-term sun damage leads to a loss of elasticity of skin and the development of pre-cancerous lesions. Many years later cancers may develop. There is the milder basal cell carcinoma, if detected early, can be treated by cutting it out or freezing it. The much nastier malignant melanoma may have already spread to bone and brain at the time that it is first noticed.

Sun protection

Prevention Sun screen. SPF stands for Sun Protection Factor. It is measured by determining how long a given person takes to 'burn' with and without the sunscreen product on. So, if it takes 10 times longer to burn with the sunscreen product applied, then that product has an SPF of 10. If it only takes twice as long then the SPF is 2. The higher the SPF the greater the protection. However, do not just use higher factors just to stay out in the sun longer. 'Flash frying' (desperate bursts of excessive exposure), as it is called, is known to increase the risks of skin cancer. Follow the Australians' with their Slip, Slap, Slop campaign.

Dengue fever

Symptoms This disease can be contracted throughout Vietnam. In travellers this can cause a severe flu-like illness which includes symptoms of fever, lethargy, enlarged lymph glands and muscle pains. It starts suddenly, lasts for 2-3 days, seems to get better for 2-3 days and then kicks in again for another 2-3 days. It is usually all over in an unpleasant week. The local children are prone to the much nastier haemorrhagic form of the disease, which often leads to their death.

Cures The traveller's version of the disease is self-limiting and forces rest and recuperation on the sufferer.

Prevention The mosquitoes that carry the Dengue virus bite during the day, unlike the malaria mosquitoes. Which sadly means that repellent application and covered limbs are a 24-hour issue. Check your accommodation for flower pots and shallow pools of water, since these are where the dengue-carrying mosquitoes breed.

Hepatitis

Symptoms Hepatitis means inflammation of the liver. Viral causes of the disease can be acquired anywhere in Vietnam. The most obvious symptom is a yellowing of your skin or the whites of your eyes. However, prior to this, all you may notice is itching and tiredness.

Cures Early on, depending on the type of hepatitis, a vaccine or immunoglobulin may reduce the duration of the illness.

Prevention Pre-travel hepatitis A vaccine is the best bet. Hepatitis B (for which there is a vaccine) is spread through blood and unprotected sex. Both can be avoided. Unfortunately there is no vaccine for hepatitis C, or the increasing list of other Hepatitis viruses.

Lung fluke (paragonimiasis)

The lung fluke occurs in Vietnam. A fluke is a sort of flattened worm. In the Sin Ho district the locals like to eat undercooked or raw crabs, my advice is to leave them to it. The crabs contain a fluke which, when eaten, travels to the lungs.

Symptoms The lung fluke may cause a cough, coughing 'blood', fever, chest pain and changes on your X-ray which will puzzle a British radiologist.

Cures The same drug that cures Schistosomiasis (another fluke which can be acquired in some parts of the Mekong delta) can be used for the lung fluke. However, this infestation takes longer and is more difficult to treat.

Prevention Avoid infected waters, be careful with unwashed vegetables (especially in the Altiplano) and check the CDC, WHO websites and a travel clinic specialist for up-to-date information on the whereabouts of the disease.

Tuberculosis

This old disease is still a significant problem in Ho Chi Minh and many other areas. The bus driver coughing as he takes your fare could expose you to the mycobacterium.

Symptoms Cough, tiredness, fever and lethargy.

Cures At least six months treatment with a combination of drugs is required.

Prevention Have a BCG vaccination before you go and see a doctor early if you have a persistent cough, cough blood, fever or unexplained weight loss.

Sexual health

If you do stray, consider getting a sexual health check on your return home

The range of visible and invisible diseases is awesome. Unprotected sex can spread HIV, Hepatitis B and C, Gonorrhea (green discharge), chlamydia (nothing to see, but may cause painful urination and later female infertility), painful recurrent herpes, syphilis and warts, just to name a few. You can cut down the risk by using condoms. Commercial sex workers in Vietnam have high levels of HIV.

The health section was written by **Dr Charlie Easmon** MBBS MRCP MSc Public Health DTM&H DOccMed Director of Travel Screening Services.

Hanoi

Hanoi

64 **Ins and outs**

64 Getting there

64 Getting around

64 Orientation

64 Tourist information

64 Background

68 Sights

81 Excursions

86 **Essentials**

86 Sleeping

90 Eating

94 Bars

94 Cafés

94 Entertainment

95 Shopping

96 Tour operators

97 Transport

99 Directory

Hanoi

Hanoi is the capital of the Socialist Republic of Vietnam. It lies nearly 100 km from the sea on a bend in the Red River. From this geographical feature the city derives its name – Hanoi means 'within a river bend'. It is a city of broad, tree-lined boulevards, lakes, parks, weathered colonial buildings, elegant squares and some of the newest office blocks and hotels in Southeast Asia. The history of the city must be the most confusing of any oriental capital: established as a defensive citadel in the eighth century it has had at least seven names since then and has served a country of fluctuating borders.

Hanoi is the capital of the world's 14th most populous country. Nevertheless, in an age of urban sprawl, the city remains small and compact, historic and charming. Hanoians may be dour and xenophobic and their leaders austere but the large diplomatic community brings a cosmopolitan feel. And a younger generation has proved willing to engage with the outside world. Consequently the feel of Hanoi is very different – and pleasantly so – from what it was just 10 years ago. "At Saigon one exists; at Hanoi one lives." This was the opinion of one 19th-century visitor (Joleaud-Barral) and it is a view increasingly echoed today.

Hanoi has a wealth of historical sights lying as it does at the heart of a region rich in history and landscapes. There is a huge amount to explore and few can hope to see it all, so careful planning is necessary.

Ins and outs

Getting there

Phone code: 04
Colour map 1, grid B4
Population: 2,841,700

See Transport,
page 97, for further
details and Airport
Information in
Essentials, page 33

While Hanoi may be Vietnam's capital city, it is not as well connected as Saigon in the south. The airport is 50 km from the city, about a 1-hr drive. There are taxis and a mini-bus service that drops passengers at their hotels. Hotels also have their own buses.

There are regular flights to a number of international destinations as well as connections with six towns and cities within Vietnam. The train station is central, about a 5-10-min taxi ride from the Old Quarter of the city north of Hoan Kiem Lake. There are regular trains to Saigon, and all points on the route south, as well as to Haiphong and Lao Cai in the north. There are also 4 trains each day to Kunming, the capital of China's Yunnan Province. There is not just 1 bus terminal but several serving destinations in the north and major towns all the way south to Saigon.

Getting around

Hanoi is getting more frenetic by the minute as wealth is invested in the internal combustion engine. With its elegant, tree-lined boulevards walking and bicycling can be delightful. If you like the idea of being pedalled, then a *cyclo* is the answer – but be prepared for some concentrated haggling. There are also motorbike taxis (*xe ôm*), self-drive motorbikes for hire as well as a fleet of metered taxis.

Orientation

Hanoi can be parcelled up into a number of districts each with its own feel and function. At the heart of the city is Hoan Kiem Lake. The majority of visitors make straight for the Old City or 36 Streets area north of the lake, which is densely packed and bustling with commerce. The French Quarter, which still largely consists of French buildings, is south of the lake. Here are the Opera House and the grandest hotels, shops and offices. A large block of the city west of Hoan Kiem Lake (Ba Dinh District) represents the heart of government and the civil and military administration of Vietnam. Imposing colonial architecture, the mark of authority of the French administration, is now occupied by Vietnamese government ministries. All around this district colonial villas are occupied by foreign embassies. To the north of the city is the West Lake, Tay Ho District, fringed with the suburban homes of the new middle class. Away to the southern and eastern edges of the city are the industrial and residential zones.

Tourist information

There are numerous travel cafés which offer plenty of advice, tours and transport to travellers. See under Travel Cafés, page 94.

Background

The original village on the site of the present city was located in a district with the local name of Long Do. The community seems to have existed as a small settlement as early as the third century AD, although the early history of the Red River Delta largely passed it by. At the beginning of the eighth century a general named Lu Yu became so enchanted with the scenery around the village of An Vien (close to Long Do), that he decided to move his headquarters there. Here he built a shrine to the Emperor Hsuan Tsung, erected an

24 hours in the city

Little Hanoi is a great place to start the day: delicious coffee and breakfast. Thus fortified, try to cover as many of Hanoi's sites as you can, but not at too rapid a pace for it is important to soak up the charm and atmosphere and take frequent stops for coffee and refreshments at the cafés. Out of respect for the great man perhaps we should begin at **Ho Chi Minh's Mausoleum**. From the Mausoleum it is a short walk to **Ho's house** and the engaging **One Pillar Pagoda**. Of considerable historical interest is the **Temple of Literature** which can be reached comfortably on foot.

Right behind is the **Fine Arts Museum**, one of many beautifully housed historical collections in Hanoi. This or the **History Museum** (a taxi or cyclo ride away) are well worth looking at. Close to the **History Museum** is Hanoi's **Opera House** which is spectacular even from the outside. Pop into the historic *Metropole Hotel* for coffee or something a little stronger or stroll back to one of several cafés around Hoan Kiem Lake which makes the delightful **Ngoc Son Pagoda** on an island in the lake the next obvious port of call.

There are so many good restaurants to choose from for lunch that decisions will be tricky. Vietnamese people eat simply, cheaply and well so follow them into what looks like a popular restaurant and you will not be disappointed.

In the afternoon the **36 Streets** area of the Old City are great to explore on foot. Many are still functioning commercial streets, it is fascinating to observe the pattern of daily life and trade: others are more geared to tourists and have clothes and souvenirs for sale. Wander along the shops on Hang Gai Street and down into Ly Quoc Su and Nha Tho streets where there are some interesting galleries and boutiques.

An early evening visit to the water puppet show at the theatre near Hoan Kiem Lake will amuse and entertain. Then a great range of Vietnamese, Italian or French restaurants is at your disposal for dinner but be quick as some (particularly Vietnamese) close quite early.

After dinner the best place to head is Hang Hanh Street. Here there are countless cafés and bars from which to choose. They tend to close early (midnight is the current edict) in which case make your way to *Apocalypse Now* or cruise around the Old City looking for a late night bowl of *pho*.

inscribed tablet, and dedicated a statue of the local earth spirit on which was inscribed a poem extolling the beauty of the spot.

The origins of Hanoi as a great city lie with a temple orphan, Ly Cong Uan. Ly rose through the ranks of the palace guards to become their commander and in 1010, four years after the death of the previous King Le Hoan, was enthroned, marking the beginning of the 200-year-long Ly Dynasty. On becoming king, Ly Cong Uan moved his capital from Hoa Lu to Dai La, which he renamed **Thang Long** or 'Soaring Dragon'. Thang Long is present-day **Hanoi**. During the Ly Dynasty the heart of Thang Long was the king's sanctuary in the Forbidden City (Cam Thanh). Drawing both spiritual and physical protection, as well as economic well-being from their proximity to the king and his court, a city of commoners grew-up around the walls of Cam Thanh. The Ly kings established a Buddhist monarchical tradition, which mirrored other courts in Southeast Asia. A number of pagodas were built at this time – most have since disappeared, although the One Pillar Pagoda and the Tran Vu Temple both date from this period (see below).

Thang Long, renamed **Tay Do** (Western Capital), was to remain the capital of Vietnam until 1400 when the Ho Dynasty (1400-07) established a new

Hanoi

Hanoi's names:
(AD 200-present)

Long Bien	AD 200
Dai La	900-1010
Thang Long	1010-1400
Tay Do	1400-1428
Dong Kinh	1428-1789
Bac Thanh	1789-1831
Hanoi	1831-

capital at Thanh Hoa. But soon afterwards, the focus of power shifted back to Thang Long which, in turn, was renamed **Dong Kinh** (Eastern Capital) and **Bac Thanh** (Northern Citadel). It is from Dong Kinh that the French name for Northern Vietnam – Tonkin – is derived. The present name of the city dates from 1831 when the Nguyen Emperor Tu Duc (1847-83) made it the capital of the province of Hanoi.

Colonial era During the period of French expansion into Indochina, the Red River was proposed as an alternative trade route to that of the Mekong. Francis Garnier, a French naval officer, was dispatched to the area in 1873 to ascertain the possibilities of establishing such a route. Despite having only a modest force of men under arms, when negotiations with Emperor Tu Duc failed in 1882, Garnier attacked and captured the citadel of Hanoi under the dubious pretext that the Vietnamese were about to attack him. Recognizing that if a small expeditionary force could be so successful, then there would be little chance against a full-strength army, Tu Duc acceded to French demands. At the time that the French took control of Annam, Hanoi could still be characterized more as a collection of villages than a city. As late as the 1870s, the French scholar André Masson, for example, argued that Hanoi "was not a city but a composite agglomeration where an administrative capital, a commercial town and numerous villages were juxtaposed". Indeed, the oldest name for Hanoi seems to have been *Ke Cho*, which means, 'a place where markets are'.

From 1882 onwards, Hanoi, along with the port city of Haiphong, became the focus of French activity in the north. Hanoi was made the capital of the new colony of Annam, and the French laid out a 2 sq km residential and business district, constructing mansions, villas and public buildings incorporating both French and Asian architectural styles. Many of these buildings still stand to the south and east of the Old City and Hoan Kiem Lake – almost as if they were grafted onto the older Annamese city. In the 1920s and 1930s, with conditions in the countryside deteriorating, there was an influx of landless and dispossessed labourers into the city. In their struggle to feed their families, many were willing to take jobs at subsistence wages in the textile, cigarette and other industries that grew up under French patronage. Before long, a poor underclass, living in squalid, pathetic conditions, had formed. At the end of the Second World War, with the French battling to keep Ho Chi Minh and his forces at bay, Hanoi became little more than a service centre. By 1954 there were about 40,000 stallholders, shopkeepers, peddlars and hawkers operating in the city – which at that time had a population of perhaps 400,000. It has been calculated that one out of every two families relied on the informal sector for their livelihoods.

War damage After the French withdrew in 1954, Ho Chi Minh concentrated on building up Vietnam and in particular Hanoi's industrial base. At that time the capital had only eight, small, privately-owned factories. By 1965, more than 1,000 enterprises had been added to this figure. However, as the US bombing of the north intensified with Operation Rolling Thunder in 1965, so the authorities began to evacuate non-essential civilians from Hanoi and to disperse industry

Beautiful Hanoi needs a miracle, says British MP

When the French were unceremoniously bundled out of Vietnam in 1954 they did not leave much behind in the way of infrastructure, but they did leave Hanoi – one of the world's most beautiful cities. Built around more than 20 lakes, Hanoi consists of avenues lined with tamarind trees, elegant villas and magnificent public buildings. Decades of war and years of economic stagnation brought terrible decay, but not destruction. Hanoi has survived almost intact.

Alas the end is nigh. The arrival of the free market means that the planners now have the resources to succeed where the B-52 bombers failed. Unless a miracle occurs, Hanoi is about to be destroyed.

Already concrete monstrosities are rising in the most unlikely places. By Hoan Kiem lake in the city centre a ghastly confection of concrete and marble now dominates the skyline amid the yellow stucco and green wooden shutters of the public buildings left by the French. It is the new city hall. In this building dwell the very planners whose job is to regulate the development of the city. It is hard to think of a more ominous portent.

What is most lacking is not funds but political will. Government and local authority leaders pay lip service to the preservation of old Hanoi, but there has been little in the way of action. A ban on private cars in the old city would be a good start. Strict controls over new building would be another.

If the political will existed, it would not be hard to generate foreign support. "There is not one of my colleagues who has not raised this with the Vietnamese Government," an ambassador wrote to me. Another said, "I say to the Vietnamese, when you can demonstrate the will to preserve your city, I will find funds to pay for a consultant to advise how it might be done."

What irony. A country that has suffered so much at the hands of rapacious foreigners is now on the point of surrender to a culture at least as foreign and at least as destructive as that which it paid such a high price to defeat.

Source: Extracted from an article written by Chris Mullin, MP, for the Vietnam Investment Review.

into smaller, less vulnerable, units of operation. Between 500,000 and 750,000 people were evacuated between 1965 and 1973, representing 75% of the inner-city population. When hostilities ended in 1973, one Soviet reporter estimated that a quarter of all buildings had been destroyed. Nevertheless, the cessation of hostilities led to a spontaneous migration back into the capital. By 1984 the population of the city had reached 2.7 million, and today it is in excess of three million.

Urban renewal Although Saigon has attracted the lion's share of Vietnam's foreign inward investment, Hanoi, as the capital, also receives a large amount. But whereas Saigon's investment tends to be in industry, Hanoi has received a great deal of attention from property developers, notably in the hotel and office sectors. Much of the development has been in prestigious and historical central Hanoi and included the construction of a huge office complex on the site of the notorious 'Hanoi Hilton' prison, much to the mortification of Vietnamese war veterans, see page 74. Some commentators applauded the authorities for this attempt at putting the past behind them.

British MP Chris Mullin has written an impassioned attack on some architecturally insensitive schemes (see box above) and drawn attention to Vietnamese politicians' disturbing haste to redevelop prime, historical sites.

Fortunately Hanoi attracts a large number of foreigners, both expats (mainly diplomats and professionals) and tourists. Numerous old colonial villas have been tastefully restored as bars, restaurants and homes to cater to this large and generally discerning market, with a very positive effect on Hanoi's architectural heritage.

Pollution levels in Hanoi have soared as a result of the construction boom: dust from demolition, piling, bricks and tiles and sand blown from the back of trucks add an estimated 150 cu m of pollutants to the urban atmosphere every day. But while asthmatics may wheeze, Hanoi's army of builders grows daily ever stronger. Hundreds of farmers join the urban job market each week and one can see bands of men standing around at strategic points waiting to be recruited; on Duong Thanh Street, for example, carpenters with their tool boxes wait patiently for the call to a day's work. But can Hanoi's economy keep pace with the rate of migration in from the countryside? Against the background of the Asian financial crisis of the late 1990s the situation looked ominous but the stage now seems set for a period of sustained growth. In addition, by means of a strict system of residential permits the Party is able to control the rate at which people settle in the capital. Without the proper papers stamped with a round red seal children cannot go to school. As education is one of the highest priorities for many Vietnamese parents it curbs their enthusiasm for moving to the city. It also helps explain the bands of boys who roam the banks of Hoan Kiem Lake selling postcards or looking for shoes to shine.

Sights

Much of the charm of Hanoi lies not so much in the official 'sights' (some of which can be decidedly uninspired) but in the unofficial and informal: the traffic, small shops, stalls, the bustle of pedestrians, clothing, parents treating their children to an ice cream, an evening visit to Hoan Kiem Lake. Like China when it was 'opening-up' to Western tourists in the late 1970s, the primary interest lies in the novelty of exploring a city which, until recently, has opted for a firmly socialist road to development and has been insulated from the West.

Hanoi's sights are centred in two main areas: around Hoan Kiem Lake and in the vicinity of Ho Chi Minh's Mausoleum. There are also some sights which fall outside these two areas.

Hoan Kiem Lake & Central Hanoi Hoan Kiem Lake (the Lake of the Restored Sword), or Ho Guom as it is more commonly referred to in Hanoi, is named after an incident that occurred during the 15th century. Emperor Le Thai To (1428-33), following a momentous victory against an army of invading Ming Chinese, was sailing on the lake when a golden turtle appeared from the depths to take back the charmed sword which had secured the victory and restore it to the lake from whence it came. Like the sword in the stone of British Arthurian legend, Le Thai To's sword assures Vietnamese of divine intervention in time of national crisis and the story is graphically portrayed in water puppet theatres across the country. There is a modest and rather dilapidated tower (the Tortoise Tower) commemorating the event on an islet in the southern part of the lake. In fact, the lake does contain large turtles; one captured in 1968 was reputed to have weighed 250 kg. The creatures that inhabit the lake are believed to be a variety of Asian softshell tortoise. The park that surrounds the lake is used by the residents of the city every morning for jogging and tai chi (Chinese shadow boxing) and is regarded by locals as one of the city's beauty spots. When the French arrived in Hanoi at the end of the 19th century, the lake was an unhealthy lagoon surrounded by so many huts that it was impossible to see the shore.

The northeast corner is *the* place to have your photo taken, preferably with the **Ngoc Son (Jade Hill) Pagoda** (see illustration) in the background. The pagoda was built in the early 19th century on a small island and is linked to the shore by a red, arched wooden bridge – the **The Huc (Sunbeam) Bridge** constructed in 1875. The temple is dedicated to Van Xuong, the God of Literature, although the 13th-century hero Tran Hung Dao, the martial arts genius Quan Vu and the physician La To are also worshipped here. Shrouded by trees and surrounded by water, the pagoda's position is its strongest attribute. ■ *12,000d.*

Old City & 36 Streets

Hanoi

Stretching north from the lake is the **Old City**. Previously, it lay to the east of the citadel, where the emperor had his residence, and was squalid, dark, cramped and disease-ridden. This part of Hanoi has survived surprisingly intact, and today is the most beautiful area of the city. Narrow streets, each named after the produce that it sells or used to sell (Basket Street, Paper Street, Silk Street etc), create an intricate web of activity and colour. Another name for the area is **36 Streets** or **36 Pho Phuong**. By the 15th century there were 36 short lanes here, each specializing in a particular trade and representing one of the 36 guilds. Among them, for example, were the Phuong Hang Dao or Dyers' Guild Street, and the Phuong Hang Bac, the Silversmiths' Street. The 36 streets have interested European visitors since they first started visiting Hanoi. Samuel Bacon, in 1685, for example, noted how "all the diverse objects sold in this town have a specially assigned street", remarking how different this was from "companies and corporations in European cities". The streets in question not only sold different products, but were usually also populated by people from different areas of the country – even from single villages. They would live, work and worship together because each of the occupational guilds had its own temple and its own community support networks.

Some of this past is still in evidence: at the south end of Hang Dau Street, for example, is a mass of stalls selling nothing but shoes, while Tin Street is still home to a community of tinkers. Generally, however, the crafts and trades of the past have given way to new activities – karaoke bars, video rental and tourist shops – but it is remarkable the extent to which the streets still specialize in the production and sale of just one type of good. The dwellings in this area are known as 'tube houses' (*nha ong*); they are narrow, with shop fronts sometimes only 3 m wide, but can be up to 50 m long. The house at No 97 Hang Dao Street, for example, is a mere 1.6 m wide. In the countryside the dimensions of houses were calculated on the basis of the owner's own physical dimensions; in urban areas no such regulations existed and tube houses evolved so that each house owner could have an, albeit very small, area of shop frontage facing onto the main street. The houses tend to be interspersed by courtyards or 'wells' to permit light into the house and allow some space for outside activities like washing and gardening. As geographers Brian Shaw and R Jones note in a paper on heritage conservation in Hanoi, the houses also had a natural air-conditioning

Ngoc Son Pagoda

| Pavilion of the stele | Hall of cult | Sanctuary of Van Xuong | Sanctuary of Kouan Ti |

Hanoi

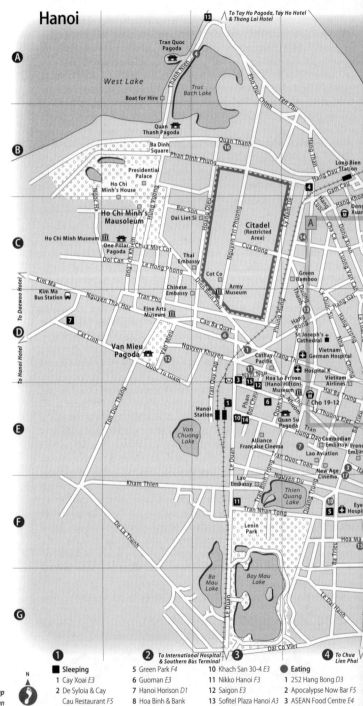

Hanoi

To Tay Ho Pagoda, Tay Ho Hotel & Thang Loi Hotel

Tran Quoc Pagoda

West Lake

Thanh Nien

Truc Bach Lake

Pho Duc Chinh

Yen Phu

Boat for Hire

Quan Thanh Pagoda

Quan Thanh

Hang Than

Hang Dau Station

Long Bien Station

Gam Cau

Hang Khoai

Ba Dinh Square

Phan Dinh Phung

Dong Xuan

Presidential Palace

Ho Chi Minh's House

Ngoc Ha

Bac Son

Dai Liet Si

Nguyen Tri Phuong

Ly Nam De

Citadel (Restricted Area)

Cua Dong

Hang Ma

Cha Ca

Luong Van Can

Hang Gai

Ho Chi Minh's Mausoleum

Ho Chi Minh Museum

One Pillar Pagoda

Chua Mot Cot

Doi Can

Le Hong Phong

Thai Embassy

Cot Co

Green Bamboo

Hang Quat

Nha Tho

Le Thai To

Kim Ma

Kim Ma Bus Station

To Daewoo Hotel

Nguyen Thai Hoc

Tran Phu

Fine Arts Museum

Diep Bien Phu

Chinese Embassy

Army Museum

Cao Ba Quat

Quoc Tu Giam

Nguyen Khuyen

Hang Bong

St Joseph's Cathedral

Vietnam-German Hospital

Hospital K

Vietnam Airlines

Cat Linh

To Hanoi Hotel

Van Mieu Pagoda

Van Mieu

Cathay Pacific

Trang Thi

Nam Ngu

Hoa Lo Prison (Hanoi Hilton) Museum

Hai Ba Trung

Ton Duc Thang

Quoc Tu Giam

Tran Quy Cap

Phan Boi Chau

Ly Thuong Kiet

Cho 19-12

Hanoi Station

Van Chuong Lake

Quan Su Pagoda

Tran Hung Dao

Cambodian Embassy

French Embassy

Lao Aviation

Alliance Française Cinema

Tran Quoc Toan

Kham Thien

Lao Embassy

Nguyen Du

New Age Cinema

Ba Trieu

Le Duan

Thien Quang Lake

Tran Nhan Tong

Eye Hospital

Lenin Park

Hoa Ma

De La Thanh

Le Dai Hanh

Ba Mau Lake

Bay Mau Lake

Le Duan

Dai Co Viet

To International Hospital & Southern Bus Terminal

To Chua Lien Phai

Detail map A Hoan Kiem, page 87

N

0 metres 200
0 yards 200

■ **Sleeping**
1 Cay Xoai E3
2 De Syloia & Cay Cau Restaurant F5
3 Dong Loi D3
4 Galaxy B4
5 Green Park F4
6 Guoman E3
7 Hanoi Horison D1
8 Hoa Binh & Bank of America E5
9 Hoan Kiem F5
10 Khach San 30-4 E3
11 Nikko Hanoi F3
12 Saigon E3
13 Sofitel Plaza Hanoi A3
14 Thu Do E3
15 Villa Bleue D3

● **Eating**
1 252 Hang Bong D3
2 Apocalypse Now Bar F5
3 ASEAN Food Centre E4
4 Banh Tom Ho Tay A3
5 Bistrot E5

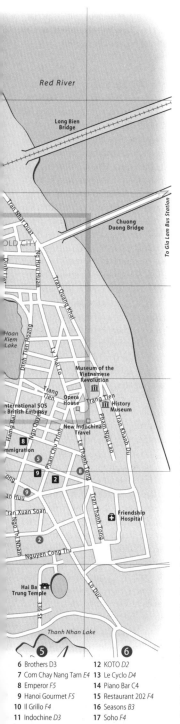

Red River

Long Bien
Bridge

Chuong
Duong Bridge

To Gia Lam Bus Station

OLD CITY

Tran Nhat Duat

Dinh Tien

Ng Huu Huan

Tran Quang Khai

Hoan
Kiem
Lake

Hang Ma

Dinh Tien Hoang

Ly Thai To

Trang
Tien

Opera
House

Trang Tien

Ngo Quyen

Phan Chu Trinh

Le Thanh Tong

Tran Thanh Tong

Phan Dinh Du

Tran Khanh Du

Ngo Thi Nham

Nguyen Cong Tru

Hai Ba
Trung Temple

To Duc

Thanh Nhan Lake

Museum of the
Vietnamese
Revolution

History
Museum

New Indochina
Travel

Friendship
Hospital

International SOS
British Embassy

Immigration

Hai Huu

6 Brothers *D3*
7 Com Chay Nang Tam *E4*
8 Emperor *F5*
9 Hanoi Gourmet *F5*
10 Il Grillo *F4*
11 Indochine *D3*

12 KOTO *D2*
13 Le Cyclo *D4*
14 Piano Bar *C4*
15 Restaurant 202 *F4*
16 Seasons *B3*
17 Soho *F4*

Hanoi

system: the difference in ambient temperature between the inner courtyards and the outside street created air flow, and the longer the house the greater the velocity of the flow. The older houses tend to be lower; commoners were not permitted to build higher than the Emperor's own residence. The structures were built of bricks 'cemented' together with sugar-cane juice.

A fear among conservationists is that this unique area will be destroyed as residents who have made small fortunes with the freeing-up of the economy, redevelop their houses insensitively. The desire is understandable: the tube houses are cramped and squalid, and often without any facilities. **48 Hang Ngang Street** is the spot where Ho Chi Minh drew up the Vietnamese Declaration of Independence in 1945, unashamedly and ironically modelled on the US Declaration of Independence (Hang Ngang Street is at the north end of Hang Dao Street, before it becomes Hang Duong Street). It now houses a small museum with black and white photographs of Uncle Ho. A walk through **Hang Be Market** (actually on Gai Ngu Street) reveals just how far Hanoi has developed over the past decade. There is a wonderful variety of food on sale - live, dead, cooked and raw. Quacking ducks, newly plucked chickens, saucers of warm blood, pigs trotters, freshly picked vegetables as well as pickled ones: the quality of produce is remarkable and testimony to the rapid strides Vietnamese agriculture has made. In this market and surrounding streets beautiful cut flowers are on sale.

Venturing further north, is the large and varied **Dong Xuan Market**, on Dong Xuan Street. This large, covered market was destroyed in a disastrous fire in 1994. Stall holders lost an estimated US$4.5 mn worth of stock and complained bitterly at the inadequacy of the fire services;

one fire engine arrived with no water. The market has been rebuilt. It specializes mainly in clothes and household goods.The Old City is also a good area to eat, with a multitude of small and cheap eating houses (see page 90).

South & east of Hoan Kiem Lake To the south and east of Hoan Kiem Lake is the proud-looking French-era **Opera House**. It was built in 1911 by François Lagisquet and is one of the finest French-colonial buildings in Hanoi. Work began in 1901. Some 35,000 bamboo piles were sunk into the mud of the Red River to provide foundations for the lofty edifice. The exterior is a delightful mass of shutters, wrought iron work, little balconies and a tiled frieze. The top balustrade is nicely capped with griffins. Inside, there are dozens of little boxes and fine decoration evocative of the French era. Having suffered years of neglect the Opera House was eventually lavishly restored, opening in time for the Francophone Summit held in 1997. Original drawings in Hanoi and Paris were consulted and teams of foreign experts were brought in to supervise local craftsmen. Slate was carried from Sin Ho to re-tile the roof, Italians oversaw the relaying of the mosaic floor in the lobby and French artists repainted the fine ornamental details of the auditorium. The restoration cost US$14 million, a colossal sum to spend on the reappointment of a colonial edifice. A Hanoi planning department architect explained that although the Opera House was French in style it was built by Vietnamese hands and represented an indelible part of Vietnamese history.

Behind the Opera House on Tran Quang Khai Street is the **Museum of the Vietnamese Revolution** (Bao Tang Cach Mang). It is a museum of the Vietnamese Revolution, tracing the struggle of the Vietnamese people to establish their independence. The rooms are arranged chronologically beginning on the first floor, and as the first recounts the story of the destruction of the Mongol Chinese fleet at the mouth of the Bach Dang River in the autumn of 938 (see Halong Bay, page 158), it becomes clear that the American involvement in Vietnam has been just one episode in a centuries-long struggle against foreign aggressors. Also on display is a French guillotine and an interesting room on the ground floor tracing the anti-war movement in the West. The final rooms show the peace and prosperity of reunification: bountiful harvests, the opening of large civil engineering projects, and smiling peasants. ■ *Tue-Sun 0800-1145, 1330-1615, 10,000d, 216 Tran Quang Khai St.*

A short distance south of the Museum of the Vietnamese Revolution, at 1 Trang Tien Street, is the **History Museum** (Bao Tang Lich Su). It is housed in a splendid building, completed in 1931. It was built as the home of the École Française d' Extrême-Orient, a distinguished archaeological, historical and ethnological research institute, by Ernest Hébrard. Hébrard, who was responsible for so many fine colonial era buildings in Vietnam, here employed a distinctly Indochinese style appropriate to its original and, indeed, its current function. The museum remains a centre of cultural and historical research. The *École française d' Extrême-Orient* played an important role in the preservation and restoration of ancient Vietnamese structures and temples many of which were destroyed or came under threat of demolition by the French to enable the growth of their colonial city. The museum remains a centre of cultural and historical research. The collection spans Vietnamese history from the neolithic to the 20th century of Ho Chi Minh. Unfortunately many labels are in Vietnamese only but the collection is arranged in chronological order. Galleries lead from the Neolithic (Bac Son) represented by stone tools and jewellery; the Bronze Age (Dong Son) with some fine bronze drums (see page 404); Funan and the port of Oc-Eo; Champa is represented by some fine stone carvings of apsaras, mythical dancing girls. There are relics such as

Syndicated loans keep the sharks away

Throughout Vietnam, and indeed across the world wherever there are large numbers of Vietnamese, one will find hui in operation. Hui is a credit circle of 10 to 20 people who meet every month; the scheme lasts as many months as there are participants. In a blind auction the highest bidder takes home that month's capital. Credit is expensive in Vietnam, partly because there are few banks to make personal loans, so in time of crisis the needy have to borrow from money-lenders at crippling rates of interest. Alternatively they can join a hui and borrow at more modest rates.

It works like this: the hui is established with members agreeing to put in a fixed amount, say 100,000d, each month. Each month the members bid according to their financial needs, entering a zero bid if they need no cash. If, in month one, Mr Nam's daughter gets married he will require money for the wedding festivities and, moreover, he has to have the money so he must bid high, maybe 25,000d. Assuming this is the highest bid he will receive 75,000d from each member (ie 100,000d less 25,000d). In future months Mr Nam cannot bid again but must pay 100,000d to whoever collects that

month's pot. Towards the end of the cycle several participants (those whose buffalo have not died and those whose daughters remain unmarried) will have taken nothing out but will have paid in 100,000d (minus x) dong each month; they can enter a zero bid and get the full 100,000d from all participants and with it a tidy profit.

There is, needless to say, strategy involved and this is where the Vietnamese love of gambling ("the besetting sin of the Vietnamese" according to Norman Lewis) colours the picture. One day, Mr Muoi wins one million dong on the Vinh Long lottery. He lets it be known that he intends to buy a Honda Dream, but to raise the necessary purchase price he must 'win' that month's hui and will be bidding aggressively. In the same month Thuy, Mrs Phuoc's baby daughter, celebrates her first birthday so Mrs Phuoc needs money to throw a lavish thoi noi party (see box on page 397). She has heard of old Muoi's intentions but does not know if he is serious. In case he is, she will have to bid high. On the day, nice Mrs Phuoc enters a knock out bid of 30,000d but wily old Muoi was bluffing all along and he and the others make a lot of interest that month.

bronze temple bells and urns of successive royal dynasties from Le to Nguyen. Unfortunately some of the pieces are reproductions, for instance a number of the stelae. The curators will sometimes give visitors personal tours of the museum (for a small gratuity). ■ *Tue-Sun 0800-1100, 1330-1630, 15,000d.*

To the west of Hoan Kiem Lake in a little square stands the rather sombre twin-towered neo-gothic **Saint Joseph's Cathedral**. Built in 1886, the cathedral is important as one of the very first colonial era buildings in Hanoi finished, as it was, just one year after the Treaty of Tientsin which gave France control over the whole of Vietnam (see page 358). Some fine stained-glass windows remain.

West of Hoan Kiem Lake

About 100 yards in front of the cathedral on Nha Tho Street is a much older religious foundation, **Chua Ba Da** or **Stone Lady Pagoda**, down a narrow alley. It consists of an old pagoda and a Buddhist school. On either side of the pagoda are low buildings where the monks live. Although few of the standing buildings are of any antiquity it is an ancient site and a tranquil and timeless atmosphere prevails. Originally built in 1056 as Sung Khanh Pagoda, by the late 15th century it needed rebuilding. In the foundations a stone statue of a woman was found which was worshipped in the pagoda. By

1767 the walls needed rebuilding. Each time they were built they collapsed. The foundations were dug deeper and the stone statue was found again. Since then the walls have held fast. Although now a pagoda for the worship of Buddha it is clear that the site has had a mixed spiritual history in a way that is quite typical in Vietnam.

South of Hoan Kiem Lake On Hai Ba Trung Street is the **Cho 19-12**, a market linking Hai Ba Trung with Ly Thuong Kiet Street and selling primarily fresh fruit, vegetables and meat (including dog). A block to the west of the market is the site of the Hoa Lo Prison better known as the **Hanoi Hilton**, the prison where US POWs were incarcerated, some for six years, during the Vietnamese War. Up until 1969, prisoners were also tortured here. Two US Airforce officers, Charles Tanner and Ross Terry, rather than face torture, concocted a story about two other members of their squadron who had been court-martialled for refusing to fly missions against the north. Thrilled with this piece of propaganda, visiting Japanese Communists were told the story and it filtered back to the US. Unfortunately for Tanner and Terry they had called their imaginary flyers Clark Kent and Ben Casey (both TV heroes). When the Vietnamese realized they had been made fools of, the two prisoners were again tortured. The final prisoners were not released until 1973, some having been held in the north since 1964. At the end of 1992 a US mission was shown around the prison where 2,000 inmates were housed in cramped and squalid conditions. Despite pleas from war veterans and party members, the site was sold to a Singapore-Vietnamese joint venture and is now a hotel and shopping complex, *Hanoi Towers*. As part of the deal the developers had to leave a portion of the prison for use as a museum, and quite a good one it is too. Maison Centrale, reads the legend over the prison's main gate which leads in to the museum. Unfortunately none of the captions are in English, which is a pity as there are plenty of interesting-looking displays. There are recreations of conditions under colonial rule when the barbarous French incarcerated patriotic Vietnamese: by 1953 they were holding 2,000 prisoners in a space designed for 500. Less prominence is given to the role of the prison for holding American pilots, but Douglas 'Pete' Peterson, the first post-war American Ambassador to Vietnam (1997-2001), who was one such occupant has his mug-shot on the wall. The conditions the Viet Cong held their captives in were, fortunately, recorded on film. ■ *Daily 0800-1100, 1330-1600, 10,000d.*

Nearby at 73 Quan Su Street is the **Quan Su** or **Ambassadors' Pagoda**. In the 15th century there was a guesthouse here for visiting Buddhist ambassadors. The current structure was built between 1936 and 1942. Chinese in appearance from the exterior, the temple contains some fine stone sculptures of the past, present and future Buddhas. It is very popular and crowded with scholars, pilgrims, beggars and incense sellers. The pagoda is one of the centres of Buddhist learning in Vietnam: at the back is a school room which is in regular use, students often spill-over into the surrounding corridors to listen.

A short distance south from the Ambassador's Pagoda, is **Thien Quang Lake** and **Lenin Park**. Not surprisingly, the park contains a statue of Lenin, together with the wreckage of a US B-52 bomber. You may be charged anything between 1,000d and 10,000d to enter depending on the entrance you use and how wealthy you look. Nearby, on Le Duan Street south of the railway station, stalls sell a remarkable array of US, Soviet and Vietnamese army-surplus kit.

Ho Chi Minh's Mausoleum (Lang Chu Tich Ho Chi Minh) is 2 km to the west of Hoan Kiem Lake. Before entering the Mausoleum, visitors must leave cameras and possessions at the office (*Ban To Chuc*) on the corner of Doi Can (which becomes Le Hong Phong Street) and Ngoc Ha streets, a few minutes walk from the Mausoleum. Most *cyclo* drivers and locals will point it out. Visitors march in file to see Ho's embalmed corpse. The Vietnamese have made his body a holy place of pilgrimage. This is contrary to Ho's own wishes: he wanted to be cremated and his ashes placed in three urns to be positioned atop three unmarked hills in the north, centre and south of the country. He once wrote that "cremation is not only good from the point of view of hygiene, but it also saves farmland". Visitors must be respectful: dress neatly, walk solemnly, and do not talk.

Ho Chi Minh's Mausoleum & surrounding sights

Hanoi

The **Mausoleum**, built between 1973 and 1975, is a massive, square, forbidding structure and must be among the best constructed, maintained and air-conditioned (for obvious reasons) buildings in Vietnam. Opened in 1975, it is a fine example of the mausoleum genre and modelled closely on Lenin's Mausoleum in Moscow. Ho lies, with a guard at each corner of his bier. The embalming of Ho's body was undertaken by the chief Soviet embalmer Dr Sergei Debrov who also pickled such Communist luminaries as Klenient Gottwald (President of Czechoslovakia), Georgi Dimitrov (Prime Minister of Bulgaria) and Forbes Burnham (President of Guyana). Debrov was flown to Hanoi from Moscow as Ho lay dying, bringing with him two transport planes packed with air conditioners (to keep the corpse cool) and other equipment. To escape US bombing, the team moved Ho to a cave, taking a full year to complete the embalming process. Russian scientists still check-up on their handiwork, servicing Ho's body regularly. Their embalming methods and the fluids they use are still a closely guarded secret, and in a recent interview, Debrov noted with pleasure the poor state of China's Chairman Mao's body, which was embalmed without Soviet help. ■ *Tue-Thu, Sat and Sun 0730-1100. Closed in Sep and Oct.*

From the Mausoleum, visitors are directed to **Ho Chi Minh's house** built in the compound of the former **Presidential Palace**. The Palace, now a Party guesthouse, was the residence of the Governors-General of French Indochina and was built between 1900 and 1908. In 1954, when North Vietnam's struggle for independence was finally achieved, Ho Chi Minh declined to live in the palace, saying that it belonged to the people. Instead, he stayed in what is said to have been an electrician's house in the same compound. Here he lived from 1954-58, before moving to a new house built on the other side of the small lake (Ho Chi Minh's 'Fish Farm', swarming with massive and well-fed carp). This modest house is airy and personal, and immaculately kept. Ho conducted meetings under the house, which is raised up on wooden pillars and slept and worked above (his books, slippers and telephones are still here). The typewriter on which it is said he typed the Declaration of Independence is on display. Built by the army, the house mirrors the one he lived in while fighting the French from his haven near the Chinese border. Behind the house is Ho's bomb shelter, and behind that, the hut where he died in 1969. ■ *Tue-Thu, Sat and Sun, 0730-1130.*

Behind Ho Chi Minh's house is the **One Pillar Pagoda** (**Chua Mot Cot**), one of the few structures remaining from the original foundation of the city. It was built in 1049 by Emperor Ly Thai Tong, although the shrine has since been rebuilt on several occasions, most recently in 1955 after the French destroyed it before withdrawing from the country. The Emperor built the pagoda in a fit of religious passion after he dreamt that he saw the goddess

The story of Quan Am

Quan Am was turned onto the streets by her husband for some unspecified wrong-doing and, dressed as monk, took refuge in a monastery. There, a woman accused her of fathering, and then abandoning, her child. Accepting the blame (why, no one knows), she was again turned out onto the streets, only to return to the monastery much later when she was on the point of death – to confess her true identity. When the Emperor of China heard the tale, he made Quan Am the Guardian Spirit of Mother and Child, and couples without a son now pray to her.

Quan Am's husband is sometimes depicted as a parakeet, with the Goddess usually holding her adopted son in one arm and standing on a lotus leaf (the symbol of purity).

Quan Am (Vietnam's equivalent of the Chinese goddess Kuan-yin) sitting on a lotus and holding a young boy, whom she handed to the Emperor. On the advice of counsellors who interpreted the dream, the Emperor built this little lotus-shaped temple in the centre of a water-lily pond and shortly afterwards his queen gave birth to a son. As the name suggests, it is supported on a single (concrete) pillar with a brick and stone staircase running up one side. The pagoda symbolizes the 'pure' lotus sprouting from the sea of sorrow. Original in design, with dragons running along the apex of the elegantly-curved tiled roof, the temple is one of the most revered monuments in Vietnam. But the ungainly concrete pillar and the pond of green slime in which it is embedded detract considerably from the enchantment of the little pagoda. Adjacent is the inhabited Dien Huu Pagoda, a sign says they don't like people in shorts but actually they're quite friendly and it has a nice courtyard.

Ho Chi Minh Museum Overshadowing the One Pillar Pagoda is the **Ho Chi Minh Museum** – opened in 1990 in celebration of the centenary of Ho's birth. Contained in a large and impressive modern building, it is the best arranged and most innovative museum in Vietnam. But, apart from newspaper clippings in French, everything is in Vietnamese. The displays trace Ho's life and work from his early wanderings around the world to his death and final victory over the south. There are also traditional Vietnamese music performances. One of the guides may speak English. ■ *Tue-Thu, Sat 0800-1100, 1330-1600; Sun 0730-1100, 1330-1600.*

Ba Dinh Square From Ho Chi Minh's Mausoleum walk north up Hung Vuong Street which leads onto **Ba Dinh Square** where Ho read out the Vietnamese Declaration of Independence on 2 September 1945. Following Ho's declaration, 2 September became Vietnam's National Day. Coincidentally 2 September was also the date on which Ho died in 1969, although his death was not officially announced until 3 September in order not to mar people's enjoyment of National Day in the beleaguered North.

In front of Ho Chi Minh's Mausoleum on Bac Son Street is the **Dai Liet Si**, a memorial to the heroes and martyrs who died fighting for their country's independence. It appears to be modelled as a secular form of stupa and inside is a large bronze urn.

Van Mieu Pagoda South from Ho Chi Minh's Museum on Nguyen Thai Hoc are the walls of the **Temple of Literature** or Van Mieu Pagoda. The entrance to the pagoda is at the south end of this long and narrow block on Quoc Tu Giam Street. The Temple of Literature is the largest, and probably the most important, temple

The examination of 1875

The examinations held at the Temple of Literature and which enabled, in theory, even the most lowly peasant to rise to the exalted position of a Mandarin, were long and difficult and conducted with great formality. André Masson quotes Monsieur de Kergaradec, the French Consul's, account of the examination of 1875.

"On the morning of the big day, from the third watch on, that is around one o'clock in the morning, the big drum which invites each one to present himself began to be beaten and soon students, intermingled with ordinary spectators, approached the Compound in front of the cordon formed around the outer wall by soldiers holding lances. In the middle of the fifth watch,

towards four or five o'clock in the morning, the examiners in full dress came and installed themselves with their escorts at the different gates. Then began the roll call of the candidates, who were thoroughly searched at the entrance, and who carried with them a small tent of canvas and mats, cakes, rice, prepared tea, black ink, one or two brushes and a lamp. Everyone once inside, the gates were closed, and the examiners met in the central pavilion of the candidates' enclosure in order to post the subject of the composition. During the afternoon, the candidates who had finished withdrew a few at a time through the central gate, the last ones did not leave the Compound until midnight."

Doctor Laureate on his way home. From an illustration by H Oger in 1905

Going to the examination camp with apparatus (bamboo bed, writing box, bamboo tube for examination papers). From an illustration by H Oger in 1905

Hanoi

complex in Hanoi. It was founded in 1070 by Emperor Ly Thanh Tong, dedicated to Confucius who had a substantial following in Vietnam, and modelled, so it is said, on a temple in Shantung, China, the birthplace of the sage. Some researchers, while acknowledging the date of foundation, challenge the view that it was built as a Confucian institution pointing to the ascendancy of Buddhism during the Ly Dynasty. Confucian principles and teaching rapidly replaced Buddhism, however, and Van Mieu subsequently became the intellectual and spiritual centre of the kingdom as a cult of literature and education spread amongst the court, the mandarins and then among the common people. At one time there were said to be 20,000 schools teaching the Confucian classics in northern Vietnam alone.

The temple and its compound are arranged north-south, and visitors enter at the southern end from Quoc Tu Giam Street. On the pavement two pavilions house stelae bearing the inscription *ha ma* (climb down from your horse), a nice reminder that even the most elevated dignitaries had to proceed on foot. The main Van Mieu Gate (Cong Van Mieu Mon) is adorned with 15th-century dragons. Traditionally, the large central gate was opened only on ceremonial occasions. The path leads through the Cong Dai Trung to a second courtyard and the Van Khue Gac Pavilion which was built in 1805 and dedicated to the Constellation of Literature. The roof is tiled according to the *yin-yang* principle.

Beyond lies the Courtyard of the Stelae at the centre of which is the rectangular pond or Cieng Thien Quang (Well of Heavenly Clarity). More important are the stelae themselves, 82 in all, on which are recorded the names of 1,306 successful examination scholars (*tien si*). Of the 82 that survive (30 are missing) the oldest dates back to 1442 and the most recent to 1779. Each stela is carried on the back of a tortoise, symbol of strength and longevity but they are arranged in no order; three chronological categories, however, can be identified. 14 date from the 15th and 16th centuries; they are the smallest and embellished with floral motifs and *yin-yang* symbols but not dragons (a royal emblem). Twenty five stelae are from the 17th century and ornamented with dragons (by now permitted), pairs of phoenix and other creatures mythical or real. The remaining 43 stelae are of 18th-century origin; they are the largest and decorated with two stylized dragons, some merging with flame clouds. Passing the examination was not easy: in 1733, out of some 3,000 entrants only eight passed the doctoral examination (*Thai Hoc Sinh*) and became Mandarins – a task that took 35 days. This tradition was begun in 1484 on the instruction of Emperor Le Thanh Tong, and continued through to 1878, during which time 116 examinations were held. The Temple of Literature was not used only for examinations, however: food was also distributed to the poor and infirm, 500 g of rice at a time. In 1880, the French Consul Monsieur de Kergaradec recorded that 22,000 impoverished people came to receive this meagre handout.

Continuing north, the **Dai Thanh Mon** or Great Success Gate leads on to a courtyard flanked by two buildings which date from 1954, the originals having been destroyed in 1947. These buildings were reserved for 72 disciples of Confucius. Facing is the **Dai Bai Duong** (Great House of Ceremonies) which was built in the 19th century but in the earlier style of the Le Dynasty. The carved wooden friezes with their dragons, phoenix, lotus flowers, fruits, clouds and *yin-yang* discs are all symbolically charged, depicting the order of the universe and by implication reflecting the god-given hierarchical nature of human society, each in his place. It is not surprising that the Communist government has hitherto had reservations about preserving a temple extolling such heretical doctrine. Inside is an altar on which sit statues of Confucius and his closest disciples. Adjoining is the **Dai Thanh (Great Success) Sanctuary** which also contains a statue of Confucius.

To the north once stood the first university in Vietnam, Quoc Tu Giam, which from the 11th to 18th centuries educated first the heir to the throne and later sons of mandarins. It was replaced with a temple dedicated to Confucius' parents and followers, which was itself destroyed in 1947. ■ *Mon-Sun, 0830-1600, 12,000d.*

Not far from the northern walls of the Van Mieu Pagoda at 66 Nguyen Thai Hoc Street is the **Fine Arts Museum** (Bao Tang My Thuat) contained in a large colonial building. The oriental roof was added later when the building was converted to a museum. The ground floor galleries display pre-20th century art – from Dong Sonian bronze drums to Nguyen Dynasty paintings and sculpture, although many works of this later period are on display in the Museum of Royal Fine Arts in Hué. There are some particularly fine stone Buddhas. The first floor is given over to folk art. There are some lovely works from the Central Highlands and engaging Dong Ho woodblock prints – one block for each colour – and Hang Trong woodblock prints, a single black ink print which is coloured in by hand. There are also some fine lacquer paintings. The top floor contains 20th-century work including some excellent water colours and oil paintings. Contemporary Vietnamese artists are building a significant reputation for their work (see box, Modern Vietnamese Art, page 406). There is a large collection of overtly political work, posters and propaganda (of great interest to historians and specialist collectors) which remind us that the freedoms of today's artists are new, precious and fragile. ■ *Tue-Sun 0915-1700, 10,000d.*

Fine Arts Museum

A five-minute walk east from the Fine Arts Museum, situated at 30 Dien Bien Phu Street is the **Army Museum** (Bao Tang Quan Doi). Across the road from the front entrance is a statue of Lenin. Tanks, planes and artillery fill the courtyard. Symbolically, an untouched Mig-21 stands at the museum entrance while wreckage of B52s, F1-11s and Q2Cs is piled up at the back. The museum illustrates battles and episodes in Vietnam's fight for independence from the struggles with China (there is a good display of the Battle of Bach Dang River of AD 938) through to the resistance to the French and the Battle of Dien Bien Phu (illustrated by a good model). Inevitably, of course, there are lots of photographs and exhibits of the American war and although much is self evident unfortunately all explanations are in Vietnamese. In the precincts of the museum is a flag tower, the **Cot Co**, raised up on three platforms. Built in 1812, it is the only substantial part of the original citadel still standing. There are good views over Hanoi from the top. The walls of the citadel were destroyed by the French in 1894-97 presumably as they symbolized the power of the Vietnamese emperors. The French were highly conscious of the projection of might, power and authority through large structures which helps explain their own remarkable architectural legacy. Other remaining parts of the citadel are in the hands of the Vietnamese army and out of bounds to visitors. ■ *Tue-Sun, 0800-1130, 1330-1630, 10,000d.*

Army Museum

North from the Old City is **Truc Bach (White Silk) Lake**. Truc Bach Lake was created in the 17th century by building a causeway across the southeast corner of Ho Tay. This was the site of the 11th century **Royal Palace** which had, so it is said, 'a hundred roofs'. All that is left is the terrace of Kinh Thien with its

Outer Hanoi

dragon staircase, and a number of stupas, bridges, gates and small pagodas. Judging by the ruins, the palace must have been an impressive sight. At the southwest corner of the lake, on the intersection of Hung Vuong, Quan Thanh and Thanh Nien streets is the **Quan Thanh Pagoda**, originally built in the early 11th century in honour of Huyen Thien Tran Vo (a genie) but since much remodelled. Despite renovation, it is still very beautiful. The large bronze bell was cast in 1677. ■ *5,000d.*

To the east of here the Long Bien and Chuong Duong bridges cross the Red River. The former of these two bridges was built as a road and rail bridge by Daydé & Pillé of Paris and named **Paul Doumer Bridge** after the Governor General of the time. Construction was begun in 1899 and it was opened by Emperor Thanh Thai on 28 February 1902. Today it is used by trains, bicycles and pedestrians. Over 1.5 km in length, it was the only river crossing in existence during the Vietnam War, and suffered repeated attacks from US planes only to be quickly repaired. The Chuong Duong Bridge was completed at the beginning of the 1980s.

The much larger **West Lake** or **Ho Tay** was originally a meander in the Red River. The **Tran Quoc Pagoda** can be found on an islet on the east shores of the lake, linked to the causeway by a walkway. It was originally built on the banks of the Red River before being transferred to its present site by way of an intermediate location. The pagoda contains a stela dated 1639 recounting its unsettled history. A few kilometres north on the tip of a promontory stands **Tay Ho Pagoda**, notable chiefly for its setting. It is reached along a narrow lane lined with stalls selling fruit, roses and paper votives and a dozen restaurants serving giant snails with noodles (*bun oc*) and fried shrimp cakes.

But West Lake is fast losing its unique charm as development spreads northwards. The nouveau riche of Hanoi are rapidly turning the area into a middle-class suburb. New houses go up in an unplanned and unco-ordinated sprawl. Nguyen Ngoc Khoi, director of the Urban Planning Institute in Hanoi, estimates that the area of the lake has shrunk by 20%, from 500 ha to 400 ha, as residents and hotel and office developers have reclaimed land. The lake is also suffering encroachment by water hyacinths which are fed by organic pollutants from factories (especially a tannery) and untreated sewage. The view from Nghi Tam Road which runs along the Red River dyke presents a contrasting spectacle of sprawling houses interspersed with the remaining plots of land which are intensively and attractively cultivated market gardens supplying the city with flowers and vegetables.

To the west The **Vietnam Museum of Ethnology**, some distance west of the city centre in Cau Giay District (Nguyen Van Huyen Road), opened in November 1997 in a modern purpose-built structure. The collection here of some 25,000 artefacts and 15,000 photographs is excellent and, more to the point, is attractively and informatively presented with labels in Vietnamese, English and French. It displays the material culture (textiles, musical instruments, jewellery, tools, baskets and the like) of the majority Kinh people as well as Vietnam's 53 other designated minority peoples. While much is historical, the museum is also attempting to build up its contemporary collection. There is a shop attached to the museum. ■ *Tue-Sun 0830-1230, 1330-1630, 10,000d. Getting there: catch the No 14 minibus from Dinh Tien Hoang St, north of Hoan Kiem Lake, to the Nghia Tan stop. Turn right and walk down Hoang Quoc Viet St for 1 block, before turning right at the* Petrolimex *station down Nguyen Van Huyen. The museum is down this street, on the left or take a taxi.*

The Trung sisters

Vietnamese history honours a number of heroines, of whom the Trung sisters are among the most revered. At the beginning of the Christian era, the Lac Lords of Vietnam began to agitate against Chinese control over their lands. Trung Trac, married to the Lac Lord Thi Sach, was apparently of a 'brave and fearless disposition' and encouraged her husband and the other lords to rise up against the Chinese in AD 40. The two sisters often fought while pregnant, apparently putting on gold plated armour over their enlarged bellies.

Although an independent kingdom was created for a short time, ultimately the uprising proved fruitless; a large Chinese army defeated the rebels in AD 43, and eventually captured Trung Trac and her sister Trung Nhi, executing them and sending their heads to the Han court at Lo-yang. An alternative story of their death has it that the sisters threw themselves into the Hat Giang River to avoid being captured, and turned into stone statues. These were washed ashore and placed in Hanoi's Hai Ba Trung Temple for worship.

Down Hue Street is the hub of motorcycle sales, parts and repairs. Off this street, for example along Hoa Ma, Tran Nhan Tong and Thinh Yen are numerous **stalls and shops**, each specializing in a single type of product – TVs, electric fans, bicycle parts and so on. It is a fascinating area to explore. At the intersection of Thinh Yen and Pho 332 people congregate to sell new and second-hand bicycles, as well as bicycle parts. Not far away is the venerable Hai Ba Trung Temple, **Den Hai Ba Trung** – the temple of the two Trung Sisters – overlooking a lake. The temple was built in 1142, but like others, has been restored on a number of occasions. It contains crude statues of the Trung sisters, Trung Trac and Trung Nhi (see box above), which are carried in procession once a year during February.

South of the city centre

Further south still from the Hai Ba Trung, is another pagoda – **Chua Lien Phai**. This quiet pagoda which can be found just off Bach Mai Street, was built in 1732, although it has since been restored.

Excursions

Compared with Saigon and the south, Hanoi and its surrounds are rich in places of interest. Not only is the landscape more varied and attractive, but the 1,000-year-old history of Hanoi has generated dozens of sights of architectural appeal, many of which can be visited on a day trip.

Co Loa Citadel is the third-century capital 16 km north of Hanoi, built by King An Duong with walls in three concentric rings, the outer of which is 8 km in circumference. It is an important Bronze Age site and thousands of arrow heads and three bronze ploughshares have been excavated here. Today there is little to see as electricity sub-stations and farms have obliterated much of archaeological interest. ■ *Getting there: drive north up Highway 3, Co Loa is signposted to the east.*

To the north

The Hung Kings' Temples, **Phong Chau**, south of Yen Bai and approximately 100 km northwest of Hanoi near the industrial town of Viet Tri in Vinh Phu Province is popular with Vietnamese visitors especially during the Hung Kings' Festival. In purely topographical terms the site is striking, an almost perfectly circular hill rising unexpectedly out of the monotonous Red River floodplain with two lakes at the bottom. Given its peculiar physical setting it is easy to understand how the site acquired its mythical reputation as the birthplace of the Viet people and why the Hung Vuong kings chose it as the capital of their kingdom.

In this place, myth and historical fact have become intertwined. Legend has it that the Viet people are the product of the union of King Lac Long Quan, a dragon, and his fairy wife Au Co. Au Co gave birth to a pouch containing 100 eggs which hatched to produce 50 boys and 50 girls. Husband and wife decided to separate in order to populate the land and propagate the race, so half the children followed their mother to the highlands and half remained with their father on the plains, giving rise to the Montagnards and lowland peoples of Vietnam. Historically easier to verify is the story of the Hung kings (Hung Vuong). They built a temple in order to commemorate the legendary progenitors of the Vietnamese people.

The **museum** is a hideous, Soviet-inspired piece but there are on display interesting items excavated from the province. Exhibits include pottery, jewellery, fish hooks, arrow heads and axe heads (dated 1000-1300 BC) but of particular interest are the bronze drums dating from the Dongsonian period (see page 404). The Dongsonian was a transitional period between the neolithic and bronze ages and the drums are thought to originate from around the fifth to the third centuries BC. Photographs show excavation in the 1960s when these items were uncovered. ■ *Daily 0800-1130, 1300-1600.*

Ascending the hill, a track leads to a **memorial to Ho Chi Minh**. Ho said he hoped that people would come from all over Vietnam to see this historic site. Nearby is the **Low Temple** dedicated to Au Co, mother of the country and supposedly the site where the 100 eggs were produced. At the back of the temple is a statue of the Buddha of a thousand arms and a thousand eyes. Continuing up the hill is the **Middle Temple** where Prince Lang Lieu was crowned seventh Hung king and where the kings would play chess and discuss pressing affairs of state. Prince Lang Lieu was (like the English King Alfred) something of a dab hand in the kitchen and his most enduring

The Hung Kings' Temples

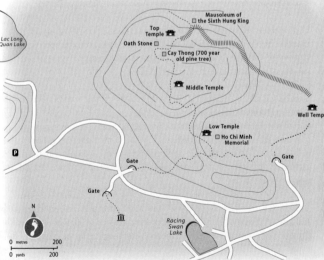

creation is a pair of cakes, *banh trung* and *banh day*, which to this day (unlike Alfred's) remain popular delicacies, eaten at Tet. This temple has three altars and attractive murals.

Further on, towards the top of the hill is the **oath stone** on which the 18th Hung king, Thuc Phan, swore to defend the country from its enemies. Adjacent is the **Top Temple** dating from the 15th century. The roof is adorned with dragons and gaudily painted mural warriors stand guard outside. A not particularly ancient drum hangs from the ceiling but smoke rising from burning incense on the three altars helps add to the antiquity of the setting. Here it was that the kings would supplicate God for peace and prosperity.

Steps lead from the back right-hand side of this temple down the hill to the **mausoleum of the sixth Hung king**. These steps then continue down the far side of the hill to the **Well Temple** built in memory of the last princess of the Hung Dynasty. Inside is a well in the reflection of which this girl used to comb her hair. Today worshippers throw money in and, it is said, they even drink the water. Turn right to get back to the car park.

Hung Kings' festival, on the 10th day of the third lunar month, is a two-week celebration when the temple site comes alive as visitors from all over Vietnam descend on the area, as Ho Chi Minh encouraged them to. The place seethes with vendors of all descriptions and food stalls and fairground activities spring up. There are racing swan boats on one of the lakes.

■ *Getting there: turn off Highway 2 about 12 km north of Viet Tri: a morning or afternoon's excursion by car from Hanoi.*

Tam Dao
Phone code: 0211

Tam Dao lies in a mountain range of the same name, a chain of three mountains whose peaks constitute a natural border between Vinh Phu and Thai Nguyen provinces. Protruding from the clouds, the three peaks are said to resemble three islands, hence the name Tam Dao which means 'three islands'.

To describe Tam Dao's setting as stunning is an understatement. The town nestles in a giant rock bowl seemingly bitten out of the side of the mountain. All around steep cliffs soar high above, clad in a glorious jungle of trees entangled with lianas; early morning mist and cloud slowly burn off as the sun rises and the forest comes alive with the sound of bird call, animal cries and the humming of insects. It is said that the gods came down from heaven to play chess here. On a good day there are clear views over the plains below. Scrambling through the overgrowth one stumbles over colonial remains rather like discovering the remnants of some ancient classical civilization in the wilderness – crumbling walls, mysterious flights of steps, forlorn bridges, rocky balustrades and charming gateways. And because of all this beauty Tam Dao is a tragedy. Most hotels are filthy and horribly managed. The people are unpleasant, rapacious and slovenly. Holiday makers tend to be little better: their habits consist solely of being photographed, eating wild animals, getting drunk, karaoke and sex – funds permitting.

Construction of the town started in 1904; in 1915 the church, a post office, tennis courts and a swimming pool were added. As in Sapa, a mansion was built for the Governor General which, with its eight roofs, was the largest such villa in Indochina. And the 130-room *Metropole Hotel* was built to cater to the needs of the steady stream of affluent expatriates who came here to escape the summer heat of the Red River Delta. Tam Dao was almost completely razed to the ground during the First Indochina War of 1945-54; all that now remains of the original 200-plus French colonial buildings are the foundations of old villas and the shell of the old church building; the latter now functions as the clubhouse of the Tam Dao Trades Union.

During the summer Tam Dao is a very busy resort – the month of July is the real high season for Vietnamese visitors – but from October through to March the weather can become quite cold and the majority of its hotels and restaurants shut for the winter. If you wish to stay overnight there are numerous hotels and guesthouses but few, if any, that can be recommended. The **C** *Cay Thong*, T0211-824271, F824256, is a Japanese joint-venture hotel with 16 rooms all with adjoining bathroom, there's also a restaurant and the price includes breakfast. The **D** *Cong Doan* (*Trades Union*), T0211-824210, offers basic accommodation. In the restaurants expect boar, bear, porcupine, civet cat, bamboo rat, deer and jungle fowl to appear on the menu. There is a tourist office, *Tam Dao Tourism,* which can be reached on T0211-824213.

A 20-30-minute walk from the town centre is the **Silver Waterfall** (Thac Bac) which descends 45 m. It is reached by way of a path and some slippery old steps, lined with irritating vendors.

■ *Getting there: by car only, 2½ hrs. All vehicles travelling along Highway 28 to Tam Dao are stopped at a checkpoint 11 km before the town where a fee of 50,000d is levied from each foreign visitor. Thereafter the road climbs through some beautiful mountain scenery to the former colonial hill station, 930 m above sea level.*

Around Hanoi

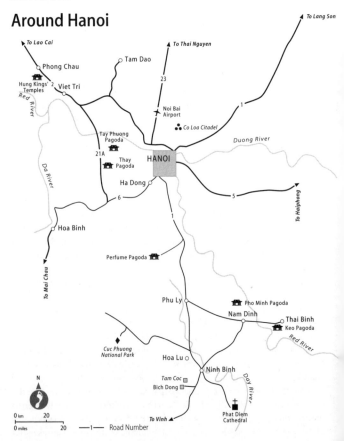

The **Perfume Pagoda** (Chua Huong or Chua Huong Tich) is 60 km southwest of Hanoi. Dedicated to Quan Am (see page 76), it is one of a number of shrines and towers built amongst limestone caves and is regarded as one of the most beautiful spots in Vietnam. The stone statue of Quan Am in the principal pagoda was carved in 1793 after Tay Son rebels had stolen and melted down its bronze predecessor to make cannon balls. Emperor Le Thanh Tong (1460-97) described it as 'Nam Thien de nhat dong' or 'foremost cave under the Vietnamese sky'. It is a popular pilgrimage spot, particularly during the festival months of March and April. A sampan takes visitors along the Yen River, a diverting 4-km ride through a flooded landscape to the Mountain of the Perfume Traces. From here it is a 3-km hike up the mountain to the cool, dark cave wherein lies the Perfume Pagoda. ■ *The US$7 fare includes the return boat trip. Getting there: a half day excursion, hire a car or take a tour.*

Keo Pagoda is 7 km outside the town of Thai Binh, which lies to the southeast of Hanoi. This pagoda was built during the 11th century and is a fine example of Vietnamese provincial architecture. ■ *Getting there: by car or on a tour.* **Thien Truong** and **Pho Minh pagodas** (see page 166), **Doi Son** and **Doi Diap pagodas** (see page 166).

Cuc Phuong National Park is about 160 km south of Hanoi. This can be done as day trip or over-nighter from Hanoi or as an excursion from Ninh Binh (see page 169 for details).

Tay Phuong Pagoda is about 6 km from the Thay Pagoda in the village of Thac Xa. It may date back to the eighth century, although the present structure was rebuilt in 1794. Constructed of ironwood, it is sited at the summit of a hill and is approached by way of a long stairway. The pagoda is best known for its collection – all 74 of them – of 18th-century *arhat* statues (statues of former monks). They are thought to be among the best examples of the woodcarver's art from the period. ■ *Getting there: by tour or hire car.*

Thay Pagoda (Master's Pagoda), also known as Thien Phuc Tu Pagoda, lies 40 km southwest of Hanoi in the village of Sai Son, in Ha Son Binh Province. Built in the 11th century, the pagoda honours a herbalist, Dao Hanh, who lived in Sai Son village. It is said that he was reborn as the son of Emperor Le Thanh Tong after he and his wife had come to pray here. The pagoda complex is divided into three sections. The outer section is used for ceremonies, the middle is a Buddhist temple, while the inner part is dedicated to the herbalist. The temple has some fine statues of the past, present and future Buddhas with gold faces and lacquered red garments, as well as an impressive array of demons. Water puppet shows are performed during holidays and festivals on a stage built in the middle of the pond at the front of the pagoda (see page 414). Dao Hanh, who was a water puppet enthusiast, is said to have created the pond. It is spanned by two bridges built at the beginning of the 17th century. There are good views from the nearby Sai Son Hill – a path leads upwards from the pagoda. ■ *Getting there: by tour or hire-car.*

Other possible day trips are excursions to **Haiphong** (see page 146), **Ninh Binh** (see page 166), **Hoa Lu** (see page 167), **Tam Coc** (see page 168), **Phat Diam Cathedral** (see page 169), **Hoa Binh** (see page 104) and **Mai Chau** (see page 106)

Essentials

Sleeping

There has been a spate of hotel building and renovation in Hanoi in recent years and accommodation of all standards and at all prices is available. The more expensive hotels offer a range of business services with IDD and satellite TV. Cheaper hotels tend to be found in the Old Quarter of the city, north of Hoan Kiem Lake.

City centre: south of Hoan Kiem Lake
■ *on maps, pages 70 and 87*
Phone code: 04
Price codes: see inside front cover

LL-L *Hilton Hanoi Opera*, 1 Le Thanh Tong St, T9330500, F9330530, hanhitw@fpt.vn Opened in Feb 1999. Built adjacent to and architecturally sympathetically with the Opera House it is a splendid building and provides the highest levels of service and hospitality. But whereas the *Metropole* is normally busy the *Hanoi Opera* is usually quiet. **LL-L** *Sofitel Metropole*, 15 Ngo Quyen St, T8266919, F8266920, sofitel@sofitelhanoi.vnn.vn Graham Greene stayed here in the 1950s. The only hotel in its class in central Hanoi and often full it boasts the *Met Pub*, restaurants, a business centre, useful bookshop and a small pool with attractive poolside bar. The hotel has retained most of its business despite competition from newer business hotels away from the city centre and remains a hub of activity. **LL-A** *Melia Hanoi*, 44B Ly Tuong Kiet St, T9343434, F9343344, solmelia@meliahanoi.com.vn A huge tower block in Central Hanoi. The lobby is fearfully cluttered with primitive art. Small swimming pool. Well-appointed rooms but not a welcoming feel. **L-A** *Guoman*, 83A Ly Thuong Kiet St, T8222800, F8222822, guomanhn@hn.vnn.vn Proving to be one of the most popular business hotels: an attractive building, with pleasing decor, 152 comfortable rooms and a tip-top location. Friendly staff and highly efficient.

A *De Syloia*, 17A Tran Hung Dao St, T8245346, F8241083, desyloia@hn.vnn.vn Very attractive and friendly small boutique, business hotel with 33 rooms and suites. The popular *Cay Cau* restaurant specializes in Vietnamese dishes and the daily set-lunch is excellent value. **A** *Green Park*, 48 Tran Nhan Tong St, T8227725, F8225977, greenpark@hn.vnn.vn 40 rooms, not an attractive building, but quite nice location, quite efficient with business facilities. **A-B** *Dan Chu*, 29 Trang Tien St, T8254937, F8266786, danchu@hn.vnn.vn Good restaurant, very pleasant, friendly state-run hotel with clean and spacious rooms. Older rooms overlooking Trang Tien St are cheapest, rooms in a new building set well back from the street cost more. **A-B** *Hoa Binh*, 27 Ly Thuong Kiet St, T8253315, F8269818, kshoabinh@hn.vnn.vn A/c, rambling old state-run hotel with quite large rooms. Renovated, but rather shoddy finish – poorly laid carpets, cracked doors. Discounts negotiable, but at US$100 per night guests would probably expect fresh rather than plastic flowers. *Le Splendide* French restaurant attached. **A-B** *Thuy Nga*, 4 Ba Trieu St, T9341256, F9341262, thuyngahotel@hn.vnn.vn Privately owned hotel with 24 rooms in a prime position – front rooms overlook Hoan Kiem Lake – or would if it weren't for the trees. All mod cons, satellite TV, etc, well maintained and polished, attentive and engaging staff, breakfast included. **B** *Eden*, 78 Tho Nhuom St, T9423273, F9424619, eden@hn.vnn.vn Good location but small rooms: nevertheless popular and handy for *A Little Italian* restaurant. **B-C** *Hoan Kiem*, 25 Tran Hung Dao St, T9434204, F9438690, hoankiemhotel@fpt.vnn State-run hotel, a/c, big rooms, clean but overpriced.

C *Bac Nam*, 20 Ngo Quyen St, T8257067, F8268998. Fairly average hotel but a good restaurant which is popular with local people. **C** *Trang Tien*, 35 Trang Tien St, T8256115, F8251416. Some a/c, hot water, central, government-run and still operating the dual pricing system, but still quite good value though often full, staff are not known

Hoan Kiem

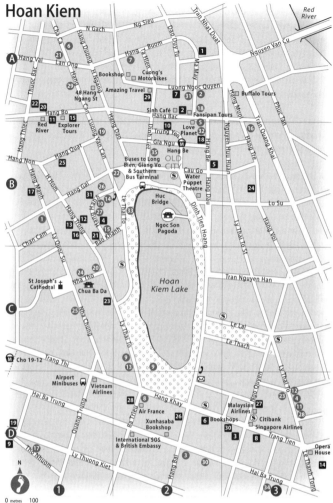

Hanoi

■ **Sleeping**
1 Anh Dao *A2*
2 A-Z Queen Café & Guesthouse (65 Hang Bac) *A2*
3 Bac Nam *D3*
4 Bao Khanh *B1*
5 Binh Minh *B2*
6 Bodega *D2*
7 Camellia *A2*
8 Dan Chu *D3*
9 Eden & A Little Italian Restaurant *D1*
10 Especen 4 *B2*
11 Especen 8 *A1*
12 Freedom *B1*
13 Hang Trong *B1*
14 Hilton Hanoi Opera *D3*
15 Hoa Linh *A1*
16 Ho Guom *B1*
17 Hong Ngoc *B1*
18 Mai Phuong & Kim Café *B2*
19 Melia Hanoi *D1*
20 My Lan *A1*
21 Nam Phuong *B1*
22 Ngoc Diep *A1*
23 Phu Gia & Rendez-Vous Café *C1*
24 Prince *B3*
25 Real Darling Café *B1*
26 Sofia *D2*
27 Sofitel Metropole & Le Beaulieu Restaurant *D3*
28 Thuy Nga (Ba Trieu St) *D2*
29 Thuy Nga (Ta Hien St) *A2*
30 Trang Tien *D3*
31 Win *B1*

● **Eating**
1 2B Ly Quoc Su St *B1*
2 69 Bar *A2*
3 Al Fresco's *D2*
4 Au Lac *D3*
5 A-Z Queen Café (13 Hang Bac) *B2*
6 Baan Thai *A1*
7 Bit Tet *A2*
8 Bobby Chinn *D2*
9 Bon Mua *C2*
10 Café des Arts & Stop Café *B1*
11 Club Opera *D3*
12 Diva *D3*
13 Fanny Ice Cream *C2*
14 Funky Monkey Bar *B1*
15 GC Bar *B1*
16 Highway 4 *B3*
17 Hoa Sua *D1*
18 Ily Café *A2*
19 Jazz Club *B1*
20 La Brique *C1*
21 La Vong (Cha Ca) *A1*
22 Little Hanoi *B2*
23 Met Pub *D3*
24 Moca Café *C1*
25 No Noodles *C1*
26 Peace Café *B1*
27 Polite Pub *B1*
28 Press Club *D3*
29 Restaurant 22 *A1*
30 Spotted Cow Bar *D2*
31 Tamarind & Handspan Adventure Travel *A2*
32 Tandoor *B2*
33 Thuy Ta *B2*
34 Verandah *D3*
35 Whole Earth & Handspan Adventure Travel *B2*

Related map
Hanoi, page 70

for their friendliness. **C-D** *Bodega*, 57 Trang Tien St, T8252241, F8267787. A/c, small 16-room hotel above coffee shop and restaurant, quite well run and clean but not much English spoken. **D** *Sofia*, 6 Hang Bai St, T8259893, F9345671. This hotel will have much resonance with travellers in the 1980s as it was one of the few where foreigners could stay. Cramped stairways, surly service, indifferent standards of cleanliness and little English spoken: in the new era of anonymous international hotels these annoyances may seem like positive virtues.

Centre: north of Hoan Kiem Lake In the Old Quarter buildings are tightly packed and rooms small, sometimes without windows. Hotels in this area offer the best value for money, most budget travellers head straight for this area.

A-B *Galaxy*, 1 Phan Dinh Phung St, T8282888, F8282466, galaxyhtl@netnam.org.vn Well-run 3-star business hotel (built in 1918) with full accessories including the all-important bedside reading lights which too many expensive hotels forget, 50 rooms. **B** *Ho Guom*, 76 Hang Trong St, T8243565, F8243564, hoguomtjc@hn.vnn.vn Very near the lake and set back from the road in a quiet courtyard, nice position, 34 rooms. **B** *Hong Ngoc*, 34 Hang Manh St, T8285053, F8285054, hongngochotel@ hn.vnn.vn This is a real find. Small, family-run hotel, the rooms and bathrooms are huge and comfortable. Well-positioned writing desk, bath tub, spotlessly clean throughout and a cheerful and helpful staff. **B-C** *Phu Gia*, 136 Hang Trong St, T8255493, F8259207, phugia@fpt.vn Behind the popular *Rendezvous Café*, 44 rooms, some with a/c, no frills, 12 best rooms have views over Hoan Kiem Lake, others are arranged around an internal courtyard so quiet, cheapest rooms may have no window. **B-C** *Win*, 34 Hang Hanh St, T8267150, F8247448, lamt76@yahoo.com Cheaper rooms are on the top (4th) floor, fair size double rooms with bath. **B-D** *Hoa Linh*, 35 Hang Bo St, T8243887, F8243886, hoalinhhotel@hn.vnn.vn Plumb in the centre of the bustling 36 Streets area, attractive lobby and willing staff. **B-D** *Prince*, 34 Hang Tre St, T9349063, F9349064, ngoxuanthang@hn.vnn.vn 10 decent a/c rooms with satellite TV in this relatively quiet street. Quite an attractive-looking hotel and friendly reception.

C *Anh Dao*, 37 Ma May St, T8267151, F8282008, anhdao@camellia-hotels.com A/c, large clean rooms, hot water, bath tubs in all rooms, the more expensive rooms have breakfast included, excellent value, popular. Recommended. **C** *Bao Khanh*, 3 Bao Khanh St, T8250271, F9285207. Simple rooms, a/c, hot water, fair price, near *Polite Pub*. **C** *Freedom*, 57 Hang Trong St, T8267119, F8243918, freedomhotel@hn.vnn.vn Not far from Hoan Kiem lake and the cathedral. Fairly plain but clean. **C-D** *Camellia*, 13 Luong Ngoc Quyen St, T8283583, F8244277, camellia@hn.vnn.vn Sister hotel of *Anh Dao* and perfectly adequate but slightly shabbier (when were the curtains last washed?), a DIY breakfast is included. **C-D** *Hang Trong*, 54-56 Hang Trong St, T8251346, F8285577, hangtronghotel@yahoo.fr A/c, a few unusual and quite decent rooms set back from the road, good position. **C-E** *My Lan*, 70 Hang Bo St, T8245510, hotelmylan@ yahoo.com, opposite Red River. Go through the dentist's surgery, elderly French-speaking doctor has 10 rooms to rent, a/c in summer, rather tightly packed but light and breezy; 1 nice roof-top apartment with kitchen and terrace.

D *Nam Phuong*, 16 Bao Khanh St, T8258030, F8258964, hiennd@netnam.org.vn Pleasant position near Hoan Kiem Lake, 8 a/c rooms but some a little airless and cramped. **D** *Red River*, 73 Hang Bo St, T8268427, F8287159, redrivertour@hotmail.com Part of the *Red River* travel business, 10 quite decent rooms, a/c, hot water, restaurant and internet. **D** *Thuy Nga*, 24C Ta Hien St, T8266053, F8282892, thuyngahotel@ hotmail.com A/c, hot water, very cramped, but friendly and quite good value. **D-E** The *Espacen Hotels*, once so numerous and so good, have collapsed to a rump of about three. All are small with a/c and fan rooms offering decent value, English spoken. *Especen 4*, 16 Trung Yen, T8253069. *Especen 8*, 67 Hang Bo St, T8251474, F9231054, oldquarterhn@fpt.vn *Especen 11*, 28 Tho Xuong St, T8244401, F8269612, especen@fpt.vn **D-E** *Mai Phuong*, 32 Hang Be St, T/F8265341, dunglucky@ hotmail.com All a/c and hot water, slightly cramped but friendly and clean.Also booking office for *Kim Café*. **D-F** *Real Darling Café*, 33 Hang Quat, T8269386, F9285007, darling_cafe@hotmail.com Travellers' café which has 16 rooms, some a/c and some dormitory rooms. **E** *A-Z Queen Café and Guesthouse*, 65 Hang Bac, T8260860, F8260300, queenaz@fpt.vn Shared bathrooms, fan rooms, basic but OK, good tour operator. **E** *Binh Minh*, 50 Hang Be St, T8267356, F8247183, queenaz@fpt.vn Some a/c. **E** *Ngoc Diep*, 83 Thuoc Bac St, T/F8250020. Just around the corner from *Red River*, cheaper rooms have fan, hot water and TV, more expensive rooms a/c and breakfast included, popular.

B *Dong Loi*, 94 Ly Thuong Kiet St, T9422721, F8267999, dongloitour@netnam.vn On the corner of Le Duan St. Spectacular building but does not represent particularly good value. **B** *Saigon*, 80 Ly Thuong Kiet St, T9424499, F9422631, saigonhotelhn@fpt.vn Renovated, expensive, state-run business hotel. **B** *Villa Bleue*, 82 Ly Thuong Kiet St, T9424733, F9424676. A/c, cable TV, nice villa, more expensive rooms are spacious and have bath tub but the place is not sufficiently well-kept or managed to merit these prices. **B-C** *Cay Xoai* (*Mango*, formerly *Railway*), 118 Le Duan St, T9423704, F8243966. Adjacent to station, *bia hoi* and *pho* stalls in the compound. Expensive for what it is. Busy, noisy area but quite friendly. **C** *Thu Do*, 109 Tran Hung Dao St, T9421268, F9421121. State-run hotel not offering particularly good value. **D** *Khach San 30-4*, 115 Tran Hung Dao St, T9420807, F8223025. Opposite railway station, cheap and good value, cheaper fan rooms shared bathroom facilities. **D** *Nhat Phuong*, 39 Le Duan St, T9423035, F9423131. A/c, hot water, reasonably priced.

Railway station area

Hanoi's relatively small central district means that some new office complexes and hotels have tended to open a short distance out of the centre.

Out of town

LL-L *Hanoi Daewoo*, 360 Kim Ma St, T8315000, F8315010, info@ hanoi-daewoohotel.com Giant hotel with 411 rooms and suites opened in 1996. Adjoining apartment complex and office tower. The hotel is one of Vietnam's most luxurious with a large pool, shops and 4 excellent restaurants, Chinese, Japanese, Italian and international. The hotel has also accumulated a large collection of Vietnamese modern art. **LL-L** *Hanoi Horison*, 40 Cat Linh St, T7330808, F7330888, saleshorison@netnam.vn A tall chimney stack stands in front of the hotel, a relic of the brickworks that once stood on the site. As in many capital cities around the world the service sector in Hanoi is gradually replacing manufacturing and occasionally, as here, preserving elements of the past. The hotel is busy and popular. It has quite a decent round pool but in rather an exposed position. All amenities and comforts for the business visitor and traveller alike. Chinese restaurant. **LL-L** *Nikko Hanoi*, 84 Tran Nhan Tong St, T8223535, F8223555, sales@hotelnikkohanoi.com.vn Rather a forbidding appearance from the outside but a tranquil marble lobby. Somewhat impersonal but a nice pool and good Japanese restaurant. Particularly popular with Japanese businessmen. **LL-A** *Sofitel Plaza Hanoi*, 1 Thanh Nien St, T8238888, F8293888, sofitel@ sotifelplazahn.com.vn 322-room hotel overlooking the West Lake, which opened just in time for the Asian Crisis. Having weathered that, it switched hands to the *French Accor Sofitel* group. Italian and Chinese restaurants, excellent business facilities and a large all-weather swimming pool with retractable roof. **A** *Hanoi*, D8 Giang Vo, Ba Dinh District, T8452270, F8459209, kshanoi@hn.vnn.vn Refurbished 11-storey building, efficient, but expensive and unfriendly state-run business hotel overlooking Giang Vo

Hanoi

Lake. **A-B** *Tay Ho*, 58 Tay Ho, T8232380, F8232390, thohotel@hn.vnn.vn Even further out of town, its 3 concrete stumps ruin a gorgeous spot on West Lake; pool and reasonable facilities, state-run. **A-B** *Thang Loi*, Yen Phu, T8294211, F8293800, thangloihtl@ hn.vnn.vn Occupies a wonderful position on West Lake but unsympathetic Cuban architecture, inconvenient location 4 km north of town, state-run, and mosquitoes are a problem; pool.

Eating

● *on maps, pages 70 and 87*

Hanoi has Western-style coffee bars, restaurants and watering holes that stand up well to comparison with their equivalents in Europe. It also has a good number of excellent Vietnamese restaurants catering both to local people and foreigners. In short, there is a super-abundance of food in Hanoi: shortage of time means most people will only sample a few of the places we recommend below.

A few words of caution: dog (*thit chó* or *thit cay*) is an esteemed delicacy in the north – 'who can resist a steaming bowl of broth with a pair of dogs paws?' demands one restaurateur – but dog is usually served only in specialist outlets so is unlikely to be ordered inadvertently. Secondly, old habits die hard: Communist ideals and recreational eating remain uncomfortable bed-fellows and, inevitably, at some stage you will suffer inedible food ungraciously served up in dingy surroundings.

Vietnamese **Expensive** *Brothers*, 26 Nguyen Thai Hoc St, T7333866. Set in a delightfully restored villa, part of the pleasure of dining here is the sumptuous surroundings. An extensive menu of delicious Vietnamese food. Visitors may well be inclined to try the *Brothers* restaurant in Hoi An. *Club Opera*, 59 Ly Thai To St, T8246950. Good restaurant with extensive menu in an attractive setting. *Emperor*, 18b Le Thanh Tong St, T8268801. Popular with diplomats and businessmen. Nicely restored French villa, very good food and attentive service. Bar stays open until 2400. *Indochine*, 16 Nam Ngu St, T9424097. Excellent Vietnamese food served by elegantly attired staff, dinner for 2 for around US$25. Lunchtimes and evenings until 2200. *Seasons*, 95B Quan Thanh, T8435444. This admirable restaurant has, inevitably, become very well known. We rate this one of the most agreeable dining experiences in Hanoi. The building is a finely restored and authentically furnished colonial villa, food is fresh and delicious and service attentive. At around US$5 per dish prices are also very fair. Bookings recommended. Open lunchtimes and evenings until around 2200. *San Ho*, 58 Ly Thuong Kiet St, T8222184. This is Hanoi's seafood restaurant which does a set weekday lunch for US$7. Operates the popular 'first catch your lobster' system to ensure freshness.

Mid-range *Banh Tom Ho Tay*, Thanh Nien St, T8293737. Specializing in *banh tom*, tasty deep-fried shrimp cakes, in a nice location between Truc Bach and West lakes from where we hope the shrimps have not been caught. *Cay Cau*, 17A Tran Hung Dao St, T9331010. In the *De Syloia Hotel*. Good Vietnamese fare at reasonable prices. Daily set lunch at 50,000d is very good value. *Le Cyclo*, 38 Duong Thanh St, T8286844. Nicely furnished restaurant with garden bar. Vietnamese and French dishes at about 50,000d. *Highway 4*, 5 Hang Tre St, T9260639. Quite a remarkable experience. This restaurant specializes in ethnic minority dishes from the north of Vietnam (Highway 4 is the most northerly road in Vietnam running along the Chinese border and favoured by owners of Minsk motorbikes). The highlight of this place is the fruit and rice wines many flavours of which are available. For those unable to make up their minds sampler shots are available, but after a couple of these they all taste good. Fairly conventional restaurant downstairs, on the upper two floors guests sit cross legged on cushions. Plenty to eat and too much to drink need not cost two people more than US$15. *La Vong* (also *Cha Ca*), 14 Cha Ca St, T8253929. Serves one dish only, the eponymous *cha ca Hanoi*, fried fish fillets in mild

Bites but no bark in a Vietnamese restaurant

Quang Vinh's restaurant was the ideal place for the ordeal to come. The palm-thatched house near the West Lake, on the outskirts of the Vietnamese capital Hanoi, was far from the accusing eyes of fellow-Englishmen.

It was dark outside. At one table, a Vietnamese couple were contentedly finishing their meal. At another, a man smoked a bamboo pipe. A television at the end of the room showed mildly pornographic Chinese videos.

But then came the moment of truth: could an Englishman eat a dog? Could he do so without his stomach rebelling, without his thoughts turning to labradors snoozing by Kentish fireplaces, Staffordshire bull terriers collecting sticks for children, and Pekinese perched on the laps of grandmothers?

One Englishman could: I ate roast dog, dog liver, barbecued dog with herbs and a deliciously spicy dog sausage, for it is the custom to dine on a selection of dog dishes when visiting a dog restaurant. The meat tastes faintly gamey. It is eaten with noodles, crispy rice-flour pancakes, fresh ginger, spring onions, apricot leaves and, for cowardly Englishmen, plenty of beer.

I had been inspired to undergo this traumatic experience – most un-British unless one is stranded with huskies on a polar ice cap – by a conversation earlier in the week with Do Duc Dinh, a Vietnamese economist, and Nguyen Thanh Tam, my official interpreter and guide.

They were much more anxious to tell me about the seven different ways of cooking a dog, and how unlucky it was to eat dog on the first five days of the month, than they were to explain Vietnam's economic reforms. "My favourite," began Tam, "is minced intestines roasted in the fire with green beans and onions." He remembered proudly how anti-Vietnamese protesters in Thailand in the 1980s had carried placards saying "Dog-eaters go home!"

During the Vietnam war, he said, a famous Vietnamese professor had discovered that wounded soldiers recovered much more quickly when their doctors prescribed half a kilogram of dog meat a day. Dinh insisted I should eat dog in Hanoi rather than Saigon. "I went to the south and ate dog, but they don't know how to cook it like we do in the north," he said. I asked where the dogs came from. "People breed it, then it becomes the family pet." And then they eat it? "Yes," he said with a laugh.

I told myself that the urban British, notorious animal lovers that they are, recoil particularly at the idea of eating dogs only because most of them never see the living versions of the pigs, cows, sheep and chickens that they eat in meat-form every day. And the French, after all, eat horses.

Resolutely unsentimental, we put aside our dog dinner and went to Vinh's kitchen. Two wire cages were on the floor; there was one large dog in the first and four small dogs in the second. Two feet away, a cauldron of dog stew steamed and bubbled. Vinh told us about his flourishing business. The dogs are transported from villages in a nearby province. A 10 kg dog costs him about 120,000 Vietnamese dong, or just over US$10. At the end of the month – peak dog-eating time – his restaurant gets through about 30 dogs a day.

The restaurant, he said, was popular with Vietnamese, Koreans and Japanese. Squeamish westerners were sometimes tricked into eating dog by the Vietnamese friends, who would entertain them at the restaurant and tell them afterwards what it was they had so heartily consumed.

Source: Extracted from an article by Victor Mallet, Financial Times

Hanoi

spice and herbs served with noodles (see page 297), popular with visitors and locals alike. 60,000d per dish. Open lunchtimes until 1400 and evenings until 2200. *Piano Bar and Restaurant*, 50 Hang Vai St, T8284423. Vietnamese and Chinese cuisine, live music. *Restaurant 202*, 202A Hue St, T9760487. Vietnamese and French menu, superb food, prices have edged up steadily, but it still represents excellent value. *69 Bar Restaurant*, 69 Ma May St, T9260452. Set in a nicely restored colonial era house this is an atmospheric experience. Good menu and well prepared food.

Cheap *Bit Tet* (Beefsteak), 51 Hang Buom St, T8251211. If asked to name the most authentic Vietnamese diner in town it would be hard not to include this on the list. The soups and steak frites are simply superb: it's rough and ready and you'll share your table, as at around US$3 per head it is understandably crowded. Evenings only, last orders around 2100. *Bodega*, 57 Trang Tien St. The ground floor is a popular coffee shop and ice cream parlour, behind is a traditional restaurant with rather poor service but stays open until 2230. *Com Chay Nang Tam*, 79A Tran Hung Dao St, T9424140. This popular little a/c restaurant is down an alley off Tran Hung Dao St, serves excellent and inexpensive vegetarian dishes. Closes around 2130. *Nos 11-25 Ta Hien St* represent a good selection of small local and inexpensive restaurants, some even have internet. *2B Ly Quoc Su St* is famous for its excellent *pho*: queue, pay, sit and eat. *Restaurant 22*, 22 Hang Can St, T8267160. Good menu, popular and tasty Vietnamese food, succulent duck. At just a couple of dollars per main course it represents brilliant value. Open 1200-2100.

Other Asian *ASEAN Food Centre, Mother's Pride*, 6C Phan Chu Trinh St, T8262168. Noodles and Malaysian dishes, slightly scruffy, but alright and not too pricey. *Baan Thai*, 3B Cha Ca St, T8288588. Authentic Thai fare, has received some good notices. *Bobby Chinn*, 1 Ba Trieu St, T9348577. One of Hanoi's better known and more expensive 'fusion' restaurants blending Western and Asian ingredients and flavours. *Edo*, Daewoo Hotel, 360 Kim Ma St, T8315000. Japanese restaurant, considered the finest in town. *Tandoor*, 24 Hang Be St, T8245359. In *Thuy Loi Hotel*, Indian food as good as any in Manchester or Bradford, popular with the expat community.

International **Expensive** *Al Fresco's*, 23L Hai Ba Trung St, T8267782. A popular Australian grill bar serving steak, pasta, pizza and fantastic salads. Giant portions, lively atmosphere, a memorable experience. Recommended. *Le Beaulieu*, 15 Ngo Quyen St, T8266919. In the *Metropole Hotel*. A good French and international restaurant open from 0630 until 2300. Its Sun buffet is regarded as one of the best in Asia. A great selection of French seafood, cold meats and cheese. For a modest extra payment this great lunch includes a free flow of champagne. *The Deli*, T8255337. Keep *The Deli* delivery

menu by the telephone for pizza, pasta, salads and sandwiches. *Il Grillo*, 116 Ba Trieu St, T8227720. Despite stiff competition from newer places this remains a popular choice. Some find it over-rated and some over-priced at US$30+ per head. Open until 2300. The *Library Bar* stocks a good range of cigars and whiskies. *Press Club*, 59A Ly Thai To St, T9340888, F9340899, www.hanoi-pressclub.com There are 3 good food outlets in this stylish complex directly behind the *Sofitel Metropole* Hotel: *The Restaurant*, has remained consistently one of the most popular dining experiences in Hanoi. Fine wine list.

Mid-range *A Little Italian*, 78 Tho Nhuom St (Eden Hotel), T9424167. Reasonable prices for European dishes and cocktails, generous servings. *Au Lac*, 57 Ly Thai To St, T8257807. Nice garden café, coffee, drinks and light meals. *Bistrot*, 34 Tran Hung Dao St, T8266136, new polished granite entrance but the same erratic service and unpriced menu; paper table cloths alas now gone but still excellent French food. Dinner for 2 excluding wine costs around US$15. Steak rocquefort and duck are always good and so is the pâté and charcuterie. Open until 2130. *Café des Arts* and *Stop Café*, 11b Bao Khanh St, T8287207. These two places are pretty much one and the same. *Café des Arts* is a very good informal French restaurant with menus at US$7, US$10 and US$18 plus full a la carte. Decent wine list. Popular among the French community. *Stop Café* is a more snacky type of place. *Diva*, 57 Ly Thai To St, T9344088. Attractive garden bar and restaurant, popular with expats. Open 0700-2400. *Hanoi Gourmet*, 1B Ham Long, T9431009. Not a restaurant but delicatessen with a couple of tables at the back. Even in Europe this would be a place to rave about. For lovers of fine wine, cheese and cold cuts, *Hanoi Gourmet* is paradise. Find a free afternoon, go short on breakfast, then go for a long leisurely lunch. Freshly restocked from France every 2 weeks. US$3 and US$5 sandwiches delivered free. Open until 2100. *Ily Café*, 97 Ma May St, T8260247. Trendy Western café restaurant in the Old City with a diverse menu. Special daily promotions are good value. *La Brique*, 6 Nha Tho St, T9285638. Trendy bare brickwork setting, fish and pasta dishes, popular with the French community. *Little Hanoi*, 21 Hang Gai St, T8288333. An excellent little place. An all-day restaurant/café, open 0730-2300. The sandwiches are particularly outstanding for US$2-3 but then so too are the cappucinos, the home-made yoghurt with honey and the apple pie. *Moca Cafe*, 14-16 Nha Tho, T8256334. From cinnamon flavoured cappuccino to smoked salmon, from dry martinis to Bengali specials. Its high open space, wafting fans and cool, marble-topped tables are hugely inviting. Open 0700-2400. *Rendez-Vous*, 136 Hang Trong St, T8289705. This is a good café overlooking the Hoan Kiem Lake. Ice creams, coffees and a good food menu. Buffet lunches are good value. *Soho*, 57 Ba Trieu St, T9436555. Low-key but stylish deli/café. Main courses, sandwiches and salads to titillate the most jaded of palates. Around US$5 for main courses. Also delivers. Open until 2200. *Verandah*, 9 Nguyen Khac Can St, T9348489. Open for lunch and dinner until 2200. A good selection of prawn, goat cheese, chicken, duck and lamb. Starters around the US$7 mark, mains around US$14. Set lunch is US$6. Attractive lemon yellow villa.

Cheap *Hoa Sua*, 81 Tho Nhuom St, T9424448. French training restaurant for disadvantaged youngsters (opposite *Eden Hotel*) where visitors can eat cheaply and well sitting around an attractive courtyard, popular. *KOTO*, 61 Van Mieu St, T7470337. A similar sort of training restaurant for underprivileged young people. Right next to the Temple of Literature, pop in for lunch after a morning's sightseeing.

Bars

The Bao Khanh and Hang Hanh area is packed with bars and music cafés. A very lively place all day and evening but like most places in Hanoi it shuts around midnight

Apocalypse Now, 5C Hoa Ma St, T9712783. Like its Saigon counterpart popular with a wide cross section of society. Music, pool and dancing, open until early morning. **Funky Monkey**, 15B Hang Hanh St. Stylish décor, good music and a good atmosphere. Attracts travellers and younger expats. **Library Bar**, *Press Club*, 59 Ly Thai To St, T9340888. Tranquil setting in which to tipple a few malts while smoking a fine Havana. **Met Pub**, back of the *Sofitel Metropole*, 56 Ly Thai To St, T8266919. Excellent pub food and a good evening buffet. All the major sporting events screened. Happy Hour 1700-1900, closes at 2300. **Polite Pub**, 5 Bao Khanh St, T8250959. Good bar snacks and cocktails, pool table, popular expat haunt merged with *GC* next door. **Spotted Cow**, 23C Hai Ba Trung St, T8241028. Cheerful and lively pub. Open 1130-0300. Happy hour until 1800, food until 2400. The Hash House Harriers bus leaves from here (see page 95).

Cafés

Bon Mua, 38-40 Le Thai To St, popular ice cream shop on the west bank of Hoan Kiem Lake. **Bon Mua**, southwest corner of Hoan Kiem Lake, lovely spot under the trees overlooking the lake. Great place for a coffee or cold drink. **Fanny Ice Cream**, 48 Le Thai To St. Nice refreshing ice cream and sorbet. 35 Trang Tien St remains a popular ice cream outlet with the Vietnamese. **No Noodles**, 20 Nha Chung St, T9285969. As they say it is Hanoi's original sandwich bar in a new location. Delicious and inexpensive (nearly all under US$2) sandwiches so big you can't fit them in your mouth, free delivery in central Hanoi. Why can't Saigon have one? **Thuy Ta**, 1 Le Thai To St, T8286290. Nice setting on northwest corner of Hoan Kiem Lake, popular meeting place for Vietnamese and travellers, snacks, ice creams and drinks. **252 Hang Bong**. Actually in what is now Cua Nam St. Excellent pastries, yoghurt and crème caramel, very popular for breakfast, 'frequented by Catherine Deneuve' er, yes, during the filming of *Indochine* a number of years ago.

Travel cafés **A-Z Queen Cafe**, 13 and 65 Hang Bac St, T9261115, T8260860, respectively. Pretty awful food but it is more a place to meet, book tours and e-mail from than a place to lunch or dine. Dormitory accommodation available. See under Sleeping. **Peace Café**, 12 Hang Hanh St T8286505. Seems to concentrate more on the café than tour side of the business which probably suits most people. Open until 2230. **Real Darling Café**, 33 Hang Quat St, popular rendezvous with backpackers, serves snacks. See also under Sleeping. **Red River**, 73 Hang Bo St. Reasonably good food, tours and accommodation. **Tamarind**, 80 Ma May St, T9260580. *Handspan Adventure Travel* office. This sets a whole new standard in travel café food. There is a comfortable café at the front and a smart restaurant behind. Very upmarket but reasonable prices. Lengthy vegetarian selection. **Whole Earth**, 7 Dinh Liet, T9260696. *Handspan Adventure Travel* booking office. Extensive vegetarian menu includes, somewhat surprisingly, pork, chicken and shrimps. In fact they are made of tofu but look like meat. This is a recurring and slightly bizarre theme in Vietnamese vegetarian restaurants. Nevertheless the real vegetable dishes are good as are the real meat dishes and the shakes.

Entertainment

Cinemas **Alliance Française**, 42 Yet Kieu St, T8266970. French films. See *Vietnam News* for current showings at all cinemas. **Fansland**, 84 Ly Thuong Kiet St, T8257484. Often with and sometimes without Vietnamese dubbing. **New Age**, 45 Hang Bai St, T8262954. Vietnamese and western films.

The *Opera House* is housed in an impressive French-era building at the east end of Trang Tien St (see page 72). A variety of Vietnamese and Western concerts, operas and plays are staged, check listings in *Vietnam News* or at the box office. **Dance & theatre**

Jazz Club (CLB Jazz), 31 Hang Quat St. Live jazz every night. **Music**

At the *Water Puppetry House*, 32 Truong Chinh St. Set up in 1956 by Ho Chi Minh, weekly performances have been staged almost continually since (see page 414). In 1984 the Australian government provided the theatre with wet suits and water resistant paints, and in recent years the troupe has performed in Japan, Australia and Europe. Entrance 20,000d. Performances every evening at 1830, 2000 and 2115 with live music (admission 20,000d-40,000d, camera 10,000d, video 50,000d). Fabulous performances, exciting music, the technical virtuosity of the puppeteers is astonishing. The theatre is some 7 km south of the centre, take a taxi. Also in the grounds of the Temple of Literature. A second water puppet theatre at 57 Dinh Tien Hoang St at the northeast corner of Hoan Kiem Lake is also good. **Water puppet theatre**

Healthclubs *Sofitel Metropole* and the *Daewoo* boast the best facilities. *Army Club*, 19 Hoang Dieu St. Pool and tennis courts open to the public. *Khuc Hao*, 1B Le Hong Phong St. Tennis courts. *Van Phuc and Trung Tu Diplomatic Compounds*, priority to diplomats but available to the public. **Hanoi Hash House Harriers:** Sat afternoons, for details check flyers at Spotted Cow, www.wso.net/hhhh **Sports**

Jan/Feb *Dong Da Hill festival* (5th day of Tet). Celebrates the battle of Dong Da in which Nguyen Hue routed 200,000 Chinese troops. Processions of dancers carry a flaming dragon of straw. **Sep** *National Day* (2nd). Features parades in Ba Dinh Square, boat races on Hoan Kiem Lake. **Festivals**

Shopping

One seasoned traveller was of the opinion that the city was a 'shopper's paradise' with cheap silk and good tailors, handicrafts and antiques. Hang Gai St is well geared to the foreign souvenir hunter and stocks an excellent range of clothes, ethnographia, fabrics and lacquerware. Hats of all descriptions abound.

Along Hang Khay and Trang Tien streets, south edge of Hoan Kiem Lake. Shops sell silver ornaments, porcelain, jewellery and carvings – much is not antique, not all is silver; bargain hard. **Antiques**

Abound near Hoan Kiem Lake, especially Trang Tien St and on Dinh Tien Hoang St at northeast corner. **Art galleries**

At the second-hand bike market at the intersection of Thinh Yen St and Pho 332, south of the city centre and on Ba Trieu St south of junction with Nguyen Du St. **Bicycles**

On Trang Tien St. For example, at No 61 is the *Foreign Language Bookshop* and No 40 is the *State Bookshop*. The alley by the side of Foreign Languages Bookstore sells copies of books otherwise out of stock. Private booksellers operate on Trang Tien St and have pavement stalls in the evening; be sure to bargain. *The Gioi*, publisher's bookshop is at 46 Tran Hung Dao. Many travel cafés operate book exchanges. Also *Book Shop*, 35 Hang Giay St, T9283186. Books sold (US$4), exchanged (2 for 1) or rented (3,000d per day). *Xunhasaba*, the state book distributor, has a shop at 32 Hai Ba Trung. **Books**

Hanoi

Handicrafts **Hang Khay St**, on southern shores of Hoan Kiem Lake, and **Hai Gai St**. A range of hand-woven fabrics and ethnographia from the hill tribes.

Maps From stalls and shops along Trang Tien St and outside post office.

Photo shops Processing and film is available all around Hoan Kiem Lake. Slide film is available for sale in a few shops but it is recommended that you do not have it processed in Vietnam.

Shoes Walking boots, training shoes, flip flops and sandals, many of which are Western sizes, are on sale in the shops around the northeast of Hoan Kiem Lake. Most are genuine brand name items and having 'fallen off the back of a lorry' are remarkably inexpensive – but do bargain.

Silk Countless shops on and around Hang Gai St; cheap tailoring services available. Smart boutiques on Nha Tho St in front of the cathedral.

Souvenirs Hang Gai St and around. For unusual souvenirs visit the shop making wooden percussion instruments at 76 Hang Bon St, great value at around US$3 each.

Tour operators

The most popular option for travellers are the budget cafés that offer reasonably priced tours and accommodation, and an opportunity to meet fellow travellers. While an excellent way to make friends, these tours do tend to isolate the visitor from local people. Operators match their rival's prices and itineraries closely and indeed many operate a clearing system to consolidate passenger numbers to more profitable levels.

Amazing Travel, 24D Ta Hien St, T/F9261126, amazingtravel@hotmail.com Small operation offering standard services and trekking around Sapa. *A-Z Queen Travel*, 13 and 65 Hang Bac St, T9261115, F8260300, queenaz@fpt.vn A well-connected and quite large organization capable of handling tailor-made as well as standard tours for individuals as well as small groups, visas. *Buffalo Tours*, 11 Hang Muoi St, T8280702, F8269370, info@buffalotours.com Well-established and well-regarded organization tending now to larger groups rather than individual budget travellers. *Exotissimo*, 26 Tran Nhat Duat, T8282150, F8282146. Specialize in more upmarket tours, good nationwide service. *Explorer Tours*, 49 Hang Bo St, T9230713, F9230835, info@explorevietnam.net Useful for both individual travel needs and small groups. *Fansipan Tours*, 24A Hang Bac St, T/F9260910, fansipantour@hotmail.com Small operator organizing tours of Sapa and the north. *Green Bamboo*, 2A Duong Thanh St, T8286504, F9231210, www.greenbambootravel.com Another well-established leader in the budget market, organizes tours of Halong Bay and Sapa. *Handspan Adventure Travel*, 80 Ma May St, T9260581, F9260445, handspan@hn.vnn.vn A reputable and well-organized business with several offices in Hanoi. Specializes in adventure tours, trekking in the north and kayaking in Halong Bay. They have their own junk in Halong Bay and kayaks. *Kim Café*, 32 Hang Be, T8265341, dunglucky@hotmail.com Small operation which offers standard tours. Car rental at reasonable prices. *Love Planet*, 25 Hang Bac St, T8284864, loveplanet8@hotmail.com Individual and small group tours; also organizes visas. *New Indochina Travel*, 4C Dang Thai Than, T9330599, F9330499, new-indochina@fpt.vn Specialists in youth travel. Cheapest student airfares out of Vietnam. *Real Darling Café*, 33 Hang Quat St, T8269386, F8256562, darling_café@hotmail.com Long-established and efficient, concentrates on tours of the north and has a visa service. *Red River Tours*, 73 Hang Bo St, T8268427, F8287159, redrivertours.hn.vn@fpt.vn Its operation seems to be

Tearaways terrorize townsfolk

A recent trend in contemporary society has manifested itself in the form of young male Hanoians racing each other on powerful motorbikes around the city streets.

Up to 400 racers take part and, to add to the frisson, the more reckless cut their brake cables. The participants are drawn chiefly from the families of the nouveau riche, some the sons of senior party members.

A number of racers and spectators have died and police have so far proved unable to prevent the clandestinely organized events. Now a team of police riders equipped with fast bikes, guns and electric cattle prods has been assembled to maintain order.

The Hanoi People's Committee has (a little naïvely) put forward the suggestion of building a special race track – presumably with the hope that legalizing and managing the 'sport' will help to control it.

Hanoi

dwindling fast; standard small group tours. **Sinh Café**, 52 Hang Bac St, T9260646, vnopentour@hn.vnn.vn One of the most successful operations in the country. Most cafés in Hanoi seem to act as agents for *Sinh Café*. Perfectly good for individual off-the-peg tours and with their wide range of contacts pretty well geared to offer more specialist travel.

Transport

The traffic in Hanoi is becoming more frantic – and lethal – as each month goes by. Bicycles, *cyclos*, mopeds, cars, lorries and buses fight for space with little apparent sense of order, let alone a highway code. At night, with few street lamps and some vehicles without lights, it can seem positively murderous. Pedestrians should watch out.

Bicycle is the most popular form of local mass transport and is an excellent way to get around the city; they can be hired from the little shops at 29-33 Ta Hien St and from most tourist cafés and hotels, expect to pay about US$1 per day. For those staying longer, it might be worth buying a bicycle (see Shopping above).

Local
91 km from Ninh Binh,
103 from Haiphong,
153 from Thanh Hoa,
165 from Ha Long Bay,
420 from Dien Bien
Phu, 658 from Hué,
763 from Danang,
1,710 from Saigon

Cyclo Hanoi's *cyclo* drivers must be among the most over-optimistic in Vietnam. They have obviously heard through the *cyclo* grapevine from Saigon that foreigners pay more than locals, but have taken this to extremes; prices quoted are usually 500% more than they should be. Drivers also have a disturbing tendency to forget the agreed fare and ask for more: be firm, some travellers even ask that the price be written down if communication is a problem. A trip from the railway station to Hoan Kiem Lake should not cost more than 15,000d. The same trip on a *xe ôm* would be 10,000d.

Motorbike Hiring a motorbike is a good way of getting to some of the more remote places. Tourist cafés and hotels rent a variety of machines for US$5-8 per day. Note that hire shops insist on keeping the renter's passport. As hotels also want to keep visitors' passports it can be hard to rent other than at your hotel. **Cuong's Motorbike Adventure**, 40 Luong Ngoc Quyen St, T8266586. Buy, sell, rent and repair Minsks only. Ideal off-road bikes for those planning more adventurous tours of the mountains. 70 Hang Bac St, T9260931. Open 24 hrs.

Taxi and private car There are plenty of metered taxis in Hanoi: **City Taxi**, T8222222. **Hanoi Taxi**, T8535252. **Mai Linh Taxi**, T8222666. **Airport Taxi**, T8733333. Private cars can be chartered from most hotels and from many tour operators, see page 96.

Road to nowhere

Symptomatic of Vietnam's traffic woes is the motorway between Hanoi and Noi Bai airport. It is the daily scene of violent clashes between ancient and modern modes of transport. Within days of its opening it was the scene of utter carnage as pedestrians, cyclists and buffalo exercised their right, laid down in black and white, to cross the road on zebra crossings in front of speeding traffic. Brazen hand-cart pushers obstinately cling to the fast lane swerving only to avoid the parked motorbikes of spectators squatting on the central reservation admiring the view; one journalist on Vietnam News reported seeing five accidents on a single journey to the airport. Although motorists might touch speeds of over 100 km per hour the road ends in such a remote part of Hanoi that it can take almost an hour to reach the city centre. Locals displayed their contempt for the scheme by hacking up the surface to excavate and sell the foundation sand and by cutting down and selling for scrap the metal handrails.

Long distance

Air There are direct international air connections with Bangkok, Beijing, Dubai, Guangzhou, Hong Kong, Kuala Lumpur, Kunming, Moscow, Seoul and Taipei. Connections with Singapore, Paris, Melbourne and Los Angeles via Saigon. Domestic air connections with Saigon (US$127), Danang (US$67), Nha Trang (US$97), Dien Bien Phu, Hué (US$67) and Na San. See timetable, page 40.

Transport to & from the airport

The official *Airport Taxi* charges a fixed price of 150,000d. Minibus is US$2. Journey time is approximately 45 mins-1 hr. The minibus service will try to get foreigners to stay at certain hotels. In order to avoid problems it is recommended that passengers alight at the *Vietnam Airlines* office and take a taxi to their booked hotel from there. Chartering a taxi from a hotel to the airport should cost no more than around US$9. Hotels normally charge around US$3 per person by bus and US$4 per person by car. Meter taxis may cost over US$15 and will charge an additional road toll of 10,000d. Minibuses leave for the airport from the *Vietnam Airlines Office* at 1 Quang Trung St, US$2, running a service at regular intervals from 0415 but check bus departure times at the *Vietnam Airlines* office.

Road

Bus: Hanoi has a number of bus stations. The **Southern bus terminal** is out of town, but linking buses run from the northern shore of Hoan Kiem Lake. The terminal serves destinations south of Hanoi: Saigon, Buon Ma Thuot, Vinh, Danang, Thanh Hoa, Nha Trang, Dalat, Qui Nhon, Ninh Binh and Nam Dinh. Express buses usually leave at 0500; advance booking is recommended. The **Kim Ma station** is on Nguyen Thai Hoc St (opposite No 168), just past Giang Vo St, and serves destinations to the northwest: Son Tay, Trung Ha, Phu To, Hat Lot, Moc Chau, Bat Bat, Tan Hong, Da Chong, Hoa Binh, Son La, Dien Bien Phu and Yen Bai. Buses and minibuses to Haiphong leave regularly from **Gia Lam station** (over Chuong Duong Bridge), 2½ hrs, 20,000d. Buses can be flagged down on Tran Quang Khai St before they cross the bridge. **Ha Dong station** in the southwest suburbs has buses to Hoa Binh. Take a local bus or *xe ôm* to the bus station. **Giap Bat station** on Giai Phong St serves destinations south.

Train

The central station (Ga Hanoi) is at 126 Le Duan St, at the end of Tran Hung Dao St (a 10-min taxi ride from the centre of town). For trains to Saigon and the south enter the station from Le Duan St. For trains to Haiphong, Lao Cai and China enter the station from Tran Quy Cap St. It is possible to walk across the tracks if you go to the wrong part. Regular daily connections with Saigon (see timetable, page 46). Advance booking is required. There are 4 trains daily to Haiphong, 1 from the central station, 3 from Long Bien station. There are 4 trains daily to China via Lang Son and Lao Cai. **Long Bien station** is at the western end of Long Bien Bridge near the Red River. Get there by taxi or *xe ôm*.

Directory

Air France, 1 Ba Trieu St, T8253484, F8266694. *Aeroflot*, 360 Kim Ma St, T7718742, **Airline offices**
F7718522. *Cathay Pacific*, 49 Hai Ba Trung St, T8267298 (Noi Bai, T8261113),
F8267709. *China Airlines*, 18 Tran Hung Dao St, T8242688, F8242588. *China Southern
Airlines*, 360 Kim Ma St, T7716611, F7716600. *Japan Airlines*, 63 Ly Thai To St,
T8266693, F8266698. *Lao Aviation*, Quang Trung St, T/F8229951. *Malaysian Airlines*,
15 Ngo Quyen St, T8268820, F8242388. *Pacific Airlines*, 100 Le Duan, T8515356.
Singapore Airlines, 17 Ngo Quyen St, T8268888, F8268666. *Thai*, 44B Ly Thuong Kiet
St, T8266893, F8267394. *Vietnam Airlines*, 1 Quang Trung St, T8320320, F8248989.
Open daily 0700-1800 for both domestic and international bookings.

Commission is charged on cashing TCs into US dollars but no longer if cashing directly **Banks**
into dong. It is better to withdraw dong from the bank and pay for everything in dong.
Most hotels will change dollars, often at quite fair rates. *ANZ Bank*, 14 Le Thai To St,
T8258190. Open Mon-Fri 0830-1600, provides full banking services including cash
advances on credit cards, 2% commission on TCs, 24-hr ATM. *Bank of Foreign Trade*,
47-49 Ly Thai To St. *Citibank*, 17 Ngo Quyen St, T8251950. Only cashes TCs into dong.
Commercial & Industrial Bank, 37 Hang Bo St, T8285359. Dollar TCs can be changed
here, with 1.25% commission for converting dollars cash. *Foreign Exchange Centre*, 2
Le Lai St. *National Bank*, 10 Le Lai St, T8249042. Open 0800-1100 and 1300-1600.
VID Public Bank, 2 Ngo Quyen St, T8266953. Charge 1.5% on TCs. *Vietcombank*, 198
Tran Quang Khai St, T8243108. 2% commission if converted to dollars cash.

Internet: internet access and emailing is cheap and easy in Hanoi. Most of the hotels **Communica-**
listed here with email addresses allow their customers to use it. Failing that, all the **tions**
travel cafés now have internet services. Many allow people who book tours through
them a short period of internet access free of charge. Rates vary: hotels which may
have just one or two terminals naturally have to charge more than internet cafés which
may have 20 computer terminals but only one telephone connection. The cheapest
rates are about 3,000d per hr, the most expensive rates are around 200-300d per min.
Post office: *GPO*, 75 Dinh Tien Hoang St. **Express Mail Service** at the GPO. International telephone, telex and fax services also available at the PO at 66-68 Trang Tien St
and at 66 Luong Van Can St and at the PO on Le Duan next to the railway station. *DHL*,
in GPO. Also at 778 Duong Lang, T7750144 and 49 Nguyen Thai Hoc St, T7332086. *TNT
International Express*, 25D-25E Lang Ha St, T5142575. *UPS*, 4C Dinh Le St, T8246483.

Algeria, 13 Phan Chu Trinh St, T8253865, F8260830. **Australia**, 8 Dao Tan St, T8317755, **Embassies &**
F8317711. **Belgium**, 49 Hai Ba Trung St, T9346179, F9346183. **Brazil**, T72-14 Thuy **consulates**
Khue St, T8432544, F8432542. **Burma**, A3 Van Phuc Diplomatic Compound, T8453396,
F8452404. **Cambodia**, 71 Tran Hung Dao St, T9424789, F9423225. **Canada**, 31 Hung
Vuong St, T8235500, F8235333. **China**, 46 Hoang Dieu St, T8453736, F8232826. **Cuba**,
65 Ly Thuong Kiet St, T9422426, F9422621. **Czech Republic**, 13 Chu Van An St,
T8454131, F8233996. **Denmark**, 19 Dien Bien Phu St, T8231888, F8231999. **Egypt**, 336
Nghi Tam St, T8294999, F8294997. **Finland**, Central Building, 31 Hai Ba Trung St,
T8266788, F8266766. **France**, 57 Tran Hung Dao St, T8252719, F8264236. **Germany**,
29 Tran Phu St, T8430245, F8453838. **Hungary**, 360 Kim Ma St, T7715714, F771716.
India, 58-60 Tran Hung Dao St, T8244989, F8244998. **Indonesia**, 50 Ngo Quyen St,
T8253353, F8259274. **Israel**, 68 Nguyen Thai Hoc St, T8433140, F8435760. **Italy**, 9 Le
Phung Hieu St, T8256256, F8267602. **Japan**, 27 Lieu Giai St, T8463000, F8463043. **Laos**,
22 Tran Binh Trong St, T9424576, F8228414. **Malaysia**, 6B Lang Ha St, T8313400,
F8313402. **Netherlands**, 360 Kim Ma, T8315651, F8315655. **Philippines**, 27B Tran
Hung Dao St, T9437938, F9439292. **Poland**, 3 Chua Mot Cot St, T8452027, F8236914.

Romania, 5 Le Hong Phong St, T8452014, F8430922. **Russia**, 191 De La Thanh St, T8336991, F8336996. **Singapore**, 41-43 Tran Phu St, T8233965, F8233992. **South Korea**, 360 Kim Ma St, T8315111, F8315117. **Sweden**, Van Phuc Diplomatic Compound, T8454824, F8232195. **Switzerland**, 44B Ly Thuong Kiet St, T9346589, F9346591. **Thailand**, 63-65 Hoang Dieu St, T8235092, F8235088. **UK**, Central Building, 31 Hai Ba Trung St, T8252510, F8265762. **USA**, 7 Lang Ha St, T8431500, F8431510.

Medical services   Hospitals: *Eye Hospital*, 85 Ba Trieu St, T8263966. *Friendship Hospital*, 1 Tran Khanh Du St, T9722231. *Hanoi Family Medical Practice*, 109-112 Van Phuc, T8430748. 24-hr medical service, including intensive care, also dental care. *Hospital Bach Mai*, Giai Phong St, T8693731. English-speaking doctors. Also dental service. *Hospital K*, 43 Quan Su St, T8252143. *International Hospital*, Giai Phong St, T5740740. *International SOS*, Central Building, 31 Hai Ba Trung St, T9340555. 24-hr, emergencies and medical evacuation. Dental service too. *Swedish Clinic*, Lang Thuong St., T8343176. *Vietnamese-German Hospital*, 40 Trang Thi St, T8255934. Dental treatment also available.

Useful address   Immigration Dept, 40A Hang Bai St, T8266200.

www.footprintbooks.com
A new place to visit

On the road? About to go? Complete introductions to all footprint destinations – great for planning and inspiring. Join the Footprint travel hub for news/messages/competitions. Adventure highs & wildlife wows. What's your view? Write in and tell us how you got on.

The North

4

The North

104	**The Northwest**
104	Hanoi to Dien Bien Phu and Sapa
111	Dien Bien Phu
121	Sapa
131	**The Northeast**
136	Cao-Bac-Lang
138	Cao Bang
141	The Northeast Frontier

146	Hanoi to Haiphong, Do Son, Cat Ba Island and Halong Bay
146	Haiphong
152	Do Son
154	Cat Ba Island
158	Halong Bay
161	Halong City
165	Hanoi to Ninh Binh
166	Ninh Binh and around

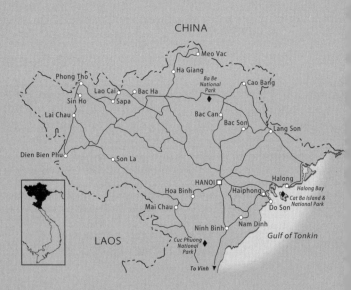

To many the Northwest represents the finest Vietnam has to offer. In terms of scenery, colour, human interest and for the thrill of discovering the unknown, it is unrivalled. Nor is the region without wider significance – the course of world history was altered at Dien Bien Phu in 1954. It is, in short, that myth of travellers' folklore – unspoilt Vietnam.

There are good reasons why this is so. The distance, rugged environment and primitive infrastructure have all contributed to placing the Northwest at the edge of Vietnamese space. But for those who wish to avoid the backpacker trail and are prepared to put up with a little discomfort, the rewards are great. Pockets of the north have already been discovered – Sapa, for example, is no longer a secret, but it is no less lovely for that.

The fertile river valleys dividing the mountain ranges of North Vietnam have long been inhabited by people of the Austro-Asiatic language family, including forebears of the modern Vietnamese and their upland cousins the Mường. They are thought to have migrated into the area from southern China during the latter half of the first millennium BC; there they joined other groups including the ancestors of the Mon-Khmer speaking peoples.

The North

The Northwest

Hanoi to Dien Bien Phu and Sapa

The road from Hanoi to Dien Bien Phu winds its way for 420 km into the Annamite mountains that mark the frontier with the Lao People's Democratic Republic. The round trip from Hanoi and back via Dien Bien Phu and Sapa is about 1,200 km and offers, perhaps, the most spectacular scenery anywhere in Vietnam. Opportunities to see something of the lives, customs and costumes of some of Vietnam's ethnic minorities (page 395) abound. The loop can be taken in a clockwise or anti-clockwise direction; the advantage of following the clock is the opportunity to recover from the rigours of the journey in the tranquil setting of Sapa.

Highway 6 leads southwest out of Hanoi to Hoa Binh. Setting off in the early morning (this is a voyage of dawn starts and early nights) the important arterial function of this road to Hanoi can be clearly seen. Ducks, chickens, pigs, bamboo and charcoal all pour in – the energy and building materials of the capital – a remarkable volume of it transported by bicycle. Beyond the city limit the fields are highly productive, with bounteous market gardens and intensive rice production.

The geology of much of Northwest Vietnam is limestone; the effect on this soft rock of the humid tropical climate and the resulting numerous streams and rivers is remarkable. Large cones and towers (hence tower karst), sometimes with vertical walls and overhangs, rise dramatically from the flat alluvial plains. Dotted with bamboo thickets, this landscape is one of the most evocative in Vietnam; its hazy images seem to linger deep in the collective Vietnamese psyche and perhaps symbolize a sort of primaeval Garden of Eden, an irretrievable age when life was simpler and more innocent.

Hoa Binh

Phone code: 018
Colour map 1, grid B4

It's about 75 km from Hanoi

Hoa Binh, on the banks of the Da (Black) River, marks the southern limit of the interior highlands. Hoa Binh is 75 km from Hanoi, a journey of about 2½ hours. A newly opened Hoa Binh Province museum (**Bao Tang Tinh Hoa Binh**) contains items of archaeological, historical and ethnographical importance. Relics of the First Indochina War, including a French amphibious landing craft, remain from the bitterly fought campaign of 1951-52 which saw Viet Minh forces successfully dislodge the French. ■ *0800-1030, 1400-1700, 5,000d.* Major excavation sites of the Hoabinhian prehistoric civilization (10,000 BC) were found in the province, which is its main claim to international fame. In 1979, with Russian technical and financial assistance, work began on the Hoa Binh Dam and hydro-electric power station, which 15 years later was complete. The reservoir has a volume of nine billion cubic metres: it provides two functions, to prevent flooding on the lower reaches of the Red River (that is Hanoi) and to generate power. Vietnam is so dependent on Hoa Binh for its electricity that when water levels fall below critical thresholds in the dry season large areas of the country are blacked out. More than 4,000 households had to be moved from the valley floor to rugged, infertile hillsides where ironically they are too poor to afford electricity.

People of the north

Ethnic groups belonging to the Sino-Tibetan language family such as the Hmong and Dao, or the Ha Nhi and Phu La of the Tibeto-Burman language group are more recent arrivals. Migrating south from China only within the past 250-300 years, these people have lived almost exclusively on the upper mountain slopes, practising swidden agriculture and posing little threat to their more numerous lowland-dwelling neighbours, notably the Thai.

Thus was established the pattern of human and political settlement which would persist in North Vietnam for over 1,000 years right down to the colonial period – a centralized Viet state based in the Red River Delta area, with powerful Thai vassal lordships dominating the North West. Occupying lands located in some cases almost equidistant from Hanoi, Luang Prabang and Kunming, the Thai, Lao, Lu and Tày lords were obliged during the pre-colonial period to pay tribute to the royal courts of Nam Viet, Lang Xang (Laos) and China alike, though in times of upheaval they could and frequently did play one power off against the other for their own political gain.

Considerable effort was thus required by successive Viet kings in Thang Long (Hanoi) and later in Hué to ensure that their writ and their writ alone ruled in the far north. To this end there was ultimately no substitute for the occasional display of military force, but the enormous cost of mounting a campaign into the northern mountains obliged most Viet kings simply to endorse the prevailing balance of power there by investing the most powerful local lords as their local government mandarins, resorting to arms only when separatist tendencies became too strong.

Such was the political situation inherited by the French colonial government following its conquest of Indochina in the latter half of the 19th century. Its subsequent policy towards the ethnic minority chieftains of North Vietnam was to mirror that of the Vietnamese monarchy whose authority it assumed; throughout the colonial period responsibility for colonial administration at both local and provincial level was placed in the hands of seigneurial families of the dominant local ethnicity, a policy which culminated during the 1940s in the establishment of a series of ethnic minority 'autonomous zones' ruled over by the most powerful seigneurial families.

The North

Hoa Binh is a possible stopping off point en route for Son La but those who make an early start can press on to Mai Chau for lunch.

Muòng and **Dao minority villages** are accessible from Hoa Binh. **Xom Mo** is around 8 km from Hoa Binh and is a village of the Muòng minority. There are around 10 stilt houses, where overnight stays are possible, and there are nearby caves to visit. Duong and Phu are villages of the Dao Tien (Money Dao), located 25 km up river. Boat hire (US$25) is available from *Hoa Binh Tourism*. Permit required for overnight stay (see Hoa Binh Tourist Co). It is also possible to arrange a tour to the nearby **hydropower station**, most of which is built underground for strategic rather than environmental reasons – but at vast expense.

B *Hoa Binh 1*, 54 Phuong Lam, T852051, F854372. On Highway 6 out of Hoa Binh towards Mai Chau, clean and acceptable standards, some rooms built in minority style, also an ethnic minority dining experience complete with rice drunk through bamboo straws. The *Hoa Binh Ethnic Minority Culture Troupe* put on 1-hr shows featuring dance and music of the Muòng, Thái, Hmông and Dao in the hotel. Gift shop stocks ethnic produce, so for those venturing no further stock up now. **B** *Hoa Binh 2*, 160 An Duong Vuong, T852001. As above but no restaurant.

Sleeping
Phone code: 018

Eating   *Thanh Toi*, 22a Cu Chinh Lan, T853951. Local specialities, wild boar and stir-fried egg-plant, prices from US$1 to US$3 per dish.

Transport **Road** **Bus**: bus station on Tran Hung Dao St. Morning departures from Hanoi's Kim Ma terminal, 2 hrs.

Directory **Post office:** Tran Hung Dao St. **Tourist offices** *Hoa Binh Tourist Co*, Song Da, T854122. Can arrange boat hire and visits to minority villages.

Mai Chau

Phone code: 022
Colour map 1, grid B3

It is about 75 km from Hoa Binh

After leaving Hoa Binh, Highway 6 heads in a south-southwest direction as far as the Chu River. Thereafter it climbs through some spectacular mountain scenery before descending into the beautiful Mai Chau valley.

During the first half of this journey, the turtle-shaped roofs of the Mường houses predominate, but after passing Man Duc the road enters the territory of the Thái, Northwest Vietnam's most prolific ethnic minority, heralding a subtle change in the style of stilted-house architecture. Whilst members of the Thái ethnic minority will be encountered in great abundance on this circuit, it is their Black Thái sub-ethnic group which will be seen most frequently. What makes the Mai Chau area interesting is that it is one of the few places en route where travellers can encounter their White Thái cousins.

An isolated farming community until 1993, Mai Chau has undergone significant change in just a few short years. Its tranquil valley setting, engaging White Thái inhabitants and superb rice wine make Mai Chau a very worthwhile pit-stop, and an alternative overnight stop for those wishing to give Hoa Binh a miss.

The growing number of foreign and domestic tourists visiting the area in recent years has had a significant impact on the economy of Mai Chau and the lifestyles of its inhabitants. Some foreign visitors complain that the valley has already gone a long way down the same road as Chiang Mai in northern Thailand, offering a manicured hill-tribe village experience to the less adventurous tourist who wants to sample the quaint lifestyle of the ethnic people without too much discomfort. There may be some truth in this allegation, yet there is another side to the coin.

Since the region first opened its doors to foreign tourists in 1993, the Mai Chau People's Committee has attempted to control the impact of tourism in the valley. Lac is the official tourist village to which tour groups are led, and although it is possible to visit and even stay in the others, by 'sacrificing' one village to tourism it is hoped to limit the impact. Income generated from tourism by the villagers of Lac has brought about a significant enhancement of lifestyles, not just in Lac but also throughout the entire valley, enabling many villagers to tile their roofs and purchase consumer products such as television sets, refrigerators and motorbikes. Of course, for some foreign visitors the sight of a television aerial or a T-shirt is enough to prove that an ethnic village has already lost its traditional culture, but in Lac they are wily enough to conceal their aerials in the roof space.

Mai Chau is proving popular with young Hanoians who tend to arrive in large groups at the weekend. They appear not to have read widely on responsible tourism and appear oblivious to the impact their presence makes. The slatternly women totter around in six inch platform shoes while their loutish men shatter the peace with their ghetto blasters. The dignity and elegance of the Thái is all the more evident by contrast.

Lac is easily accessible from the main road – go a few hundred metres past the *People's Committee Guesthouse* then take a track to the right directly into the village of Lac, the village most popular with day-trippers and overnight visitors from Hanoi. Turning into the village one's heart may sink: minibuses are drawn up and stilt houses in the centre of the village all sport stickers of Hanoi tour operators. But before you turn and flee take a gentle stroll around the village, find a non-stickered house and by means of gestures, signs, broken English and the odd word of Vietnamese ask whether you can spend the night.

Lac, White Thái village

Borrow or rent a bicycle from your hosts and wobble across narrow bunds to the neighbouring hamlets, enjoying the ducks, buffaloes, children and lush rice fields as you go. It is one of the most delightful of experiences. If you are lucky you will be offered a particularly refreshing tea made from the bark of a certain tree. About 5 km south of Mai Chau on Route 15A is the Naon River on which, in the dry season, a boat can be taken to visit a number of large and **impressive grottoes**. Others can be reached on foot. Ask your hosts or at the *People's Committee Guesthouse* for details.

Grottoes

The North

D *People's Committee Guesthouse*, T851812. Fan rooms, basic, no restaurant. Competition from the *Ethnic Houses* means the *Guesthouse* does not always operate. **E** *Ethnic Houses*, visitors can spend the night in a White Thái house on stilts. Mat, hard pillow, mosquito net, basic washing facilities (cold tap or a well) and sometimes fan provided. This is particularly recommended as the hospitality and easy manner of the people is a highlight of many visitors' stay in Vietnam. Food and local rice wine provided. Avoid the large houses in the centre if possible. Dinner, bed and breakfast should cost 50,000d.

Sleeping
Phone code: 022

Most people will eat with their hosts. Mai Chau town itself has a couple of simple *com pho* places near the market. The rice wine in Mai Chau is excellent, particularly when mixed with local honey.

Eating

Mai Chau Ethnic Minority Dance Troupe, Thái dancing culminating in the communal drinking of sweet, sticky rice wine through straws from a large pot. This troupe performs most nights in Lac in one of the large stilt houses, admission included as part of the package for people on tours or otherwise a small contribution.

Entertainment

Villagers offer a range of woven goods and fabrics on which they are becoming dependent for a living. There are also local paintings and wicker baskets, pots, traps and pouches all well made. Mai Chau is probably the best place for buying handicrafts in the Northwest.

Shopping

Road Bus: connections with **Hoa Binh** (2 hrs) and with **Hanoi**'s Kim Ma station (4 hrs), and onward buses northwest to **Son La**. While it is quite easy and cheap to get here using the public bus most people visit on an **organized tour**. Hanoi tour operators run tours on Mon, Wed and Sat for around US$20. The cost of a tour for two people on other days is outrageously expensive. The cost of renting a car for a night and two days should be no more than about US$60: accommodation, as described above, is cheap.

Transport

Son La

What the road to Son La lacks in comfort is more than compensated for by the scenery and superb **Black Thái** and **Muòng villages**. The road passes close to several particularly attractive villages each with a suspension footbridge and fascinating hydraulic works. Mini hydro-electric generators on the river supply houses with enough power to run a light or television and water power is

Phone code: 022
Colour map 1, grid B2

It is about 310 km northwest of Hanoi

also used to husk and mill rice. The succession of picturesque little villages located just across the river to the left-hand side of the road between 85 and 78 km from Son La, affords an excellent opportunity to view Black Thái stilt-house architecture. **Cuc Dua village** at the 84 km mark is highly photogenic. Typically there is a suspension bridge over the incised river in which you can see fish traps and swimming children as clouds of butterflies flutter by on the breeze.

It was not until the 18th century, under the patronage of the Black Thái seigneurial family of Ha, that Son La began to develop as a town. During the late 1870s the region was invaded by renegade Chinese Yellow Flag bands taking refuge after the failed Taiping Uprising. Allying himself to Lin Yung-fu, commander of the pursuing Black Flag forces, Deo Van Tri, Black Thái chieftain, led a substantial army against the Yellow Flags in 1880, decisively defeating and expelling them from the country. Thus Tri established hegemony over all the Black and White Thái lords in the Son La area, enabling him to rely on their military support in his subsequent struggle against the French – indeed, the chieftains of Son La were to take an active role in the resistance effort between 1880 and 1888.

As the French moved their forces up the Da River valley during the campaign of 1888, the chieftains of the area were one by one obliged to surrender. A French garrison was quickly established at Son La. As elsewhere in the Northwest, the French chose to reward the chieftains of Son La district for their new-found loyalty by reconfirming their authority as local government mandarins, albeit now on behalf of a colonial rather than a royal master.

While large-scale resistance to French rule in the Northwest effectively ceased after 1890, sporadic uprisings continued to create problems for the colonial administration. The French responded by establishing detention centres throughout the area which were known to the Thái as *huon mut* (dark houses). The culmination of this policy came in 1908 with the construction of a large penitentiary designed to incarcerate resistance leaders from the Northwest and other regions of Vietnam. Just one year after the opening of the new Son La Penitentiary, prisoners staged a mass breakout, causing substantial damage to the prison itself before fleeing across the border into Laos.

During the final days of colonial rule Son La became an important French military outpost, and accordingly an air base was built at Na San, 20 km from the town. Both Na San air base and the colonial government headquarters in Son La town were abandoned to the Viet Minh in November 1953, on the eve of the Battle of Dien Bien Phu.

Sights Contemporary Son La is undergoing a facelift, with gleaming new government buildings under construction in the centre of this provincial capital.

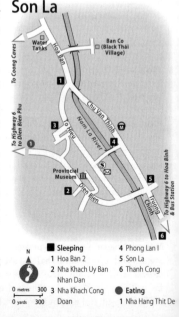

Son La

To Coong Caves

Water Tanks

Hoa Ban

Ban Co (Black Thái Village)

To Highway 6 to Dien Bien Phu

Chu Van Thinh

Nam Ta River

To Hieu

Provincial Museum

Dien Bien

To Highway 6 to Hoa Binh & Bus Station

Truong Chinh

N

0 metres 300
0 yards 300

■ **Sleeping**
1 Hoa Ban 2
2 Nha Khach Uy Ban Nhan Dan
3 Nha Khach Cong Doan
4 Phong Lan I
5 Son La
6 Thanh Cong

● **Eating**
1 Nha Hang Thit De

There is little to see other than the **Son La Provincial Museum** on Youth Hill, just off Highway 6 and near the centre of town. The museum building is in fact the town's old French Penitentiary, constructed in 1908, damaged in 1909, bombed in 1952, and now partially rebuilt for tourists. The original 3-m-deep dungeon and tiny cells complete with food-serving hatches and leg-irons, can be seen together with an exhibition illustrating the history of the place and the key individuals who were incarcerated here. ■ *Daily 0800-1030, 1400-1700, although a man with a key can normally be found at other times, 5,000d.*

Excursions

To reach the **Coong Caves** – or Tham Coong – walk or drive to the north end of town, after a few hundred metres are the tanks of the Son La Water Company; turn left and follow the stream or take the path and yomp across the bunds of the rice fields. There are two caves, the wet cave is now fenced off but a scramble up the limestone face brings you to a dry cave (entrance 5,000d if the man is there) from which are lovely views. As you have probably come to expect by now in Vietnam, the caves are nothing, the walk a never-ending joy – with wet feet. The fields, ponds and streams below the caves are a miracle of inventiveness and beauty: stilt houses, gardens, hibiscus hedgerows, and a range of colours and smells that are particularly appealing in the late-afternoon sunlight. Fish are bred in the ponds, which are covered with water cress (*salad soong*) and what looks like a red algal bloom, but it actually a small floating weed (*beo hoa dau*) which is fed to ducks and pigs.

Ban Co is a Black Thái village and a visit here can be combined with a trip to Tham Coong. Returning from the caves, rejoin the road then turn left and take a track across the fields to the village of Co. The village is a largeish and fairly ordinary Black Thái settlement but a diverting twilight hour can be spent watching its inhabitants returning from the fields with a fish or duck for the pot and a basket of greens, washing away the day's grime in the stream and settling down to a relaxing evening routine that has changed little in the last few hundred years.

For these and the other inhabitants of Son La, however, it will be not just the evening routine that changes: the government is flooding the whole valley by damming the Da River. Presumably they have judged it prudent to get on with the large scale dam business before the population wises up to 'green' issues and an environmental movement evolves. The dam and reservoir will be three times bigger than the Hoa Binh complex, currently the biggest in Southeast Asia, and as many as 100,000 people could be displaced. For a rather paltry sum of money and a promise of a plot of land the government appears to have bought grudging acquiescence – at least from the people interviewed by *Vietnam News*. The Son La authorities claim to be willing to sacrifice part of their land for the greater good of the country, although quite how widely this altruistic view is held is by no means clear. The effects of the dam will be felt all the way up the Da River to Lai Chau.

There are **hot springs** in Mong village 5 km south of Son La. However, they are not up to much.

Sleeping
■ *on map*
Phone code: 022
Price codes:
see inside front cover

C *Hoa Ban 2*, Hoa Ban St, T852395, F852712. A/c or fan, hot water, clean and fairly comfortable, slightly pricy. **C** *Nha Khach Uy Ban Nhan Dan (People's Committee Guesthouse)*, Highway 6, T852080. Signed *Nha Khach* just off Highway 6, a/c, fan, renovated and now the pick of the bunch, lovely setting overlooking hillsides and villages. **C** *Phong Lan 1*, T853515, F852318. Opposite Central Market. A/c, clean and ordinary. **C** *Thanh Cong*, 278 Truong Chinh St, T856421, F855023. On the road in from Mai Chau, new and stark. **D** *Nha Khach Cong Doan (Trade Union Guesthouse)*, Chieng Le St,

The North

T852804, F855312. A/c, fan rooms, basic, some English spoken. **D** *Son La*, Quang Thang St, opposite bus station, T852702. A/c and fan rooms, basic accommodation, restaurant.

Eating *Nha Hang Thit De*, near the bridge, TT852394. Goat specialities. *Nha Hang Thit Vit*, also near the bridge. Duck specialities.

Transport **Air**: 3 flights per week from **Hanoi**, Wed and Fri 0930, Sun 1030, 45 mins. Returning same days at 1105 and 1205 respectively. Son La airport is at Na San, 20 km southeast of Son La on Highway 6. *Vietnam Airlines* office in the airport, T845102. **Road** **Bus**: connections with **Hanoi**'s Kim Ma station and, en route to Hanoi, with Mai Chau and Hoa Binh. Continuing north from Son La, there are regular bus connections with Dien Bien Phu and Lai Chau.

Directory **Bank** *Vietcombank*, 57 To Hieu St. **Communications** Post office: 43 To Hieu St.

West to Dien Bien Phu or north to Lai Chau from Son La

The scenery on leaving Son La is breath-taking. Reds and greens predominate – the red of the soil, the costumes and the newly tiled roofs, and the green are the trees, the swaying fronds of bamboo, and the wet-season rice. Early morning light brings out the colours in their finest and freshest hues, and as the sun rises colours transmute from orange to pink to ochre.

Around every bend in the road is a new visual treat. Most stunning are the valley floors, blessed with water throughout the year. Here generations of ceaseless human activity have engineered a land to man's design. Using nothing more than bamboo technology and human muscle, terraces have been sculpted from the hills: little channels feed water from field to field illustrating a high level of social order and common purpose. Water powers devices of great ingenuity – water wheels for raising water from river level to field level, rice mills and huskers and mini electrical turbines. And, quite inadvertently, these people, who for centuries have been isolated from outside perceptions of beauty, have produced a fusion of natural and human landscape that cannot fail to please the eye. Shape, form, scale and colour blend and contrast in a pattern of sympathy and understanding wholly lost to the modern world. Then the road climbs away from the river to a village dependent on rain for its water: the grey and red dust and the meagre little houses indicate great poverty and makes one realize the importance of a constant water supply.

There is a small and colourful market village 25 km from Son La and 10 km further on is **Thuan Chau**, another little market town. In the early morning these two places are good for photographing people of different minorities in traditional dress bartering and trading. Thuan Chau is a good spot for breakfast and for buying headscarves. The settlements along this route nicely illustrate the law which describes the inverse relationship between the size of a place and the proportion of the population traditionally garbed. The road is remarkably good with crash barriers, mirrors positioned strategically on hair-pin bends and warning signs, which, considering the precipitous nature of the terrain from Thuan Chau to Tuan Giao and that visibility is often obscured by cloud and fog, is just as well.

Tuan Giao is 75 km and approximately three hours from Son La. From Tuan Giao travellers have the choice of either proceeding north across the mountains direct to Lai Chau, or taking the longer route via Dien Bien Phu.

Highway 6 from Tuan Giao heads north across the Hoang Lien Son Range direct to Lai Chau. This journey of around 100 km takes five hours. From

Tuan Giao, the road climbs up through some spectacular scenery reaching altitudes of around 1,800-1,900 m. Red and White Hmông villages are passed en route. It is the option taken by those who do not have time on their hands.

The journey from Tuan Giao to Dien Bien Phu on Highway 279 is 80 km and takes around four hours and is chosen by those with a strong sense of Vietnamese history.

Dien Bien Phu

Situated in a region where even today ethnic Vietnamese still represent less than one-third of the total population, Dien Bien Phu lies in the Muong Thanh valley, a heart-shaped basin 19 km long and 13 km wide, crossed by the Nam Yum River.

Phone code: 023
Colour map 1, grid B1

For such a remote and apparently insignificant little town to have earned itself such an important place in the history books is a considerable achievement. And yet the Battle of Dien Bien Phu in 1954 was a turning point in colonial history. It marked the end of French involvement in Indochina and heralded the collapse of its North African empire. Had the Americans, who shunned French appeals for help, taken more careful note of what happened at Dien Bien Phu they might have avoided their own calamitous involvement just a decade later.

110 km from Son La,
345 from Hoa Binh,
420 from Hanoi

The North

Ins and outs

Dien Bien Phu is deep in the highlands of Northwest Vietnam, close to the border with Laos and 420 km from Hanoi (although it feels much further). The airport is 2 km north of town and there are 4 connections a week with Hanoi. Buses snake their way up from Hanoi via Hoa Binh and Son La, and there are also connections onward with Lai Chau, Sapa and Lao Cai. Expect overland journeys to be slow and sometimes arduous in this mountainous region – but the discomfort is more than compensated for by the sheer majesty of the landscapes. The road to Son La has been significantly upgraded over recent years but the route to Sapa is still poor.

Getting there
See Transport,
page 115,
for further details

The town of Dien Bien Phu with its neat streets is quite easy to negotiate on foot. The battlefield sites, most of which lie to the west of the Nam Yum River, are, however, a bit spread out and best visited by car or by motorbike. Since the majority of visitors arrive in Dien Bien Phu in their own transport this is not normally a problem.

Getting around

History

Modern Dien Bien Phu is a growing town. This reflects the decision to make it the provincial capital of Lai Chau Province and attempts to develop it as a tourist destination. But tucked away in one of Vietnam's remotest corners, where only the most determined of travellers will find it, Dien Bien Phu's dreams of tapping the tourist dollar have been left largely unfulfilled.

Settled from an early date, Muong Thanh valley has been an important trading post on the caravan route between China and Burma for 2,000 years. Over the years numerous fortifications were constructed in and around Muong Thanh, the best-known being the fabled Citadel of the Thirty Thousand (Thanh Tam Van) built by the Lu during the 15th century. Remnants of this citadel can still be seen today, near Xam Mun.

The early years of the 18th century were a period of acute political instability throughout Vietnam. During this time the Northwest was overrun by armies of the Phe from China's southern Yunnan Province who committed

The Battle of Dien Bien Phu

On 20 November 1953, after a series of French successes, Colonel Christian de Castries and six battalions of French and French-colonial troops were parachuted into Dien Bien Phu. The location, in a narrow valley surrounded by steep wooded peaks, was chosen specifically because it was thought by the French strategists to be impregnable. From there, they believed, their forces could begin to harry the Viet Minh close to their bases as well as protect Laos from Viet Minh incursions. At the centre of the valley was the all-important airstrip – Colonel de Castries' only physical link with the outside world. In his history of Vietnam, Stanley Karnow describes de Castries thus: "Irresistible to women and ridden with gambling debts, he had been a champion horseman, dare-devil pilot and courageous commando, his body scarred by three wounds earned during the Second World War and earlier in Indochina."

In response, the famous Vietnamese General Giap moved his forces, some 55,000 men, into the surrounding area, manhandling heavy guns (with the help, it is said of 200,000 porters) up the impossibly steep mountainsides until they had a view over the French forces. The French commander still believed, however, that his forces would have the upper hand in any set-piece confrontation, and set about strengthening his position. He created a series of heavily fortified strongholds, giving them women's names: Anne-Marie, Françoise, Huguette, Béatrice, Gabrielle, Dominique, Claudine, Isabelle and Eliane. It is said that they were named after de Castries' numerous mistresses.

As it turned out, de Castries was not luring the Viet Minh into a trap, but creating one for himself and his men. From the surrounding highlands, Giap had the French at his mercy. The shelling started in the middle of March, and the strongholds fell

one-by-one; Béatrice first and then Gabrielle and Anne-Marie by mid-March until de Castries' forces were concentrated around the airstrip. Poor weather, which prevented the French from using their air power, and human-wave attacks gradually wore the French troops down. By this time, de Castries had withdrawn to his bunker and command had effectively been taken over by his junior officers. A furious bombardment by the heavy guns of the Viet Minh from 1 May led to the final massed assault five days later. On the final night, the Viet Minh taunted the French defenders by playing the 'Song of the Partisans', the theme of the French Resistance, over the garrison's radio frequencies. The colonel's HQ fell on 7 May at 1730 when 9,500 French and French-colonial troops surrendered. A small force of paratroopers at the isolated southern position, Isabelle, continued to resist for a further 24 hours.

This humiliation at Dien Bien Phu led the French to sue for peace at a conference in Geneva. On 20 July 1954, it was agreed that Vietnam should be divided in two along the 17th parallel: a Communist north and a capitalist south. In total, 20,000 Viet Minh and over 3,000 French troops were killed at Dien Bien Phu. The Geneva agreement set terms so that the dead from both sides would be honoured in a massive ossuary. But when Ngo Dinh Diem, the President of the Republic of South Vietnam, symbolically urinated over Viet Minh dead in the South rather than bury them with honour, Giap and Ho Chi Minh decided to leave the French dead to lie where they had fallen. Over the nine years of war between the Viet Minh and the French, the dead numbered between a quarter of a million and one million civilians, 200,000-300,000 Viet Minh and 95,000 French-colonial troops. Who was to guess another 20 years of warfare lay ahead.

unspeakable acts of barbarism against the inhabitants of the area. In 1751, however, a Vietnamese peasant leader from the Red River Delta named Hoang Cong Chat, whose army had retreated into the region to escape from royal troops, rallied local Lu, Lao and Thái chieftains to his cause and expelled the Phe back across the border to China. Building a new fortress at Ban Phu, Chat set himself up as lord of a large area including most of modern Son La and Lai Chau provinces, winning the hearts of the local people by carrying out important land and taxation reforms.

The town of Dien Bien Phu itself only came into existence in 1841 when, in response to continued Lao, Siamese and Chinese banditry in the area, the Nguyen dynasty ordered the establishment of a royal district governed from a fortified settlement at Muong Thanh.

Occupied by French forces during the course of their major Northwest campaign of 1888-89, Dien Bien Phu was subsequently maintained as a garrison town. The town fell briefly to Thái insurgents during the latter stages of the 1908 Son La Penitentiary uprising (prompting the suicide of Dien Bien Phu's French commander) and again during the course of the 1914-16 uprising of Son La chieftains, but perhaps the most serious threat to French rule in the region came in 1918 when the Hmông rebelled against the harsh fiscal policies of the new Governor General Paul Doumer, by refusing to pay taxes in silver coins or to supply opium to the French and taking up arms against the garrison. The insurrection quickly spread east to Son La and south across the Lao border into Samneua, and although the French responded ruthlessly by devastating rebel areas, destroying food crops to provoke famine and setting a high price on the heads of prominent rebels, the revolt persisted until March 1921.

In Vietnam, as elsewhere in Asia, the defeat of the European Allies during the early years of the Second World War utterly shattered the image of western colonial supremacy, fuelling the forces of incipient nationalism. French attempts to resume their authority in the region in 1945 thus encountered stiff resistance from Viet Minh forces, and in the nine years of fighting which followed, the Northwest became a cradle of national resistance against French colonialism.

Following the French defeat at Hoa Binh in 1952 the Vietnamese Army went on the offensive all over the Northwest, forcing the French to regroup at their two remaining strongholds of Na San (Son La) and Lai Chau. Early the following year, acting in conjunction with Pathet Lao forces, the Viet Minh overran Samneua in upper Laos and proceeded to sweep north, threatening the Lao capital of Luang Prabang. By November 1953 the French colonial government headquarters at Lai Chau, just 110 km north of Dien Bien Phu, had also come under siege.

Dien Bien Phu was the site of the last calamitous battle between the French and the forces of Ho Chi Minh's Viet Minh, and was waged from March to May 1954. The French, who under Vichy rule had

Dien Bien Phu battle site

The French Garrison, 13 March 1954 shortly before the siege began

GABRIELLE

Ford

Pavie Track

Ban Kéo

ANNE-MARIE

Nam Yum River

BEATRICE

HUGUETTE

Rt 41

DOMINIQUE

FRANÇOISE

ELIANE

CLAUDINE

Phony Hill

Ban Ong Pet

Baldy Hill

Ban Hong Lech Cang

Ban Na Loi

Ban Papé

MARCELLE Evacuated

Ban Ten

Ban Palech

Ban Bom La

Ban Nhong Nhai

Ban Kho Lai

Auxiliary Airstrip

Ban Hong Cum

N

ISABELLE

WIEME

0 km   1
0 miles   1

CLAUDINE French strong points
······ Barbed-wire systems

accepted the authority of the Japanese during the Second World War, attempted to regain control after the Japanese had surrendered. Ho, following his Declaration of Independence on 2 September 1945, thought otherwise, heralding nearly a decade of war before the French finally gave up the fight after their catastrophic defeat here. The lessons of the battle were numerous, but most of all it was a victory of determination over technology. In the aftermath, the French people, much like the Americans two decades later, had no stomach left for a war in a distant, tropical and alien land.

Sights

On the sight of the battlefield **General** (as he was by the end of the battle) **de Castries' bunker** has been rebuilt and eight of the 10 French tanks (known as bisons) are scattered over the valley, along with numerous US-made artillery pieces. On **Hill A1** (known as Eliane 2 to the French and scene of the fiercest fighting) is a bunker, the bison named Gazelle, a war memorial dedicated to the Vietnamese who died on the hill, and around at the back is the entrance to a tunnel dug by coal miners from Hon Gai. Their tunnel ran several hundred metres to beneath French positions and was filled with 1,000 kg of high explosives. It was detonated at 2300 on 6 May as a signal for the final assault. The huge crater is still there. The hill is a peaceful spot and a good place from which to watch the sun setting on the historic valley. After dark there are fireflies. Both places are fenced off so those wishing to get inside should check with the Historic Victory Exhibition Museum first.

Historic Victory Exhibition Museum The Historic Victory Exhibition Museum (Nha Trung Bay Thang Lich Su Dien Bien Phu) has a good collection of assorted Chinese, American and French weapons and artillery in its grounds. There are photographs and other memorabilia together with a large illuminated model of the valley illustrating the course of the campaign. While every last piece of Vietnamese junk is carefully catalogued, displayed and described (in Vietnamese only, of course) French relics are heaped into tangled piles. It is interesting to note that while ordinary Vietnamese people forgive and forget so disarmingly readily, the

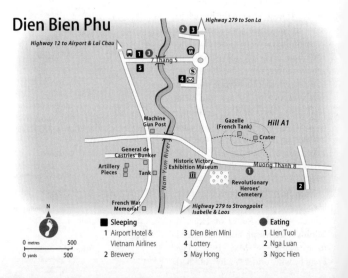

Dien Bien Phu

Highway 279 to Son La

Highway 12 to Airport & Lai Chau

7 Thang 5

Machine Gun Post

Gazelle (French Tank)   Hill A1

Crater

General de Castries' Bunker

Artillery Pieces   Tank

Historic Victory Exhibition Museum

Muong Thanh 8

Revolutionary Heroes' Cemetery

French War Memorial

Highway 279 to Strongpoint Isabelle & Laos

Nam Yum River

N

0 metres   500
0 yards   500

■ **Sleeping**
1 Airport Hotel & Vietnam Airlines
2 Brewery
3 Dien Bien Mini
4 Lottery
5 May Hong

● **Eating**
1 Lien Tuoi
2 Nga Luan
3 Ngoc Hien

The North

Communist propaganda machine gloats over its victory of almost half a century ago as though it were yesterday. ■ *Daily 0730-1130, 1330-1630, 5,000d.*

The Revolutionary Heroes' Cemetery, located directly opposite the Exhibition Museum adjacent to Hill A1, contains the graves of some 15,000 Vietnamese soldiers killed during the course of the Dien Bien Phu campaign. Located close to the sight of de Castries' command bunker is the **French War Memorial** (Nghia Trang Phap). It consists of a white obelisk surrounded by a grey concrete wall and black iron gates sitting on a bluff overlooking the Nam Yum River – unloved, unkempt and forgotten.

Revolutionary Heroes' Cemetery

Essentials

Virtually all the hotels are state run: customers mean extra work which hotel keepers on minimal salaries could do without. Expect a cool reception and to pay way over the odds for a very ordinary room.

Sleeping
■ *on map*
Phone code: 023
Price codes:
see inside front cover

The North

C *Dien Bien Mini Hotel*, 7A 7 Thang 5 St, T824319, F825836. Newish building with 23 rooms, a/c, fan rooms, restaurant, breakfast included. **C** *May Hong*, T826300. Opposite *Vietnam Airlines* booking office, a/c, hot water, new and possibly the smartest in town but soulless. **D** *Airport*, T825052, F826060. 6 rooms, a/c, hot water, fairly basic, near the bus station, *Vietnam Airlines* booking office is in the hotel and *Ngoc Hien Restaurant* is next door. **D** *Brewery*, 62 Muong Thanh 10 St, T824635. 10 rooms, out beyond Hill A1 at the east end of town. While not exactly welcoming we found them at least amenable to bargaining, basic fan and a/c rooms, no restaurant but, as the name suggests, beer and plenty of it. A little *bia hoi* is next to the gate and fresh cool beer at 1,500d a glass slips down very easily – it gets our vote for the best in the Northwest. **D** *Lottery*, just off 7 Thang 5 St, T825789, F825931. Centrally located with just 5 rooms, basic accommodation.

Lien Tuoi, 27 Muong Thanh 8 St, next to the Vietnamese cemetery and Hill A1, T824919. Delicious local fare in a family run restaurant, dishes cost US$2-3. The family sits down to eat at 2000, don't expect much service (or food) after that. *Nga Luan*, near the market. Unpretentious canteen-type eatery serving honest fodder. *Ngoc Hien*, next to *Airport Hotel*. Plain, ordinary but tasty food.

Eating
● *on map*

Air The airport (T824416) is 2 km north of town, off Highway 12. There are 4 flights a week to Hanoi.

Transport

Road Bus: the bus station is close to the centre of town, on Highway 12. It is an easy walk to the hotels. There are now direct bus connections with **Hanoi**'s Kim Ma station, depart 0430, 75,000d; **Son La**, 38,000d; and **Lai Chau**, 5 buses per day, 25,000d. Note that road transport in the mountains is arduous. **Hire car**: roads via Son La are generally good (in the dry season) but via Sapa so bad in places that a 4WD vehicle is highly recommended, if not essential. Russian-made army jeeps are ideal and can be hired, with driver, from hotels or tour operators in Hanoi (see page 96); expect to pay around US$300 for a 4- or 5-day round trip (1,200 km via Sapa), quite reasonable if split between four. For those willing to pay more, Japanese land cruisers offer higher levels of comfort.

Banks *Vietcombank* and *Nong Nghiep Bank*.

Directory

The road to Lai Chau

It is 104 km on Highway 12 from Dien Bien Phu to Lai Chau. The road was originally built by an energetic French district governor, Auguste Pavie, and was used by soldiers fleeing from the French garrison at Lai Chau to the supposed safety of the garrison at Dien Bien Phu in 1953. Viet Minh ambushes along the Pavie Track meant that the French were forced to hack their way through the jungle and those few who made it to Dien Bien Phu found themselves almost immediately under siege again.

Within a few kilometres of Dien Bien Phu what has until then been a pleasant ride on decent metalled roads becomes a jarring, exhausting slog along particularly uncomfortable farm tracks. The five-hour journey is scenically interesting and the few minority villages – Kho Mu and Thái on the valley floors and Hmông higher up – divert attention from the discomfort.

The scenery is different from any you will have encountered so far. What draws gasps of amazement around Son La is the exquisite human landscape. From Dien Bien Phu to Lai Chau what impresses is the scenery in its natural state. It is unfriendly but spectacular. The agents at work here are rivers, rain, heat and gravity, and the raw materials are rock and trees. There are no rice terraces but forested hills in which slash-and-burn farming takes place. This is the land of rockslide and flood. It is geologically young and dangerous – the steep slopes of thinly bedded shales collapse after heavy rain, in contrast to the more solid limestone bands of Son La. The density of population is low and evidence abounds that the living here is harsh. A less romantic side to minority-village life is evident here: tiny children of four stagger along with a baby strapped to their back, there is no colourful dress or elaborate costume, just ragged kids in filthy T-shirts.

Pu Ka village, 46 km from Lai Chau, is a White Hmông settlement newly established by the authorities to transplant the Hmông away from their opium fields.

Lai Chau

Phone code: 023
Colour map 1, grid B2

*It is 103 km from
Dien Bien Phu*

If Son La is notable for the colour of its minorities and Dien Bien Phu for its history, then Lai Chau, should be noted for the splendour of its trees. The town occupies a majestic setting in a deep and wide valley which is cloaked in dense tiers of forest. For various reasons the trees have not been felled and the

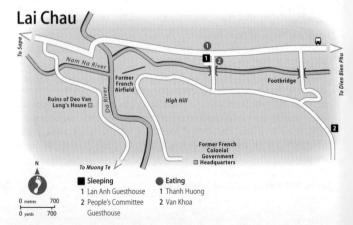

Lai Chau

To Sapa · Nam Na River · Former French Airfield · Footbridge · To Dien Bien Phu · Da River · Ruins of Deo Van Long's House · High Hill · Former French Colonial Government Headquarters · To Muong Te

N

0 metres 700
0 yards 700

■ **Sleeping**
1 Lan Anh Guesthouse
2 People's Committee Guesthouse

● **Eating**
1 Thanh Huong
2 Van Khoa

beauty they confer on Lai Chau presumably extended over a much wider reach of country in an age gone by.

Much of the present town of Lai Chau dates from 1969-72, when it was expanded to accommodate the large numbers of Chinese engineers posted here to upgrade the road from Dien Bien Phu to the Chinese border (the Friendship Road). In 1993 the status of capital of Lai Chau Province was transferred from Lai Chau town to Dien Bien Phu, partly in recognition of the latter's growing importance as a hub of economic and tourist activity and partly in deference to plans to drown the entire Lai Chau valley. The floods of 1996 drove another nail into the coffin of this unhappy but lovely town: 29 people were killed and 4,000 lost their homes – flood damage can still be seen in the town centre. Many more than 4,000 will lose their homes for good over the next 10 years as the Son La hydro-electric power scheme is completed and the Da River is dammed (see page 109 for further details.)

The history of Lai Chau is inextricably entwined with that of the Black Thái **History** seigneurial family of Deo who had achieved ascendancy over the former White Thái lords of Muong Lay by the first half of the 15th century. In 1451 the Vietnamese King Le Thai To is recorded as having led a campaign against the Deo family of Muong Lay (today a village 13 km south of the town) for its disloyalty to the crown.

The Deo family in fact comprised a number of separate Black Thái lineages dotted around what is now Northwest Vietnam and the Yunnan Province of China, but it was the marriage during the 1850s of Deo Van Xeng, a wealthy merchant from Yunnan, to the daughter of a Mường Lay Deo chieftain, which established the most notorious line of the Deo family. When his father-in-law died, Xeng seized control of the Muong Lay dominions and, with the support of the royal court in Luang Prabang and the mandarinate of Yunnan, quickly established himself as one of the most powerful lords in the Northwest.

Deo Van Xeng's eldest son, the energetic Deo Van Tri, continued his father's expansionist policies. Allying himself with Chinese Black Flag commander Lin Yung-fu, Tri succeeded in expelling a Chinese Yellow Flag occupation force from Son La, instantly winning the respect and allegiance of the Black and White Thái chieftains of that area. Apart from a small number who stayed and were subsequently integrated into the Thái community, the Black Flags also left the country shortly after this, enabling Tri to assume suzerainty over a large area of Northwest Vietnam.

When French forces launched their campaign to pacify the Northwest, Tri initially took an active part in the resistance, leading a joint Black and White Thái force against the colonial army at the battle of Cau Giay in 1883. Consequently, king-in-exile Ham Nghi appointed Tri military governor of 16 districts. But the garrisoning of French troops at Lai Chau during the campaign of 1888-89 marked a turning point in the war of resistance and Tri was ultimately obliged to surrender to the French at Lai Chau in 1890.

As elsewhere in the north, the French moved quickly to graft their colonial administrative systems onto those already established by the Nguyen court, and they ensured Deo Van Tri's future co-operation by awarding him the hereditary post of Supreme Thái Chieftain.

After his death in 1915, Tri was succeeded as Governor of Lai Chau by his son Deo Van Long who later took office as mandarin of the colonial government in 1940. However, as the Viet Minh war of resistance got under way in 1945, the colonial government sought to ensure the continued allegiance of ethnic minority leaders by offering them a measure of self-government.

Accordingly, in 1947 Mường, Thái, Tày, Hmông and Nung Autonomous Regions were set up throughout the Northwest and, in Lai Chau, Deo Van Long was duly installed as king of the Thái.

King Deo Van Long is remembered with loathing by most older inhabitants of the Lai Chau area. By all accounts he was a tyrant who exercised absolute authority, striking fear into the hearts of the local people by occasionally having transgressors executed on the spot. The overgrown ruins of Long's mansion lie just across the river from Doi Cao (High Hill) and may be visited either by boat or by road (see below).

During the latter days of French rule, as the security situation began to deteriorate throughout the Northwest, Lai Chau became an important French military base; older citizens of the town remember clearly the large numbers of Moroccans, Algerians and Tunisians who were posted here between 1946 and 1953. The French were finally forced to abandon Lai Chau during the winter of 1953 on the eve of the momentous battle of Dien Bien Phu. Bereft of his colonial masters, a discredited Deo Van Long fled to Laos and then to Thailand, whence he is believed to have emigrated to France. A few remaining relatives still live in the area, but have wisely changed their family name to Dieu.

Sights The excellent little **Lai Chau Museum**, just a stone's throw from the *People's Committee Guesthouse* seems to have been closed and its exhibits transfered to Dien Bien Phu. Former **French Colonial Government Headquarters** are used as offices and house the local hospital. To get there walk up High Hill past the hospital and fork left up a track leading to the crest of the hill 500 m further along. Also, on a terrace above the river, is a former airfield (Sang Bay Phap). A very pleasant couple of hours can be whiled away pottering around the largely overgrown and derelict French remains. In trying to identify French areas any budding Indiana Jones can put botanical archaeology to good use. The French were fond of ornamental trees and planted many exotic types: straight rows of huge century-old trees (*muong*) fringe what may have been a former parade ground or playing field; the vivid colours of the flame trees (*phuong*) flag the nascent archaeologist up flights of decaying steps and balustrades towards what looks to have been the sanitorium.

The ruins of **Deo Van Long's House**, originally a plush colonial mansion, lie on Road 127 to Muong Te on the opposite bank of the Da River from High Hill (Doi Cao). The remains are wonderfully overgrown with creeper and strangling figs. Older inhabitants of the six or seven remaining houses recall that for many years Deo Van Long and his family lived in great luxury with a large retinue of servants. Some say that before fleeing the country in 1953, Long had all his servants poisoned so they could not inform the advancing Viet Minh forces of his whereabouts. Beware of precarious piles of loose masonry and deep vaults (dungeons or wine cellars, who can be sure) covered with only a matting of creeper. ■ *Getting there: by boat from below High Hill (not when river levels are too high or too low), or a circuitous 8-km road trip, crossing one especially rickety suspension bridge.*

Excursions **Phi Hay White Hmông village** makes an interesting morning's excursion for those who made the detour via Dien Bien Phu. It offers a snapshot of the stunning scenery along the more direct Lai Chau-Tuan Giao mountain route. Phi Hay village is very old and comprises some 50 houses. ■ *Getting there: take Highway 6 in the direction of Tuan Giao for 13 km, stop next to a group of small shops as the road begins to level out, and walk up the path to the left of the road for a further 2 km.*

C *Lan Anh Guesthouse*, T/F852370. Fan and a/c rooms in the main part of town, not far from the treacherous Da River, a new block has wisely been built on stilts. Clean, comfortable, helpful staff, restaurant. **D-E** *People's Committee Guesthouse*, Nghe Toong, T852456. North of People's Committee Bridge (Cau Uy Ban Nhan Dan) and then up the zig-zag road, a/c and fan rooms, basic, clean and quiet accommodation with rock-hard beds, no restaurant. *Ethnic Houses*, overnight stays in ethnic houses are currently not possible.

Sleeping
■ *on map*
Phone code: 023
Price codes:
see inside front cover

Lan Anh Guesthouse (see above). *Thanh Huong*, on the main road nearly opposite bridge, and *Van Khoa*. Expect no menu or English, just point, mime and hope – or use the food glossary, see Footnotes.

Eating
● *on map*

Road **Bus**: connections south with **Dien Bien Phu**, 4 hrs (and from there to Hanoi via Son La and Hoa Binh) and north and east with Sapa. Following the 1996 floods, the bus station was moved several kilometres west of the town; try to get dropped off by the bridge in the town centre. The People's Committee Bridge is no longer open to traffic.

Transport

The North

Sin Ho

When you announce your intention to visit Sin Ho your driver will inform you of the latest outbreak of bubonic plague in the town, the absence of water and electricity and, when that does not dissuade you, he will remind you of the bus which plunged off the road in 1995 killing all 27 passengers. But your mind is made up and off you go. Your driver dodged American bombs, shells and napalm in the war and he applies the same degree of resolve and resignation to the hazardous task of negotiating the hairpin bends and precipitous drops which characterize the road to Sin Ho. Unfortunately, the views from the back of a Russian army jeep are highly restricted so if the weather is clear you would be strongly advised to walk some stretches to appreciate the full majesty of the scenery. It will also give you a chance to absorb the delicious cool air, the forest sounds and smells and the wayside flowers. You also have the opportunity to witness the extraordinary perpendicular fields and to wonder how it is that local farmers can actually harvest slopes on which most people could not even stand. And your driver can have a cigarette to settle his shattered nerves.

Phone code: 023
Colour map 1, grid A2

The first 20 km towards Sin Ho off the main highway is possibly the most spectacular and terrifying drive in Vietnam. After 20 km the road levels off and meanders over the Sin Ho plateau passing hamlets of Red, White and Flower Hmông and Dao minorities. Sin Ho provides little that won't have been seen already, although the **Sunday morning market** is worthy of note. As with other markets in the region, the Sunday market is an important social occasion – after their transactions are done, the men of various ethnic minorities gather around drinking wine and unattached boys and girls seek partners.

D *People's Committee Guesthouse*. In a competitive field this is one of the grottiest holes to spend a night in. Too late you realize your driver was not joking. The town is powered by a feeble generator that comes on at dusk providing just enough wattage to broadcast the Communist Party's latest propaganda over the public tannoy system and to excite light bulbs up to the equivalent of two guttering candles. One or two drips of water may be coaxed from the tap but more likely the woman in charge will deliver two buckets of unclean water while muttering about the current drought and El Niño. The sheets have not been washed for months and while the mosquito nets *are* adequate for approximately half a bed the beds have to be manoeuvered in order to lie under the net.

Sleeping
Phone code: 023

Eating Eat early at one of the little cafés around the market. May only have instant noodles at night and eggs for breakfast. But washed down with the delicious local rice wine (purple or white and often sweetened with honey) it tastes like a feast. Wine costs less than US$0.50 a bottle. Bottled water and biscuits can be bought as can the local runny honey – but not much to eat with it.

Transport Sin Ho is a 40-km detour off Highway 12. **Road Bus**: connections with **Lai Chau** and **Phong Tho**.

Directory **Communications Post office:** near the market.

Phong Tho

Phone code: 023
Colour map 1,
grid A2

A small market town, Phong Tho will detain no one for long but is a pleasant enough lunch stop or adequate overnighter for those with engine problems. The surrounding hamlets are home to the White Thái, Ha Nhi and Dao Tuyen ethnicities who can be encountered either at home or in Phong Tho's early morning market.

Sleeping **D** *Phung Tam*, on the main drag, 1 branch on either side of the road. **D** *Tam Duong*, on
& eating the same street but further up, T875288. A surprisingly clean and comfortable little place, 8 fan rooms, hot water and a cheerful welcome. A jolly good little road-sider opposite *Tam Duong Hotel* will knock up a delicious meal, seemingly out of nothing.

Transport **Road Bus**: daily bus connections with **Sapa** and **Lao Cai**; foreigners get charged double the 35,000d local fare for the journey to Lao Cai. Also bus connections with Lai Chau.

Tam Duong

Phone code: 023
Colour map 1, grid A2

The chief attraction of Tam Duong is the colour and costume of the minority people, White and Flower Hmông, Dao Khau, Giay and White and Black Thái. There are some interesting walks to Na Bo, a Pu Na minority village, Giang (Nhang minority) and Hon minority villages. Pu Na and Nhang people are similar in culture and costume. Na Bo is 7 km from Tam Duong from which Giang is a further 1½ km and Hon a further 5 km. Alternatively a motorbike and driver can be hired for around 80,000d.

About 35 km southeast of Tam Duong, Highway 4D swings sharply to the northeast and the altitude climbs abruptly into the Hoang Lien Son range. Here is harsh mountain scenery on a scale previously unencountered on this circuit of Northwest Vietnam. The geology is hard and crystalline as is the skyline, with sharp jagged peaks punching upwards into the sky. Vertical cliffs drop below and soar above, friendly rolling scenery has been replaced by 3,000-m-high mountains.

Sleeping **D** *Phuong Thanh*, T875235, F875158. A/c and fan rooms, hot water, clean, comfortable,
& eating lovely views. **D-E** *People's Committee Guesthouse*. Some a/c, basic, clean. **E** guesthouse at the bus station. For eating there is *Hong Nhung*, and others near the bus station.

Transport From Lai Chau, Highway 12 heads almost due north following the picturesque Na river valley towards the Chinese border. At Pa So, 10 km from China (border crossing closed), take Highway 4D, southeast. Tam Duong is in fact a collection of three small settlements, all new. **Road Bus**: connections with **Sapa** and **Lao Cai** and south with **Lai Chau**.

Sapa

Despite the countless thousands of tourists who have poured in every year for the past decade Sapa retains great charm. Its beauty derives from two things: the impressive natural setting high on a valley side with Fan Si Pan, Vietnam's tallest mountain either clearly visible or brooding in the mist; and the clamour and colour of ethnic minorities selling jewellery and clothes.

Phone code: 020
Colour map 1, grid A2

Perhaps the beauty of the town is a little compromised by the new hotels sprouting up everywhere. Certainly none of the new ones can compare with the lovely old French buildings – pitched roofs, window shutters and chimneys each with their own neat little garden of temperate flora, foxgloves, roses, apricot and plum trees, carefully nurtured by generations of gardeners. Weekends are peak tourist time but during the week the few visitors who remain will have the town to themselves – the sight of winsome Hmông girls, long quiet walks and the pick of the hotels.

Ins and outs

You get to Sapa in one of two ways, either by road as part of the Northwest loop or by overnight train from Hanoi, via Lao Cai. A fleet of minibuses ferries passengers from Lao Cai railway station to Sapa. There are numerous classes of seat or berth on the trains and the *Victoria Sapa Hotel* and *Royal Hotel* have their own private carriages. (see Sleeping, page 125 for details). It is quite easy to make the travel arrangements yourself, except that you can only buy a one-way ticket in Hanoi and need to book the return as soon as you get to Lao Cai (the station ticket office only opens in the afternoon) or Sapa. A railway office in Sapa sells tickets for the journey back to Hanoi (although you have to use their minibus to Lao Cai). Tour operators in Hanoi sell tours from 3 to 5 days duration which include treks of various lengths.

Getting there
See Transport, page 127, for further details

Sapa is a charming town, small enough to walk around easily. From Sapa there are a great many walks and treks and the tracks and paths are fun to explore on a Minsk.

Getting around

At 1,650 m Sapa enjoys warm days and cool evenings in the summer but gets very cold in winter. Snow falls on average every couple of years and settles on the surrounding peaks of the Hoang Lien Son Mountains. Rain and cloud can occur at any time of year but the wettest months are May-Sep with nearly 1,000 mm of rain in Jul and Aug alone, the busiest months for Vietnamese tourists. Dec and Jan can be pretty miserable with mist, low cloud and low temperatures. Spring blossom is lovely but even in Mar and Apr a fire or heater may be necessary in the evening.

Best time to visit

Background

Originally a Black Hmông settlement, Sapa was first discovered by Europeans when a Jesuit missionary visited the area in 1918. By 1932 news of the quasi-European climate and beautiful scenery of the Tonkinese Alps had spread throughout French Indochina. Like Dalat in the south it served as a retreat for French administrators when the heat of the plains became unbearable. By the 1940s an estimated 300 French buildings – including a sizeable prison and the summer residence of the Governor of French Indochina – had sprung up. Until 1947 there were more French than Vietnamese in the town, which became renowned for its many parks and flower gardens. However, as the security situation began to worsen during the latter days of French rule, the expatriate community steadily dwindled, and by 1953 virtually all had gone. Immediately following the French defeat at Dien Bien Phu in 1954, victorious Vietnamese forces razed a large number of Sapa's French buildings to the ground.

Sapa was also one of the places to be invaded by the Chinese in the 1979 border skirmish. Chinese soldiers found and destroyed the holiday retreat of the Vietnamese Communist Party Secretary-General, Le Duan, no doubt infuriated by such uncomradely display of bourgeois tendencies.

The huge scale of the Fan Si Pan range gives Sapa an Alpine feel and this impression is reinforced by *haut savoie* vernacular architecture with steep pitched roofs, window shutters and chimneys. But in an alluring blend of European and Vietnamese vegetation the gardeners of Sapa cultivate their foxgloves and apricot trees alongside thickets of bamboo and delicate orchids, just yards above the paddy fields.

Ethnic minorities

Distinctly oriental but un-Vietnamese in manner and appearance are the Hmông, Dao and other minorities who come to Sapa to trade. Interestingly the Hmông (normally so reticent) have been the first to seize the commercial opportunities presented by tourism; they are engaging but persistent vendors of hand-loomed indigo shirts, trousers and skull caps and other handicrafts. Of the latter, particularly notable is a little brass and bamboo Jew's-harp. The Dao have also now started to latch on to the commercial opportunities presented by these tall, red-haired and red-faced strangers and have altered their weaving looms accordingly. In fact, as a close inspection will reveal, almost all the clothes on sale are second-hand with patches and embroidered panels reworked onto new items. The women, their hands stained purple by the dye, sell clothing, sitting on street corners stitching while they wait for a foreigner to pounce upon. The girls roam in groups, bracelets, earrings and necklaces jingling as they walk. '*Jolie, jolie*' they say as they push bracelets into your hand and it is hard to disagree. '*Mua mot cai di, mua mot cai di*' (buy one, buy one) the little ones sing and most people do.

Saturday night is always a big occasion for Black Hmông and Red Dao teenagers in the Sapa area, as youngsters from miles around come to the so-called **Love Market** to find a partner. The market proved so popular with tourists that the teenagers now arrange their trysts and liaisons in private. The regular market is at its busiest and best on Sunday morning when most tourists scoot off to Bac Ha.

Sights

Sapa is a pleasant place to relax in and unwind, particularly after the arduous journey from Dien Bien Phu. Being comparatively new it has no important sights but several French buildings in and around are worth visiting.

Sapa church Most spectacular is the **church** in the centre of Sapa built in 1930. Recently rebuilt, the church was wrecked in 1952 by French artillerymen shelling the adjacent building in which Viet Minh troops were billeted. In the churchyard are the tombs of two former priests, including that of Father Thinh, who was brutally murdered. In the autumn of 1952, Father Thinh confronted a monk named Giao Linh who had been discovered having an affair with a nun at the Ta Phin seminary. Giao Linh obviously took great exception to the priest's interference, for shortly after this, when Father Thinh's congregation arrived at Sapa church for mass one foggy November morning, they discovered his decapitated body lying next to the altar.

Ham Rong or **Dragon's Jaw Hill**, on which the district's TV transmitter is stuck, is located immediately above Sapa town centre and can be climbed by following the steps behind the *Ham Rong Hotel*. Apart from offering excellent views of the town, the path winds its way through a number of interesting limestone outcrops and miniature grottoes as it nears the summit. **Dragon's Jaw Hill**

This is located near the row of restaurants. The museum houses ethnic minority costumes and other ethnological exhibits relating to the Sapa region. ■ *0800-1130, 1330-1600 Sat and Sun only, at other times contact Service of Culture and Information opposite, 5,000d.* **Sapa Museum**

Excursions

Near Ta Phin, is this derelict seminary, where the names of the Bishop who consecrated it and the presiding Governor of Indochina can be seen engraved on stones at the west end. Built in 1942 and under the ecclesiastical jurisdiction of the Parish of Sapa, the building was destroyed 10 years later by militant Vietnamese hostile to the intentions of the order. **Abandoned French seminary**

Beyond the seminary the path descends into a valley of beautifully sculpted rice terraces past Black Hmông settlements, with their shy and retiring inhabitants, to Ta Phin. ■ *Getting there: take the road 8 km east towards Lao Cai then a track left up towards Ta Phin, 3 km to monastery 4 km further to Ta Phin.* **Ta Phin Red Dao village**

At a height of 3,143 m, Vietnam's highest mountain is a three-day trek from Sapa. It lies on a bearing of 240° from Sapa; as the crow flies it is 9 km but by track it is 14 km and involves dropping to 1,200 m and crossing a rickety bamboo bridge before ascending. Enquire at *Auberge* or *Cat Cat* guesthouses (see Sleeping, page 125) for a local guide. A three-day expedition is recommended. There are few suitable spots for camping other than at the altitudes suggested below. **Mount Fan Si Pan**

Day 1: depart Sapa (1,650 m) 0800. Lunch at 1,400 m, 1200. Camp at 2,285 m.
Day 2: reach summit late afternoon. Return to camp at 2,800 m.
Day 3: descend to Sapa.

Camping equipment is not available for hire but rucksacks, boots, fleeces and waterproofs can be bought in Hanoi. Porters are unwilling to carry more than about 6 kg and are therefore of little use. The ascent involves some steep scrambles which are quite nasty in wet conditions. Only the very fit will make it to the summit.

This is a round trip of 20 km taking in minority villages and beautiful scenery. Head out of town in a southeast direction (past the *Auberge Guesthouse* – see Around Sapa map), Lao Chai is 6 km on the far valley side. Follow the track leading from the right-hand side of the road down to the valley floor, cross the river by the footbridge (*cau may*), see box, page 125, and then walk up through the rice fields into Lao Chai village. You will find Ta Van 2 km further on. **Lau Chai village of the Black Hmông, Ta Van village of the Zay**

A leisurely stroll through these villages could well be the highlight of a trip to Vietnam. It is a chance to observe rural life led in reasonable prosperity. Wet rice forms the staple income, weaving for the tourist market puts a bit of meat on

The North

the table. Here nature is kind, there is rich soil and no shortage of water. Again it's possible to see how the landscape has been engineered to suit man's needs. The terracing is on an awesome scale (in places more than 100 steps), the result of centuries of labour to convert steep slopes into level fields which can be flooded to grow rice. Technologically, and in no sense pejoratively, the villages might be described as belonging to a bamboo age. Bamboo trunks carry water huge distances from spring to village; water flows across barriers and tracks in bamboo aqueducts; mechanical rice huskers made of bamboo are driven by water requiring no human effort; houses are held up with bamboo; bottoms are parked on bamboo chairs; and tobacco and other substances are inhaled through bamboo pipes. Any path chosen will lead to some hamlet or other; the Hmông in villages further from Sapa tend to be more reserved and suspicious – their fields and houses are often securely fenced off.

Cross back to the north side of the river by the suspension bridge. A dip in the deep pools of the Muong Hoa river is refreshingly invigorating. **Engraved stones** are a further 2 km southeast (away from Sapa, that is) by the side of road; they are believed to be inscribed in ancient Hmông. It is to be hoped they survive the current road repair and widening. The return walk to Sapa

Around Sapa

With acknowledgment to Mr Dang Trung

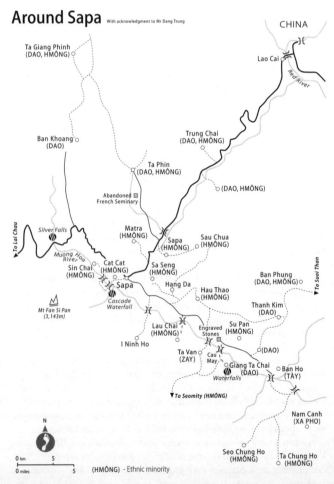

from the inscribed stones is a steady 10-km uphill climb. Exhausting work but stimulated by the views and the air and fuelled by hard-boiled eggs and warm Lao Cai beer from roadside shacks, and the prospect of cold beer at home, it is a pleasure, not an ordeal. In the late afternoon sun the rice glows with more shades of green than you would have thought

Bridge of confusion

Cau may *means rattan bridge; it can also be translated as cloudy bridge. Originally all the bridges were rattan, today only one is. Villagers all refer to their own bridges as* cau may *and insist that theirs is the only true one.*

possible and the lengthening shadows cast the entire landscape into vivid three-dimensional relief – even through a camera lens.

The track heading west from Sapa through the market area offers either a short 5-km round-trip walk to Cat Cat Black Hmông village or a longer 10-km round-trip walk to Sin Chai Black Hmông village; both options take in some beautiful scenery. Foreigners now have to pay an iniquitous 5,000d fee for taking the track. The path to Cat Cat leads off to the left of the Sin Chai track after about 1 km, following the line of pylons down through the rice paddies to Cat Cat village; beyond the village over the river bridge you can visit the **Cascade Waterfall** (from which the village takes its name) and an old French hydro-electric power station that still produces electricity. Sin Chai village is 4 km northwest of here.

Cat Cat & Sin Chai villages

The North

The **Silver Falls** are 12 km west of Sapa on the Lai Chau road, spectacular following rain. Hardly worth a special visit but if passing it's quite nice to stop for a paddle in the cold pools.

Essentials

A host of guesthouses has sprung up to cater for Sapa's rejuvenation. Prices tend to rise Jun-Oct to coincide with northern hemisphere university vacations and at weekends. Hoteliers are accustomed to bargaining; healthy competition ensures rates in Sapa are fair market prices.

Sleeping
■ *on map*
Phone code: 020
Price codes:
see inside front cover

L-A *Victoria Sapa*, T871522, F871539, victoriasapa-fo@hn.vnn.vn Opened in 1998 with 76 rooms, a nice position above the town and a pleasant aspect: this hotel is easily the best in town. Comfortable, well-appointed rooms, it is a lovely place in which to relax and enjoy the peace. In winter there are lovely open fires in the bar and dining rooms. The hotel has private sleeper carriages on the train from Hanoi to Lao Cai. Contact the hotel for further details.

B-C *The Gecko*, T871504, F871898, the-gecko-sapa@hn.vnn.vn This new, French-run hotel and restaurant occupies what used to be the Observatory, near the weather station. With just 5 rooms the emphasis is on comfort and pleasure in a way the French do very well. Prices rise at the weekend but include a full American breakfast.
B-D *Auberge Guesthouse*, T871243, F871666, auberge@fpt.vn Mr Dang Trung, the French-speaking owner, shows guests his wonderful informal garden with pride: sweet peas, honeysuckle, snap dragons, foxgloves, roses and irises – all familiar to visitors from temperate climes – grow alongside sub-Alpine flora and a fantastic collection of orchids. A recent extension in traditional style shows what can be done if owners make an effort. The rooms are simply furnished but clean and boast bath tubs, and log fires in winter. Restaurant on a lovely terrace and internet terminals.

C *Green Bamboo*, T871411, F871214, greenbamboo@sapaonline.com A lovely secluded valley-side location 200 m beyond *Auberge* and down the steps. All 28 rooms in this nice old building have wonderful views and have electric heaters in winter. Breakfast is included in the price. **C** *Ham Rong Guesthouse*, T871251, F871303, hamrongsapa@hn.vnn.vn French colonial villa, accommodation now looking a little rundown. Quite good (but expensive) restaurant. **C-D** *Cat Cat*, T871946, F871387, catcatht@hn.vnn.vn On the Cat Cat side of town through the market. The guesthouse has expanded up the hillside, with new terraces and small bungalows with balconies all with views down the valley. A friendly and popular place, its 28 rooms span the price range but all represent good value for money. The hotel has a good restaurant and, like most others, arranges tours and provides useful information. **C-D** *Darling*, T871349. It's a short walk from town to this secluded building but for those seeking peace worth every step of the way, simple, clean and a warm welcome, stunning views and a colourful garden, the top floor is a dormitory. A new wing has 12 rooms, rather more expensive but comfortable, and again, all with fabulous views. **C-D** *Royal*, T871313, royalhotel-sapa@yahoo.com A not particularly attractive and quite large (30 rooms) new hotel which spoils some views, although it is friendly enough and quite popular. Cheaper rooms overlook the town more expensive rooms are rewarded with magnificent views of the valley. The hotel has a special train for US$14 one-way Hanoi to Lao Cai.

D *Forestry Guesthouse*, T871230, F820080. All 10 rooms have private bathrooms, hot water and good views, up a steep drive. **D** *Post Office Guesthouse*, T871244. In town, not particularly spectacular views, but comfortable enough, hot water and clean. **D** *Phuong Nam Guesthouse* , nice views and reasonable food. **E** *Lotus* (formerly

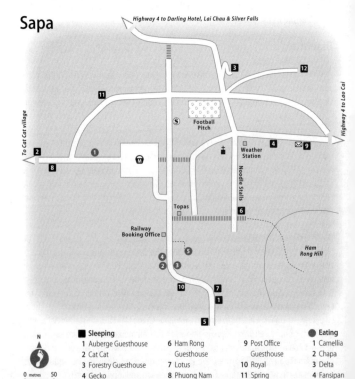

Sapa

Sleeping		Eating
1 Auberge Guesthouse	6 Ham Rong Guesthouse	9 Post Office Guesthouse	1 Camellia
2 Cat Cat	7 Lotus	10 Royal	2 Chapa
3 Forestry Guesthouse	8 Phuong Nam Guesthouse	11 Spring	3 Delta
4 Gecko		12 Victoria Sapa	4 Fansipan
5 Green Bamboo			5 Mimosa

y *Student*), T871308. A small guesthouse next to *Auberge* with a pleasant outlook and a nice terrace. **E** *Spring*, T871380. Newish, family-run guesthouse with 12 rooms. Comfortable, clean and good value.

Nha San Dan Toc (Ethnic Houses). It is possible to spend the night in one of the ethnic houses in the Sapa district. Those of the Black Hmông are probably the best bet, though facilities are considerably more basic than in the Muòng and Thái stilted houses of Hoa Binh, Mai Chau and Son La, and travellers will need to bring their own bedding materials and mosquito net. A contribution of around 30,000d should be made or more if dinner included.

Auberge. Popular terrace, a lovely breakfast setting, full menu including vegetarian and several types of rice wine, also sells film and camera batteries. *Camellia*, just through market on the right, T871455. Long menu, delicious food and rice, and fruit wine. They actually warm the rice bowls for you in winter. The beef steak is rather like dried buffalo, the grilled deer is good and the Camellia salad is spicy and excellent, the apple wine warm and strong (much better value by the bottle than by the glass) and the apple cake unusual, but with local honey very tasty. *Chapa*, T871245. Over-lit. Rather grubby and erratic service, but decent food and popular with local Vietnamese. *Delta*, T871799. Sapa's Italian restaurant serving good portions of pasta and pizzas, US$4-5. *Fansipan*. Good food and fruit wine. *Gecko*, T871504. New and attractive, well-lit dining room. Good French as well as Vietnamese food. Pizzas for US$5, main courses around US$7. Delicious with the restaurant's home-made bread. The daily set lunch at US$10 is good value. Decent wine list. *Mimosa*, T871377, is a small family-run restaurant in an old house up a small path off the road. Sit cosy indoors or in the fresh air on a small terrace. Long menu of good Western and Asian dishes. Open until 2400.

Eating
● *on map*

There are rice and noodle stalls in the market and along the path by the church

Sapa is the place for buying ethnic clothes. Nowhere in Vietnam has the range of shirts, baggy trousers, caps, bags and other garments of Sapa. Sold by vendors or in shops, a lot is used but all the more authentic for that. Note that it is not possible to buy walking shoes, rucksacks, coats or jackets or any mountaineering equipment in Sapa. Quite a good range is available in Hanoi. Temperate fruit, plums and apricots, also delicious baby pineapples, 1,000d each or 15 for a dollar!

Shopping

Topas and *Phu Thinh*, T871331, F871596, info_topas@fpt.vn A combined Danish and Vietnamese operator offering treks varying from fairly leisurely one-day walks to an arduous four-day assault on Mount Fan Si Pan. They also organize bicycling tours and family tours.

Tour operators

Road Roads to Sapa have been improved but heavy rain and trucks can destroy a good surface very quickly. **Bus**: frequent connections with **Lao Cai** 25,000d, 1½ hrs. *Honda ôm*, jeep (US$3 per person). **Train** Connections from Hanoi to Lao Cai depart Hanoi 0530 arrive Lao Cai 1535; depart Hanoi 2020 arrive Lao Cai 0610. From Lao Cai to **Hanoi** depart 0940, arrive Hanoi 2015, depart Lao Cai 1830, arrive Hanoi 0445. Cost 155,000-180,000d depending on comfort level. Tickets from Lao Cai can be booked at the railway booking office in Sapa, 0730-1130 and 1300-1600. Passengers buying tickets from here are obliged to use the railway minibus to Lao Cai, 25,000d.

Transport

Banks The bank will change money US$ cash, as will most hotels but at poor rates. Convert before you travel: as elsewhere in the Northwest beads and gold go further than plastic. **Communications** Post office: 2 in Sapa from where international phone calls can be made. **Internet:** many of the better hotels have email and allow their customers to use it, normally for around 500d per min.

Directory

The North

No man's land

Travellers with the correct exit visa for one country and the incorrect entry visa have often found themselves stranded on the bridge at Lao Cai marking the border. This is particularly serious as most travellers have only single entry visas and can't get back into the country they've just left. Local traders are now accustomed to the almost

daily battle of wills between the two sets of immigration officials as forlorn visitors plead with these uniformed guards to release them from their Kafkaesque nightmare. Vietnamese officials usually prove the most intransigent. Keep a few dollar bills handy. Land travellers to Cambodia and Laos also take note.

Lao Cai

Phone code: 020
Colour map 1, grid A2

It is about 38 km from Sapa, 347 from Hanoi

Lao Cai is the most important border crossing with China. A two-way flow of people and trade cross through the town each day. But whereas the balance of human traffic is roughly equal the value of traded goods is highly one-sided: an endless flow of products from China's modern factories wreaks havoc on Vietnam's hapless state-owned enterprises struggling to fill quotas of shoddy goods that no one wants to buy.

The border crossing   This crossing is open to railway passengers and pedestrians with the correct exit and entry visas for both countries (see box No Man's Land above). From Ha Khau (Hekou) on the Chinese side there are rail connections with Kunming (20 hours). Visas into Vietnam must be obtained in Hong Kong or Beijing and specify the Lao Cai crossing; they normally take a week to process and are not obtainable at the border. Visas for China must be obtained in Hanoi and must specify the Lao Cai crossing. Travellers crossing on foot must report to the Customs House south of the bridge and near the level crossing for passport stamping and customs clearance, and also to buy a 2,000d bridge ticket.

An important north-south transit stop for traders with caravans of pack oxen or horses since time immemorial, Lao Cai has changed hands many times over the past thousand years as rival Chinese, Vietnamese and ethnic minority chieftains fought for ascendancy in the region. The town itself dates back at least to 1463, when the Viet kings established it as the capital of their northernmost province of Hung Hoa.

Lao Cai fell to the French in 1889 and thereafter served as an important administrative centre and garrison town. The direct rail link to Hanoi was built during the first decade of this century, a project remarkable for the 25,000 Vietnamese conscripted labourers who died during its seven-year construction period.

Following the Vietnamese invasion of Cambodia in late 1978, China, Cambodia's ally, responded in February 1979 by launching a massive invasion of northern Vietnam, 'to teach the Vietnamese a lesson'. Over 600,000 Chinese troops were deployed occupying territory from Phong Tho in the Northwest to Cao Bang and Lang Son in the Northeast. From the start of the campaign, however, the poorly trained Chinese forces encountered stiff resistance from local militia, and as the Vietnamese Army got into gear the Chinese invasion force ground to a halt. After two weeks Chinese troops had penetrated no more than 30 km into Vietnamese territory and, with an estimated 20,000 casualties already incurred by the People's Army, the Chinese Government withdrew its troops, declaring the operation 'a great success'.

Trade with China, much of it illegal, has turned this small town into a community of (dong if not dollar) millionaires and Lao Cai is experiencing something of a construction boom. Huge boulevards flanked by enormous local government buildings are sprouting up in the main part of town, west of the Red River. Other than for border-crossers Lao Cai holds little appeal.

Owing to the essentially ephemeral nature of Lao Cai's visitors, hotels tend to be not much more than a bed for the night. The hotels are clustered in the border end of town, convenient for pedestrians but less so for rail travellers.

Sleeping & eating
■ on map
Phone code: 020
Price codes:
see inside front cover

D *Binh Minh*, 39 Nguyen Hue, T830085, F823469. Perhaps the priciest of the hotels listed here but not necessarily any better, a/c, hot water, fridge and TV in top end rooms. Fan only in the cheaper ones. **D** *Hanoi*, 16 Nguyen Hue, T832486, F832488. 9 rooms all with a/c, hot water and fridge, perfectly alright. **D** *Hong Ha*, 26 Nguyen Hue, T830007, F830073. Sign outside just says 'Hotel', 10 a/c rooms, 4 fan rooms, next to bank and opposite post office. **D** *Petrolimex*, 67 Nguyen Hue, T831540. On a busy corner, 10 rooms, a/c, hot water, fridge. **D** *Song Hong*, facing border, near bridge, T830004. Simple but clean, 13 rooms overlooking China, a/c, hot water, quiet, probably the pick of the bunch. **E** *Ngoc Chung*, 27 Nguyen Hue, T832199, F830137. Just 6 rooms, quite busy, a/c, hot water and fridge, neat and clean.

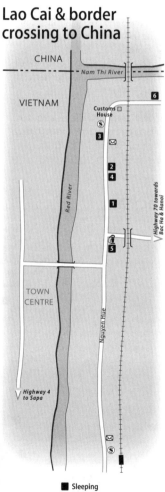

Lao Cai & border crossing to China

CHINA

— Nam Thi River —

VIETNAM

Customs House

6

3

2
4

1

Red River

Highway 70 towards Bac Ha & Hanoi

Nguyen Hue

TOWN CENTRE

Highway 4 to Sapa

■ **Sleeping**
1 Binh Minh
2 Hanoi
3 Hong Ha
4 Ngoc Chung
5 Petrolimex
6 Song Hong

N

0 metres   300
0 yards   300

Transport

Road Bus: connections with **Sapa** (2 hrs) and **Hanoi**. Bus station on Hong Ha St. **Train** Trains from Hanoi to Lao Cai depart Hanoi 0530 arrive Lao Cai 1535; depart Hanoi 2020 arrive Lao Cai 0610. From Lao Cai to **Hanoi** depart 0940, arrive Hanoi 2015; depart Lao Cai 1830, arrive Hanoi 0445. Cost 155,000-175,000d depending on comfort level. There is a twice-weekly train service between Hanoi and Kunming (Con Minh) in each direction (one Vietnamese and one Chinese train) depart Mon and Sat. Depart Hanoi 2130, arrive Lao Cai 0730; depart Lao Cai 0920 arrive Kunming 0500 next day. Hanoi-Kunming is 277,000d soft sleeper on the Vietnamese train but only 222,000d on the Chinese train; hard sleeper 199,000d Vietnamese and 159,000d Chinese. The station is about 2 km south of the hotel area so those arriving from China will need to take a *xe ôm* (around 10,000d).

The North

Directory **Banks** Next to railway station, cash only and just south of the border opposite the post office on Nguyen Hue St. **Communications** Post office: opposite railway station and just south of border on Nguyen Hue St. **Internet:** 44 Hoang Lien St.

Bac Ha

Phone code: 020
Colour map 1, grid A3

Bac Ha is really only notable for one thing and that is its Sunday market. That 'one thing', however, is very special. Hundreds of local minority people flock in from the surrounding districts to shop and socialize, while tourists from all corners of the earth pour in to watch them do it. Otherwise there is very little of interest and neither the appeal or comforts of Sapa.

The Sunday market (0700-1300) draws in the Flower Hmông, Phu La, Dao Tuyen, La Chi and Tày – the latter being Vietnam's largest ethnic minority. It is a riot of colour and fun. While the women trade and gossip, the men consume quantities of rice wine. By late morning they can no longer walk so are heaved onto donkeys by their wives and led home.

There are a number of walks to outlying villages. Pho village of the Flower Hmông is around 4 km north; Thái Giang Pho village of Tày is 4 km east; and Na Hoi and Na Ang villages also of the Tày are 2-4 km west.

Sleeping **C-D** *Tran Sin*, T880240. Opposite market, clean and comfortable, restaurant.
■ *on map* **D** *Anh Duong*, T880329. Opposite market, 12 rooms with toilet and shower. **D** *Dang*
Price codes: *Khoa*, T880290, F880285. 14 rooms, basic but clean. **D** *Sao Mai*, T/F880288. Probably
see inside front cover the best, a short hike from the centre, quiet, clean, 20 fan rooms with hot water.

Eating A couple of the hotels have restaurants,
● *on map* otherwise there is *Cong Phu*, don't use
the menu – most dishes are 'off', look in
the pots in the kitchen, no fridge, no ice.

Transport **Train** From Lao Cai or Hanoi (10 hrs) to
Pho Lu, bus up to Bac Ha. **Road** The drive
from Sapa to Hanoi is very long – those
intending just a quick detour to Bac Ha on
the way home face a gruelling day – Sapa
to Bac Ha is 3 hrs, Bac Ha to Hanoi around
10 hrs. Bus to **Lao Cai** departs 0500; 2
buses daily to **Pho Lu**, 0900 and 1100,
15,000-20,000d. **Bus**: simplest, as so
often is the case, is to buy a tour from a
Hanoi travellers' café: early departure for
Bac Ha to see the market. Some hotels in
Sapa run a Sun morning minibus excursion to Bac Ha.

Routes **From Lao Cai to Hanoi** the road begins
in a beautiful valley, home to the
colourfully-dressed minorities, rice, cinnamon (in places the air is scented) and tea.
By **Viet Tri** it has become a drab industrial
landscape and remains so all the way
back. Tam Dao (see page 83) is a detour
that can be taken en route back to Hanoi.

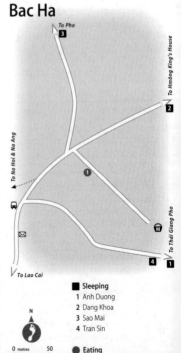

Bac Ha

To Pho
To Hmông King's House
To Na Hoi & Na Ang
To Thái Giang Pho
To Lao Cai

■ **Sleeping**
1 Anh Duong
2 Dang Khoa
3 Sao Mai
4 Tran Sin

● **Eating**
1 Cong Phu

0 metres 50
0 yards 50
N

The Northeast

Rugged, but lacking the lofty grandeur of Northwest Vietnam, the scenery of the Northeast consists of limestone hills dissected by fast-flowing streams – tributaries of the Gam and Red rivers – hurrying south with their burden of silt. Altitudes decline towards the coast, and the river systems of the eastern quarter flow north into China and the You Jiang River. Once densely wooded, centuries of slash-and-burn cultivation and logging have taken their toll on the region and little tree cover remains. Localized landscapes draw admiration but extensive tracts are unremarkable. Hilltribe minorities, particularly the Dao, Nung and Tày are much in evidence.

Despite its sparse population, Northeast Vietnam features prominently in the annals of nationalist and revolutionary history: decisive victories over invading Chinese, armed resistance against the French and momentous events in the founding of the Vietnamese Communist Party took place here.

Unlike Northwest Vietnam which has so conveniently aligned its attractions along one road circuit, Northeast Vietnam is somewhat fragmented and until important roads are built or improved, the traveller wishing to see everything must be prepared to double back over quite long distances. For those wishing to make forays from Hanoi into Northeast Vietnam the situation is better. Broadly speaking, there is a choice: Ha Giang and the far north, or the Bac-Cao-Lang region.

The road to Ha Giang

Ha Giang can be reached comfortably in a day. Having acquired a special permit issued by the authorities there, it is possible to continue further north to the remote Dong Van-Meo Vac region. Beyond Meo Vac the road is impassable to motorized vehicles, and travellers must therefore return to Tuyen Quang before proceeding to other destinations in Northeast Vietnam such as Cao Bang and Lang Son (although see box, Off-road in the Northeast, page 132, for an exception to this rule).

For much of its length the well-maintained Highway 2 follows the Lo River northwards through some delightful scenery. During the early stages of the journey as the road travels past the eastern shores of the Thac Ba Lake, tea plantations may be seen everywhere, but northwards from Ham Yen, 41 km beyond Tuyen Quang, it is orange plantations which carpet the hillsides.

Tuyen Quang Province has a large ethnic minority population, and not long after leaving the provincial capital travellers will begin to see people from the two main ethnic groups of this province, the Tày and the Dao (pronounced 'Zao'). The delightful little town of **Vinh Tuy**, near the banks of the Lo River, is a possible lunch stop. Boats may be seen on the river most days, dredging the bed for gold.

Bac Quang is a sizeable market town located some 60 km before Ha Giang at the junction with Highway 279, the mountain road west to Bao Yen in Lao Cai Province. Unfortunately this road is currently impassable to motorized transport.

The North

Off-road in the Northeast

*Those with sufficient faith in their Minsks and in their own ability to make running repairs to their bike can take an alternative route through some wild and unexplored country which will enable them to press forward without doubling back; but only in the dry season. The road from **Ha Giang** to **Bao Lac** (Highway 34) is passable by motorbike or jeep until Bac Me, although there are a couple of rivers to ford which will be impassable in the rainy season. From **Bac Me** on to **Bao Lac** is also very hard going, and from Bac Me only motorcycles can continue over the rickety suspension bridges and through narrow jungle trails. Bao Lac*

from Ha Giang is about 12 hours and only worth it if you enjoy off-road biking. Bao Lac is a small town but visitors can put up for the night at the People's Committee Guesthouse. There is a busy morning market but this far from anywhere and food is limited (no coffee or bread).

*From **Bao Lac** to **Tinh Tuc** takes a whole day; a very difficult road, again only for experienced bikers. Tinh Tuc is a tin mining town in a pretty valley. It has a simple but adequate hotel next to the post office; there's also a canteen-type diner with very cold beer. **Tinh Tuc** to **Cho Ra** (for Ba Be Lake) is passable, scenic and rewarding.*

Ha Giang

Phone code: 019
Colour map 1, grid A3

Ha Giang lies 333 km north of Hanoi

The provincial capital of Ha Giang lies on the banks of the Lo River just south of its confluence with the River Mien, perched picturesquely between the beautiful Cam and Mo Neo mountains. Like Cao Bang and Lang Son, Ha Giang was badly damaged during the border war with China in 1979 and has since undergone extensive reconstruction.

Archaeological evidence unearthed at Doi Thong (Pine Hill) in Ha Giang town indicates that there was human settlement in the region at least 30,000 years ago. It was during the Bronze Age, however, that the most important flowering of early culture took place under the Tay Vu, one of the most important tribes of the Hung kingdom of Van Lang, whose centre of power was in the Ha Giang region. Some of the most beautiful Dong Son bronze drums were found in Ha Giang Province, most notably in the Meo Vac region, where the tradition of making bronze drums for ceremonial purposes continues even to this day amongst the Lo Lo and Pu Peo ethnic minority communities.

The original settlement in Ha Giang lay on the east bank of the Lo River and it was here that the French established themselves following the conquest of the area in 1886. The town subsequently became an important military base, a development confirmed in 1905 when Ha Giang was formally established as one of four North Vietnamese military territories of French Indochina.

The Ha Giang area saw a number of important ethnic minority rebellions against the French during the early years of the colonial period, the most important being that of the Dao who rose up in 1901 under the leadership of Trieu Tien Kien and Trieu Tai Loc. The revolt was quickly put down and Trieu Tien Kien was killed during the fighting, but in 1913 Trieu Tai Loc rose up again, this time supported by another family member known as Trieu Tien Tien, marching under the slogans: 'No corvees, no taxes for the French, – Drive out the French to recover our country, – Liberty for the Dao'.

Carrying white flags embroidered with the four ideograms *To Quoc Bach Ky* (White Flag of the Fatherland) and wearing white conical hats (hence the French name 'The White Hat Revolt'), the rebels launched attacks against Tuyen Quang, Lao Cai and Yen Bai and managed to keep French troops at bay until 1915 when the revolt was savagely repressed. Hundreds of the insurgents were subsequently deported and 67 condemned to death by the colonial courts.

Sights

The **Ha Giang Museum** is next to Yen Bien Bridge in the centre of town. It contains important archaeological, historical and ethnological artefacts from in and around the region, including a very helpful display of ethnic minority costumes. Unfortunately the museum is normally locked and it is not always possible to visit.

Located close to the east bank of the River Lo in the old quarter of the town, **Ha Giang Market** is a daily market although it is busiest on Sunday. Tày, Nung and Red Dao people are always in evidence here, as are members of northern Ha Giang Province's prolific White Hmông ethnic minority.

Doi Thong or **Pine Hill** lies just behind the main Ha Giang Market. The pine trees are newly planted but the hill itself is an area of ancient human settlement believed to date back some 30,000 years to the Son Vi period. Many ancient axe-heads and other primitive weapons were discovered on the hill during land clearance; these are now in the local museum and in the History Museum in Hanoi.

The North

Sleeping
Phone code: 019

D *Electricity Company Guesthouse*, Tran Hung Dao St, T866317. 10 a/c rooms with adjoining shower/toilet. **D** *Huong Giang*, Tran Hung Dao St, T866015. 6 a/c and fan rooms, basic but comfortable accommodation. **D-E** *Ha Giang*, 517 Nguyen Trai St, T868229. 15 rooms, some a/c, some fan with outside shared facilities, basic with adjacent restaurant, steam bath/massage. **D-E** *River Mien*, Nguyen Trai St, T866746. Picturesque setting on a hill overlooking the river, 13 a/c and fan rooms, all with adjoining shower/toilet. It seems foreigners are no longer allowed to stay. **D-E** *Yen Bien*, 517 Nguyen Trai St, T866333. Part of the *Ha Giang Hotel*. The biggest hotel in town, 36 a/c and fan rooms, all have shower/toilet, restaurant.

Eating

Tourist Company Quan Com Pho, Tran Hung Dao St. The most traveller-friendly place to eat in Ha Giang, located next to the *Ha Giang Hotel*. Another restaurant next door. There are also numerous other small places to eat located down side streets off Tran Hung Dao and on the other side of town near the main market.

Shopping

Tea is the speciality produce of the region, which grows many different varieties including green, yellow, black and flower-scented. Best known is *Shan Tuyet* tea, a flavoursome variety which is exported.

Tour operators

Ha Giang Tourist Company, Tran Hung Dao St, T867054. Permits for Dong Van-Meo Vac region obtainable here, 150,000d, may take a day to issue.

Transport

Road Bus: the bus station is on Nguyen Trai St. Early morning departures from Hanoi's Long Bien terminal, 6 hrs. 4WD vehicle recommended in the far north, whatever the season.

Directory

Banks *Nong Nghiep Bank*, Nguyen Trai St. **Communications** Internet: Tran Phu St, T868599. **Post office**: Nguyen Trai St.

Dong Van-Meo Vac Region

This is the northernmost tip of Vietnam, close to the Chinese border and just 30 km south of the Tropic of Cancer. The primary tourist attraction of the area are the colourful costumes of the ethnic people and the fabulous mountainous scenery which compensate for the rather arduous journey along very bumpy roads. One particular highlight of the trip is the Ma Phi Leng Pass between Dong Van and Meo Vac, an area of breathtaking natural beauty.

Ins & outs All foreign visitors are required to obtain a special permit before proceeding beyond Ha Giang into the remote Dong Van/Meo Vac area on the Chinese border. This can be obtained either directly from the local police or alternatively through the *Ha Giang Tourist Company* (see above) – one possible advantage of booking a tour in Hanoi as they do it for you. Local bus services are infrequent and slow. The roads north of Ha Giang are in extremely poor condition and the going is very hard. A 4WD vehicle is highly advisable. Ha Giang to Dong Van via Yen Minh is 148 km, 7½ hrs; Dong Van to Meo Vac, 22 km, 1½ hrs. Returning from Meo Vac to Ha Giang head straight to Yen Minh via Highways 176 and 180 by-passing Dong Van and cutting off 22 km. Since both Dong Van and Meo Vac are located very close to the Chinese border, hill-walking by foreigners around both towns is forbidden, making the number of things to do in Dong Van and Meo Vac somewhat limited.

Local villages **Quan Ba** is 45 km from Ha Giang. The road climbs up the Quan Ba Pass to 'Heaven's Gate' – identifiable by the TV transmitter mast to the left of the summit – from where there are wonderful views of the Quan Ba valley with its extraordinary row of uniformly shaped hills. Quan Ba has a Sunday market, one of the largest in the region, which attracts not only White Hmông, Red Dao, Dao Ao Dai and Tày people but also members of the Bo Y ethnic minority who live in the mountains around the town.

Yen Minh is located 98 km northwest of Ha Giang and is a convenient place to stop for lunch on the way to Dong Van and Meo Vac – a possible overnight stop for those planning to spend a little longer in the region. It too has a bustling Sunday market where in addition to the ethnic groups mentioned above can be seen Giay, Pu Peo, Co Lao, Lo Lo and the local branch of Red Dao.

The White Hmông village of **Lang Si** lies at the top of the Lang Si Pass (117 km from Ha Giang); an ethnic minority market visited mainly by White Hmông people is held here every six days. Just above the village, near the crest of the hill heading over towards Sa Phin, travellers can see sections of the substantial wall built by the French army at the end of the last century in order to delineate the westernmost frontier of the former White Hmông kingdom. Apiaries dot the hillside in this famed honey-producing area.

Sleeping **D** *People's Committee Guesthouse*, T019-852032. Basic rooms although some are reported now to have a/c and hot water.

Sa Phin

Phone code: 019 Crossing the old border into the former demesne of the White Hmông kings the very distinctive architecture of the White Hmông houses of the area becomes apparent; it is quite unlike the small wooden huts characteristic of Hmông settlements elsewhere in North Vietnam. These are big, two-storey buildings, constructed using large bricks fashioned from the characteristic yellow earth of the region and invariably roofed in Chinese style. But it is not only the Hmông who construct their houses in this way – the dwellings of other ethnic minorities of the area such as the Co Lao and the Pu Peo are of similar design, no doubt a result of their having lived for generations within the borders of the former Hmông kingdom.

The remote Sa Phin valley is just 2 km from the Chinese border. Below the road lies the village of Sa Phin, a small White Hmông settlement of no more than 20 buildings from which loom the twin, white towers of the Hmông royal house, at one time the seat of government in the Dong Van-Meo Vac region.

While it is clear that people of the Hmông ethnic minority have lived in the Dong Van-Meo Vac border region for many centuries, the ascendancy of White Hmông in the area is believed to date from the late 18th century, when the powerful Vuong family established its seat of government near Dong Van. In subsequent years the Vuong lords were endorsed as local government mandarins of Dong Van and Meo Vac by the Nguyen kings in Hué and later, following the French conquest of Indochina, by their colonial masters.

The Hmông Kings of Sa Phin

Keen to ensure the security of this key border region, the French authorities moved to further bolster the power of the Vuong family. Accordingly, in 1900 Vuong Chi Duc was recognized as king of the Hmông, and Chinese architects were brought in to design a residence befitting his newly elevated status. A site was chosen at Sa Phin, 16 km west of Dong Van; construction commenced in 1902 and was completed the following year.

During the early years of his reign, Vuong Chi Duc remained loyal to his French patrons, participating in numerous campaigns to quell uprisings against the colonial government. In 1927 he was made a general in the French army; a photograph of him in full military uniform may be seen on the family altar in the innermost room of the house. But, as the struggle for Vietnamese independence got underway during the 1930s, Duc adopted an increasingly neutral stance. Following his death in 1944, Duc was succeeded as king of the Hmông by his son, Vuong Chi Sinh, who the following year met and pledged his support for President Ho Chi Minh.

Built between 1902 and 1903, the **house of the former Hmông king** faces south in accordance with the geomantic principles which traditionally govern the construction of Northeast Asian royal residences, comprising four, two-storey sections linked by three open courtyards. The building is surrounded by a moat, and various ornately carved tombs of members of the Vuong family lie outside the main gate. Both the outer and cross-sectional walls of the building are made of brick, but within that basic structure everything else is made of wood. The architecture, a development of late-19th-century Southern Chinese town-house style, features *mui luyen* or *yin-yang* roof tiles.

No accommodation available here but there is a guesthouse in Dong Van, 16 km away (see below).

Sleeping

Dong Van

This remote market town is itself nothing special (situated 16 km from Sa Phin) but is set in an attractive valley populated mainly by Tày people. Dong Van has a Sunday market, but is very quiet at other times of the week. Since the town is only 3 km from the Chinese border, foreigners are not permitted to walk in the surrounding hills or visit villages in the vicinity. (Interestingly no two maps of this part of Vietnam tell the same story.) There is a simple government guesthouse in town.

Phone code: 019
Colour map 1, grid A4

E *People's Committee Guesthouse*, T856189, F856295. Very basic, although it appears there is now some a/c and hot water.

Sleeping

Meo Vac

Phone code: 019
Colour map 1, grid A4

Passing through the **Ma Phi Leng Pass** around 1,500 m above the Nho Que River, the scenery is simply awesome. Like Dong Van, Meo Vac is a restricted border area, and foreigners are not permitted to walk in the surrounding hills or visit villages outside the town. A small **market** is held every day in the town square, frequented mainly by White Hmông, Tày and Lo Lo people. Meo Vac is also the site of the famous Khau Vai 'Love Market' held once every year on the 27th day of the third month of the lunar calendar, which sees young people from all of the main ethnic groups of the region descending on the town to look for a partner. The highly colourful Lo Lo ethnic minority make up a large proportion of the town's population. A **Lo Lo village** is nearby, up the hill from the town centre.

Sleeping   **E** *People's Committee Guesthouse*, T871176, F871239. Very basic, but hot water at least.

Cao-Bac-Lang

The three provinces of Cao Bang, Bac Can and Lang Son – the famous Cao-Bac-Lang resistance zone of the 1947-50 Frontier Campaign – form the heartland of the Viet Bac (literally North Vietnam), a mountainous region heavily populated by members of the Tày and Nung ethnic minorities which became the cradle of the revolution during the twilight of the French colonial period.

Ins & outs
Tours available from Hanoi

It is possible to tour this beautiful area by way of a circuit which leads north along Highway 3 from Thai Nguyen to Bac Can, making a small diversion to Ba Be National Park before continuing north to Cao Bang and the historic border district of Pac Bo. From here, Highway 4, scene of some of the most bitter fighting during the First Indochina War, leads south to the important frontier town of Lang Son. The return journey from Lang Son to Hanoi may then be made either directly along Highway 1A or across the mountains along Highway 1B. Although it is possible to reach the larger centres by bus from Hanoi's Long Bien Terminal, the going is tough and detours are not possible. A 4WD vehicle (Russian jeep) is recommended.

Bac Can

Phone code: 0281
Colour map 1, grid A4

The market town and eponymous capital of Bac Can Province lies on the River Cau. Bac Can acquired enormous strategic significance during the First Indochina War as the western-most stronghold of the Cao-Bac-Lang battle zone. The town was captured by the Viet Minh in 1944 and its recovery was considered crucial to the success of the 1947 French offensive against the Viet Bac resistance base. Although colonial troops did succeed in retaking Bac Can, and built military outposts along Highway 3 in the autumn of 1947, guerilla attacks on the town's garrison subsequently became so frequent that the French were forced to abandon the town two years later.

Bac Can's **daily market** is frequented by all of the main ethnic minority groups of the region, which include not only Tày but also local branches of the White Hmông and Red Dao in addition to Coin Dao (*Dao Tien*) and Tight-trousered Dao (*Dao Quan Chet*).

D-E *Bac Can* or *Huong Son*, T870375, F871428. Better rooms have a/c and adjoining shower/toilet, cheaper rooms have fan and shared outside facilities. *Thin Vien Restaurant*, serves simple local fare. Shuts early.
Sleeping & eating

The bus station Is on Duc Xuan St.
Transport

Banks *Nong Nghiep Bank*, Phung Chi Kien St. **Communications** Internet: Minh Khai St, T871859, 450d per min. **Post office:** Phung Chi Kien St.
Directory

Ba Be National Park

Ba Be National Park (Vuon Quoc Gia Ba Be) was established in 1992. It is Vietnam's eighth National Park and comprises 23,340 ha of protected area plus an additional 8,079 ha of buffer zone. The park centre is located on the eastern shore of Ba Be Lake.
Phone code: 0281
Colour map 1, grid A4

The park is centred on the beautiful Ba Be Lake (*ba be* means 'three basins'), 200 m above sea level. The lake is surrounded by limestone hills carpeted in tropical evergreen forest. The park itself contains a very high diversity of flora and fauna, including an estimated 417 species of plant, 100 species of butterfly, 23 species of amphibian and reptile, 110 species of bird and 50 species of mammal. Amongst the latter are 10 seriously endangered species, including the Tonkinese snub-nosed monkey (*Rhinopitecus avunculus*) and the black gibbon (*Hylobates concolor*). Within the park there are a number of villages inhabited by people of the Tày, Red Dao, Coin Dao and White Hmông ethnic minorities.
The area

The national park centre runs many different tours led by English-speaking guides with an expert knowledge of the area and its wildlife. These tours range from two-hour boat trips to two-day mountain treks staying overnight in Tày or Dao ethnic minority villages and visiting caves, waterfalls and other local beauty spots.

D *Ba Be National Park Guesthouse*, T0281-876127/876131. 5 guesthouses each of 3 twin rooms with adjoining bathroom, prices rise in the summer, basic but comfortable accommodation. Meals available in the park office. About 15 km east of Ba Be National Park, Cho Ra has accommodation in the form of the **C** *Ba Be Hotel*, Nguyen Cong Quynh St, T876115, F876257. 9 twin, fan rooms with hot water, shower/toilet, in the event that the National Park Guesthouse is full. The hotel manager can arrange a whole-day boat trip for US$20; the trip includes 2 hrs on the river to the lake passing a small ethnic community homestead where you will be fed and filled with rice wine for 20,000d. Opposite the hotel is a 5-day market for Dao and Tày people, some of whom will have walked through the night to get there.
Sleeping & eating

Ba Be National Park lies 44 km west of Na Phac on Highway 279, 1 hr. 15 km before the park is a checkpoint where a fee of 40,000d is levied.
Transport

The North

Cao Bang

Phone code: 026
Colour map 1, grid A5

Cao Bang stands in a valley on a narrow peninsula between the Bang Giang and Hien rivers, which join just to the northwest of the town. Cao Bang was badly damaged during the 1979 border war with China and has since been extensively rebuilt. At the time of writing, many new government buildings, hotels and commercial developments are taking shape in and around the town; the market here is one of the largest in the country.

Ins and outs

See Transport,
page 141,
for further details

Na Phac to Cao Bang is 83 km, 1½ hrs along a well-metalled road. The Cao Bac Pass runs between 39 km and 29 km before Cao Bang, with stunning scenery all the way and breathtaking views at its summit. Arriving in Cao Bang, fork left over a bridge and keep going until the *Bang Giang Hotel* appears straight in front of you.

History

Tày-Thai settlement in the area began at a very early date, leading to the emergence of the powerful Tay Au kingdom here during the Bronze Age. The Tay Au kings moved their capital south to Co Loa in the Red River Delta where, over the ensuing centuries, they gradually succumbed to the dominant Viet culture.

In the mid-10th century the Viet kings set about establishing fortifications in and around Cao Bang owing to its strategic position near the Chinese border, but the region continued to pose a significant security problem throughout the feudal era, as indicated by the revolts of Tày lords, Be Khac Thieu and Nung Dac Thai, against the Le Dynasty during the 1430s.

During the late 16th and early 17th centuries Cao Bang became a hotbed of revolt against royal authority. The essential background to the events of that period was the usurpation of the Le throne in 1527 by the Mac; although the Le kings were reinstated in 1592, members of the Mac family subsequently seized Cao Bang and proceeded to rule the region as an independent kingdom for a further 75 years. The ruins of a temple which once functioned as the palace of the Mac kings may still be seen today near the small market town of Cao Binh, 12 km northwest of Cao Bang town.

Before the arrival of the French, the market town of Cao Binh served as the administrative headquarters of Cao Bang Province. However, the Cao Bang peninsula had also been settled from an early date, and following the French conquest of the area in 1884 the colonial authorities decided to transfer the provincial capital to the current site. A substantial fortress was subsequently constructed on the hill overlooking the town centre – the outer walls of this fortress still stand today, although what's left of the fortress itself currently serves as a base for the People's Army and is therefore off-limits to visitors.

From the late 1920s onwards Cao Bang became a cradle of the revolutionary movement in the north. The following years saw the establishment of many party cells through which a substantial programme of subversive activity against the colonial regime was organized. It was thus no accident that in 1940, when he returned to Vietnam after his long sojourn overseas, Ho Chi Minh chose to make remote Cao Bang Province his revolutionary headquarters during the crucial period from 1940 to 1945.

Sights

There is not a lot to see in the town. A few late-19th-century French buildings have survived the ravages of war and redevelopment in the old quarter of town which stretches down the hill from the fortress to the Hien River Bridge, making that area worth exploring on foot. **Cao Bang Exhibition Centre**, Kim Dong St, located just behind the new market, records the history of the revolutionary struggle in Cao Bang Province, with particular reference to the years leading up to the establishment of the Democratic Republic of Vietnam when Ho Chi Minh's headquarters were based at Pac Bo, 56 km north of Cao Bang. Pride of place in the exhibition hall is given to Ho's old staff car, registration number 'BAC 808'. Unfortunately all information is in Vietnamese only.

Excursions

Ky Sam Temple This temple honours the memory of Nung Tri Cao, Nung lord of Quang Nguyen, who led one of the most important revolts of the ethnic minority people against the Vietnamese monarchy during the 11th century.

The story of Nung Tri Cao began in 1039 when Nung Tri Cao's father Nung Ton Phuc and his elder brother Nung Tri Thong rose in rebellion against Le Thai Tong. An expeditionary force was swiftly assembled by the Viets and the rebels were caught and summarily executed. However, two years later Nung Tri Cao himself gathered an army, seizing neighbouring territories and declaring himself ruler of a Nung kingdom which he called Dai Lich. He too was quickly captured by Viet troops, but having put his father and elder brother to death two years earlier, King Le Thai Tong took pity on Nung Tri Cao and let him return to Quang Nguyen. For the next seven years peace returned to the area, but in 1048, Nung Tri Cao rose up in revolt yet again, this time declaring himself 'Emperor of Dai Nam' and seizing territories in southern China. For the next five years he managed to play the Viet and Chinese kings off against each other until Le Thai Tong finally captured and executed him in 1053.

There has been a temple in the village of Ngan for many centuries, but the one standing today dates from the 19th century. It comprises two buildings, the outer building housing an altar dedicated to one of Nung Tri Cao's generals, the inner sanctum originally containing statues of the king, his wife and his mother; unfortunately these statues were stolen many years ago. The poem etched onto the walls in the outer building talks of Nung Tri Cao's campaigns and declares that his spirit is ever ready to come to the aid of his country in times of need. ■ *Getting there: Ky Sam Temple 18 km north of Cao Bang town on Highway 203 to Pac Bo. It is located in the Nung village of Ngan, 200 m east of Highway 203.*

Ruins of Cao Binh Church Constructed in 1906, Cao Binh Church was one of three churches administered from Cao Bang during the French period, the others being those of Cao Bang and That Khe. There used to be many French houses in the vicinity of the church, but the majority of those that survived the French war were destroyed in 1979. However, the former vicar's house still stands relatively intact, adjacent to the ruins of the church. The family which currently occupies it runs one of the Cao Bang region's most famous apiaries. ■ *Getting there: 5 km north of Ky Sam Temple along Highway 203 to Pac Bo, fork left at a junction; the ruins are 500 m from the junction.*

The North

Mac Kings' Temple Cao Binh is situated on the east bank of the Dau Genh river, a tributary of the Bang Giang River. On the opposite bank of the river lies Lang Den (Temple village), which takes its name from the ruined 16th-century palace of the Mac Dynasty located on a hill just above the village.

This structure is believed to have been built during the early 1520s by Mac Dang Dung, a general of the Le army who in 1521-22 seized control of the kingdom, forcing the 11-year-old King Le Chieu Tong into exile and setting up his younger brother Le Thung as king. Two years later Mac Dang Dung forced Le Thung to abdicate, declaring himself king of Dai Viet.

The Mac Dynasty retained control of Dai Viet for 65 years, during which period representatives of the deposed Le Dynasty mounted numerous military campaigns against the usurpers. The Le kings were finally restored to power in 1592 by the powerful Trinh family, but in that year a nephew of Mac Mau Hop, the last Mac king, seized Cao Bang and set up a small kingdom there. Over the next 75 years three successive generations of the Mac family managed to keep the royal armies at bay, even managing to launch two successful attacks on Thang Long (Hanoi) before Cao Bang was finally recaptured by Trinh armies in 1667.

It is clear that this building was originally constructed as a small royal residence; the original cannon placements may still be seen on the hill in front of the main entrance. ■ *Getting there: 1½ km beyond Lang Den (Temple village), located on the west bank of the Dau Genh River, opposite Cao Binh. Accessible either on foot or by 4WD capable of fording the river.*

Pac Bo On 28 January 1941 Ho Chi Minh crossed the Sino-Vietnamese border, returning home to take charge of the resistance movement after 30 years overseas. In the days which followed, he and his colleagues set up their revolutionary headquarters in a cave in the Pac Bo valley. Of interest primarily to scholars of the fledgling Vietnamese Socialist Party, Pac Bo is the sort of pilgrimage spot that model carpet-weavers or revolutionary railwaymen might be brought to as a reward.

The road to Ba Dinh Square Taking advantage of the surrender of the French administration to the Japanese Ho Chi Minh returned to Vietnam setting up his HQ at Pac Bo, an area populated mainly by the Nung ethnic minority. It was from here that Ho Chi Minh – dressed in the traditional costume of the Nung people – guided the growing revolutionary movement, organizing training programmes for cadres, translating *The History of the Communist Party in the USSR* into Vietnamese and editing the revolutionary newspaper *Independent Vietnam*.

The eighth Congress of the Communist Party Central Committee, convened by Ho Chi Minh at Pac Bo from 10-19 March 1941, was an event of great historic importance which saw the establishment of the Vietnam Independence League (*Vietnam Doc Lap Dong Minh Hoi*), better known as the Viet Minh. This Congress also speeded up preparations for the future armed uprising, establishing guerilla bases throughout the Viet Bac.

The years from 1941 to 1945 were a period of severe hardship for the Vietnamese people, as the colonial government colluded with Japanese demands to exploit the country's natural resources to the full in order to support the Japanese war effort. But, by 1945, the Vichy Government in France had fallen and the French colonial administration belatedly drew up plans to resist the Japanese. However, on 9 March 1945, their plans were foiled by the Japanese who set up a new government with King Bao Dai as head of state.

At this juncture, Viet Minh guerilla activity was intensified all over the country with the result that by June 1945, almost all of the six provinces north of the Red River Delta were under Communist control. On 13 August Japan surrendered to the Allied forces; three days later Ho Chi Minh headed south from Pac Bo to Tan Trao near Tuyen Quang to preside over a People's Congress which declared a general insurrection and established the Democratic Republic of Vietnam. The August Revolution which followed, swept all in its wake; within a matter of weeks the three major cities of Hanoi, Hué and Saigon had fallen to the Viet Minh and King Bao Dai had abdicated. On 2 September 1945 President Ho Chi Minh made an historic address to the people in Hanoi's Ba Dinh Square, proclaiming the nation's independence.

The **Pac Bo Exhibition Centre** houses artefacts concerning the revolution and Ho Chi Minh's part in it. ■ *0800-1700, 5,000d.*

Coc Bo Cave is where Ho lived and worked after his return from overseas. The area is not unattractive with its streams and trees, but the charm is rendered somewhat comic by the commemorative plaques which festoon the place, complete with names dubbed by Ho: Karl Marx mountain, Lenin stream and so on. ■ *Getting there: The road from Cao Bang to Pac Bo passes through 56 km of stunning scenery, 1½ hrs. Despite its proximity to China, no special permit is needed, but walking outside the area is not permitted.*

Ban Doc (Ban Zop), Vietnam's most recently discovered **waterfall**, and apparently the highest, is about 80 km due north of Cao Bang. *Cao Bang Guesthouse* (see below) can provide details. They also reckon to be able to arrange permits for three-day trips into China but quite what there is to see and whether you can get back in to Vietnam you will have to find out for yourself.

Essentials

B-C *Bang Giang Hotel*, Kim Dong St, T853431, F854984. New 80-room building, 1st floor a/c, 2nd floor fan, all with adjoining bathroom. **C** *Cao Bang Guesthouse*, Hoang Nhu St, T851023. 28 rooms a/c and fan. **C** *Duc Trung Mini*, Be Van Dan St, T853424. 6 a/c rooms. **D** *Phong Lan*, 83 Be Van Dan St, T852260, F852258. 40 rooms, better ones a/c, cheaper fan and shared facility. **D** *Phuong Dong*, 136 Bac Po St, T853178. On Bang Giang River opposite town centre, 8 rooms fan and a/c, restaurant. — **Sleeping** *Phone code: 026*

Bac Lam, Kim Dong St, T852697. Local dishes, open 1000-2000. *Thanh Truc*, 278 Vuon Cam St, T852798. Serves basic local fare from 0800 until 2000. — **Eating**

The bus station is on Kim Dong St. — **Transport**

Bank *Nong Nghiep Bank*, Kim Dong St. **Communications** Post office: on Be Van Dan St. — **Directory**

The Northeast Frontier

From Cao Bang to Lang Son along Highway 4 is a journey of 135 km; the road is in relatively poor condition and the going can be quite hard, taking 3½ hours, but it is not without its rewards.

About 10 km south of Dong Khe, Highway 4 climbs up to the infamous **Lung Phay Pass**. From here to the village of Bong Lau the wonderful mountain scenery makes it difficult to imagine the carnage which took place between 1947 and 1950, when convoy after convoy of French supply trucks ran into carefully planned Viet Minh ambushes. The War Heroes' Cemetery at Bong Lau is sited on a hill where a French military outpost once stood and marks the border between Cao Bang and Lang Son provinces.

About 30 km south of That Khe the road passes through more towering limestone outcrops before commencing its climb up through another of the Frontier Campaign's infamous battle zones, the beautiful **Bo Cung Pass**.

The Frontier Campaign of 1947-50

The government established by Ho Chi Minh in September 1945 soon found itself in a cleft stick. The terms of the Potsdam Conference had provided for the surrender of Japanese forces to be accepted south of the 16th parallel by British-Indian forces and north of that line by the Chinese Kuomintang (Nationalist Party) troops of Chiang Kai-shek. In the south, General Gracey promptly freed thousands of French troops detained in the wake of the Japanese coup.

Unable to confront both the French and the Chinese, Ho Chi Minh decided to negotiate with the French, concluding, as we have already seen, that they were the lesser of the two evils. In February 1946 the French signed a treaty with the Chinese Nationalists which secured their withdrawal from Vietnamese territory. The following month a Franco-Vietnamese agreement confirmed the status of Vietnam as a free state within the French Union and the Indochinese Federation.

After consolidating their positions in the Red River Delta, the French resolved to launch a major offensive against the Viet Bac in October 1947 with the objective of destroying the resistance leadership. Their plan involved a pincer movement of two armed columns – one under Colonel Communal moving by water up the Red and Lo rivers to attack and occupy Tuyen Quang and Chiem Hoa, the other under Colonel Beaufre travelling to Lang Son and then north along Highway 4 to That Khe, Dong Khe and Cao Bang before heading southwards to Bac Can. The offensive was intended to take the Viet Minh by surprise but, just six days after the attack had begun, an aircraft carrying the French chief of staff was shot down near Cao Bang, allowing the plans to fall into the hands of the Viet Minh High Command.

Sailing up the Lo River, Communal's column fell into a Viet Minh ambush suffering a humiliating defeat and losing some 38 gunboats before being forced to retreat to Tuyen Quang. Meanwhile, Beaufre's forces suffered repeated ambushes at the hands of Viet Minh before finally managing to recapture the fortresses of Cao Bang and Bac Can in late October 1947. Having failed to achieve the objective of their offensive, the French were now obliged to dig-in for a long and costly war.

The position of the French became steadily more and more precarious. Supply convoys travelling from Lang Son to Cao Bang and Bac Can were ambushed repeatedly, particularly along Highway 4. Thousands of colonial troops lost their lives whilst travelling along, what French press dubbed the 'Road of Death', the most dangerous stretches of which were the Lung Phay Pass 10 km south of Dong Khe and the Bo Cung Pass 30 km south of That Khe.

Despite massive subsidy from the United States under the emerging Truman doctrine of containing communism, the cost of air-dropping supplies into the region was becoming an intolerable burden. The French High Command finally concluded that their position in the Viet Bac was no longer tenable and began to draw up plans for the abandonment of Cao Bang.

Before these plans could be implemented, however, the Viet Minh launched a surprise attack on Dong Khe, capturing the post. Taken aback by

The border crossing

About 12 km north of Lang Son, Highway 4 meets Highway 1. From this junction it is just 8 km to the Dong Dang Friendship Gate (Cua Khau Huu Nghi Dong Dang), the border with China.

The border is open in both directions to those with the correct entry and exit visas specifying the Friendship Crossing. Visas cannot be obtained at the border and must be picked up in Saigon/Hanoi or Hong Kong/Beijing. Vietnamese visas normally specify air routes only; a special stamp for land crossings must be obtained from the immigration police or travel agents.

Crossing from China *From the border town of Ping Xiang in China, catch a minibus near the main bus station (¥3 per person) to the border. Tell the driver you want to go to YuteLarm GorGwarn (Cantonese for Vietnam border). At the drop-off point you will be greeted by a crowd of willing motorbike drivers who can take you to the border, a 5-10 minute drive, for around ¥5 per person. He will take you to the policed border-gate leaving you*

to walk the 500 m or so down an almost deserted road before reaching the Chinese Immigration Building. After paying ¥10 for the privilege of leaving China at this border point and other obligatory stages of red tape, you have to continue, unescorted, down the same road for another five minutes with the occasional truck going past, but little else. The silence is quite eerie and out-of-place for a border point. On average only about 20 or 30 people cross at this point per day.

Reaching Vietnam *The Vietnamese border control looks more like a restaurant and the Vietnamese guards are relaxed and cheeky (a contrast to the stern Chinese!). From Dong Dang, the trip to Lang Son itself is easily managed, as hordes of hopefuls wait outside the Immigration Building with vans, cars and bikes. They will also change money at terrible rates. The journey to Lang Son takes about 30 minutes and will cost around US$5 for a van which can hold five or six people.*

this bold move and desperate to secure the speedy and safe retreat of its Cao Bang garrison, the French High Command ordered the post's commander, Colonel Charton, to withdraw to Lang Son.

Leaving Cao Bang on 3 October 1950, Charton's column made it no further than Nam Nang, 17 km south of the town, before running into a Viet Minh ambush. Travelling northwards from That Khe to rendezvous with Charton, Lepage's forces were also intercepted in the vicinity of Dong Khe. The subsequent battle in the hills to the west of Highway 4 resulted in a resounding Viet Minh victory, in the aftermath of which, on 8 October, some 8,000 French troops had been either killed or taken prisoner. Within days the French had abandoned all their remaining posts on Highway 4.

The Viet Minh victory on Highway 4 was a major turning point in the war, which threw the colonial forces throughout the north into complete disarray. During the following two weeks the French were obliged to withdraw all their forces from Lang Son, Thai Nguyen and Tuyen Quang, while in the northwest, the French garrisons at Hoa Binh and Lao Cai were also driven out. Thus was the scene set for the final stage of the First Indochina War, which would culminate four years later in the momentous battle at Dien Bien Phu (see page 112).

Lang Son

The town of Lang Son lies on the Ky Lung River in a small alluvial plain surrounded by 1,000-m-high mountains. Like Cao Bang, Lang Son was badly damaged during the border war of 1979 and has since been substantially

Phone code: 025
Colour map 1, grid B5

rebuilt. But, the old quarter of the town, south of the Ky Cung River still contains a number of interesting historic buildings and the town's markets see regular visits from ethnic minority people.

Ins & outs
See Transport, page 145, for further details

The direct route from Hanoi is along Highway 1A via Chi Lang and Bac Giang, 154 km, 3½ hrs. Chi Lang Pass is the site of Le Loi's historic victory over 100,000 Ming invaders in 1427, effectively bringing to an end 1,000 years of Chinese hegemony. The longer, more scenic route is along Highway 1B via Bac Son and Thai Nguyen, 237 km, 7 hrs. The road passes through some delightful highland countryside settled by Tày, Nung and Dao ethnic people. There are early morning bus departures from Hanoi's Long Bien terminal. Two trains run daily from Hanoi and back – one during the day, one overnight – from Dong Dang (Border Gate) and Dong Kinh (Lang Son Central) to Hanoi.

History   Lang Son rose to prominence as early as the Bronze Age, when emergent trade routes between India and China turned it into an important transit stop on the main road from the Red River Delta through Nanning to Guangzhou.

Between 1527 and 1592 the Mac devoted considerable attention to the task of fortifying the strategically important Lang Son border region. Vestiges of a number of Mac Dynasty fortifications may still be seen today in Lang Son Province, the best preserved of which is the citadel which lies on a limestone outcrop to the west of the present town.

By the time of its seizure by French troops in 1885 Lang Son had developed into a sizeable and prosperous market town. In subsequent years it became a French military base second in importance only to Cao Bang.

Sights   **Dong Kinh Market** has been recently rebuilt and is chock-full of Chinese consumer goods brought through Dong Dang. Although rebuilt many times and finally sidelined by the gleaming new structure at Dong Kinh, **Ky Lua Market** is the oldest in Lang Son and still sees a trickle of trading activity every day. Members of the Tày and Nung ethnicity are regular visitors here. **Lang Son Citadel** comprises a large section of the ancient city walls, dating back to the 18th century, of which can still be seen. The former Lang Son monastery once stood on the other side of the city walls. ■ *Getting there: south down Nguyen Thai Hoc St from the old quarter to My Son junction.*

Excursions   The east- and west-facing walls of the imposing 16th-century **Mac Dynasty Citadel** are located on a limestone outcrop west of Lang Son. ■ *Getting there: head out of town past the 6-way junction on the Tam Thanh rd.*

A poem by Ngo Thi Sy (1726-80), military commander of the Lang Son garrison, who first discovered the **Tam Thanh Cave** and other caves in the area, is carved on the wall near the entrance. There are three chambers; the outer one functions as a pagoda with two shrines and the second one contains a fresh water pool. ■ *10,000d. Getting there: on the road to the Mac citadel.*

Nhi Thanh, perhaps the best known of Lang Son's caves, is located south of Tam Thanh Cave. There are in fact two separate caves here – the one on the right contains the Tam Giao Pagoda, established in 1777 by Ngo Thi Sy, in which are six shrines, whilst the one on the left follows the Ngoc Tuyen stream deep into the mountain: the latter is particularly dramatic. More of Ngo Thi Sy's poetry adorns the walls. The ladies who sit in front of the pagoda are lovely and very friendly, they will offer visitors tea and bananas. ■ *10,000d. Getting there: from the 6-way junction take the Nhi Thanh road.*

Sleeping
Phone code: 025

C *A1 Guesthouse*, 32 Dinh Tien Hoang St, T812221. The only hotel in the old quarter of town, 30 twin rooms all with adjoining bathroom, basic. **C** *Anh Dao*, 1 Nhi Thanh St, T870543, F870419. 16 twin a/c rooms all with bathroom, restaurant. **C** *Bac Son*, 41 Le Loi St, T871849, F871507. 22 rooms, all with adjoining bathroom, pricier rooms have a/c. **C** *Hoa Binh*, 127 Tran Dang Ninh St, T870807, F871506. 12 rooms all a/c, adjoining bathroom, comfortable accommodation. **C** *KDN*, 233 Tran Dang Ninh St, T871272. 18 a/c rooms, own bathroom, comfortable enough with *Gia Canh Restaurant* next door. **C** *Kim Son*, 3 Minh Khai St, T870378, F872118. Comfortable Chinese joint-venture hotel, 29 rooms all a/c, adjoining bathroom, *Quang Chau* Chinese restaurant. **C** *Tam Thanh*, 117 Tran Dang Ninh St, T870979, F871507. 18 a/c and fan rooms all with adjoining bathroom, basic, comfortable but rather overpriced accommodation next to *Tam Thanh* restaurant. **D** *Dong Kinh*, 25 Nguyen Du St, T870166, F872186. Near market, better rooms with own bathroom, a/c, fridge etc, cheapest rooms shared facilities, basic but comfortable accommodation, restaurant.

Eating

A number of hotels have restaurants attached, see above. Also *Cua Hang An Uong*, corner of Le Loi and the market street, looks like a 1970s-built English clubhouse, but serves fantastic *lau* (steamboat) at good prices.

Transport

Road Bus station is at 28A Ngi Quyen St. A main highway links Lang Son with Hanoi and public buses travel along this route. More interesting is the road via Bac Son and Thai Nguyen. It is possible to return (on a *Minsk*) via Halong Bay and the coast; the road to Tien Yen is a shocker, and carry lunch and spare fuel with you as there are no supplies en route. From Tien Yen the road improves but as it passes through the dusty coal-mining areas of Quang Ninh you will end up as black as a miner. **Train** Railway station is on Le Loi St. One daytime and one nighttime train connects each day with **Hanoi**.

Directory

Banks *Nong Nghiep Bank*, 1 Tran Hung Dao St. *Vietcombank*, 1 Quang Trung St. **Communications** Internet: 40 Phai Ve St, 6,000d per hr. **Post office:** 49 Le Loi St.

Bac Son

Phone code: 025
Colour map 1, grid B5

Settled mainly by members of the Tày and Nung ethnicity, this small market town has two important reasons to claim significance in the history of the Vietnamese nation.

The first derives from the very large number of prehistoric artefacts unearthed here by archaeologists. The so-called Bac Son period (5000-3000 BC) was characterized by the development of pottery and the widespread use of refined stone implements, including distinctive axes with polished edges known as Bacsonian axes.

The second is the Bac Son Uprising. In September 1940, revolutionaries detained in Lang Son prison, seized the opportunity afforded by the Japanese attack on the town to escape, heading northwest across the mountains to Bac Son. With the support of the local Communist Party organization they fomented a general insurrection in the town, disarming the fleeing French troops and taking over the district centre to set up the first revolutionary power base in the Viet Bac.

The following year French forces responded by launching a campaign of terror in the Viet Bac, forcing the leaders of the uprising to retreat into the mountains. The Bac Son uprising did, however, prove to be an important milestone in the revolutionary struggle and, in the years which followed, the tide turned steadily against the French throughout the region.

Museum of the Bac Son Rebellion On the way into the town the road passes an unmarked white building on stilts with a Vietnamese flag fluttering on its roof – this is the Museum of the Bac Son Rebellion which contains a small collection of prehistoric axe-heads and other tools dating from the Bac Son period plus a large display of artefacts relating to the Bac Son Uprising. These include the weapons and personal effects of those involved in the uprising, plus letters and other documents written by Ho Chi Minh and leading revolutionaries such as Hoang Van Thu. ■ *0700–1600, free, no English translation unfortunately.*

Transport **Road Bus**: connections with **Hanoi** and **Lang Son**.

Hanoi to Haiphong, Do Son, Cat Ba Island and Halong Bay

The 100 km road from Hanoi to Haiphong, the north's principal port, passes through the flood-prone riceland of the Red River Delta. In places the land lies below sea-level and an elaborate system of dykes and bunds has been built-up over the centuries to keep the river in place. Haiphong was heavily bombed during the American War, but still retains a surprising amount of French-era architecture. From Haiphong it is just a 40-minute drive to the resort town of Do Son or a one hour hydrofoil ride to Cat Ba Island, one of Vietnam's more accessible national parks. Cat Ba's rugged scenery and forests make it an attractive place in which to spend a few days. It is also an ideal spot from which to explore the wonderful scenery of Halong Bay.

Haiphong

Phone code: 031
Colour map 1, grid B5
Population: 1.6 million

The port of Haiphong was established in 1888 on the Cua Cam River, a major distributory of the Red River. It is the largest port and the second-largest city in the north. Over and above its natural attributes Haiphong is blessed with a go-ahead and entrepreneurial People's Committee (no surprises that the district sports Vietnam's only casino) and this attitude is reflected in the bustle of the town and the industry and vitality of the population. Haiphong's prosperity looks set to redouble with heavy investment in port and communications infrastructure and major investment from overseas in manufacturing plant. Despite this (from the tourists' viewpoint) seemingly inauspicious framework, central Haiphong remains remarkably attractive and its people open and warm. Although its role in the tourist trade is unlikely to exceed by far the provision of a bed for those who have missed the last ferry to Cat Ba, there is sufficient in and around Haiphong to justify a closer look.

Ins and outs

Getting there
See Transport, page 151, for further details

As the north's second city after Hanoi, and the region's premier port, Haiphong is well connected. Cat Bi, Haiphong's airport, is 7 km from the city and there are 5 departures a week for Saigon (but none with Hanoi). The road from Hanoi is now excellent (for Vietnam) and there are frequent bus and minibus connections from Long Bien bus station, 25,000d. Choose a big bus in the interests of comfort and safety. There are 5 trains each day between the two cities. Haiphong is the departure point for Cat Ba Island and from there with Ha Long Bay.

Central Haiphong is sufficiently compact for most sights to be visited on foot. But the **Getting around** distance from, for example, the railway station to port merits a taxi, cyclo or *xe ôm* as do the outer temples. Because Haiphong does not receive many Western tourists it is not normally possible to rent a motorbike for independent exploring. To rent a motorbike and driver should only cost around US$4-5 per day, that is about the same as renting just a motorbike in most other places.

History

Haiphong witnessed the initial arrival of the French in 1872 (they occupied Hanoi a year later) and, appropriately, their final departure from the north at 1500 in the afternoon of 15 May 1955. As the major port of the north, it was subjected to sustained bombing during the War. To prevent petrol and diesel fuel reaching the Viet Cong, nearly 80% of all above-ground tanks were obliterated by US bombing in 1966. The US did not realize that the North Vietnamese, anticipating such an action, had dispersed much of their supplies to underground and concealed tanks. This did not prevent the city from receiving a battering, although Haiphong's air defence units are said to have retaliated by shooting down 317 US planes.

Sights

Much of outer Haiphong is an ugly industrial sprawl that will win no environmental beauty contests. But, considering the bombing the city sustained, there is still a surprising amount of attractive **colonial-style architecture** in the city centre. Central Haiphong is pleasantly green with tree-lined streets.

Right in the heart of town, where Tran Hung Dao and Quang Trung streets **Great Theatre** meet, is the Great Theatre. It was built in 1904 using imported French materials, with a colonnaded front, facing a wide tree-lined boulevard. In November 1946, 40 Viet Minh fighters died here in a pitched battle with the French, triggered by the French government's decision to open a customs house in Haiphong. A plaque outside commemorates the battle. The streets around the theatre support the greatest concentration of foodstalls and shops.

The museum (Bao Tang Hai Phong), at 66 Dien Bien Phu Street, is an impres- **Museum** sive colonial edifice in a wash of desert-sand red, and contains records of the city's turbulent past. ■ *Tue, Wed, Sun 0800-1100, 1400-1630.*

There are a number of **street markets** and **flower stalls** off Cau Dat Street, **Markets** which runs south from the theatre, along Tran Nhat Duat and Luong Khanh Thien streets. **Sat Market** is to be found in the west quarter of town, at the end of Phan Boi Chau Street. A market has stood on this site since 1876. The present building is a huge concrete edifice of six storeys that has never quite taken off.

Near the centre of town on Me Linh Street is the Nghe Pagoda built at the **Nghe Pagoda** beginning of the 20th century. The pagoda is dedicated to the memory of heroine General Le Chan who fought with the Trung sisters against the Chinese. A festival is held on the eighth day of the second lunar month to commemorate her birthday and offerings of crab and noodles, her favourite foods, are made.

The North

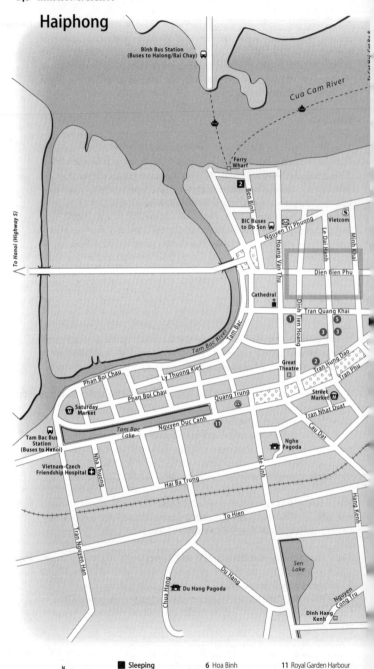

Haiphong

The North

To Hanoi (Highway 5)

Binh Bus Station
(Buses to Halong/Bai Chay)

Cua Cam River

Ferry
Wharf

Ben Binh

BIC Buses
to Do Son

Nguyen Tri Phuong

Le Dai Hanh

Minh Khai

Vietcom

Hoang Van Thu

Dien Bien Phu

Cathedral

Tran Quang Khai

Dinh Tien Hoang

Tam Bac River

Tam Bac

Tran Hung Dao

Tran Phu

Great
Theatre

Phan Boi Chau

Ly Thuong Kiet

Phan Boi Chau

Quang Trung

Street
Market

Tran Nhat Duat

Cau Dat

Saturday
Market

Tam Bac Bus
Station
(Buses to Hanoi)

Tam Bac
Lake

Nguyen Duc Canh

Nghe
Pagoda

Nha Thuong

Me Linh

Hang Kenh

Vietnam-Czech
Friendship Hospital

Hai Ba Trung

To Hien

Sen
Lake

Tran Nguyen Han

Chua Hang

Du Hang

Du Hang Pagoda

Nguyen Cong Tru

Dinh Hang
Kenh

N

0 metres 200
0 yards 200

■ Sleeping	6 Hoa Binh	11 Royal Garden Harbour
1 Bach Dang	7 Hoang Yen	View
2 Ben Binh	8 Hong Bang	12 Thang Nam
3 Cat Bi	9 Huu Nghi	
4 Dien Bien	10 Phuong Dong	● Eating
5 du Commerce		1 Formosa Tea House

Dien Bien Phu Street detail

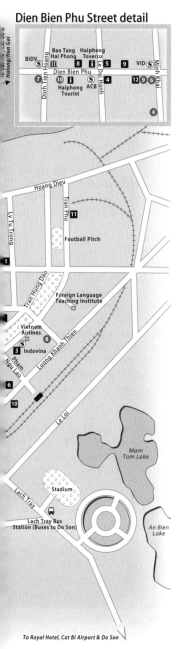

One kilometre south of the city centre, on Chua Hang Street, is the Du Hang Pagoda. Originally built in 1672 by wealthy mandarin turned monk Nguyen Dinh Sach, it has been renovated and remodelled several times since. Arranged around a courtyard, this small temple has some fine traditional woodcarving. ■ *Getting there: by* xe ôm, *along a pot-holed road, past workers' cottages.* — **Du Hang Pagoda**

Also 2 km south of the centre, at 51 Nguyen Cong Tru Street, is Dinh Hang Kenh (Hang Kenh communal house or *dinh*) which dates back to 1856. Although built as a communal house, its chief function today is as a temple. The main building is supported by 32 columns of ironwood and the wood carvings in the window grilles are noteworthy. From the outside, the roof is the most dramatic feature, tiled in the fishscale style, and ornamented with a number of dragons. The corners of the roof turn up and it appears that the sheer weight is too much as they are now propped up on bricks. There are a number of *dinh* around Haiphong reflecting the traditional importance of Chinese in the area. Today Taiwanese businessmen are some of the major investors in Haiphong. — **Dinh Hang Kenh**

The Foreign Language Teaching Institute is in Ngo 10 in Nguyen Duc Canh Street, and has a crowd of eager young Vietnamese students more than willing to chat to you for an afternoon and show you around Haiphong in exchange for practising their English. — **Foreign Language Teaching Institute**

The North

2 Hoa Bien
3 Hoa Dai
4 Lucky
5 M&N Club
6 Maxim's Bar
7 Saigon Café
8 Saigon Thien Bao
9 Sake
10 Thien Nhat
11 Trong Khach

Essentials

Sleeping
■ *on map*
Phone code: 031
Price codes:
see inside front cover

Haiphong offers plenty of accommodation to meet the demands of industrialists and expats rather than travellers, therefore standards tend to be fairly good but prices a little high. There is value to be found, however.

L-A *Royal Garden Harbour View*, 4 Tran Phu St, T827827, 827828, royalgarden@ hn.vnn.vn Haiphong's newest, largest (just) and most luxurious hotel. Near the river, this 127-room hotel has a restaurant and bar, it is well managed and comfortable. Daily buffet lunch starting at US$7.

A-B *Huu Nghi*, 60 Dien Bien Phu St, T823310, F823245, huunghihotel@ hn.vnn.vn Central, and at 11 storeys and 126 rooms one of Haiphong's largest. It's efficient enough and prices have been reduced to sensible levels. Popular with Chinese tour groups, breakfast included. **A-B** *Royal*, 275 Lach Tray St, T847857, F843368. On the airport/Do Son road, 3 km south of centre, new, comfortable, well appointed and good value (breakfast included), particularly recommended for longer stays.

B *Dien Bien*, 67 Dien Bien Phu St, T842264, F842977. Similar to most in this area, fairly large rooms but somewhat plasticky decor. **B** *Hoang Yen*, 7 Tran Hung Dao St, T842383, F842205. A very attractive French colonial building centrally located. Quite whether the architectural charm is worth these prices remains to be seen. Breakfast included. **B** *Hotel du Commerce*, 62 Dien Bien Phu St, T842706, F842560. Attractive colonial style, renovated but still atmospheric, large rooms, restaurant. **B-C** *Cat Bi*, 30 Tran Phu St, T921837, F921181. Short distance south of centre, all a/c, a range of rooms, 20 in all, more expensive ones with bath tub. **B-C** *Thang Nam*, 55 Dien Bien Phu St, T823460, F841019. 18 rooms all a/c, central, well run, fair value. **B-D** *Bach Dang*, 42 Dien Bien Phu St, T842444, F841625. Newly renovated with 34 rooms at a range of prices, central location, restaurant, breakfast included.

C *Ben Binh*, 6 Ben Binh St, T842260, F842524. Haiphong City guesthouse, set in a garden opposite the ferry dock, a/c, hot water, fridge in more expensive rooms, could be cleaner. The staff seem to have lost their interest. **C** *Hong Bang*, 64 Dien Bien Phu St, T842229, F841044. Colonial façade, 1970s renovation, largeish rooms. With *Chie* Japanese restaurant.

D *Phuong Dong*, 19 Luong Khanh Thien St, T855391. Immediately in front of the railway station, clean, good value for money. **D-E** *Hoa Binh*, 104 Luong Khanh Thien St, T846909, F846907. Opposite station, with some very basic, but clean, fan rooms and others a little smarter with a/c.

Eating
● *on map, page 148*

Foreign business influence is reflected in the form of at least two Japanese restaurants and several Chinese/ Taiwanese restaurants

Hoa Bien, 24 Tran Hung Dao St, T745633. Excellent Vietnamese fare with Chinese influence in a street-side setting. All dishes served fresh and piping hot. Lunch for two will cost around US$3-4. *Hoa Dai*, 39 and 40 Le Dai Hanh St, T822098. Popular with well-off locals. Good Vietnamese food, particularly busy at lunchtime. Service leaves something to be desired. *Lucky*, 22 Minh Khai St. Next to *Quang Minh Hotel*. Popular locally, Chinese food, mid-price. *Saigon Thien Bao*, 6 Tran Binh Trong St, T859152. South of town centre, reckons to be the town's top venue, cavernous and somewhat intimidating to the lone diner, Vietnamese and Western dishes, rather bland food and erratic service, staff are more absorbed in the latest twist in the current TV soap than in their customers' vain wishes for more rice. Hence bills for one can be kept below US$7. *Sake*, 55 Dien Bien Phu St. Next to *Thang Nam Hotel*, Japanese food at fair prices. *Thien Nhat*, 97 Dien Bien Phu St, T823327. Another well-regarded Japanese restaurant.

Trong Khach, 35 Nguyen Duc Canh St, T737677. Chinese-style restaurant, seafood, rather expensive.

Formosa Tea House, 25 Tran Quang Khai St, T810302. Smart, pale-blue and white **Bars** décor. A wonderful selection of tea and coffee and cocktails too. Good music. Open 0800-2400. *M & N Club or Haiphong Club*, 17 Tran Quang Khai St, T822603. Vast and normally vacant but at least it's there serving up beer, Baskin Robbins ice cream and music from pirated CDs. *Maxim's*, 51B Dien Bien Phu St, T822934. Bar café with live music in the evening. Also serves Asian and European food. *Saigon Café*, 107 Dien Bien Phu St, T822195. Colourful bar, café and restaurant.

Haiphong Toserco, 64 Dien Bien Phu St, T747332, F745415, haiphongtour@ **Tour operators** yahoo.com *Haiphong Tourist*, 87 Dien Bien Phu St, T842709. *Vietnam Tourism*, 15 Le Dai Hanh St, T842989, F842674. All these offices have cars for rent and will arrange tours to Halong Bay, Cat Ba and the like but nothing that cannot be done by most individuals for considerably cheaper.

Local Mai Linh Taxi, T833666, cyclos or *xe ôm*. **Transport**

Air Cat Bi, Haiphong's airport, lies 7 km southeast of town, the only air connections are with **Saigon**, daily except Mon and Fri.

Ferry Connections with Cat Ba and Hon Gai from the wharf on Ben Binh St. Ticket office open 1 hr before departures. Departures for **Cat Hai** and **Cat Ba** at 0630 and 1330, 60,000d, 4 hrs. Depart for **Cat Hai** and **Hon Gai** at 0900, 50,000d. **Express boat**, a/c to **Cat Ba** depart 0900 and 1400, 90,000d, 1 hr. From Cat Ba, express boat to Haiphong dept 1130 and 1600.

Road Bus: Highway 5 has been newly relaid (with a little help from our Japanese friends) and is now a fast motorway connecting capital with coast. There are regular bus departures from Hanoi. Minibuses from Hanoi's Tran Quang Khai St. Buses to **Hanoi** leave from Tam Bac bus station in front of Sat Market. From **Bai Chay** to Binh bus station north of Cua Cam River, 3 hrs, and then ferry into town. Buses to **Do Son** leave from the Lach Tray Bus Station, see under Do Son for details.

Train There are 5 train departures daily from Hanoi; 0600 from central station (Tran Qui Cap St entrance); 0820, 1000, 1500 and 1705 depart from Long Bien station on Gam Cau St, 22,000d, 2½ hrs.

Airline offices *Vietnam Airlines*, 30 Tran Phu St, T921242, F859497. **Banks** *ACB*, 69 **Directory** Dien Bien Phu St. Changes US$ cash only. *BIDV*, 68-70 Dien Bien Phu St. Cash major currencies but no TCs. *Indovina Bank*, 30 Tran Phu St. Cash TCs 0.2% commission US$ and 0.1% commission VND, but no other currency can be cashed here apart US$. *VID Bank*, 56 Dien Bien Phu St. Changes US$, Sing $ and Malay $, TCs and cash. *Vietcombank*, 11 Hoang Dieu St. Cashes TCs. **Communications** GPO: 5 Nguyen Tri Phuong St. Full international telephone and fax services and *DHL* and *EMS* offices, T842596. **Medical facilities** *Vietnam-Czech Friendship Hospital*, 1 Nha Thuong St, T846236.

The North

Do Son

Phone code: 031
Colour map 1, grid B5

Do Son, which boasts Vietnam's only casino, is a tourist resort 21 km southeast of Haiphong sitting on the southern end of the Do Son peninsula. It is also known for its buffalo fights whose gore and guts thousands flock to witness. Not really a 'Pattaya' it would, nevertheless, desperately love to become one. It is primarily a Vietnamese holiday and weekend destination that has not caught on with foreigners. Indeed, it is likely to be a while before it does but anyone caught in Haiphong with a day to spare would find Do Son a refreshing break.

Orientation

See Transport, page 154, for further details

Do Son is regimented into three zones or *khu*. Khu 1 is nearest Do Son town. It has a prom and a front with waves and several huge hotels; it is the least attractive of the three zones so if it does not appeal press on. Khu 2 is better geared to tourists from overseas: there are a couple of quite attractive small hotels, the beach is nothing special but there are plenty of restaurants and it is breezy and fresh. Khu 3 at the end of the peninsula is the least developed and most wooded zone. Hotels here tend to be small and there is a fairly secluded beach. Right at the southern tip is the casino, formerly *Hotel de la Pointe*. Honda *ôms* are available for local transport.

Sights

The Do Son Peninsula was originally developed as a resort by the French and it is currently experiencing a renaissance as joint ventures are signed, old hotels renovated and *Haiphong Tourist* cranks the marketing machine into action. The small **Ba De Temple** on Doc Mountain, at the north end of the peninsula, honours a young girl who threw herself to her death after spending a night with a courtier. (This theme is a popular one in Vietnam – the idea of honourable maidens choosing death in preference to despoilation is seen as highly romantic; although in this case the poor girl got both). Buffalo fights are held on the ninth day of the eighth lunar month at Do Son village.

The North

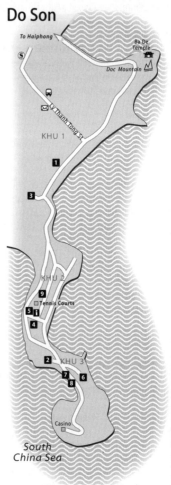

Do Son

To Haiphong
Ba De Temple
Doc Mountain
Ly Thanh Tong St
KHU 1
KHU 2
Tennis Courts
KHU 3
Casino
South China Sea

N
0 metres 500
0 yards 500

■ **Sleeping**
1 Cong Doan

2 Doi Tien
3 Forestry
4 Garden Resort
5 Hai Au
6 Hoa Sua
7 Huong Dua
8 Truc Lam
9 Van Thong

Preparation for the fights takes months – the normally docile bulls are fed special diets and kept in isolation. The fighting takes place at the end of the fishing season and attracts thousands of drinking and gambling visitors. The buffaloes charge each other, smashing skulls and gouging each other with horns. The victor is electrocuted and sliced up for everyone to enjoy. The festival celebrates delivery from a huge storm in the 15th century and honours the great bird king (Diem Tuoc Dai Vuong) who saved them.

Do Son does have potential as a resort and it does have charm but these attributes need working on. Considering what it is (a Vietnamese holiday resort four hours drive from Hanoi) it could be a lot worse. The beaches are quite white and, off season, quite clean but rather than being fringed by gently swaying palms are lined by austere sea-pines which shed sharp needles; the sea itself is an unappealing rust colour from silt discharged into the sea by the Red River. The peninsula is too narrow to permit space to roam and escape but there are secluded spots to deeply breath the fresh air blowing in from the South China Sea, or the Eastern Sea as the Vietnamese would prefer we call it. It has a friendly and relaxed feel as sea-side retreats invariably do.

Essentials

There are one or two hotels which Westerners would feel relaxed in. Most hotels are concrete monoliths owned by trade unions, state enterprises or utilities and geared to providing holidays for 100 factory workers and their families at a time. Prices can rise quite sharply in the summer holidays, above the levels indicated here.

Sleeping
■ *on map*
Phone code: 031
Price codes:
see inside front cover

Khu 1 C *Cong Doan (Trade Union)*, T861300. 100 rooms, cheaper on higher floors, fan only and no lift, simply furnished but clean, Party conference venue rather than riotous holiday getaway. **C** *Forestry*, T861104, F861105. Grim concrete block, 76 rooms all with a/c and hot water.

Khu 2 B-C *Garden Resort*, T861226, F861186. A series of villas set in well kept and wooded grounds, each with 2 large and 2 small rooms, a/c, hot water, fridge, IDD, TV etc, larger rooms have bath tub, smaller ones shower only, clean, friendly. Recommended. Prices here, as at many other hotels in Do Son, rise by 50% Fri-Sun. **B-C** *Hai Au*, T861221, F861186. Nothing special about the hotel, large and slightly forbidding aspect, but set among trees and has tennis court at rear. **C** *Van Thong*, T861331, F861131. Clean, but relatively small, a/c rooms around a nice courtyard setting at back, like a number of other Do Son hotels this one offers 'Thai massage'. The *BIC* bus to Haiphong begins here.

Khu 3 D *Doi Tien*, T861182. 14 fan rooms on a slight rise, no hot water, views but pretty grotty buildings, poorly maintained and managed. **D** *Hoa Sua*, T861202. 12 a/c rooms with hot water, in a concrete block that could be Le Corbusier in one of his darker moods. Although some rooms have a view, not all do, and one side is dangerously near a karaoke strip, a common enough hazard in Do Son. **D** *Huong Dua*, T861181, F861174. Small, colonial-style buildings in yellow wash overlooking a secluded beach, nice and airy, well maintained and clean, simple, some a/c some fan, restaurant. Recommended. **D** *Truc Lam*, T862176. Next to Huong Dua, last hotel before the casino. All rooms have a/c and hot water.

Many of the hotels have restaurants but the best option is to dive into one of the countless restaurants offering seafood specialities (*dac san bien*) which line the roads. All fairly indistinguishable but not undistinguished. Khu 2 offers the more attractive options for eating.

Eating

Entertainment **Casino** Located at the very southern tip in Khu 3 occupying the former *Hotel de la Pointe*, T861888. Open 1100-0500, no Vietnamese allowed, passport needed for entrance, restaurant.

Tour operators *Do Son Tourism Company*, Khu 2, T861330, F861186. In *Hai Au Hotel*. Rare among state tourism offices for its high level of enthusiasm and eagerness to help, but a limited range of services – chiefly a very expensive boat to Cat Ba or a cheaper one to the small island of Dau, just off the southern tip of the peninsula.

Transport **Road** **Bus**: Do Son bus station is a couple of kilometres inland from Khu 1. There are frequent bus services between **Haiphong**'s post office and Do Son, 45 mins, 10,000d. The *BIC* bus goes as far *as Van Thong Hotel*, Khu 2. *Xe ôm*: US$2 one-way from Haiphong.

Directory There is a **post office** and **bank** in Do Son town, but for sophisticated financial transactions Haiphong is not far away.

Cat Ba Island

Phone code: 031
Colour map 1, grid B5

Whilst not quite the tropical island of our dreams – it is too rocky, and too cold in winter to be idyllic – Cat Ba nevertheless matches the highest expectations. It occupies a stunning setting in the south of Halong Bay. Much of the island and the seas around are designated a national park and, while perhaps not quite teaming with wildlife (already eaten), it is pleasantly wild and green. Cat Ba's remoteness (it only plugged into mains electricity in 1999) keeps the hordes away, but progress it must: a new ferry is about to open a new line of communication with the mainland.

Cat Ba Island & Halong Bay

Ins and outs

Getting there
See Transport,
page 158,
for further details

There are usually 2 hydrofoils a day and 2 ferries a day, both departing from Haiphong, taking 1 hr and 4 hrs respectively. **Express boat** From Cat Ba express boats to Haiphong depart 1130 and 1600. **Ferry** From Cat Ba to Haiphong, departs 0600 and 1300. For travelling from Cat Ba to Hon Gai; most hotels on the island offer tours of Halong Bay that will drop off passengers in Hon Gai.

Getting around

Either by tour organized by local hotel or tour operator in Hanoi. *Xe ôm* (US$3 should get you anywhere on the island) or hire a motorbike, usually a Russian Minsk for around US$5 per day. There is a bus service between Cat Ba town and Phu Long along the new road. Boats usually use the new Cat Ba pier in the middle of town but when strong westerly winds are blowing they use the old harbour. From the old harbour it is a 10-min bus ride or *xe ôm* around to the hotels.

**Best time
to visit**

Cat Ba is at its wettest Jul-Aug, driest and coolest (15°C) Nov-Jan and busiest (and most expensive – hotel rates double) during school summer holidays May-Sep.

The Island

Cat Ba is the largest island in a coastal archipelago which includes over 350 limestone outcrops. It is adjacent to and geologically similar to the islands and peaks of Halong Bay but separated by a broad channel as the map illustrates. The islands around Cat Ba are larger than the outcrops of Halong Bay and generally more dramatic. Cat Ba is the ideal place from which to explore the whole coastal area: besides the quality of its scenery it is a more agreeable town in which to stay, although the countless new hotels springing up are slowly eroding the difference.

The island is rugged and sparsely inhabited. Outside Cat Ba town there are only a few small villages. Perhaps the greatest pleasure is to hire a motorbike and explore, a simple enough process given the island's limited road network. Half of the island forms part of a national park, see below.

For an island of its size Cat Ba has remarkably few **beaches** – only two within easy access, creatively named **Cat Co One** and **Cat Co Two**. These lie just to the east of town behind a steep hill in the southern fringes of the national park. They are popular with locals and visitors alike, especially in the late afternoon and at weekends but are also tending to attract tourist paraphernalia and litter, national park status notwithstanding. It's a 2-km walk to the first and a further 1-km to the second which is quieter and cleaner; there is an entrance fee of 5,000d. There are cold drinks and peanutty snacks for sale, tyres for hire, showers and toilets.

Excursions

Cat Ba National Park
Colour map 1, grid B5

The national park (Vuon Quoc Gia Cat Ba), established in 1986, covers roughly half the island. Of this area, a third consists of coast and inland waters. Home to 109 bird and animal species, and of particular importance is the world's last remaining troupe of white-headed langur (around 200 animals). These elusive creatures are rarely spotted and then only from the sea as they inhabit wild and remote cliff habitats. There are also several types of rare macaque (rhesus, pig-tailed and red-faced) and moose deer. Vegetation ranges from mangrove swamps in sheltered bays and densely wooded hollows, to high, rugged limestone crags sprouting caps of hardy willows.

The marine section of the park is no less bounteous: perhaps less fortunate is the high economic value of its fish and crustacea populations which keeps the local fishing fleet hard at work and prosperous. In common with other coastal areas in the region the potential for snorkelling here is zero.

Visitors are free to roam through the forest but advised not to wander too far from the path. Many hotels arrange treks from the park gate through the forest to Ao Ech (Frog Lake) on to the village of Viet Hai for a light lunch then down to the coast for a boat ride home. This takes the best part of a day and costs around US$10. It is a good way to see the park but those preferring solitude can go their own way or go with a park guide, US$5 for half a day, US$10 for the full day. July to October is the wet season when leeches are a problem and mosquitoes are at their worst. Bring leech socks if you have them and plenty of insect repellent. Collar, long sleeves and long trousers advisable. Fauna and flora enthusiasts who fancy staying longer and chatting to the friendly park wardens can put up at one of the several species of *Park Guesthouse* (**D-E**). Park office 0700-1130, 1140-1730. Alternatively visitors can bring tents and camp in the park. ■ *US$1. Town to park gate 30 mins on a motorbike.*

Cat Ba Town

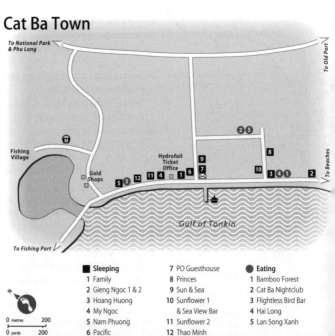

To National Park & Phu Long

To Old Port

Fishing Village

To Beaches

Gold Shops

Hydrofoil Ticket Office

Gulf of Tonkin

To Fishing Port

0 metres 200
0 yards 200

■ **Sleeping**	7 PO Guesthouse	● **Eating**
1 Family	8 Princes	1 Bamboo Forest
2 Gieng Ngoc 1 & 2	9 Sun & Sea	2 Cat Ba Nightclub
3 Hoang Huong	10 Sunflower 1	3 Flightless Bird Bar
4 My Ngoc	& Sea View Bar	4 Hai Long
5 Nam Phuong	11 Sunflower 2	5 Lan Song Xanh
6 Pacific	12 Thao Minh	

Halong Bay is the most famous and most dramatic excursion from Cat Ba. **Halong Bay**
Almost all hotels in Cat Ba offer tours as do the touts along the seafront. It is
better to use a service provided by a reputable hotel (as listed below), as you
are less likely to be left stranded or charged extra for lunch. **Monkey Island** is
closer and a four-hour excursion in a small boat costs around US$12. There
are six bungalows on the island for those wishing to stay overnight costing
around US$3 in the off season and US$5 in summer. It is also possible to pitch
a tent here but take plenty of drinking water and mosquito repellent.

Kayaking and junk cruises in Halong Bay and Lan Ha Bay are now regular fea- **Kayaking &**
tures, especially in the summer months. For these it is probably best to go via **junk cruises**
one of the better established tour operators in Hanoi, such as *Handspan*, but
Family Hotel and *My Ngoc Hotel* in Cat Ba (see below) also have kayaks. These
are best taken out on a larger boat and paddled from the open sea. *My Ngoc
Hotel* is building a junk to give passengers a chance to experience leisurely
wind-powered travel. Junks have disappeared from Halong Bay over the past
15 years as declining fish stocks have forced fishermen to travel further afield.

Essentials

Currently a boom town, there are already dozens of hotels and guesthouses and more **Sleeping**
are completed every month. In the summer, prices may well be double those indicated ■ *on map*
here, but during quieter periods substantial discounts can and should be negotiated. *Phone code: 031*
There are no addresses, and to confuse matters further many hotels claim the same *Price codes:*
name (*Gia Dinh* or *Family* is the current favourite). A small selection of the better *see inside front cover*
accommodation is listed below.

C *PO Guesthouse*. *Central and clean*. **C** *Princes*, T888892, F888899,
princeshotel@yahoo.com This is currently the best appointed and most comfortable
hotel in Cat Ba. The rooms are nice and light and airy and, unlike all the vertical
shoe-box hotels, this one has made an effort to look decent and has an open courtyard
at the back with a little waterfall promised. Well-furnished rooms and friendly reception. It is quite large, 50 rooms, takes credit card and breakfast is included in the price.
C *Sun and Sea*, past the post office on the right, T888315, F888475. One of the plushest
in town, 20 rooms, all mod cons including satellite TV, tall, but no seaview, slightly
tacky finish but enthusiastic owners. **C** *Sunflower 1*, T888429, 888451,
sunflowerhotel@hn.vnn.vn This is quite a good new hotel with 30 rooms, from some
the sea is visible, which is not quite the same as a sea view. Some family rooms, clean,
comfortable, price includes breakfast. *The Sea View Bar* located on the 9th floor has a
real sea view and very loud music. **D** *Family* (*Quang Duc*), just west of pier, T888231.
The original 'Family' Hotel, fan, hot water, spotlessly clean, views from most rooms, a
very well-run little hotel, owners are knowledgeable on local matters and helpful, restaurant. Recommended. **D** *Gieng Ngoc 1 and 2*, east of the pier, T888286. Among the
best of the budget hotels, quiet (a rare commodity in Cat Ba town), front rooms overlook sea, fair-sized rooms, basic, but clean, fan only, hot water in winter. *Gieng Ngoc 1* is
the smaller, older and cheaper of the two, but both are being renovated.
D *Hoang Huong*, near pier, T888274. Clean and central. **D** *Nam Phuong*, T888473. 10
rooms down towards the fishing port end of town, all a/c, hot water and sea view, restaurant. **D** *Pacific*, opposite PO, T888331, F888325, pacifichotel@hn.vnn.vn 12 rooms,
popular with tour groups, friendly and efficient. Expensive internet service.
D *Sunflower 2*, west of pier in the busiest part of town (karaoke is a real menace here),
T888215, F888451, sunflowerhotel@hn.vnn.vn 14 rooms, 10 with sea view, a/c and
comfortable, good restaurant. **D** *Thao Minh*, west of pier, T888408, F888630. 50 rooms

The North

some with a/c and sea view, all with hot water. Clean, tour group type hotel, popular restaurant. **E** *My Ngoc*, T888199, F888422. Quite central, not far from the ferry pier, 18 rooms, a/c in summer, hot water. Restaurant and tours arranged, try to speak to the helpful Mr Tuan. Immediately opposite the ferry pier is a hotel under construction. It is being built by a young Australian and when finished will be known as the *Noble House*.

Eating
● *on map*

After dark there is a charged atmosphere along the front as tanned Westerners crowd into small restaurants to quaff large bottles of chilled beer, consume fresh seafood and strike up lively conversations and friendships. Some hotels listed above have restaurants. Of particular note are *Family* (*Quang Duc*), *Thao Minh*, *My Ngoc* and *Sunflower*. East of the pier are 2 good restaurants *Hai Long*, T888635 which specializes in seafood, shrimp, squid and crab for aroound US$3 per dish and *Truc Lam* or *Bamboo Forest*, T888654, truclamrestaurant@yahoo.com Mr Dau, the owner, is a relative newcomer to Cat Ba, but knowledgeable and can arrange tours. His restaurant serves the usual seafood and also vegetarain dishes. There are many other restaurants along the seafront serving seafood, Vietnamese/Chinese and vegetarian.

Bars

Cat Ba Nightclub, not far from *Princes Hotel* has a bar and pool tables. The next door *Lan Song Xanh* is more of a disco with very loud music. *Flightless Bird*, T888517, is on the seafront and run by Graeme Moore, a New Zealander, the only real pub in town, also a book exchange. Open 1730-2400, closed on Sun. *Sea View Bar* on top of *Sunflower Hotel 1* (no lift) screens sporting events.

Transport

The **hydrofoil**, a/c, from Haiphong departs twice a day, 90,000d, 1 hr. The timings vary seasonally but usually there are 2 boats in the morning, at 0800 and 0900. If it is not running late the 0600 train from Hanoi will get you to Haiphong just in time to *xe ôm* across town to catch the 0900. The question of taking a tour or making your own way to Cat Ba is an interesting one. For while the do-it-yourself method is easy and cheap, by the time you add in all the little incidental costs and the cost of a boat excursion from Cat Ba it may be just as cheap to take a tour. **Ferry** From Haiphong (usually crowded) depart 0630 and 1330, 60,000d, 4 hrs. Alternatively take the Hon Gai ferry at 0900 stopping off at Cat Hai; from there small boat to Phu Long on the west of Cat Ba Island and *xe ôm* or bus (erratic service) to Cat Ba town. **Minibus** At the time of writing a new car ferry service is shortly to be introduced from Haiphong which will mean through buses from Hanoi to Cat Ba.

Directory

Banks None, hotels will exchange US$ cash at poor rates. Alternatively there are a couple of gold shops at the west end of the town. **Communications** Internet: email access is available, but it is expensive. A couple of hotels have email and allow their guests to use it for around 2,000d per min. *Bamboo Forest Restaurant* is cheaper at 1,000d per min and the post office cheapest of all at 500d per min, but expect these prices to come down. **Post office:** in town centre, opposite pier. International calls and faxes, may also change money.

Halong Bay

Colour map 1, grid B6
Halong Bay is a
UNESCO World
Heritage Site

Halong means 'descending dragon', and an enormous beast is said to have careered into the sea at this point, cutting the fantastic bay from the rocks as it thrashed its way into the depths. Vietnamese poets (including the 'Poet King' Le Thanh Tong) have traditionally extolled the beauty of this romantic area with its rugged islands that protrude from a sea dotted with sailing junks; and artists have been just as quick to draw inspiration from the crooked islands seeing the forms of monks and gods in the rock faces and dragon's lairs and fairy lakes in the depths of

The Battles of Bach Dang River (AD 938 and AD 1288)

The battles of Bach Dang River were both won in a style prefiguring many of the battles that would much later be fought against the US.

In AD 938, unable to confront the powerful Chinese fleet on equal terms, the Vietnamese General Ngo Quyen sunk sharpened poles tipped with iron into the bed of the river that the Chinese were about to sail up. When the Chinese fleet appeared off the mouth of the river, Quyen sent a small flotilla of shallow draught boats to taunt the Chinese. Rising to the

bait they attacked and, as the tide fell, their heavy ships were impaled on the stakes that lay just below the surface. Over half the Chinese, including the Admiral Hung-ts'ao were drowned.

In 1288, apparently not having learnt the lessons of history, another Mongol Chinese fleet of 400 ships appeared off the coast. This time the famous Vietnamese general Tran Hung Dao laid the trap, again luring the enemy onto sunken stakes. In both instances, the victories were so emphatic as to terminate the Chinese invasion plans.

The North

the caves. Another myth says that the islands are dragons sent by the gods to impede the progress of an invasion flotilla. Historically more believable, if substantially embellished, the area was the location of two famous sea battles, in the 10th and 13th centuries (*see box, Battles of Bach Dang River, above*).

Ins and outs

There are 2 bases from which to explore Halong Bay – Halong City or Cat Ba. Traditionally, visitors went direct to Halong City and took a boat from there. This is still a valid option, especially for those who are short of time. But Cat Ba is becoming increasingly popular as a springboard to Halong Bay, largely because Cat Ba itself is interesting. **Getting there**

Boat tours of the bay can be booked in Halong City and Cat Ba Town. To see the bay properly allow 4-5 hrs. See the end of this section for details and the separate entries on Cat Ba town and Halong City for local transport. **Getting around**

Karsts and caves in Halong Bay

Geologically the tower-karst scenery of Halong Bay is the product of millions of years of chemical action and river erosion working on the limestone to produce a pitted landscape. At the end of the last ice age, when glaciers melted, the sea level rose and inundated the area turning hills into islands. The islands of the bay are divided by a broad channel: to the east are the smaller outcrops of Bai Tu Long while to the east are the larger islands with caves and secluded beaches.

Among the more spectacular caves are **Hang Hanh** which extends for 2 km. Tour guides will point out fantastic stalagmites and stalactites which, with imagination, become heroes, demons and animals. **Hang Luon** is another flooded cave which leads to the hollow core in a doughnut or Polo-shaped island. It can be swum or navigated by coracle. **Hang Dau Go** is the cave wherein Tran Hung Dao stored his wooden stakes prior to studding them in the bed of the Bach Dang River in 1288 to destroy the boats of invading Mongol hordes. **Hang Thien Cung** is a hanging cave, a short 50-m haul above sea level, with dripping stalactites, stumpy stalagmites and solid rock pillars. ■ *All these and more – Grotto of Wonders, Customs House Cave and Surprise Grotto – charge US$1.* Many are a disappointment with harrying vendors, mounds of litter and disfiguring graffiti. Many are lit but some are not so bring a torch. Rocks can be treacherously slippery, so sensible footwear is advised. A good boatman (and some speak English) will take you to more secluded islands where you can swim and rest free of charge and free of hassles while he knocks up a delicious seafood lunch (not free of charge).

Tours & **Boat tours** can be booked from hotels although it may be cheaper to organize
transport the trip independently; try the tourist wharf opposite *Van Hai Hotel*. You will
from Halong be approached by numerous touts along the seafront in Bai Chay, most are
prepared to bargain. Because it takes about one hour to get into the bay
proper, one long trip represents better value than two short ones. A tour of the
bay including a cave or two and a swim needs four to five hours. Charter rates
are around 50,000-80,000d per hour for a boat that will accommodate eight to
10, food extra. Boats can be hired overnight for upwards of 400,000d, which,
considering the saving on hotel bills is fairly economical (take warm clothes).
The *Huong Hai Junk Halong Company* operates in the bay. Further information from 1 Vuon Dao St, Bai Chay-Halong, Quang Ninh, T845042,
F846263, www.vietnamtourism.com/huonghai-junk

   Tourist cafés in Hanoi offer tours of the bay with one night in Bai Chay, at
prices ranging from US$16-35 plus the US$3 tax which Quang Ninh Province
in its wisdom has started to levy on all foreign visitors (how Haiphong and Cat
Ba must be rubbing their hands). This is alright for those short of time but
more economical and fun to do it yourself.

The North

Cat Ba is an increasingly popular alternative springboard to Halong Bay. The **Tours &**
chief advantage is that there is a lot to see on the island: unlike Bai Chay it is an **transport**
attractive destination in its own right. From Cat Ba there are two further **from Cat Ba**
options: either return to Hanoi via Halong City (tours of Halong Bay from
Cat Ba may drop passengers off in Hon Gai if specially requested) or double
back via Haiphong. But the journey from Halong to Hanoi is wretched, and
the minibus operators, some of the least pleasant in the country (and note the
last bus to Hanoi from Bai Chay leaves at 1600). The preferred alternative,
therefore, is to arrive and depart Cat Ba via Haiphong and take a one-day or
half-day tour of the bay, thus cutting out Halong City altogether. The final nail
in the coffin for Halong City is that all foreign visitors to this wretched town
are taxed US$3 through the compulsory purchase of a 'sightseeing ticket'. A
one-day tour of Halong Bay costs US$10 per person plus US$2 for lunch but
groups can bargain.

Halong City

The route from Hanoi passes newly industrializing satellite towns whose facto- Phone code: 033
ries, petrol stations and houses spill onto what were recently paddy fields. After Colour map 1, grid B6
Uong Bi, the scenery improves with the limestone hills which rise out of the allu-
vial plain giving a foretaste of the better things to come. Following the admission
of Halong Bay to UNESCO's hallowed roll of World Heritage Sites, the two small
towns of Bai Chay and Hon Gai were in 1994 collectively elevated in status by the
government and dubbed Halong City, a moniker largely ignored by locals.

The North

Ins and outs

There are regular bus connections from Hanoi's Gia Lam terminal to Bai Chay, across the **Getting there**
water from Hon Gai, 4-5 hrs, 35,000d. The Bai Chay station is on the waterfront, near the See Transport,
post office. Or you can take the train to Haiphong and get a bus or ferry from there. page 164,
for further details

Given the paucity of sites in the town, pretty much anywhere of relevance can be reached **Getting around**
on foot. For venturing further afield the town has the usual gangs of *xe ôm* drivers.

The town

It was at Halong that, arguably, Vietnam's fate under the French was sealed. In
late 1882 Captain Henri Rivière led two companies of troops to Hon Gai to
seize the coal mines for France. Shortly afterwards he was ambushed and
killed and his head paraded on a stake from village to village. His death persuaded the French parliament to fund a full-scale expedition to make all of
Vietnam a protectorate of France. As the politician Jules Delafosse remarked
at the time: "Let us, gentlemen, call things by their name. It is not a protectorate you want, but a possession."
    The twin towns, Bai Chay to the west and Hon Gai to the east, separated by
a river estuary and linked by a ferry, could not be more different. Few visitors
make the short crossing to Hon Gai which, with its port and adjacent coal-
mines, could fairly be described as the industrial end of town.
    Bai Chay has made great efforts and not a little progress towards turning
itself into an attractive destination rather than merely a dormitory for those
visiting Ha Long Bay. At huge expense a narrow beach has been constructed

in front of the hotels; casuarina, palm and flame trees have been planted along the prom, old hotels renovated and new ones built. There is no denying the effect, an attractive feel, a seaside town. But the charm is not likely to work its magic with travellers from abroad in the same way that it does with Vietnamese who are drawn in huge numbers, rapidly swamping the little beach every weekend. Several large and attractive modern hotels have been built, including the *Halong Plaza*, one of the most luxurious in the country. But quite who is going to occupy all these junior and executive suites is a problem the marketing men appear to have overlooked.

A five-minute, 500d ferry ride takes you to the bustling port of **Hon Gai**. The Vietnamese government would dearly like to bridge the estuary which divides the town but owing to the listed status of Halong Bay must first obtain UNESCO's approval. As mining areas go, this is quite a nice one, but it does not live up to the 'natural wonderland' image *Quang Ninh Tourism* is trying to promote. The port of Hon Gai is busy with plenty of little bamboo and resin coracles (*thung chai*) which are used by the fishermen as tenders to get out to their boats and to bring ashore the catch. There is a thriving market and near the ferry dock is the 106-m-high **Poem Mountain** (Nui Bao Tho) so named following a visit in 1486 by King Le Thanh Tong who was so taken by the beauty of Ha Long Bay that he composed a poem celebrating the scenery and carved his verse into the rock. It is quite a scramble up the hill and finding the right path may require some help. At the foot of the mountain nestles the little **Long Tien Pagoda** which dates from earlier this century. Twenty minutes' walk north up from Hon Gai is a **ruined colonial church** damaged by a bomb in 1972 but the site affords lovely views. About 1 km east of central Hon Gai is a small **museum** on Coc 3 Street.

Excursions

Yen Tu Mountains The Yen Tu Mountains are 14 km northwest of Uong Bi and climb to a maximum elevation of 1,068 m. Peppered with pagodas from the 13th-16th centuries, much has been lost to the ravages of war and climate but stupas and temples of more recent foundation survive. The site has attracted pilgrims

Halong City

Vuon Dao

Mini Hotels

BAI CHAY

Vietnam Airlines **13**

9

Buses to Hanoi

Tourist Wharf

Buses to Haiphong

1

6

Halong

Restaurants

12

7

11

Minimart

5

4

3

To Saigon Halong Hotel

Halong Bay

N

0 metres 300
0 yards 300

■ **Sleeping**
1 Bach Dang
2 Halong Guesthouse

3 Ha Long 1
4 Ha Long 2
5 Ha Long 3

6 Halong Plaza
7 Heritage Halong
8 Hien Cat

since the 13th century when King Tran Nhan Tong abandoned the throne in favour of a spiritual life. He washed the secular dust from his body in the Tam stream and entered the Cam Thuc (Abstinence) Pagoda. His 100 concubines traced him here and tried to persuade him of the folly of his ways but despite their undoubted allure he resisted all appeals and clung to his ascetic existence. Distraught by their failure, the poor women drowned themselves. Tran Nhan Tong later built a temple to their memory. Climbing the hills, visiting the temples and admiring the views can take a full day.

Essentials

The past couple of years have seen an explosion in the number of hotels and guest-houses in Bai Chay and Hon Gai; this reflects the popularity of Halong Bay as a destination for both Vietnamese and foreign visitors. The enthusiasm of the hotel builders has, for the time being at least, outstripped demand, so owners are having to accept hard bargaining as an uncomfortable fact of life. Many of the newer hotels are badly built and, apart from the fact that some of the taller ones look structurally unsound, are hideously damp and musty; check the room first.

Sleeping
■ on map, page 162
Phone code: 033
Price codes:
see inside front cover

Hon Gai There are few hotels here but they tend to be more competitively priced than those in Bai Chay. **C** *Queen*, 70 Le Thanh Tong St, T826193, F827268. A/c, hot water, bathrooms attached, smallish rooms but clean and well run, disco on Sat evenings – finishes early. **D** *Halong Guesthouse*, 80 Le Thanh Tong, T826509. Just 8 rooms, but a/c, hot water, private bathroom, clean and good value. Several other guesthouses on Le Thanh Tong St. **D** *Hien Cat*, 252 Ben Tau St, T827417. Nearest to the ferry wharf, cheapest and possibly the best, only 5 rooms, the best is at the top, airy, breezy, clean, fan only, outside bathroom, hot water, the family will invite guests to join them for meals. Recommended.

Bai Chay There are 2 main groups of hotels, 2 km apart. Most are to be found at the west end on the way in to town, set back a little from the sea front and include Vuon Dao St composed entirely of 5-8 room mini hotels. 2 km further on, near the ferry to Hon Gai is a smaller group some of which have good views.

The North

9 Minh Tuan	**12** Thu Trang	● **Eating**
10 Queen	Vuon Dao	1 Kem Mely
11 Thanh Nien	**13** Van Hai	

Ferry end L-A *Halong Plaza*, 8 Halong Rd, T845810, F846867, plazaqn@hn.vnn.vn A Thai joint venture with 200 rooms and suites and fantastic views over the sea, especially from upper floors, luxuriously finished, huge bathrooms, every comfort and extravagance as the Thais do so well, swimming pool, restaurants and engaging staff, a lovely hotel by any standards. **A-B** *Bach Dang*, 2 Halong Rd, T846330, F845892, bachdanghotelqn@hnhn.vnn.vn Old but a clean and well-run establishment, a/c, sea views and restaurant. **B** *Van Hai*, Halong Rd, T846403, F846115. Opposite tourist wharf, beginning to show its age, furnishings of flimsy construction and public areas rather shabby, but staff are friendly. **D** *Minh Tuan*, Ho Xuan Huong St, T846200. Up a quiet lane 50 m before the bus station, 14 a/c rooms with bathroom, clean, well managed.

West end L-A *Ha Long 1*, Halong Rd, T846014, F846318. A converted French villa with stacks of charm set amongst frangipani, some of the 23 rooms have sea outlook, huge bathrooms, bathtubs, bidets etc. **L-A** *Heritage Halong*, 88 Halong Rd, T846888, F846999, heritagehl.qn@hn.vnn.vn A Singapore joint venture lacking the opulence of the *Plaza* but nevertheless extremely comfortable and cheaper, all rooms have sea views. 24-hr coffee shop, disco and pool. **A** *Saigon Halong*, Halong Rd, T845845, F845849, sahahotel@hn.vnn.vn Newly built and run by *Saigon Tourist*, 23 rooms in 5 'villas', comfortable, all mod cons, set back from the road on the way into town, relaxed and attractive surroundings, ring in advance to negotiate discount or package. **B** *Thu Trang Vuon Dao*, Halong Rd, T846370, F846287. Set at the top of a drive, large concrete edifice but fairly breezy and airy, restaurant, breakfast included. **C** *Ha Long 2 & 3*, Halong Rd, T846014, F846318. Set behind *Ha Long 1*, some large and some smaller blocks that chiefly cater for the Vietnamese market, not particularly clean or comfortable. **C** *Thanh Nien*, Halong Rd, T846715, F845739. Occupies a nice spot on a little promontory jutting into the sea but can be a bit noisy from surrounding cafés etc, attractive bungalow accommodation, a/c, hot water. **D** *Huong Tram*, Halong Rd, T846365, F845930. Up a track off Halong Rd, 500-m east of post office, nice views from the top floor of this a/c mini hotel, helpful with advice for local walks and boat trips.

Vuon Dao St A plethora of mini hotels all offering similar accommodation at similar prices (**C-D**) and all willing to bargain during quiet periods.

Eating
Seafood is fresh and abundant and fairly priced

Hon Gai Le Qui Don St has good seafood restaurants. *Kem Mely*, 90 Le Thanh Tong St has ice cream and cakes but since *Walls* have made their ice cream available almost everywhere in Vietnam such places, while useful, have lost the importance they once had.

Bai Chay Other than the hotels, Halong Rd, near the junction with Vuon Dao St is lined for several hundred metres with restaurants all much of a muchness and all pretty good. *Café Indochine* is useful for local information as well as the usual *ca phe sua da*. At the ferry end there is a decent restaurant opposite the tourist wharf.

Entertainment Discos in *Heritage Halong*, Bai Chay and *Queen Hotel*, Hon Gai.

Shopping Quang Ninh traditional coal sculpture available in Hon Gai.

Tour operators *Quang Ninh Tourism*, near *Halong Hotel*, Bai Chay, T846274. *Vietnam Tourism*, 2 Le Thanh Tong St T827250, near Hon Gai bus station.

Transport **Road Bus**: regular connections from Bai Chay bus station on Halong St to **Hanoi** from 0700, last bus departs 1600. Buses are slow, crowded, uncomfortable and full of pickpockets. Bai Chay bus station demands foreigners pay double the published fare (35,000d), bus operators will demand triple. Regular connections with **Haiphong**'s Binh bus station 0900-1500, 20,000d (published fare).

Sea Charter boat: to and from **Cat Ba** try the tourist wharf opposite *Van Hai Hotel*. **Ferries**: depart for **Haiphong** from Hon Gai 0600, 0830, 1100 and 1600, 45,000d, 3 hrs. The trip itself is worthwhile; the ferry is packed with people and their produce and threads its way through the limestone islands and outcrops that are so characteristic of the area, before winding up the Cua Cam River to the port of Haiphong. For Cat Ba take the Haiphong ferry to Cat Hai and either transfer to the Haiphong-Cat Ba ferry or hop over to Phu Long and take a *xe ôm* from there.

Banks *Vietcombank* 172 Le Thanh Tong offers same rates as Hanoi. Nong Nghiep Bank, **GPO** also changes money. **Communications GPO**: in Hon Gai, Le Thanh Tong St. Open 0700-2000, international telephone and fax. In Bai Chay at junction of Halong Rd and Vuon Dao St and opposite Hon Gai ferry. **Internet**: Many hotels and cafés provide email services at reasonable prices, should be around 200d per min and upwards. **Post office**: in Hon Gai has email service, 210d per min. **Medical facilities** *Bai Chay Hospital*, T846557. *Hon Gai Hospital*, T825499.

Directory

Hanoi to Ninh Binh

From Hanoi, the route south runs through the rather grey, industrial towns of Ha Nam, Nam Dinh and Ninh Binh. The last few years have brought rapid expansion to these industrial centres which are being convulsed with change: road widenings and realignments, wholesale demolition of old buildings to make way for new, huge industrial zones and factories gobbling up prime 'ricefield' sites. The traffic is dominated by trucks and buses which sweep bicycles, pedestrians and hand cart pushers into the ditch. Communities which for centuries were divided by nothing more than a dirt track now find themselves rent asunder by four-lane highways, but ancient ties of kith and kin and tradition have yet to adjust. Thus you see gaggles of little children dodging the wheels of juggernauts, racing to get to school on time and a little old lady trying to avoid spilling the three delicately balanced, steaming bowls of noodle soup in her hands destined for the officers of the Planning and Investment Committee of Ward No 8, while simultaneously trying to dodge the oncoming Hanoi to Vinh express bus. The bus is accelerating to overtake the Ha Nam to Ninh Binh stopping bus, which in turn has swerved to avoid the heavy truck of Construction Company No 17 of Ha Tay Province whose driver has pulled up to enable his mate to jump down and buy two 555 cigarettes (and while he's at it to have a pee); and all the time, coming up from the south, a similar contingent of fast- and slow-moving vehicles duel to overtake all in their path while desperately trying to prevent anything else from getting in front.

Nam Dinh

Nam Dinh is a large and diverse industrial centre, with a reputation for its textiles. The Nam Dinh Textile Mill was built by the French in 1899, and is still operating (which says a lot for the state of Vietnamese industry and Vietnamese resourcefulness).

Phone code: 0350
Colour map 1, grid C5
Population: 300,000

Excursions **Thien Truong and Pho Minh Pagodas** – both highly regarded – are to be found in the village of Tuc Mac (My Loc district), 3 km north of Nam Dinh. Also here are the few remains of the Tran Dynasty. Thien Truong was built in 1238 and dedicated to the kings of the Tran family; Pho Minh was built rather later, in 1305, and contains an impressive 13-storey tower.

Doi Son and **Doi Diep Pagodas** are situated on two neighbouring mountains (Nui Doi Son and Nui Doi Diep). The former was originally built at some point during the early Ly Dynasty (AD 544-602). When the Emperor Le Dai Hanh (980-1005) planted rice at the foot of the mountain, legend has it that he uncovered two vessels, one filled with gold and the other with silver. From that season on, the harvests were always bountiful.

North of the main channel of the Red River, 10 km southwest of Thai Binh is the site of the 11th-century **Keo Pagoda**, which was destroyed in a flood. The present building dates back to the 17th century but has been remodelled several times. Its chief architectural attraction is a wooden, three-storey campanile containing two bronze bells.

■ *Getting to the pagodas: either by* xe ôm *from Nam Dinh or as part of a day trip by car (including Hoa Lu) from Hanoi.*

Sleeping **B-C** *Son Nam*, 26 Le Hong Phong St, T645617, F846287. A range of accommodation in
& eating 3 buildings. **B-C** *Vi Hoang*, 115 Nguyen Du St, T849290, F646704. Somewhat uncared for, restaurant.

Transport At the eastern apex of the Ha Nam, Nam Dinh, Ninh Binh growth triangle; cut off by
About 80 km Highway 1, but the railway detours two sides of the triangle to get there. **Road Bus**:
south of Hanoi regular connections with **Hanoi**'s Southern terminal, 3 hrs, and with **Haiphong** on Highway 10, 4 hrs. **Train** 5 daily connections with **Hanoi**, 2-3 hrs, also with **Ninh Binh**.

Directory **Communications Post office:** 4 Ha Huy Tap St. **Internet:** in post office, 600d per min.
Tourist information *Nam Dinh Tourist*, 115 Nguyen Du St, T849439.

Ninh Binh and around

Phone code: 030 Ninh Binh is capital of the densely populated and newly formed province of Ninh
Colour map 1, grid C4 *Binh. It marks the most southerly point of the northern region. The town itself has little to commend to the tourist but it is a useful and accessible hub from which to*
The site is 94 km *visit some of the most interesting and attractive sights in the north. Within a short*
south of Hanoi on *drive lie the ancient capital of Hoa Lu with its temples dedicated to two of Viet-*
Highway 1 and the *nam's great kings; the exquisite watery landscape of Tam Coc, an 'inland Halong*
main north-south *Bay', where sampans carry visitors up a meandering river, through inundated*
railway line *grottoes and past verdant fields of rice; the Catholic landscape around Phat Diem*
See map, Around *Cathedral, spires and towers, bells and smells; and the lovely Cuc Phuong*
Hanoi, page 84 *National Park with its glorious butterflies, flowers and trees.*

Ins and outs

See Transport, It is an easy 3-hr journey from Hanoi by bus or by train. There are frequent connections.
page 170, Most visitors get to the places around Ninh Binh as a day trip from Hanoi through tour
for further details agencies. Taxis, motorbikes and cyclos can be hired for getting around.

Excursions

Hoa Lu was the capital of Vietnam from AD 968 to AD 1010, during the Dinh and Early Le dynasties. Prior to the establishment of Hoa Lu as the centre of the new kingdom, there was nothing here. But the location was a good one in the narrow valley of the Hong River – on the 'dragon's belly', as the Vietnamese say. The passes leading to the citadel could be easily defended with a small force, and defenders could keep watch over the plains to the north and guard against the Chinese. The kings of Hoa Lu were, in essence, rustics. This is reflected in the art and architecture of the temples of the ancient city: primitive in form, massive in conception. Animals – elephants, rhinoceros, horses – were the dominant motifs, monumentally carved in stone. The inhabitants were not, by all accounts, sophisticated aesthetes.

Much of this former capital, which covered over 200 ha, has been destroyed, although archaeological excavations have revealed a great deal of historical and artistic interest. The two principal temples of Hoa Lu are those of Dinh Bo Linh who assumed the title King Dinh Tien Hoang on ascending the throne (reigned 968-980) and Le Hoan who assumed the title King Le Dai Hanh on ascending the throne (ruled 980-1009). The **Temple of Dinh Tien Hoang** was originally constructed in the 11th century but was reconstructed in 1696. It is arranged as a series of courtyards, gates and buildings. The inscription on one of the pillars in the temple, in ancient Vietnamese, reads 'Dai Co Viet', from which the name 'Vietnam' is derived. The temple also contains statues of various animals, often crude, which came to represent higher beings. The back room of the temple is dedicated to Dinh Tien Hoang, whose statue occupies the central position, surrounded by those of his sons. In the 960s, Dinh Tien Hoang managed to pacify much of the Red River plain, undermining the position of a competing ruling family, the Ngos, who eventually accepted Dinh Tien Hoang's supremacy. However, this was not done willingly, and banditry and insubordination continued to afflict Hoang's Kingdom. He responded by placing a large kettle and a tiger in a cage in the courtyard of his palace and decreed: 'those who violate the law will be boiled and gnawed'. An uneasy calm descended on Dinh Tien Hoang's kingdom, and he could concern himself with promoting Buddhism and geomancy, arranging strategic marriages, and implementing administrative reforms. But, by making his infant son Hang Lang heir apparent, rather than Dinh Lien (his only adult son), he sealed his fate. History records that the announcement was followed by earthquakes and hailstorms, a sign of dissension in the court, and in 979 Lien sent an assassin to kill his younger brother Hang Lang. A few months later in the same year, an official named Do Thich killed both Dinh Tien Hoang and Dinh Lien as they lay drunk and asleep in the palace courtyard. When Do Thich was apprehended, it is said that he was executed and his flesh fed to the people of the city.

Hoa Lu

Colour map 1, grid C4

Hoa Lu lies about 13 km from Ninh Binh near the village of Truong Yen

The North

Hoa Lu & the Temple of Dinh Tien Hoang

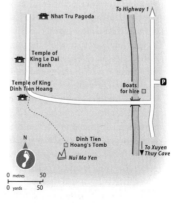

The **Temple of King Le Dai Hanh** is dedicated to the founder of the Le Dynasty who seized power after the regicide of Dinh Tien Hoang. In fact Le Dai Hanh took not only Hoang's throne but also his wife, Duong Van Nga, and representations of her, Le Dai Hanh and Le Ngoa Trieu (Hanh's eldest son) each sit on their own altar in the rear temple.

A short walk beyond Le Dai Hanh's temple is Nhat Tru Pagoda, a 'working' temple. In front of it stands a stone pillar engraved with excerpts from the Buddhist bible (*Kinh Phat*). Adjacent to Dinh Tien Hoang's temple is a small hill, Nui Ma Yen, at the top of which is Dinh Tien Hoang's tomb. Local children will tell you it is 265 steps to the top. There are also boat trips on the river to Xuyen Thuy cave (15,000d), less spectacular than Tam Coc. ■ *US$1. Getting there: by bicycle or* xe ôm, *6 km north of Ninh Binh and 6 km west of Highway 1, follow signs to Truong Yen. From Hanoi, by chartered car, 2 hrs, or on an organized tour. Cheaper, especially for three or four persons, and more flexible to hire a car with driver, no need for a guide.* **Sleeping B-C** *Van Xuan*, just off Highway 1 (T030-860648, F030-860647). New hotel, a/c, hot water, clean, restaurant.

Tam Coc
Some 10 km south of Ninh Binh a few kilometres west of Highway 1

Tam Coc means literally 'three caves'. The highlight of this excursion is an enchanting boat ride up the little Ngo Dong River through the eponymous three caves. Those who have seen the film *Indochine*, some of which was shot here, will be familiar with the nature of the bee-hive type scenery created by limestone towers, similar to those of Halong Bay. The exact form varies from wet to dry season; when flooded the channel disappears and one or two of the caves may be drowned. In the dry season the shallow river meanders between fields of golden rice. Women row and punt pitch-and-resin tubs that look like elongated coracles through the tunnels. It is a most leisurely experience and a chance to observe at close quarters the extraordinary method of rowing with the feet. Take plenty of sun cream and a hat. The villagers have a rota to decide whose turn it is to row and to supplement their fee will try and sell visitors embroidered table cloths and napkins. Enterprising photographers snap you setting off from the bank and will surprise you 1 km up-stream with copies of your cheesy grin already printed. On a busy day the scene from above is like a two way, nose to tail procession of waterboatmen, so to enjoy Tam Coc at its best – make it your first port of call in the morning.

Bich Dong

A short drive to the south is Bich Dong. This is much harder work, so not surprisingly it is a lot quieter than Tam Coc. Bich Dong consists of a series of temples and caves built into, and carved out of, a limestone mountain. The temples date from the reign of Le Thai To in the early 15th century. It is typical of many Vietnamese cave temples but with more than the average number of legends attached to it, while the number of interpretations of its rock formations defies belief. The cliff face into which the lower temple is built is beautifully covered with the roots and trunks of banyan trees. Next to the temple is a pivoted and carved rock that resonates beautifully when tapped with a stone. Next see Buddha's footprints embedded in the rock (size 12, for the curious) and the tombs of the two founding monks. Leading upwards is the middle temple, an 18th-century bell, a memorial stone into which are carved the names of benefactors and a cave festooned with rock forms. Here, clear as can be, are the likenesses of Uncle Ho, a turtle and an elephant. More resonant rock pillars follow and a rock which enables pregnant women to choose the sex of their baby: touch the top for a boy and the middle for a girl. But best of all scramble right to the pinnacle of the peak for a glorious view over the whole area. ■ *US$2 plus US$1.50 per person for the boat ride (tip or purchase will be requested). Getting there: the turning to Tam Coc and Bich Dong is 4 km south of Ninh Binh on Highway 1. A small road leads 2-3 km west to Tam Coc and a further 2 km to Bich Dong. Can easily be reached by bicycle or* xe ôm *from Ninh Binh, or by car from Hanoi (on a day trip including Hoa Lu); again the same reservations about taking an organized tour apply.*

The Red River Delta was the first part of the country to be influenced by Western missionaries: Portuguese priests were proselytizing here as early as 1627. Christian influence is still strong despite the mass exodus of Roman Catholics to the south in 1954 and decades of Communist rule. Villages (which are built of red brick, often walled and densely populated) in these coastal provinces may have more than half-a-dozen churches, all with packed congregations, not only on Sundays. It is hard to escape the feeling visiting some of these Roman Catholic villages that it is the trappings of the religion that are the objects of worship rather than the founder of the religion. The churches, the shrines, the holy grottoes, the photographs of the parish priest on bedroom walls and the holy relics clearly assume huge significance in people's lives.

Phat Diem Cathedral

Phat Diem Cathedral is the most spectacular of the church buildings in the area, partly for its scale but also for its remarkable oriental style. Completed in 1891, it boasts a bell tower in the form of a pagoda behind which stretches for 74 m the nave of the cathedral held up by 52 ironwood pillars. ■ *There are several services daily. Getting there: 24 km southwest of Ninh Binh in the village of Kim Son. The journey takes in a number of more conventional churches, waterways and paddy fields. Motorbike from Ninh Binh or hire a car from Hanoi. Hoa Lu, Tam Coc and Phat Diem can all be comfortably covered in 1 day.*

This is probably the second most accessible of Vietnam's national parks, and for nature lovers not intending to visit Cat Ba island, it is worthy of consideration. Located in an area of deeply-cut limestone and reaching elevations of up to 800 m, the park is covered by 22,000 ha of humid tropical montagne forest. It is home to an estimated 1,880 species of flora including the giant *parashorea, cinamomum* and *sandoricum* trees. Wildlife has been much depleted by hunting, only 64 mammal and 137 bird species are thought to remain. The government has resettled a number of the park's 30,000 Mường minority people although Mường villages do remain and can be visited. April and May sees fat grubs and pupae metamorphosing into swarms of beautiful butterflies that mantle the forest in fantastic shades of greens and yellows.

Cuc Phuong National Park
Colour map 2, grid A1

Accommodation is available at the Park Gate (**B** fan or a/c, hot water) or in the interior (**B-C** hot water, no a/c). ■ *US$5. One- or two-day treks can be arranged with a guide (US$10 per day). Park office T866085. Getting there: around 120 km south of Hanoi and 45 km west of Ninh Binh. Can be done as a day trip from Ninh Binh, or from Hanoi (early start). Access by car only. Organized tour from Hanoi may be a sensible option for lone travellers or pairs, otherwise charter a car.*

Essentials

B-D *Hoa Lu*, Tran Hung Dao St, T871217, F874126. On Highway 1 towards Hanoi, 120 rooms at a range of prices for a range of standards, cars and motorbikes for rent, tours arranged, including hunting, friendly. **C-D** *Thuy Anh*, 55A Truong Han Sieu St, T871602, F876934, thuyanhhotel@hn.vnn.vn 8 a/c rooms, with fridge etc in this spotless hotel, 30 additional rooms in their sister hotel, car for hire 300,000d per day,

Sleeping & eating
Phone code: 030

The North

motorbike 60,000d per day and bicycle, will arrange tours, useful source of information and a good restaurant. **D** *Queen*, Hoanh Hoa Tham St, T871874. Near station, simple but clean.

Tour operators See under Sleeping and under Hanoi tour operators, page 96.

Transport **Road** **Bus**: there are regular bus connections from Ninh Binh's bus station at 207 Le Dai Hanh St with **Hanoi**'s Southern terminal, 3 hrs, and also to **Haiphong**, once daily at 0530, 20,000d. The journey to Haiphong involves a ferry crossing and change of bus. Make sure you are issued a ticket and keep it otherwise you may find yourself having to buy another. **Train** There are regular local train connections with **Hanoi**, 3 hrs, soft seats 48,000d, hard seats 38,000d. 13 hrs from **Hué**, soft seats 213,000d. It may be difficult getting connections on from Ninh Binh because of Ninh Binh's limited allocation of tickets. In case of difficulty, board the train and negotiate once under way.

Directory **Bank** *Vietcombank*, Tran Hung Dao St. Cashes TCs. **Communications** GPO: Tran Hung Dao St. **Internet:** Thuy Anh Hotel.

The North

The Central Region

5

The Central Region

174 Thanh Hoa to Hué

177 Hué

202 Danang

212 Hoi An

221 Quang Ngai to Phan Rang via
     Nha Trang

224 Central Highlands

234 Nha Trang

249 Dalat

259 Dalat to Saigon

260 Vung Tau

The Central Region extends over 1,000 km north to south. It includes the mountains of the Annamite chain which form a natural frontier with Laos to the west and in places extend almost all the way to the sea, in the east. Many of Vietnam's hill peoples are concentrated in these mountains. The narrow coastal strip, sometimes only a few kilometres wide, supported the former artistically accomplished kingdom of Champa.

The narrow central region is traversed by Highway 1 which runs all the way from Hanoi to Saigon. Along much of its route, the road runs close to the coast, passing through a succession of interesting, though rather unattractive, towns. These northern provinces – such as Nghe Tinh – are among the poorest in the country but their inhabitants are among the friendliest. Villagers here grow barely enough to feed themselves. Some 654 km south of Hanoi and 1,071 km north of Saigon, is the former imperial capital of Hué. Though devastated during the Vietnam War, the Imperial Palace and tombs represent the most impressive collection of historical sights in Vietnam.

Thanh Hoa to Hué

Thanh Hoa

Phone code: 037
Colour map 2, grid A2
153 km from Hanoi

The **citadel of Ho** was built in 1397 when Thanh Hoa was the capital of Vietnam. Much of this great city has been destroyed, although the massive city gates are preserved. Art historians believe that they rival the finest Chinese buildings, and the site is in the process of being excavated. This town and province mark the most northerly point of the central region.

The 160-m-long **Ham Rong Bridge** or 'Dragon's Jaw' which crosses the Ma River south of Thanh Hoa was a highly significant spot during the Vietnam War. The bridge, a crucial transport link with the south, was heavily fortified and the US lost 70 planes in successive abortive raids from 1965. Eventually, in 1972, they succeeded using laser-guided 'smart' bombs – at which point the Vietnamese promptly built a replacement pontoon bridge. Significantly, however, during the attack in 1972, as well as one at the same time using the same technology against the Paul Doumer Bridge in Hanoi, no US aircraft were lost. About 15 km east of Thanh Hoa lies the coastal resort of **Sam Son**. This is truly a bizarre place catering mainly for the holidaying Vietnamese. The place is teeming with karaoke cafés and commercial sex workers. The beach is long and crowded with deckchairs. It is impossible to stroll around without the hirers of these chairs following you. If you walk south along the beach and over the hill you can find a deserted cove (walk past the temple). This beach is full of tiny crabs.

Sleeping **B-C** *Thanh Hoa*, 25 Quang Trung St, T852517, F853963. 93 rooms offering everything from a/c and satellite TV to sauna and massage. **C** *Hoa Hong*, 102 Trien Quoc Dat St, near the post office and railway station, T855195. Satellite TV, a/c and restaurant.

Transport **Bus** Bus station is on Ba Trieu St, regular connections with Hanoi's Ha Dong bus station, 4 hrs, Ninh Binh, Vinh and other towns on Highway 1. **Train** Express trains to and from Hanoi and Saigon stop here, 4¼ hrs from Hanoi.

Directory **Banks** *Nong Nghiep Bank*, 11 Phan Chu Trinh St. **Communications** Internet: *Ha Anh Tuan*, 491 Le Hoang St, 5,000d per hr. **Post office**: 33 Tran Phu St. **Tourist information** *Thanh Hoa Province Tourism* in *Thanh Hoa Hotel* and at 34 Le Loi St, T854140.

Vinh

Phone code: 038
Colour map 2, grid B2

Vinh is a diversified industrial centre and the capital of Nghe Tinh Province. It was damaged by the French before 1954, and then suffered sustained bombing by US and ARVN (Army of the Republic of Vietnam) aircraft from 1964 through to 1972. In the process it was virtually razed. Vinh lies at the important point where the coastal plain narrows, forcing roads and railways to squeeze down a slender coastal strip of land. The town has since been rebuilt with assistance from the former East Germany, in startlingly unimaginative style. The dirty-brown apartment blocks make Vinh one of the most inhuman and uninspired cities in Vietnam. The province of Nghe Tinh also happens to be one of the poorest, and the mini-famine of 1989 struck hard.

There is nothing of historical interest here, unless socialist architecture can be thought of as such. The **Central Market**, at the south end of Gao Thang Street (the continuation of Quang Trung Street), is a bustle of colour and activity.

Kim Lien village, 14 km west of Vinh, is the birthplace of Ho Chi Minh, who was born here in 1890. There is a reconstruction of the house Ho was born in together with a memorial altar. **Sen** is another village close to Kim Lien, where Ho lived with his father from the age of six. Although the community and surrounding area were hardly wealthy, Ho was fortunate to be born into a family of modest means and his father was highly educated. The house where he lived (in fact a replica built in 1955) may be thatched and rude, but it was a great deal better than the squalor that most of his countrymen had to endure (see page 360, for a short account of Ho's life). The province of Nghe Tinh has a reputation for producing charismatic revolutionary leaders; not only Ho Chi Minh but also Phan Boi Chau – another fervent anti-colonialist – was born here (see page 374). ■ *Getting there: take a motorbike.*

Excursions

Cua Lo is a beach 20 km from Vinh. It boasts 8 km of white sandy beach and is a very popular (if slightly downmarket) holiday spot with the locals. There are a number of hotels but finding a room during the holiday period (June-August) can be tricky and the prices are double what they are at other times. Accommodation is available at the **B-C** *Thai Binh Duong*, 92 Binh Minh St, T824164, F824692. All with a/c and hot water. Restaurant and breakfast included. ■ *Getting there: take a motorbike.*

A-C *Kim Lien*, 25 Quang Trung St, T844751, F838898. Perhaps the best in town with a/c and hot water in all rooms. **B-D** *Giao Te*, 9 Ho Tung Mau St, T843175. A/c, large and unattractive, massage and karaoke. **C** *Hong Ngoc*, 86B Le Loi St, T841314, F841229. Mini hotel offering comfortable accommodation with a/c. Prices can be bargained to reasonable levels. **C** *Nghe An Guesthouse*, 4 Phan Dang Luu St, T846112. A/c. **D-E** *Railway Station Hotel*, 2 Le Nin St (adjacent to the station), T853754. All rooms have a/c and hot water. **D-E** *Song Lan*, 13 Quang Trung St, T840603, F843635. 20 rooms, some a/c, all with hot water.

Sleeping
Phone code: 038

Because so few visitors stay in Vinh, hotel rates can be bargained down considerably

Local *Honda ôm*. Cars available from *Vinh Tourist* or most hotels. **Bus** The bus station is at 2 Le Loi St. Express buses leave for **Hanoi**, **Saigon** and **Danang** at 0500. **Train** The station is in the west quarter of town, 3 km from the central market. Connections with **Hanoi** and all points south to **Saigon**. Express trains stop here.

Transport
197 km from Dong Hoi, 291 from Hanoi, 368 from Hué

Banks *Nong Nghiep Bank*, 364 Nguyen Van Cu St. *Vietcombank*, 9 Nguyen Si Sach St. **Communications** Internet: 61 Le Hong Phong St. **Post office**: 2 Nguyen Thi Minh Khai St. **Tourist information** *Nghe An Tourist Office* is at 13 Quang Trung St, T844692, F843635.

Directory

Ngang Pass or Porte d'Annam

Running between the Central Highlands and the coast is a small range of mountains, the Hoanh Son, which neatly divides the north from Central Vietnam. In French times the range marked the southern limit of Tonkin and northern limit of Annam. The mountains which reach up to 1,000 m have a marked effect on climate, blocking cold northerly winds in winter and receiving up to 3,000 mm of rain. During the reign of Minh Mang a gate was built, the Hoanh Son Quan. Subsequently, Emperor Thieu Tri on a visit north composed a poem which is inscribed on a nearby rock.

Dong Hoi

Phone code: 052
Colour map 2, grid A2

Travelling either south from Vinh towards Hué, or north to Vinh, there is little to entice the traveller to stop. Along this stretch of coastal plain, which crosses from the province of Nghe An to Ha Tinh to Quang Binh then to Quang Tri and on to Thua Thien Hué, the inhabitants have been struggling against floods and encroaching sand dunes for years. During the Vietnam War, the area was pounded by bombs and shells, and sprayed with defoliants. Unexploded bombs still regularly maim farmers (1,000,000 bombs have been unearthed since the end of hostilities), and it is claimed that the enduring effects of Agent Orange can be seen in the high rates of physical deformity in both animals and humans.

The town of Dong Hoi can be used as a stopping-off point on the way north or south. It was virtually annihilated during the war as it lies just north of the 17th parallel, marking the border between North and South Vietnam. Just south of the town is the **Hien Luong Bridge** which spans the Ben Hai River – the river forming the border between the two halves of former North and South Vietnam.

Excursions **Phong Nha Cave** is about 50 km from Dong Hoi. It is a true speleological wonder – if not of the world then certainly of Vietnam. Visitors are taken only 600 m into the cave by boat and are dropped off to explore. The brick foundations of a Cham temple remain in one of the chambers. There are stalagmites and stalactites and those with a powerful torch can pick out the form of every manner of ghoul and god in the rocks. A team of British divers explored 9 km of the main cave system in 1990 but less than 1 km is accessible to visitors. ■ *US$6 including boat ride. Getting there: north on Highway 1 for 20 km, 30 km west to the Son River landing stage. Take a motorbike.*

Sleeping **C** *Phuong Nam*, 36 Ly Thuong Kiet St, T052-823194. A/c, restaurant but not very friendly.
& eating

Transport
522 km from Hanoi,
166 from Hué,
197 from Vinh

Bus The bus station is on Tran Hung Dao St. Buses travelling up Highway 1 linking Saigon with Hanoi pass through Dong Hoi. **Train** Regular connections with **Hanoi** and **Saigon**.

Directory **Banks** *Nong Nghiep Bank*, 2 Me Sut St. **Communications** Post office: 2 Tran Hung Dao St.

Dong Ha

Phone code: 053

Dong Ha sits on the junction of Highways 1 and 9 and is prospering from the growth of trade with Laos. Dong Ha is a convenient overnight stop for those crossing into or coming from Laos. Travellers have reported successfully hitching lifts with trucks bound for Laos.

Excursions **The Demilitarized Zone (DMZ)**, **Khe Sanh** and the **Ho Chi Minh Trail** lie to the south of Dong Hoi. These war-time sights are normally visited on a tour from Hué and are described in detail on page 193. About 94 km south, at Dong Ha, Highway 9 branches off the main coastal Highway 1 and proceeds to the border with Laos. Along this route is Khe Sanh (now called Huong Hoa) – one of the most evocative names associated with American involvement in Vietnam (see page 193). Close to Khe Sanh are parts of the famous Ho Chi Minh Trail along which supplies were ferried from the north to the south (see page 194). Highway 9 has been extensively improved in recent years to provide land-locked Laos with an alternative access route to the sea.

This border crossing to Savannakhet is open to foreigners with the appropriate visa for the **Lao Bao Crossing**. The crossing is 2 km beyond Lao Bao village. There are bus connections from Hué to Khe Sanh, also from Khe Sanh to Lao Bao village (where there is accommodation at the **E** *Mountain*, simple, clean, friendly). *Honda ôm* from Khe Sanh to the border, costs US$3, or from Lao Bao village to the border US$1. Those crossing into Vietnam may be able to get a ride with the DMZ tour bus from Khe Sanh back to Hué (see page 193), in the late afternoon. **International border crossing**

C-D *Ngan Ha Guesthouse*, 1B Le Quay Don St, T852806. Some a/c and hot water. **F** *Thai Son Guesthouse*, 142 Le Duan St, T852181. Fan only, but does have hot water. Good restaurant nearby. **Sleeping**

The bus station is on Le Duan St. Bus to **Vinh**, 12 hrs. Dong Ha is 74 km from Hué and 80 km from Lao Bao border crossing. **Transport**

Banks *Nong Nghiep Bank*, 1 Le Quy Don St. **Communications** Internet: 88 Le Duan St, 300d per min. **Post office**: 20 Tran Hung Dao St. **Directory**

Hué

Hué, an imperial city that housed generations of the country's most powerful emperors was built on the banks of the Huong Giang, or 'Perfume River', 100 km south of the 17th parallel. The river is named after a scented shrub which is supposed to grow at its source. *Phone code: 054*
Colour map 3, grid A4

Hué does, in many respects, epitomize the best of Vietnam and in a country that is rapidly disappearing under concrete, Hué represents a link with the past where the people live in old buildings and don't lock their doors. Whether it is the royal heritage or the city's Buddhist tradition, the people of Hué are the gentlest and, apart from the odd cyclo driver throwing a tantrum, the least aggressive in the country. They speak good English and drive their motorbikes more carefully than anyone else.

Just south of the city are the last resting places of many Vietnamese emperors (see page 185). A number of war relics in the Demilitarized Zone (DMZ) can be easily visited from Hué (see page 193).

Ins and outs

Hué's Phu Bai airport is a 40-min drive from the city. There are daily connections with Hanoi and Saigon. The 2 bus stations and 1 railway station are more central and there are connections north to Hanoi and south to Saigon – and all points between. The trains tend to fill up, so advance booking is recommended, especially for sleepers. Many foreign visitors arriving by road do so on tourist minibuses. **Getting there** *See Transport, page 198, for further details*

For the city itself, walking is an option – interspersed, perhaps, with the odd *cyclo* journey. However, most guesthouses hire out bicycles and this is a very pleasant and slightly more flexible way of exploring Hué and some of the surrounding countryside. **Getting around**

A motorbike provides even more flexibility: it makes it possible to fit so much more into a day and this, in Hué, is very important. Boats are available for hire on the river (a pleasant way of getting to the tombs) and there is also the usual array of *xe ôm* motorbike taxis.

Best time to visit Hué has a reputation for its bad weather. The rainy season runs from Sep to Jan and rainfall is particularly heavy between Sep and Nov; the best time to visit is therefore between Feb and Aug. However, even in the 'dry' season an umbrella is handy, especially when venturing out of town to the pagodas and tombs. Rainfall of 2,770 mm has been recorded in a single month. Humidity levels can be gauged from the trees along Le Loi Street by the Perfume River which sprout mossy ferns from their trunks and branches. Temperatures in Hué can also be pretty cool in winter compared with Danang, Nha Trang and other places to the south as cold air tends to get bottled here, trapped by mountains to the south. For several months each year neither fans nor air-conditioning are required.

Nguyen Dynasty Emperors (1802-1945)

Gia Long	1802-1819
Minh Mang	1820-1840
Thieu Tri	1841-1847
Tu Duc	1847-1883
Duc Duc	1883
Hiep Hoa	1883
Kien Phuc	1883-1884
Ham Nghi	1884-1885
Dong Khanh	1885-1889
Thanh Thai	1889-1907
Duy Tan	1907-1916
Khai Dinh	1916-1925
Bao Dai	1925-1945

History

Ancient capital Hué was the capital of Vietnam during the Nguyen Dynasty and is one of the cultural cores of the country. The Nguyen Dynasty ruled Vietnam between 1802 and 1945, and for the first time in Vietnamese history a single court controlled the land from Yunnan (southern China) southwards to the Gulf of Siam. To link the north and south – over 1,500 km – the Nguyen emperors built and maintained the Mandarin Road (Quan Lo), interspersed with relay stations. Even in 1802, when it was not yet complete, it took couriers just 13 days to travel between Hué and Saigon, and five days between Hué and Hanoi. If they arrived more than two days late, the punishment was a flogging. There cannot have been a better road in Southeast Asia, or a more effective incentive system.

The city of Hué was equally impressive. George Finlayson, a British visitor in 1821-22 wrote that its "style of neatness, magnitude, and perfection" made other Asian cities look "like the works of children". Although the Confucian bureaucracy and some of the dynasty's technical achievements may have been remarkable, there was continual discontent and uprisings against the Nguyen emperors. The court was packed with scheming mandarins, princesses, eunuchs and scholars writing wicked poetry. The female writer Ho Xuan Huong, wrote of the court and its eunuchs:

> "Why do the twelve midwives who cared for you hate each other? Where have they thrown away your youthful sexual passions? Damned be you if you should care about the twitterings of mice-like lovers, or about a bee-like male gallant caressing his adored one ... At least, a thousand years from now you will be more able to avoid the posthumous slander that you indulged in mulberry-grove intrigues."

In 1883 a French fleet assembled at the mouth of the Perfume River, not far from Hué, and opened fire. After taking heavy casualties, Emperor Hiep Hoa sued for peace, and signed a treaty making Vietnam a protectorate of France. As French influence over Vietnam increased, the power and influence of the Nguyen waned. The undermining effect of the French presence was compounded by significant schisms in Vietnamese society. In particular, the spread of Christianity was undermining traditional hierarchies. Despite the impressive imperial tombs and palace (see Sights, page 180), many scholars maintain that the Nguyen Dynasty was simply too short-lived to have ever had a 'golden age'. Emperor Tu Duc may have reigned for 36 years (1847-83), but by then the imperial family had grown so large that he had to contend with a series of damaging attempted coups d'état as family members vied for the throne. Although the French, and then the Japanese during the Second World War, found it to their advantage to maintain the framework of Vietnamese imperial rule, the system became hollow and, eventually, irrelevant. The last Nguyen Emperor, Bao Dai, abdicated on 30 August 1945.

Unfortunately for art lovers, the relative peace which descended upon Hué at the end of the Second World War was not to last. During the 1968 Tet offensive, Viet Cong soldiers holed up in the Citadel for 25 days. The bombardment which ensued, as US troops attempted to root them out, caused extensive damage to the Thai Hoa Palace and other monuments. During their occupation of Hué, the NVA forces settled old scores, shooting, beheading and even burning alive 3,000 people, including civil servants, police officers

The Central Region

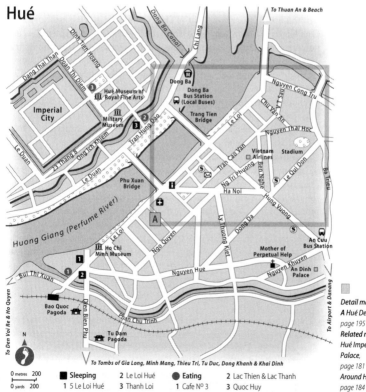

Hué

Detail maps
A Hué Detail, page 195
Related maps
Hué Imperial Palace, page 181
Around Hué, page 184

0 metres 200
0 yards 200

■ **Sleeping** 2 Le Loi Hué ● **Eating** 2 Lac Thien & Lac Thanh
1 5 Le Loi Hué 3 Thanh Loi 1 Cafe Nº 3 3 Quoc Huy

and anyone connected with, or suspected of being sympathetic to, the government in Saigon. This action lent support to the notion that should the north ever achieve victory over the south it would result in mass killings. The irony was that this series of atrocities was not remarked on in the US: at the time the Western media were pre-occupied with the infamous My Lai massacre by American troops (see page 221).

Sights

The Imperial City The **Imperial City** at Hué is built on the same principles as the Forbidden Palace in Peking. It is enclosed by 7-10-m-thick outer walls, the **Kinh Thanh**, along with moats, canals and towers. Emperor Gia Long commenced construction in 1804 after geomancers had decreed a suitable location and orientation for the palace. The site enclosed the land of eight villages (for which the inhabitants received compensation), and covers 6 sq km; sufficient area to house the Emperor and all his family, courtiers, bodyguards and servants. It took 20,000 men to construct the walls alone. Ten gates pierce the four walls of the citadel, although many are in poor condition. Not only has the city been damaged by war and incessant conflict, but also by natural disasters such as floods which, in the mid-19th century, inundated the city to a depth of several metres.

Chinese custom decreed that the 'front' of the palace should face south (like the Emperor) and this is the direction from which visitors approach the site. Over the outer moat, a pair of gates pierce the outer walls: the **Hien Nhon** and **Chuong Duc** gates. Just inside are two groups of massive cannon; four through the Hien Nhon Gate and five through the Chuong Duc Gate. These are the Nine Holy Cannon (**Cuu Vi Than Cong**), cast in 1803 on the orders of Gia Long from bronzeware seized from the Tay Son revolutionaries. The cannon are named after the four seasons and the five elements, and on each is carved its name, rank, firing instructions and how the bronze of which they are made was acquired. They are 5 m in length, but have never been fired. Like the giant urns outside the Hien Lam Cac (see page 182), they are meant to symbolize the permanence of the empire. Between the two gates is a massive **flag tower**. The flag of the National Liberation Front flew here for 24 days during the Tet Offensive in 1968 – a picture of the event is displayed in Hué's Ho Chi Minh Museum.

Northwards from the cannon, and over one of three bridges which span a second moat, is the **Ngo Mon**, or Royal Gate (**1**), built in 1833 during the reign of Emperor Minh Mang. The ticket office is just to the right. The gate, remodelled on a number of occasions since its original construction, is surmounted by a pavilion from where the emperor would view palace ceremonies. Of the five entrances, the central one – the Ngo Mon – was only opened for the emperor to pass through. UNESCO has thrown itself into the restoration of Ngo Mon with vigour and the newly finished pavilion atop the gate now gleams and glints in the sun; those who consider it garish can console themselves with the thought that this is how it might have appeared in Minh Mang's time. On an upper floor are photographs showing Ngo Mon before and after restoration.

North from the Ngo Mon, is the **Golden Water Bridge** (**2**) - again reserved solely for the emperor's use - between two tanks (**3**), lined with laterite blocks. This leads to the **Dai Trieu Nghi**, the Great Rites Courtyard (**4**), on the north side of which is the **Thai Hoa Palace**, the Palace of Supreme Harmony, constructed by Gia Long in 1805 and used for his coronation in 1806. From here, sitting on his golden throne raised up on a dais, the emperor would receive ministers, foreign emissaries, mandarins and military officers during formal ceremonial occasions. In front of the palace are 18 stone stelae, which stipulate the arrangement of the nine mandarinate ranks on the Great Rites Courtyard: the upper level was for ministers, mandarins and officers of the upper grade; the lower for those of lower grades. Civil servants would stand on the left, and the military on the right. Only royal princes were allowed to stand in the palace itself, which is perhaps the best-preserved building in the Imperial City complex. Its red and gold columns, tiled floor, and fine ceiling have been restored and the rear of the palace is now a tourist shop.

North of the Palace of Supreme Harmony is the **Tu Cam Thanh** (the Purple Forbidden City). This would have been reserved for the use of the emperor and his family, and was surrounded by 1-m-thick walls: a city within a city. Tragically, the Forbidden City was virtually destroyed during the 1968 Tet offensive. The two **Mandarin Palaces** and the **Royal Reading Pavilion** (**10**) are all that survive.

At the far side of the Thai Hoa Palace, are two enormous **bronze urns** (Vac Dong) decorated with birds, plants and wild animals, and weighing about 1,500 kg each. To either side of the urns are the **Ta** (**6**) and **Huu Vu** (**7**) pavilions – one converted into a souvenir art shop, the other a mock throne room in which tourists can pay US$5 to dress up and play the part of king for five

The Central Region

Hué Imperial City

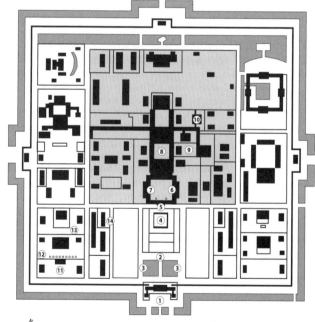

0 metres 100
0 yards 100

1 Ngo Mon (Noon Gate)
2 Golden Water Bridge
3 Tanks
4 Dai Trieu Nghi (Great Rites Courtyard) & Thai Hoa Palace (Throne Hall)
5 Red Gate
6 Ta Pavilion
7 Huu Vu Pavilion
8 Central Pavilion, private apartments of the Emperor
9 Quang Minh Palace
10 Royal Reading Pavilion
11 Hien Lam Cac
12 9 Bronze urns
13 Thé Temple
14 Waiting Pavilion, (Huu Ta Dai Lam Vien)

☐ Tu Cam Thanh (Purple Forbidden City)

minutes. The Royal Reading Pavilion has been rebuilt but, needless to say, has no books. On the far side of the palace are the outer northern walls of the citadel and the north gate.

Most of the surviving buildings of interest are to be found on the west side of the palace, running between the outer walls and the walls of the Forbidden City. At the southwest corner is the well-preserved and beautiful **Hien Lam Cac** (**11**), a pavilion built in 1821, in front of which stand nine massive **bronze urns** (**12**) cast between 1835 and 1837 on the orders of Emperor Minh Mang. It is estimated that they weigh between 1,500 kg and 2,600 kg, and each has 17 decorative figures, animals, rivers, flowers and landscapes representing between them the wealth, beauty and unity of the country. The central, largest and most ornate urn is dedicated to the founder of the empire, Emperor Gia Long. Next to the urns walking northwards is **Thé Temple** - the Temple of Generations (**13**). Built in 1821, it contains altars honouring 10 of the kings of the Nguyen Dynasty (Duc Duc and Hiep Hoa are missing) behind which are meant to be kept a selection of their personal belongings. It was only in 1954, however, that the stelae depicting the three Revolutionary emperors Ham Nghi, Thanh Thai, and Duy Tan were brought into the temple. The French, perhaps fearing that they would become a focus of discontent, prevented the Vietnamese from erecting altars in their memory. North of the The Temple is **Hung Temple** built in 1804 for the worship of Gia Long's father, Nguyen Phuc Luan, the father of the founder of the Nguyen Dynasty. The temple was renovated in 1951.

UNESCO began the arduous process of renovating the complex in 1983: Vietnam at that time was a pariah state due to its invasion of Cambodia in 1978-79 and the appeal for funds and assistance fell on deaf ears. It was, therefore, fitting testimony to Vietnam's rehabilitation in the eyes of the world that in 1993 UNESCO declared Hué a World Heritage Site. Although it is the battle of 1968 which is normally blamed for the destruction, the city has in fact been gradually destroyed over a period of 50 years. The French shelled it, fervent revolutionaries burnt down its buildings, typhoons and rains have battered it, thieves have ransacked its contents, and termites have eaten away at its foundations. In some respects it is surprising that as many as a third of the monuments have survived relatively intact. ■ *Daily 0630-1730, entrance to the Imperial City US$5.*

Museums   Hué has a number of museums. The best is the **Hué Museum of Royal Fine Arts,** at 3 Le Truc Street. Housed in the Long An Palace, the museum contains a reasonable (although unlabelled) collection of ceramics, furniture, screens and bronzeware. In the front courtyard are stone mandarins, cannon, gongs and giant bells. The building itself is worthy of note for its elegant construction, built by Emperor Thieu Tri in 1845 it was dismantled and erected on the present site in 1909. ■ *Daily 0800-1600, 22,000d.*

Directly opposite the Royal Fine Arts museum is the **Royal College,** at 2 Le Truc Street, established in 1803 and moved to this site in 1908. It is now fully open to visitors but lamentably short of exhibits. ■ *Free.* Immediately in front, at 23 Thang 8 Street (between Dinh Tien Hoang and Doan Thi Diem streets), is the **Military Museum**. Missiles, tanks and armoured personnel carriers fill the courtyard. On the south side of the river, at 7 Le Loi Street, is the requisite **Ho Chi Minh Museum** which displays pictures of Ho's life plus a few models and personal possessions. The 'tour' begins at the end of the corridor on the second floor. Some interesting photographs (for example of Ho as a cook's assistant at the Carlton Hotel in London), but does not compare with the Ho Chi Minh Museum in Hanoi. ■ *Daily 0730-1130, 1330-1630.*

On the north bank of the river next to the Dong Ba bus station, on Tran Hung Dao Street, is the covered **Dong Ba Market**. The **Bao Quoc Pagoda** (just off Dien Bien Phu Street to the right, over the railway line), is said to have been built in the early 18th century by a Buddhist monk named Giac Phong. Note the 'stupa' that is behind and to the left of the central pagoda and the fine doors inscribed with Chinese and Sanskrit characters. Further along Dien Bien Phu Street, at the intersection with Tu Dam Street, is the **Tu Dam Pagoda**. According to the Hué Buddhist Association this was originally founded in 1690-95 but has been rebuilt many times. The present day pagoda was built shortly before the Second World War. In August 1963, the Diem government sent its forces to suppress the monks here who were alleged to be fermenting discontent among the people. The specially selected forces – they were Catholic – clubbed and shot to death about 30 monks and their student followers, and smashed the great Buddha image here.

The Perfume River is spanned by two bridges; downstream is the ill-fated **Trang Tien Bridge**, named after the royal mint that once stood at its northern end. It was built in 1896 and destroyed soon after by a typhoon; after having been rebuilt it was then razed once more in 1968 during the Tet Offensive. Upstream is Phu Xuan bridge, built by the US Army in 1970. This carries Highway 1, in other words the main north-south highway, but traffic levels in Hué will fall dramatically when the new bypass is completed with a huge new river crossing 10 km upriver.

The skyline of modern Hué is adorned by the striking pagoda-like tower of the **Church of Mother of Perpetual Help**. This three-storey, octagonal steel tower is 53 m high and an attractive blend of Asian and European styles. The church was completed in 1962 and marble from the Marble Mountain in Danang was used for the altar. The church lies at the junction of Nguyen Hue and Nguyen Khuyen streets.

Other sights

Excursions

As the geographical and spiritual centre of the Nguyen Dynasty, Hué and the surrounding area is the site of numerous pagodas and seven imperial tombs, along with the tombs of numerous other royal personages and countless courtiers and successful mandarins. Few visitors will have time to see them all – visitors are taken to two or three perennial favourites so, time permitting, do try to see one or more of the less popular: whatever is lacking in architectural splendour is more than made up for in quietude and solitude. For tours and tour operator details see page 198.

Thien Mu Pagoda (the Elderly Goddess Pagoda), also known as the Thien Mau Tu Pagoda, and locally as the **Linh Mu Pagoda** (the name used on most local maps), is the finest in Hué. It is beautifully sited on the north bank of the Perfume River, about 4 km upstream from the city. It was built in 1601 by Nguyen Hoang, the governor of Hué, after an old woman appeared to him and said that the site had supernatural significance and should be marked by the construction of a pagoda. The monastery is the oldest in Hué, and the seven-storey **Phuoc Duyen** (Happiness and Grace Tower), built later by Emperor Thieu Tri in 1844, is 21 m high, with each storey containing an altar to a different Buddha. The summit of the tower is crowned with a water pitcher to catch the rain, water representing the source of happiness. Arranged around the tower are four smaller buildings one of which contains the **Great Bell** cast in 1710 under the orders of the Nguyen Lord, Nguyen Phuc Chu, and weighing 2,200 kg. Beneath

Thien Mu Pagoda

The Central Region

another of these surrounding pavilions is a monstrous **marble turtle** on which is a 2.6-m-high stela recounting the development of Buddhism in Hué, carved in 1715. Beyond the tower, the entrance to the pagoda is through a triple gateway patrolled by six carved and vividly painted guardians – two on each gate. The roof of the sanctuary itself is decorated with jataka stories. At the front of the sanctuary is a brass laughing Buddha. Behind that are an assortment of gilded Buddhas and a crescent-shaped gong cast in 1677 by Jean de la Croix. The first monk to commit suicide through self immolation, Thich Quang Duc, came from this pagoda (see page 282) and the grey Austin in which he made the journey to his death in Saigon is still kept here in a garage in the temple garden. In May 1993, a Vietnamese – this time not a monk – immolated himself at Thieu

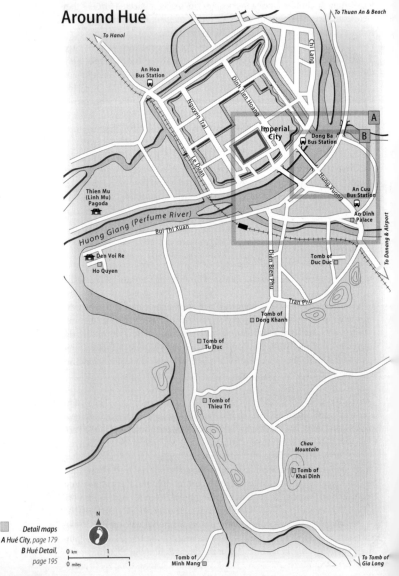

Around Hué

To Thuan An & Beach

To Hanoi

An Hoa
Bus Station

Chi Lang

Dinh Tien Hoang

Nguyen Tri

Le Duan

Imperial
City

Dong Ba
Bus Station

A

B

Hung Vuong

An Cuu
Bus Station

Thien Mu
(Linh Mu)
Pagoda

An Dinh
Palace

Huong Giang (Perfume River)

Bui Thi Xuan

To Danang & Airport

Den Voi Re

Ho Quyen

Dien Bien Phu

Tomb of
Duc Duc

Tran Phu

Tomb of
Dong Khanh

Tomb of
Tu Duc

Tomb of
Thieu Tri

Chau
Mountain

Tomb of
Khai Dinh

N

Detail maps
A Hué City, page 179
B Hué Detail,
page 195

0 km   1
0 miles   1

Tomb of
Minh Mang

To Tomb of
Gia Long

Mu. Why is not clear: some maintain it was linked to the persecution of Buddhists; others that it was because of the man's frustrated love life. ■ *Getting there: it is an easy 4-km bicycle (or cyclo) ride from the city, following the north bank of river upstream (west).*

After the Imperial Palace, the tombs of the former emperors which dot the countryside to the south of the city are Hué's most spectacular tourist attraction (see map). Each of the tombs follows the same stylistic formula, although at the same time they reflect the tastes and predilections of the emperor in question. The tombs were built during the lifetime of each emperor, who took a great interest in their design and construction - after all they were meant to ensure his comfort in the next life. Each mausoleum, variously arranged, has five design elements: a courtyard with statues of elephants, horses and military and civil mandarins (originally, usually approached through a park of rare trees); a stela pavilion (with an engraved eulogy composed by the king's son and heir); a Temple of the Soul's Tablets; a pleasure pavilion; and a grave. Geomancers decreed that they should also have a stream and a mountainous screen in front. The tombs faithfully copy Chinese prototypes, although most art historians claim that they fall short in terms of execution. ■ *Daily 0630-1800, entrance to the popular tombs US$5, others free. An extra US$5 is charged for video cameras. Getting to and around the Imperial Tombs is easiest by motorbike or car as they are spread over a large area. Most hotels and cafés organize tours either by minibus or by boat. A cyclo for the day should cost about 40,000-50,000d (with some walking up the hills), bicycle hire about US$1 (see Local transport page 198). Set out early if bicycling; all the tombs are accessible by bicycle. It is also possible to go on the back of a motorcycle taxi (Honda ôm). Finally, boats can be chartered to sail up the Perfume River – the most peaceful way to travel, but only a few of the tombs can be reached in this way (see Tours, page 198). Also see for details under each individual tomb*

The Tomb of Emperor Gia Long is the most distant and the most rarely visited – it is accessible by bicycle or motorbike (which can be taken by boat across the Perfume River) – but is well worth the effort. The tomb is overgrown with venerable mango trees, the only sound is bird call and, occasionally, the wind in the trees: otherwise a blessed silence. Devoid of tourists, touts and ticket sellers it is the most atmospheric of all the tombs, and as the political regime in Vietnam is not a fan of Gia Long it is likely to remain this way. However, given the historical changes that were to be wrought by the dynasty Gia Long founded, it is arguably the most significant tomb in Hué. It was built between 1814 and 1820 (see box, page 186, for an account of the emperor's burial). Being the first of the dynasty, Gia Long's mausoleum set the formula for the later tombs. There is a surrounding lotus pond

Tomb of Emperor Gia Long

Tomb of Emperor Gia Long

Vinh Mau Tomb

▲ *To River Crossing*

Hoang Co Tomb

Thoai Thanh Tomb
Quang Hung Tomb
Thoai Thanh Temple

Tomb of Gia Long's second wife

Gia Thanh Temple

Truong Phong Tomb

Minh Thanh Temple
Gia Long's Tomb
Stela House

N

Obelisks

Not to scale

The death and burial of Emperor Gia Long (1820)

When the Emperor Gia Long died on 3 February 1820, the thread on the ancestors' altar (representing his soul) was tied. The following day the corpse was bathed and clothed in rich garments, and precious stones and pearls were placed in his mouth. Then a ritual offering of food, drink and incense was made before the body was placed in a coffin made of catalpa wood (bignonia catalpa) – a wood impervious to insect attack. At this time, the crown prince announced the period of mourning that was to be observed – a minimum of three years. Relatives of the dead emperor, mandarins and their wives each had different forms and periods of mourning to observe, depending upon their position.

Three days after Gia Long's death, a messenger was sent to the Hoang Nhon Pagoda to inform the Empress, who was already dead, of the demise of her husband. Meanwhile, the new Emperor Minh Mang had the former ruler's deeds recorded and engraved on golden sheets which were bound together as a book. Then astrologers selected an auspicious date for the funeral, picking 27 May after

some argument (11 May also had its supporters). On 17 May, court officials told the heaven, the earth, and the dynastic ancestors, of the details for the funeral and at the same time opened the imperial tomb. On 20 May, the corpse was informed of the ceremony. Four days later the coffin left the palace for the three-day journey to its final resting place. Then, at the appointed time, the coffin was lowered into the sepulchre – its orientation correct – shrouded in silk cloth, protected by a second outer coffin, covered in resin, and finally bricked in. Next to Gia Long, a second grave was dug into which were placed an assortment of objects useful in his next life. The following morning, Emperor Minh Mang, in full mourning robes, stood outside the tomb facing east, while a mandarin facing in the opposite direction inscribed ritual titles on the tomb. The silk thread on the ancestors' altar – the symbol of the soul – was untied, animals slaughtered, and the thread then buried in the vicinity of the tomb.
(This account is adapted from James Dumarçay's The palaces of South-East Asia, 1991.)

and steps lead up to a courtyard with the Minh Thanh ancestral temple, rather splendid in its red and gold. To the right of this is a double, walled and locked burial chamber where Gia Long and his wife are interred (the Emperor's tomb is fractionally the taller). The tomb is perfectly lined up with the two huge obelisks on the far side of the lake. Ask the custodian for admittance to the burial chamber for which he will request a small contribution. Beyond this is a courtyard with five now headless mandarins, horses and elephants on each side; steps lead up to the stela eulogizing the Emperor's reign, composed, presumably, by his eldest son, Minh Mang, as was the custom. This grey monolith engraved in ancient Chinese characters remained miraculously undisturbed during two turbulent centuries.

Gia Long's geomancers did a great job finding this site: with the mountainous screen in front it is a textbook example of a final resting place. Interestingly, despite their getting first choice of all the possible sites, it is also the furthest tomb from the palace: clearly they took their task seriously.

Nguyen Anh, or Gia Long as he was crowned in 1802, came to power with French support. Back in 1787, Gia Long's son, the young Prince Canh, had caused a sensation in French salon life when, along with soldier/missionary Georges Pigneau de Béhaine, he had sought military support against the Tay Son from Louis XVI. In return for Tourane (Danang) and Poulo Condore, the French offered men and weapons – an offer that was subsequently withdrawn.

Pigneau then raised military support from French merchants in India and in 1799 Prince Canh's French-trained army defeated the Tay Son at Qui Nhon.

Gia Long's reign was despotic – to his European advisers who pointed out that encouragement of industry would lead to the betterment of the poor, he replied that he preferred them poor. The poor were virtual slaves – the price for one healthy young buffalo was one healthy young girl. Flogging was the norm - it has been described as the 'bamboo's golden age'. One study by a Vietnamese scholar estimated that there were 105 peasant uprisings between 1802 and 1820 alone. For this, and the fact that he gave the French a foothold in Vietnam, the Vietnamese have never forgiven Gia Long. Of him they still say "*cong ran can ga nha*" (he carried home the snake that killed the chicken).

■ *Getting there: by bicycle or motorbike. Take Dien Bien Phu St out of town past the railway station. After a couple of kilometres turn right at the T-junction and follow the road along the river bank. The road passes the new river crossing (under construction) and becomes a track. A short distance beyond the Ben Do 1 km milestone is a red sign reading Gia Long Tomb. Down a steep path a sampan is waiting to ferry passengers across this tributary of the Perfume River (bargain but expect to pay US$2 return); on the far side follow the track upstream for about 1km. By a café with 2 billiard tables turn right and then almost immediately turn left. Keep on this path. Ask for directions along the way.*

The Tomb of Emperor Minh Mang is possibly the finest of all the imperial tombs. Built between 1841 and 1843, it is sited among peaceful ponds, about 12 km from the city of Hué. In terms of architectural poise and balance, and richness of decoration, it has no peer in the area. The tomb's layout, along a single central and sacred axis (*Shendao*), is unusual in its symmetry; no other tomb, with the possible exception of Khai Dinh (see page 190), achieves the same unity of constituent parts, nor draws the eye onwards so easily and pleasantly from one visual element to the next. The tomb was traditionally approached through the **Dai Hong Mon** – today visitors pass through a side gate – a gate which leads into the ceremonial courtyard containing an array of

Tomb of Emperor Minh Mang

The Central Region

Tomb of Emperor Minh Mang

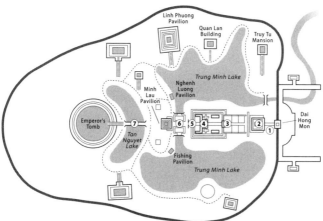

1 Ceremonial courtyard
2 Stela Pavilion
3 Hien Duc Gate
4 Sung An Temple
5 Hoang Trach Gate
6 Trung Dao Bridge
7 Thong Minh Chinh Truc Bridge

statuary. Next is the stela pavilion in which there is a carved eulogy to the dead Emperor composed by his son, Thieu Tri. Continuing downwards through a series of courtyards there is, in turn, the **Sung An Temple** dedicated to Minh Mang and his Empress, a small garden with flower beds that once formed the Chinese character for 'longevity', and two sets of stone bridges. The first consists of three spans, the central one of which (**Trung Dao Bridge**) was for the sole use of the Emperor. The second, single bridge leads to a short flight of stairs with naga balustrades, at the end of which is a locked bronze door. The door leads to the tomb itself which is surrounded by a circular wall. ■ *Getting there: by bicycle or motorbike, as for Gia Long's tomb but visitors must cross the Perfume River by boat several kilometres before the Gia Long crossing.*

Tomb of Thieu Tri   The Tomb of Thieu Tri (7 km southwest of Hué in the village of Thuy Bang) was built in 1848 by his son Tu Duc, who took into account his father's wishes that it be 'economical and convenient'. Thieu Tri reigned for just seven years and unlike his forebears did not start planning his mausoleum the moment he ascended the throne. Upon his death his body was temporarily interred in Long An Temple (now the Hué Museum of Royal Fine Arts, see page 182). The tomb is in two adjacent parts, with separate tomb and temple areas; the layout of each follows the symmetrical axis arrangement of Minh Mang's tomb which has also inspired the architectural style. The memorial temple area is to the right and reached via a long flight of steps. A gatehouse incorporates Japanese triple-beamed columns (as seen in the Japanese Bridge in Hoi An) and at the back of the courtyard beyond is the temple dedicated to Thieu Tri. A ticket is required only for admission beyond the gatehouse.

The stela pavilion and tomb are a few hundred yards to the left, unmissable with the two obelisks. Just like his father, Thieu Tri is buried on a circular island reached by three bridges beyond the stela pavilion.

Tomb of Tu Duc   The Tomb of Tu Duc is 7 km from the city and was built between 1864 and 1867 in a pine wood. It is enclosed by a wall within which is a lake. The lake, with lotus and water hyacinth, contains a small island where the king built a number of replicas of famous temples – which are now rather difficult to discern. He often came here to relax, and from the pavilions that reach out over the lake, composed poetry and listened to music. The **Xung Khiem Pavilion,** built in 1865, has recently been restored with UNESCO's help and is the most attractive building here (although it is usually overrun with Vietnamese picnickers). The tomb complex follows the formula described above: ceremonial square, mourning yard with pavilion, and then the tomb itself. To the left of Tu Duc's tomb are the tombs of his Empress, Le Thien Anh and adopted son, Kien Phuc. Many of the pavilions are crumbling and ramshackle – lending the tomb a

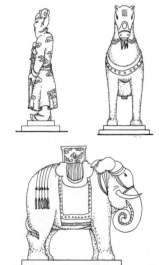

Statues in the front courtyard of Minh Mang's Tomb

rather tragic air. This is appropriate: though he had 104 wives, Tu Duc fathered no sons. He was therefore forced to write his own eulogy, a fact which he took as a bad omen. The eulogy itself recounts the sadness in Tu Duc's life. A flavour of its sentiment can be gleaned from a confession he wrote in 1867 following French seizure of territory (see box, page 191). It was shortly after Tu Duc's reign that France gained full control of Vietnam.

The Tomb of Duc Duc is the closest to Hué, 2 km south of the city centre, on Tan Lang Street. Despite ruling for just three days and then dying in prison, Emperor Duc Duc (1852-83) has a tomb, built posthumously by his son, Thanh Thai, in 1889 on the spot where, it is said, the body was dumped by gaolers. Emperors **Thanh Thai** and **Duy Tan** are buried in the same complex. Unlike Duc Duc, though, both were strongly anti-French and were, for a period, exiled in Africa. Although Thanh Thai later returned to Vietnam and died in Vung Tau in 1953, his son Duy Tan was killed in an air crash in central Africa in 1945. It was not until 1987 that Duy Tan's body was repatriated and interred alongside his father Thanh Thai. The tomb is in three parts: the Long An Temple; Duc Duc's tomb to the south; and Thanh Thai and Duy Tan's tombs adjacent to each other. **Tomb of Duc Duc**

The Tomb of Dong Khanh is 500 m from Tu Duc's tomb: walk up the path on the other side of the road from the main entrance to Tu Duc's tomb – the path is partly hidden in amongst the stalls. Built in 1889, it is the smallest of the imperial mausoleums, but nonetheless one of the most individual. Unusually, it has two separate sections. One is a walled area containing the usual series of pavilions and courtyards and with an historically interesting collection of personal objects that belonged to the Emperor. The second, 100 m away, consists **Tomb of Dong Khanh**

The Central Region

Tomb of Tu Duc

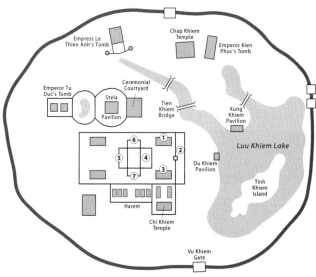

1 Le Khiem House
2 Khiem Cung Gate
3 Phap Khiem House
4 Hoa Khiem Palace
5 Luong Khiem Palace
6 Minh Khiem Royal Theatre
7 On Khiem Mansion

of an open series of platforms. The lower platform has the honour guard of mandarins, horses and elephants along with a stela pavilion; the third platform is a tiled area which would have had an awning; and the highest platform is the tomb itself. The tomb is enclosed within three open walls, the entrance protected by a dragon screen (to prevent spirits entering).

Tomb of Khai Dinh

The Tomb of Khai Dinh is 10 km from Hué and was built between 1920 and 1932. It is the last of the mausoleums of the Nguyen Dynasty, and by the time Khai Dinh was contemplating the afterlife brick had given way in popularity to the concrete that is now beginning to deteriorate. Nevertheless, it occupies a fine position on the Chau Mountain facing southwest towards a large white statue of Quan Am, also built by Khai Dinh. The valley, used for the cultivation of cassava and sugar cane, and the pine-covered mountains, make this one of the most beautifully sited and peaceful of the tombs. Indeed, before construction could begin, Khai Dinh had to remove the tombs of Chinese nobles who had already selected the site for its beauty and auspicious orientation. A total of 127 steep steps lead up to the Honour Courtyard with statuary of mandarins, elephants and horses. An octagonal Stela Pavilion in the centre of the mourning yard contains a stone stela engraved with a eulogy to the Emperor. At the top of some more stairs, are the tomb and shrine of Khai Dinh, containing a bronze statue of the Emperor sitting on his throne and holding a jade sceptre. The body is interred 9 m below ground level (see box, page 192, for a description of Khai Dinh's interment). The interior is richly decorated with ornate and colourful murals (the artist incurred the wrath of the emperor and only just escaped execution), floor tiles, and decorations built up with fragments of porcelain. It is the most elaborate of all the tombs and took 11 years to build. Such was the cost of construction that Khai Dinh had to levy additional taxes to fund the project. The tomb shows distinct European stylistic influences.

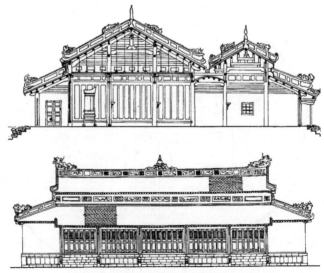

Two views of Sung An Temple, Minh Mang's Tomb:
a cross section through the temple (top) and the southern elevation (bottom)

Tu Duc's lament

"Never has an era seen such sadness, never a year more anguish. Above me, I fear the edicts of heaven. Below, the tribulations of the people trouble my days and nights. Deep in my heart I tremble and blush, finding neither words or actions to help my subjects.

Alone, I am speechless. My pulse is feeble, my body pale and thin, my beard and hair white. Though not yet 40, I have already reached old age, so that I lack the strength to pay homage to my ancestors

every morning and evening. Evil must be suppressed and goodness sought. The wise must offer their counsel, the strong their force, the rich their wealth, and all those with skills should devote them to the needs of the army and the kingdom. Let us together mend our errors and rebuild.

Alas! The centuries are fraught with pain, and man is burdened by fear and woe. Thus we express our feelings that they may be known to the world."
(Taken from Vietnam, *S Karnow.)*

Ho Quyen (Amphitheatre) lies about 4 km upstream of Hué on the south bank of the Perfume River. It was built in 1830 by Emperor Minh Mang as a venue for the popular duels between elephants and tigers. This royal sport was in earlier centuries staged on an island in the Perfume River or on the river banks, but by 1830 it was considered desirable for the royal party to be able to observe the duels without placing themselves at risk from escaping tigers. The amphitheatre is said to have been last used in 1904 when, as was usual, the elephant emerged victorious: "The elephant rushed ahead and pressed the tiger to the wall with all the force he could gain. Then he raised his head, threw the enemy to the ground and smashed him to death," wrote Crosbie Garstin, in *The Voyage from London to Indochina*. The walls of the amphitheatre are 5 m high and the arena is 44 m in diameter. At the south side, beneath the royal box, is one large gateway (for the elephant) and, to the north, five smaller entrances for the tigers. The walls are in good condition and the centre is filled either with grass or immaculately tended rows of vegetables, depending on the season.

Ho Quyen

The Central Region

Den Voi Re, the Temple of the Elephant Trumpet, dedicated to the call of the fighting elephant, is a few hundred metres away. It is a modest little place with a pond in front and contains two small elephant statues. Presumably this is where elephants were blessed before battle or perhaps where the unsuccessful ones were mourned. ■ *Getting there: by bicycle or motorbike; about 3 km west of Hué railway station on Bui Thi Xuan Street. Turn left up a paved track opposite 203 Bui Thi Xuan St. The track for the Elephant Temple runs in front of the amphitheatre.*

Thanh Toan Covered Bridge is 8 km west of Hué. Built in the reign of King Le Hien Tong (1740-86) by Tran Thi Dao, a childless woman as an act of charity hoping that God would bless her with a baby. The bridge, with its shelter for the tired and homeless, attracted the interest of several kings who granted the village immunity from a number of taxes. The original yin-yang tiles have been replaced with ugly green enamelled tube tiles, unfortunately, but the structure is still in good condition.

Thanh Toan Bridge

Thuan An town and beach is 13 km to the northeast of Hué. Six kilometres in length, it offers swimming in both a protected lagoon (into which flows the Perfume River) and in the South China Sea. The beach is nothing special,

Thuan An Beach

The funeral of a King

On 6 November 1925, Dai-Hanh-Hoang-Khai-Dinh, King of Annam, 'mounted the dragon's back,' or, to put it briefly, died. Seven diamonds were put in the mouth of the corpse, which was washed, embalmed, dressed in state robes, placed in a huge red and gold lacquer coffin and covered over with young tea-leaves. Ten days later official mourning was inaugurated with the sacrifice of a bullock, a goat and a pig. A portrait of the late monarch, painted on silk, was placed on the throne. Paper invocations were burnt, massed lamentations rent the air four times daily for 60 days.

All Annam was in Hué, dressed in its best and brightest. Sampans swarmed about the bridge, packed with expectant people. Gay shrines lined the way, hung with flowers and paper streamers. Bunting, citron and scarlet, fluttered in the breeze. Route-keepers in green and red held the crowds in check, chasing small boys out of the way, wacking them over their mushroom hats – chastisement that produced a maximum of noise with a minimum of pain.

At the head of the column were two elephants, hung with tassels and embroidered cloths and topped with crimson howdahs and yellow umbrellas. Never have I seen animals so unutterably bored. They lolled against each other, eyes closed – and slumbered. But for an occasional twitch of an ear or tail they might have been dead. Their boredom was understandable when you came to think of it. An elephant is a long-lived beast. No elephant gets his photograph in the papers on reaching the century: it is far too common an occurrence. These two were full-grown; elderly, even. It is possible that they featured at the obsequies of Thieu-Tri, and there have been innumerable royal funerals since. At one period kings weren't stopping on the throne of Annam long enough to get the cushions warm. What was a very novel and splendid exhibition to me was stale stuff to these beasts.

"All very fine for you, mister", they might have said. "First time and all that. Can drop out and buy yourself a drink any time you like. All very well for you, Henry, in a feather-weight gent's suiting; but what about us, tight-laced front and back with about a ton of passengers, brollies, flags and furniture up top?"

An old bearded mandarin in a gorgeous coat of royal blue struck with a wooden hammer on a silver gong. The procession began to shuffle slowly forward – somebody in front had found means to rouse the elephants, apparently. One-hundred-and-sixty trained porters, clad in black and white, crouched under the red lacquer poles of the giant bier – slips of bamboo had been placed between their teeth to stop them from chattering.

Slowly, steadily, keeping the prescribed horizontal, the huge thing rose. Six tons it weighed and special bridges had to be built to accommodate it. Slowly, steadily it moved towards us, preceded by solemn-stepping heralds in white; flagbearers in sea-green carrying dragon banners of crimson and emerald, blue and gold.

The second day was spent in getting the coffin from Nam-Gio to the mausoleum and was a mere repetition of the first. The actual interment took place on the morning of the third day. In a few minutes the mourners were out in the daylight again and the vault doors were being sealed. The spirit of Khai-Dinh was on its way to the Ten Judgement Halls of the Infernal Regions, to pass before the Mirror of the Past wherein he would see all his deeds reflected, together with their consequences; to drink the Water of Forgetfulness, and pass on through transmigration to transmigration till he attained the Pure Land and a state of blessed nothingness. And Bao-Dai – weeping bitterly, poor little chap – reigned in his stead.

(Adapted from The Voyage from London to Indochina, *Crosbie Garstin*.)

The battle at Khe Sanh (1968)

Khe Sanh (already the site of a bloody confrontation in April and May 1967) is the place where the North Vietnamese Army (NVA) tried to achieve another Dien Bien Phu (see page 361); in other words, an American humiliation. One of the NVA divisions, the 304th, even had Dien Bien Phu emblazoned on its battle streamers. Westmoreland would have nothing of it, and prepared for massive confrontation. He hoped to bury Ho Chi Minh's troops under tonnes of high explosive and achieve a Dien Bien Phu in reverse. But, the American high command had some warning of the attack: a North Vietnamese regimental commander was killed while he was surveying the base on 2 January and that was interpreted as meaning the NVA were planning a major assault. Special forces long-range patrols were dropped into the area around the base and photo reconnaissance increased. It became clear that 20,000-40,000 NVA troops were converging on Khe Sanh.

With the US Marines effectively surrounded in a place which the assistant commander of the 3rd Marine Division referred to as "not really anywhere", there was a heavy exchange of fire in January 1968. The Marine artillery fired 159,000 shells, B-52s carpet-bombed the surrounding area, obliterating each 'box' with 162 tonnes of bombs. But, despite the haggard faces of the Marines, the attack on Khe Sanh was merely a cover for the Tet offensive – the commanders of the NVA realized there was no chance of repeating their success at Dien Bien Phu against the US military. The Tet offensive proved to be a remarkable psychological victory for the NVA – even if their 77-day seige of Khe Sanh cost many 1,000s (one estimate is 10,000-15,000) of NVA lives, while only 248 Americans were killed (43 of those in a C-123 transporter crash). Again, a problem for the US military was one of presentation. Even Walter Cronkite, the doyen of TV reporters, informed his audience that the parallels between Khe Sanh and Dien Bien Phu were "there for all to see".

The Central Region

however. Accommodation is available at the **C** *Dong Hai Hotel*, T866115. About 1 km from the beach, new and clean. **C-D** *Thuan An Hotel* is 100 m from the beach, dirty and unhelpful. ■ *Getting there: local buses leave for Thuan An from the Dong Ba bus station; boats can be chartered from the dock behind the Dong Ba Market, 1 hr (30,000-40,000d). Alternatively a ½-hr motorbike ride. At the main gate to the beach there is a bicycle park which charges 5,000d for a bicycle.*

The incongruously named Demilitarized Zone (DMZ), scene of some of the fiercest fighting of the Vietnam War, lies along the Ben Hai River and the better-known 17th Parallel. The DMZ was the creation of the 1954 Geneva Peace Accord, which divided the country into two spheres of influence prior to elections that were never held. Like its counterpart in Germany the boundary evolved into a national border separating communist from capitalist, but unlike its European equivalent it was the triumph of communism that saw its demise. A number of wartime sights can be seen on a single, rather gruelling, day's tour from Hué. ■ *Getting there: most visitors visit the sights of the DMZ, including Khe Sanh and the Ho Chi Minh Trail, on a tour. But buses do leave for the town of Khe Sanh from the An Hoa bus station; the site of the US base is 3 km from Khe Sanh bus station. From here it is possible to arrange transport to the Ho Chi Minh Trail and to other sights, but it is probably more trouble than it is worth. A 1-day tour of all the DMZ sights can be booked from a number of Hué hotels. The cost is around US$10; depart 0600, return 1900.*

The Demilitarized Zone (DMZ)

Khe Sanh is the site of one of the most famous battles of the war. The battleground lies along Highway 9 which runs west towards Laos, to the north of Hué, and south of Dong Hoi and is 3 km from the village of the same name. There is not much to see here; it is of most interest to war veterans.

Ho Chi Minh Trail is another popular but inevitably disappointing sight, given that its whole purpose was to be as inconspicuous as possible. Anything you see was designed to be invisible – from the air at least; rather an artificial 'sight' but a worthy pilgrimage considering the sacrifice of millions of Vietnamese porters and the role it played in the American defeat (see box, page 193). A section of the trail runs close to Khe Sanh.

The tunnels of Vinh Moc served a similar function to the better known Cu Chi tunnels. They evolved as families in the heavily bombed village dug themselves shelters beneath their houses and then joined up with their neighbours. Later the tunnels developed a more offensive role when Viet Cong soldiers fought from them. Some visitors regard these tunnels as more 'authentic' than the 'touristy' tunnels of Cu Chi. Offshore is **Con Co Island**, an important supply depot and anti-aircraft stronghold in the war. Life for ordinary peasants in the battle zone just north of the DMZ was terrifying: some idea of conditions (for revolutionary peasants at least) can be gained from the 1970 North Vietnamese film *Vinh Linh Steel Ramparts*. ■ *Getting there: 6 km north of Ben Hai River turn right in Ho Xa village. Vinh Moc is 13 km off Highway 1.*

The Rock Pile is a 230-m-high limestone outcrop just south of the DMZ. It served as a US observation post. An apparently unassailable position, troops, ammunition, Budweiser and prostitutes all had to be helicoptered in. The sheer walls of the Rock Pile were eventually scaled by the Viet Cong. Jon Swain, the war correspondent, describes in his memoirs, *River of Time*, how his helicopter got lost around the Rock Pile and nearly came to disaster in this severely contested zone. The **Hien Luong Bridge** on the 17th parallel which marked the boundary between north and south (see page 176) is included in most tours. As all war paraphernalia has been stripped from the DMZ the visit is more of a 'pilgrimage' than a visual experience. Those who are short of time should visit one or two tombs instead. For details of tours and tour operators see page 198.

Essentials

Sleeping
■ *on maps,*
pages 179 and 195

Most hotels lie to the south of the Perfume River, although there are a couple to the north in the old Vietnamese part of town. Conditions in many hotels have improved and it is pleasing to note the fairly dramatic reduction in prices at many hotels, which have come to realize that they can make money from renting motorbikes and selling tours to their guests.

L-A *Saigon Morin*, 30 Le Loi St, T823526, F825155, sgmorin@dng.vnn.vn Recognizable as the fine hotel originally built by the Morin brothers in the 1880s. Arranged around a courtyard with a small pool, the rooms are large and comfortable. All a/c, satellite TV and hot water. The courtyard, lit with candles, is a delightful place to sit in the evening and enjoy a quiet drink. Despite minor drawbacks (nylon towels, hot-water tank too small to fill a bath etc) the service is friendly and the overall effect most agreeable. Recommended.

A *Huong Giang* (*Perfume River Hotel*), 51 Le Loi St, T822122, F845555, hghotel@dng.vnn.vn Gorgeous position on the river, comfortable rooms - despite the heavy wooden, lacquered 'royal' furniture many Hué hotels do insist on using - and efficient service. Only some rooms (the pricier ones) overlook the river. There's quite a good pool but the top-floor restaurant is for emergencies only. Breakfast included. **A-B** *Century Riverside*, 49 Le Loi St, T823390, F823394, cnhuevn@dng.vnn.vn Fabulous river views and technically satisfactory but service is held to be poor. Tends to be used by less discriminating tour operators. Breakfast included. **A-C** *Le Loi Hué*, 5 Le Loi St, T822155, F828816, 5leloihotel@dng.vnn.vn Large yellow-wash and green-shuttered French villa on the river, expansive rooms and high ceilings mean it is naturally cool and large windows make it bright. Room 15 at the top of the building has the best views in all Hué. It also has a large roof terrace but, like the rest of the hotel, rather shabby furniture. Right by the river, in the rainy season rooms can be dank and chilly. A new wing has recently been opened, bringing the total to 35 rooms.

B *Hoa Hong 2*, 1 Pham Ngu Lao St, T824377, F826949, hoahonghotel@dng.vnn.vn Large and a little impersonal but popular with tour groups, breakfast included. **B-C** *Thuan Hoa*, 7 Nguyen Tri Phuong St, T822553, F822470. Large and not particularly appealing place, restaurant and dancing. **B-D** *Dong Loi*, 19 Pham Ngu Lao St, T822296, F826234, interser@dng.vnn.vn Well situated and surrounded by internet cafés, shops and restaurants, this is a bright, breezy, airy and comfortable hotel, all rooms with a/c and hot water and all except the cheapest rooms have a bathtub. Family run, friendly and helpful service. Has the *Why Not Bar* and *La Carambole Restaurant*. **B-D** *Duy Tan*, 12 Hung Vuong St, T825001, F826477. Large building, spartan rooms, in bustling part of town.

The Central Region

Hue detail

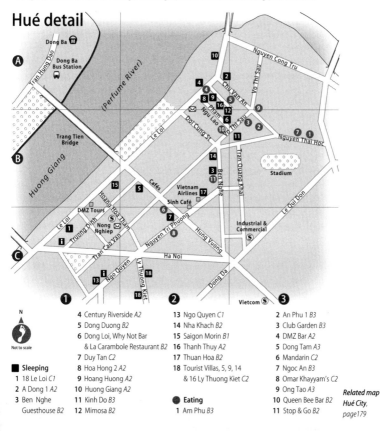

N
Not to scale

■ Sleeping
1 18 Le Loi *C1*
2 A Dong 1 *A2*
3 Ben Nghe
   Guesthouse *B2*

4 Century Riverside *A2*
5 Dong Duong *B2*
6 Dong Loi, Why Not Bar
   & La Carambole Restaurant *B2*
7 Duy Tan *C2*
8 Hoa Hong 2 *A2*
9 Hoang Huong *A2*
10 Huong Giang *A2*
11 Kinh Do *B3*
12 Mimosa *B2*

13 Ngo Quyen *C1*
14 Nha Khach *B2*
15 Saigon Morin *B1*
16 Thanh Thuy *A2*
17 Thuan Hoa *B2*
18 Tourist Villas, 5, 9, 14
   & 16 Ly Thuong Kiet *C2*

● Eating
1 Am Phu *B3*

2 An Phu 1 *B3*
3 Club Garden *B3*
4 DMZ Bar *A2*
5 Dong Tam *A3*
6 Mandarin *C2*
7 Ngoc An *B3*
8 Omar Khayyam's *C2*
9 Ong Tao *A3*
10 Queen Bee Bar *B2*
11 Stop & Go *B2*

Related map
Hué City,
page179

C *Kinh Do*, 1 Nguyen Thai Hoc St, T823566, F821190. Architecturally unattractive and smallish rooms – 50 in total – but comfortable and quiet with friendly staff. **C** *Ngo Quyen*, 9 Ngo Quyen St, T823278, F828372, nqhotel@yahoo.com Cheaper rooms have fan and shared bathroom, better rooms have a/c, bathtub and hot water, breakfast included, quite good value. **C-D** *A Dong 1*, 1 bis Chu Van An St, T824148, F849419, adongcoltd@dng.vnn.vn 7 rooms in this friendly hotel, a/c, fridge and bathtub; an attractive upstairs terrace. **C-D** *Dong Duong*, 2 Hung Vuong St, T823866, F825910, indochinahotel@dng.vnn.vn Priciest rooms in the old villa in front, the building behind is modern and sterile, cheapest rooms around the back. Indochina restaurant. **C-D** *Le Loi Hué*, 2 Le Loi St, T822153, F824527, leloihotel@dng.vnn.vn Not far from the station, consists of 6 blocks of differing comfort, some a/c, clean, hot-water showers, good value. **C-D** *Thanh Loi*, 7 Dinh Tien Hoang St, T524803, F525344. North of the river, almost opposite Lac Thien Restaurant, newish building, rather flimsy fittings, a bit run down. **C-D** *Tourist Villa*, 14 Ly Thuong Kiet St, T825461. Unsigned. Privately run, 4 spacious rooms, lovely garden, good breakfast (not included). **C-D** *Tourist villas* on Ly Thuong Kiet St, T823945, F825814, huetc@dng.vnn.vn Run by *Hué Tourist*. All a little shabby, but have atmosphere, a/c, hot water and include breakfast in the price. *No 5*, 5 Ly Thuong Kiet St. Nice colonial façade, one room has a lovely balcony. *No 9*, 9 Ly Thuong Kiet St. Large and small rooms (all the same price), curtains consist of nylon sheets pocked with cigarette burns. *No 16*, 16 Ly Thuong Kiet St. Several large rooms, friendly.

D *18 Le Loi*, 18 Le Loi St, T823720, F825814. Nice position not far from the river, 10 rooms, avoid downstairs and try the larger airy 1st floor rooms, all a/c, hot water. Bicycles for rent.

E *Ben Nghe Guesthouse*, 4 Ben Nghe St, T889106. Some quite comfortable rooms, 14 in all, fan and a/c, offering good value. Attached is the *Stop and Go Café*. **E** *Nha Khach*, 2 Ben Nghe St, T889158. Externally an attractive French building but sadly the insides have been allowed to run down. No English spoken.

The little *hem* (alley) opposite the *Century Riverside* has some really nice rooms in comfortable and cheerful guesthouses in what is easily the best value accommodation in Hué. Particularly recommended are: **D** *Mimosa*, 46/6 Le Loi St, T828068, F823858. 6 rooms, a/c, hot water, bathtub, quiet, simple and clean, French spoken. **D-E** *Hoang Huong*, 46/2 Le Loi St, T828509. Some a/c, cheaper room with fan, friendly and helpful family guesthouse. **D-E** *Thanh Thuy*, 46/4 Le Loi St, T824585. Another small, peaceful, clean and friendly family-run guesthouse, with only 4 rooms, a/c and hot water. Can arrange car hire at good rates.

Eating
● on map, page 179
Hué specialities are excellent and although a few years ago they were quite hard to obtain in Hué the situation has improved greatly. The influence of the royal court on Hué cuisine is evident in a number of ways: there are a large number of dishes served – it tends to be 'nibble' food – each dish being relatively light. Hué food is delicately flavoured and requires painstaking preparation in the kitchen: in short, a veritable culinary harem in which even the most pampered and surfeited king could find something to tickle his palate. Other Hué dishes are more robust, notably the famed *bun bo Hué*, round white noodles in soup with slices of beef and laced with chilli oil of exquisite piquancy.

Among the hotels the **Saigon Morin** does excellent barbecues for around US$5 a plate in a lovely garden setting. *Am Phu* (*Hell*), 35 Nguyen Thai Hoc St. Do not confuse with An Phu – we'd suggest you spell it for your *cyclo* driver rather than rely on your Vietnamese pronunciation. Excellent Vietnamese dishes in this spit-and-sawdust type eatery. Popular with locals which is always a good sign, two will dine and drink for less than US$5. *An Dinh Palace*, 97 Phan Dinh Phung St (Front Gate) or 78A Nguyen Hue St (Back Gate), T833019. This place is a bit like a garden hut. Being set in the grounds of a minor palace is not really sufficient justification but those who have eaten here say it is quite good. Come to look at the lovely palace in daytime. *An Phu 1*, 18 Chu Van An St. Slightly more polished and therefore favoured by cautious tour leaders. Decent enough food, Western and local, but lots of pestering kids selling postcards. *Café No.3*, 3 Le Loi St. Near the train station and opposite *Le Loi Hué Hotel*, a cheap and popular café serving standard Vietnamese, Western and vegetarian food, useful source of information, bikes for rent. *Club Garden*, 12 Vo Thi Sau St, T826327. A relaxed and attractive setting, Vietnamese and fairly ambitious Western menu, the food is alright.

Dong Tam, 48/7 Le Loi St, T828403. Tucked away in the little *hem* opposite *Century Riverside* this is Hué's vegetarian restaurant. Sit in a pleasant and quiet little yard surrounded by plants and topiary while choosing from the very reasonably priced menu. Its credentials are reflected in its popularity with the city's monkish population. *Huong Giang* sometimes offers special Hué banquets but these are normally for large groups and tours only. *Lac Thien* and *Lac Than*, 6 Dinh Tien Hoang St. Arguably Hué's most famous restaurants. Run by schismatic branches of the same deaf-mute family in adjacent buildings. You go to one or the other: under no circumstances should clients patronize both establishments. 12 years ago providence took us to *Lac Thien* which serves excellent dishes from a diverse and inexpensive menu, its Huda beers are long and cold, the family is riotous and entertaining and we have never looked back. (Recently one of the daughters set up the *Lac Thien Restaurant* in Saigon.) Similar reports have been heard about *Lac Thien* next door but it's not possible to believe it's as good. *Mandarin*, 12 Hung Vuong St, T821281. Backpacker food at its worst. Everything comes swimming in its own little pond of liquid or grease. Fly-blown grunge, but nevertheless popular. Travel services and bike rental. *Ngoc An*, 29 Nguyen Thai Hoc St. Yet another fine diner in this end of town. Some Western, but Vietnamese dishes are what it's best at. Cheap and cheerful.

Omar Khayyam's or *Nha Hang An Do*, 10 Nguyen Tri Phuong St, T821616. Hué's Indian restaurant. Pretty authentic tandoor dishes and curries. Decent portions. *Ong Tao*, 96 Chu Van An St. A not particularly atmospheric restaurant located in the eating quarter, but serves excellent Vietnamese dishes at very fair prices. *Quoc Huy*, 43 Dinh Cung Trang. Not far from the Northeast Gate of the Imperial Palace this is an ideal place for lunch after a morning's royal sight-seeing, well prepared food at fair prices. *Stop and Go*, 4 Ben Nghe St, T889106. Travel café run by the silver haired Mr Do. His specialities include rice pancakes and the Hué version of spring rolls which are excellent and cheap.

Cafés   There are plenty on Hung Vuong St opposite *Dong Duong Hotel*, all pretty much alike in serving excellent snacks, fried noodles and breakfasts etc at low prices.

DMZ Bar, 44 Le Loi St, T822585. Hué's first bar, cold beer and spirits at affordable prices   **Bars** and budget travellers around a pool table. *Queen Bee*, 21 Vo Thi Sau St. Slightly arty café bar, just in the process of opening so it remains to be seen how popular it will be.

The old open-air water-puppet theatre, which local people used to love, has been   **Entertainment** demolished and replaced with a 'Festival' tourist complex geared to tour groups and not to locals, which makes it all rather a tourist gimmick rather than a genuine cultural experience. It's at 11 Le Loi St, on the river bank near the Trang Tien Bridge. Otherwise rent a dragon boat and sail up the Perfume River with your own private singers and musicians. Tour offices and major hotels will arrange groups.

The Central Region

Shopping There is a much wider range of goods on sale in Hué now than was the case in the past, no longer just the *Non bai tho* or poem hats. These are a form of the standard conical hat, *Non Lá*, which are peculiar to Hué. Made from bamboo and palm leaves, love poetry, songs, proverbs or simply a design are stencilled on to them, which are only visible if the hat is held up to the light and viewed from the inside. Shops around the Huong Giang Hotel, for example Le Loi and Pham Ngu Lao streets, sell ceramics, silk and clothes. There are a number of new art galleries. Perfectly decent stuff but not the range of Hoi An where visitors are advised to shop. No Vietnamese visitor would shake the dust of Hué off his feet without having previously stocked up on *me xung*, a sugary, peanut and toffee confection coated in sesame seeds: quite a pleasant energy booster to carry while cycling around the tombs, and with the significant advantage over Mars Bars, that while it may pull your teeth out it won't melt in your pocket.

Tour operators The more expensive hotels organize bus and boat tours to the **Imperial Tombs**. It is also possible to charter boats to the tombs (the most romantic way to visit them) and to **Thuan An Beach** (see page 191). Local tour operators charge around US$3 per person to visit Linh Mu Pagoda, Tu Duc, Minh Mang and Khai Dinh's Tombs, departing at 0800, returning 1500. Boats are available on the stretch of river bank between the *Huong Giang Hotel* and the Trang Tien Bridge, and also from the dock behind the Dong Ba Market. From Hué, there are also tours organized to some of the **sights of the Vietnam War**. Tour operators (see below) charge around US$10 for a day's programme, taking in nine sights including Vinh Moc tunnels and museum, the Ho Chi Minh Trail and Khe Sanh, depart 0600, return 2000. Those wishing to travel overland to Laos can arrange to be dropped off in Khe Sanh and pay less.

New provincial hostilities are reportedly hotting up in the DMZ as Quang Tri Province, in which the DMZ lies, and which technically has jurisdiction over the DMZ sights, is losing out from the tourist trade. Tours begin in Hué, Thua Thien-Hué Province, so it is the tour operators from here that gain all the benefit.

Café no 3, 3 Le Loi St. Provides a small range of tours at competitive prices. *DMZ Tours*, 26 Le Loi St, T825242, F824806. They know the area well and run tours of the DMZ (all-day tour, around US$10), boat trips on the river to see the tombs and temples, and sell tickets to onward destinations like Danang, Hoi An, Saigon etc. *Hué City Tourism*, 1 Truong Dinh St, T823577. *Le Van Tam*, 126 Phan Chu Trinh St, T826848. Rents out cars at reasonable prices (US$26-30 to Hoi An). *Sinh*, 7 Nguyen Tri Phuong St, T845022, sinh5hue@dng.vnn.vn Offers a very similar package at matching prices. *Thua-Thien Hue Tourism*, 9 Ngo Quyen St, T823288. Neither is very helpful from the information and map perspective but can arrange tours, the latter to other parts of the province too.

Transport **Local** Bicycles and motorbikes can be hired from most hotels, guesthouses and cafés or from the men who hang around outside the *Huong Giang Hotel*; bicycles are about a dollar a day, motorbikes around US$6 per day. **Boat hire** Boats can be hired through tour agents, from outside the Huong Giang Hotel and from any berth on the south bank of the river, east of Trang Tien Bridge. Good for either a gentle cruise, with singers in the evening, or an attractive way of getting to some of the temples and mausoleums. *Cyclo* and *xe ôm* are available everywhere. The latter is the speedier way to see the temples as the terrain south of town is quite hilly. *Cyclos* are fine for visiting the more central attractions. **Taxi** *Hué Taxi* T833333; *Thanh Do Taxi*, T858585; *Gili Taxi*, T828282; *Mai Linh Taxi*, T898989.

Air Phu Bai Airport is a 40-min drive south of Hué - *Vietnam Airlines* run a bus service in to town which costs 25,000d or you can take a taxi for 90,000d. There are two connections daily with Hanoi (70-105 mins, depending on aircraft type) and two with Saigon

(90-120 mins). A new Daewoo bus ferries passengers the whole 30 m from the aeroplane to the airport terminal – presumably a Korean aid project. This is kinder than it sounds as descending out of the cloudy murk the pilot usually only sees the runway at rooftop altitude. Phu Bai airport has no landing aids whatsoever. Interestingly, when the old but perfectly sound landing system from Hanoi's recently upgraded Noi Bai airport was offered to them the authorities here refused it fearful, perhaps, of losing out on any 'benefits' they might have received had they bought a brand-new system.

Road Bus: The An Cuu station at 43 Hung Vuong St serves destinations south of Hué. The An Hoa station up at the northwest corner of the citadel serves destinations north of Hué. The Dong Ba station serves local villages and Thuan An Beach. **Minibus** These can be booked to major destinations from hotels or from most of the agencies listed above.

Train The station is at the west end of Le Loi St, and serves all stations south to Saigon and north to Hanoi. Advance booking, especially for sleepers, is essential. The 4-hr journey to **Danang** is especially recommended for its scenic views.

Airline offices *Vietnam Airlines* (in the *Thuan Hoa Hotel*), 7 Nguyen Tri Phuong St, **Directory** T/F8824709. **Banks** *Industrial & Commercial Bank*, 2A Le Quy Don St. 0700-1130 and 1330-1700, closed Thu afternoon. *Vietcom Bank*, 78 Huong Vuong St. *Nong Nghiep Bank*, 10 Hoang Hoa Tham St. The post office (see below) also changes money. **Communications** Internet: given its well-educated population Hué has probably the highest rate of internet users, per capita, in the country. Access to the internet is via the portal in Danang so charges are not the lowest, but at around 200d per min, is still very cheap. There are internet cafés everywhere and most hotels listed here offer internet services. Pham Ngu Lao and Doi Cung streets each have several internet cafés. **Post office**: 8 Hoang Hoa Tham St. Open 0630-2100. International telephone and fax, poste restante and money changing facilities. **Medical services** Hué **General Hospital**, 16 Le Loi St, T822325.

Bach Ma National Park and Hill Station

The French established a great many hill stations in Vietnam. Dalat was the only one to really develop as a town. Others, like Sapa, were rejuvenated a few years ago and yet others, like Bach Ma, had been forgotten about until very recently. Only now are the ruins of villas being uncovered, flights of steps unearthed and old gardens and ponds cleared. Bach Ma was established as a hill station in 1932 when the construction of a road made it accessible. By the outbreak of the Second World War there were 139 villas and a hotel. Recognising its natural beauty and biological diversity the French gave it protected status. In 1991 the Vietnamese government classified it as a National Park with 22,031 ha at its core and a further buffer zone of 21,300 ha. The area is rugged granite overlain in places by sandstone rising to an altitude of 1448 m at the summit of Bach Ma. There are a number of trails past cascades, through rhododendron woods and up the summit trail overlooking the remains of colonial villas.

The mammal species of the park have yet to be comprehensively surveyed and so far only 48 species of mammal have been confirmed. Included in this figure, however, are some species of special interest such as the red-shanked douc langur and the buff-cheeked or white-cheeked gibbon.

Birdlife here is particularly interesting. Four restricted range species are the Annam partridge, crested argus, short-tailed scimitar babbler and the grey-faced tit babbler. The most characteristic feature of Bach Ma's birdlife is the large number of pheasants. Of the twelve species of pheasant recorded in Vietnam, seven have been seen in the park. A subspecies of the silver pheasant lives in the park and Edwards' pheasant, believed extinct until it was rediscovered in 1996, was seen just outside the park buffer zone in 1998. There are many other species of interest including the red-collared woodpecker, Blyth's Kingfisher and the coral-billed ground cuckoo. ■ *National park entry 10,500d. Best time to visit: climatically it is at least 7°C colder than the coastal plain and annual rainfall of 8,000mm falls mainly Sep–Jan which is when the leeches are most active. It is busiest on summer weekends, and Mar and Apr are particularly worthwhile for the rhododendron blossom.*

Sleeping There are three guesthouses, one near the park gate (**D-E**) and the other two near the summit (**C-D**). Near the gate there is some a/c, near the summit it tends to be fireplaces. T054 871330, F054 871329, www.bachma.vnn.vn

Transport Using your own transport go south down Highway 1 from Hué. Turn off at the small
45 km from Hué town of Cau Hai. From here it is about 3 km to the park entrance. About 4 km off High-
65 from Danang way 1 is the National Park office. Visitors must report here. A variety of cars and mini-buses are available from here for around US$20 per tour.

Hué to Danang

Between Hué and Danang a finger of the Truong Son Mountains juts eastwards, extending all the way to the sea: almost as though God were somewhat roguishly trying to divide the country into two equal halves. This barrier to north-south communication has resulted in some spectacular engineering solutions: the railway line closely follows the coastline (fortunately it is single track and narrow gauge) sometimes almost hanging over the sea – while Highway 1 winds its way equally precariously over the Hai Van Pass. The road is littered with broken-down trucks and buses for whom the long haul up to the summit is just too much: drivers seem to spend more time on their backs under their vehicles than they do behind the steering wheel. Work has begun on a tunnel through the mountains which should improve the chances of elderly vehicles reaching their destination.

The difficult terrain means that much remains wooded, partly because the trees are too inaccessible to cut down and partly because of government edicts preventing the clearance of steep slopes. The hilly woodlands of **Bach Ma National Park** stretch from the Lao border right down to the coast and although little is virgin forest quite a lot of bird and animal life flourishes within its leafy branches (see page 199).

Lang Co The road passes through many pretty, red-tiled villages, compact and surrounded by clumps of bamboo and fruit trees which provide shade, shelter and sustenance. And, for colour, there's the bougainvillea – which through grafting produces pink and white leaves on the same branch. Windowless jalopies from the French era trundle along picking up passengers and their bundles while station wagons from the American era provide an inter-village shared taxi service. Just north of Hai Van Pass lies the idyllic fishing village of **Lang Co** (about 65 km south of Hué), which has a number of cheap and good seafood restaurants along the road. Shortly after crossing the Lang Co lagoon, dotted with coracles and fish traps, the road begins the long haul up to Hai Van Pass.

Apparently, in the first year of his reign Emperor Khai Dinh visited Lang Co and was so impressed that he ordered the construction of a summer

By train from Hué to Danang

The train journey from Hué to Danang is regarded as not just one of the most scenic in Vietnam, but in the world. Paul Theroux in his book The Great Railway Bazaar *recounts his impressions as the train reached the narrow coastal strip, south of Hué and approaching Danang.*
"The drizzle, so interminable in the former Royal Capital, gave way to bright sunshine and warmth; 'I had no idea,' I said. Of all the places the railway had taken me since London, this was the loveliest. We were at the fringes of a bay that was green and sparkling in bright sunlight. Beyond the leaping jade plates of the sea was an *overhang of cliffs and the sight of a valley so large it contained sun, smoke, rain, and cloud – all at once – independent quantities of colour. I had been unprepared for this beauty; it surprised and humbled me ... Who has mentioned the simple fact that the heights of Vietnam are places of unimaginable grandeur? Though we can hardly blame a frightened draftee for not noticing this magnificence, we should have known all along that the French would not have colonized it, nor would the Americans have fought so long, if such ripeness did not invite the eye to take it."*
(Penguin, London, 1977)

palace. This, it seems, was never carried out not even by his son Bao Dai who was so fond of building palaces. Unfortunately the Huong Giang Tourist Company has taken this noble task upon itself and built the *Lang Co Beach Resort* in heavy Hué style complete with imitation dynastic urns and other tat. The whole place is crass and insensitive not to say a colossal and tragic waste of public funds and unspoilt beach. At prices of up to US$200 per night no one stays here and despite the charm of the hapless staff, it seems unlikely they ever will.

If you want to stay overnight there are a couple of options. **L** *Lang Co Beach Resort*, T054-873555, F873504, langco@dng.vnn.vn Pool, restaurant and bar. All rooms have a/c. **D** *Lang Co Hotel*, T054-874426, has a few simple rooms at the top of the dunes looking down to the sea, some a/c and hot water, some fan and cold water (and that sporadically) only. The beach here is wide, clean and usually deserted, but somewhat spoilt by the high voltage power lines which run its length.

Hai Van Pass (Deo Hai Van) 'Pass of the Ocean Clouds' or, to the French, Col **Hai Van Pass** des Nuages lies 497 m above the dancing white waves that can be seen at its foot. In historic times the pass marked the border between the kingdoms of Vietnam and Champa. The mountains also act as an important climatic barrier trapping the cooler, damper air-masses to the north and bottling it up over Hué, which accounts for Hué's shocking weather. They also mark an abrupt linguistic divide, with the Hué dialect (the language of the royal court) to the north the source of bemusement to many southerners.

The pass is peppered with abandoned pillboxes and crowned with an old fort, originally built by the dynasty from Hué and used as a relay station for the pony express on the old Mandarin Road. Subsequently used by the French, today it is a pretty shabby affair collecting wind-blown litter and sometimes used by the People's Army for a quiet brew-up and a smoke. Looking back to the north, stretching into the haze is the littoral and lagoon of Lang Co. To the south is Danang Bay and Monkey Mountain, and at your feet lies a patch of green paddies which belong to the leper colony, accessible only by boat. Hai Van Pass will not detain anyone long, unless their engine has blown up, the litter and vendors will see to that.

Highway 1 passes through the village of **Nam O**, once famous for firework manufacture. Pages of old school books were once dyed pink, laid out in the sun to dry, rolled up and filled with gunpowder. But, alas, no more. Like other pyrotechnical villages, Nam O has suffered from the government's ban on firecrackers. Just south of Nam O is **Xuan Thieu Beach**, dubbed 'Red Beach II' by US Marines who landed here in March 1965, marking the beginning of direct intervention by the US in the Second Indochina War. The tarmac and concrete foundations of the military base still remain.

Danang

Phone code: 0511
Colour map 3, grid A5

Danang is yet another name to conjure with. It is a city with a history. Originally Danang was known as Cua Han ('Mouth of the Han River'). When the French took control they renamed it Tourane, a rough transliteration of Cua Han. Then it acquired the title Thai Phien, and finally Danang. The city is sited on a peninsula of land at the point where the Han River flows into the South China Sea. An important port from French times, Danang gained world-wide renown when two US Marine battalions landed here in March 1965 to secure the airfield. They were the first of a great many more who would land on the beaches and airfields of South Vietnam.

Today it is Vietnam's third-largest port and a commercial and trading centre of growing importance. The city has a frenetic buzz but no real charm and no sense of permanence. Only a few French buildings survive, along near the river. Few cities in the world, however, have such spectacular beaches on their doorstep let alone three (including Hué) UNESCO World Heritage sites within a short drive.

Ins and outs

Getting there
See Transport, page 211, for further details

The airport is on the edge of the city. There are three connections each week with Bangkok and daily connections with Hanoi and Saigon and less regularly with Buon Ma Thuot, Dalat, Pleiku and Nha Trang. A taxi into town is US$2 and takes 5-10 mins. Danang is on the north-south railway line linking Hanoi and Saigon and there are also regular bus and minibus connections with all major cities in the south as far as Saigon, and in the north as far as Hanoi. The border with Laos at Lao Bao is open to foreign travellers and daily buses leave Danang for the Lao town of Savannakhet, on the Mekong. Visas are available from the Lao consulate in Danang.

Getting around
Danang is a sizeable town – rather too large to explore on foot – and there is abundant public transport including *cyclos*, taxis and *Honda ôm*. Bicycles and motorbikes are available for hire from most hotels and guesthouses.

Background

Danang lies in a region of great historical significance. Fairly close to the city – but often not particularly easy to reach – lie ruins of the powerful kingdom of Champa, one of the most glorious in ancient Southeast Asia (see page 354). The Cham were probably of Indonesian descent, and Chinese texts give the date AD 192 as the year when a group of tribes formed a union known as Lin-Yi, later to become Champa. The polytheistic religion of Champa was a fusion of Buddhism, Sivaism and local elements – and later Islam – producing an abundance of religious (and secular) sculptures and monuments. The goddess Uroja is of central importance; the 'mother' of the nation, she is normally represented as a breast and nipple. Siva is represented as a linga (see Glossary, page 435). The kingdom reached its apogee in the 10th and 11th centuries but, unlike the Khmers, Champa never had the opportunity to create a capital city matching the magnificence of Angkor. For long periods the Cham were compelled to pay tribute to the Chinese, and after that they were dominated in turn by the Javanese, Annamese (the Vietnamese) and then the Khmers. The Cham nation was finally eradicated in 1471, although there are still an estimated 90,000 Cham living in central Vietnam (mostly Brahmanists and Muslims). Given this turbulent history, it is perhaps surprising that the

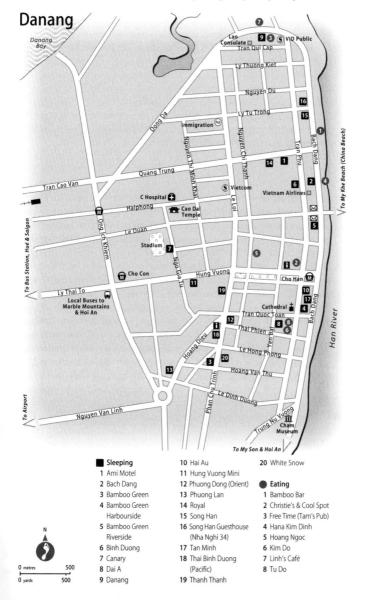

Danang

The Central Region

Sleeping		
Sleeping	10 Hai Au	20 White Snow
1 Ami Motel	11 Hung Vuong Mini	
2 Bach Dang	12 Phuong Dong (Orient)	● **Eating**
3 Bamboo Green	13 Phuong Lan	1 Bamboo Bar
4 Bamboo Green	14 Royal	2 Christie's & Cool Spot
Harbourside	15 Song Han	3 Free Time (Tam's Pub)
5 Bamboo Green	16 Song Han Guesthouse	4 Hana Kim Dinh
Riverside	(Nha Nghi 34)	5 Hoang Ngoc
6 Binh Duong	17 Tan Minh	6 Kim Do
7 Canary	18 Thai Binh Duong	7 Linh's Café
8 Dai A	(Pacific)	8 Tu Do
9 Danang	19 Thanh Thanh	

Cham found any opportunity for artistic endeavours. It should perhaps be added that since the demise of the kingdom, the number of Cham sculptures has grown enormously as forgers have carved more of these beautiful images.

Danang today has a population of 700,000, making it the fourth largest city in Vietnam. Its position, roughly equidistant between Hanoi and Saigon, gives Danang strategic significance. Danang Bay is a marvellous natural harbour and the port is the third busiest in the country after Saigon and Haiphong. Danang represents modern Vietnam and is a pointer to the way many of Vietnam's towns will look in not so many years to come. Its transformation in the past 10 years has been quite remarkable. It has undergone a whirlwind-like period of growth and continues to expand at a phenomenal rate. The city is ringed by huge dual carriageways and new roads have been driven out into the empty spaces beyond. Within months of the new roads' arrival they are fleshed out with factories, shops and houses. The new River Han Bridge has opened up the Son Tra peninsula for commercial development, which has added a major new dimension to Danang's expansion. The Han River is large enough to take passenger cruise liners which are arriving in greater numbers. Danang and its region need sensitive development from a far-sighted and disciplined authority if both its commercial and tourist potential is to be realized. Currently commercial interests are dominant and risk swamping irreplacable tourist attractions.

Sights

Cham Museum The Cham Museum is at the intersection of Trung Nu Vuong and Bach Dang streets. It was established by academics of the École française d'Extrême Orient, and contains the largest display of Cham art anywhere in the world (see page 403 and Excursions, to My Son). The museum buildings alone are worth the visit: constructed in 1916 in a beautiful setting, the complex is open-plan in design, providing an environment in which the pieces can be exhibited to their best advantage. There are a number of rooms each dedicated to work from a different part of Champa, Tra Kieu, My Son and Dong Duong. Because different parts of Champa flowered artistically at different times from the fourth to the fourteenth centuries the rooms show the evolution of Cham art and prevailing outside influences from Cambodia to Java. The Cham were polytheistic, they worshipped many gods. Uroja was the mother goddess and was regarded as mother of the nation. She was represented as a breast and the perfectly rounded female breast and nipple adorn many sculptures in the museum. Hindu gods were important in Cham religion although Buddhism flourished at certain periods of Champa's history.

Tra Kieu was the earliest Cham capital sacked by the Chinese in the fifth century. Some 40 km southwest of Danang little remains today but the pieces on display at the museum testify to a lively and creative civilization. An altar is inscribed with scenes from the wedding story of Sita and Rama from the Ramayana, a Hindu epic. There are plenty of pieces from My Son which illustrate the Hindu trinity, Brahma the Creator, Vishnu the Preserver and Siva the Destroyer. Ganesh, the elephant headed son of Siva, was a much-loved god and is well represented here. At the end of the ninth century Dong Duong replaced My Son as the centre of Cham art. It was at this time that Buddhism became the dominant religion of court although it never fully replaced Hinduism. The Dong Duong room of the museum is illustrated with scenes from the life of Buddha. From this period faces become less stylistic and more human and the bodies of the figures more graceful and flowing. The subsequent period of Cham art is known as the late Tra Kieu style and dates from the late 10th century. In this section of the museum there are apsaras, celestial dancing maidens whose fluid and animated forms are exquisitely captured in stone. Thereafter Cham sculpture went into artistic decline. Sculptors appeared to lose their flair and artistic creativity and later works were often derivative and conservative. One problem with the display is the lack of any background information. The museum booklet (10,000d) has been written as an art history, not as a guide to the collection, and is of little help. The pieces are wonderful, but the visitor may leave the museum rather befuddled by the display. ■ *Daily 0700-1800.*

Danang's **Cao Dai Temple** is at 35 Haiphong Street and is the second-largest temple in Vietnam. The priest here is particularly friendly and informative – especially regarding Cao Dai-ism and its links with other religions. Services are held at 0600, 1200, 1800 and 2400 (see also page 419). **Danang Cathedral**, single-spired with a sugary-pink-coloured wash and built in 1923, can be found at 156 Tran Phu Street. The stained-glass windows were made in Grenoble, in 1927, by Louis Balmet who was also responsible for the windows of Dalat Cathedral (see page 250). The city has a fair array of markets. There is a covered **general market** (**Cho Han**) in a new building at the intersection of Tran Phu and Hung Vuong streets. Another market, **Cho Con**, is at the intersection of Hung Vuong and Ong Ich Khiem streets. The stalls close by sell basketwork and other handicrafts. On Haiphong Street, running east from the railway station, there is a **street market** selling fresh produce.

Excursions

Once a fabled resort celebrated in rock songs, China Beach is now a quiet seashore, with souvenir and food stalls. Of course, it retains the white sand and surf that brought it such popularity with American soldiers. At times too, there is a strong and dangerous cross-current and undertow. China Beach was the GI name for this US military R & R retreat during the Vietnam War. Since 1975 it has been called T20 Beach. T20 was the military code by which the North Vietnamese Army referred to the beach and still today the whole area and the hotels (like much of Danang) belongs to the Vietnamese Army. The local Vietnamese name is My Khe. My Khe is a real 'undiscovered', and certainly undeveloped, asset despite being only 20 minutes from the centre of Danang. It has the potential to transform Danang into the Río de Janeiro of Asia. Miles and miles of fine white sand, clean water and a glorious setting - the hills of Monkey Mountain to the north and the Marble Mountains clearly visible to the south. There is a merciful absence of vendors, no litter and a number of excellent seafood restaurants.

China Beach (My Khe Beach)

Currently there are only two hotels but others will surely follow. **B** *Tourane*, T932666, F844328, touranehotel@dng.vnn.vn A new 'resort' type hotel with accommodation in not unattractive villa-type blocks. 30 rooms all with a/c and hot water. **C-D** *My Khe Beach*, T836125, F836123. Accommodation here is in rather austere looking blocks set among the sea pines. All a/c and hot water and price includes breakfast. *Conroy's Bar* is on the ground floor of the block nearest the sea. The many restaurants are virtually indistinguishable and it is impossible to single any one out for special mention. They all have excellent fish, prawn, crab, clams and cuttlefish, grilled, fried or steamed. Two can eat well for US$7-10 including local beers. The one restaurant that differs from this formula is the *My Khe Restaurant* or *Conroy's Pub*, T847067, which, besides its seafood, serves the city's expats

The Central Region

with sandwiches, hamburgers and cold beer. ■ *Getting there: with the opening of the new River Han Bridge, My Khe Beach is just a short ride from the centre of Danang. Bicycle or motorbike (15-20 mins) across the bridge, turn right then take the first big turning on the left which is Nguyen Cong Tru St. Go straight to the end.*

Bac My An Beach Two kilometres south of China Beach and 8 km from the centre of Danang is Bac My An Beach, next to the *Furama Resort*. This is a clean and attractive beach with some seafood stalls. Most visitors here go direct from the airport to the *Furama Resort*. **LL-L** *Furama Resort*, 68 Ho Xuan Huong St, T847333, F847666, furamadn@hn.vnn.vn Has 200 rooms and suites beautifully designed and furnished. Cool and comfortable and with a private beach. Watersports facilities, mountain biking, pool and tennis. Surprisingly the price does not include breakfast.

Marble Mountains Marble Mountains (or Ngu Hanh Son) overlook the city of Danang and its airfield, about 12 km to the west. The name was given to these five peaks by the

Around Danang

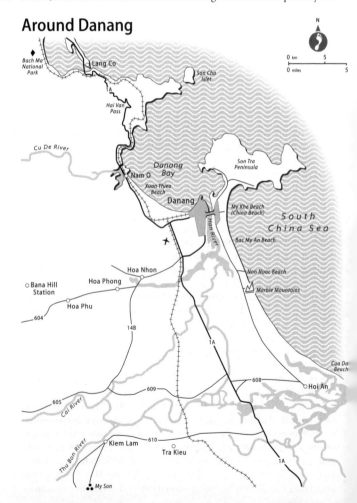

Nguyen Emperor Minh Mang on his visit in 1825 – although they are in fact limestone crags with marble outcrops. They are also known as the mountains of the five elements (fire, water, soil, wood and metal). An important religious spot for the Cham, the peaks became havens for communist guerrillas during the war owing to their commanding view over Danang airbase. From here, a force with sufficient firepower could control much of what went on below, and the guerrillas harried the Americans incessantly. The views from the mountain sides, overlooking Danang Bay, are impressive. On the Marble Mountains are a number of important sights, often associated with caves and grottos formed by chemical action on the limestone rock.

At the foot of the mountains is a village with a number of shops selling marble carvings. Of the mountains, the most visited is **Thuy Son**. There are several grottos and cave pagodas in the mountain which are marked by steps cut into the rock. The **Tam Thai Pagoda**, reached by a staircase cut into the mountain, is on the site of a much older Cham place of worship. Constructed in 1825 by Minh Mang, and subsequently rebuilt, the central statue is of the Buddha Sakyamuni (the historic Buddha) flanked by the Bodhisattva Quan Am (a future Buddha and the Goddess of Mercy), and a statue of Van Thu (symbolizing wisdom). At the rear of the grotto is another cave, the **Huyen Khong Cave**. Originally a place of animist worship, it later became a site for Buddhist pilgrimage. The entrance is protected by four door guardians. The high ceiling of the cave is pierced by five holes through which the sun filters and, in the hour before midday, illuminates the central statue of the Buddha Sakyamuni. In the cave are various natural rock formations which, if you have picked up one of the young cave guides along the way, will be pointed out as being stork-like birds, elephants, an arm, a fish and a face.

A few hundred metres to the south on the right is a track leading to Chua Quan The Am, which has its own grotto complete with stalactites, stalagmites and pillars. Local children will point out formations resembling the Buddha and an elephant. There are many shops selling marble carvings. Touts try to inveigle tourists into "their" shop. Do not follow then: it is not their shop but they get paid commission. Go into whichever shop you fancy.

■ *Entrance to Marble Mountain, US$2. Guides, usually young girls, are useful for pointing out the various caves dotted over the mountain but complaints of harassment from tourists seem to have ended this useful service. Getting there: 12 km from Danang 20 km from Hoi An, red-and-white bus to Hoi An from Danang's local bus station opposite 350 Hung Vuong St, 25 mins, or take a* xe ôm. *Many visitors stop off at Marble Mountain en route to Hoi An.*

Non Nuoc Beach is a 1-km walk from Marble Mountain. A huge, white sandy beach, it was developed as a beach resort for Russians after 1975, which perhaps explains the ugliness of the concrete Non Nuoc Beach Resort. Visitors are charged for using the beach (2,000d) and the usual rate for bike parking (2,000d). If you wish to stay there is **D** *Non Nuoc Beach Resort*, T0511-836216, F836335. Three blocks, some a/c, restaurants, breakfast included in the price. Also some cheap guesthouses.

Hoi An is a beautiful, historic town (see page 212), situated 32 km south of Danang. Although a few years ago most visitors saw the town as an excursion from Danang, the roles are now reversed, most people stay in Hoi An and make an excursion to Danang. ■ *Getting there: by bus from 350 Hung Vuong St, look for a red-and-white bus with the Hoi An sign at the front, 1 hr; the last bus returns at about 1700.*

Hoi An

The Central Region

Bana Hill Station Bana is a recently rehabilitated hill station in Vietnam. It is 38 km west of Danang on Chua Mountain (Nui Chua). The mountain rises to a height of 1,467 m, while Bana itself is tucked in to the hillside at an altitude of 1,200 m. The view in all directions is spectacular, the air is fresh and cool and encompassed into each day are four seasons: morning is spring, noon the summer, afternoon is autumn and night the winter. Bana was founded in 1902 by the French, who brought their febrile and palsied here to convalesce in a more benevolent clime. Flora and fauna are diverse and interesting, and villas have been fashioned from the foundations of former French fabrications, some of which accept guests. Rather tragically, this once attractive little place is heading the way of Tam Dao, the old French hill station outside Hanoi, as karaoke bars and similar establishments open. ■ *10,000d per person, 5,000d per motorbike. Basic guesthouse accommodation available. Getting there: head south through Danang towards Highway 1 then take road 604 to Hoa Nhon, Hoa Phong and Hoa Phu. Easily accessible by motorbike from Danang.*

My Son

Colour map 3, grid A5 Declared a World Heritage site by UNESCO in 1999, My Son is one of Vietnam's most ancient monuments. Weather, jungle and years of strife have wrought their worst on My Son. But arguably the jungle under which My Son remained hidden to the outside world provided it with its best protection, for more has been destroyed in the past forty years than the previous four-hundred. Today, far from anywhere, My Son is a tranquil archaeological treasure. Not many visitors have time to make an excursion to see it which makes it all the more appealing to those that do. The thin red bricks of which the towers and temples were built have been beautifully carved and the craftsmanship of many centuries remains abundantly transparent today. The trees and creepers have been pushed back but My Son remains cloaked in green; shoots and saplings sprout up everywhere and one senses that were its custodians to turn their backs for even a short time My Son would be quickly reclaimed by the ever vital and inexorable forces of nature.

Tra Kieu, My Son and Dong Duong are the three most important centres of the former Cham Kingdom (see page 354). My Son is located about 60 km south of Danang (28 km west of Tra Kieu) and consists of over 70 monuments spread over a large area. The characteristic Cham architectural structure is the tower, built to reflect the divinity of the king: tall and rectangular, with four porticoes, each of which is 'blind' except for that on the west face. Because Cham kings were far less wealthy and powerful than the deva-rajas (god kings) of Angkor, the monuments are correspondingly smaller and more personal. Orginally built of wood (not surprisingly, none remains), they were later made of brick, of which the earliest (seventh century) are located at My Son. These are so-called Mi-Son E1 - the unromantic identifying sequence of letters and numbers being given, uncharacteristically, by the French archaeologists who rediscovered and initially investigated the monuments in 1898. Although little of these early examples remains, the temples seem to show similarities with post-Gupta Indian forms, while also embodying Chen-La stylistic influences. Bricks are exactly laid and held together with a form of vegetable cement probably the resin of the day tree. It is thought that on completion, each tower was surrounded by wood and fired over several days in what amounted to a vast outdoor kiln.

It is important to see My Son in the broader context of the Indianisation of Southeast Asia. Not just architecture but spiritual and political influences are echoed around the region. Falling as it did so strongly under Chinese influence it is all the more remarkable to find such compelling evidence of Indian culture and iconography in Vietnam. Indeed this was one of the criteria cited by UNESCO as justification for its listing. Nevertheless one of the great joys of Cham sculpture and building is its unique feel, its graceful lines and unmistakable form. Angkor in Cambodia is the most famous example but Bagan in Burma, Borobudur in Java and Ayuthaya in Thailand, with all of which My Son is broadly contemporaneous, are temple complexes founded by Hindu or Sivaist god kings. In all these places Buddhism appeared in the seventh century and by the eleventh century was in the ascendent with the result that, My Son excepted, these are all widely regarded as Buddhist holy sites. The process whereby new ideas and beliefs are absorbed into a pre-existing culture is known as syncretism. The Hindu cult of deva-raja was developed by the kings of Angkor and later employed by Cham kings to bolster their authority. The king was the earthly representative of the god Siva. Sivaist influence at My Son is unmissable. Siva is one of the Hindu holy trinity, destroyer of the universe. Siva's timeless dance of destruction is the very rhythm of existence and hence also of rebirth. Siva is often represented, as at My Son and other Cham relics thoughout Vietnam, by the lingam, the phallus. My Son was obviously a settled city whose maximum population is unknown but it seems to have had a holy or spiritual function rather than being the seat of power and it was, very probably, a burial place of its god kings.

Much that is known of My Son was discovered by French archaeologists of the École française d' Extrême-Orient. Their rediscovery and excavation of My Son revealed a site that had been settled from the early eigth to the fifteenth centuries, the longest uninterrupted period of development of any monument in Southeast Asia. My Son architecture is notable for its use of red brick which has worn amazingly well. Sandstone plinths are sometimes used as are sandstone lintels, the Cham seemingly - like the Khmer of Angkor - never having learnt the art of arch building, one of the few architectural techniques in which Europe was centuries ahead of Asia. Linga and yoni, the female receptacle into which the carved phallus was normally inserted, are also usually made of sandstone. Overwhelmingly, however, brick is the medium of construction and the raw material from which Hindu, Sivaist and Buddhist images and ornaments are so intricately carved.

Unfortunately, My Son was a Viet Cong field headquarters and therefore located within one of the US 'free fire' zones and was extensively damaged - in particular, the finest sanctuary in the complex was demolished by US sappers. Of the temple groupings, Groups A, E and H were badly damaged in the war. Groups B and C have largely retained their temples but many statues, altars and linga have been removed to the Cham Museum in Danang.

Nevertheless My Son is well worth a visit. Apart from its historical importance it is a truly lovely setting and the difficulty in getting there make an excursion more of an expedition of discovery rather than just another temple visit.

■ *Daily 0800-1800, 50,000d. Getting to My Son: from Danang, drive south on Highway 1 and turn right towards Tra Kieu after 34 km (some 2 km after crossing the Thu Bon River). Drive through Tra Kieu to the village of Kiem Lam. Turn left; the path to My Son is about 6 km further along this road. At this point is the ticket office, a short bamboo bridge crossing and a 2-km jeep ride (included in the ticket price) with a short walk at the end to My Son. It is not clear how thoroughly the area has been de-mined so it is advisable not to stray too far from the road and path. Take a hat, sun cream and water - it is hot and dry. My Son can be reached just as easily from Hoi An, 2 hrs each way by Honda ôm (US$7) or by boat (US$15), which takes all day. Tour operators in Hoi An offer tours to My Son.*

Dong Duong, 20 km from My Son, supplanted My Son as the centre of Cham art and culture when King Indravarman II built a large Buddhist monastery there at the end of the ninth century. Artistically, little changed - the decoration of the towers simply became more ornate, flamboyant and involved, and the reliefs more deeply cut. There is a room in the Cham Museum in Danang devoted to sculptures from Dong Duong, including carved Buddha images. Cham Buddhism saw its finest artistic flowering in the 10th century. Then, in the early 10th century, the focus of Cham art returned to My Son once again under the patronage of Indravarman III (so-called Mi-Son A1 style). Here, a new and far more elegant architecture, evolved. The towers became taller and more balanced, and the decoration purer and less crude.

Tra Kieu, which today is a non descript little place en route to My Son was, in fact, the first Cham capital in the fourth century. That it supported a flourishing artistic and religious life can be gleaned from the exhibits in the Cham Museum in Danang. Tra Kieu was sacked by the Chinese in the fifth century but appears to have flourished again in the late 10th century. Today, alas, there is little to see.

Essentials

Sleeping
■ *on map, page 203*

A number of new hotels have opened and, together with renovated hotels, Danang now offers reasonable accommodation at a range of prices. As a general rule hotels in Danang are purely functional and lack character or atmosphere.

A-C *Song Han*, 36 Bach Dang St, T822540, F821109, kssonghan@dng.vnn.vn 60 rooms, a/c and more expensive rooms with nice river views. Breakfast included for all but the cheapest rooms. **B** *Phuong Dong (Orient)*, 97 Phan Chu Trinh St, T821266, F822854, phdong@dng.vnn.vn A/c, still rather grand, good-size rooms. Breakfast included. **B** *Bach Dang Hotel*, 50 Bach Dang St, T823649, F821659, bdhotel@dng.vnn.vn Large and centrally located hotel, rooms rather cramped for the price, some with river views, cheaper rooms in an older building at the back, all have satellite TV and bath tub. Quite a good restaurant. **B** *Bamboo Green*, there are 3 hotels in this chain: *Bamboo Green Central*, 158 Phan Chu Trinh St, T822996, F822998; *Bamboo Green Harbourside* (a somewhat tenuous claim), 177 Tran Phu St, T822722, F824165; and *Bamboo Green Riverside*, 68 Bach Dang St, T832591, F382593. All share the bamboogreen@dng.vnn.vn email address. All are well-run, well-equipped, comfortable, business-type hotels with efficient staff and in central locations offering excellent value for money. Riverside has a particularly attractive outlook. **B** *Royal* (formerly *Marco Polo*), 17 Quang Trung St, T823295, F827279, royalhotel@dng.vnn.vn With its discounted rates (breakfast included) this 28 room hotel offers quite good value. There's a restaurant and nightclub.

B *Hai Au*, 177 Tran Phu St, T822722, F824165. Central with large rooms, friendly reception, but indifferent restaurant. **B-C** *Ami Motel*, 7 Quang Trung, T824494. Clean, friendly. **B-C** *Binh Duong*, 30, 32 Tran Phu St, T821930, F827666. Clean and friendly. **B-C** *Danang*, 1-3 Dong Da St, T821986, F823431, dananghotel@dng.vnn.vn Large hotel with 160 rooms, some around a courtyard at the back with balconies. Restaurant and tour services, now merged with the old *Marble Mountain* hotel next door. **B-C** *Thai Binh Duong (Pacific)*, 92 Phan Chu Trinh St, T822137. A/c, large and central but rather characterless. **B-C** *White Snow*, 177 Phan Chu Trinh St, T834333, F834332. Considered to be one of the best hotels in Danang; good breakfasts.

C *Canary*, 30 Ngo Gia Tu St, T829800, F828900. A/c, all have bath tub and hot water, good value. **C** *Dai A*, 51 Yen Bai St, T827532, F825760, daiahotel@dng.vnn.vn Another of Danang's rather characterless but perfectly functional and clean hotels. Central location and efficient staff. **C** *Phuong Lan*, 142 Hoang Dieu St, T820373, F820382. A/c, satellite TV, hot water, good value (after some bargaining), free airport pick-up, motorbikes for rent. **C-D** *Tan Minh*, 142 Bach Dang St, T827456, F830172. On the riverfront, a well-kept small hotel, friendly and intelligent staff speak good English.

D *Hung Vuong Mini*, 95 Hung Vuong St, T823967. 10 rooms, some a/c, hot water, bicycles, motorbikes and cars for hire at competitive prices. **D** *Thanh Thanh*, 54 Phan Chu Trinh St, T830684, F829886. Some a/c, a bit run down but good location. **E** *Song Han Guesthouse (Nha Nghi 34)*, 34 Bach Dang St, T822732. Nine small and simple rooms around a quiet courtyard by the river. Some rooms have a/c. No English spoken but good value.

Seafood is good here, and Danang has its own beers, Da Nang 'Export' and Song Han. There are a number of cafés and restaurants along Bach Dang St, overlooking the river. Bread in Danang is particularly good which makes banh mi ôp la (fried egss and bread) a particularly good start to the day.

Eating
● *on map, page 203*

Bach Dang Hotel, 50 Bach Dang St. Informal, glimpses of river and decent food. *Christie's* and *Cool Spot*, 112 Tran Phu St, T824040, ccdng@dng.vnn.vn The old premises were demolished in the construction of the River Han Bridge, the new location is one block in from the river and has merged forces with the *Cool Spot* bar. Frequented by expats from Danang and outlying provinces. Small bar downstairs, restaurant upstairs. Cold beer and Western and Japanese food. *Hana Kim Dinh*, 7 Bach Dang St. Restaurant on a small pier shaped like a boat, opposite *Bach Dang Hotel*, Western and Vietnamese menus, mainly seafood. Rather expensive. *Hoang Ngoc*, 106 Nguyen Chi Thanh St, T821214. Extensive menu, good food and welcoming atmosphere, popular. *Kim Do*, 174 Tran Phu St, T821846. Now a huge Chinese restaurant on the site of the popular old restaurant. Typical Chinese menu, reasonable food at fair prices. Popular with tour groups. *Tu Do*, 172 Tran Phu St. Extensive menu and excellent food.

Bars and cafés *Bamboo*, 5 Bach Dang St, T837175. Overlooks the river. Popular with the 'vodka and Red Bull' backpacker set and young locals. Serves food, pool table. *Christies and Cool Spot*, 112 Tran Phu St. Expat-type place. *Free Time* (*Tam's Pub*), 1 Dong Da St, T819535. Run by the eponymous Tam, whose business plan is to get old customers to return, which, because of her good travel advice, they do. Mixed Western and Vietnamese menu, good value. *Linh's Café*, 4 Dong Da St, T820401. Opposite *Danang Hotel*. A little far from the centre for many visitors. Popular for its pool table, also serves food. Their travel services are not always reliable.

There is a nightclub at the *Royal Hotel*, 17 Quang Trung St, T823295 (see Sleeping, page 210).

Nightclubs

Marble carvings Available from shops in town, but particularly from the stalls around the foot of Marble Mountain (see Excursions, page 206). There are many touts at the Marble Mountains who will invite you into 'their' shop. Do not follow them as you will end up paying their commission. Just take yourself into any shop and bargain.

Shopping

Danang Tourist Office, 76 Hung Vuong St, T821423, F822854, also at 92A Phan Chu Trinh St, arranges cars and guides, and *Vietnamtourism*, 158 Phan Chu Trinh St, T822990.

Tour operators

Local Bus: local buses to **Hoi An** run from the station at the west end of Hung Vuong St, opposite Con Market. Bicycles available from many hotels from around US$1 per day. Some cafés and hotels also rent motorbikes for US$5-7 per day. Otherwise the usual *cyclo* or *Honda ôm*. **Taxis** *Airport Taxi*, T825555, *Dana Taxi*, T815815.

Transport
*108 km from Hué,
130 from
Quang Ngai*

The Central Region

Air The airport is 2½ km southwest of the city. There are 2-3 connections daily from **Saigon** and **Hanoi**, 70-85 mins; connections with **Buon Ma Thuot** (65 mins) and **Dalat** (85 mins) 3 times a week; and with **Nha Trang** (80 mins) 5 days a week. Direct flights to **Bangkok** on *Thai Airways* and *Vietnam Airlines*, Tue, Thu and Sat, depart 1110 arrive 1245, US$170 one way. *Thai International*, in the airport, T656060. The airport at Danang is probably the easiest airport in Vietnam to negotiate and has a particularly good restaurant – facing the main terminal.

Road Bus: the inter-province bus station is on Dien Bien Phu St, about 3 km from town, from which there are connections with all major cities.

Train The train station is on Haiphong St, 2 km west of town, and there are express trains to and from **Hanoi**, **Saigon** and **Hué**.

International connections It is possible to get a visa for Laos in Danang from the Lao consulate here (US$25 for a 7-day transit visa), it takes 1 day. See address under Embassies and consulates, below. There are daily departures for the Lao town of Savannakhet, on the Mekong River. The road runs west from Dong Ha into the Annamite mountains and crosses the border at Lao Bao, not far from the former battlefield of Khe Sanh.

Directory **Airline offices** *Vietnam Airlines Booking Office*, 35 Tran Phu St, T821130, F832759. **Banks** *VID Public Bank*, 2 Tran Phu St. *Vietcombank*, 104 Le Loi St. Will change most major currencies, cash and TCs. **Communications** Internet: Danang is one of only 3 cities in Vietnam to have its own internet portal with the outside world. There are numerous internet cafés all over town catering to the enthusiastic young internet surfing population at rates as low as 50d per min. Most hotels listed also offer internet services to their customers but at slightly higher rates. **TNT International:** T821685. **Post office:** 60 Bach Dang St, corner of Bach Dang and Le Duan streets. Telex, fax and telephone facilities here. Poste restante at 62 Bach Dang St. **Embassies and consulates** Lao Consulate, 12 Tran Qui Cap St, T821208, F822628, open 0800-1100, 1400-1600. **Medical services** Hospital: C Hospital, 74 Haiphong St, T821480. **Useful addresses** Immigration Police: Nguyen Thi Minh Khai St, opposite *Hai Van Hotel*.

Hoi An

Phone code: 0510
Colour map 3, grid A5

The ancient town of Hoi An (formerly Faifo) lies on the banks of the Thu Bon River. During its heyday two hundred years ago, when trade with China and Japan flourished, Hoi An became a prosperous little port. Much of the merchants' wealth was spent on family chapels and Chinese clan houses which remain little altered today. Today Hoi An is seeing a late but much deserved revival: the river may be too shallow for shipping but it is perfect for tourist boats; the silk merchants may not export any produce but that's because all they can make leaves town on the back of satisfied customers.

Hoi An's tranquil riverside setting, its diminutive scale (you can touch the roof of many houses), friendly and welcoming people and its wide array of shops and galleries have made it one of the most popular destinations for foreign travellers. There is plenty to see of historical interest, there is a nearby beach and, as if that were not enough, it has superb and inexpensive restaurants, possibly the best in the country.

Ins and outs

There are direct minibus connections with Saigon, Hanoi, Hué and Nha Trang. The quickest way of getting from Hanoi or Saigon is by flying to Danang and then getting a taxi from the airport direct to Hoi An, US$9, 40 mins. **Getting there** *See Transport, page 220, for further details*

Hoi An is compact and quite busy – best explored on foot. Guesthouses hire out bicycles. **Getting around**

The town

Hoi An is divided into five quarters, or 'bangs', each of which would traditionally have had its own pagoda and supported one Chinese clan group. The Chinese, along with some Japanese, settled here in the 16th century and controlled trade between the islands of Southeast Asia, East Asia (China and Japan) and India. Portuguese and Dutch vessels also docked at the port. During the Tay Son rebellion (1771-88) the town was almost totally destroyed, although this is not apparent to the visitor. By the end of the 19th century the Thu Bon River had started to silt up and Hoi An was gradually eclipsed by Danang as the most important port of the area.

Hoi An has emerged as one of the most popular tourist destinations in Vietnam and there has been no diminution in its status, in fact quite the reverse. Walking along Tran Phu Street more Western than Vietnamese faces can be seen.

Hoi An's historic character is being slowly submerged by the rising tide of tourism. Although remaining physically intact, virtually every one of its fine historic buildings either markets some aspect of its own heritage or touts in some other way for the tourist dollar; increasingly it is coming to resemble the 'Vietnam' pavilion in a Disney theme park. Nevertheless, visitors to Hoi An are charmed by the gentleness of the people and the sedate pace of life. The tempo has picked up in recent years, however, and although the police are vigilant in guarding Hoi An's morals (try getting even a foot massage here), every boat and café owner by the river will attempt to press passers-by into using their services. Hoi An also has a number of highly praised restaurants and the nearby Cua Dai Beach, see page 217.

Boat rides are available on the Thu Bon River. Local boatwomen charge a dollar or so an hour, a tranquil and relaxed way of spending the early evening.

Sights

Most of Hoi An's more attractive buildings and assembly halls (known as *hoi quan*) are found either on, or just off, Tran Phu Street. Tran Phu stretches west to east from the Japanese Covered Bridge to the market, running parallel to the river. The best way to explore this small, intimate town is on foot. People are friendly and will generally not mind inquisitive, but polite, foreigners. A day is needed to see the town properly. Entrance to most buildings is by **sightseeing ticket**, 50,000d for four separate sights, on sale at *Hoi An Tourist Office* at the junction of Phan Chu Trinh and Nguyen Hue streets, and also at Hoi An Museum. Tokens for additional sights cost 10,000d.

At the west end of Tran Phu Street is Hoi An's most famous landmark: the covered bridge – variously known as the Pagoda Bridge, the Faraway People's Bridge and, popularly, as the Japanese Covered Bridge (*Cau Nhat Ban*). The bridge was built in the 16th century, perhaps even earlier. On its north side **Japanese Covered Bridge**

The Central Region

there is a pagoda, Japanese in style, for the protection of sailors. At the west end of the bridge are statues of two dogs, and at the east end, of two monkeys – it is said that the bridge was begun in the year of the monkey and finished in the year of the dog. Some scholars have pointed out that this would mean a two-year period of construction, an inordinately long time for such a small bridge; they maintain that the two animals represent points of the compass, WSW (monkey) and NW (dog). Father Benigne Vachet, a missionary who lived in Hoi An between 1673 and 1683, notes in his memoirs that the bridge was the haunt of beggars and fortune tellers hoping to benefit from the stream of people crossing over it. Its popular name – the Japanese Covered Bridge – reflects a long-standing belief that it was built by the Japanese, although no documentary evidence exists to support this. One of its other names, the Far-away People's Bridge, is said to have been coined because vessels from far away would moor close to the bridge. ■ *1 token – keep your ticket to get back.*

Just south of the Covered Bridge is **Bach Dang Street** which runs along the bank of the Thu Bon River. Here there are boats, activity and often a cooling

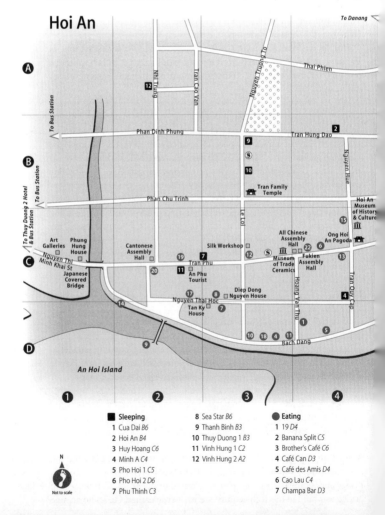

Hoi An

To Danang

Sleeping
1 Cua Dai *B6*
2 Hoi An *B4*
3 Huy Hoang *C6*
4 Minh A *C4*
5 Pho Hoi 1 *C5*
6 Pho Hoi 2 *D6*
7 Phu Thinh *C3*
8 Sea Star *B6*
9 Thanh Binh *B3*
10 Thuy Duong 1 *B3*
11 Vinh Hung 1 *C2*
12 Vinh Hung 2 *A2*

Eating
1 19 *D4*
2 Banana Split *C5*
3 Brother's Café *C6*
4 Café Can *D3*
5 Café des Amis *D4*
6 Cao Lau *C4*
7 Champa Bar *D3*

N
Not to scale

breeze. The road loops round to the Hoi An Market (see below). The small but interesting **French quarter** around Phan Boi Chau St is worth taking time over; it's not on the regular 'tourist circuit' and requires no entry fee. The colonnaded fronts are particularly attractive. As everywhere in historical quarters in Vietnam visitors should raise their gaze above street level to appreciate the architectural detail of upper floors, which is more likely to have survived, and less likely to be covered up.

Chinese traders in Hoi An (like elsewhere in Southeast Asia) established self-governing dialect associations or clan houses which owned their own schools, cemeteries, hospitals and temples. The clan houses *(hoi quan)* may be dedicated to a god or an illustrious individual and may contain a temple but are not themselves temples. There are five hoi quan in Hoi An, four for use by people of specific ethnicities: Fukien, Cantonese, Hainan, Chaozhou and the fifth for use by any visiting Chinese sailors or merchants.

Assembly Halls

The Central Region

Strolling east from the Covered Bridge down Tran Phu Street all the assembly halls can be seen. Merchants from Guangdong would meet at the **Cantonese Assembly Hall**, or **Quang Dong Hoi Quan**, at 176 Tran Phu Street. This assembly hall is dedicated to Quan Cong, a Han Chinese general and dates from 1786. The hall, with its fine embroidered hangings, is in a cool, tree-filled compound and is a good place to rest. ■ *Admission, 1 token.*

Next is the **All Chinese Assembly Hall** or **Ngu Bang Hoi Quan**, sometimes referred to as **Chua Ba** (Goddess Temple), at 64 Tran Phu St. Unusually for an assembly hall, it was a mutual aid society open to any Chinese trader or seaman, regardless of dialect or region of origin. Chinese vessels tended to visit Hoi An during the spring, returning to China in the summer. The assembly hall would help ship-wrecked and ill sailors and perform the burial rites of merchants with no relatives in Hoi An. Built in 1773 as a meeting place for all five groups (the four listed above plus Hakka) and also for those with no clan house of their own, today it accommodates a Chinese School, *Truong Le Nghia*, where children of the diaspora learn the language of their forebears. ■ *Admission, 1 token.*

The **Fukien Assembly Hall**, or **Phuc Kien Hoi Quan**, at 46 Tran Phu St, founded around 1690, served Hoi An's largest Chinese ethnic

8 Christie's *C3*
9 Dong An *D2*
10 Dong Phuong *D3*
11 Du Port *D3*
12 Fai Fo *C3*
13 Fukien *C4*
14 Han Huyen *D2*
15 Ly Cafeteria 22 *C4*
16 Nhu Y *C5*
17 Tam Tam Café *C2*
18 Thanh *D3*
19 Treats Bar *C2*
20 Vinh Hung *C2*
21 Win's Café *C5*
22 Yellow River *C4*

group, those from Fukien. It is an intimate building within a large compound and is dedicated to Thien Hau, goddess of the sea and protector of sailors. She is the central figure on the main altar, clothed in gilded robes, who, together with her assistants, can hear the cries of distress of drowning sailors. Immediately on the right on entering the temple is a mural depicting Thien Hau rescuing a sinking vessel. Behind the main altar is a second sanctuary which houses the image of Van Thien whose blessings pregnant women invoke on the lives of their unborn children. ■ *Admission, 1 token.*

With a rather more colourful history comes the **Hainan Assembly Hall**, or **Hai Nam Hoi Quan**, 100 m further east at 10 Tran Phu St. Founded in 1883 in memory of the more than 100 sailors and passengers who were killed when three ships were plundered by an admiral in Emperor Tu Duc's navy. In his defence the admiral claimed the victims were pirates and some sources maintain he even had the ships painted black to strengthen his case. ■ *Admission, 1 token.*

Exquisite wood carving is the highlight of the **Chaozhou**, or **Trieu Chau Assembly Hall**, at 157 Nguyen Duy Hieu St. The altar and its panels depict images from the sea and women from the Peking court, presumably intended to console homesick traders. ■ *Admission, 1 token.*

Merchants' Houses

Tan Ky House, which can be visited at 101 Nguyen Thai Hoc St, dates from the late 18th century. Built by later generations of the Tan Ky family (they originally arrived in Hoi An from China two hundred years earlier), it reflects not only the prosperity the family had acquired but also the architecture of their Japanese and Vietnamese neighbours, whose styles had presumably worked their influence on the aesthetic taste and appreciation of the younger family members.

At the east end of Tran Phu Street, at No 24, close to the intersection with Nguyen Hue Street, is the **Ong Hoi An Pagoda**. This temple is in fact two interlinked pagodas built back-to-back: *Chua Quan Cong*, and behind that *Chua Quan Am*. Their date of construction is not known, although both certainly existed in 1653. In 1824 Emperor Minh Mang made a donation of 300 luong (1 luong being equivalent to 1.5 oz of silver) for the support of the pagodas. They are dedicated to Quan Cong and Quan Am, respectively.

Virtually opposite the Ong Hoi An Pagoda, is the **Hoi An Market** (*Cho Hoi An*). The market extends down to the river and then along the river road (Bach Dang Street). At the Tran Phu Street end it is a covered market selling mostly dry goods. Numerous cloth merchants and seamstresses will produce made-to-measure shirts in a few hours for US$5, but not all to the same standard. Mr Thuc, *Tran Quy Cap and Yaly*, 27 Tran Qui Cap have been recommended by visitors, also at 60 Le Loi Street. The riverside of the market is the local **fish market** which comes alive at 0500-0600 as boats arrive with the night's catch.

On the junction of Le Loi and Phan Chu Trinh streets stands the **Tran Family Temple** which has survived for 15 generations; the current generation has no son which means the lineage has been broken. The building exemplifies well Hoi An's construction methods and the harmonious fusion of Chinese and Japanese styles. It is roofed with heavy *yin* and *yang* tiling which requires strong roof beams; these are held up by a triple-beamed support in the Japanese style (seen in the roof of the covered bridge). Some beams have Chinese-inspired ornately carved dragons. The outer doors are Japanese, the inner are Chinese. On a central altar rest small wooden boxes which contain the photograph or likeness of the deceased together with biographical details;

beyond, at the back of the house, is a small, raised Chinese herb, spice and flower garden with a row of bonsai trees. As with all Hoi An's family houses guests are received warmly and courteously and served lotus tea and dried coconut. ■ *1 token.*

Diep Dong Nguyen House, at 80 Nguyen Thai Hoc Street, with two Chinese lanterns hanging outside, was once a Chinese dispensary. The owner is friendly, hospitable and not commercially minded. He takes visitors into his house and shows everything with pride and smiles.

Just east of the Japanese Bridge is **Phung Hung House**, at 4 Nguyen Thi Minh Khai Street. Built over 200 years ago it has been in the same family for eight generations. The house, which can be visited, is constructed of 80 columns of ironwood on marble pedestals. During the floods of 1964, Phung Hung House became home to 160 locals who camped upstairs for three days as the water rose to a height of 2.5 m.

Museums

Adjacent to Ong Hoi An Pagoda is **Hoi An Museum of History and Culture**, at 7 Nguyen Hue St, housed in a former pagoda. The museum sets the history of the town in its trading context with sections on all the main cultural influences. ■ *Admission, 1 token.* The **Museum of Trade Ceramics**, at 80 Tran Phu St, was opened with financial and technical support from Japan; it contains an interesting range of ancient wares, some of them from shipwrecks in surrounding waters. There are also detailed architectural drawings of various houses in Hoi An. Upstairs, from the front balcony, there is a fascinating roofscape. ■ *Admission, 1 token.*

Excursions

Cua Dai Beach, which is 5 km from Hoi An, east down Tran Hung Dao Street, is a pleasant 20-minute bicycle ride. Alternatively, a quieter route is to set off down Nguyen Duy Hieu Street. This peters out into a footpath which can be cycled. It is a lovely path past paddy fields and ponds. Nothing is signed but those with a good sense of direction will make their way back to the main road a kilometre or so before Cua Dai. Those with a poor sense of direction can come to no harm. For accommodation see under Sleeping, page 218.

As travellers now tend to make Hoi An their base for a couple of days it is the natural place from which to visit the Marble Mountains, see page 206 and My Son, see page 208. Although it is slightly further to My Son from Hoi An than it is from Danang there are many operators offering tours from here. This is the easiest way of getting to My Son. Some tours include a visit to the Cham Museum in Danang in the itinerary and this is well worth doing preferably on the same day as many of the carvings in the museum came from My Son.

Essentials

There has been a dramatic increase in the number of hotel rooms available in Hoi An and so the chances of being left bedless for the night have fallen dramatically. It is still as well to book in advance, however. During slack periods discounts can be reckoned on.

Sleeping
■ *on map, page 214*
Phone code: 0510

Town B-C *Pho Hoi 2*, Cam Nam Island, T862628, F862626, phohoiht@dng.vnn.vn South of Cam Nam Bridge, a new and rather unattractive 45-room hotel, all a/c, bathtubs and satellite TV, some rooms have river view, motorbikes and sampans for rent.

B-C *Vinh Hung 1*, 143 Tran Phu St, T861621, F861893, quanghuy.ha@dng.vnn.vn An attractive old building with a splendid and ornate reception room decorated with dark wood in Chinese style. 12 rooms at a range of prices, some large and traditionally furnished, others rather small and lacking a window. Popular. **B-C** *Vinh Hung 2*, Nhi Trung St, T863717, F864094, uanghuy.ha@dng.vnn.vn A new sister hotel with 40 rooms, a short walk away, built in traditional style, with a pool and all mod cons but lacking the atmosphere of the original. **B-D** *Hoi An*, 6 Tran Hung Dao St, T861445, F861636, www.hoiantourist.com Attractive colonial building set well back from the road in spacious grounds, cheaper rooms have fan and shared bathroom, staff are not particularly welcoming.

C-D *Cua Dai*, 18A Cua Dai St, T862231, F862232. On the beach road, a little way from town but comfortable, clean, well-run and a friendly reception, perhaps can be charmed into including breakfast. **C-D** *Huy Hoang*, 73 Phan Boi Chau St, T861453. 19 a/c rooms, bath, hot water, nice terrace on the river for breakfast, clean and friendly. A decent hotel spoilt by the noise from the neighbours, which affects the cheaper downstairs rooms in particular. **C-D** *Minh 4*, 2 Nguyen Thai Hoc St, T861368. This is a very special little place. An old family house with just four guestrooms, all different and all different prices. Guests are made to feel part of the family. All rooms have hot water and fan. Right next to the market in a busy part of town. **C-D** *Pho Hoi 1*, 7/2 Tran Phu St, T861633, near the market. Some a/c, cheaper rooms share facilities. **C-D** *Sea Star (Sao Bien)*, 15 Cua Dai St, on the road to the beach, T861589, F861382. A newish, privately run hotel, all with a/c and hot water. Travel services, bicycle, motorbike and car hire on offer. Efficient and popular but possibly starting to get a little complacent.

D *Phu Thinh*, 144 Tran Phu St, T861297, F861757, minhthaoha@dng.vnn.vn Behind an attractive Chinese-looking façade stands a very ordinary 1970's hotel. Except for a couple of rooms upstairs all rooms are on a long internal corridor. Rather dark and airless but efficient staff. **D** *Thanh Binh*, 1 Le Loi St, T861740, vothihong@dng.vnn.vn A new hotel with 15 rooms, follows the common (and good value) Hoi An standard of price and quality. **D** *Thuy Duong 1*, 11 Le Loi St, T861574, F861330, thuyduongco@dng.vnn.vn 10 rooms, some a/c, friendly. Downstairs is a popular internet café charging 200d per min. **D** *Thuy Duong 2*, 68 Huynh Thuc Khang St, T861394, F861330. All a/c with bath tub and hot water, friendly and a short walk out of the centre so rather quiet, near the bus station.

Cua Dai Beach **LL-L** *Hoi An Resort*, T927040, F927041, fo-victoriaha@dng.vnn.vn A charming and attractive addition to the *Victoria Hotel* group chain, this newly built resort is right on the beach. It has 100 rooms and 55 bungalows all facing the sea, some with balconies. There is a large but slightly exposed pool (the trees have not had much time to grow), restaurants and charming service. Do not be surprised to see a long line of craters running down the beach, they belong to the hotel's pet elephant, Darling, which ambles up and down the beach giving rides. Actual prices are not always as high as the published figures suggest. A free shuttle bus runs between the hotel and the town. The **L** *Hoi An Riverside Resort*, Cua Dai Road, T864800, F864900, hoianriver@dng.vnn.vn is neither fish nor fowl and is a slightly strange place neither on the beach nor in town. A short five-minute cycle ride from the beach and a 15-minute pedal from town, the resort is right on the road, admittedly not a busy one but slightly exposed to passing traffic. The accommodation is comfortable and the views overlooking the river are lovely. There is a dark slate-lined pool. There is also the **L-A** *Hoi An Beach Resort*, run by the *Hoi An Tourist Service Company*, T927011, F927019, www.hoiantourist.com

A Hoi An speciality is *cao lau* – a special noodle soup with slices of pork and croutons and traditionally made with water from one particular well. Fresh seafood is also readily available. The quality of food in Hoi An, especially the fish, is outstanding and the value for money is not matched by any other town in Vietnam. Bach Dang St is particularly pleasant in the evening when tables and chairs are set up almost the whole way along the river.

Eating
● *on map, page 214*

Banana Split, 53 Hoang Dieu St, T861136. A good little corner café with a range of dishes at low prices. Good fish and fried noodles. Fruit shakes are recommended and very cheap. *Brother's Café*, 27 Phan Boi Chau St, T914150. It is excellent news that these little cloistered French houses should have been put to such good use and renovated in such exquisite taste. The house and garden leading down to the river are beautifully restored. The menu is strong on Vietnamese specialities, especially seafood, and at US$6 the daily set menu offers very good value. *Café Can*, 74 Bach Dang St. Good Vietnamese and Western menu, seafood specialities in an attractive setting by the river. *Café des Amis*, 52 Bach Dang St, near the river, T861616. Choose fish and seafood or vegetarian, the set menu changes daily and is widely acclaimed; at about US$5 for 5 dishes and 2 local beers it is also excellent value. The owner, Mr Nguyen Manh Kim, spends several months a year cooking in Europe. Highly recommended. *Cao Lau*, 42 Tran Phu St. For the best *cao lau* and cheap. Recommended. *Christie's*, 88 Nguyen Thai Hoc St, T861576. Rather like the parent restaurant in Danang this new addition concentrates on Western dishes, pizza, pasta, burgers and shakes. *Dong An*, 65 Cong Dong, An Hoi, T862132. Actually located at the end of the footbridge leading to An Hoi island, this is a good place to sit and look at the sun setting on Hoi An. Their speciality is the very good fish in a banana leaf. *Dong Phuong*, 88 Bach Dang St, T861346. Right on the corner of Le Loi Street overlooking the river this is slightly cheaper than some. *Du Port*, 70 Bach Dang St, T861768. Success has bred a complacent attitude in service to customers but the fish is outstanding. *Fai Fo*, 104 Tran Phu St. Especially good for breakfast and ice cream. *Fukien*, 31 Tran Phu St. Family run Chinese restaurant. *Han Huyen (Floating Restaurant)*, Bach Dang St, T861462. Just east of the footbridge to An Hoi island. Excellent seafood. *Ly Cafeteria 22*, 22 Nguyen Hue St. Cheap, cheerful and very popular. *Nhu Y (aka Miss Vy's or Mermaid)*, 2 Tran Phu St. Miss Vy turns out all the local specialities as well as some of her own. The 5-course set dinner is particularly recommended. *Tam Tam Café*, 110 Nguyen Thai Hoc. This is a great little café in a renovated tea house. Cocktails, draft beer, music, book exchange, plus attached restaurant serving French and Italian cuisine. A relaxing place for a drink, expresso or meal. *Thanh*, 76 Bach Dang St. A charming old house overlooking the river which is recognizable by its Chinese style and being draped in creeper; the shrimp is excellent. *Vinh Hung*, 147 Tran Phu St, T862203. Belongs to the hotel of the same name. Another attractive building finely decked with Chinese lanterns and traditional furniture. An excellent range of seafood dishes and Vietnamese specials at fair prices. *Win's Café*, 5 Tran Phu St, T862270. Service here is not a strength but prices are low and it has internet access at 200d per min. *Yellow River*, 38 Tran Phu St. Good Hoi An family restaurant, fried wanton is recommended, especially for francophones. *19*, 19 Hoang Van Thu St. Serves locally brewed fresh beer at just 3,000d per glass and simple inexpensive dishes.

Champa, 75 Nguyen Thai Hoc St, T862974. This is a rambling place with pool tables and an upstairs cultural show in the evenings. Downstairs hits from the 60s and 70s predominate. *Tam Tam Café*, 110 Nguyen Thai Hoc St, also has a good bar. *Treats (Triets)*, 158 Tran Phu St, T861125. One of Hoi An's few bars and a very well run one. Two pool tables, airy, attractive style: popular happy hour.

Bars

The Central Region

Shopping

Hoi An is a shopper's paradise – Tran Phu and Le Loi streets being the main shopping areas

Two items stand out, paintings and clothes. Countless galleries sell original works of art. Vietnamese artists have been inspired by Hoi An's old buildings and a Hoi An school of art has developed. Hoi An buildings are instantly recognizable even distorted into a variety of shapes and colours on canvas or silk. Galleries are everywhere but in particular the more serious galleries are to be found in a cluster on Nguyen Thi Minh Khai Street west of the Japanese Bridge. *Co*, 18 Nguyen Thi Minh Khai St, T862123, is in a particularly lovely building. Hoi An's tailors are famed – there are now reckoned to be more than 140 – and will knock up silk or cotton clothing in 24 hrs. The quality of the stitching varies from shop to shop so see some samples first. The range of fabrics is limited so many people bring their own. A suit can cost anywhere from US$30-100 depending on fabric and quality of workmanship. Hoi An silk is quite coarse. The shop at 41 Le Loi Street is a silk workshop where the whole process from silkworm to woven fabric can be seen and fabrics purchased. Hoi An is the place to buy handbags and purses and attractive Chinese silk lanterns, indeed anything that can be made from silk, including scarves and shoes.

There is also a lot of quite nice chinaware available, mostly modern, some reproduction and a few antiques. There is blue and white and celadon green, the ancient Chinese pale green glaze, here often reproduced with fine cracks. Note, however, that it is illegal to take items more than 200 years old out of the country and the customs officials are likely to confiscate anything that takes their fancy.

Tour operators

An Phu Tourist, 141 Tran Phu St, T861447, anphu18@hotmail.com They have several offices in town and offer a wide range of tour services. *Hoi An Tourist Office*, 12 Phan Chu Trinh St, T861276. English-speaking, car and minibus hire and guides to Hoi An. *Mr Tung*, 21 Cua Dai St, T861517, is a small, one-man operation but does a good job booking bus tickets and arranging tours to My Son etc. Tours to My Son cost only US$1.50 by bus or US$4 by bus and boat. The admission fee of 50,000d is extra. *My Son Tours*, 17/2 Tran Hung Dao St, T861121. Cheap minibus tickets to Hué (US$3). Nha Trang (US$5) and Saigon (US$15) plus car and motorbike hire and useful advice.

Transport

Local Hoi An itself is best explored on foot, but for venturing further abroad, hotels have 2- and 4-wheel vehicles for hire, bicycle hire is only 5,000d per day, motorbike US$4 per day.

Long distance Air Flights to **Danang** from Saigon and Hanoi. A taxi from Danang airport to Hoi An will cost about US$15 or less (bargain hard), 40 mins. Car from Hoi An to Danang is US$6.

Road Bus: the bus station is about 1 km west of the centre of town. There are regular connections from Danang's local bus station, 1 hr. If on a day's excursion from **Danang**, the last bus returns at about 1700. Special **tourist buses** cost around US$10 to **Hanoi** and US$12 to **Saigon**. Book through local tour operators (see above).

Directory

Banks *Hoi An Bank*, 4 Hoang Dieu. Exchanges cash and TCs. **Communications** Internet: widely available, in cafés and hotels, usually 200d per min. **Post office:** 5 Tran Hung Dao St, next to *Hoi An Hotel*. Has poste restante, international telephone and fax service. **Medical services** Hospital: 4 Tran Hung Dao St.

The Son My (My Lai) Massacre

The massacre at Son My was a turning point in the American public's view of the war, and the role that the US was playing. Were American forces defending Vietnam and the world from the evils of communism? Or were they merely shoring up a despotic government which had lost all legitimacy among the population it ostensibly served?

The massacre occurred on the morning of 16 March 1968. Units from the 23rd Infantry Division were dropped into the village of Son My. The area was regarded as an area of intense communist presence – so much so that soldiers referred to the villages as Pinkville. Only two weeks beforehand, six soldiers had been killed after stumbling into a mine field. The leader of the platoon that was charged with the job of investigating the hamlet of My Lai was 2nd Lieutenant William Calley. Under his orders, 347 people, all unarmed and many women and children, were massacred. Some of Calley's men refused to participate, but most did. Neil Sheehan, in his book A Bright Shining Lie, describes wrote:

"One soldier missed a baby lying on the ground twice with a .45 pistol as his comrades laughed at his marksmanship. He stood over the child and fired a third time. The soldiers beat women with rifle butts and raped some and sodomized others before shooting them. They shot the water buffalos, the pigs, and the chickens. They threw the dead animals into the wells to poison the water. They tossed satchel charges into the bomb shelters under the houses. A lot of the inhabitants had fled into the shelters. Those who leaped out to escape the explosives were gunned down. All of the houses were put to the torch".

In total, over 500 people were killed at Son My; most in the hamlet of My Lai, but another 90 at another hamlet (by another platoon) in the same village. The story of the massacre was filed by Seymour Hersh, but not until 13 November – eight months later. The subsequent court-martial only convicted Calley, who was by all accounts a sadist. He was sentenced to life imprisonment, but had served only three years before President Nixon intervened on his behalf (he was personally convicted of the murder of 109 of the victims). As Sheehan argues, the massacre was, in some regards, not surprising. The nature of the war had led to the killing and maiming of countless unarmed and innocent peasants; it was often done from a distance. In the minds of most Generals, every Vietnamese was a potential Communist; from this position it was only a small step to believing that all Vietnamese were legitimate targets.

Quang Ngai to Phan Rang via Nha Trang

This 500-km stretch of Highway 1 runs along the coast, sometimes within sight of the sea. Areas of lowland suitable for rice cultivation are few, and the soils generally poor. The beach resort of Nha Trang is situated in the heartland of the former Cham Kingdom and along this stretch of Vietnam's central region are innumerable Cham towers, most unrestored and only rudimentarily studied. The former US Navy base at Cam Ranh Bay lies 50 km south of Nha Trang, and another 55 km south from here is the town of Phan Rang. Phan Rang is notable for the group of Cham Towers that lie just outside the town. From here the road divides: Highway 1 and the railway continue southwards to Phan Thiet and from there to Saigon, a total of 318 km; another road runs northwest for 110 km to Dalat.

My Lai – 30 years on

It was thought that pretty much everything that happened that awful day in My Lai was known. Thirty years ago Hugh C Thompson Jr and Lawrence Colburn received medals for heroism under enemy fire, but in 1998 the US Army corrected an oversight: there was no enemy in My Lai; or rather, the enemy was the US.

Thompson, a 24-year-old helicopter pilot, Colburn, his gunner, and a third man, Glenn U. Andreotta (who was later killed in action) stopped the My Lai massacre before more people were killed. Thompson spotted

women and children hiding in a bunker and put his helicopter down between them and advancing American soldiers. He called up another chopper and between them they evacuated the 10 civilians. At the same time Thompson reported the massacre to his CO who called off all action in the sector, thus ending the killing.

On 7 March 1998, at the Vietnam Veterans Memorial in Washington, the two survivors, Thompson and Colburn, were awarded the highest medal for bravery not involving conflict with an enemy.

Quang Ngai

Phone code: 055
Colour map 3, B6

Quang Ngai is a modest provincial capital on Highway 1, situated on the south bank of the Tra Khuc River. Few people stay here as facilities are still pretty basic. Its greatest claim to fame is its proximity to **Son My** – the site of the **My Lai massacre** (see above). There is an extensive **market** running north from the bus station, along Ngo Quyen Street (just east of Quang Trung Street or Highway 1). Also in the city is a **citadel** built during the reign of Gia Long (1802-19). The town is 130 km from Danang.

Excursions   **Son My (My Lai)** lies 13 km from Quang Ngai. Just over 1 km north of town on Highway 1, soon after crossing the bridge over the Tra Khuc River, is a plaque indicating the way to Son My. Turn right, and continue for 12 km to the subdistrict of Son My where one of the worst, and certainly the most publicized, atrocities committed by US troops during the Vietnam War occurred (see box, page 221). The massacre of innocent Vietnamese villagers is better known as the My Lai Massacre – after one of the four hamlets of Son My. In the centre of the village of Son My is a memorial with a military cemetery 400 m beyond. There is an exhibition of contemporaneous US military photos of the massacre and a reconstruction of an underground bomb shelter; the creek where many villagers were dumped after being shot has been preserved. A sign prohibits photographs from being taken, but permission may be given by the informative English-speaking guide. There is no charge but visitors are invited to contribute to the upkeep of the memorial. The track to Son My from the main road is in poor condition (difficult except in a four-wheel drive vehicle) but is under reconstruction.

Sleeping   **C** *Nha Khach Uy Ban*, 54 Hung Vuong St, T822873, F828195. Situated west of the post office, a/c and has a restaurant. **E** *Khach San So 2*, 41 Huong Vuong St, T823610. Some a/c and some hot water.

Transport   **Road Bus**: the bus station is on Le Thanh Ton St. **Train** The station is about 3 km west of town. There are regular connections with **Hanoi** and **Saigon** and all stops between the two.

Directory   **Banks** *Vietcombank*, 345 Hung Vuong St. *Nong Nghiep Bank*, 114 Tran Hung Dao St. **Communications** Internet: 141 Hung Vuong St. Post office: 80 Phan Dinh Phung St.

The Tay Son Rebellion (1771-88)

At the time of the Tay Son rebellion in 1771, Vietnam was in turmoil and conditions in the countryside were deteriorating to the point of famine. The three Tay Son brothers found a rich lode of dissatisfaction among the peasantry, which they successfully mined. Exploiting the latent discontent, they redistributed property from hostile mandarins to the peasants and raised a motley army of clerks, cattle-dealers, farmers, hill people, even scholars, to fight the Trinh and Nguyen lords. Brilliant strategists and demonstrating considerable skills of leadership, the brothers and their supporters swept through the country extending the area under their control south as far as Saigon and north to Trinh.

The Chinese, sensing that the disorder and dissent caused by the conflict gave them an opportunity to bring the entire nation under their control, sent a 200,000-strong army southwards in 1788. In the same year, the most intelligent (by all accounts) of the brothers, Nguyen Hue, proclaimed himself emperor under the name of Quang Trung and began to prepare for battle against the cursed Chinese. On the fifth day of Tet in 1789, the brothers attacked the Chinese near Thang Long catching them unawares as they celebrated the New Year. (The Viet Cong were to do the same during the Tet Offensive nearly 200 years later.) With great military skill, they routed the enemy, who fled in panic back towards China. Rather than face capture, one of the Chinese generals committed suicide. This victory at the Battle of Dong Da is regarded as one of the greatest in the annals of Vietnamese history. Quang Trung, having saved the nation from the Chinese, had visions of recreating the great Nam Viet Empire of the second century BC, and of invading China. Among the reforms that he introduced were a degree of land reform, a wider programme of education, and a fairer system of taxation. He even tried to get all peasants to carry identity cards with the slogan 'the great trust of the empire' emblazoned on them. These greater visions were not to be however: Quang Trung died suddenly in 1792, failing to provide the dynastic continuity that was necessary if Vietnam was to survive the impending French arrival.

As a postscript to the Tay Son rebellion, in 1802 the new Emperor Gia Long ordered his soldiers to exhume the body of the last of the brothers and urinate upon it in front of the deceased's wife and son. They were then torn apart by four elephants. Quang Trung and the other Tay Son brothers – like many former nationalist and peasant leaders – are revered by the Vietnamese and honoured by the Communists.

Quy Nhon

Quy Nhon, the capital of Binh Dinh Province, has a population of nearly 250,000 and is situated on a spur just 10 km off Highway 1. The town, established by royal decree in 1898, is taking a breather after a flurry of economic growth based on the export of logs and smuggling, so don't expect much from the hotels or restaurants. It can be used as a stopping-off point on the long journey north or south between Danang and Nha Trang. A seaside town, it has reasonable swimming off the sandy **Quy Nhon Beach** and a number of sights in the vicinity. A leper colony was founded here in 1929 by a French priest, Paul Maheu, and patients and their families were cared for by nuns. The colony survives (at the western end of Nguyen Hue St) but is now run by the health department.

Phone code: 056
Colour map 3, grid C6

Thap Doi Cham towers are situated on the edge of town. The area around Quy Nhon was a focus of the Cham Empire, and a number of monuments

Excursions

(13, it is said) have survived the intervening years. The two impressive Cham towers are about 3 km from the centre of town. ■ *Getting there: walk or bicycle northwest on Tran Hung Dao St, past the bus station, and after 2 km turn right onto Thap Doi St. The towers are a short distance along this street.*

Tay Son District is about 50 km from Quy Nhon off Highway 19, running west towards Play Ku. It is famous as the place where three brothers led a peasant revolt in 1771 (see box, page 223). The Vietnamese have a penchant for celebrating the exploits of the poor and the weak, and those of the Tay Son brothers are displayed in the **Quang Trung Museum**. ■ *Getting there: take a bus from the station on Tay Son St.*

Hoang De Citadel (also known as Cha Ban) is situated about 27 km north of Quy Nhon. Originally a Cham capital which was repeatedly attacked by the Vietnamese, it was taken over by the Tay Son brothers in the 18th century and made the capital of their short-lived kingdom. Not much remains except some **Cham ruins**, within the citadel walls, in the vicinity of the old capital. Fifty kilometres south of Quy Nhon is the small town of Song Cau, 2 km north of which is the *Sao Bien Restaurant,* recommended for its crab.

Transport *174 km from Quang Ngai, 223 from Buon Ma Thuot, 238 from Nha Trang, 304 from Danang, 412 from Hué*

Air The airport is 35 km to the north, 3 connections weekly with **Saigon**, 1 hr. Take a motorbike or taxi to the airport. **Road Bus**: the bus station is on Tay Son St. Express buses leave at 0500 for **Hanoi**, **Saigon**, **Nha Trang**, **Danang**, **Dalat**, **Hué**. **Train** The station is just over 1 km northwest of the town centre, on Hoang Hoa Tham St which runs off Tran Hung Dao St. Express trains do not stop here. To catch the express, take the shuttle train to Dieu Tri, 10 km away.

Directory **Airlines** *Vietnam Airlines,* Nguyen Tat Thanh St, T823125, F821280. **Banks** *Vietcombank*, 152 Le Loi St. Changes US$, cash and TCs. *Nong Nghiep Bank*, 44 Le Thanh Ton St. **Communications** Internet: 245 Le Hong Phong St, 5,000d per hr. **Post office:** Phan Boi Chau St. **Medical services** General Hospital, 102 Nguyen Hue St, T822722. **Tourist information** *Binh Dinh Tourism Company*, at 4 Nguyen Hue St, T822524.

Central Highlands

Despite its many splendours the Central Highlands does not match, in terms of rugged scenery, botanical diversity, and ethnic colour, the huge attractions of the mountainous north. Nevertheless, it has vibrant markets, exotic traditions and extraordinary vernacular architecture. A national park, mountain and high-plateau scenery, wild animals – all can be seen in the 250 km span that separates Kontum in the north from Buon Ma Thuot in the south. At elevations high enough to produce cool evenings, the Central Highlands offers the additional advantage to the visitor that the warm coastal plain and beaches of Nha Trang are only a few hours away.

Best time to visit
In the dry season (Dec-May) it is normally clear and sunny. Temperatures are pleasantly warm in the daytime and cooler at night, when a jacket is needed. In the wet season the sky is grey and the ground turns to oozing clay.

Background

French missionaries were active among the minorities of the Central Highlands (the colonial administration prevented ethnic Vietnamese from settling here) although with uneven success. Bishop Cuenot dispatched two missionaries from Quy Nhon to Buon Ma Thuot where they received a hostile reception from the M'nong, so travelled north to Kontum where among the Bahnar they found more receptive souls for their evangelizing. Today many of the ethnic minorities in the Central Highlands are Roman Catholic, although some are Protestant (Ede around Buon Ma Thuot, for instance).

While their compatriots were busy proselytizing, servants of the *Compagnie d'Haute Plateau d'Indochine* (CHPI), and many other smaller enterprises, were hard at work establishing plantations. Rubber and coffee were the staple crops. The greatest difficulty they faced was getting sufficient labour. Men and women of the ethnic minorities were happy in their villages drinking rice wine and cultivating their own small plots. They were poor but content in their poverty and saw no reason to accept the hard labour and slave wages of the plantation owners. Norman Lewis travelled in the Central Highlands and describes the situation well in his book, *A Dragon Apparent*.

Since 1984 there has been a bit of a free-for-all and a scramble for land. Ethnic Vietnamese, who the French kept out of the Central Highlands, have encroached on minority land and planted it with coffee, pepper and some fruit trees. From the air you can see neat rows of crops and carefully tended plots, interrupted only by large areas of scrub which are too dry to cultivate. The scene is reinforced at ground level where the occasional tall tree is the only reminder of the formerly extensive forest cover. As an indicator of progress, Vietnam is now the second largest producer of coffee in the world, although it produces the cheaper robusta rather than arabica coffee. The way of life of the minorities is disappearing with the forests – there are no trees to build their stilt houses from or shady forests in which to live and hunt. It is feared the fate the government has in mind for them is no more than the 'exotic' element of package holidays.

Play Ku

Play Ku (commonly known as Pleiku) was HQ to II Corps, one of the four military tactical zones into which South Vietnam was divided during the American war. John Vann (see Neil Sheehan's *Bright Shining Lie*, page 429) controlled massive B52 bombing raids against the encroaching NVA from here and, in June 1972, he was killed in a helicopter crash just outside Play Ku.

Phone code: 059
Colour map 3, grid B5

The town, with a population of 35,000, is located high on the Play Ku Plateau, one of many such structural features in the Central Highlands. It is the capital of Gia Lai Province which, with a population density of just 34 people per sq km, is one of the most sparsely inhabited areas of Vietnam. Historically, this was a densely forested part of the country and it remains home to a large number of hill tribes.

The town itself has little to offer the tourist; during the monsoon the streets turn into muddy torrents and chill damp pervades hotel rooms and bedding. There is a small **museum** at 28 Quang Trung St which houses little of interest. The attractions of the area lie outside the town on the road north to Kontum, which is a pleasant drive by motorbike, especially early in the year when the white coffee blossom is attractive and exudes a lovely jasmine-like scent.

There are a number of places to visit on the Kontum road. **Bien Ho** is a large volcanic lake and the main source of water for Play Ku, so no fishing or swimming. A raised platform on a promontory jutting out into the lake is a good place from which to appreciate the beauty and peace of the setting. ■ *1,000d. Getting there: by car or xe ôm, 5 km north of Play Ku turn right on to the Quy*

Excursions

Nhon road (Highway 19) and after a further 2 km turn left past a derelict ARVN barracks.

Bien Ho tea factory which occupies an unlovely concrete building 14 km north of Play Ku sometimes allows visits. About 2 km further is the turn left to the once spectacular **Yaly Falls**. Now that there is a hydro-electric plant to which the water is diverted there is not much to see, but along the road are several **Jarai villages** which are worth a visit. It would appear that foreigners no longer need a licence to do so. For the sake of preserving the traditional way of life it would seem sensible to stick to those villages. The first such village is **Plei Mrong**, about 2 km on the left. This is the least interesting of the three as it has no *rong* (see Glossary page 435) or communal house or graveyard statues, but it still affords a glimpse of Jarai life to those in a hurry. **Plei Fun** is about 20 km along the Yaly road and is the village *Gia Lai Tourist* will take you to if you book a tour through them. The local villagers have wised up to tourism and may try and charge you 30,000d to see their graveyard. The graves are covered by tiled or wooden roofs which shelter the worldly possessions of the deceased – bottles, bowls, even the odd bicycle. Carved hardwood statues guard the graves, a peculiarly Jarai tradition. Push on to **Plei Mun**, another 5 km down the road and left 2 km down a dirt road, for some even finer examples. There is also a traditional wooden rong house with a corrugated iron roof.

Sleeping

Play Ku has something of a shortage of hotel accommodation and some hotels still do not accept foreigners. Don't expect any bargains either

B-C *Pleiku*, 124 Le Loi St, T824628, F822151. Recently revamped, but no getting away from the Soviet 'ethnic' concrete architectural style. Some perfectly satisfactory rooms with satellite TV and cheaper ones that represent good value. **C** *Hung Vuong*, 215 Hung Vuong St, T824270, F827170. Actual entrance to the hotel is at 2 Le Loi Street. A/c, fridge and TV in every room, friendly staff, may be possible to negotiate a discount. **C-D** *Ialy*, 89 Hung Vuong St, T824843, F827619, ialyhotel@dng.vnn.vn The cheapest rooms are on the top floor and quite good value for Play Ku, Asian restaurant, breakfast included. **C-D** *Movie Star*, 6 Vo Thi Sau St, T823855. Very friendly and comfortable. **C-E** *Thanh Lich*, 86 Nguyen van Troi St, T824674, F828319. A typical Play Ku Hotel, discuss the price before staying.

Play Ku

Sleeping
1 Hung Vuong
2 Ialy
3 Movie Star
4 Pleiku
5 Thanh Lich

Eating
1 My Tam
2 Nguc Huong

There are noodle restaurants along Nguyen Van Troi St and the occasional low cost **Eating**
com binh dan. *Ialy Hotel*, 89 Hung Vuong St. Decent Vietnamese and Western fare.
My Tam, 63 Quang Trung St. Serves good Vietnamese staples, chicken rice and noodles. *Ngoc Huong*, 76 Hung Vuong St, serves decent northern Vietnamese dishes.
Thanh Lich. Spotless restaurant with a good choice of dishes, meals for under US$3.

In the *Hung Vuong Hotel*. Expensive, but quite helpful. Organize some specialist veter- **Tour operators**
ans and trekking tours. The independent tourist should try ringing Mr Nhung of
Nhung's Tours, 48 Hung Vuong St, T822666 or 827563. Very friendly, knowledgeable
one-man outfit which can organize all sorts of programmes at reasonable (although
not always the cheapest) prices. Mr Nhung speaks good English.

Air There are daily connections with **Saigon**, 3 per week with **Vinh** and **Danang**. For **Transport**
passengers travelling light, just take a *xe ôm* from the airport for around US$1. Taxis *Play Ku is 186 km from*
wait at the airport and charge US$4. **Road Bus**: Regular connections with **Saigon**, *Quy Nhon, 197 from*
Quy Nhon, **Buon Ma Thuot** (Dak Lak), **Dalat** and **Kontum**. **Minibuses**: depart from *Buon Ma Thuot*
the market. **Taxi** *Pleiku Taxi,* 11B Nguyen Van Troi St, T757575. Also rent cars, for
example 500,000d to Buon Ma Thuot, T828877.

Airlines *Vietnam Airlines*, 55 Quang Trung St, T823058. **Banks** *Vietcombank*, 12 **Directory**
Tran Hung Dao St. The only place in town that changes TCs (as there's nowhere in
Kontum this is probably the most compelling reason to stop in Play Ku at all). **Commu-**
nications Internet: 57A Nguyen Du St. 350d/ min. **Post office:** 87 Hung Vuong St.
Tourist information *Gia Lai Tourist*, is at 2 Le Loi St, T824271, F824891,
gialaitourist@fpt.net.com

Kontum

Kontum is the administrative capital of Kontum Province. There are two good *Phone code: 060*
reasons for visiting Kontum, to see some lovely old churches and to visit Bahnar *Colour map 3, grid B5*
minority villages. Otherwise the town itself is rather dull. It is 49 km north of
Play Ku with a population of 35,000, many of whom are from ethnic minorities.

About 12 km south of Kontum the road crosses the **Chu Pao Pass**, the former site of a US and ARVN base. There is nothing to see in particular, but one
can imagine its strategic importance with its commanding views over the
Kontum Plateau. The road descends past sugar cane plantations before crossing the Dakbla River – the lighter soil of Kontum is much more suitable for
sugar than the red loam of Play Ku, which is best for coffee and rubber.

In town there is the **Tan Huong Church** on Nguyen Hue Street, whose
whitewashed façade bears an interesting depiction of St George and the dragon.
Built 150 years ago, this little church alone is worth a visit to Kontum. It is not
immediately evident that the church is built on stilts, but crouch down and look
under one of the little arches that run along the side and the stilts, joists and
floorboards are clear. The glass in the windows is all old, as the rippling indicates, although one of the two stained-glass windows over the altar has required
a little patching up. Unfortunately the roof is a modern replacement, but the
original style of fishscale tiling can still be seen in the tower. The interior of the
church is exquisite, with dark wooden columns and a fine vaulted ceiling made
of wattle and daub. The altar is a new, but rather fine addition, made of a
jackfruit tree, as is the lectern. Set into the altar is an old plaque which commemorates the French priests and missionaries slain by Emperor Tu Duc in the
mid-to-late 19th century. If the church is shut a kindly old one-legged verger
will gladly open it and show visitors around. He lives in the adjacent house.

The Central Region

Further east on the same street is the superb **Wooden Church**, well worth a visit. Built by the French with Bahnar labour in 1913, it remains largely unaltered, with the original wooden frame and wooden doors. Inside, the blue walls combine with the dark-brown polished wood to produce a very serene effect. Unfortunately the windows are modern tinted-glass and the paintings on them depicting scenes from Christ's life as well as a couple of Old Testament scenes with Moses are a little crude. In the grounds to the right stands a *rong* house and a statue of Stephano Theodore Cuenot, the first Catholic bishop of East Cochin China diocese. He died, a victim of Emperor Tu Duc's implacable stance against missionaries, in prison in Binh Đinh on 14 November 1861, the day before the beheading instructions arrived. Every year a fête is held to commemorate him. Cuenot was beatified Saint Etienne-Théodore Cuenot in 1909. The **Bishop's Palace** still stands and is the finest building in Kontum, although not open to the public. It is at 56 Tran Hung Dao Street at the junction with Nguyen Van Troi Street.

Kontum Prison, the former residence of several prominent revolutionaries, is now being added to visitors' itineraries by *Kontum Tourist*. In fact it was completely demolished and has been rebuilt from scratch, so if it's authenticity you're after, don't bother.

Excursions There are scores of Bahnar villages around Kontum that can be reached by motorbike, and at least one that is easily accessible on foot. **Play To Ngia** is at the westerly end of Phan Chu Trinh Street down a dusty track. Wattle and daub houses, mostly on stilts, can be seen and the long low white building on short stilts is the church. In the evening the elderly folk of the village go for communal prayers while the young people gather at the foot of their longhouses for a sunset chat. In and around the village are small fields heavily fortified with thorns and barbed wire, which seems a little strange considering the Bahnar do not lock their doors. In fact the defence is not against poachers but the village's large population of rooting, snuffling, pot-bellied pigs. Every family has a few pigs which roam loose. The pigs are sometimes given names and recognize the voice of their owner, coming when called.

Most houses are on stilts, with the animals living underneath. They are built from wattle and daub around a wooden frame, although brick is starting to appear, and modern tile is beginning to replace the lovely old fishscale tiling. The shortage of

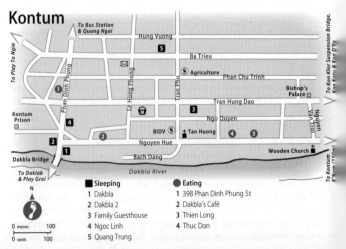

Kontum

To Bus Station & Quang Ngai

Hung Vuong

Ba Trieu

Agriculture

Phan Chu Trinh

Bishop's Palace

Tran Hung Dao

Ngo Quyen

Tan Huong

Nguyen Hue

Bach Dang

Dakbla Bridge

Dakbla River

To Daklak & Play Groi

To Play To Ngia

Phan Dinh Phung

Le Hong Phong

Tran Phu

Nguyen Van Troi

Kontum Prison

BIDV

Wooden Church

To Kon Klor Suspension Bridge, Kon Kotu & Kon D'Re

N

0 metres 100
0 yards 100

■ **Sleeping**
1 Dakbla
2 Dakbla 2
3 Family Guesthouse
4 Ngoc Linh
5 Quang Trung

● **Eating**
1 39B Phan Dinh Phung St
2 Dakbla's Café
3 Thien Long
4 Thuc Don

trees in the Central Highlands means that newer buildings are constructed without stilts. Considering the tiny spaces in which most Vietnamese live, these houses are positively palatial. There is a large living room in the centre, a kitchen (with no chimney) at one end and bedroom at the other. On the inside, the half-timbered effect with hunting trophies hanging on the walls creates the impression of a baronial mansion, particularly as the smoke of decades darkens the wood and impregnates the house with a rich fragrance. **Kon D'Re** is a fine example of a community almost untouched by modern life. A perfect *rong* communal house dominates the hamlet, and all other dwellings in the village are made from bamboo, or mud and reeds. The Bahnar *rong* is instantly recognizable by its tall thatched roof. The height of the roof is meant to indicate the significance of the building and make it visible to all. It is a focal point of the village for meetings of the village elders, weddings and other communal events. The stilt house nearest the well is in fact a small Roman Catholic church. Nearby **Kon Kotu** is similar. ■ *Getting there: follow Nguyen Hue St and turn right into Tran Hung Dao St, cross the suspension bridge (Kon Klor Bridge) over the Dakbla River (built in 1997 after a flood washed the old one away). After a few hundred metres turn left (just before the centre for traditional medicine) and continue for 3 km bearing left for Kon Kotu and right for Kon D'Re.*

A more lively Bahnar community can be found at **Kontum K'Nam**. Turn right off Nguyen Hue past the Wooden Church. Here the stilt houses are crowded close together and the village bustles with activity. The village of **Play Groi** is about 1 km south of Dakbla Bridge. Its *rong* house is past its best, roofed with corrugated sheets, but the people are friendly. ■ *Getting there: go south down Highway 14, approximately 1 km after Dakbla bridge turn left immediately before a petrol station and continue down this lane.*

The Central Region

Sleeping

B-D *Dakbla*, 2 Phan Dinh Phung St, T863333, F863336. Some a/c, all hot water, satellite TV, friendly welcome. **B-D** *Dakbla 2*, near the old bus station. Upstairs rooms have a nice view over the river and surrounding countryside but cheaper rooms have no hot water. Usually empty, even charm will fail to produce a discount. **C-D** *Quang Trung*, 168 Ba Trieu St, T862249. Some a/c, all rooms have hot water, cheaper rooms in a small block at the back. It may be possible to charm them into lowering the price. **D-E** *Family Guesthouse*, 55 Tran Hung Dao St, T865748. A new and privately run guesthouse offering good value for money. **D-E** *Ngoc Linh*, 12 A Phan Dinh Phung St, T864560. All a/c, even the dormitory rooms, clean, good value.

■ *on map, page 228*
Phone code: 060

Not a lot of choice and not particularly good value. Few foreigners stay here

Eating

Not a lot of choice but the best restaurants are to be found along Nguyen Hue Street. *Dakbla Restaurant*, under the *Dakbla Hotel*. Some good Vietnamese and Western dishes. *Dakbla's Café*, 168 Nguyen Hue St, T862584. Café and souvenir shop with English menu and friendly staff. Recommended. *Thien Long*, 40 Nguyen Hue St, T864198. Decent Vietnamese menu but check the prices before ordering. *Thuc Don*, 90 Nguyen Hue St, T862594. Enormous menu broken down into sections – 'à la carte', 'lunch', 'special' and 'celebration' – good food. Noodles and noodle soup are served at *39B Phan Dinh Phung St*.

● *on map, page 228*

Tour operators

The offices of *Dakbla Tourist* can be found in *Dakbla Hotel*, T863333.

Transport

Road Kontum is reached via Play Ku (Pleiku) on Highway 14 by bus (regular departures), car or motorbike. Coming from Danang it is possible to cut across via the road 10 km south of Quang Ngai, but only by 4WD. Surrounding villages are best toured by motorbike. **Motorbike rental:** bicycles and motorbikes can be hired at *Dakbla's Café*.

Directory

Banks *Agriculture Bank* is on the corner of Tran Phu and Phan Chu Trinh, but doesn't cash TCs. *BIDV*, Tran Phu St. **Communications** Post office: 205 Le Hong Phong St.

Buon Ma Thuot

Buon Ma Thuot is sited on the Daclac Plateau at an altitude of about 1,000 m. The unofficial capital of the Central Highlands, it is surrounded by plantations and large numbers of *montagnards* – the ethnic minorities of the hills or hill tribes. It is rarely visited by tourists as it lies off the main tourist trail, but it is not hard to get to. It is the capital of Dac Lac Province with a population of 100,000, and not far from the Cambodian border.

Within a short drive is a National Park, where rare white elephants are said to roam, and several accessible minority villages where visitors can spend the night. Coffee has long been the mainstay of the local economy and the fortunes of the area, including employment prospects, are highly dependent on the price of coffee. Buon Ma Thuot has a number of graduates

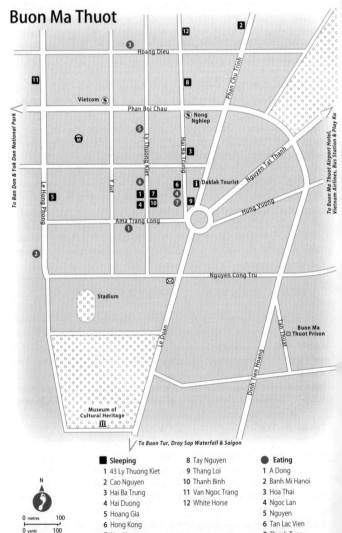

Buon Ma Thuot

■ Sleeping
1 43 Ly Thuong Kiet
2 Cao Nguyen
3 Hai Ba Trung
4 Hai Duong
5 Hoang Gia
6 Hong Kong
7 Huy Hoang
8 Tay Nguyen
9 Thang Loi
10 Thanh Binh
11 Van Ngoc Trang
12 White Horse

● Eating
1 A Dong
2 Banh Mi Hanoi
3 Hoa Thai
4 Ngoc Lan
5 Nguyen
6 Tan Lac Vien
7 Thanh Tuan

0 metres 100
0 yards 100

and when coffee prices are low a job as a hotel receptionist is the best they can hope for.

History

Since reunification in 1975, areas of this part of Vietnam have been designated New Economic Zones. 'Excess' population from the rural areas around Saigon and from the overpopulated lands of the Red River Delta have been resettled in new villages and the forest has been cleared. Many of the resettlement communities have been unsuccessful – the poor quality of the land was not fully appreciated and yields of crops have been disappointingly low. There has also been some friction between the settlers and the minority ethnic groups (mostly Ede) who live in the area, who have been discriminated against for many years. Indeed, there are suggestions that the mass inwards migration of ethnic Vietnamese into upland areas is as much about politics as economics. In 2001 there were serious disturbances in the area resulting in the closure of the Central Highlands to all foreigners. Many minority people fled to Cambodia in fear of their lives.

Sights

There is a **Museum of Cultural Heritage**, at 4 Nguyen Du St, in Bao Dai's old palace; it contains a smallish collection of clothes, tools and other artefacts of the various minority groups (*montagnards*) that live in the area, and admission is free. **Buon Ma Thuot prison** is at 18 Tan Thuat Street and is worth a visit. Here you can see guardrooms, watch towers and the tiny cells where revolutionaries from the 1930s to the 1970s were imprisoned. A small museum in the former governor's residence contains paintings of prison life and photographs of distinguished former inmates. The buildings are grim but the compound is actually a rather peaceful place with well-tended and attractive gardens. ■ *Free, but if the caretaker has to open it up especially for you, a small donation is appreciated.*

Excursions

Many people get to these sites on a tour from Nha Trang

The serene **Lak Lake** is about 50 km southeast of Buon Ma Thuot. It is an attraction in its own right but all the more compelling a visit on account of the surrounding **M'nong villages**. Early morning mists hang above the calm waters and mingle with the columns of woodsmoke rising from the longhouses. The lake can be explored by dugout (about US$3 per hour). The canoes are painstakingly hollowed out from tree trunks by axe. The M'nong have been famed as elephant catchers for hundreds of years, although the elephants are now used for tourist rides rather than in their traditional role for dragging logs from the forest. It is possible to stay overnight at a M'nong village, **Buon Juin** (Buon means village), indeed it is the only way to watch the elephants taking their evening wallow in the cool waters and to appreciate the tranquility of sunrise over the lake. The M'nong number about 50,000 and are matriarchal. An evening supping with your hosts, sharing rice wine and sleeping in the simplicity of a M'nong longhouse is an ideal introduction to these genial people. ■ *It costs US$3-5 to stay in a longhouse.*

Unfortunately, Lak Lake has been developed as a tourist attraction and Buon Juin is rather touristy now. For those going on a tour there is little choice as to where to go, but for the independent traveller on a motorbike there are plenty of villages, both ethnic Vietnamese and minority, to visit, but do not expect any English to be spoken. ■ *Getting there: take Highway 27 (the Dalat road) turn right down a track just before a sign advising 'Dalat 156 km'.*

Yet another of Bao Dai's hunting lodges overlooks the lake about 3 km from Buon Juin: whatever his other faults the last emperor was blessed with a good eye for location. The building looks nothing like a palace now, having long ago been stripped of the precious woods with which it was panelled. In fact, the rather ugly concrete shell is now a television broadcasting station, hence the large aerial. A quick climb to the top of the stairs inside, however, brings its reward in the form of superb views of the lake and surrounding plateau.

The lake can be explored by dugout (US$10 per hour through *Daklak Tourist*, see page 234, or for less than one third if arranged independently). **Krong Kmar Falls** are popular locally but it is dubious whether their attraction warrants the 14-km detour off Highway 27. This applies particularly in the holiday season when they are strewn with litter. ■ *5,000d.*

The best **Ede village** to visit is **Buon Tur**. Apart from the odd TV aerial, life has remained unchanged in this community of 20 stilt houses and, despite the efforts of the government to stop it, Ede is still taught in school. The village headman was born in 1916, he speaks no English or Vietnamese so if he invites you for tea under his house the conversation will have to be conducted in French. Visitors used to be able to stay overnight in the village, but the local police have put a stop to this pleasant and harmless practice. This is for our own safety, they explain in their customary thoughtful way, because the doors on Ede houses have no locks. ■ *Getting there: 15 km southwest of Buon Ma Thuot on Highway 14.*

A further 6 km on is **Dray Sap waterfall**, a low but 100-m-wide cascade, particularly spectacular in the wet season when it fully justifies its name 'waterfall of smoke'. It's a beautiful spot with huge trees and lush greenery. A new, red barrier replaces the painted line beyond which you venture at your peril. ■ *Admission to the waterfall, 5,000d. Getting there: take Le Duan St south of town. This becomes Highway 14, the main road to Saigon, so exercise particular care in driving.*

Yok Don National Park is a 58,000 ha wildlife reserve about 40 km northwest of Buon Ma Thuot. The park contains at least 63 species of animals and 196 species of birds and is thought to be the home of several rare white elephants. There are treks and tours, some of which can be undertaken on the back of an elephant: a two-day elephant safari costs US$180 for two people, trekking deep into the park and staying in tents near Yok Don mountain. This is probably the only chance of seeing wildlife of any great rarity but, alas, the rare become rarer with each passing year. The less adventurous (or those with smaller elephant-trekking budgets) will have to make do with one-hour rides at US$15 or simply watching one of the village's elephants at work. Accommodation is available at the **D** *Park Guesthouse*, T853110. Four rooms near the park gate. ■ *Admission to the park, US$5.*

About 3 km beyond the park gate is **Ban Don village**, a harmonious, multi-racial village. It is home to Ede, M'nong, Lao, Thai, Khmer and a few Giarai people. The village has a long tradition of taming the forest's elephants, and beyond the third sub-hamlet is the tomb of Khun Ju-Nop, known as the king elephant catcher, who died in 1924. His tomb is the square one next to the taller white stupa commemorating his brother, also a famous elephant

Around Buon Ma Thuot

To Play Ku & Kontum

Ban Don

Yok Don National Park

Buon Ma Thuot

Buon Tur

Dray Sap Waterfall

To Saigon

Buon Jun

Lak Lake

Krong Kmar Falls

To Nha Trang

14

26

14

27

To Dalat

0 km   10
0 miles   10

catcher, who died in 1950. Both of these men were of Lao origin. Behind these is a more modern tomb of a M'nong elephant catcher, Y Pum B'Ya, a son of Khun Ju-Nop. ■ *Getting there: take Phan Boi Chau St west out of town.*

Daklak Tourist operates 7 hotels in town, all demanding US$ cash-in-hand and plenty of it from foreigners, and not much room for bargain. There are now a few rival operations including a couple of private hotels.

B *Cao Nguyen*, 65 Phan Chu Trinh St, T851913, F851912. Price includes breakfast. All rooms have satellite TV and bath. There are 6 truly enormous suites for which it would seem worth paying the extra US$5. **B** *Thang Loi*, 1 Phan Chu Trinh St, T857615, F857622, daklaktour@dng.vnn.vn All mod cons, comfortable, restaurant. **C** *Hai Ba Trung*, 8-10 Hai Ba Trung St, T852407, F853113. Comfortable and cheerful but overpriced. **C** *Tay Nguyen*, 110 Ly Thuong Kiet St, T851010, F852250. All rooms have a/c, hot water etc. Breakfast included but even so it is horribly overpriced. **D** *Hong Kong*, 35 Hai Ba Trung St, T852630. Some a/c, all hot water, in need of renovation. Since there is a wider choice in Buon Me Thuot now, it is pricey for what it offers. **D-E** *43 Ly Thuong Kiet*, 43 Ly Thuong Kiet St, T853921. Fan only, some hot water, grotty and cheap. **E** *Hoang Gia*, 80 Le Hong Phong St, T852161. Fan only, some decent-sized but shabby rooms.

The following independent hotels offer far better value for money and charge foreigners the same price as Vietnamese. **B-C** *White Horse*, 50-54 Hai Ba Trung St, T850379, F852121. All rooms a/c, hot water, IDD, satellite TV. Friendly and good value. **C-D** *Hoa Polang*, Km 8, Highway 14, T863444, F863046, hiepphuc@dng.vnn.vn A truly amazing pink edifice built on the profits of coffee. A short way out of town on the Play Ku road. Large rooms all with a/c, hot water and every amenity, including comfortable firm beds (rare in Vietnam). Visitors may regard this as sufficient compensation for the noise of the karaoke (which admittedly stops at 2200). In the grounds of the hotel are a local amusement park and pool. **D** *Buon Ma Thuot Airport*, 65-67 Nguyen Tat Thanh St, T952266, F956265. All a/c, a little way out of town but nice rooms with bath, and friendly staff. Vietnam Airlines office is in the hotel. **D** *Thanh Binh*, 24 Ly Thuong Kiet St, T853812, F811511. Clean, all rooms with a/c, good value. **D** *Van Ngoc Trang*, 269 Le Hong Phong St, T853945. Newly built to a high standard, all rooms have hot water and bath tub, some have a/c. **D-E** *Huy Hoang*, 30 Ly Thuong Kiet St, T/F858020. Newly built, efficient staff. **E** *Hai Duong*, 33 Ly Thuong Kiet St, T857790. Nice rooms, shared bathroom with hot water, a/c rooms are very good value.

Thang Loi Hotel has a good restaurant, as does the *White Horse*, whose seafood is particularly good. *Banh Mi Hanoi*, 17-19 Le Hong Phong St. Bakery selling sandwiches, drinks and a range of goodies such as cheese and Mars Bars, ideal picnic provisions. *A Dong*, 29 Ama Trang Long St. Has a range of Vietnamese, Chinese, Thai and western foods. *Hoa Thai*, 70 Hoang Dieu St. Serves good Vietnamese and Chinese food. *Ngoc Lan*, 27 Hai Ba Trung St. Simple and tasty Vietnamese food. *Tan Lac Vien*, 61 Ly Thuong Kiet St. Serves local Vietnamese fare. *Thanh Tuan*, 21 Hai Ba Trung St. Cheap rice dishes. *Nguyen*, 55 Hai Ba Trung St. Very cheap and reputedly does the best *pho* in town.

Local Most independent travellers visit the sites by motorbike but should be warned that local standards of driving are atrocious even by Vietnamese standards. Parents drape their infants over the handlebars of their new US$300, Chinese fall-apart- in-2-day-motorbikes and hurtle around in an appalling massacre of the innocents.

The Central Region

Air Daily connections with **Saigon**, 55 mins; 3 flights weekly from **Danang**, 65 mins. Taxi or motorbike to airport, 15 mins. **Road** It's possible to take a 4WD from Dalat over the mountain road. **Bus**: regular connections with **Saigon** (4 hrs by minibus via the upgraded Highway 14), **Nha Trang** and **Quy Nhon**. The bus terminal is about 2½ km northeast of the town centre. **Motorbike rental**: there are no official motorbike rental shops in Buon Ma Thuot but most hotels will rent them and many *Honda ôm* drivers will happily rent you their bike for US$5-8 per day. Note, however, that to hire the driver too will cost little more. **Taxi**: *Buon Ma Thuot Taxi*, T813813, 811811.

Directory **Airlines** *Vietnam Airlines*, 65-67 Nguyen Tat Thanh St, T955055. **Banks** *Vietcombank*, 92-94 Y Jut St. Changes TCs. Jewellers shops in Y Jut St also change US$ cash. *Nong Nghiep Bank*, 37 Phan Boi Chau St. **Communications** Internet: cyber cafés still yet to make an appearance, one or two hotels have email and allow access to their customers. **Post office**: *GPO*, 6 Le Duan St. **Tourist information** *Daklak Tourist*, 3 Phan Chu Trinh St, T852108, F852865, has quite expensive tours, but is helpful and usually has maps.

Nha Trang

Phone code: 058 *Nha Trang is Vietnam's only real seaside town. It nestles amid the protective*
Colour map 4, *embrace of the surrounding hills and islands. The long golden beach, which*
grid A6 *only a very few years ago was remarkably empty, fills up quickly these days, and it is easy to see why. The light has a beautifully radiant quality and the air is clear: colours are vivid, particularly the blues of the sea, sky and fishing boats berthed on the river.*

An important Cham settlement, NhaTrang retains distinguished and well-preserved Cham towers. It is a centuries-old fishing town established in the sheltered mouth of the Cai Estuary. A port was built here in 1924 which can handle small coastal traders. Its clear waters and offshore islands won wide acclaim in the 1960s and its new-found prosperity is based firmly on tourism.

Ins and outs

Getting there Nha Trang's airport is on the southern edge of town – a 5-min ride from the centre.
See Transport, There are daily flights to Hanoi and Saigon and 5 departures a week for Danang. The
page 241, town is on the main north-south railway line and there are trains to Saigon and Hanoi –
for further details and stops between. The main bus terminal is west of the town centre. Note that inter-provincial buses do not go into Nha Trang but drop off on Highway 1 which bypasses the town. *Xe ôms* take passengers into town.

Getting around Nha Trang is negotiable on foot – just. But there are bicycles and motorbikes for hire everywhere and the usual *cyclos*. Some hotels and the tour companies have cars for out-of-town excursions.

The town

Word has spread, and Nha Trang's days as an undiscovered treasure are over. Nha Trang is a firmly established favourite of Vietnamese as well as foreign visitors and Nha Trangites of all backgrounds and persuasions endeavour to ease the dollar from the traveller's sweaty paw. Nevertheless, there is a permanent relaxed holiday atmosphere, the streets are not crowded and the motorbikes cruise at a leisurely pace.

The name Nha Trang is thought to be derived from the Cham word *yakram*, meaning bamboo river, and the surrounding area was a focal point of the Cham Kingdom – some of the country's best-preserved Cham towers lie close by (see below). Nha Trang was besieged for nine months during the Tay Son rebellion in the late 18th century (see page 223), before eventually falling to the rebel troops. There are, in reality, two Nha Trangs: popular Nha Trang, which is a sleepy, sedate seaside town consisting of a long, palm and casuarina-fringed beach and one or two streets running parallel to it, and commercial Nha Trang to the north of Yersin Street, which is a bustling city with an attractive array of Chinese shophouses.

The Central Region

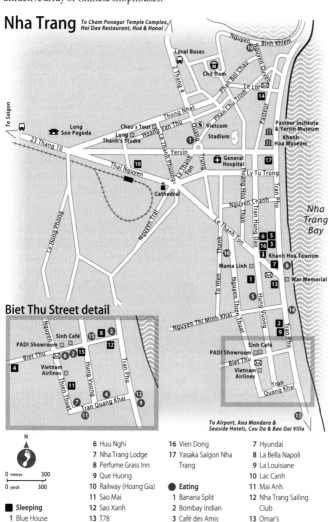

Nha Trang

N

0 metres 300
0 yards 300

■ **Sleeping**
1 Blue House
2 Hai Quan
3 Hai Yen
4 Hanoi
5 Hoc Vien Luc Quan
6 Huu Nghi
7 Nha Trang Lodge
8 Perfume Grass Inn
9 Que Huong
10 Railway (Hoang Gia)
11 Sao Mai
12 Sao Xanh
13 T78
14 Thang Loi
   (Hotel La Frégate)
15 Truc Linh
   & Restaurant
16 Vien Dong
17 Yasaka Saigon Nha
   Trang

● **Eating**
1 Banana Split
2 Bombay Indian
3 Café des Amis
4 Candlelight Café
5 Chau Café
6 Good Morning
   Vietnam & Baan Thai
7 Hyundai
8 La Bella Napoli
9 La Louisiane
10 Lac Canh
11 Mai Anh
12 Nha Trang Sailing
   Club
13 Omar's
14 Rainbow Bar
15 Shorty's
16 Thanh Thanh

Sights

Cham Ponagar Temple complex On a hill just outside the city is the Cham Ponagar Temple complex, known locally as Thap Ba. Originally the complex consisted of eight towers, four of which remain. Their stylistic differences indicate that they were built at different times between the seventh and 12th centuries. The largest (at 23 m high) was built in AD 817 and contains a statue of Lady Thien Y-ana, also known as Ponagar (who was the beautiful wife of Prince Bac Hai), as well as a fine and very large lingam. She taught the people of the area weaving and new agricultural techniques, and they built the tower in her honour. The other towers are dedicated to gods: the central tower to Cri Cambhu (which has become a fertility temple for childless couples); the northwest tower to Sandhaka (wood cutter and foster-father to Lady Thien Y-ana); and the south tower to Ganeca (Lady Thien Y-ana's daughter). The best time to visit the towers is in the late afternoon, 1600-1700. ■ *5,000d. Getting there: either walk or catch a cyclo. Take 2 Thang 4 St north out of town; Cham Ponagar is just over the second of two bridges (Xom Bong bridge), a couple of km from the city centre.*

En route to the towers, the road crosses the **Cai River estuary** where there is a diversity of craft – including Nha Trang's elegant fleet of blue fishing boats, lined with red and complete with painted eyes for spotting the fish, and coracles (*cái thúng*) for getting to the boats and mechanical fish traps. The traps take the form of nets which are supported by long arms; the arms are hinged to a platform on stilts and are raised and lowered by wires connected to a capstan which is turned, sometimes by hand but more commonly by foot.

Long Son Pagoda The best known pagoda in Nha Trang is the Long Son Pagoda, built in 1963, which can be found at 23 Thang 10 Street (the west extension of Yersin Street). Inside the sanctuary is an unusual image of the Buddha, backlit with natural light (ask a monk for access if the building is closed). Murals depicting the jataka stories decorate the upper walls. To the right of the sanctuary, stairs lead up to a 9-m-high white Buddha, perched on a hill top, from where there are fine views. The pagoda commemorates those monks and nuns who died demonstrating against the Diem government – in particular those who, through their self-immolation, brought the despotic nature of the Diem regime and its human rights abuses to the attention of the American public.

Nha Trang Cathedral Granite-coloured (though built of concrete) and imposing, the cathedral was built in 1933 on a small rock outcrop. The cathedral has a single, crennelated tower, with stained glass in the upper sections of its windows and pierced metal in the lower. The path to the cathedral runs off Nguyen Trai Street. Daily mass is said here.

Yersin Museum The Yersin Museum, at 8 Tran Phu Street, south of the post office, is contained within the colonnaded **Pasteur Institute** founded by the great scientist's protégé, Dr Alexandre Yersin. Swiss-born Yersin first arrived in Vietnam in 1891 and spent much of the rest of his life in Nha Trang (see box, page 237). The museum contains the lab equipment used by Yersin, his library and stereoscope through which visitors can see in 3-D the black-and-white slides, including shots taken by Yersin on his visits to the highlands. The curator is helpful and friendly, and fluent in French and English. ■ *Mon-Sat 0730-1100, 26,000d.*

Alexandre Yersin

Alexandre John Emille Yersin was born in 1863 in Canton Vaud, Switzerland. He enrolled at the University of Lausanne and completed his medical education in Paris where he became an assistant to Louis Pasteur. In 1888, Yersin adopted French citizenship. To the astonishment of all he became a ship's doctor; he visited the Far East and in 1891 landed in Nha Trang.

Two years later, as part of his exploration of Vietnam he 'discovered' the Dalat Plateau which he recommended for development as a hill resort owing to its beauty and temperate climate. The following year, in 1894, he was urged to visit Hong Kong to assist in an outbreak of the plague. He identified the baccilus which was named Yersinia pestis.

In 1895 he set up a laboratory in Nha Trang which, in 1902, became a Pasteur Institute, the first to be established outside France. Here he developed an anti-serum for the treatment of plague. He established a cattle farm for the production of serum and vaccines and for the improvement of breeding stock at Suoi Dau, 25 km south of Nha Trang. Yersin was responsible for the introduction to Vietnam of commercial crops such as coffee, rubber and the cinchona (quinine) tree.

In his retirement he indulged his passions, astrology, photography and observation of the hydrographic conditions of Nha Trang Bay.

Yersin died in 1943 and was buried at Suoi Dau. His tombstone, simply engraved 'Alexandre Yersin 1863–1943', can be seen today at Suoi Dau. Take Highway 1, 25 km south of Nha Trang, look for the sign 'Tombeau de Alexandre Yersin'. The key to the gate is kept with a local family. The tomb is 1.5 km from the gate.

The Khanh Hoa Museum is at 16 Tran Phu Street. It contains a Dongson bronze drum and a Palaeolithic stone xylophone. There is a room of ethnographics and, of course, a Ho Chi Minh room which contains several items of interest. English-speaking curators will be pleased to show you around and should be tipped.

Khanh Hoa Museum

The **Cho Dam** (central market) close to Nguyen Hong Son Street is a good place to wander and browse and it is quite well-stocked with useful items. In the vicinity of the market, along **Phan Boi Chau Street** for example, are some bustling streets with old colonial-style shuttered houses.

Central market

Long Thanh is one of Vietnam's most distinguished photographers. He works only in black and white. Many of his famous pictures are taken in and around his native Nha Trang. Long Thanh is one of the most sensitive of photographers and captures the full gamut of human emotions. His cheerful children (often the ethnic minority Cham) frolicking in the rain and wistful old men and women who have witnessed generations of change in a single lifetime stand out as do his pictures of young women. Long Thanh has won a series of international awards and recognition for his work. He speaks English and welcomes visitors to his **studio** at 126 Hoang Van Thu Street not far from the railway station, T824875.

Long Thanh's studio

Excursions

Cau Da is a small fishing port 5 km south of Nha Trang along the beach road (*Tran Phu*). Attractively sited on a small promontory outside Cau Da with magnificent views on all sides, is yet another villa of the last emperor of Vietnam, Bao Dai, which is now a hotel. Born into an era of air travel Dai took

South of Nha Trang

The Central Region

advantage of this mode of travel to enjoy the most enchanting places in Vietnam. With his penchant for fresh air this must have been one of his favourites.

Cau Da is home to the **Institute of Oceanography**. Built in 1922, it is the only institute of its kind in Vietnam: it contains a selection of poorly displayed marine fauna in pickling jars and glass cases and in the front courtyard are tanks of live fish, turtles and seahorses. The institute conducts research and tries to promote marine conservation but wages an uphill struggle against the powerful fishing industry, which dynamites and trawls its way through the bay with little heed for tomorrow. ■ *Daily 0730-1130, 1330-1630. 20,000d.*

Islands　From Cau Da pier, boats can be taken to the islands in Nha Trang Bay. Prices vary according to the number of passengers. To Tri Nguyen, for example, costs US$16. Probably easiest is to book via one of the tour operators listed below.

Mieu Island boasts the **Tri Nguyen aquarium**, a series of tanks in which fish and crustacea are reared, ostensibly for scientific purposes, but as the adjacent restaurant makes plain it is the science of the tummy that is being served. Not a particularly noteworthy trip.

Other nearby islands are **Hon Mun**, **Hon Tam** and **Hon Mot**. The islands are usually a bit of an anticlimax for, as so often in Vietnam, to travel is better than to arrive: it's often a case of lovely boat trip, disappointing beach. The best part is anchoring offshore and jumping into the exquisitely cool water while your skipper prepares a sumptuous seafood feast and the beers chill in the ice bucket. These islands are sometimes known as the **Salangane** islands after the sea swallows that nest here in such profusion. The sea swallow (*yen* in Vietnamese) produces the highly prized bird's nest from which the famous soup is made (see box on page 52). **Hon Yen** (Swallow Island) is out of bounds and strictly government controlled, presumably to deter any would-be private nest collectors. ■ *Getting there: the best known are the tours run by* Hanh's Green Hat *(Mama Hanh was locked up a few years ago) and* Mama Linh. *These tours (see Tour operators, page 241) depart at 0900; it's best to book the night before. They have established US$7 as the benchmark price for a day trip, which should include a seafood lunch and snorkelling equipment: cold beers (not unreasonably) cost extra. A number of other captains and their wives are keen to cash in on the trade and for those seeking a little more solitude in Nha Trang Bay or something a little less routine it may be preferable to negotiate terms – but establish exactly what those terms are before setting sail as some hapless travellers have been charged extortionate sums for their lunch.*

North of town　**Hon Chong Headland,** or Husband Rocks, lie a short distance north of Ponagar Towers from where they can be reached easily on foot. Proceed a few hundred yards north then turn off to the right down to the sea. The water of the crescent-shaped bay is clear and calm although the beach is rather dirty. At the south end of the bay is Non Chong Promontory. The rock perched at the end of the promontory has a large, rather pudgy indentation in it – said to have been made by the hand of a male giant. It looks more like a paw print and is disfigured with grafitti. There are numerous cafés here but the appeal of the whole area, saga and all, is distinctly Vietnamese. Westerners would probably have a better day advancing no further north than Ponagar then taking a leisurely seafood lunch on the way back into town.

Ba Ho is the name given to a sequence of three pools and rapids to be found in a remote and attractive woodland setting. Huge granite boulders have been sculpted and smoothed by the dashing torrent, but it is easy enough to find a lazy pool to soak in. ■ *Getting there: 20 km north up Highway 1, followed by a 2-km hike.*

Tour operators in Nha Trang now run one-, two- or three-day excursions to **Buon Ma Thuot**, see page 241, and the **Central Highlands**. For those who prefer all arrangements to be made this is quite a good option.

West of Nha Trang

Essentials

There has been a considerable increase in the number of hotel rooms available in Nha Trang but even so rooms in the more popular hotels get snapped up quickly, often long in advance by tour groups. Best to book before arriving.

Sleeping
■ *on map, page 235*
Phone code: 058

LL-L *Ana Mandara*, Tran Phu St, T829829, F829629, salesana@dng.vnn.vn Nha Trang's beach resort, where those who can afford it relax in unashamed and exquisitive luxury. Simple but elegant designs are set against cool woods, wafting fans and icy a/c – all pitched in battle against the scorching sun that blazes down on the beach outside. Pool, restaurants and every conceivable facility in this enchanting retreat.

L-A *Nha Trang Lodge*, 42 Tran Phu St, T810500, F828800. A 14-storey monster overlooking the beach that it so shamefully distorts. Comfortable with all mod-cons, pool, tennis court and restaurant. **L-A** *Yasaka Saigon Nha Trang*, 18 Tran Phu St, T820090, F820000, sg-nthotel@dng.vnn.vn Another appalling insult to the beach front. This grotesque hotel is for package tour guests only. Has a/c, IDD and pool.

A-B *Bao Dai's Villas*, Tran Phu St (just before Cau Da village), T590147, F590146, baodai@dng.vnn.vn A/c, several villas of former Emperor Bao Dai, with magnificent views over the harbour and outlying islands, sited on a small promontory, with large elegant rooms. An additional 40 rooms in assorted buildings that lack the scale and elegance, not surprisingly, of the emperor's own quarters. Overrun with sightseers during holiday periods. **A-B** *Vien Dong*, 1 Tran Hung Dao St, T821606, F821912, viendonghtl@dng.vnn.vn A/c, hot water, suites, pool (open to outsiders for 15,000d), tennis, cheapest rooms are good value, popular and sometimes booked up weeks ahead. **A-C** *Hai Yen*, 40 Tran Phu St, T822974, F821902. Large rooms, some a/c, characterless but comfortable and friendly, some rooms with bathtub, sea view, access to *Vien Dong's* pool. **A-C** *T78*, 44 Tran Phu St, T822445, F825395. Formerly the *Grand* and now bizzarely named with a code. Large colonial mansion with spacious, elegant rooms overlooking the sea, cheaper fan rooms at the back. Lethargic service.

B *Que Huong*, 60 Tran Phu St, T825047, F825344, quehuong60@dng.vnn.vn New hotel built on the site of the old one, balconies with seaview, swimming pool. Restaurant, clean, friendly but a bit pricey, although the price includes breakfast. **B-D** *Thang Loi* or *Hotel La Frégate*, 4 Pasteur St, T822523, F821905, 4pasteur@dng.vnn.vn Some a/c, newly renovated, clean, friendly, arranged around courtyard, bicycles and motorbikes for rent. Internet service.

C *Seaside*, 96B Tran Phu St, T821178, F828038. South of the airport on the way to Cau Da. All a/c, views of the beach. **C-D** *Hai Quan*, 58 Tran Phu St, T822997. A navy-run guesthouse with a barrack-like block at the back for sailors and their families. Overpriced. **C-D** *Sao Mai*, 99 Nguyen Thien Thuat St, T827412, saomaiht@dng.vnn.vn Popular with travellers but success has made the owners complacent. A/c and fan rooms, hot water and kept clean.

The Central Region

D *Perfume Grass Inn*, 4A Biet Thu St, T826345, huanaz@dng.vnn.vn Only 8 rooms in this friendly and popular family run hotel. Restaurant and internet service downstairs. Book in advance. **D** *Sao Xanh*, 1B Biet Thu St, T826447, quangc@dng.vnn.vn Another popular, clean and friendly family run hotel, free coffee and bananas. Near the beach and in a popular area. **D-E** *Blue House*, 12/8 Hung Vuong St, T824505. Down a little alley in a quiet setting. Some a/c and some fan rooms in a small blue building. Excellent value for money. **D-E** *Hanoi*, 31/1C Biet Thu St, T824127. In a quiet cul-de-sac at the end of the road this hotel has some a/c and some fan rooms. **D-E** *Hoc Vien Luc Quan*, 36 Tran Phu St, T822534. Another navy-run establishment. All a/c with hot water, renovated guesthouse in a courtyard with a restaurant. Price negotiable and depends on season. **D-E** *Huu Nghi*, 3 Tran Hung Dao St, T822246, F827416. Formerly *Hung Dao*. A range of rooms, some a/c, some satellite TV, friendly. **D-E** *Truc Linh*, 11 Biet Thu St, T825742, internet_bt@yahoo.com Best known for its restaurant, this establishment is popular with budget travellers. Some rooms a/c and all hot water.

E *'Railway' Hotel or Hoang Gia*, 40 Thai Nguyen St, T822298, F813728. Some a/c and some hot water, a little decrepit, but cheap.

Eating
● *on map,*
page 235

There are a number of seafood restaurants and cafés along the beach road and a wide range of restaurants elsewhere, particularly Indian and Italian. A local speciality is *nem nuong* which is grilled pork wrapped in rice paper with salad leaves and bun, fresh rice noodles. The French bread in Nha Trang is excellent.

Banana Split, 58 Quang Trung St. Excellent breakfasts, delicious banana, chocolate and nut pancakes, popular meeting place. *Bombay Indian*, 15 Biet Thu St, T812557. Very good paratha and chicken curry for just under US$2. *Café des Amis*, 2D Biet Thu St, T813009. Off-shoot of its Hoi An parent, good for breakfast, vegetarian and seafood dinners. *Candlelight Café*, 6 Tran Quang Khai St. Attractive and popular in the evening. Wide range of dishes. *Chau Café*, 42 Hung Vuong St, T826336. A diverse menu includes Indian and Japanese dishes. The lady owner is friendly and helpful. *Good Morning Vietnam & Baan Thai*, 19B Biet Thu St, T815071. Italian and Thai have combined forces here in a popular restaurant that believes in offering choice. *Hai Dao*, 304 2 Thang 4 St, T822995. North of town on the way to Ponagar Towers and a great place to stop off for lunch on the way back from sight-seeing. Located on an island from where there are views over the river and the Cham towers. The food is good and the seafood recommended, but service is erratic. *Hyundai*, 24 Tran Quang Khai St, T811652. Korean restaurant. *La Bella Napoli*, Tran Phu St, T829621. On the beach near the war memorial. Good Italian restaurant, slightly higher prices. *La Louisiane*, Tran Phu St, T812948. Opposite the turning for the airport. Open 0700-2400. This is a large and popular place right on the beach which also has a small swimming pool. Serves a range of Western dishes and seafood as well as home-made ice cream and French patisserie. Cocktail bar. *Lac Canh*, 44 Nguyen Binh Khiem St, T821391. Serves excellent Chinese and Vietnamese food, with seafood specialities, best are the meats, squid and prawns barbecued at your table, smoky atmosphere and can be hard to get a table. Recommended. *Mai Anh*, 1/26 Tran Quang Khai St, T815920. Specializes in pizza (30,000-50,000d) but does other dishes well. Lovely refreshing lemon juice for 4,000d, nice salad and the club sandwiches look good. Well-run, clean and friendly restaurant. *Nha Trang Sailing Club*, 76 Tran Phu St. Bar and restaurant are in two separate sections; slump back in a rattan chair enjoying sun-downers then walk over to the Italian/Vietnamese restaurant. The bar attracts a lively crowd. Music and dancing. *Omar's*, 96A/7 Tran Phu St. A popular Indian restaurant near the beach. Indian chef, excellent food and friendly service. US$8 for a filling dinner for two. *Thanh Thanh*, 10 Nguyen Thien Thuat St, T824413.

Specializes in Italian food. Rather charming with its oil lamps. Like most Nha Trang restaurants also dispenses tour information. *Truc Linh*, 11 Biet Thu St, T825742. Deservedly popular, sensible prices, 3,000-5,000d for good fruit shake, 8,000d for *op la* (fried eggs). Service a little slow but plenty to observe while waiting. *Vien Dong Hotel*. Poolside restaurant, candle-lit at night, entertainment, a bit touristy but good food. For some excellent and inexpensive beef steaks there are a couple of *Bo Ne* restaurants at the western end of Hoang Van Thu St (that is, away from the beach) that serve beef napoleon and chips. A little way from the centre but worth a visit.

Bars *Rainbow Bar*, 52 Tran Phu St. On the beach behind the Ferris Wheel. Friendly staff and good atmosphere. They serve reasonably priced beer and the food isn't bad – pizzas and barbecue – kebabs are available until 0200. Pool table and Happy Hour 2100-2200. *Sailing Club*, 76 Tran Phu St. Lively bar, especially on Sat nights when a wide spectrum of ex-pats, locals and tourists congregate to enjoy pool, cold beer and music. *Shorty's*, 4E Biet Thu St, T810985. A popular bar with a pool table, run by an Englishman. Interesting menu which includes shepherd's pie and burgers. Open until 0200. Second-hand books for sale.

Shopping **Book exchanges** *Mr Lang* has been operating from near the War Memorial for many years. Second-hand paperbacks, but not cheap. *Shorty's*, 4E Biet Thu St. Has a range of second-hand books which are also sold by boys lugging them around in boxes.

Seashells, **coral** and **shell jewellery** Mounted marine life (lobsters, horseshoe crabs, turtles etc) – environmentalism and conservation are not words on the lips of many Vietnamese.

Sport **Diving** Takes place during the dry season only (Jan-May). To judge by the plethora of signs one would think that diving is the only activity in Nha Trang. *Rainbow Divers*, which claims to be the best, operates from the *Rainbow Bar*, the *Sailing Club* and from the *PADI Showroom*, 14 Biet Thu St, T829946, F826166. It runs a full range of dives from beginner to advanced divers of varying durations. **Fishing** Boats and equipment can be hired from Cau Da Pier; contact *Khanh Hoa Tourism*, 1 Tran Hung Dao St, for more information.

Tour operators *Chau's Tour* is run by the engaging Chau (Captain Cook), 22 Le Thanh Phuong St, T0903598159, havanchau@hotmail.com He is highly entertaining, knowledgable, speaks excellent English and runs a good ship. His tours are pitched at a slightly higher level than the standard (US$8-10 per day) but are worth the extra. *Hanh's Green Hat*, 44 Ly Thanh Ton St, T821309, F825117. Branch office at 2A Biet Thu St. Boat trips (US$7 including lunch and pick-up from hotel). Also other local tours, car, motorbike and bicycle hire. *Khanh Hoa Tourism*, 1 Tran Hung Dao St, T822226, F821092. *Mama Linh*, 2A Hung Vuong StT826693. Organizes standard boat trips for US$7 and sells minibus tickets to Hoi An, Phan Thiet, Saigon and Dalat. *Sinh Café*, Biet Thu St. Offers the usual Sinh Café formula. Sinh Café buses arrive and depart from here. Many travel cafés and hotels also advertise and can arrange trips to Buon Ma Thuot and the Central Highlands.

Transport **Local** Bicycles and motorbikes can be hired from almost every hotel and every café in Nha Trang for around 10,000d per day for a bicycle and 60,000d per day for a motorbike. *Mr Vu*, 5L Hung Vuong and from opposite *Truc Linh Café* on Biet Thu St. **Car hire** From *Vien Dong Hotel*, 1 Tran Hung Dao St, or one of the tour operators listed above.

Nha Trang lies 105 km from Phan Rang, 215 from Dalat, 445 from Saigon

The Central Region

Air 3 connections daily with **Saigon**, 65 mins, daily with **Hanoi**, 2 hrs 40 mins, and 5 per week with **Danang**, 80 mins. The airport is just south of town and taxis, *xe ôms* and *cyclos* run from here. It is so central that the lightly laden traveller could easily walk.

Road Bus The long-distance bus station (*ben xe lien tinh*) is west out of town at 23 Thang 10 St (23rd October St) and has connections with **Saigon, Phan Rang, Danang, Quy Nhon, Buon Ma Thuot, Dalat, Hué** and **Vinh**. Note that inter-province buses do not go into Nha Trang, they drop off at junctions on Highway 1 from where a *xe ôm* will deliver you to your destination (pay no more than US$1). The *Sinh Café bus* departs from the *Sinh Café* (see Tour operators above). **Taxi** *Khanh Hoa Taxi*, T810810.

Train There are regular train connections with **Hanoi** and **Saigon** and all stops between the two. The station is a yellow-wash colonial building with blue shutters on Thai Nguyen St, T822113.

Directory **Airline offices** *Vietnam Airlines*, 91 Nguyen Thien Thuat St, T826768, F825956. Open 0700-1100 and 1330-1615. **Banks** *Vietcombank*, 17 Quang Trung. Will change most major currencies, cash, TCs (2% commission), and arrange cash advances on some credit cards. There's a *Vietcombank* exchange bureau at 8A Biet Thu St. Gold shops near Dam market will also change money. **Communications** Internet: there are email cafés are all over town, particularly in Biet Thu St. Expect to pay around 100d per min. **Post office:** *GPO* 2 Le Loi St. Also 50 Le Thanh Ton St, opposite *Vien Dong Hotel* (international calls and faxes). Also in Biet Thu St, near Nguyen Thien Thuat St. **Medical services** General Hospital, 19 Yersin St, T822168. Dr Catherine Bonnotte, 37B Dong Da St, T090 3583602.

Cam Ranh Bay

Colour map 4, grid A6 Cam Ranh Bay is one of the world's largest natural harbours, lying 50 km south of Nha Trang. Highway 1 skirts around the bay – once an important US naval base and subsequently taken over by the Soviets. In fact the Soviets, or at least the Russians, were here before the Americans: they used it for re-provisioning during the Russo-Japanese war of 1904, which they emphatically lost. After re-unification in 1975, the Vietnamese allowed the Soviets to use this fine natural harbour once again as part-payment for the support (political and financial) that they were receiving. However, from the late 1980s, the former Soviet fleet began to wind down its presence here as Cold War tensions in the area eased and economic pressures forced the former USSR to reduce military expenditure. Now the port is almost deserted.

Cam Ranh is also a centre for Vietnam's salt industry; for miles around the scenery is white with salt pans (looking like wintry paddy fields) producing pure, crystalline sea salt. There is a modest **Cao Dai Church** near the intersection of Highway 1 and the road leading towards the Bay (Da Bac Street). Continuing east along Da Bac Street, the road leads to a thriving fish market (down a pair of narrow alleys) and then to a busy boatyard producing small fishing vessels. At 120 Da Bac Street is **Chua Phuoc Hai**, an attractive little Buddhist temple. There is nowhere to stay in Cam Ranh, but 2 km south along Highway 1 is *Hotel Restaurant Nguyen Quang*, which has two rooms on stilts over a lake. ■ *Getting there: by bus from the local station opposite 115 2 Thang 4 St.*

Phan Rang

Few tourists stop at Phan Rang, a small seaside town of about 150,000 people and the capital of Ninh Thuan Province. Phan Rang was once the capital of Champa, when it was known as Panduranga, and there are a number of **Cham towers** (*Thap Cham*) nearby. The town and surrounding area are still home to a small population of **Cham**. In the centre of town, at 305 Thong Nhat Street (Highway 1), is a large salmon-pink **pagoda** with fine roof decoration. South from the pagoda, opposite 326 Thong Nhat Street, is the entrance to **Phan Rang Market** (*Cho Phan Rang*). The beach here is beautiful and, no doubt, prospective developers have their eye on creating another Nha Trang, but for now it remains unspoilt.

Phone code: 068
Colour map 4, grid A6

*For the route
Phan Rang to Dalat,
see page 248*

Po Klong Garai is a group of three Cham towers on the road towards Dalat, 6 km from Phan Rang. Other than My Son, they are perhaps the best Cham relics in the country. Built during the 13th century, they are located on a cactus and boulder-strewn hill with commanding views over the surrounding countryside. Raised up on a brick base, the towers have been extensively renovated. The central tower has a figure of dancing Siva over the main entrance and, tucked inside the dimly lit main chamber full of incense smoke, Siva's vehicle, the bull Nandi and other statues. ■ *5,000d. Getting there: bicycle or take a xe ôm (US$1-2) or local bus towards Dalat; 2 km beyond the village of Thap Cham turn right when a concrete water tank comes into view. The towers are visible a short distance along this track. The temple complex has been looked after by a Cham caretaker since 1968.*

Excursions

Po Ro Me is another group of more-recently constructed Cham buildings, which can be seen in the distance from Po Klong Garai, rising up from the valley floor. Po Ro Me was the last king of independent Champa (1627-51), and he died a prisoner of the Vietnamese. ■ *Getting there: it is not easy: drive south on Highway 1 from Phan Rang towards Saigon; the towers are a 5-km walk from the road. Ask for Thap Cham Po Ro Me.*

Finally, there is a **third group of Cham towers**, in poor condition, 16 km north of town right at the side of Highway 1.

Tuan Tu is a small Cham village, about 5 km south of Phan Rang. Like most Cham these villagers have renounced Hinduism in favour of Islam and their names reflect this, boys are called Mo Ham Mat, Su Le Man and so on.

About 6-7 km northeast of Phan Rang is **Ninh Chu Beach**. Overall it's not a bad beach – at least it's fairly quiet. There are several cafés along the beach which rent chairs and umbrellas in addition to selling drinks. For accommodation there's the **B-C** *Ninh Chu Hotel*, T873900, F873023. A nice beach hotel with some concrete bungalows scattered

Phan Rang

To Hanoi &
Nha Trang

Tran Phu

To Ninh Chu Beach

To Thap Cham, Railway Station & Dalat

Huong Vuong

Thong Nhat

To Saigon

N

Not to scale

■ **Sleeping**
1 Huu Nghi 1   3 Ninh Thuan
2 Huu Nghi 2   4 Thong Nhat

The Central Region

about. Prices start at a reasonable level but can rise pretty high for rooms with a/c, satellite TV, hot water tub and so on. The usual karaoke and massage services are available, and there's a decent, reasonably priced restaurant and a small post office nearby. Some of the staff now speak English and credit cards are accepted.

Sleeping Most hotels in Phan Rang are either old dumpy things that look like prisons, or newly finished, 'modern' mini-hotels. Basically expensive and poor. Eventually someone will figure out that a renovated, old-style, French building with modern conveniences would be a real hit, but until then it might be a good idea to stay somewhere near the beach.

B *Ninh Thuan*, 1 Le Hong Phong, T827100, F822142. Fan and a/c rooms, restaurant. **B-C** *Thong Nhat*, 343 Thong Nhat St, T827201, F822943. One of the mini-hotels with all the modern conveniences but absolutely no charm or character. Clean but overpriced, restaurant and all the usual karaoke, sauna and massage paraphernalia. **D** *Huu Nghi 1, 2* and *3*, 13, 194 and 354 Thong Nhat St, T822606, F873023. Maybe the Russians felt at home with the neo-gulag styling, 'looks like a prison', depressing and filthy. No hot water.

Eating As is usually the case in towns of this size, there are no cafés or restaurants catering to backpackers. There are, however, quite a few *pho* stands and *bia hoi* joints on the west end of Quang Trung St, as well as some rice stalls near the bus station and the usual local cafés scattered around town. If you're feeling lucky just point to something randomly on the menu and enjoy the surprise of seeing what you get.

Transport **Road** **Bus**: the bus station is on the east side of Thong Nhat, near the post office. Local
105 km from Nha buses, however, leave from the south side of town. Regular connections with **Saigon**,
Trang, 110 from Dalat, **Dalat** and **Nha Trang. Train** The closest stop is **Thap Cham**, about 5 km west of town.
318 from Saigon

Directory **Banks** The foreign exchange service is at 334 Thong Nhat St. *Nong Nghiep Bank*, 540 Thong Nhat St. Most hotels and jewellery shops will change US$ cash, but cashing TCs may be a bit difficult. **Communications** Internet: *T & T*, 31 16 Thang 4 St. **Post office:** is at 217, the north end of Thong Nhat St, near the turn-off to Ninh Chu. **Tourist information** Ninh Thuan Tourist, at 505 Thong Nhat St, T822722.

Ca Na

Phone code: 068 This is just a wide place in the road between Phan Thiet and Phan Rang. It's about 36 km south of Phan Rang, nestled between boulder-strewn hills to the west and wild rocky surf to the east. There are a couple of small restaurants selling decent road-food and drinks and a couple of guesthouses that are as close to the highway as they are to the beach. It's worth a stop for fried noodles with seafood and a quick walk up the hill to see the small pagoda that is visible from the road, and maybe a stroll on the beach.

Sleeping **D** *Ca Na*, T861320, F861320. A few rooms between the road and beach, simple but clean, some even have a/c now but still no hot water. **D** *Hai Son*, T861322, F861339. Similar but better, does at least extend to hot water and a/c throughout.

Phan Thiet

Phan Thiet is a little fishing town at the mouth of the Ca Ty River. Despite its modest appearance and unassuming nature it is the administrative capital of Binh Thuan Province. For the traveller the real attraction lies east of town in the form of the 20-km sweep of golden sand of Mui Ne. Here can be found Vietnam's finest collection of coastal resorts and one of Vietnam's most attractive golf courses.

There are still significant numbers of Cham (50,000) and Raglai (30,000) minorities, who until a few hundred years ago, were the dominant groups in the region. There are a number of relics of the Cham era, the best and easiest to find being *Po Shanu*, two **Cham towers** dating from the late eighth century on a hill on the Mui Ne road. They are now somewhat broken down but the new road leading up to them makes a nice evening ride to watch the sun set and from this vantage point one can see the physical make-up of the coastal plain and estuaries to the south and the Mui Ne headland with its beaches to the north. Driving up the long climb towards Mui Ne the towers are on the right hand side of the road and quite unmissable. Like Cham towers elsewhere in this part of the country they were constructed of brick bound together with resin of the *Day* tree. Once the tower was completed timber was piled around it and ignited; the heat from the flames melted the resin which solidified on cooling.

Phone code: 062
Colour map 4,
grid B5

The Central Region

Phan Thiet

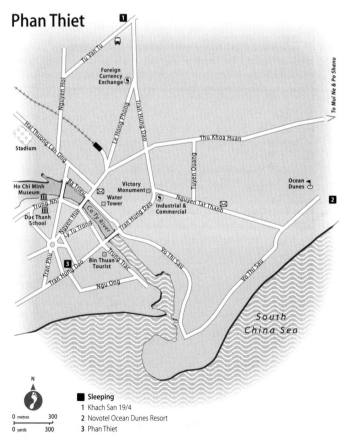

Sleeping
1 Khach San 19/4
2 Novotel Ocean Dunes Resort
3 Phan Thiet

The most distinctive landmark in town is the municipal **water tower** completed in 1934. It is an elegant structure and its pagoda-like roof suggests a spiritual rather than utilitarian purpose. The tower icon features in the logos of many local businesses and agencies. There are a few **Ho Chi Minh relics**, including a museum on Nguyen Truong To Street and the Duc Thanh school next door, where Ho Chi Minh taught in 1911, but otherwise nothing of interest. It would appear that even the local tourist authority would admit as much by listing a lighthouse 45 km distant as one of the town's attractions.

Mui Ne (or Cape Ne) is the name of the famous sandy cape and the small fishing village that lies at its end. Mui Ne's two claims to fame are its *nuoc mam* (fish sauce) and its beaches. The cape is dominated by some impressive sand dunes; some are golden but in other parts quite red, a reflection of the underlying geology. Around the village visitors may notice a strong smell of rotting fish. This is the unfortunate but inevitable by-product of fish sauce fermenting in wooden barrels. The *nuoc mam* of Phan Thiet is made from anchovies as *cá com* on the label testifies. The process takes a year but to Vietnamese palates it is worth every day. *Nuoc mam* from Phan Thiet is regarded highly but not as reverentially as that from the southern island of Phu Quoc.

Overwhelmingly, Phan Thiet is a place in which to enjoy a thoroughly relaxing seaside holiday. The almost total absence of historical sites means that one can do so without any guilt at missing cultural treasures. Phan Thiet's 18-hole **golf course**, designed by Nick Faldo, is regarded by golfers as one of the best in Vietnam. Golfers come from all around the region to play it.

Excursions Those interested in learning more about the Cham might care to visit the **house of Nguyen Thi Them**, a Cham princess who died in 1998. The house where she lived is 60 km north of Phan Thiet in Phan Thanh village, Bac Binh, commune where a few vestigial treasures from the past are kept.

Hon Rom is the name of the undeveloped bay north of Mui Ne and accessible only from Mui Ne. It is a weekend destination for Vietnamese people and towards the northern end of the beach road there are cheap huts with primitive facilities. The beach up here is dirty and the smell of fish is strong but further south there are acres of unspoilt golden beach. It is parched and arid in the dry season. ■ *Getting there: about 15 km by motorbike or bicycle from Mui Ne.*

Sleeping **Phan Thiet town** Accommodation in town is nothing special but there are a few
Phone code: 062 hotels for those needing to stay here. **C** *Phan Thiet*, 276 Tran Hung Dao St, T819907, F821695. The first hotel in town if driving in from the south. 21 rooms all with a/c and

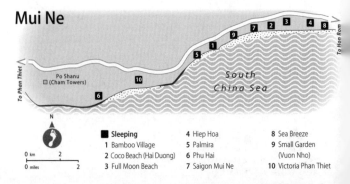

Mui Ne

■ **Sleeping**
1 Bamboo Village
2 Coco Beach (Hai Duong)
3 Full Moon Beach
4 Hiep Hoa
5 Palmira
6 Phu Hai
7 Saigon Mui Ne
8 Sea Breeze
9 Small Garden
   (Vuon Nho)
10 Victoria Phan Thiet

hot water, phone and TV in a fairly non-descript state-run hotel. Reception is some-what chaotic and not much English is spoken, a reflection of how few foreigners stay in town. MasterCard and Visa are accepted. **C-D** *Khach San 19/4*, 1 Tu Van Tu St, T821794, F825184. Right at the northern end of town it is convenient for the bus station and little else. Some fan, some a/c, all hot-water.

Mui Ne Beach High season is dry season, Nov to May, when prices rise by around 20-30%. Weekends tend to be busier as Mui Ne is a popular escape for expats from Saigon.

L-A *Coco Beach (Hai Duong)*, T847111-3, F847115, paradise@cocobeach.net The European owners live here and ensure the place is well run. Not luxurious but friendly and impeccably kept. Wooden bungalows and a few larger two-bedroom 'villas' facing the beach. Beautiful setting, lovely pool, relaxing. Good restaurant and a beachclub on the beach. *Coco Beach* was the first resort on Mui Ne and it is pleasing how, despite a little competition, it remains easily the best. Its rates are a bit high but include quite a decent buffet breakfast. **L-A** *Novotel Ocean Dunes Resort*, T823393, F825682, novpht@hcm.vnn.vn Strictly speaking not really on Mui Ne but it does have a beach setting. Comfortable and with good facilities, 2 pools, 2 restaurants, bar, tennis courts and gym, guests enjoy a 20% discount on green fees at the adjacent *Ocean Dunes Golf Club*. **L-A** *Phu Hai*, T812799, F812797, phuhairesort@hcm.vnn.vn A brand-new resort on a vast scale. Villas and other types of room set around a giant and rather exposed pool with mini waterfall. It remains to be seen who it will attract and how well trained its staff are. **L-A** *Victoria Phan Thiet*, T847171, F847174, victoriapt@hcm.vnn.vn Part of the French-run Victoria Group, the resort has 50 thatch-roof bungalows of different sizes in an attractive landscaped setting. It is well equipped with restaurants, several bars, an attractive pool and health club.

A *Saigon Mui Ne*, T847303, F847307, saigonmuineresort@hcm.vnn.vn This is a *Saigontourist* resort, perfectly professional but lacking flair and imagination. Bunga-lows, pool, restaurant and beach. **A-B** *Bamboo Village*, T847007, F847095, bam-boo_village@hcm.vnn.vn 20 attractive, simple hexagonal bamboo huts and 9 larger thatch villas in a lovely shady spot at the top of the beach. More expensive rooms have a/c and hot water showers. An excellent restaurant and attractive swimming pool. **B** *Palmira*, T847004, F847006, cocogarden@palmiraresort.com One's heart would slightly sink as one's transport drew up outside the white rotunda which houses the reception to this resort. The place is perfectly OK in its specifications and amenities but it generates no atmosphere and is usually only sparsely occupied. Large pool area lacks shade. **B** *Sea Breeze*, T847373, F847430. This far north the beach is getting a bit narrow and the road is a little close to some of the rooms for comfort. Although they are slightly pricier, insist on the sea-view rooms of which there are 2 categories. The place is well kept, clean and comfortable, breakfast is included. Motorbike and bicycle rental. **B-C** *Full Moon Beach*, T847008, F847160, fullmoon@windsurf-vietnam.com Visitors are assured of a friendly reception by the French and Vietnamese couple who own and run the place. Accommodation is in a variety of types: some rooms are spacious, others a little cramped, some brick, some bamboo. The most attractive rooms have a sea view and constant breeze. There is a good restaurant.

C *Hiep Hoa*, T847262. This is an attractive and simple little place. Only 7 rooms, fan and cold water only but quiet, clean and with its own stretch of beach. Small restaurant. **C-D** *Small Garden (Vuon Nho)*, T874012. Run by a Vietnamese woman with her Swiss husband, it consists of simple and cheap accommodation. Although lacking in ameni-ties it is in a good part of the beach with plenty of cafés and restaurants nearby.

The Central Region

Eating As you would expect, fish is the speciality in Phan Thiet. There are many restaurants in town, look for signs that say 'nha hang' or 'quan an'. If the place looks busy, the food is probably pretty good. Hotel restaurants tend to be a little expensive, especially compared with the small restaurants and cafés on the opposite side of the road. Of these no one stands out; they all serve fairly similar fare of decent standard, not much English is spoken and they all charge similar prices. Most people tend to go to the restaurant nearest their hotel and venture a little further each day.

Sport **Golf**: *Ocean Dunes Golf Club*, T823366, F821511. This *IMG*-managed, 18-hole, 6746-yd course is highly regarded. It has a fully equipped club house with bar and restaurant. Green fee US$80, caddy US$15. **Tennis**: at *Novotel*. **Beach sports**: wind surfing and other watersports are offered by the resorts.

Transport
198 km from Saigon,
250 from Nha Trang,
146 from Phan Rang,
247 from Dalat

Local *Cyclos* and *xe ôms* are abundant in Phan Thiet town. A *xe ôm* from town to **Mui Ne** should cost under US$2. *Binh Thuan Tourist*, 82 Trung Trac St, can arrange car hire, as can the larger hotels. Bicycles (US$2 per day) and motorbikes (normally US$7 per day) can be rented from most hotels and represent the best way to explore the vicinity.

Road **Bus**: the bus station is a few kilometres north of town past the Victory monument on Tran Hung Dao St. Connections with all neighbouring towns. A local bus plies the Phan Thiet bus station to Mui Ne route, 8,000d each way, as do taxis. The *Sinh Café* bus from Saigon will drop travellers off at their resort on **Mui Ne**, US$6.

Train Although Phan Thiet has a station it connects only with **Muong Man**, 12 km to the west. From Muong Man there is 1 train daily south to **Saigon** and 1 north to **Hanoi**.

Directory **Banks** *The Foreign Currency Exchange*, on Tran Hung Dao, is open from 0730 to 1630, but they do not cash TCs. *Industrial and Commercial Bank*, 2 Nguyen Tat Thanh St, near the Victory Monument, cashes TCs. The larger hotels will exchange money. **Communications** **Internet**: there are no internet cafés but almost all hotels offer internet access to their guests. Prices are quite high, partly because of lack of competition but also because the nearest service provider is in Saigon. **Post office:** 2 Le Hong Phong St. **Tourist information** *Binh Thuan Tourist*, 82 Trung Trac St, T816821, F817139, can arrange tours and car rentals.

Phan Rang to Dalat

The 100-km trip between Dalat and Phan Rang is spectacular but sometimes excruciatingly uncomfortable by bus. The narrow strip of land between the highlands and the coast is an area of intensive rice, tobacco and grape cultivation. Winding upwards, the road passes under a massive pipe carrying water from the mountains down to the turbines of a hydropower plant in the valley. It then works its way through the dramatic Ngoan Muc Pass to the Dalat Plateau.

Dalat

Dalat is situated on a plateau in the Central Highlands, at an altitude of almost 1,500 m. The town itself, a former French hill station, is centred on a lake – Xuan Huong – amidst rolling countryside. To the north are the five volcanic peaks of the Lang Biang mountains, rising to 2,400 m. In the vicinity are forests, waterfalls, and an abundance of orchids, roses and other temperate flora.

Phone code: 063
Colour map 4, grid A5
Population: 130,000

Ins and outs

Dalat airport is 30 km from town and there are multiple daily connections with Saigon. There is an airport bus into town to the *Vietnam Airlines* office, 40,000d. However, most people arrive here by road from Saigon, a 6-hr journey. There are also bus connections with Nha Trang via Phan Rang (4 hrs) and direct buses to Buon Ma Thuot, another hill station to the north.

Getting there
See Transport,
page 258,
for further details

Walking is the best way to see the town. Mountain bikes and motorbikes are available for hire and represent the best way to visit the palaces and surrounding countryside, and there are also motorcycle taxis and ordinary taxis for those less sure of their directions.

Getting around

Nights are cool throughout the year in Dalat and can be quite cold during the winter months between Dec and Feb. On clear winter days it is possible to be burnt by the sun then enveloped in mist whilst you shiver in bed at night. Take suncream, insect repellent and a fleece. May is the warmest month when the average daytime temperature reaches nearly 20°C. It is also wettest during the summer and autumn, May to Oct.

Best time to visit

The Central Region

Background

The city was founded in 1897 after the site had been discovered by Dr Alexandre Yersin. A hill station was established to give sick and wounded soldiers a cooler climate in which to convalesce. By 1935, a railway line had been laid linking it with Saigon, via Phan Rang. Colonial servants and their families took the chance to escape from the stultifying heat of the lowlands. At that time, when the only respite from heat was the ice in a citroen pressé, it is easy to imagine the relief they felt on arriving in Dalat. The French built timber-framed houses to remind them of home and colonial children from all over Indochina were hustled off to the distinguished lyceés in Dalat, especially during the summer.

Dalat is a city in the European sense that it has a cathedral, a university, a research institute (nuclear physics) and a royal history (although neither a long nor particularly proud one). But in reality it appears to be nothing so much as a large market town (although rather a grand one). The modern economy of Dalat owes much to the prosperity generated by sales of vegetables and flowers to lowland Vietnam. Several international agribusinesses have set up in Dalat to develop the huge potential the region offers – cut flowers from Dalat are to be found ornamenting all the leading hotels in Saigon.

Dalat's economy is also heavily dependent on tourism (of which nine-tenths or more is Vietnamese) and there are countless guesthouses, restaurants and shops to serve this trade. Despite investment in the tourist sector Dalat has not really taken off as a destination with foreigners in the way it should have. Business at the top end of the market will undoubtedly grow now that the reputation of the excellent golf course and the two newly renovated hotels is becoming more widely known. At the other end of the spectrum opportunities for trekking, visiting minority villages and so on have been curtailed by the state-run *Dalat Tourism* whose monopoly suffocates initiative and stifles enterprise. Fortunately, Dalat's appeal is more enduring and the independent traveller can find plenty of diversion as well as peace and quiet to fill a couple of pleasant days.

Sights

Xuan Huong Lake The central Xuan Huong Lake (originally the Grand Lake – renamed in 1954) was created in 1919 after a small dam was constructed on the Cam Ly River. A road runs round the perimeter of the lake, a pleasant and easy bicycle ride. In general, however, the hills and the dispersed nature of Dalat's sights make hiring a motorbike a more popular option.

Dalat Flower Garden At the northeast end of the lake is the Dalat Flower Garden. Established in 1966, it supports a modest range of temperate and tropical plants including orchids (in the orchid house), roses, camelias, lilies and hydrangeas. It has recently been extended. ■ *Daily 0730-1600, 10,000d.*

Dalat Cathedral Visible from the lake, and next to the *Novotel resort*, is the single-spired Dalat Cathedral. Construction began in 1931, although the building was not

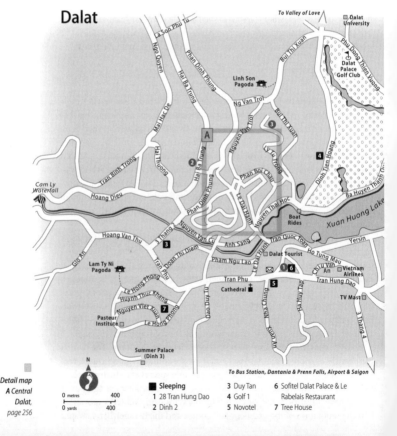

Dalat

To Valley of Love
Dalat University
La Son Phu Tu
Ngo Quyen
Phan Dinh Phung
Hai Ba Trung
Bui Thi Xuan
Phu Dong Thien Vuong
Dalat Palace Golf Club
Linh Son Pagoda
Ng Van Troi
Mai Hac De
Ha Thuong
Nguyen Van Troi
Bui Thi Xuan
Ly Tu Trong
A
Tran Binh Trong
Hai Ba Trung
Phan Boi Chau
Dinh Tien Hoang
Cam Ly Waterfall
Hoang Dieu
Phan Dinh Phung
Le Dai Hanh
Nguyen Thai Hoc
Ba Huyen Thanh
Nguyen Van Cu
Boat Rides
Xuan Huong Lake
Hoang Van Thu
3 Thang 4
Anh Sang
Le Dai Hanh
Tran Quoc Toan
Ho Tung Mau
Yersin
Gio An
Tran Phu
Phan Ngu Lao
Dalat Tourist
Luu Van An
Vietnam Airlines
Lam Ty Ni Pagoda
Le Hong Phong
Huynh Thuc Khang
Nguyen Viet Xuan
Tran Phu
Cathedral
Tran Hung Dao
Pasteur Institute
Le Hong
Nha Chung
Xuan An
Ha Huy Tap
TV Mast
Summer Palace (Dinh 3)
N
3 Thang 4

To Bus Station, Dantania & Prenn Falls, Airport & Saigon

Detail map A Central Dalat, page 256

0 metres 400
0 yards 400

■ Sleeping
1 28 Tran Hung Dao
2 Dinh 2
3 Duy Tan
4 Golf 1
5 Novotel
6 Sofitel Dalat Palace & Le Rabelais Restaurant
7 Tree House

completed until the Japanese 'occupation' in the 1940s. The stained-glass windows, with their vivid colours and use of pure, clean lines, were crafted in France by Louis Balmet between 1934 and 1940. Sadly, most have not survived the ravages of time or revolution. Lining the nave are blocks of woodcarvings of Jesus and the crucifixion. ■ *Mass is held twice a day at 0515 and 1715 Mon-Sat, and 0515, 0700, 0830, 1430 and 1600 on Sun. The cathedral has a good choir and attracts a large and enthusiastic congregation.*

Many of the large colonial villas – almost universally washed in pastel yellow – are 1930s and 1940s vintage. Some have curved walls, railings and are almost nautical in inspiration; others are reminiscent of houses in Provençe. Many of the larger villas can be found along Tran Hung Dao Street. Sadly many of the villas have fallen into a very sorry state and are looking decidedly unloved. Given their architectural significance this is a great pity. Perhaps the largest and most impressive house on Tran Hung Dao is the **former residence of the Governor General** at 12 Tran Hung Dao Street – now the *Hotel Dinh 2*. 1930s in style, with large airy rooms and uncomfortable furniture, it occupies a magnificent position set among mountain pines and overlooking the town. The house is a popular place for domestic tourists to have their photographs taken with the requisite stuffed animals. It is possible to stay here although it is often booked up by state enterprises and is popular with members of Lam Dong People's Committee.

Colonial villas

To Thien Vuong Pagoda

● Eating
1 Le Café de la Poste
2 Saigon Nite Bar
3 Stop & Go Café

Vietnam's last emperor, Bao Dai, had a Summer Palace on Le Hong Phong Street, about 2 km from the town centre and now known as **Dinh 3**. Built on a hill with views on every side, it is Art Deco in style both inside and out, and rather modest for a palace. The palace was built between 1933 and 1938. The stark interior contains little to indicate that this was the home of an emperor – almost all of Bao Dai's personal belongings have been removed. The impressive dining-room contains an etched-glass map of Vietnam, while the study has Bao Dai's desk, a few personal ornaments and photographs, and a small collection of his books (Shakespeare's comedies, Voltaire, Brontë and the Bible). The Emperor's bedroom and bathroom are open to public scrutiny as is the little terrace from his bedroom where, apparently, on a clear night he would gaze at the stars. The family drawing room is open together with a little commentary on which chair was used by whom. According to US reports, by 1952 Bao Dai was receiving an official stipend of US\$4 mn per

Summer Palace

The Central Region

year. Much of this was ferreted away in US and Swiss bank accounts – insurance against the day when his reign would end. The rest was spent on his four private planes, leaving little to lavish on his home. The palace is very popular with Vietnamese tourists who have their photographs taken wherever they can. The gardens are colourful and well maintained. ■ *5,000d. Visitors have to wear covers over their shoes to protect the wooden floors.*

Bao Dai also had a **hunting lodge**, which was recently restored as a museum and opened to the public by the *Sofitel* hotel. Now known as **Dinh 1**, the lodge sports 1930s furniture, antique telephone switchboards, and although it is not sumptious, nevertheless has a feel of authenticity. The gardens are green but lacking in intimacy, although as very few tourists visit at least you can have the place to yourself and scribble a diary entry while sitting unobserved on the foot of the late emperor's bed. ■ *Daily 0700-1130, 1300-1630, 10,000d.*

Municipal splendour Not far from the Summer Palace is the **Pasteur Institute**. This was built to produce vaccines for keeping the colonial population healthy. The yellow-wash institute was opened in 1935. Although small and modest it is quite an attractive building fashioned in a series of cubes. Notice how the corners of all the cubes have been bevelled.

Dalat Railway Station, off Quang Trung Street, was opened in 1938, five years after the completion of the rack-and-pinion track from Saigon, and was closed in 1964. Dalat station is the last in Vietnam to retain its original French Art Deco architecture – the coloured-glass windows remain intact. Its steep pitched roofs could handle the heaviest of Alpine snowfalls for which, presumably, they were designed. The waiting room, formerly segregated by race, is in good condition. Despite the fact it is virtually unused, the building is surprisingly well maintained and beds of geraniums flourish under the sun and the careful hand of an unseen gardner. In 1991, a 7-km stretch to the village of Trai Mat was reopened and every day a small Russian-built diesel car makes the journey (see Excursions, page 254). There is also an old steam engine which is occasionally fired up and a Renault diesel car.

Some of the finest buildings in town are educational. The **Dalat Teacher Training College** is the old Lycée Yersin, still to be found on Yersin Street. The long curved wall of the school can be seen from the outside. It ends in a blind tower the top of which can be seen from miles away. Sadly the college has neglected its architectural heritage and many of the buildings are abandoned and overgrown. The track that skirts around the side of the college has an interesting row of modest houses, perhaps originally for teachers.

Dalat University Out near the golf course, on Phu Dong Thien Vung Street, is **Dalat University**, founded as a Roman Catholic University in 1957 and taken over by the government in 1975. It currently provides for 8,000 students from central and southern Vietnam. It is strong on English teaching and science and has links with the Nuclear Research Institute. Symbolic of the change in political fortunes, a huge red Communist star atop the obelisk in the University's grounds actually conceals a crucifix.

Lam Ty Ni Pagoda Lam Ty Ni Pagoda is down a track off Le Hong Phong Street. Unremarkable save for a charming monk, Vien Thuc, who lives here. The main sanctuary was built in 1961 and contains an image of the Buddha with an electric halo. Vien Thuc arrived in 1968 and in 1987 he finished the gateway that leads up through a garden to the figure of Quan Am. Vien Thuc originally named his garden – which is almost Japanese in inspiration – An Lac Vien, or Peace Garden, but has now decided that Divine Calmness Bamboo Garden has a better ring to it. Vien Thuc is a scholar, poet, artist, philosopher, mystic, divine and entrepreneur but is best known for his paintings of which, by his own reckoning, there are more than 100,000. And wandering through the maze of rustic huts and shacks tacked on to the back of the temple one can easily believe this: the walls are lined deep with hanging sheets which bear his simple but distinctive calligraphy and philosophy: "Living in the present how beautiful this very moment is", "Zen painting destroys millennium sorrows", "The mystique, silence and melody universal of love" and so on. Vien Thuc shows visitors around with a mixture of pride "I work very hard" and self-deprecating modesty, chuckling to himself as if to say "I must be mad". His work is widely known. He has exhibited in Paris, New York and Holland as well as on the web. His paintings and books of poetry are for sale at prices that are creeping up to levels high enough for you to wish you could buy shares in him.

Tree House The slightly wacky theme is maintained at the nearby Tree House, 3 Huynh Thuc Khang, leading many to wonder what they put in the water for this corner of Dalat to nurture so many creative eccentrics. Doctor Dang Viet Nga has, over a period of many years, built up her hotel in organic fashion. The rooms and gardens resemble scenes taken from the pages of a fairy story book. Guests sleep inside mushrooms, trees and giraffes and sip tea under giant cobwebs. There is a honeymoon room, an ant room and plenty more. It is not a particularly comfortable place to stay and privacy is limited by the number of visitors but it is a sight well worth the 4,000d entrance ticket. See Sleeping, page 255.

Linh Son Pagoda The Linh Son Pagoda is at 120 Nguyen Van Troi Street, just up from the intersection with Phan Dinh Phung Street. Built in 1942 it is kept in immaculate condition. Perched on a small hillock, the sanctuary is fronted by two dragon balustrades, themselves flanked by two ponds with miniature mountain scenes. To the right is a military-looking turret. Behind is a flourishing school of Buddhist studies attended by dozens of young, grey-clad men and women.

Thien Vuong Pagoda Four kilometres from the centre of town, at the end of Khe Sanh Street, is the Thien Vuong Pagoda. Begun in the 1950s, this stark pagoda has recently been expanded and renovated. In the main sanctuary are three massive bronze-coloured, sandalwood, standing figures with Sakyamuni, the historic Buddha, in the centre. The pagoda, though in no way artistically significant, is popular with local visitors and stalls nearby sell local jams, artichoke tea, cordials and dried mushrooms.

Dalat Market Dalat Market (*Cho Dalat*) is at the end of Nguyen Thi Minh Khai Street and sells, to the eyes of an average lowland Vietnamese, a dazzling array of exotic fruits and vegetables grown in the temperate climate of the area – plums, strawberries, carrots, potatoes, loganberries, cherries, apples, onions and avocados. The forbidding appearance of the market is masked by the riot of colour of the flowers on sale, including gladioli, irises, roses, chrysanthemums and marigolds.

Excursions

The area surrounding Dalat was a beautiful wilderness until fairly recently. It is still beautiful, but no longer a wilderness. It is said that during the War, US

The Central Region

soldiers would come to hunt tiger, leopard, stag, bear and other game, only to find that they themselves were being hunted – not by the animals, but by the Viet Cong who lived and fought in the forests and mountains. Despite the admonitory posters, the authorities have not controlled deforestation in the Dalat area: the land on either side of the road up from Saigon is almost entirely cleared, except for a narrow band of pine forest around Dalat itself and on the steeper slopes.

Cam Ly Waterfall The landscape around Dalat is characterized by fast-flowing rivers and water-falls. Cam Ly Waterfall is the closest waterfall to Dalat, 2 km west of the town centre, on Hoang Van Thu Street. Not exactly spectacular but relatively uncluttered and not overrun. ■ *Daily 0700-1800.* **Dantania Falls** are along a track, 5 km out of town on the road towards Saigon. The path leads steeply downwards into a forested ravine; it is an easy hike there, but tiring on the return journey. The falls – really a cascade – are hardly spectacular, but few people come here except at weekends so it is usually peaceful. **Prenn Falls** are also on the route to Saigon, next to the road, 15 km from Dalat. The falls were dedicated to Queen Sirikit of Thailand when she visited them in 1959. Bur-dened with tourist tat, swan boats, stuffed animals and vendors of everything you could ever conceivably not want, Prenn tends to appeal more to the dra-matic than the international market. There is also a restaurant here. ■ *10,000d. Getting there: by motorbike or by bus en route towards Saigon.*

Lake of Sighs The Lake of Sighs lies 5 km northeast of Dalat. The lake is said by some to be named after the sighs of the girls being courted by handsome young men from the military academy in Dalat. Another unlikely theory is that the name was coined after a young Vietnamese maiden, Mai Nuong, drowned herself in the lake in the 18th century. The story is that her lover, Hoang Tung, had joined the army to fight the Chinese who were mounting one of their periodic invasions of the country, and had thoughtlessly failed to tell her. Devastated, and thinking that Hoang Tung no longer loved her, she committed suicide in the lake. Not long ago the lake was surrounded by thick forest; today it is a thin wood. Souve-nir shops, incredibly, sell stuffed tigers (no environmental movement here), while Montagnard 'cowboys' with plastic guns and holsters lead horses along the forest trails. The area is busy at weekends. The **Valley of Love**, or Thung Lung Tinh Yeu, is 5 km due north of Dalat. Boats can be hired on the lake here, there is horse 'riding' and a few refreshment stands. ■ *8,000d or free if you take a path to the side. Getting to the waterfalls and lakes: because of the cool climate, it is very pleasant to reach the lakes, forests and waterfalls around Dalat by bicycle. In fact a day spent travelling is probably more enjoyable than the sites themselves.*

Trai Mat Village & others Trai Mat Village can be reached by train from Dalat. In 1991 a 7-km stretch of track from Dalat railway station to the village of Trai Mat was reopened after 15 years of inoperation, and every day at 1400 a small Russian-built diesel car makes the return journey (US$5). The train can be hired at other times for a negotiable cost. The journey to Trai Mat village takes you near the Lake of Sighs and past immaculately tended vegetable gardens; no space on the valley floors or sides is wasted and the high intensity agriculture is a marvellous sight. Trai Mat is a prosperous market village with piles of produce from the sur-rounding area. Walk 300 m up the road and to the left a narrow lane leads down to Chua Linh Phuoc, an attractive Buddhist temple more than 50 years old. It is notable for its huge Buddha and mosaic adorned pillars. The mosaics are made of broken rice bowls and fragments of beer bottle. ■ *Getting there: by* *train or motorbike, follow Tran Hung Dao St which becomes Hung Vuong St, past SOS Village on the left, and keep going.*

In the vicinity of Dalat are a number of **villages**, both of **tribal minorities**, and of **migrants** who have been relocated here by the authorities. The best known group of such villages are the **Lat** communities, 10 km northwest of town. At present, local officials are not keen to have foreigners visiting the villages.

Essentials

Dalat has a large number of hotels and guesthouses most of which cater for Vietnamese visitors only. Most cheaper hotels for foreigners are controlled by the state and therefore tend not to represent particularly good value for money. Dalat's chilly evenings make cold showers an uninviting prospect, the hotels listed below all have hot water and, by the same token, no a/c. Prices tend to rise in the high season (Oct-May).

Sleeping
■ *on map, pages 250 and 256*
Phone code: 063

LL-L *Sofitel Dalat Palace*, 12 Tran Phu St, T825444, F825666, sofitel@bdvn.vnd.net This rambling old building was built in 1922 and in 1995 was restored to its former glory. Those that knew it before restoration will be amazed: the renovation is superb, curtains, furniture, statues, gilt mirrors and chandeliers adorn the rooms which are tastefully arranged as the French do best. The view over Xuan Huong Lake to the hills beyond is lovely and the extensive grounds of the hotel are beautifully laid out. One of the finest hotels in Vietnam. The hotel offers guests special green fees on the nearby golf course.

L-A *Empress Hotel*, 5 Nguyen Thai Hoc St, T833888, F829399, empress@hcm.vnn.vn This is a particularly attractive hotel in a lovely position overlooking the lake. All rooms are arranged around a small courtyard which traps the sun and is a great place for breakfast or to pen a postcard. The rooms are large, comfortable and the more expensive ones have luxurious bathrooms – try and get a room upgrade. Attentive and courteous staff.

A *Novotel*, 7 Tran Phu St, T825777, F825888, novotel@bdvn.vnd.net Formerly the *Dalat Hotel*, opposite the post office and near the *Sofitel* with which it shares its management and many facilities. Rooms nicely restored and comfortably furnished. No restaurant but breakfast served here and *Café de la Poste* is just over the road. **A-B** *Golf 3*, 4 Nguyen Thi Minh Khai St, T826042, F830396, golf3hot@hcm.vnn.vn Smart new centrally located hotel, comfortable rooms, cheaper rooms have showers only. Nightclub and restaurant. **A-B** *Tree House (Hang Nga)*, 3 Huynh Thuc Khang St, T822070, F831480. If you fancy a fantasy night in a mushroom, a tree or a giraffe then this is the place for you. Most unusual but rather overrun by visitors, restaurant.

B *Anh Dao*, 50-52 Hoa Binh Square, T823577, F823570. 27 rooms, central location, plasticky furnishings, cheaper rooms have no window. **B** *Dinh 2*, 12 Tran Hung Dao St, T822092, F825885. Formerly the residence of the French Governor General. 3 buildings, 22 rooms in all. Lovely setting but not a particularly welcoming place. **B** *Duy Tan*, 83 3 Thang 2 St, T822216, F822677. Low-rise buildings arranged around a courtyard, all the usual amenities at this price, satellite TV, fridge, bath tub etc, but not particularly good value. **B** *Golf 1*, 11 Dinh Tien Hoang St, T821281, F824945. A little way from centre, opposite the golf course, popular with golfers, clean, comfortable quiet, busy at weekends, book in advance.

C-D *Thanh The*, 118 Phan Dinh Phung St, T822180. Prices vary seasonally and you should bargain if it's not full. A bit of a rabbit warren, clean but nothing special, restaurant. **C-D** *28 Tran Hung Dao*, 28 Tran Hung Dao St, T822764, F835639. Further up the road from *Dinh 2*, about 2 km from the centre. A lovely old villa that has seen better days, comfort levels not great but nice views and a friendly welcome. 14 irregular rambling rooms – some wood-panelled – airy and clean, small garden at the back, ideal for those looking for peace and relaxation. Some dorm rooms at US$5 per person, breakfast included. On Thu and Fri it is largely taken over by a tour group.

D *Cam Do*, 81 Phan Dinh Phuong St, T822482, F830273. A friendly place with good English spoken. Clean but rather tatty furniture. Restaurant, breakfast included. **D** *Hoa Binh 1*, 64 Truong Cong Dinh St, T822787. Good location, one of the better low-cost places, 15 rooms including 5 at the back around a small yard, quiet but not much view, rooms at the front have a view but can be a bit noisy, furniture a bit battered but a friendly place and has an all-day café. **D** *Hoa Binh 2*, 67 Truong Cong Dinh St, T822982. Almost opposite its sister hotel, rather an attractive 1930s building. Clean and some rooms have small balconies. **D** *Mimosa*, 170 Phan Dinh Phung St, T822656.

Dalat centre

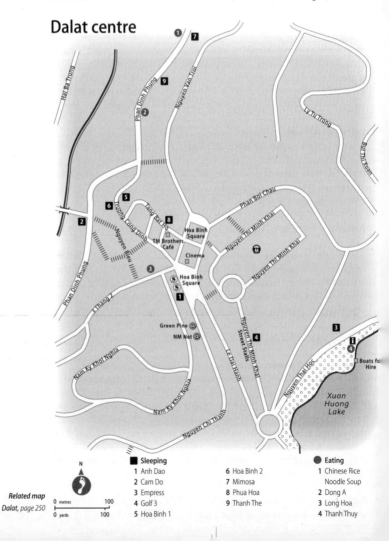

Sleeping		Eating
1 Anh Dao	6 Hoa Binh 2	1 Chinese Rice
2 Cam Do	7 Mimosa	Noodle Soup
3 Empress	8 Phua Hoa	2 Dong A
4 Golf 3	9 Thanh The	3 Long Hoa
5 Hoa Binh 1		4 Thanh Thuy

Related map
Dalat, page 250

0 metres 100
0 yards 100

TRAVELBAG

Adventures

Off the beaten track...

Over 100 trips in

Argentina
Bali
Belize
Bhutan
Bolivia
Botswana
Brazil
Cambodia
Canada
Canaries
Chile
China
Costa Rica
Corsica
Cuba
Ecuador
Egypt
Finland
France
Greece
Guatemala
Iceland
India
Iran
Italy
Japan

WIN A FREE TRIP TO South Africa

Win an adventure safari for two from Jo'Burg to Cape Town worth over £3000. You'll see superb wildlife at Kruger, explore exotic Swaziland and Zululand, walk in the dramatic Drakensberg mountains and travel along the stunning Wild Coast and Garden Route on the way to stunning Cape Town. International flights, all transport and accommodation, plus a group leader included. Simply fill in and return this form to enter.

To receive a copy of our full colour brochure tick here ☐

Which Footprints guide did you take this from? _____

Mr/Mrs/Miss/Ms/Dr First name _____ Surname _____

Address _____

Postcode _____ Email Address _____

Conditions: Draw will be held April 2003. Closing date for entries 01 Mar 2003. Winners will be notified by post. The prize is subject to availability and must be taken before December 2003. It is not transferable or redeemable for cash and may not be taken in July, August or December. Winners must accept Travelbag Adventures standard booking conditions.

A bit like all the other unremarkable *Dalat Tourist* hotels in this area, fairly central, not terribly quiet at the front, 30 rooms, showers, fridge, TV. **D** *Phu Hoa*, 16 Tang Bat Ho St, T822194, F833956. Central, simple but clean, 32 rooms, rear-facing ones are quieter but still within range of the propaganda loudspeakers which blast out from the cinema in Hoa Binh Square every morning. Popular with large groups of Vietnamese.

A number of popular eateries have closed and sadly few have sprung up to replace them, a result of lean times in the tourist trade. Cafés and, in the evening, street stalls line Nguyen Thi Minh Khai St, leading to Dalat market, which is itself the ideal place to buy picnic provisions. There are lakeside cafés and restaurants which may look attractive places to eat but they are badly staffed and serve indifferent food.

Eating
● *on map, page 256*

Chinese Rice Noodle Soup, 217 Phan Dinh Phung St, opposite *Mimosa Hotel*. Pretty self-explanatory really, steaming soups with or without *wan tun*. *Dong A Family Restaurant*, 82 Phan Dinh Phung St, T821033. Vegetarian, Vietnamese and Western dishes on offer. *Hoa Binh 1*, 67 Truong Cong Dinh St. An all-day eatery serving standard back-packer fare – fried noodles, vegetarian dishes and pancakes at low prices. *Le Café de la Poste*, 12 Tran Phu St. Adjacent to the *Sofitel* and under the same management, international food and a not very well-stocked deli but spot-on if you are craving cheese. Bar and nightclub upstairs. *Le Rabelais*, Sofitel Dalat Palace, 12 Tran Phu St, T825444. French specialities, superb dining room with views down to the lake, starters around US$12, main courses US$25, excellent. *Long Hoa*, 6 3 Thang 2, T822934. In the best traditions of French family restaurants, delicious food, super breakfasts, popular with Dalat's few ex-pats and visitors alike, fairly priced. Chicken soup and beefsteak, just over US$2, are particularly recommended. Do sample Madam's home-made strawberry wine which can be bought by the bottle for around US$6. Service is highly erratic, don't be surprised if your main course arrives with your starter. Get there well before 2200. *Stop and Go Café*, 2A Ly Tu Trong St, T828458. Rather hard to know which category to put this under. It's a café and art gallery run by the locally distinguished poet, Mr Duy Viet. Viet was born in the house, which fills with the early morning sunlight. Sit inside or on the terrace as he bustles around rustling up breakfast pulling out volumes of visitors' books and his own collected works. The garden is an attractively overrun wilderness where tall fir trees sigh in the breeze. *Thanh Thuy*, 2 Nguyen Thai Hoc St. On the lakeshore. Lovely setting and good for an evening drink (take a jacket) but food is not its forté. There are *Pho* and *banh mi* stalls on **Tang Bat Ho St** in front of *Phu Hoa* Hotel. Noodle soup and filled baguettes (paté, cold cuts or Vache Qui Rit) available from early morning until late in this little side street.

Bakery *Le Café de la Poste*, part of *Sofitel/Novotel*, pastries, coffee etc, European style. The top end of 3 Thang 2 St is crowded with sandwich sellers in the evening.

Dancing *PK's Nightclub*, upstairs at *Le Café de la Poste*, more for Vietnamese cha cha cha couples than Western clubbers. Entrance ticket 30,000d, free to guests. *Golf 3 Hotel* is slightly more racy, but the small floor is packed out with a forest of chairs. Probably the best is the disco in *Hai Son* Hotel close to the Dalat market.

Entertainment

Bars *Larry's Bar* in the *Sofitel* is not exactly a theme pub but resembles a European dungeon. *Saigon Nite*, 6 Nguyen Chi Thanh St, T820007. This is the longest-running bar in Dalat by far, and bar none. It is a popular and friendly, family-run establishment now in a new location. Pool table and good sounds but no food. Stays open late.

Golf *Dalat Palace Golf Club*, T823507. *IMG*-managed, 18-hole golf course originally developed by Emperor Bao Dai and rebuilt in 1994. Rated by some, including Gordon

Sport

The Central Region

Simmonds, as the finest in Vietnam and one of the best in the region. Beautiful setting overlooking Xuan Huong Lake. Green fee US$85 reduced to US$50 after 1500, US$60 at weekends, US$10 caddy fee. **Tennis** 2 courts at *Sofitel Dalat Palace*. **Boat rides** On the lake. Pedaloes from 30,000d per hour by the side of *Thanh Thuy Restaurant*.

Shopping Wood carvings, minority handicrafts, fabrics etc from shops on Hoa Binh Square. Local delicacies include jams, artichoke teas, cordials and dried mushrooms; also local fruit wines, smooth and fiery.

Tour operators *Action Dalat*, 114 3 Thang 2 St, T829422, F820532. Trekking, boat rides, camping, climbing and abseiling on Lang Bian mountain and excursions to minority villages. A number of set pieces from around US$20 per day including lunch; English-speaking guide. *Dalat Tourist*, 9 Le Dai Hanh St, T/F822479, and 4 Tran Quoc Toan St, T822125. Provide no information, just offer 2 standard tours of Dalat and surrounds taking in waterfalls, lakes, ethnic villages from US$7-13. Another branch at 2 Nguyen Thai Hoc St, T822520, dalattou@hcm.vnn.vn, is slightly more forthcoming. *TM Brother's Café*, 9 Tang Bat Ho St, T828383, dalat_tmbrother@yahoo.com Provides a full range of tour services including buses to Saigon and Nha Trang, local tours and internet services.

Transport **Local** For short hops and longer excursions motorbike taxi (*xe ôm*) is probably the
110 km from simplest option. Negotiate the fare in advance but expect to pay around 5,000d for a
Phan Rang, short distance, 80,000d for a day. For those desiring a little more independence, moun-
210 from Nha Trang, tain bikes and motorbikes can be rented from many hotels and from the kiosks along
299 from Saigon, Nguyen Thi Minh Khai St in front of *Golf 3 Hotel* and the market, 20,000d per day for the
1,505 from Hanoi former, 80,000d per day for the latter. Shared taxis available to outlying villages from Hoa Binh Square or the roundabout by the dam. For metered taxis try *TL Taxi*, T835533, *Dalat Taxi*, T830830.

Air Lien Khuong airport is 30 km south of Dalat, a 40-min drive. There are daily con-nections from Saigon. The *Vietnam Airlines* airport bus costs 40,000d. It gets departing passengers to the airport in good time, sufficient to allow for a drink in the café set up under the remains of the old YAK 40, a lethal 3-engined Russian jet, which skidded off the end of the runway in 1994 and now serves as a specialist karaoke room. Fortu-nately, the security guards at Lien Khuong airport are well equipped with electric cattle prods which enables them to deal with the 50 or so passengers they receive every day.

Road **Bus**: long-distance buses and minibuses arrive at Dalat bus station (Ben Xe Dalat) on 3 Thang 4, the main road in from the south. From here take a *xe ôm* the 2 or so km into town. Inter-province buses (*xe lien tinh*) for major destinations depart from 0500 onwards, check times the evening before. **Minibuses**: these ply the **Saigon** (US$6, 6 hrs) and **Nha Trang** (US$5, 4 hrs) routes, and are bookable from most hotels. Direct connection with **Buon Ma Thuot**.

Directory **Airlines** *Vietnam Airlines*, 40 Ho Tung Mau St, in front of *Sofitel*, T822895. **Banks** *Incombank*, 46-48 Hoa Binh Square. Mon-Fri 0700-1100, 1300-1600 and Sat 0700-1100. Changes cash also £, US$, AU$, CA$, TCs at 1% commission. *BIDV*, 42 Hoa Binh Square. Stays open until 1630 on Sat. **Communications** Internet: there are now a few internet cafés in Dalat which offer connections to the outside world at fair prices, 6,000d per hr, via Saigon. *NM Net*, 6 Nguyen Chi Thanh St. *Green Pine*, 2 Nguyen Chi Thanh St, T828232. A 3-in-1 internet café providing email, refreshments and tour ser-vices. **Post office**: 14 Tran Phu St, opposite *Novotel*. **Medical services** 4 Pham Ngoc Thach St, T822154.

Dalat to Saigon

*For the first 20 km out of Dalat on Highway 20 to Saigon the land is forested. But as the road descends on to the Bao Loc Plateau the forest is replaced by tea planta- tions and fruit orchards. Many of the farmers on the plateau settled here after flee- ing from the north following partition in 1954. At the centre of the plateau is the town of Bao Loc (180 km from Saigon, 120 km from Dalat). About 20 km north of Bao Loc are the **Dambri Falls** considered the most impressive in southern Vietnam and worth an excursion for those who have time (open July-November only; get an xe ôm from Bao Loc to get there).*

Nam Cat Tien National Park

This newly created national park is about 150 km north of Saigon, off High- way 20, en-route for Dalat. The park is one of the last surviving areas of natural bamboo and dipterocarp forest in southern Vietnam. It is also one of the few places where populations of large mammals can be found in Vietnam – tiger, elephant, bear and the last few remaining Javan rhino (see page 423). There are also 300 species of bird, smaller mammals, reptiles and butterflies. The park is managed by 20 rangers who besides helping protect the flora and fauna also conduct research and show visitors around. They do not speak English. ■ *A 2-hr trek with guide costs around US$3, full-day and 2-day treks (sleeping out in hammocks) are also possible. Take tough, long-sleeved and long-legged clothing, jungle boots and leech socks if possible and plenty of insect repellent.*

E The park has very primitive lodgings for about 20, 4 beds per room, mosquito nets provided, outside toilet-block with sink and cold shower, limited food available (instant noodles) and beer. **Sleeping & eating**

About 50 km south of Bao Loc on Highway 20 (at the small town of Tan Phu) turn off to Nam Cat Tien, which is about 25 km down a rough road, not well sign-posted. Some of the larger tour operators in Saigon offer 2-day trips to Nam Cat Tien, see Saigon Tour operators, page 308. **Transport**

South to Saigon

Beyond Nam Cat Tien, Highway 20 works its way down from the plateau through scrub bamboo forest towards the rolling landscape around Saigon, heavily cultivated with rubber and fruit trees. About 30 km before Highway 20 joins Highway 1 the road crosses **La Nga Lake**. Fishermen live in floating houses on the lake; besides fishing in conventional ways they also keep fish in cages under their houses. The road between Dalat and Saigon is good. At the important industrial centre of Bien Hoa, 26 km northeast of Saigon, a road runs south to the resort town of Vung Tau.

The Central Region

Vung Tau

Phone code: 064
Colour map 4, grid B4

www.vungtau
vietnam.com

Vung Tau is the hub of the country's oil industry, a significant port and home to a major fishing fleet. Despite earlier successes it is now rather a downmarket seaside resort and, as gas is piped ashore to power stations and processing plants, it is becoming a sort of oriental Teesside, an image enhanced by the opening of Vung Tau's greyhound racing track.

Ins and outs

Getting there
See Transport, page 266, for further details

Vung Tau is a painless 2-3 hr road journey from Saigon. The bus and minibus stations are both relatively central and there are regular connections with Saigon. There is an even quicker hydrofoil service from central Saigon and for those who find even that too demanding to contemplate, a helicopter can get you here in just 30 mins.

Getting around

Vung Tau has the normal fleet of *Honda ôms* and a good number of taxis but rather few *cyclos*. Distances within town are quite short and much can be covered comfortably on foot: from the hydrofoil to central hotels, for example.

Background

Before the 17th century, Vung Tau was under the control of the Khmer kings of Cambodia. A large dam and reservoir to the north was built by one of the Cambodian kings to water his horses and elephants. In the 17th century, the Vietnamese annexed the surrounding territory, and later still the French gained control. The town began to develop as a seaside resort at the beginning of the 20th century when roads linking it to Saigon were constructed. At this time it was known as Cap Saint-Jacques and considered a fairly fine resort by the French; adequate, at least, for the Governor General of Indochina to build himself a retreat here.

Vung Tau is situated on a rocky and hilly promontory that juts into the sea. This is the last piece of solid coastal geology until Hon Chong near Cambodia, which gives some indication of the vast expanse of mud of the Saigon and Mekong river deltas that lie to the south. The town nestles between two hills, Nui Lon (Big Mountain) to the north and Nui Nho (Small Mountain) to the south. It is now a popular resort town for Vietnamese day-trippers and enjoys a relatively high level of prosperity, its wealth based on oil, trade and its role as provincial capital of Ba Ria-Vung Tau Province.

Oil was found off the coast of Vung Tau in the 1970s and after 1975 the Russians moved in to help develop the fields. Then, in what now seem the heady days of the early 1990s, British, Japanese and Canadian oil companies poured vast sums of money into the search for more of the black stuff. But, with the exception of relatively minor gas deposits, not much was found and most oilmen have packed their kitbags and gone to prospect in more promising strata. Some cling on but more from inertia than any real sense of optimism. As a result the construction boom and easy riches which poured into the town have come to an end. In addition the Russians, while not exactly the biggest of spenders, are also coming to an end: from 5,000 in 1996 the contingent was down to 1,000 in 1998 and are now no more than a couple of hundred.

Sadly for Vung Tau the development of other coastal resort towns means very few foreign tourists now ever reach Vung Tau. Nearby Long Hai, for instance, is packed with visitors every weekend for the simple reason that it has clean sandy beaches. But Vung Tau should not be dismissed lightly; it is a short hydrofoil ride from Saigon and a good place to take a non-beachy seaside break. With its cooling breezes and quiet streets it is pleasantly relaxing after the stresses of Saigon.

Sights

Being a beach resort one would expect good beaches but with the exception of Back Beach or Bai Sau they are poor – narrow, with little or no sand, no coral and second-rate swimming. Even the Back Beach can be a pretty grubby affair: it is narrow and not particularly clean and the colour of the water is not inviting. In the town itself is **Bai Truoc**, or Front Beach, lined with kiosks and restaurants and really not a beach at all. Freighters moor offshore and the bay

The Central Region

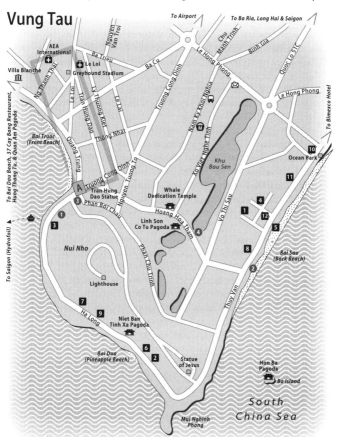

Vung Tau

South China Sea

N

Not to scale

■ Sleeping	7 Nha Nghi 104	● Eating
1 Dang Gia Trang	8 Nha Nghi 117	1 Bi Ti
2 Halong	9 O Cap	2 Cuu Long Café
3 Hai Au	10 Sammy	3 Hai Dang Internet Café
4 Hien Hoa	11 Thang Muoi	4 Ngoc Thuy
5 Jonah	12 Thien Nhien	
6 Neptune		

Detail map
A Vung Tau
Centre, page 264

and beach are home to Vung Tau's substantial fishing fleet. South from town, taking the coast road (Halong Street), is **Bai Dua** (Pineapple Beach, formerly Roches Noires Beach) and a collection of guesthouses and hotels. Again, the beach is poor. At Bai Dua there are two temples, one with a **large Buddha** looking out to sea. Also at Bai Dua is **Niet Ban Tinh Xa**, a pagoda built on a hill in 1971. It is said to be one of the largest temples in Vietnam, and contains a 5,000 kg bronze bell and a 12 m-long reclining Buddha.

Around the headland is a small and peaceful cove with good surf – **Mui Nghinh Phong** (formerly Au Vents Beach); swimming can be dangerous here. Northeast from the headland, on Thuy Van Street, and just past the **island pagoda of Hon Ba**, is the longest stretch of sand – **Bai Sau** (Back Beach). Bai Sau is about 2 km southeast from the centre of town, taking Hoang Hoa Tham Street. This is a beach in the usual sense of the word, comprising 5 km of sand. It is exposed to the wind and the South China Sea and the surf is usually good, sometimes ferocious. Overlooking the South China Sea at the south end of Bai Sau is, somewhat surprisingly, a **giant statue of Jesus** with arms outstretched – not on the same scale as that in Río de Janeiro but impressive nevertheless. Behind the figure, on Small Mountain, Nui Nho, is a **lighthouse** built in 1910 which can be reached either from Halong Street (near the *Hai Au Hotel*) up Hem 150 or from the southern end of Bai Sau. It is a pleasant walk or motorbike ride in the late afternoon. Many local people do the walk for exercise. At a shade under 200 m it is sufficiently high to be perceptibly cooler than sea level and there are good views of the town, bays and sea.

North of town, at 12 Tran Phu Street (the coast road), is **Bach Dinh** (Villa Blanche) built in the early part of this century as a summer residence for Governor General Paul Doumer on the site of an old fort. King Thanh Thai was kept here from 1906-17 prior to being sent into exile on the island of Reunion, and it was later used by President Thieu. The house and gardens are open to visitors. The house is now a museum housing a sample of what the Vietnamese call the Hon Cau ceramics but what the rest of the world calls the Vung Tau ceramics. Whatever, these are Ching Dynasty ceramics salvaged in 1990-91 from a Chinese trading junk which sank near Con Dao island around 1690. The ceramics were auctioned at Christies in Amsterdam for US$7.3 mn in 1992. The find was highly significant not only for its size, consisting of 48,000 pieces, but also because it represents some of the first pieces of standing as opposed to flat ceramics to come from China. The collection here consists of vases, goblets and small statues; some are encrusted with coral and some retain their original elegant blue and white glaze. The building itself is rather fine with a glorious outlook and lovely gardens with colourful *cay su* trees, a type of Vietnamese rhododendron. ■ *Daily 0700-1700, 5,000d.* **Bai Dau Beach** is 3 km northwest of town at the fishing village of Ben Dinh (now geared primarily to the demands of domestic tourists). Again, the beach is nothing special, but it is the quietest spot on the peninsula. The pagoda on the hill here is called **Hung Thang Tu**.

Although there are numerous pagodas and churches in Vung Tau none is particularly noteworthy. At the south end of Tran Hung Dao Boulevard is a massive and rather crude **statue of General Tran Hung Dao** who defeated a Chinese invasion force in the mid-13th century (see page 159). At 104 Hoang Hoa Tham Street, on the way to Bai Sau, is the 100-year-old **Linh Son Co Tu Pagoda**. Not far away on the other side of the road from the Linh Son Pagoda, at 77A Hoang Hoa Tham Street, is the **Lang Ca Ong**, or Whale Dedication Temple, sumptuously adorned in red and gold, and dedicated to the whale, the patron god of Vung Tau fishermen (worship of the whale was inherited from the Cham). It was built in 1911 and contains a number of whale skeletons

Superior God of the Southern Sea

The whale has long been worshipped in Vietnam. Ever since the days of the early Champa the whale has been credited with saving the lives of drowning fishermen. The Cham believed that Cha-Aih-Va, a powerful god, could assume the form of a whale in order to rescue those in need. Emperor Gia Long is said to have been rescued by a whale when his boat sank. After he ascended the throne, Gia Long awarded the whale

the title Nam Hai Cu Toc Ngoc Lam Thuong Dang Than, 'Superior God of the Southern Sea'. Coastal inhabitants always try to help whales in difficulty and cut them free of their nets.

If a whale should die a full funeral is arranged. The person who discovered its dead body is considered to be the whale's 'eldest son' and will head the funeral procession dressed in white as if it were his own father's funeral.

displayed in cabinets behind the main altar. The cabinet to the right of the altar contains a skeleton dating from 1931, while the central skeleton is believed to date from 1848. Whale and dolphin bones are brought to the temple and worshipped before being cremated: they are credited with saving drowning sailors and fishermen. Photographs show the annual Whale Dedication ceremony. Rather quaintly the Vietnamese regard large sea mammals as big fish: the whale is **cá voi** (jumbo fish) and the dolphin **cá heo** (pig fish). **Vung Tau market** is on Nam Ky Khoi Nghia Street just down from the bus station.

Essentials

Many hotels belong to state-owned corporations and staff are not as welcoming as they might be. Vietnamese work outings tend to head for Vung Tau and therefore many hotels place more emphasis on massage and karaoke than on a decent night's sleep.

Sleeping
■ *on maps, pages 261 and 264 Phone code: 064*

In town L-B *Petro House*, 63 Tran Hung Dao St, T852014, F852015, petro.htl@hcm.vnn.vn New, central, comfortable and full of amenities including a decent pool, a business centre and *Ma Maison*, a good French restaurant. Generally regarded as the best in town. **L-B** *Royal* (formerly *Canadian*), 36 Quang Trung St, T859852, F859851, rht@hcm.vnn.vn Occupies a prime seafront site, some rooms have spectacular views; *Oilmen's Pub* and a pool shared with the adjoining *Rex Hotel*. **A** *Rang Dong Orange Court*, 5 Le Qui Don St, T854933, F858306, orangecourt@ hcm.vnn.vn Comfortable new serviced apartment complex, apartments available by the day or for longer stays. Large pool, tennis court and all rooms come with fully equipped kitchen. **A-B** *Rex*, 1 Duy Tan St, T852135, F859862. Not far from the beach but good views from the upper floors; restaurant and swimming pool but rather grumpy service. **A-C** *Hai Au*, 100 Ha Long St, T856178, F856868, haiauhotel@ hcm.vnn.vn Sea view overlooking hydrofoil jetty, short walk into town centre, rooms on higher floors cost more, breakfast included, restaurant, small pool, dancing. **A-C** *Palace*, 11 Nguyen Trai St, T856411, F856878. Offers a wide range of business and recreational services, swimming pool. **B-C** *Grand*, 26 Quang Trung St, T852469. Occupies a nice position overlooking the sea, offers the usual entertainments. **B-C** *Sea Breeze*, 11 Nguyen Trai St, T856392, F856856. Spartan rooms, a place to spend the night, pool and the popular Cajun restaurant and bar attached. **B-C** *Song Hong*, 3 Hoang Dieu St, T852137, F852452, songhongvtu@hcm.vnn.vn Decent rooms, large downstairs restaurant. **C** *Lan Rung*, 2 Tran Hung Dao St, T810707. A lovely French villa, recently renovated, not, alas, with a great deal of skill. Eight palatial rooms miserably furnished with tacky plastic. All a/c and hot water but not much English spoken.

For much of the year there are far more rooms than customers. Therefore it is rare that a discount cannot be negotiated although prices do tend to rise in the summer holidays when Vietnamese families pour into town

The Central Region

Vung Tau centre

AEA International

Nguyen Thanh That

Thu Khoa Huan

Greyhound Stadium

Le Loi

Nguyen Van Troi

Hoang Dieu

Tran Van Ky

Quang Trung

Duy Tan

Le Loi

Ba Cu

Tran Hung Dao

Ly Tu Trong VCJSB

Hollywood Club BIDV

Minibus

Thong Nhat

Bai Truoc (Front Beach)

Quang Trung

Nguyen Du

Nguyen Trai

Truong Cong Dinh

Tran Hung Dao Statue

N

Not to scale

■ **Sleeping**
1 Cong Doan
2 Grand
3 Lan Rung
4 Palace
5 Petro House
6 Rang Dong Orange Court
7 Rex
8 Royal
9 Sea Breeze
10 Song Hong

● **Eating**
1 Cajun
2 Ettamogah Bar
3 Hot Gossip Bar
4 Hue Anh
5 Huu Nghi
6 Oasis
7 Purple Night Bar
8 Snafu
9 Sweetheart Bar
10 Thanh Tam
11 Viet An Halal
12 Whispers

Related map
Vung Tau,
page 261

Bai Dau C-D Quiet accommodation (*nha nghi* and *nha tro*) along Tran Phu St, eg nos 28, 29, 47, 142 (about 6-7 of them), catering mostly to Vietnamese.

Bai Sau (Back Beach) There are hundreds of guesthouses on both sides of the road, mostly catering to Vietnamese families. Properties on the beach side of the road are under threat of demolition to make way for larger, and supposedly smarter, new tourist facilities but no one seems to know when. The government is offering only paltry compensation to owners. **A-B** *Sammy*, 157 Thuy Van St, T854755, F854762, sammyhotel@hcm.vnn.vn Large and very comfortable new hotel, somewhat glitzy but easily the best along the Back Beach with decent service, good views, business facilities and good Chinese restaurant; customers get use of the *Ocean Park* swimming pool opposite at reduced prices. **C-D** *Bimexco*, Thuy Van St (far north end of Bai Sau St), T859916, F853470. Bungalows in casuarina-filled compound, mainly on beach side of the road, some a/c, all with hot water. **C-D** *Cong Doan*, 4 Tran Hung Dao St, T856500. Large, some a/c and private bathrooms, friendly, but characterless. **C-D** *Dang Gia Trang*, 26 Pho Duc Chinh St, T859249. 100 m up a small track off Thuy Van St, some large a/c rooms, clean and well run. **C-D** *Hien Hoa*, 6 Phan Van Tri St, T522364. Slightly chaotic but clean, with decent-sized, comfortable rooms. **C-D** *Thang Muoi*, 151 Thuy Van St, T852665, F859876. Low-terraced bungalows in a casuarina and palm-filled compound. A/c villas and simple, clean fan rooms, large restaurant, small pool (not always filled). **D** *Nha Nghi 117*, 117 Thuy Van St, T522158. Fan rooms and cold water showers only in a few small bungalows, not much English spoken. **D-E** *Jonah Guesthouse*, 29 Thuy Van St, T853481. Under threat of demolition at time of writing so may no longer exist. Friendly, English spoken, fan rooms on beach. Their new guesthouse on the opposite side of the road is the perfectly functional **D-E** *Thien Nhien*, 145A Thuy Van St, T853481. A/c and fan rooms, hot water, balcony, kept spick and span.

Bai Dua There are a number of smaller hotels and guesthouses in this quiet, almost Mediterranean, enclave. **B-C** *O Cap*, 78-80 Halong St, T810360. A splendid setting and attractive appearance but service is not one of the strengths of this police-owned hotel. Clean and spacious. **B-D** *Neptune Hotel*, 36 Halong St, T856192, F856439, neptune@hcm.vnn.vn Large and friendly hotel despite its off-putting exterior, with some superb suites overlooking the sea, competent and reliable service. Restaurant and roof-top terrace also with good views, private (rather rocky) beach across the road. **D** *Halong*, 34 Halong St, T856286. Striking blue-wash exterior to this rather military looking building with a lovely outlook. Clean but a little spartan. **D** *Nha Nghi 104*, 86 Halong St, T850060. A clean, well-ordered and breezy guesthouse with nice views. All 33 rooms have a/c and hot water. More expensive rooms have a small living room with fridge.

In town (Front Beach) Owing to the power of the expat pocket, prices tend to be a little higher here than elsewhere. *Bi Ti*, 138 Halong St, T856652. Attractive restaurant swathed in greenery, extensive Vietnamese menu and views over the bay. *Cajun*, 11 Nguyen Trai St. Spicy Deep South specials and bar are popular with the expat crowd *Ettamogah Pub*, 15 Quang Trung St, 510173. Serves substantial breakfasts and decent bar food throughout the day. *Hai Dang Internet Café*, 154A Halong St, T510584. Does excellent 'Italian' and Vietnamese coffee as well as light snacks and breakfasts. *Hue Anh*, 446 Truong Cong Dinh St, T856663. *Hue Anh* has a bigger sister inside the *Sammy Hotel*. Chinese with healthy portions at middle-of-the-road prices. *Huu Nghi*, 14 Tran Hung Dao St, T852017. Chinese/Vietnamese menu popular with locals. *Oasis*, 1 Le Loi St, T858088. Fairly large Western and Vietnamese menu, decent pizzas. *Snafu*, 14 Nguyen Trai. A bar adjoining *Whispers*, it shares the same kitchen and serves excellent bar food including *wiener schnitzel* at US$7 and sandwiches. *Thanh Tam*, 13 Quang Trung St, T856144. Decent Vietnamese fare at reasonable prices. *Viet An Halal*, 40 Quang Trung St, T853735. (Despite the address, actually just around the corner at 11 Ba Cu St). A range of excellent curries for around the US$3 mark prepared by an Indian/Vietnamese chef; popular with the expat community and highly recommended. *Whispers*, 12 Nguyen Trai St, T856028. Extensive Western menu and excellent food, including foreign imported beef. Sun lunch recommended. There are a number of cafés along the seafront, eg *Thanh Nien*, 55 Quang Trung St.

Bai Sau Two places in this area deserve special mention, however. *Ngoc Thuy*, 63/3 Hoang Hoa Tham St, T859188. Interesting setting, backing onto and over the Khu Bau Sen Lake, gigantic Vietnamese menu. *Cuu Long Café*, 57 Thuy Van St. Cheap café with bicycles and motorbikes for hire.

On Bai Dau *Cay Bang*, 69 Tran Phu St, T838522. Vung Tau's most celebrated seafood restaurant and well worth a detour. People travel for miles just for this: packed on Sun, busy the rest of the week. Crab, prawn, squid and fish specialities in a rough-and-ready setting over the sea. *37 Cay Bang*, 37 Tran Phu St, T832123. Same name and concept, a no frills, good seafood derivative.

There are 3 or 4 bars on Nguyen Trai St which are popular with expats: *Snafu*, at no 14, and *Sweetheart*, at no 18, are both a/c with cold beer, pool and Western snacks. *Hot Gossip*, 436 Trong Cong Dinh St, is just around the corner, also with a pool table. On the seafront is *Ettamogah*, 15 Quang Trung St, T510173. A friendly Australian-run bar frequented by expats. Motorbikes can be rented for just US$3 per day. *Purple Night*, 23 Quang Trung St, T810243. A good night-time hangout.

Eating
● on maps,
pages 261 and 264

Restaurants in town are often attached to hotels but there are plenty of independents

The Central Region

There are numerous seafood restaurants on the beach, all of which are much of a muchness

Bars

Going to the dogs

Vung Tau Greyhound stadium was the brainchild of an Australian, Bevan Williamson. Finance for the 400 m track and stadium, the air-conditioned kennels, laser timing mechanisms, electronic implants and virtually all the equipment all came from Australia but the beautifully swept sand on the track comes from Vung Tau beach.

There is a kennel of several hundred dogs, many of which are now owned by Vietnamese and foreign businessmen in Vung Tau and Saigon, some by foreign diplomats too. All the original stock came from Australia but many have now been bred in Vietnam. There is a huge greyhound farm complex 10 km from the stadium with capacity for 1,500 dogs. Dogs are kept in the

greatest of comfort with a four times daily training regime, massages, swimming and a special diet of kangaroo meat.

The Lam Son stadium seats 5,000 spectators and is the only place in Vietnam where Vietnamese nationals can bet legally. Every Saturday 12 races are run for a total prize pot of around US$3,000. There is a computer operated system for on course betting although it is estimated that a great deal more money changes hands (illegally) off course. A sophisticated and informative race card and form guide is available free of charge in all big VungTau hotels a few days before the next race.

The scheme is a great success and a popular spectator sport. There are plans to start a second track in Saigon.

Nightclubs **Dancing** *Hollywood Club*, 4 Ly Tu Trong St. *Rex Hotel*, 1 Duy Tan St. *Hai Au Hotel*, 100 Halong St.

Sports **Greyhound racing** 15 Le Loi St, T807309. Unlikely as it may seem this novel entertainment has been operating in Vietnam for several years. There are 12 races every Sat evening 1915-2230. The track and stand are modern and maintained to the highest standards, a great evening's entertainment. See box above for further information. **Tennis** There are courts in many of the main hotels, *Rang Dong Orange Court* etc.

Festivals *Whale festival* (*Le Nghinh Ong*) (16th day of the 8th lunar month), fishermen make offerings starting on the beach and then processing in great splendour and dignity to the Lang Ca Ong (Whale) Temple at 77A Hoang Hoa Tham St.

Shopping Shells, shell ornaments, shell jewellery, stuffed animals and lobsters, carved wood, lacquered tortoises, star fish and coral: in short, absolutely nothing of interest but all to be found on the seafront along Quang Trung St. Ba Cu St, north of Le Loi is regarded as Vung Tau's shopping belt, which has a good selection of clothes and shoes.

Tour operators *Ba Ria-Vung Tau Tourist Co*, 33-35 Tran Hung Dao St, T856445.

Transport **Air** There is a helicopter service from Saigon, Mon, Thu and Sat, 30 mins, US$20, T08-8443289. **Road Bus**: Vung Tau bus station is at 192 Nam Ky Khoi Nghia St, sandwiched between Nam Ky Khoi Nghia and Xo Viet Nghe Tinh streets. Regular connections with **Saigon**, 2½ hrs, 25,000d, **Bien Hoa** and **Binh Khanh**. **Minibuses**: these arrive and depart from Tran Hung Dao St in front of the church. Taxi or car chartered from a hotel should cost no more than US$20 to Saigon, 2 hrs. **Taxi**: *Gili Taxi*, T858585. *Mai Linh Taxi*, T822266. **Boat Hydrofoil**: operates from wharf at end of Ham Nghi St in Saigon to Halong St jetty in Vung Tau, 4 services daily in each direction, 1 hr 20 mins, US$10 each way, *Vinaexpress* T08-8253888 and 064-856530.

113 km from Saigon, 85 from Bien Hoa, 20 from Long Hai

Directory **Banks** *BIDV*, 72 Tran Hung Dao St. Changes TCs and cash. *VCJSB*, 59 Tran Hung Dao

St. Changes cash but not TCs. Most major hotels change US$. **Communications** Internet: *Hai Dang Internet Café*, 154A Halong St, and in major hotels. GPO: *PetroVietnam Towers* on Le Loi St. International phone and faxes. Poste Restante service. The PO at 45 Le Hong Phong St is more convenient for Back Beach. **Medical services** Hospital: **AEA International**, 1 Nguyen Thanh Thai St, T858776; **Le Loi Hospital**, 22 Le Loi St.

Long Hai

Long Hai is a small town a few kilometres up the coast from Vung Tau, although in order to get here from Vung Tau you have to retreat inland as far as Ba Ria. It is such a non-descript little place that you could easily pass through without realizing you had ever got there. Glimpses of the sea can be had from the road through the trees, but only just. Long expanses of clean sand and beaches far superior to Vung Tau's are the main attraction, but although the town itself is rather shabby, in recent years it has become very popular with Vietnamese tourists. Along the stretch of road that runs north of Long Hai several resorts have opened and more will surely follow to take advantage of the natural and unspoilt coast.

Phone code: 064

L *Anoasis Beach Resort*, T868227, F868229, Anoasis@hcm.vnn.vn 2-3 km east of Long Hai. It consists of bungalows in a park setting with fantastic views over the sea. It is owned and run by Anoa, the spunky French lady of Vietnamese origin who in 1992 flew her helicopter and her husband from Paris to Hanoi. Scenically, it is one of the most appealing of all Vietnam's resorts. It is attractively finished and everything is on a generous scale: each bungalow has a bath big enough for 2, comfortable and beautifully designed furnishings, a gigantic pool, a private beach and jetty. Also a good restaurant with prices which suggest they know you have no alternative but to eat in. **A** *Long Hai*, T868976, F868010. 30 rooms in this recently tarted-up hotel, all with a/c and hot water, comfortable but cannot possibly justify these prices. **C** *Palace*, T868364, F843556. Some a/c, large, wood-panelled rooms in this imposing domed mansion set amidst trees on a small hill, smacks of faded grandeur and a touch overpriced. **C-D** *Cong Doan*, T868312. Some a/c and only the more expensive rooms have hot water, many rooms have a balcony, comfortable and clean, gardens back onto the beach. **D** *Rang Dong*, T868356. Some a/c, grubby and unfriendly. **E** *Green*, T868337. Some a/c, friendly and fairly clean. **E** *Ngoc Minh*, T868429. Fan only, shared bathrooms but cleanish.

Sleeping

Apart from the restaurant at *Anoasis*, there are no noteworthy eateries, the restaurants inside the *Palace*, *Cong Doan* and *Ngoc Minh* hotels being the pick of the bunch. Seafood, naturally, is the speciality.

Eating

Road Bus: some direct services from Saigon but it's probably quicker to take the Vung Tau bus, get off at Ba Ria and catch a *xe ôm* from there. Station: 192 Nam Ky Khoi Nghia St. **Hydrofoil** Catch the Vung Tau hydrofoil and take a taxi or motorbike from there.

Transport

Banks *Nong Nghiep Bank*, 103 Nam Ky Khoi Nghia St. *Vietcombank*, 27 Tran Hung Dao St. **Communications** Internet: 535 Nguyen An Ninh St. **Post office:** 408 Le Hong Phong St. **Tourist information** *Ba Ria – Vung Tau Tourist*, 207 Vo Thi Sau St, T856445.

Directory

Thuy Duong

The coastal road from Long Hai first ducks inland past large sand dunes then rejoins the sea, winding its merry way around rocky headlands and passing

Phone code: 064

The Central Region

within a few feet of small, sandy beaches. The **caves** at **Minh Danh**, 5 km from Long Hai, are soon reached. Signposted, it is a scramble up the hill to reach them. The caves and crevices were used by Communist soldiers as a hide-out from 1948 to 1975. ■ *20,000d, if you are unlucky.*

Thuy Duong is soon reached. This amounts to nothing except a quite comfortable hotel, a few beach cafés and shelters. But at weekends the place comes alive with families from Saigon, Bien Hoa and, one suspects, Vung Tau. The beaches here are superb, gently shelving and golden; there is lovely swimming, it's safe for kids and peaceful mid-week. Even at weekends a short walk will take you well away from the crowds to coves, which romantically minded couples might have thought they had to themselves. ■ *Getting there: by car.*

Sleeping **A-C** *Thuy Duong Hotel*, T886215, F886180. A/c in the more expensive rooms, comfort-
& eating able hotel with pool, tennis court (US$5-7 per hr), restaurant. Also some cheaper bungalows which are run by the same establishment but lack hot water. The beach cafés don't look much but the food is plentiful, cheap and good.

Ho Coc

Phone code: 064 After Thuy Duong, the road turns inland again to the quaint Dat Do, rejoin-
Colour map 4, ing the main road from Ba Ria. Head east until reaching Bong Trang from
grid B4 where a straight and narrow road cuts a swathe through some lovely trees almost due south to the sea at tiny **Ho Coc**. The beach here is long and wide, another idyllic place for swimming and relaxing. This is a true escape and almost wholly undeveloped. During the week you can have the place almost to yourself but at the weekend a crush of trippers descends.

Sleeping **D** *Saigon – Ho Coc*, T878175, F871130. 6 simple A-frame huts with fan and cold-water
& eating shower. Book in advance. Other huts also available. Quite a decent restaurant.

Transport **Road** Buses from Ba Ria stop at Bong Trang, catch *Minsk ôm* from there to Ho Coc, 5,000d. Some Saigon travel cafés organize day trips (3-3½ hrs) from Saigon by car.

Binh Chau Rejoining the main road, continue a further 10 km or so east to the **hot springs** at Binh Chau. Here one can immerse oneself in a communal or a private pool, although be careful where you bathe: in places the sulphurous water bubbles out of springs at 82°C. See for yourself by buying an egg and cooking it. For those wishing to take the waters, accommodation is available at the **D-E** *Cu Mi Hotel*, T871131, F871130. Some a/c, some hot water, clean. ■ *5,000d, private pool an additional 30,000d-50,000d per hr.*

Con Dao

Phone code: 064 Con Dao is the name given to the 14 islands that make up this tiny archipelago;
Colour map 4, grid A3 the biggest and only permanently settled island is **Con Son**. The population is approximately 6,000 people. A trading post was set up here between 1702 and 1705 by the East Indies Trading Company. Because of the millions of sea birds that inhabited it, it was then called Bird Island. In 1773, it became the home of Nguyen Anh and many mandarin families who fled there after being defeated by the armies of the Tay Son. In 1832, the Con Dao archipelago was handed over to the French by Emperor Tu Duc. Prisons were built in 1863 by Admiral Bonard in which the French incarcerated their more obstinate political prisoners. Up to 12,000 people could be held in the completed prisons. The Con Dao

Vo Thi Sau

Born Ba Ria in 1933, executed Con Dao in 1952. At the precociously early age of 14 this Vietnamese revolutionary heroine developed an interest in politics and a passionate hatred for the French.

In 1949 she obtained three hand-grenades and with just one of them she killed one French soldier and injured 20 others. She became a messenger and supplied food and ammunition to the Viet Minh. In 1950 she tried to assassinate a village headman working for the French but the hand-grenade failed to go off. She was caught, tortured and sentenced to death. She was executed on 23 January 1952 at the age of 18.

prisons were later used by the government of South Vietnam to hold political prisoners. The infamous 'tiger cages' where prisoners were chained and tortured still stand. One kilometre beyond the prison is a cemetery where many of the victims of the prison are buried. The grave of Vo Thi Sau (1933-52) can be seen among them (see also box above). There is a **museum** (Bao Tang Tong Ho Tinh) in the town of Con Dao in the house of the former prison governor containing artefacts relating to the island's past. Three of the prisons are open to visitors, including one that has life-size models inside, recreating the horrific conditions in which prisoners were kept. Con Dao museum has an interesting display of old photographs, and can arrange walking tours of the old prisons. ■ *Daily 0800-1600, 1,000d, prison tour 30,000d per person.*

Con Dao National Park

In 1983 the forests on all 14 islands of the Con Dao archipelago were given official protection, and in 1993, 80% of the land area was designated a National Park. In 1997 the park boundaries were expanded to include the surrounding sea.

Con Dao is a special place ecologically, though is not the most diverse protected area in Vietnam. In 1995, with support from the World Wildlife Fund, the park began a sea-turtle conservation project. Con Dao is the most important sea-turtle nesting site in Vietnam, with several hundred female green turtles (*chelonia mydas*) coming ashore to lay their eggs every year. Park staff attach a tag to the flipper of every turtle in order to identify returning turtles, and carefully move the turtle's eggs if they are in danger of being flooded at high tide. The rest of the year the turtles migrate long distances. Recently, a turtle tagged in Con Dao was found in a fishing village in Cambodia – unfortunately the tag was insufficient protection to prevent it being eaten. Also in 1995, park staff identified the presence of dugongs. Dugongs are large, mammals that feed on seagrass and can live to more than 70 years. Unfortunately, before the national park was established dugongs were regularly caught for meat so now the population in Con Dao is very small and endangered. Current threats come from collisions with boats, entanglement in fishing nets and reduced seagrass habitat caused by sedimentation from coastal erosion.

The coral reefs surrounding the islands are among the most diverse in the country. Scientists have identified more than 200 species of coral and 200 species of coral fish. In November 1997, typhoon *Linda* struck the islands and during just four hours of strong winds many of Con Dao's coral reefs were badly damaged or destroyed.

In the forests scientists have identified more than 1,000 plant species, of which several are unique to Con Dao and include many valuable medicinal

The Central Region

and timber species. Bird life is also significant with rare species such as the pied imperial pigeon (*ducula bicolor* – Con Dao is the only place in Vietnam where you can see this bird), the red-billed tropicbird (*phaethon aethereus* – a rare bird found on only a few islands in the world), and the brown booby (*sula leucogaster* – a very rare sea bird that inhabits the park's most remote island, Egg Island, or Hon Trung). Egg Island, a one-hour speedboat ride away, is home to thousands of seabirds and cannot fail to impress even the most experienced bird enthusiast.

On some of the outer islands, park staff harvest the nests of the edible-nest swiftlet, which makes its nests in the many caves found on some of the islands' more exposed edges. The nests are sold in Saigon and some find their way to Hong Kong where they are used in making bird-nest soup (see box, page 52).

Most of the threats to the island's natural resources come from development in the form of new roads, houses and the new fishing port built in Ben Dam bay – an area of once-beautiful coral reef and mangrove forest. Local people do take some resources such as firewood from the park, but fortunately most of the land clearance takes place outside the park.

There are a number of activities that can be organized in the National Park, from snorkelling and swimming, to forest walks and birdwatching. Diving may be available in the near future, which will provide visitors with the opportunity to see some of Con Dao's underwater features, such as its caves, as well as the coral reefs. The national park will rent out snorkelling gear and you can also rent one of their speedboats if you are in a group that can share the cost.

The combination of its mountains and islands, cultural diversity as well as its biodiversity, make Con Dao quite unique. It is also one of the last-few relatively pristine areas remaining in Vietnam.

Sleeping
Phone code: 064

B-C *Saigontourist Hotel*, T064-830155. Converted French buildings on seafront. **C** *ATC Guesthouse*, T064-830267, 4 rooms in a converted French villa next to *Saigontourist* and 4 rooms in renovated North Vietnamese-style stilt houses. **C-D** *Phi Yen Hotel*, T064-830168. A state hotel opposite the fishing port. **D** *National Park Guesthouse*, T064-830437. New building located at the park HQ approximately 2 km inland.

Transport

Air Helicopter services operate from Vung Tau airport. There are 3 flights a week, leaving at 0800 on Mon, Thu and Sat and using 24-seat Russian-made Mi-17 Helicopters that also service the offshore oil industry. (This is likely to change as the Vung Tau airport runway will be extended in the future for fixed-wing aircraft.) The helicopters leave Con Dao on the same days at 1000. Ticket price is US$150 return. Tickets can be purchased from a number of sources, but none are entirely reliable. The most reliable is the *SSFC* office at the military airport (helicopter terminal, adjacent to Tan Son Nhat Airport in Ho Chi Minh City). Contact Ms Phuong T/F08-8448814. Alternatively, *ATC* tourism company have an office in District 1, Saigon, T08-9306833, and in Vung Tau, T064-856099. *ATC* do a package consisting of helicopter tickets and accommodation on the island. *Saigontourist* also sell tickets and book accommodation. Contact their office in Siagon, T08-8368542, or the hotel in Con Dao T064-830155.

Sea A larger passenger ship, *Con Dao 9*, was launched in 2000 and now plies the route between Vung Tau and Con Son. In late 2001, the ship sailed weekly, returning to Vung Tau 2 days later. Journey time: approximately 14 hrs. Tickets can usually only be purchased a few days in advance when the departure day has been confirmed. The journey is overnight and a bunk bed is included in the price. The price for foreigners is 200,000d. Two older ships are also used for this trip – *Con Dao 4* and *5*, both river boats and so can be uncomfortable. Contact the shipping office in Vung Tau at 2 Le Loi St, T064-580439.

Saigon

Saigon

274	**Ins and outs**
274	Getting there
274	Getting around
274	Safety
274	Orientation
274	History
276	Background
278	**Sights**
278	Central Saigon
284	Cholon
287	Outer Saigon
288	**Excursions**
288	Cu Chi Tunnels
289	Tay Ninh
290	Nui Ba Den/Black Lady Mountain
290	Can Gio
291	Bien Hoa
292	My Tho
292	**Essentials**
292	Sleeping
297	Eating
302	Bars
304	Entertainment
304	Shopping
306	Sport
308	Tour operators
309	Transport
312	Directory

Saigon, Pearl of the Orient, is the largest city in Vietnam. It is also the nation's foremost commercial and industrial centre. Founded as a Khmer trading and fishing port on the west bank of the Dong Nai River it fell into Vietnamese hands in the late 17th century.

Early in the 18th century the Nguyen emperors established Gia Dinh Citadel, destroyed by French naval forces in 1859. Rebuilt as a French colonial city it was named Saigon (Soai-gon – 'wood of the kapok tree'). Officially Ho Chi Minh City since 1975, it remains to most the bi-syllabic, familiar, old 'Saigon'.

Ins and outs

Getting there

Phone code: 08
Colour map 4, grid B3

See Transport,
page 309, for further
details and Airport
Information in
Essentials, page 33

Saigon may not be Vietnam's capital, but it is the economic powerhouse of the country and the largest city. Reflecting its premier economic position, it is well connected with the wider world – indeed, more airlines fly here from more places than they do to Hanoi. **Tan Son Nhat airport** is 30 mins from town. There are no buses, but taxis charge US$3-4. There are direct domestic connections with Hanoi and Haiphong in the north, Hué, Danang, Play Ku, Buon Ma Thuot, Qui Nhon and Nha Trang in the central region, and Phu Quoc and Rach Gia in the Mekong region. The **train station** is north-west of the city centre and there are regular daily connections with Hanoi and all stops on the line north. As well as international air connections, there is a bus service from Saigon to Phnom Penh (Cambodia). Buses for destinations within the country leave from two main city **bus terminals** and connect Saigon with many larger towns in the central and northern regions, and with most places in the Mekong Delta.

Getting around

See Transport,
page 309,
for further details

Saigon has abundant transport – which is fortunate, because it is a hot, large and fre-netic city. Metered taxis, motorcycle taxis and *cyclos* vie for business in a healthy spirit of competition. Many tourists who prefer some level of independence opt to hire (or even, buy) a bicycle or motorbike. See Tour operators for tourist offices, page 308.

Safety

It is not safe to carry handbags and purses on the streets of Saigon. Jewellery should not be worn. Cameras should be held tightly at all times and passports, tickets and money kept in the safe of your hotel. See the warning on Safety, page 35.

Orientation

Virtually all of Saigon lies to the west of the Saigon River. The eastern side of the river, District 2, is marshy, poor and rather squalid. Most visitors to Saigon head straight for hotels in Districts 1 or 3. Pham Ngu Lao, the backpacker area, is in District 1 not far from the city centre. Cholon or Chinatown is a couple of kilometres west of the centre. The Port of Saigon lies downstream of the city centre in districts 4 and 8. Few visitors ven-ture here although cruise ships berth in District 4. East of the river over Saigon Bridge and up Highway 1 lie Saigon's leafy suburbs in the walled residential compounds of Thu Duc.

History

Before the 15th century, Saigon was a small Khmer village surrounded by a wilderness of forest and swamp. Through the years it had ostensibly been incorporated into the Funan and then the Khmer empires, although it is hard to believe that these kingdoms had any direct, long-term influence on the inhabitants of the community. The Khmers, who called the region *Prei Nokor*, used the area for hunting.

By 1623 Saigon had become an important commercial centre, and in the mid-17th century it became the residence of the so-called Vice-King of Cam-bodia. In 1698, the Viets managed to extend their control this far south and

24 hours in the city

It is said that Saigon is a city that never sleeps. Certainly its restlessness and energy convey themselves to visitors who are invigorated by its dynamism.

Breakfast at your hotel or at a café on Le Loi or Nguyen Hue streets (with strong Vietnamese coffee) should be followed by a tour of historical and cultural sites. This would include **Cong Xa Pari** to see the French cathedral and post office. Many visitors go to the **War Remnants Museum** (although some find this a bit disturbing) and to the **Reunification Palace**, the former Presidential Palace. At the opposite end of Le Duan Street is the worthwhile little **History Museum**. From here take a *cyclo* or taxi to Cholon to see some of the **Chinese pagodas**.

The choice of restaurants for lunch is overwhelming. Vietnamese, French or almost anything else. Take your pick from whatever you fancy on Nguyen Thiep Street or Ngo Duc Ke. For simple Vietnamese food follow office workers to a canteen or popular *com binh dan* and eat well and inexpensively.

The afternoon could perhaps be set aside for some browsing and light shopping. **Ben Thanh** is the best stocked market in Saigon, the quality is high and storeholders are attuned to the needs and whims of foreigners: plenty of fabrics, clothes and souvenirs. From here it is not far to Dong Khoi Street and an hour or two can be spent leisurely looking at the shops and galleries here. Some very nice boutiques sell silk and linen clothes and there are all sorts of antiques, curios and knick knacks left behind by the French and Americans.

By early evening it is time for a drink and the first port of call should be the fifth floor terrace of the *Rex Hotel* used in the war by American officers. Another pre-prandial could be taken at *Saigon Saigon*, an attractive bar in the Caravelle Hotel from where there are splendid views of the city.

Being spoilt for choice, dinner is another dilemma. For Vietnamese food *Hoi An* or *Mandarin* restaurants are memorable as indeed is *Lemon Grass*. *Q Bar* is a stylish place to go for an after dinner drink where you can sit outside the Opera House in relative tranquility.

It would be most unfashionable to get to *Apocalypse Now* too early so don't arrive before 2300 or preferably midnight by which time the place will be swinging. You could easily spend the rest of the night here but if you feel peckish wander outside to one of the noodle carts or go in search of a bowl of *pho* on Nguyen Trai Street by the New World Hotel roundabout.

Saigon

finally Saigon was brought under Vietnamese control – and hence celebrated the city's tercentenary in 1998. By 1790, the city had a population of 50,000 and before Hué was selected as the capital of the Nguyen Dynasty, Emperor Gia Long made Saigon his place of residence.

In the middle of the 19th century, the French began to challenge Vietnamese authority in the south of Vietnam and Saigon. Between 1859 and 1862, in response to the Nguyen persecution of Catholics in Vietnam, the French attacked and captured Saigon, along with the southern provinces of Vinh Long, An Giang and Ha Tien. The Treaty of Saigon in 1862 ratified the conquest and created the new French colony of Cochin China. Saigon was developed in French style: wide, tree-lined boulevards, street-side cafés, elegant French architecture, boutiques and the smell of baking baguettes. The map of French Saigon in the 1930s was a city that owed more to Haussmann than Vietnamese geomancers.

Background

The population of Saigon today is officially six million and rising fast as the rural poor are lured by the tales of streets paved with gold. Actual numbers are thought to be considerably higher when all the recent migrants without residence cards are added. But it has been a roller-coaster ride over the last 35 years. During the course of the Vietnam War, as refugees spilled in from a devastated countryside, the population of Saigon almost doubled from 2.4 million in 1965 to around 4.5 million by 1975. With reunification in 1976, the new Communist authorities pursued a policy of depopulation, believing that the city had become too large – that it was parasitic and was preying on the surrounding countryside. Certainly, most of the jobs were in the service sector, and were linked to the United States' presence. For example, Saigon had 56,000 registered prostitutes alone (and many, many, more unregistered 'amateurs') – most of them country girls.

Vietnam's economic reforms are most in evidence in Saigon (see page 386) and average incomes here, at US$480, are over double the national average. It is here that the highest concentration of *Hoa* (ethnic Chinese) is to be found –

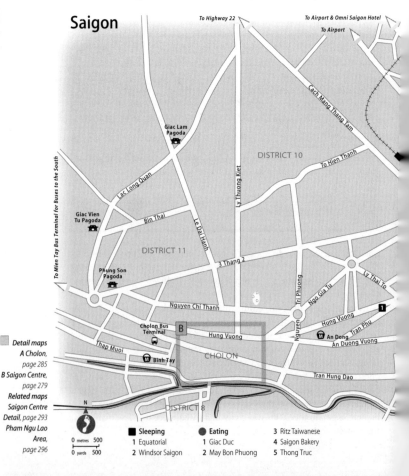

Saigon

To Highway 22
To Airport & Omni Saigon Hotel
To Airport

Cach Mang Thang Tam

Giac Lam Pagoda

DISTRICT 10
To Hien Thanh

Lac Long Quan

Ly Thuong Kiet

To Mien Tay Bus Terminal for Buses to the South

Giac Vien Tu Pagoda

Bin Thal

Le Dai Hanh

DISTRICT 11

3 Thang 2

Phung Son Pagoda

Tri Phuong

Ngo Gia Tu

Ly Thai To

Nguyen Chi Thanh

Hung Vuong

Cholon Bus Terminal

B

Hung Vuong

Nguyen

An Dong

Tran Phu

Thap Muoi

Binh Tay

CHOLON

An Duong Vuong

Tran Hung Dao

N

DISTRICT 8

Detail maps
A Cholon,
page 285
B Saigon Centre,
page 279
Related maps
Saigon Centre
Detail, page 293
Pham Ngu Lao
Area,
page 296

0 metres 500
0 yards 500

■ **Sleeping**
1 Equatorial
2 Windsor Saigon

● **Eating**
1 Giac Duc
2 May Bon Phuong

3 Ritz Taiwanese
4 Saigon Bakery
5 Thong Truc

numbering around 380,000 – and, although once persecuted for their economic success (see page 402), they still have the greatest economic influence and acumen. Most of Saigon's ethnic Chinese live in the district of Cholon, and from there control two-thirds of small-scale commercial enterprises. The reforms have encouraged the *Hoa* to begin investing in business again. Drawing on their links with fellow Chinese in Taiwan, Hong Kong, Bangkok, and among the overseas Vietnamese, they are viewed by the government as crucial in improving prospects for the economy. The reforms have also brought economic inefficiencies into the open. Although the changes have brought wealth to a few, and increased the range of goods on sale, they have also created a much clearer division between the haves and the have-nots.

In its short history Saigon has had a number of keepers. Each has rebuilt the city in their own style. First the Khmer, then the early Vietnamese, followed by the French who tore it all down and started from scratch and were succeeded by the Americans and the 'Puppet' Régime, and finally the Communist North who engineered society rather than the buildings, locking the urban fabric in a time warp.

Under the current régime, best described as crony capitalist, the city is once more being rebuilt. Ever larger holes are being torn in the heart of central

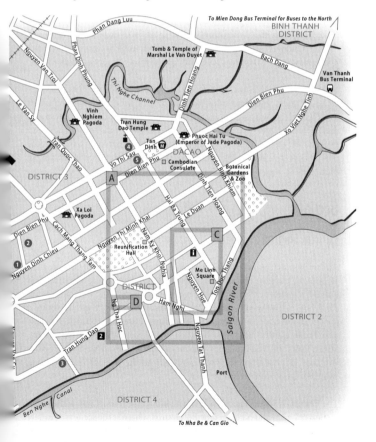

Saigon

Crossing the road

Saigon's streets may look anarchic but they are not. A strict code of conduct applies: the main difference between Vietnam's roads and those of the West is that in Vietnam the individual abdicates responsibility for his personal safety and assumes an obligation on the part of everyone else; it is the closest Vietnam has ever come to true communism!

Watch Vietnamese cross a busy street: unlike Westerners they do not wait for a lull in the traffic but launch themselves straight into the flow, chatting and laughing with their friends, eyes ahead so as to avoid walking into a passing bicycle (their sole duty), no looking left and right, no ducking and weaving – responsibility for their safety rests entirely with the oncoming cyclists. In order to make it easier for cyclists not to hit them they walk at a steady, even pace with no deviation from a clearly signalled route, as any slight change in trajectory or velocity would spell certain disaster.

Saigon. Whereas a few years ago it was common to see buildings disappear, now whole blocks fall to the wrecker's ball. From the holes left behind, concrete, steel and glass monuments emerge. There is, of course, a difference from earlier periods of remodelling of the city. Then, it was conducted on a human scale and the largest buildings, though grand, were on a scale that was in keeping with the dimensions of the streets and ordinary shophouses. French buildings in Dong Khoi Street, for example, were consistent with the Vietnamese way of life: street-level trading with a few residential floors above.

Saigon or Ho Chi Minh City is divided, administratively, into 12 urban districts, or *quan*, and nine suburban districts, or *huyen*. These are further sub-divided into wards and the wards into neighbourhoods; each district and ward has its own People's Committee or local government who guard and protect their responsibilities and rights jealously and maintain a high degree of administrative autonomy. A city-wide People's Committee, elected every four years, oversees the functioning of the entire metropolis.

Sights

Central Saigon

All the sights of Central Saigon can be reached on foot or *cyclo* in no more than 30 minutes from the major hotel areas of Nguyen Hue, Dong Khoi and Ton Duc Thang streets. Visiting all the sights described below will take several days, not that we would particularly recommend visiting them all. Quite a good first port of call, however, is the **Panorama Café** on the 33rd floor of **Saigon Trade Centre**, the tallest building in Vietnam at 37 Ton Duc Thang Street. From this vantage point you can see the whole city stretching before you, and its position and layout in relation to the river and surrounding swampland becomes strikingly clear.

Rex Hotel The *Rex Hotel*, a pre-Liberation favourite with US officers, stands at the intersection of Le Loi and Nguyen Hue Boulevards. This was the scene of the daily 'Five O'Clock Follies' where the military briefed an increasingly sceptical press corps during the Vietnam War. Fully renovated, the crown on the fifth floor terrace of the *Rex* (a good place to have a beer) is rotating once again following a number of years of immobility. Some maintain that it symbolizes Saigon's newly discovered (or rediscovered) vitality.

A short distance northeast from the *Rex*, at the end of Le Loi Boulevard, is the once impressive, French-era **Opera House**. The opera house was once home to the National Assembly and when it is functioning provides a varied programme of events: for example, traditional theatre, contemporary dance and gymnastics. At the northwest end of Nguyen Hue Boulevard, again close to the *Rex*, is the yellow and white **City Hall**, now home to Ho Chi Minh City People's Committee, which overlooks a **statue of Bac Ho** (Uncle Ho) offering comfort, or perhaps advice, to a child. This is a favourite spot for

Saigon centre

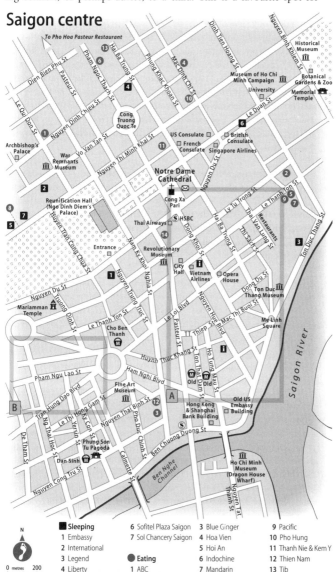

Saigon

Detail maps
A Saigon
Centre Detail,
page 293
B Pham Ngu
Lao Area,
page 296
Related map
Saigon,
page 276

N

0 metres 200
0 yards 200

■ **Sleeping**
1 Embassy
2 International
3 Legend
4 Liberty
5 Saigon Star
6 Sofitel Plaza Saigon
7 Sol Chancery Saigon

● **Eating**
1 ABC
2 Bar No 5
3 Blue Ginger
4 Hoa Vien
5 Hoi An
6 Indochine
7 Mandarin
8 Nam Son
9 Pacific
10 Pho Hung
11 Thanh Nie & Kem Y
12 Thien Nam
13 Tib
14 VY

Vietnamese to have their photograph taken, especially newly-weds who believe old Ho confers some sort of blessing. On weekend evenings literally thousands of young Saigon men and women cruise up and down Nguyen Hue and Le Loi Boulevards and Dong Khoi Street (formerly the bar-lined Tu Do Street, the old Rue Catinat) on bicycles and motorbikes; this whirl of people and machines is known as *chay long rong* 'cruising' or *song voi*, 'living fast'. There are now so many bicycles and motorbikes on the streets of Saigon that intersections seem lethally confused. Miraculously, the riders miss each other (most of the time) while pedestrians safely make their way through waves of machines (see box, page 278).

Notre Dame Cathedral North up Dong Khoi Street, in the middle of Paris Square (Cong Xa Pari), is the imposing but austere red-brick, twin-spired Notre Dame Cathedral, overlooking a grassed square in which is a statue of the Virgin Mary holding an orb. The cathedral was built between 1877 and 1880, and is said to be on the site of an ancient pagoda. A number of homeless sleep under its walls at night, as the Lord would no doubt wish; unfortunately the signs asking Vietnamese men not to treat the walls as a public urinal do not deter this unpleasant but widespread practice. Communion is celebrated here six times on Sundays and three times on weekdays. The late Sunday afternoon and evening services draw particularly large congregations.

General Post Office Facing onto the square is the General Post Office, built in the 1880s, a particularly distinguished building despite the veneer of junk that has been slapped onto it. The front façade has attractive cornices with French and Khmer motifs and the names of distinguished French men of letters and science. Inside, the high, vaulted ceiling and fans create a deliciously cool atmosphere in which to scribble a post card. Note the old wall-map of Cochin-China which has miraculously survived.

Archbishop's Palace Around this area are a number of very fine French-era buildings; some have been allowed to fall into decay but others have been nicely maintained. In particular the Archbishop's Palace on the corner of Nguyen Dinh Chieu and Tran Quoc Thao streets and the high schools, Le Qui Don at 2 Le Qui Don Street and Marie Curie on Nam Ky Khoi Nghia Street. Sadly, all three have had extensions built in the past year rather spoiling the effect, but at least the schools (unlike the archbishop) have attempted to match the new buildings with the old.

North of the Cathedral is Le Duan Street, the former corridor of power with Ngo Dinh Diem's Palace at one end, the zoo at the other and the former embassies of the three major powers France, the US and the UK in between. Quite who was aping who and who the puppet and who the master was a tangled question. Nearest the Palace is the compound of the **French Consulate**. A block away is the **former US Embassy**. After diplomatic ties were resumed the Americans lost little time in demolishing the 1960s building which held so many bad memories. The new Consulate General now stands on this site. Outside, a queue of hopeful visa supplicants forms every day come rain or shine. A plaque outside records the attack by Viet Cong special forces during the Tet offensive of 1968 and the final victory in 1975. On the other side of the road, a little further northeast at 25 Le Duan, is the former **British Embassy**, now the British Consulate General and British Council. At 2 Le Duan Street is the **Museum of Ho Chi Minh Campaign** (Bao Tang Quan Doi) with a tank and warplane in the front compound. It contains an indifferent display of photographs and articles of war. ■ *Tue-Sun 0800-1130, 1330-1600.*

At the end of Le Duan Street are the Botanical Gardens which run alongside **Botanical** Nguyen Binh Khiem Street at the point where the Thi Nghe channel flows into **Gardens & zoo** the Saigon River. The gardens were established in 1864 by French botanist Jean-Batiste Louis Pierre; by the 1970s they had a collection of nearly 2,000 species, and a particularly fine display of orchids. With the dislocations of the immediate postwar years, the gardens went into decline, a situation from which they are still trying to recover. In the south quarter of the gardens is a mediocre **zoo** with a rather moth-eaten collection of animals which form a backdrop to smartly dressed Vietnamese families posing for photographs. The latest addition to the zoo is a life size family of Vietnamese-speaking model dinosaurs. ■ *Daily 0600-2000, entrance to gardens and zoo, 10,000d, T8293728, 2 Nguyen Binh Khiem St.*

More stimulating and impressive, at 2 Nguyen Binh Khiem Street, just to the **Historical** left of the main gates to the Botanical Gardens, is the Historical Museum, for- **Museum** merly the National Museum, and before that the Musée Blanchard de la Bosse (from 1929-56). This elegant building was constructed in 1928 and is pagodaesque in style. It displays a wide range of artefacts from the prehistoric (300,000 years ago) and the Dongson periods (3,500 BC – AD 100), right through to the birth of the Vietnamese Communist Party in 1930. Particularly impressive are the Cham sculptures, of which the standing bronze Buddha dating from the fourth to sixth century is probably the finest. There are also representative pieces from the Chen-la, Funan, Khmer, Oc-eo and Han Chinese periods, and from the various Vietnamese dynasties together with some hill tribe artefacts. Little of the labelling is in English and even the English booklet available from the ticket office is of little help. Water puppet shows (see also page 414) are held here daily (10,000d). ■ *Daily 0800-1130, 1330-1630, 10,000d, T8298146, 2 Nguyen Binh Khiem St.* Opposite the Historical Museum is the **Memorial Temple**, constructed in 1928 and dedicated to famous Vietnamese. ■ *Tue-Sun 0800-1130, 1300-1600.*

The popular War Remnants Museum is on Vo Van Tan Street, close to the **War Remnants** intersection with Le Qui Don Street. In the courtyard are tanks, bombs and **Museum** helicopters, while in the museum itself are countless photographs, and a few exhibits, illustrating man's inhumanity. The display covers the Son My (My Lai) massacre on 16 March 1968 (see box, page 221), the effects of napalm and phosphorous, and the after-effects of Agent Orange defoliation (this is particularly disturbing, with bottled malformed human foetuses). Understandably, there is no record of North Vietnamese atrocities to US and South Vietnamese troops. There is also a rather laughable exhibit of such latter-day Western atrocities as heavy-metal music. This museum has gone through some interesting name changes in recent years. It began life as the Exhibition House of American and Chinese War Crimes. In 1990, 'Chinese' was dropped from the name, and in 1994 'American' was too. Since 1996 it has simply been called the 'War Remnants Museum'. Water puppet theatre can be seen here. ■ *Daily 0730-1145, 1330-1715, 10,000d, T9306325, 28 Vo Van Tan St.*

Saigon has close to 200 pagodas – far too many for most visitors to see. Many **Xa Loi Pagoda** of the finest are in Cholon (see page 284), although there is a selection closer to the main hotel area in central Saigon. The Xa Loi Pagoda is not far from the War Remnants Museum at 89 Ba Huyen Thanh Quan Street (see Saigon General map), surrounded by food stalls. If the main gate is shut, try the side entrance on Su Thien Chieu Street. Built in 1956, the pagoda contains a

Saigon

 ## The Buddhist martyrs: self-immolation as protest

In August 1963 there was a demonstration of 15,000 people at the Xa Loi Pagoda, with speakers denouncing the Diem régime and telling jokes about Diem's sister-in-law, Madame Nhu (she was later, during a speaking tour in the US, to call monks "hooligans in robes"). Two nights later, ARVN special forces (from Catholic families) raided the pagoda, battering down the gate, wounding 30 and killing seven people. Soon afterwards Diem declared martial law. The pagoda became a focus of discontent, with several monks committing suicide through self-immolation to protest against the Diem régime. The first monk to immolate himself was 66-year-old Thich Quang Du, from Hué. On 11 June 1963, his companions poured petrol over him and set him alight as he sat in the lotus position. Pedestrians prostrated themselves

at the sight; even a policeman threw himself to the ground in reverence. The next day, the picture of the monk in flames filled the front pages of newspapers around the world. Some 30 monks and nuns followed Thich's example in protesting against the Diem government and US involvement in South Vietnam. Two young US protesters also followed suit, one committing suicide by self-immolation outside the Pentagon and the other next to the UN, both in November 1968. Madame Nhu, a Catholic, is reported as having said after the monks' death: "Let them burn, and we shall clap our hands." Within five months Diem had been killed in a military coup. In May 1993, a Vietnamese man immolated himself at the Thien Mu Pagoda in Hué – the pagoda where the first monk-martyr was based (see page 183).

multi-storeyed tower, which is particularly revered, as it houses a relic of the Buddha. The main sanctuary contains a large, bronze-gilded Buddha in an attitude of meditation. Around the walls are a series of silk paintings depicting the previous lives of the Buddha (with an explanation of each life to the right of the entrance into the sanctuary). The pagoda is historically, rather than artistically, important as it became a focus of dissent against the Diem regime (see box above). ■ *Daily 0630-1100, 1430-1700.*

Reunification Hall **Ngo Dinh Diem's Presidential Palace**, now renamed Reunification Hall, or the **Thong Nhat Conference Hall**, is in a large park to the southeast of Nguyen Thi Minh Khai Street, and southwest of Nam Ky Khoi Nghia Street. The residence of the French governor was built on this site in 1868, which was later renamed the Presidential Palace. In February 1962, a pair of planes took off to attack Viet Cong emplacements – piloted by two of the south's finest airmen – but they turned back to bomb the Presidential Palace in a futile attempt to assassinate President Diem. The president escaped with his family to the cellar, but the Palace had to be demolished and replaced with a new building. One of the most memorable photographs taken during the War was of a North Vietnamese Army (NVA) tank crashing through the gates of the Palace on 30 April 1975 – symbolizing the end of South Vietnam and its government. The President of South Vietnam, General Duong Van Minh, along with his entire cabinet, was arrested in the Palace shortly afterwards. The hall has been preserved as it was found in 1975 and visitors can take a guided tour. In the *Vice President's Guest Room*, there is a lacquered painting of the Temple of Literature in Hanoi, while the *Presenting of Credentials Room* contains a fine 40-piece lacquer work showing diplomats presenting their credentials during the Le Dynasty (15th century). In the basement there are operations rooms, military maps, radios and other paraphernalia. In essence, it is a 1960s-style building filled with 1960s-style official furnishings. Visitors are shown a poorly made, but nonetheless interesting, film of the Revolution. ■ *Daily 0730-1130, 1300-1600, 15,000d, T8223652. The visitors' entrance is at 106 Nguyen Du Street. The guides are friendly, but their English is not always very good. The hall is sometimes closed for state occasions.*

Revolutionary Museum

Close by is the Revolutionary Museum. Like its equivalent in Hanoi, this is not a revolutionary museum but a museum of the revolution, with a display of photographs, a few pieces of hardware (helicopter, anti-aircraft guns) in the back compound, and some memorabilia. All the labelling is in Vietnamese, and the museum is usually filled with red-scarved school children. ■ *Daily 0800-1600, 10,000d, T8293728, 65 Ly Tu Trong Street.* Opposite the museum is a small park with an open-air café. Southeast from the Revolutionary Museum along Ly Tu Trong Street is the centre of Saigon's 'fashion' industry, selling some genuine brand names but mostly quite good fakes.

Mariamman Hindu Temple

Not far away at 45 Truong Dinh Street is the Mariamman Hindu Temple. Although clearly Hindu, with a statue of Mariamman flanked by Maduraiveeran and Pechiamman, it is largely frequented by Chinese worshippers, providing the strange sight of Chinese Vietnamese clasping incense sticks and prostrating themselves in front of a Hindu deity, as they would to a Buddha image. The Chinese have always been pragmatic when it comes to religions.

Ben Thanh Market (Cho Ben Thanh)

A large, covered central-market, Ben Thanh Market faces a statue of Tran Nguyen Han at a large and chaotic roundabout, the Ben Thanh gyratory system, which marks the intersection of Le Loi, Ham Nghi and Tran Hung Dao streets. Ben Thanh is well stocked with clothes (cheap souvenir T-shirts), household goods, a wide range of soap, shampoo and sun cream, a good choice of souvenirs, lacquerware, embroidery and so on, as well as some terrific lines in food, including cold meats, fresh and dried fruits. It is not cheap (most local people window-shop here and purchase elsewhere) but the quality is high and the selection probably without equal. It is a terrific experience just to wander through and marvel at the range of produce on offer, all the more so now most of the beggars have been eased out. Outside the north gate (*cua Bac*) on Le Thanh Ton Street are some particularly tempting displays of fresh fruit (the oranges and apples are imported) and beautiful cut flowers.

Saigon has a number of markets, but this one and the Binh Tay Market in Cholon (see page 286) are the largest. Many of the markets are surprisingly well stocked for a country which a few years ago was close to economic collapse. The people of the south, and particularly the Chinese of Saigon, have not forgotten what it is like to conduct business, and with the economic reforms, private traders have reappeared on the streets to make a quick dong or buck.

Fine Art Museum

The Fine Art Museum (*Bao Tang My Thuat*), housed in an impressive cream-coloured mansion at 97A Pho Duc Chinh Street, displays work from the classical period through to socialist realism. On the third floor is a museum of ancient art which contains artefacts from the ancient civilizations of Oc Eo. The building itself is worthy of note having been built early this century by a Chinese man whose fortune was made by selling empty bottles. ■ *Tue-Sun 0900-1700, 10,000d, T8294441.*

At 338 Nguyen Cong Tru Street is the **Phung Son Tu Pagoda**. This is a small temple built just after the Second World War by Fukien Chinese; its most notable features are the wonderful painted entrance doors with their fearsome armed warriors. Incense spirals hang in the open well of the pagoda, which is dedicated to Ong Bon, the Guardian of Happiness and Virtue.

The **War Surplus** (or **Dan Sinh Market**) is close to the Phung Son Tu Pagoda at 104 Nguyen Cong Tru Street. Merchandise on sale includes dog tags and military clothing and equipment (not all of it authentic). The market is popular with Western visitors looking for mementoes of their visit, so bargain particularly hard.

Old Market The Old Market is on Ton That Dam Street, running between Ham Nghi Street and Ton That Thiep Street. It is the centre for the sale of black market goods (particularly consumer electronics) – now openly displayed. There is also a good range of foodstalls and fruit sellers. Close by on Ben Chuong Duong Street is the old and rather splendid **Hong Kong and Shanghai Bank building**.

Ho Chi Minh Museum (Dragon House Wharf) Nguyen Tat Thanh Street runs south from here over the Ben Nghe Channel to **Dragon House Wharf**, at the confluence of the Ben Nghe Channel and the Saigon River. The building has been converted into a **museum** (predominantly on the first floor) celebrating the life and exploits of Ho Chi Minh, mostly through pictures and the odd piece of memorabilia. School children are brought here to be told of their country's recent history, and people of all ages have their photographs taken with a portrait of Bac Ho in the background. ■ *Tue-Thu & Sat 0800-1130, 1400-1800, Sun 0800-1130, 1400-2000, 5,000d.*

Ton Duc Thang Museum A short distance north up Ton Duc Thang Street from the broad Me Linh Square (in the centre of which an imposing statue of Vietnamese hero Tran Hung Dao glares down at the site vacated by the *Floating Hotel*), is the rarely visited Ton Duc Thang Museum. Opened in 1989, it is dedicated to the life of Ton Duc Thang or Bac (Uncle) Ton. Bac Ton, a comrade of Ho Chi Minh, with whom he fought, was appointed President of Vietnam following Minh's death, remaining in office until his own death in 1980. The museum contains an array of photographs and other memorabilia. ■ *Daily 0730-1130, 1330-1700, 10,000d, T8297542.*

Cholon

Chinatown Cholon (*Cho lon* or 'big market') or Chinatown is an area inhabited predominantly by Vietnamese of Chinese origin. Since 1975, the authorities have alienated many Chinese, causing hundreds of thousands to leave the country. In making their escape many have died – either through drowning, as their perilously small and overladen craft foundered, or at the hands of pirates in the South China Sea (see page 376). In total, between 1977 and 1982, 709,570 refugees were recorded by the UNHCR as having fled Vietnam. By the late 1980s, the flow of boat people was being driven more by economic, rather than political, forces; there was little chance of making good in a country as poor, and in an economy as moribund, as that of Vietnam. Today, although economic conditions for the vast majority of Vietnamese have barely changed, the stream has dried to a trickle as the opportunities for claiming refugee status and gaining asylum have disappeared. Even with this flow of Chinese out of the country, there is still a large population of Chinese Vietnamese living in Cholon, an area which encompasses the fifth and the sixth precincts, or *quan*, to the southwest of the city centre. Cholon appears to the casual visitor to be the most populated, noisiest, and in general the most vigorous part of Saigon, if not of Vietnam. It is here that entrepreneurial talent and private funds are concentrated; both resources that the government are keen to mobilize in their attempts to reinvigorate the economy.

Cholon is worth visiting not only for the bustle and activity, but also because the temples and assembly halls found here are the finest in Saigon. As with any town in Southeast Asia boasting a sizeable Chinese population, the early settlers established meeting rooms which offered social, cultural and spiritual support to members of a dialect group. These assembly halls, or *hoi quan*, are most common in Hoi An and Cholon. There are temples in the buildings which attract Vietnamese as well as Chinese worshippers, and indeed today serve little of their former purpose. The elderly meet here occasionally for a natter and a cup of tea. The sights outlined below can be walked in half a day, although hiring a *cyclo* for a few hours is a more relaxing way to get around.

The Nghia An Assembly Hall can be found at 678 Nguyen Trai Street, not far from the *Arc en Ciel Hotel*, the best hotel in Cholon. A magnificent, carved, gold-painted wooden boat hangs over the entrance. To the left, on entering the temple, is a larger than life representation of Quan Cong's horse and groom. At the main altar are three figures in glass cases: the central red-faced figure with a green cloak is Quan Cong himself; to the left and right are his trusty companions, General Chau Xuong (very fierce) and the mandarin Quan Binh respectively. On leaving note the fine gold figures of guardians on the inside of the door panels.

Nghia An Assembly Hall

The Tam Son Assembly Hall is nearby at 118 Trieu Quang Phuc Street, just off Nguyen Trai Street. The temple, built in the 19th century by Fukien immigrants, is frequented by childless mothers as it is dedicated to Chua Thai Sanh, the Goddess of Fertility. It is an uncluttered, 'pure' example of a Chinese/Vietnamese pagoda – peaceful and quiet. Like Nghia An Hoi Quan, the temple contains figures of Quan Cong, his horse and two companions (see above).

Tam Son Assembly Hall

The Thien Hau Pagoda, at 710 Nguyen Trai Street, is one of the largest in the city. Constructed in the early 19th century, it is Chinese in inspiration and is dedicated to the worship of both the Buddha and to the Goddess Thien Hau – the goddess of the sea and the protector of sailors. Two enormous incense urns can be seen through the main doors. Inside, the principal altar supports the gilded form of Thien Hau, with a boat to one side. Silk paintings depicting religious scenes decorate the walls. By far the most interesting part of the

Thien Hau Pagoda

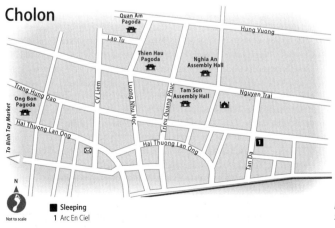

Cholon

Sleeping
1 Arc En Ciel

N

Not to scale

Related map
Saigon, page 276

pagoda is the roof, which can be best seen from the small open courtyard. It must be one of the finest and most richly ornamented in Vietnam, with the high-relief frieze depicting episodes from the Legends of the Three Kingdoms. In the post-1975 era, many would-be refugees prayed here for safe deliverance before casting themselves adrift on the South China Sea. A number of those who survived the perilous voyage sent offerings to the merciful goddess and the pagoda has been well maintained since.

Quan Am Pagoda Close to Thien Hau, at 12 Lao Tu Street (just off Luong Nhu Hoc Street), is the Quan Am Pagoda, thought to be one of the oldest in the city. The roof supports four sets of impressive mosaic-encrusted figures, while inside the main building is fronted with old, gold and lacquer panels of guardian spirits. The main altar supports a seated statue of A-Pho, the Holy Mother. In front of the main altar is a white ceramic statue of *Quan Am, the Goddess of Purity and Motherhood* (Goddess of Mercy) – see page 76. The pagoda complex also contains a series of courtyards and altars dedicated to a range of deities and spirits. Outside, hawkers sell caged birds and vast quantities of incense sticks to pilgrims.

Binh Tay Market The Binh Tay Market, sandwiched between Thap Muoi and Phan Van Khoe streets, is one of the most colourful and exciting markets in Saigon, with a wonderful array of noises, smells and colours. It sprawls over a large area and is contained in what looks like a rather decayed Forbidden Palace. Beware of pickpockets here. A new high-rise market – the five-storey **An Dong Market** – opened at the end of 1991 in Cholon. It was built with an investment of US$5 million from local ethnic Chinese businessmen.

Phung Son Pagoda A 25-minute walk from the Binh Tay Market, and set back from the road at 1408 3 Thang 2 Boulevard, is the Phung Son Pagoda, also known as **Go Pagoda**. It was built at the beginning of the 19th century on the site of an earlier Cambodian structure and has been rebuilt several times. At one time, it was decided to move the pagoda, and all the temple valuables were loaded on to the back of a white elephant. The beast stumbled and the valuables tumbled out into the pond that surrounds the temple. This was taken as a sign from the gods that the pagoda was to stay where it was. In the sanctuary, there is a large, seated, gilded Buddha, surrounded by a variety of other figures from several Asian and Southeast Asian countries.

Giac Vien Pagoda Giac Vien Pagoda (Buddha's Complete Enlightenment) can be found at the end of a narrow 200-m-long dirt road running off Lac Long Quan Street (just after No 247), set among vegetable plots. It is similar in layout, content and inspiration to Giac Lam Pagoda (see below). Visiting just one of the two pagodas would be enough for most visitors. The Giac Vien Pagoda was built in 1771 and dedicated to the worship of the Emperor Gia Long. Although restored, Giac Vien remains one of the best preserved temples in Vietnam. It is lavishly decorated, with over 100 carvings of various divinities and spirits, dominated by a large gilded image of the Buddha of the Past (Amitabha or *A Di Da Phat* in Vietnamese). It is everything a pagoda should be – demons and gods jump out around every corner, a confusion of fantastic characters. With the smoke and smells, the richness of colour, and the darkness, it assaults the senses. Among the decorations, note the 'Buddha lamp', funerary tablets, and urns with photographs of the deceased.

Giac Lam Pagoda The Giac Lam Pagoda (Forest of Enlightenment) is at 118 Lac Long Quan Street, about 2 km northeast from Giac Vien Pagoda, through an arch and down a short track about 200 m from the intersection with Le Dai Hanh Street. Built in 1744, it is the oldest pagoda in Saigon. There is a sacred Bodhi tree in the temple courtyard and the pagoda is set among fruit trees and vegetable plots. Inside Giac Lam it feels, initially, like a rather cluttered private house. In one section, there are rows of funerary tablets with pictures of the deceased – a rather moving display of man's mortality. The main altar is particularly impressive, with layers of Buddhas, dominated by the gilded form of the Buddha of the Past. Note the 49-Buddha oil lamp. The monks are very friendly and will probably offer tea. Some have good English and French as well as detailed knowledge of the history of the pagoda. It is a small haven of peace. An unusual feature is the use of blue and white porcelain plates to decorate the roof and some of the small towers in the garden facing the pagoda.

Outer Saigon

Phuoc Hai Tu (Emperor of Jade Pagoda)

The Phuoc Hai Tu (Emperor of Jade Pagoda) can be found off Dien Bien Phu Street at 73 Mai Thi Luu Street, nestling behind low pink walls, just before the Thi Nghe Channel. Women sell birds that are set free to gain merit, and a pond to the right contains large turtles. The Emperor of Jade is the supreme god of the Taoists, although this temple, built in 1900, contains a wide range of other deities. These include the archangel Michael of the Buddhists, a Sakyamuni (historic) Buddha, statues of the two generals who tamed the Green Dragon (representing the east) and the White Dragon (representing the west), to the left and right of the first altar respectively, and Quan Am (see page 76). The Hall of Ten Hells in the left-hand sanctuary has reliefs depicting the 1,000 tortures of hell.

Tran Hung Dao Temple

Not far from the Emperor of Jade Pagoda is the small Tran Hung Dao Temple at 34 Vo Thi Sau Street. Built in 1932, it was dedicated to the worship of the victorious 13th-century General Hung Dao, and contains a series of bas-reliefs depicting the general's successes, along with weapons and carved dragons (see page 159). In the front courtyard is a larger-than-life bronze statue of this hero of Vietnamese nationalism. ■ *Daily 0700-1100, 1430-1700.*

Vinh Nghiem Pagoda

To the west, on Nguyen Van Troi Street, and just to the south of the Thi Nghe Channel is another modern pagoda, the Vinh Nghiem Pagoda. It was completed in 1967 and is one of the largest in Vietnam. Built in the Japanese style, it displays a classic seven-storey pagoda in a large and airy sanctuary. On either side of the entrance are two fearsome warriors; inside is a large Japanese-style Buddha in an attitude of meditation, flanked by two goddesses. Along the walls are a series of scrolls depicting the jataka tales, with rather quaint (and difficult to interpret) explanations in English.

Tomb & Temple of Marshal Le Van Duyet

A 10-15 minute *cyclo* ride across the Thi Nghe Channel and almost into the suburbs leads to the Tomb and Temple of Marshal Le Van Duyet at 126 Dinh Tien Hoang Street. Le Van Duyet was a highly respected Vietnamese soldier who put down the Tay Son rebellion (see page 223) and who died in 1831. The pagoda was renovated in 1937 – a plaque on the left lists those who made donations to the renovation fund. The main sanctuary contains a weird assortment of objects: a stuffed tiger, a miniature mountain, whale baleen, carved elephants, crystal goblets, spears and other weapons of war. Much of the collection is made up of the Marshal's personal possessions. In front of the temple is the tomb itself, surrounded by a low wall and flanked by two guardian lions and two lotus buds. The pagoda's attractive roof is best seen from the tomb.

Saigon

Excursions

Unlike Hanoi, which is so rich in sights to visit on a day out, the Saigon region is woefully under-endowed (thank goodness the city itself has so much to offer). The Cu Chi Tunnels are the most popular day trip, followed closely by an excursion to the Mekong Delta. It is possible to get to the coast and back in a day, Vung Tau (see page 260), Long Hai (see page 267) and Ho Coc (see page 268) being the obvious candidates. Saigon does, on the other hand, have several out of town sports facilities with three golf courses and the exhilarating Saigon Water Park all within less than an hour's drive. See page 307.

Cu Chi Tunnels

Cu Chi Tunnels are about 40 km northwest of Saigon (see map, page 365). Cu Chi town is on the main road to Tay Ninh and the Cao Dai temple, and both the tunnels and the temple can be visited in a single day trip. Dug by the Viet Minh, who began work in 1948, they were later expanded by the VC and used for storage and refuge, and contained sleeping quarters, hospitals and schools. The tunnels are too narrow for most Westerners, but a short section of the 200 km of tunnels has been especially widened to allow tourists to share the experience. Tall or large people might still find it a claustrophobic squeeze.

Cu Chi was one of the most fervently Communist of the districts around Saigon and the tunnels were used as the base from which the VC mounted the operations of the Tet Offensive in 1968. Communist cadres were active in this area of rubber plantations, even before the Second World War. Vann and Ramsey, two American soldiers, were to notice the difference between this

Around Saigon

area and other parts of the south in the early 60s: "No children laughed and shouted for gum and candy in these hamlets. Everyone, adult and child, had a cold look" (Sheehan 1989, pages 539-40). When the Americans first discovered this underground base on their doorstep they would simply pump CS gas down the tunnel openings and then set explosives. Later, realizing that the tunnels might also yield valuable intelligence, they sent volunteer 'tunnel rats' into the earth to capture prisoners. Cu Chi district was a free-fire zone and was assaulted using the full battery of ecological warfare. Defoliants were sprayed and 20 tonne Rome Ploughs carved up the area in the search for tunnels. It was said that even a crow flying over Cu Chi district had to carry its own lunch.

There are in fact two sets of Cu Chi Tunnels open to visitors. Cu Chi 1 is more touristy. Visitors are shown a somewhat antique but nevertheless interesting video and invited to a firing range to try their hand with equally ancient AK47s at a buck a bang. ■ *US$5*. Cu Chi 2 has fewer tourists and more original tunnels. It also has a 'minefield' where visitors have to avoid tripwires. ■ *Daily 0700-1700, 65,000d, Dia Dao Ben Duoc. Getting there: most visitors reach Cu Chi on a tour or charter a car (about US$20-30 per day, including a visit to Tay Ninh – see below). Regular buses leave for Cu Chi town from the Mien Tay station (Cholon) and the Ham Nghi station; from Cu Chi it is necessary to take a* Honda ôm *to the tunnels or the infrequent Ben Suc bus, 10 km. It is also possible to take a motorbike the whole way from Saigon, US$10 round trip. Go up Cach Mang Thang Tam Street which turns into Highway 22 to Cu Chi. From the centre of Cu Chi the tunnels are quite well signed.*

Tay Ninh

Tay Ninh contains the idiosyncratic **Cao Dai Great Temple**, the 'cathedral' of the Cao Dai religion (see page 419 for background on Cao Daiism), and is the main reason to visit the town.   *Phone code: 066*

Tay Ninh, which is 96 km northwest of Saigon and 64 km further on from Cu Chi town, can be visited on a day trip from the city and can easily be combined with a visit to the Cu Chi tunnels. The province of the same name borders Cambodia and, before the 17th century, was part of the Khmer Kingdom. Between 1975 and December 1978, soldiers of Pol Pot's Khmer Rouge periodically attacked villages in this province, killing the men and raping the women. Ostensibly, it was in order to stop these incursions that the Vietnamese army invaded Cambodia on Christmas Day 1978, taking Phnom Penh by January 1979.

The Cao Dai Great Temple, built in 1880, is set within a large complex of schools and administrative buildings, all washed in pastel yellow. The twin-towered cathedral is European in inspiration but with distinct Oriental features. On the façade are figures of Cao Dai saints in high relief, and at the entrance to the cathedral is a mural depicting Victor Hugo flanked by the Vietnamese poet Nguyen Binh Khiem and the Chinese nationalist Sun Yat Sen. The latter holds an inkstone, symbolizing, strangely, the link between Confucianism and Christianity. Graham Greene in *The Quiet American* called it "The Walt Disney Fantasia of the East". Monsieur Ferry, an acquaintance of Norman Lewis, described the cathedral in even more outlandish terms, saying it "looked like a fantasy from the brain of Disney, and all the faiths of the Orient had been ransacked to create the pompous ritual ...". Lewis himself was clearly unimpressed with the structure and the religion, writing in *A Dragon Apparent* that "This cathedral must be the most outrageously vulgar building ever to have been erected with serious intent".

After removing shoes and hats, women enter the cathedral through a door to the left, men to the right, and they then proceed down their respective aisles towards the altar, usually accompanied by a Cao Dai priest dressed in white with a black turban. During services they don red, blue and yellow robes signifying Confucianism, Taoism and Buddhism respectively. Two rows of pink pillars entwined with green dragons line the nave, leading up to the main altar which supports a large globe on which is painted a single staring eye – the divine, all-seeing-eye. The roof is blue and dotted with clouds, representing the heavens, and the walls are pierced by open, lattice-work windows. ■ *Ceremonies are held each day at 0600, 1200, 1800 and 2400, and visitors can watch from the cathedral's balcony. NB Visitors should not enter the central portion of the nave – keep to the side aisles – and also should not wander in and out during services. If you go in at the beginning of the service you should stay until the end (one hour). Photography is allowed.* About 500 m from the cathedral (turn right when facing the main façade) is the *Doan Ket*, a formal garden.

Tay Ninh also has a good **market** and some **Cham temples** 1 km to the southwest of the town. ■ *Getting there: a tour, or charter a car in Saigon. Regular buses leave for Tay Ninh, via Cu Chi, from Mien Tay station (2½ hrs) or motorbike.*

Nui Ba Den/Black Lady Mountain

Also known as *Nui Ba Den*, Black Lady Mountain is 10 km to the northeast of Tay Ninh and 106 km from Saigon. The peak rises dramatically from the plain to a height of almost 1,000 m and can be seen in the distance, to the right, on entering Tay Ninh. The Black Lady was a certain Ly Thi Huong who, while her lover was bravely fighting the occupying forces, was ordered to marry the son of a local mandarin. Rather than complying, she threw herself from the mountain. Another version of this story is that she was kidnapped by local scoundrels. A number of shrines to the Black Woman are located on the mountain, and pilgrims still visit the site. Fierce battles were also fought here between the French and Americans, and the Viet Minh. There are excellent views of the surrounding plain from the summit. ■ *Buses to Tay Ninh go from Tay Ninh bus station on Cach Mang Tam Tang St by the western edge of Tan Son Nhat Airport. From Tay Ninh to Nui Ba Den go by* Honda ôm.

Can Gio

This mangrove forest is the green lung of Saigon. Within an hour or two of central Saigon visitors can be motoring through mile after mile of unspoilt woodland, albeit woods with a difference. For these trees grow in salty water and are inundated by rising tides twice a day (see box Rebirth of a forest, page 291). Within the forest is a monkey sanctuary and a rather poor crocodile farm. While not a day out for the kids, those of a botanical disposition will find it interesting. There are no beaches, just mud banks and food is likely to be no more than a packet of instant noodles. ■ *Getting there: easiest by motorbike. Go through District 4, past Ho Chi Minh Museum and the port and just go straight. Take a ferry from Nha Be to Binh Khanh (approx 15-20 mins) and keep driving. After three km it starts getting green. Very muddy in the wet season.*

Rebirth of a forest

About 25 km southeast of Saigon, stretching down to the coast, lies the district of Can Gio. A low-lying area, it is watered by the silty Saigon River and twice daily washed by the salty tides of the South China Sea. Conditions are ideal for mangrove forest, one of the most diverse and prolific of all woodland types, and the 30,000-ha forest in Can Gio is no exception. The forest that visitors see today is, however, less than 16 years old, having been replanted by Vietnamese forestry workers to replace the dead stumps that remained after the US Air Force defoliated the old mangroves with herbicides, chiefly Agent Orange.

Ho Chi Minh's famous dictum "Rung la vang, neu ta biet bao ve, thi rung rat quy" (forests are gold, if we know how to protect them we can be rich) was prescient; the great man understood environmental issues long before the green movement made them trendy. Happily, the Can Gio mangrove swamps reflect the truth of Ho's words, providing fertile spawning and nursery grounds for commercially valuable fish and crustacea stocks as well as providing habitat for numerous semi-aquatic and rare species such as otters.

The Rhizophora tree species (distinguished by their stilt roots, like 'flying buttresses') deliver a sustainable harvest of charcoal, building materials, fruit, edible leaves and tannin when carefully managed.

Vietnamese and international scientists have been impressed by the extent of re-colonization of the forest by wildlife because, while new flora species are slow to colonize, the fauna has developed apace: otters, crocodiles, kingfishers, storks and many other species have returned and in growing numbers. No scientific enumeration has been completed but preliminary observations look promising.

Given the fantastic achievement this represents it is dismaying that government planners have now decided to turn the mangrove forest into a Special Economic Zone. The proposals for the area sound like the rantings of a mad World Bank economist: 'infrastructure', EZ, EPZ, multi-sectoral Ips, sea-port, eco-tourism ...' in other words, long on jargon and short on coherence. The damage has begun: the central road through the forest has been widened and metalled and a bridge built at Dan Xay.

Bien Hoa

Bien Hoa is the capital of the province of Dong Nai and was established by Chinese migrants on the banks of the Dong Nai River in the late 17th century when the town, 26 km north of Saigon, was known by the name Dong Nai Dai Pho. During the war it was a massive US air base and although there is little to see today there are suggestions that it could replace Tan Son Nhat as Saigon's airport, owing to the latter's cramped site. Paul Theroux in *The Great Railway Bazaar* wrote of Bien Hoa:

Phone code: 061

> "... out here in the suburbs of Bien Hoa, created by the pressure of American occupation, the roads were falling to pieces and cholera streamed into the backyards. Planning and maintenance characterize even the briefest and most brutish empire; apart from the institution of a legal system there aren't many more imperial virtues. But Americans weren't pledged to maintain. There is Bien Hoa Station, built fifty years ago. It is falling down, but that is not the point. There is no sign that it was ever mended by the Americans; even sagging under its corona of barbed wire it looks a good deal sturdier than the hangars at Bien Hoa airbase".

■ *Frequent buses to Bien Hoa go along Nguyen Thi Minh Khai St or catch one from near Van Thanh Park just before Saigon Bridge.*

My Tho

My Tho is another town it is quite possible to visit in a day. My Tho is in the Mekong Delta about 70 km from Saigon (see page 319). While My Tho does not represent the rest of the Mekong Delta those for whom time is pressing should consider a day trip to My Tho, for while the journey there is unexciting, a trip on the river gives a taste of the huge delta region.

Essentials

Sleeping

Phone code: 08
All in District 1,
Quan 1 – Q1, unless
stated otherwise

With the opening of new hotels and the renovation and upgrading of older ones there is a good choice of places to stay. Prices have crept up over the past year or two but rates remain reasonable. Saigon offers a wide range of accommodation from glittering five-star hotels to cheap, dormitory accommodation.

Central Saigon
■ *on maps,*
pages 276 and 279
Price codes:
see inside front cover

LL-L *Caravelle*, 19-23 Lam Son Square, T8234999, F8243999, hotel@caravellehotel.vnn.vn Central and one of Saigon's top hotels. All mod cons, comfortable with well-trained and friendly staff. *Port Orient* serves a fantastic buffet lunch and dinner and *Saigon Saigon*, the roof-top bar, draws the crowds until the early hours of the morning. Recommended. **LL-L** *Legend*, 2A-4A Ton Duc Thang St, T8233333, F8232333, info@legendhotelsaigon.com The hotel boasts Saigon's most opulent foyer. Popular with businessmen, particularly Japanese, it overlooks the Saigon River and offers a full range of restaurants and business facilities. **LL-L** *Renaissance Riverside*, 8-15 Ton Duc Thang St, T8220033, F8235666, rsvn.rrhs@hcm.vnn.vn This is, in size and feel, almost a boutique hotel. Certainly very well run, comfortable and popular with its customers it also boasts Vietnam's highest atrium. Several excellent restaurants and attractive pool. **LL-L** *Saigon Prince*, 63 Nguyen Hue Blvd, T8222999, F8228745, saigon-princehtl@hcm.vnn.vn An ungainly pink giant right in the centre of town, popular with Japanese visitors. Health club (but no pool), several restaurants including Japanese. The *Grill Restaurant* serves popular Sun brunch 1100-1500. **LL-L** *Sofitel Plaza Saigon*, 17 Le Duan St, T8241555, F8241666, sofitelsgn@hcmc.netnam.vn For many this is Saigon's top hotel, smart, fashionable and comfortable, with 300 rooms, roof-top pool and gym, Provençal restaurant and coffee shop.

LL-A *Kim Do*, 133 Nguyen Hue Blvd, T8225914, F8225913, kimdohotel@fmail.vnn.vn Renovated backpacker hotel masquerading as a business hotel, absurd prices, centrality is its only redeeming feature. **LL-A** *Norfolk Hotel*, 117 Le Thanh Ton St, T8295368, F8293415, norfolk@bdvn.vnd.net A/c, satellite TV, in a bustling area near Ben Thanh market, business facilities, restaurant and excellent staff, popular with visiting and expat businessmen, especially Australians. **LL-A** *Rex*, 141 Nguyen Hue Blvd, T8292185, F8296536, rexhotel@hcm.vnn.vn A/c, satellite TV, restaurants, small pool, quite decent sized rooms with famous roof-top terrace bar, popular with journalists and upmarket tour groups.

L *Oscar*, 68A Nguyen Hue Blvd, T8231818, F8292732, rsvn.oscar@bdvn.vnd.net Friendly staff, excellent buffet lunch, coffee shop, business centre, small health club, hairdresser, central location but somewhat cramped and quite expensive rooms. **L-A** *Bong Sen*, 117-123 Dong Khoi St, T8291516, F8298076, bongsen1@hcm.vnn.vn Upgraded hotel with decent business facilities. A *Saigon-tourist* property, but considered to be well run, restaurant, price includes breakfast, central. **L-A** *Continental*,

Saigon centre detail

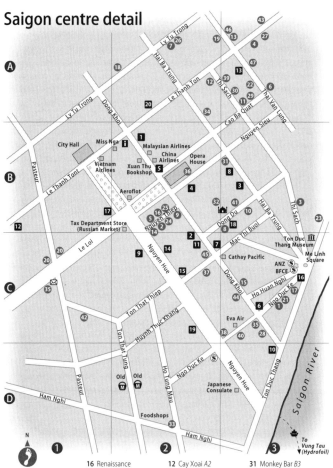

0 metres 100
0 yards 100

N

■ Sleeping
1 Asian *B2*
2 Bong Sen *C2*
3 Bong Sen 2 *B3*
4 Caravelle *B2*
5 Continental *B2*
6 Grand *C3*
7 Huong Sen *C2*
8 Khach San 69 *B3*
9 Kim Do *C2*
10 Majestic *D3*
11 Mondial *C2*
12 Norfolk *B1*
13 Orchid *A3*
14 Oscar *C2*
15 Palace *C2*
16 Renaissance
Riverside *C3*
17 Rex *B1*
18 Saigon *B3*
19 Saigon Prince *C2*
20 Spring *A2*

● Eating
1 13 Ngo Duc Ke *C3*
2 Angkor Encore *B2*
3 Apocalypse
Now Bar *B3*
4 Ashoka *A3*
5 Augustin *B2*
6 Bi Bi *A3*
7 Blue Gecko *A2*
8 Bombay *B3*
9 Brodard *B2*
10 Café Latin *B3*
11 Camargue *A3*
12 Cay Xoai *A2*
13 Chao Thai *A3*
14 Ciao Café *B2*
15 Gartenstadt *C3*
16 Globo Café *B2*
17 Hoang Yen *C3*
18 Huong Lai *A2*
19 Idecaf *A2*
20 Kem Bach Dang &
Ice Cream *C1*
21 La Fourchette *C3*
22 La Villa *A3*
23 Le Caprice *B3*
24 Le Cochon d'or Deli *B2*
25 Lemon Grass *B2*
26 Luong Son *A2*
27 Marine Club *A3*
28 Maxim's *C3*
29 Maya Bar *A3*
30 Mogambo *A3*
31 Monkey Bar *B3*
32 Mosque *B2*
33 Nhu Lan Bakery *D2*
34 O'Brien's Factory *A2*
35 Paris Deli *C1, C3*
36 Q Bar *B2*
37 Saigon Indian *C2*
38 Santa Lucia *C3*
39 Sawaddee *A3*
40 Seoul *C3*
41 Tan Nam *B3*
42 Temple Club *C1*
43 Tex-Mex *A3*
44 Underground *C3*
45 Vietnam House *C2*
46 Why Not? *A3*
47 Wild Horse Saloon *A3*

Related maps
Saigon, page 276
Saigon Centre,
page 279

Saigon

132-134, Dong Khoi St, T8299201, F8290936, continental@hcm.vnn.vn A/c, built in 1880 and an integral part of the city's history, Graham Greene stayed here and the hotel features in the book version of *The Quiet American* but not the film version (shot in 2001) which, slightly surprisingly, replicated the *Continental* in the facing *Caravelle Hotel*. Old journalists' haunt – *Continental Shelf* was "a famous verandah where correspondents, spies, speculators, traffickers, intellectuals and soldiers used to meet during the war to glean information and pick up secret reports, half false, half true or half disclosed. All of this is more than enough for it to be known as Radio Catinat". A delightful enclosed garden ("I sometimes went there for a late evening drink among the frangipani and hibiscus blossom ... It was the reverse of the frenzy of the war, and a good place to think," wrote war journalist Jon Swain), faded colonial splendour and large rooms – just ripe for the Raffles Group to renovate and run. **L-A** *Majestic*, 1 Dong Khoi St, T8295517, 8228750, F8295510, hotelmajestic@hcm.vnn.vn Built in 1925, the hotel has character and charm and has been tastefully restored. A/c, satellite TV, price includes breakfast; restaurant, small but nicely shaded pool, more expensive and large rooms have superb views over the river (pool view and quieter at the back), from the bar on the top floor there are magnificent views of the river-front, especially at night. **L-B** *Asian*, 146-150 Dong Khoi St, T8296979, F8297433, asianhotel@hcm.fpt.vn A/c, satellite TV, restaurant, breakfast included, central, rooms a little small, eclipsed by newer business hotels. **L-B** *Grand*, 8 Dong Khoi St, T8230163, F8235781, grand-hotel@fmail.vnn.vn A/c, satellite TV. Newly emerged from extensive renovation, happily the stained glass and marble staircase have largely survived the process. Lovely pool and a very reasonably priced restaurant.

A *Orchid*, 29A Thai Van Lung St, T8231809, F8292245. A/c, satellite TV, central, surrounded by restaurants and bars, now under renovation. **A-B** *Huong Sen*, 66-70 Dong Khoi St, T8291415, F8290916, huongsen@hcm.vnn.vn A/c, popular with tour groups. **A-B** *Palace*, 56-64 Nguyen Hue Blvd, T8292860, F8244230, palace@hcm.vnn.vn Government-run hotel with some decent-sized rooms. Central, restaurant, small roof-top pool, dancing, price includes breakfast. **A-B** *Spring*, 44-46 Le Thanh Ton St, T8297362, F8221383, springhotel@hcm.vnn.vn Central, comfortable, charming and helpful staff, book well in advance if you want to stay in this well-run family hotel, excellent value, breakfast included. Recommended.

B *Bong Sen 2*, 61-63 Hai Ba Trung St, T8235818, F8235816, bongsen2@hcm.vnn.vn A/c, restaurant, well managed, price includes breakfast. **B** *Embassy*, 35 Nguyen Trung Truc St, T8231981, F8231978, embassyh@hcmc.netnam.vn Rather unappealing lobby area but quite comfortable rooms, newly found favour with tour groups, moderately efficient. **B** *Mondial*, 109 Dong Khoi St, T8296291, F8296273, mondial.htl@bdvn.vnd.net.vnd.net A/c, roof restaurant, well managed, price includes breakfast, good value for downtown. **B-C** *Saigon*, 45-47 Dong Du St, T8299734, F8291466, saigonhotel@hcm.vnn.vn Some a/c, central, some rooms a bit dark and small, but popular, clean and good value.

C *Mogambo*, 20Bis Thi Sach St, T8251311, F8226031, mogambo@saigonnet.vn A/c, satellite TV, a few good rooms above this popular American run bar-diner. **C-D** *Khach San 69*, 69 Hai Ba Trung St, T8291513, F8258903, 69hotel@saigonnet.vn Some a/c, backs on to Saigon's Indian mosque, clean rooms, reasonably priced.

Edge of central Saigon These hotels are a little out of the centre – around 10-30 mins walk or a short taxi ride.

LL-L *Omni Saigon*, 251 Nguyen Van Troi St, Q Phu Nhuan, T8449222, F8449200, omnibus@hcm.vnn.vn A/c, satellite TV, pool, health club, presidential suite, restaurants, the popular *Mulligan's Bar*, full business facilities, a highly rated hair-dresser, dry-cleaning service, but inconvenient for town: a courtesy shuttle connects with town centre. **LL-A** *Equatorial*, 242 Tran Binh Trong St, Q5, T8390000, F8390011, eghcmc@hcm.vnn.vn A/c, satellite TV, a marble-cool oasis of calm with charming staff; large and lovely pool, well-equipped gym; Japanese, Chinese and Western restaurants, a bakery and the largest ball-room in Vietnam. Rather an out-of-the-way location. **LL-A** *New World*, 76 Le Lai St, T8228888, F8230710, nwhs@hcm.vnn.vn Over the years this has proved the most popular hotel with visiting businessmen. Efficient, friendly staff, large attractive pool and gym, business facilities, Chinese and Western restaurants, patisserie and bakery, dry cleaning service and nightclub.

A *Sol Chancery Saigon*, 196 Nguyen Thi Minh Khai St, Q3, T9304088, F9303988, chancery@hcm.vnn.vn Overlooks *Lao Dong Sports Club*, all the rooms are suites, comfortable, good service, popular. **A** *Windsor Saigon*, 193 Tran Hung Dao St, T8367848, F8367889, windsor.hotel@hcm.fpt.vn High-quality suites and studios, gym, restaurant, business facilities and the *Gourmet Royale*, a first-class delicatessen selling bread, pies, cheese, ham, sausages and sandwiches. Also a popular Szechuan restaurant. **A-B** *Saigon Star*, 204 Nguyen Thi Minh Khai St, Q3, T9306290, F9306300, saigonstarhotel@hcm.vnn.vn A/c, satellite TV, business centre and secretarial facilities, a friendly, well-run hotel.

B *International*, 19 Vo Van Tan St, Q3, T9304009, F9304566, international-ht@hcm.vnn.vn A/c, satellite TV, comfortable and elegant, Chinese seafood restaurant and noodle shop, business centre, breakfast included. **B** *Que Huong (Liberty 1)*, 167 Hai Ba Trung St, Q3, T8294227, F8290919, qhuong1@libertyhotel.vnn.vn Popular restaurant, decent enough rooms but a little pricey for what it offers.

D *Khach San Ga Saigon* (*Station Hotel*), 1 Nguyen Thong St, T8436189. Overlooks the railway station, noisy area, rather run down, not much English spoken. **D-F** *Miss Loi's Guesthouse*, 178/20 Co Giang St, T8367973, missloi@hcm.fpt.vn Cheap and cheerful, well kept, some a/c, breakfast included, popular. Recommended.

Most backpackers head straight for this bustling district, a 10-15 min walk from downtown. There are countless hotels, guesthouses and rooms to rent which open and close and change name or owner with remarkable speed. Shared rooms can be had for as little as US$4-5 per night and dormitory rooms for less but facilities and comfort levels at the bottom end are very basic. The area is littered with restaurants, cafés, email services, tour agencies and money changers, all fiercely competitive; there are mini-supermarkets and shops selling rucksacks, footwear, CDs and ethnic knick-knacks. The concentration of services means the area is popular with younger expats as well as with tourists.

Pham Ngu Lao
■ *on map, page 296*

L-A *Que Huong* (*Liberty 4*), 265 Pham Ngu Lao St, T8365822, F8365435, quehuong4@quehuonghotel.com.vn Formerly *Hoang Vu*, well renovated but priced way too high for this area.

A-B *Vien Dong*, 275A Pham Ngu Lao St, T8368941, F8368812, viendonghotel@hcm.fpt.vn Refurbished, marble-clad lobby which in no way justifies these room rates.

B-D *Le Le 1*, 171 Pham Ngu Lao St, T8368686, F8368787, lelehotel@hcm.fpt.vn Small rooms and rather pricey.

Saigon

C *Dai Hoang Long* (*Giant Dragon*), 173 Pham Ngu Lao St, T8369268, F8367279, gdhotel@hcm.vnn.vn With a small ground-floor area but soaring many stories into the air this type of building is sometimes known as a rocket building, we shall no doubt know in a few years whether they skimped on the cement. **C** *Que Huong* (*Liberty 3*), 187 Pham Ngu Lao St, T8369522, F8364557, qhuong3@libertyhotel.vnn.vn Less popular with travellers than previously as there is now more choice; cheapest on the upper floors, rather noisy. **C-D** *Hong Hoa*, 185/28 Pham Ngu Lao St, T836 1915, hotel@honghoavn.com A well-run family hotel with 7 rooms, all a/c, hot water and private bathroom, 3 rooms have bathtubs. Conveniently, the downstairs has banks of email terminals and a supermarket. **C-D** *Ngoc Dang*, 254 De Tham St. Clean friendly and pleasant, some a/c rooms.

D *Huong*, 40/19 Bui Vien St, T8369158. A/c and hot water, private bathrooms. **D** *Le Le 2*, 269 De Tham St, T8368585, F8368787. Rooms with fans and some a/c. **D** *Linh*, 40/10 Bui Vien St, T/F8369641, linh.hb@hcm.vnn.vn A well-priced, clean, friendly, family-run hotel with a/c and hot water. Attracts some longer-staying guests. **D** *Linh Thu Guesthouse*, 72 Bui Vien St, T8368421, linhthu72@saigonnet.vn Fan rooms with bathroom, some a/c. **D** *Mimi Guesthouse*, 40/5 Bui Vien St, T8369645, tuanviet@hcm.vnn.vn 6 rooms with private bathroom, a/c and hot water. **D** *Phuong Lan Guesthouse*, 70 Bui Vien St, T/F8369569, phanlan@hcm.vnn.vn Fan rooms, 2 shared bathrooms for 7 guest rooms, some a/c. **D** *Yen Nhi*, 283/24 Pham Ngu Lao St, T/F8367232. Hot water, bath tubs, a/c, friendly, clean, English-speaking hotel. **D** *211*, 211 Pham Ngu Lao St, T8367353, F8361883. Some a/c, clean, roof-top terrace.

D-E *Minh Chau*, 75 Bui Vien St, T8367588. Price includes breakfast, some a/c, hot water and private bathrooms, spotlessly clean, run by two sisters it has been recommended by lone women travellers. **D-E** *Tan Thanh Thanh*, 205 Pham Ngu Lao St, T8367027, F8371238. A/c and fan rooms, some dorm accommodation, roof-top bar and 'grill', best stick to the beer and enjoy the breeze. **D-E** *Thanh Huyen*, 175/1 Pham Ngu Lao St, T8370760, 3 rooms (1 a/c, 2 fan) above a small eatery, clean and, being off the main drag, quiet.

E *Thai Binh*, 325 Pham Ngu Lao St, T8369544. Basic old building, fan rooms only, cold water.

Pham Ngu Lao

Not to scale

Related maps
Saigon, page 276
Saigon Centre,
page 279

■ **Sleeping**
1 211
2 Dai Hoang Long
3 Hong Hoa
4 Huong
5 Le Le 1
6 Le Le 2
7 Linh
8 Linh Thu
   Guesthouse
9 Lucy
10 Mimi Guesthouse
11 Minh Chau
12 Ngoc Dang
13 Que Huong
   (Liberty 3)
14 Que Huong
   (Liberty 4)
15 Tan Thanh Thanh
16 Thai Binh
17 Thanh Huyen
   & Margherita
   Restaurant
18 Vien Dong
19 Yen Nhi

● **Eating**
1 Café Van
2 Cappuccino
3 Cay Bo De
4 Kim Café
5 Long Phi Bar
   & Chez Papa
6 Lost in Saigon Bar
7 Lucky
8 Saigon Café
9 Sinh Café
10 Zen

Those intending to stay a month or more might consider the furnished apartments of **Apartments**
Lucy Hotel, 61 Do Quang Dau St, T8360712, F8367281. US$250-300 per month, often full.

Few people stay in Cholon, but it does have the best pagodas in Saigon and is only a **Cholon**
short *cyclo* ride from the centre of town. **B** *Arc en Ciel* (*Thien Hong*), 52-56 Tan Da St, Q5,
T8552869, F8552424, thienhong@hcm.vnn.vn A/c, restaurant, best in Cholon with
roof-top bar, price includes breakfast.

These hotels are located several kilometres northwest of the city centre. Prices tend to **Near airport**
be marginally more competitive as a result.

L-A *Garden Plaza*, 309 Nguyen Van Troi St, Q Tan Binh, T8421111, F8424370,
gphotel2@saigonnet.vn Comfortable, well-run, business-oriented hotel just a stone's
throw from the airport. Popular bar and excellent buffet lunch. **L-A** *Saigon Lodge*, 215
Nam Ky Khoi Nghia St, Q3, T9326112, F9325070. Geared to the needs of Malay businessmen, halal food, Karaoke etc. Closed for renovation in 2002. **A-B** *De Nhat* (formerly
Chains First Hotel), 18 Hoang Viet St, Q Tan Binh, T8441199, F8444282,
first.hotel@hcm.vnn.vn A/c, new and pricey, downtown shuttle, tennis court, pool,
disco, karaoke and business services. **B** *Orient*, 261 Hoang Van Thu St, Q Tan Binh,
T8441322, F8444809, phuongdong@hcm.vnn.vn Functional and fairly priced, perfectly good for a night, breakfast included. **B-C** *Airport*, 108 Hong Ha St, Q Tan Binh,
T8445761, F8440166. Closest to the airport and reasonable value. Just 100 m east, a
café sits beneath the wings of a grounded Boeing 707. Closed for renovation in 2002.

Eating

Saigon has a rich culinary tradition. You could quite easily eat a different national cuisine every night for several weeks. There is everything from the starchy
expense-account restaurant to wayside cafés. Pham Ngu Lao, the backpacker area, is
chock-a-block with low-cost restaurants many of which are just as good as the more
expensive places elsewhere. Do not overlook street-side stalls whose staples consist of
pho (noodle soup), *bánh xeo* (savoury pancakes), *cha giò* (spring rolls) and *banh mi pate*
(baguettes stuffed with pâté and salad, all usually fresh and very cheap); *binh dân* (popular) street restaurants where food is set out on a counter – simply point to what you
want – are frequented by shop and office workers at lunch time and provide excellent
value and usually good food.

● *on maps,
pages 276, 279
and 293*

Expensive *Hoi An*, 11 Le Thanh Ton St, T8237694. This is a sister restaurant of *Manda-* **Vietnamese**
rin (see below) and meets the same exacting standards imposed by manager Frank.
The building is a good replica of a Hoi An house, a theme that is repeated in the décor
and staff uniforms. Service and food are good. *Mandarin*, 11A Ngo Van Nam St,
T8229783. One of the finest Vietnamese restaurants in Saigon. Elegant decor, exquisite
service and delicious food. Two people can have a truly enjoyable evening out here for
around US$40.

Mid-range *Binh An*, 1163 Xo Viet Nghe Tinh St, Q Binh Thanh, T8990090. Beautiful
setting by the river, immaculately kept gardens dotted with pavilions in which you can
sit and drink or dine. It is this you pay for as the food and service are not, alas, particularly memorable. Quite a long way from the centre but a lovely place to spend a Sunday
lunchtime and afternoon. *Blue Ginger* (*Saigon Times Club*), 37 Nam Ky Khoi Nghia St,
T8298676. Delicious food, courteous and discrete service, dine indoors or in a small
courtyard, menu includes *cha ca Hanoi* (see below). *Cha Ca Hanoi*, 5A Tran Nhat Duat,
T8484240. A little way out of town, beyond Tan Dinh Market, now in a new modern

and characterless building but still serving same excellent *cha ca Hanoi*. Small cubes of boneless, white fish fried in a mildly spicy sauce at the table on a charcoal burner, flavoured with dill and spring onions and eaten with rice noodles, green leaves and peanuts, a glorious fusion of flavours, around US$6 for two, but unpriced menu and an unattractive tendency to rook foreigners on the drinks. *Com Nieu Saigon*, 6C Tu Xuong St, Q3, T8203188. Well known for the theatricals which accompany the serving of the speciality baked rice. One waiter smashes the earthenware pot before tossing the contents across the room to his nimble fingered colleague standing by your table. Deserves attention for its excellent food and a good selection of soups. Four can eat well for US$12. *Givral*, 169 Dong Khoi. Café/patisserie offering convenient snacks and drinks in the city centre.

Hoang Yen, 5-9 Ngo Duc Ke St. Utterly plain setting and décor but absolutely fabulous Vietnamese dishes, as the throngs of local lunchtime customers testify, soups and chicken dishes are ravishing, you cannot go wrong at US$3-4 per head. *Indochine*, 32 Pham Ngoc Thach St, T8239256. Sister of the equally popular *Indochine* in Hanoi; staff attired in Vietnamese costume, the menu is long and covers just about all Vietnamese specialities. *Lemon Grass*, 4 Nguyen Thiep St, T8220496. Good food attractively served, set-lunch menu is good value, popular with tourists wishing to sample typical Vietnamese food, convenient location in the heart of town. *Ngu Binh*, 82 Cu Xa Nguyen Van Troi St, Q Phu Nhuan, T8447230. Specializes in Hué dishes, simple and stylish setting, turn right into a small alley just north of Nguyen Van Troi bridge on the airport road. Open 1500-2000 only. *Quan An Hué*, 7/1 Ky Dong, Q3, T9317934. Evenings only. Hué specialities. Work your way down the list sampling the many delicate dishes. Each dish is cheap but multiplied by the number of diners the cost rises more quickly than you might expect.

Tan Nam, 60-62 Dong Du St, T8298634. Another popular and central restaurant serving national dishes from an extensive menu. *Temple Club*, 29 Ton That Thiep St, T8299244. This is a most beautifully furnished club and restaurant open to non-members. The style is colonial Vietnamese and the effect is striking. Tasty Vietnamese dishes cost around US$3-4 each, excellent value. *Thanh Nien*, 11 Nguyen Van Chiem St. Popular with young Vietnamese, indoor and outdoor seating, excellent Vietnamese cooking, live music, attached is *Kem Y* (Italian ice cream café). *Thong Truc* (aka *Mongolian Barbecue*), 162B Dien Bien Phu St, Q3, T8200554. Eat what you want for around US$4, the engaging staff play the guitar and sing while you eat, fun for groups. *Tib*, 187 Hai Ba Trung St, Q3, T8297242. Quiet, good service, extensive menu, which includes a good selection of Hué specialities, nice for Sun lunch, which for two costs around US$10. *Vietnam House*, 93-95 Dong Khoi St, T8291623. Attractively restored building, waiters and waitresses wear traditional Vietnamese costume and traditional music is played on an array of exotic instruments, excellent food. *VY*, 164 Pasteur St, T8296210. Indoor and open-air sections, attractive ambience and first-class Vietnamese food. *13 Ngo Duc Ke*. Fresh, well cooked, honest Vietnamese fare, chicken in lemon grass (no skin, no bone) is a great favourite and the beef (*bo luc lac*) melts in the mouth. Open 0600-2300, popular with locals, expats and travellers alike, (a/c and one of the few places in Saigon without music).

Cheap *Giac Duc*, 492 Nguyen Dinh Chieu St, Q3. Vietnamese vegetarian restaurant. *Huong Lai*, 38 Ly Tu Trong St, T8226814. An interesting little place up the stairs, operated rather successfully by former street children. Decent food and service. *Kem Bach Dang*, 26-28 Le Loi St, on opposite corners with Pasteur St. A very popular café serving fruit juice, shakes and ice cream. Try the coconut ice cream (*kem dua*) served in a coconut. *Luong Son* (aka *Bo Tuong Xeo*), 31 Ly Tu Trong St. Noisy, smoky and chaotic, usually packed, specializes in *bo tung xeo* (sliced beef barbecued at the table served with mustard sauce – the name also refers to a gruesome torture, ask

Vietnamese friends for details). The beef, barbecued squid and other delicacies are truly superb, two people can eat and drink well for under US$8. This restaurant is also the place to sample unusual dishes such as scorpion, porcupine and cockerel's testicles. Recommended. *May Bon Phuong*, 335/5 Dien Bien Phu St, Q3. Tucked away between Dien Bien Phu St and Nguyen Dinh Chieu St, outstanding fish salad, popular with Vietnamese, a little rough-and-ready but good value. *Nam Son*, 200 bis Nguyen Thi Minh Khai St. Serves sizzling steak and chips and nothing else. Excellent and cheap. *Pacific*, 15A Le Thanh Ton St. A *bia hoi*, which is packed with locals every night. On account of its centrality it is also popular with foreigners. A decent range of simple, cheap dishes washed down with fresh beer. *Pho Hoa Pasteur*, 260C Pasteur St. Probably the best known of all *pho* restaurants, costs more than average but it serves good *pho* and is usually packed. *Pho Hung*, 46 Mac Dinh Chi St. Another highly recommended *pho* outlet.

Seafood

In **Thi Sach St** numerous restaurants specializing in seafood spill out on to the pavement – although the government ban on pavement eating has obliged many to close. One restaurant owner enthused 'customers are impressed because they see these fresh animals which minutes ago were swimming in water'. For some reason most of the restaurants are named after trees; in particular look out for *Mango* or *Cay Xoai*. *Minh Thanh*, 2 Ham Tu St, just west of the junction with Nguyen Van Cu St, Q5. Half way to Cholon this is not an easy restaurant to find. Very rough and ready, plastic chairs and stools but reckoned by some to have the most succulent crab and prawn.

Other Asian

Saigon, it is said, has the cheapest Japanese food in the world. We can certainly testify to the excellence of Saigon's Japanese restaurants – long may the Japanese salaryman live away from home. The city's Chinese population is concentrated in Cholon and a cruise through District 5 will reveal a number of good Chinese eating houses.

Expensive *Chao Thai*, 16 Thai Van Lung St, T8241457. Regarded as the best Thai restaurant in town. Attractive Thai setting and attentive service. An excellent dinner for two for under US$30. *Dynasty* (*New World Hotel*), 76 Le Lai St, T8228888. A long Chinese menu, excellent lunchtime dim sun. *Ohan*, 71-73 Pasteur St, T8244896. Japanese, decent-sized portions, welcoming atmosphere, popular with Japanese. A huge lunch will set you back US$40 for two. *Ritz Taiwanese*, 333 Tran Hung Dao St, T8324325. Superb Chinese food with, as the name suggests, specialities from its off-shore republic, but jolly expensive, not hard for four to notch up a bill for US$100. *Sawaddee*, 29B Thi Sac St, T8221402. Good Thai food at a fair price. *Seoul*, 37 Ngo Duc Ke St, T8294297. Good Korean food, extensive menu, popular with Saigon's Korean business fraternity.

Mid-range *ABC*, 172 Nguyen Dinh Chieu St, Q3,. Nightime refuge for those in need of solid Chinese fare (excellent fried noodles for around US$4 a plate). Stays open until 0300 and serves as a clearing house for girls not yet fixed up with a partner for the night. *Angkor Encore*, 5 Nguyen Thiep St, T8226278. Deservedly popular restaurant run by a local photographer serving, as its name suggests, Cambodian specialities. *Ashoka*, 17A/10 Le Thanh Ton St, T8231372. Delicious food and attractive atmosphere. Quite expensive and fair quality. *Saigon Indian*, 73 Mac Thi Buoi St, T8245671. Proving to be Saigon's most popular Indian restaurant it has a wide range of dishes from north and south with plenty of vegetarian options. Main courses around US$3 per dish. *Tandoor*, 103 Vo Van Tan St, T9304839. A popular Northern Indian restaurant. Delivery service.

Cheap *Bombay*, 49 Dong Du St, T8298354. Almost opposite the mosque; a long-established restaurant whose Halal status munificently stretches to alcohol. Quite outstanding curry sauces and *parathas* at US$1-2 per dish. *Mosque*, 66 Dong Du St, opposite *Saigon Hotel*. Walk around to the back of the mosque (infidels, women and shoes permitted), superb vegetarian and meat curries and stuffed bread, lunch only, especially popular on Fri, get there by 1200.

International   **Expensive** *Bi Bi*, 8A/8D Thai Van Lung St, T8295783. Ideal for long lunches over which affairs of the world can be discussed, which is presumably why it is so popular with diplomats and bankers. Informal atmosphere and excellent French food. *Camargue*, 16 Cao Ba Quat St, T8243148, corner of Thi Sach St. Unsigned, large French villa, lovely open-air terrace, *chic*, consistently excellent food, several bars and pool tables, dinner for two with wine won't come to much less than US$60. *Le Bordeaux*, F7-F8 D2 St, Cu Xa Van Thanh Bac, Q Binh Thanh, T8999831. If you can find it you are in for a treat. Lovely décor and warm atmosphere, receives the highest accolades for its French cuisine, expect to pay at least US$60 for two if drinking wine. *Le Caprice*, 15th Floor, Landmark Building, 5B Ton Duc Thang St, T8228337. Lovely views over the river, very expensive and thought to be a little starchy, generates more complaints than compliments. The rooftop bar is, however, well worth a visit. *Maxim's*, 13-17 Dong Khoi St, T8225554. Massive menu; the food receives mixed reviews but the floorshows are widely acclaimed. *Port Orient*, *Caravelle Hotel*, Lam Son Square, T8234999. Buffet lunch and dinner. Japanese sushi, Chinese dim sun, seafood, a range of hot dishes, cheeses and puddings galore. Weekends are especially extravagant with excellent roast beef. The free-flow of wine makes it an epicurean delight.

Mid-range *Annie's Pizzas*, 45 Mac Thi Buoi St, T8392577. Great pizzas, eat in, take away or home delivery. *Augustin*, 10 Nguyen Thiep St (between Dong Khoi St and Nguyen Hue Blvd), T8292941. Fairly priced and some of the best, unstuffy French cooking in Saigon; tables pretty closely packed, congenial atmosphere. Excellent baked clams and rack of lamb. *Brodard*, 131 Dong Khoi St, T8223966. Decades old international restaurant run in the old style. Good meals at a decent price. Bang in the centre. *Café Latin*, 25 Dong Du St, T8226363. French restaurant above, attracts the young expat trendies. *Ciao Café*, 72 Nguyen Hue Blvd, T8251203. Corner with Nguyen Thiep St, ice creams, pasta, fruit juice, coffee, popular rendezvous spot. *Gartenstadt*, 34 Dong Khoi St, T8223623. Plates of wurst and sauerkraut and draught German beer. Sadly this previously outstanding German restaurant has lost its way with the menu spoiled by an invasion of non-German dishes and quite absurd price increases. A real loss. *Globo Café*, 6 Nguyen Thiep St, T8228855. Emphasis on design: the cocktails and glittering clientele are more impressive than the food. *La Fourchette*, 9 Ngo Duc Ke St, T8298143. A truly excellent and authentic little French bistrot. Warm welcome, well-prepared dishes, generous portions, local steak as tender as any import, reasonably priced (an extravagant dinner for two need cost no more than US$20 excluding wine), booking advised. Recommended. *La Villa*, 11 Thai Van Lung St, T8223240. Minimalist décor works well in this good French restaurant. Waitresses are becoming in their *ao dais* while poor male colleagues are rather less fetching in uniforms that look like Bulgarian state railways. Nevertheless, the food is excellent and homely including exquisite *coq au vin*. Round off the meal with Irish Coffee – as much for the theatricals as the perfectly smooth flavour. *Marine Club*, 17A4 Le Thanh Ton St, T8292249. Menu is mostly French and good atmosphere, sizzling cocktails and good food (especially the pizzas), popular with racy young ex-pats. Once a month has live jazz. *Maya*, 6 Cao Ba Quat St, T8295180. Latin American restaurant serving generous helpings of delicious food; bar is very popular and frequently hosts special themed parties. *Mogambo*, 20 bis Thi Sach St, T8251311. Bar and restaurant, serves up excellent burgers, steaks, pies and fries but not the tarts that are such a popular feature of Mogambo's in Manila. *Rex Hotel*, 141 Nguyen Hue Blvd, T8292185. 5th floor restaurant and terrace bar, Western and Vietnamese food is quite good, service notoriously slow, drink prices high.

Santa Lucia, 14 Nguyen Hue Blvd, T8226562. Pleasing Italian décor and style, excellent food and service. *Tex-Mex*, 24 Le Thanh Ton St, T8295950. American and Mexican specialities, a friendly and well-run bar with pool tables, a great place to watch rugby, football or other international sporting highlights. *Thien Nam*, 53 Nam Ky Khoi Nghia St, T8223634. Was popular with US servicemen in the 1960's, but its original décor is now largely painted over or ripped out. Extensive Chinese and Western menus; worth visiting every now and again just to remind yourself how incredibly rude the Chinese waiters are and for the excellent cauliflower cheese. *Underground*, 69 Dong Khoi St, T8299079. Instantly recognisable by its London Underground symbol, this bar in its stygian gloom is an unlikely place to find Saigon's best food. The menu spans the full Mediterranean-Mexican spectrum and is superb. Portions are gigantic. Prices are very reasonable, around US$5 for a delicious pizza. It is, quite simply, a crime not to eat here. Lunchtime specials are excellent value. It *Underground* is one of the main venues for viewing live sporting events, particularly rugby. *Why Not?*, 24 Thai Van Lung St, T8226138. French bistro-type restaurant but with the departure of former owner, Thu Anh, it has lost its charm and the quality of cooking. *Wild Horse Saloon*, 8A1/2D1 Thai Van Lung St, T8251901. With its rustic exterior this bar-cum-diner would look more at home in Wyoming than in a Saigon street. Friendly and attentive service from Vietnamese cowgirls and squaws, a long menu, often with special promotions. Excellent roasts for Sun lunch.

Cheap *Chez Guido*, T8983747. An excellent delivery service with an amazingly long and varied menu, quick, efficient and very good value for money, perfect for a soaking wet monsoon night. *Hoa Vien*, 28 bis Mac Dinh Chi St, T8290585. An amazing and vast Czech bierkeller boasting Saigon's first microbrewery. Freshly brewed dark and light beer available by the litre or in smaller measures. Its food has recently improved dramatically. Grilled mackerel, pork, sausages: all are very useful for soaking up the alcohol. The building is also home to the Consulate General of the Czech Republic. *Idecaf*, 31 Thai Van Lung St, T8258465. Excellent little French café, part of the *French Cultural Institute*, eat in or out, good food, fairly priced, check out the French films being screened.

Cheap *Café Van*, 169B De Tham St, T8360636. A good little sandwich bar which also does free deliveries, try BLT or chicken curry baguette, also baked potatoes with chilli-con-carné and other tempting fillings. *Cappuccino*, 258 De Tham St, T8371467. Excellent range of well-prepared Italian food at sensible prices, US$2 for a good pizza, same for pasta dishes, they also do very good zabaglione. *Cay Bo De* (*Bodhi Tree*), 175/6 Pham Ngu Lao St. Saigon's most popular vegetarian eatery in the heart of backpacker land, excellent food and amazing prices. Mexican pancake, vegetable curry, rice in coconut and braised mushrooms are classics. It is a struggle to spend US$2 per head. Recommended. *Chez Papa*, 163 Pham Ngu Lao St, T8369319. Small and quiet French restaurant above the busy *Long Phi Bar*, limited menu but good food at fair prices, US$15 for two excluding wine. *Kim Café*, 268 De Tham St, T8368122. Wide range of food, open from early till late, popular with travellers and expats. At US$2 – with baked beans, fried eggs, pork chop and chips – Peter's breakfast must rate as one of the best value breakfasts in the country. *Lucky*, 224 De Tham St. Italian food (Japanese upstairs), bar and good breakfasts. *Margherita*, 175/1, Pham Ngu Lao St, is opposite *Bodhi Tree* and serves good Italian fare at fair prices. *Sinh Café*, 246-248 De Tham St, T8369420. Good value food and drink all day. *Zen*, 175/18 Pham Ngu Lao St, another popular vegetarian restaurant.

Pham Ngu Lao area

Anh Thu, 49 Dinh Cong Trang St, and numerous other stalls nearby on the south side of Tan Dinh market serve excellent *cha gio*, *banh xeo*, *bi cuon* and other Vietnamese street food. *Nguyen Trai St* (extreme east end of, by the *New World Hotel* roundabout) late

Foodstalls

night *pho* can be had from the stalls in this area. **Tran Cao Van St**, east of Cong Truong Quoc Te, Q3, the restaurants and stalls here serve delicious noodles of all kinds, especially noodle soup with duck (*my vit*). **362-376**, Hai Ba Trung St, just north of Tan Dinh market. Everyone has their favourite but these restaurants serve excellent chicken rice (*com ga*), 381, **Hong Phat** is particularly good. All charge just over US$2 for steamed chicken and rice (*com gà hap*) with soup. **Thinh Phat**, 177 Vo Van Tan St, Q3, also does good chicken rice.

Bakeries   The major hotels all have gourmet shops selling bread and pastries: *Equatorial*, *Omni*, *New World, Sofitel Plaza* and *Windsor* are all good.

   Brodard, 11 Nguyen Thiep St. Its cakes are a little too sweet and gooey for European tastes, as are those at **Givral**, 169 Dong Khoi St, although they look superb. **Nhu Lan**, 66-68 Ham Nghi St. If there are more delicious baguettes than these we would like to know where. Churns out freshly baked bread until 2200. **Paris Deli**, 31 Dong Khoi St, T8297533 and Saigon Centre, 65 Le Loi St, T8216127. Bread, sandwiches and patisserie, eat in café or have delivered. **Saigon Bakery**, 281c Hai Ba Trung St, Q3 (just north of Vo Thi Sau St). Delicious selection of doughnuts, tarts, bread rolls, mini quiches and other tempting savouries. **Sama**, 35 Dong Khoi St. Well known for its sandwiches.

Bars

Along with the influx of foreigners and the freeing up of Vietnamese society has come a rapid increase in the number of bars in Saigon and they cater to just about all tastes – drink, music and company-wise. At one time hotel bars were just about the only safe and legal place for foreigners to drink but now they are beginning to look much the same as hotel bars the world over. The roof-top bar at the *Rex Hotel* is an exception, it has strange fish tanks, song birds, topiary, good views, cooling breeze, snacks and meals – and a link with history. **Mulligan's**, at the *Omni Hotel*, Nguyen Van Troi St, with its 1960s theme and girls around the pool table generates a happy mood.

Countless bars have opened and countless bars have closed since the first edition of this book, but of those remaining two stand out: *Apocalypse Now* and *Q Bar*. **Apocalypse Now**, 2C Thi Sach St. Each night crowds of tourists go in search of a legend. Despite this it remains one of the most abidingly popular bars with the younger expat crowd. The crowded dancefloor gets very sticky. **Bar No 5**, 5 Ly Tu Trong St, T8256300. A nicely converted building. Attracts an interesting selection of expats. With its engaging bar staff and excellent bar food it is well worth a look. Pool table. The most sophisticated of Saigon's bars is **Q Bar**, 7 Lam Son Square, T8291299, under the Opera House. The sophisticated, intelligent, witty, rich, handsome, cute, curvaceous, camp, glittering and famous are all welcome; unwashed *tay ba lo* trying to eke out a bottle of BGI for the evening are not. Striking décor and Caravaggio murals, haunt of a wide cross-section of Saigon society, open till the small hours. Directly opposite is the towering form of the *Caravelle Hotel* which is home to the popular **Saigon Saigon** (10th floor) which is breezy and cool, has large comfortable chairs in which to loll and superb views. Strongly recommended for a glimpse into a more civilized and better past. **Underground**, 69 Dong Khoi St, T8299079. Notable for its food but as the evening wears on, tables are packed away and the space fills with drinkers and dancers. A couple of hundred yards north up Hai Ba Trung St is the admirably run **O'Brien's Pizza Factory** (formerly *Bernie's*), T8293198, which also does excellent food, especially pizzas. Around the corner is **Blue Gecko** at 31 Ly Tu Trong St, T8243483. It has been adopted by Saigon's Australian community so expect cold beer and Australian flags above the pool table.

   The Pham Ngu Lao area has a large number of reasonably priced bars, most have pool tables: **Long Phi**, 163 Pham Ngu Lao St, is one of the best, popular with expats

AIDS in Vietnam

Like the other countries of Southeast Asia, Vietnam is thought to have the potential for 'rapid increase' in the HIV/AIDS epidemic. The first case of AIDS was reported (ie admitted) in 1990. Although 30,000 cases of HIV have so far been reported it is believed that more than 100,000 people, 2,500 of whom are children, are living with HIV or AIDS, which is present in all 61 provinces. The low levels of infection reported in the early 1990s reflected the absence of research and a reluctance to admit that Vietnamese were susceptible to this 'foreign disease', rather than the absence of a problem. UNAIDS reports that while HIV incidence among the adult population is low (0.24%) rates could be as high as 65% among intravenous drug abusers. It appears, however, that the much feared crossover into the normal population is proceeding rapidly. UNICEF attributes the rapid spread of AIDS in Vietnam to the fact that it is officially classified as a 'social evil' and the stigma surrounding the disease means the infected and those at risk deny their infection or even susceptibility.

Another route of transimission is also alarming authorities who say that in Dong Nai Province tattooing is a major cause of the transmission of HIV. In 2000 all 60 cases of new infection had a tattoo. Body art is becoming fashionable with women tattooing their lips to look fresh and rosy and men getting dragons blazoned across their chests.

In the early 1990s the government launched a visible but somewhat ineffective campaign against AIDS. AIDS was always referred to in Vietnam by its French name SIDA which Vietnamese pronounce with a rather sinister hissing sound. But bowing to pressure from the similarly acronymed Swedish International Development Agency, which has been very generous to Vietnam, the government adopted the more international sounding AIDS, a word few Vietnamese can pronounce.

Star of the SIDA campaign, appearing on countless posters, was the durian fruit. With its putrid smell and perilous spikes the analogy between durian and the HIV virus was presumably considered obvious to all and sufficient warning to Vietnamese youth – while still within the strict limits of decency set by the Culture and Information Department. Inevitably, the hapless durian is now dubbed trai SIDA, 'the AIDS fruit'.

The ineffectiveness of the campaign can be gauged from the still commonly held belief that AIDS is spread by white foreign males only. Fortunately the protection offered by condoms (as mua, or 'rain coats') is generally understood although unfortunately ao mua are usually used in pre- and extra-marital relationships only – in which they are prized for their contraceptive effect. A disadvantage the maligned white male labours under is that locally sold 'rain coats' (including those exported from Japan) don't quite measure up to the task. Further complicating the matter, large quantities of good quality second-hand garments are sent from abroad to clothe the poor of Vietnam. Often these find their way into the hands of vendors and are sold on the street. Popular belief was that these were the clothes of Westerners who had died of SIDA, hence the common street sign 'Ao SIDA' advertising a second-hand clothing stall.

Saigon

who prefer Pham Ngu Lao prices. **Lost in Saigon**, 169 Pham Ngu Lao St, previously known as *Backpacker Bar*, has a pool table. **Saigon Café**, on the corner of De Tham St, attracts a good number of regulars, especially bikers, as well as visitors.

A characteristic feature of Vietnamese nightlife is *bia om*, dimly-lit bars with young **Bia ôm** female hostesses to entertain clients: this they do by rehearsing their English, or at least certain well-worn phrases, and general flirtatiousness. The girls expect to be bought drinks and should be tipped. *Bia ôm* bars spring up like mushrooms and survive until the police close them down and arrest the girls; a number are to be found in Hai Ba Trung St, notably **Monkey Bar**, at 97 (formerly *Linda's Pub*), and a clutch of others around 74 Hai Ba Trung St.

Cafés Vietnamese tend to prefer non-alcoholic drinks and huge numbers of cafés exist to cater to this market. Young romantic couples sit in virtual darkness listening to Vietnamese love songs while sipping coffee. The furniture tends to be rather small for the Western frame but these cafés are an agreeable way of relaxing after dinner in a more typically Vietnamese setting. **Thien Ha Café** at 25A Tu Xuong, Q3, which features piano and violin duets is a prime and popular example.

Entertainment

Cinemas There were 44 picture houses in Saigon at last count; Western films are beginning to be
Tickets are 5,000d shown. **Film Archive Club**, 212 Ly Chinh Thang St, District 3, T8468883. Shows a good selection of modern and classic Western movies. French films are screened at the **French Cultural Institute (Idecaf)**, 31 Thai Van Lung, T8295451. **Tan Son Nhat Cinema**, 186 Nguyen Van Troi St, Tan Binh District. Shows English language films from time to time.

Nightclubs When people think of dancing in Saigon they immediately think of *Apocalypse Now*. **Apocalypse Now**, 2C Thi Sach St. Nightclub with dance floor. Free admission. Gets going after 2300 and stays open very late. Unfortunately many clubs have been closed down for drug offences and those that remain have to close early. **Catwalk**, *New World Hotel*. **Planet Europa**, Truong Son St, near the airport. Part of the Superbowl complex. **Spaceship**, 34 Ton Duc Thang St. Built with funny money, believed to be mafia money, it is a gigantic investment with spectacular light shows and sophisticated effects. Unfortunately, like many discos in Vietnam the dance floor is half filled with tables and chairs and the music doesn't count for much. **Vasco**, 16 Cao Ba Quat St, T8243148. In the *Camargue* restaurant, this is a great spot any evening but only gets busy on Fri and Sat evenings after 2200 when a live band plays. It has a small dance floor and generates a lot of energy. Garden to sit in. Very popular with expats..

Shopping

Most visitors head straight for the so-called *Russian Market*, officially known as the **Tax Department Store** on the corner of Le Loi and Nguyen Hue streets. This offers the widest range of shopping under one roof in Saigon: CDs, DVDs (all pirate, of course) and a good selection of footwear and shirts (some pirate, genuine products from the factories manufacturing for export). In addition most other things from lacquer and linen to padlocks and pencils are on sale here.

Antiques Most shops are on Dong Khoi, Mac Thi Buoi and Ngo Duc Ke streets (the latter two both run off Dong Khoi). For the knowledgeable, there are bargains to be found, especially Chinese and Vietnamese ceramics – the difficulty is getting them out of the country (see page 30, Export restrictions). Also available are old watches, colonial bric-à-brac, lacquerware and carvings etc. For the less touristy stuff visitors would be advised to spend an hour or so browsing the shops in Le Cong Trieu St. Le Cong Trieu is not marked on any maps but runs between Nam Ky Khoi Nghia and Pho Duc Chinh streets just south of Ben Thanh Market. Among the bric-à-brac and tat are some interesting items of furniture, statuary and ceramics. Bargaining is the order of the day and some pretty good deals can be struck. **Lac Long**, 143 Le Thanh Ton St. Mr Long sometimes has some unusual items for sale even if there is nothing of interest on display.

Raid

Overwhelmed by the pent-up forces of capitalism, freer since đòi mòi, Saigon's authorities no longer exercise the degree of control over business activities that they once possessed. There are periodic assertions of police authority coupled with a crusading zeal as part of the 'social evils' campaign.

The victims of a police raid usually consist of those least able to protect themselves. Thus in Hai Ba Trung St or Pham Ngu Lao there may be a sudden rush in the street. Word flashes down the street: can sat – 'police'. Street vendors rapidly gather their stock in trade, stack their little plastic chairs, gather empty soup bowls and wheel their cigarette or noodle stall down a side street or into an accommodating neighbour's yard and hold their breath.

A typical raid is heralded by uniformed policemen on motorbikes backed up by colleagues, often not in uniform, lounging in the back of an open yellow police jeep. They proceed at a leisurely pace enjoying the fear they create. Justice is blind – usually consisting of a random strike. Into the back of a police truck goes a cigarette trolley together with its wailing elderly female owner, somebody's grandmother. A dozen plastic stools are thrown in followed by six collapsible wooden tables, a small drinks cart and another protesting granny. They are driven off and normality descends. Out pop the concealed bottles, cigarettes and the usual street furniture – business as usual.

Poor and unlicensed street vendors whose stock may represent their entire worldly wealth bear the brunt of these raids while the owners of cafés and restaurants whose furniture and customers spill onto the street, breaking every ordinance in the book, stand calmly by. They have greased the right palms. The poor have no protection and lack the wherewithall to buy it.

The other group of people to suffer are those lacking official residence papers, along with other undesirables. On one night in August 1996 around 1,900 were rounded up including "homeless children, old people and migrants from other parts of the country, many of whom were beggars and pickpockets". The official report continued, "homes would be found for the homeless, drug addicts would be sent to rehabilitation centres and prostitutes would go to education centres". And, thank goodness: "Social evils have decreased by 50-70% since the government issued the anti-social vices decision."

Bicycles From the stalls along Le Thanh Ton St close to the Ben Thanh market and Vo Thi Sau west of the junction with Pham Ngoc Thach St. US$40 for a Vietnamese bike, at least US$70 for a better built Chinese one.

Books *Bookazine*, 28 Dong Khoi St. A decent range of English-language books. *The Cat*, 243 De Tham St. Sells, buys and exchanges books, CDs, tapes; also buys cameras, Walkmans and watches from hard-up travellers. *Hong Ha*, 40 Ngo Duc Ke St, and shops at 60-62 and 56 Le Loi Blvd and 40 Nguyen Hue Blvd, sell English-Vietnamese dictionaries and phrase books and some books on Vietnam. *Lan Anh Bookshop*, 201 Dong Khoi St. For second-hand books in French and English. The bookshop, at 20 Ho Huan Nghiep sells French, English and Vietnamese books including bound photocopies of volumes. Some old books have 'US Embassy Library' stamped in the front. It doubles as a café selling some of the tastiest ice cream in Saigon. *Xuan Thu*, foreign language bookstore on Dong Khoi St, opposite *Continental Hotel*, sells books imported from England and France as well as pirated versions of Western books. All foreigners around Pham Ngu Lao and De Tham streets are game to the numerous booksellers who hawk mountains of pirate books under their arms and stagger from table to table. The latest bestsellers together with enduring classics (ie *The Quiet American*) can be picked up for a couple of dollars.

Foodstores Shops specializing in western staples (which, in Vietnam, seem suddenly luxurious) such as cornflakes, peanut butter and Marmite abound on Ham Nghi St around numbers 62 and 64 (*Kim Thanh*). They also sell baby products, nappies etc at a price. *Le Cochon d'or*, 7 Nguyen Thiep St, T8293856. Purveys an excellent range of charcuterie, cheese and delicacies, imported and local. Those wishing to sample pure yoghurt will enjoy tracking down *Hoa Sinh*, 20/10 Ho Hao Hon St, T8367181. An unsigned 'dairy', not easy to find but only 5 mins by bicycle from Pham Ngu Lao St, it sells locally produced goat and other cheeses and dairy products as well at very reasonable prices.

Handicrafts There are a number of shops along Dong Khoi St and Nguyen Hue Blvd. Handicrafts include embroidered and woven fabrics, lacquerware, mother-of-pearl inlaid screens and ceramics. Nice decorative items from *Arts and Crafts Gallery*, 26 Le Thanh Ton St. *Mai Handicrafts*, 298 Nguyen Trong Tuyen St, Q Tan Binh, T8440988. A little way out of town but sells an interesting selection of goods, fabrics and handmade paper all made by disadvantaged people in small income-generating schemes. A number of shops in De Tham St sell woven and embroidered goods including scarves, bags and clothes. *East Meets West*, 24 Le Loi Blvd. Nicely made Vietnamese and ethnic handicrafts, reasonably priced.

Lacquerware Vietnamese lacquerware has a long history, and a reputation of sorts (see page 409). Visitors to the workshop can witness the production process and, of course, buy the products if they wish. Lacquerware is available from many of the handicraft shops on Nguyen Hue Blvd and Dong Khoi St. Also from the *Lamson Laquerware Factory*, 106 Nguyen Van Troi St (opposite *Omni Hotel*). Accepts Visa and MasterCard. *Miss Nga*, 61 Le Thanh Ton St. Sells lacquer and other top quality handicrafts suitable for souvenirs from her shop.

Linen Good-quality linen table cloths and sheets are avaliable from shops on Dong Khoi and Le Thanh Ton streets.

Maps Saigon has the best selection of maps in Vietnam, at the stalls on Le Loi Blvd between Dong Khoi St and Nguyen Hue Blvd. Bargain hard – the bookshops listed above are probably cheaper.

Outdoor Gear Vietnam produces a range of equipment for climbing and camping, such as walking boots, fleeces and rucksacks. Top-quality brand name goods can be bought cheaply, especially around Pham Ngu Lao and De Tham streets.

Silk/Ao Dai Vietnamese silk and traditional dresses (*ao dai*) are to be found in the shops on Dong Khoi St and in Ben Thanh market.

War surplus From 336 Nguyen Cong Tru St.

Western newspapers & magazines Sold in the main hotels. Same day *Bangkok Post* and *The Nation* newspapers (English language Thai papers), and up-to-date *Financial Times*, *Straits Times*, *South China Morning Post*, *Newsweek* and *The Economist*, available from *Xuan Thu* bookshop on Dong Khoi St. Numerous vendors around the *Continental Hotel*.

Sport

Bowling There are 3 venues: *International Club*, 285 Cach Mang Thang Tam St, T8651709, 12 lanes, 15,000d per person per game; and the enormous *Superbowl*, 43A Truong Son St, just outside the airport, 32 lanes, 40,000d per person per game plus shoe hire, video

Horse races

"The commencement was a race of 12 horses, or rather ponies; for, however great were the prizes for competition, the rivalship had not caused them to improve the breed of their cattle; a more meagre, dwarfish, crippled, puny lot of horses, I never before beheld. Chinese horses are bad enough, but these were 10 times worse; and I think the best mode the Quong or the King could adopt to improve them would be, to have races twice or thrice a year, and give prizes to be run for, that would pay the natives to buy foreign horses, and mix the breed.

Well, these 12 animals started; but with all their whips, rattans, spurs, and shouting, they could not get more than a very slow canter out of the best of them. I pitied the poor beasts; they looked far more in want of a feed of corn, than fit to run a race. They made two or three more trials, but it was 'no go'; I could have run faster myself, weak as I was. The poor brutes broke down before they got half-way round the course; and, out of the twelve that started, only three managed to come in anything at all like 'racers'."

Taken from Cochin-China and My Experience of It *by Edward Brown, London 1861.*

arcades and fast food outlets – a great hit with the Vietnamese – book in advance, T8486405. There is bowling on the top floor of the department store in *Diamond Plaza*, Le Duan St, right behind the cathedral.

Golf *Golf Vietnam and Country Club*, Thu Duc, T8252951. Green fees Mon-Fri US$73, Sat-Sun, US$92. *Song Be Golf Resort*, 20 km from Saigon, T065-855802. An attractive course 1 hr drive from town.

Hash House Harriers *Hash House Harriers* meet Sun. The bus leaves at 1430 sharp from the *Caravelle Hotel*, www.saigon3.com

Racing The *Phu Tho Racecourse*, 2 Le Dai Hanh St, District 11. Stages races on Thu, Sat and Sun afternoons. Both the winner and the second horse have to be selected to collect. The course has been reopened with financing from an interested Chinese entrepreneur but not a lot has changed since 1858 when Edward Brown recorded his impressions of Vietnamese racing, see box, above. He would be delighted to know of plans by fellow Britons to introduce new breeding stock to Vietnam. Entrance to Turf Club, 20,000d. Beware pickpockets.

Swimming Some hotels (like the *New World* and *Equatorial*) allow non-residents to use their pool for a charge that can be pretty steep. Apart from these two, other hotels with decent pools are the *Sofitel Plaza*, *Omni*, *Grand* and *Carvelle*. *International Club*, 285 Cach Mang Thang Tam St. 20,000d Mon-Fri, 30,000d on Sat and Sun. Almost next door at 291 Cach Mang Thang Tam is the pleasant *Lan Anh Club* with nice pool and tennis courts. The *Lao Dong Club* (old *Cercle Sportif*) on the corner of Nguyen Thi Minh Khai and Huyen Tran Cong Chua St has a good size pool. *Saigon Water Park*, T8970456. A little way out but is enormous fun. Just hop in a taxi (70,000d) and ask for Saigon Water Park, 50,000d. Open daily 0900-1700 (sometimes shut Tue).

Tennis Courts at the *Lan Anh Club*, 291 Cach Mang Thang Tam St and the *Lao Dong Club* in Van Hoa Park, behind Reunification Hall. Also at the *Rex Hotel* and *New World Hotel*.

Saigon

Tour operators

Ann Tourist, 58 Ton That Tung St, T8334356, F8323866, anntourist@yahoo.com Generally excellent, knowledgeable guides. *ATLAS Tours & Voyages*, 34 thai Van Lung, Ben Nghe, District 1, T8224122, F8298604, www.AtlasToursVoyages.com *Cam On Tour*, 6 Phung Khac Khoan St, T8256074, F8298169, camoncom@hcm.vnn.vn *Cuu Long Tourist*, 97A Nguyen Cu Trinh St, T8300339, F8364820, cuulongtourist@hcm.vnn.vn Branch of Vinh Long provincial tourist authority. For tours to Mekong Delta. *Diethelm Travel*, 1A Me Linh Square, District 1, T8294932, F8294747, dtvlsgn@hcm.vnn.vn *Exotissimo*, Saigon Trade Centre, 37 Ton Duc Thang, T8251723, F8295800, info@exotissimo.com An efficient agency that can handle all travel needs

of visitors to Vietnam. Also popular with overseas tour operators for whom it handles group travel. *Far East Tourist*, 32 Dong Du St, T8225187, F8225187, fareasttour@hcm.fpt.vn *Fiditourist*, 195 Pham Ngu Lao St, T8368018, F8361922, fidi_branch@hcm.fpt.vn A rival of *Sinh* and *Kim* cafés (see below), vying for the budget traveller's dollar, has a money exchange which remains open long after the banks have closed.

Hasia, Land of Dragons, 80 Truong Dinh, District 1, T8242667, F8229105, hasia@land-of-dragons.com *Heart of Vietnam*, 251 Nguyen Van Troi, Phu Nhuan District, T8446122, F9971036, heartofvietnam@hcm.vnn.vn This is a highly regarded travel agency based in the *Omni Hotel* with a speciality in making travel arrangements for those intending to adopt Vietnamese children. *Heart of Vietnam* has been working successfully for four years in this area fraught with legal and moral difficulties and can provide legal and practical advice. *Kim Café*, 270 De Tham St, T8368122, cafekim@hcm.vnn.vn Organizes minibuses to Nha Trang, Dalat etc and tours of the Mekong, good source of information. *Saigontourist*, 49 Le Thanh Ton St, T8295834, F8224987, SGTVN@hcmc.netnam.vn Organizes expensive tours, maybe useful for advice and a few useful handouts. *Sinh Café*, 248 De Tham St, T8367338. Sinh Café now has brances and agents in all main towns in Vietnam. Its tours are generally good value but its open ticket is excellent value. For many people, especially budget travellers, Sinh Café is the first port of call. It is tempting to tour the entire country with them as they make travelling easy. *Vidotour*, 145 Nam Ky Khoi Nghia St, T9330457, F9330470, vidotour@fmail.vnn.vn *Vietnamtourism*, 234 Nam Ky Khoi Nghia St, T9327772, F9326775. Again, only helpful if booking one of its tours. *Vyta Tours*, 17A Tran Dinh Xu, District 1, T8377881, F8368385, www.vytatours.com

Transport

If staying in Saigon for any length of time (or intending to travel by bus with the bike) it might be a good idea to buy a bicycle (see Shopping, above and page 304). Bicycles and motorbikes can be hired from some of the cheaper hotels and cafés, especially in Pham Ngu Lao St. Bikes should always be parked in the roped-off compounds (*Gui xe*) that are all over town; they will be looked after for a small charge (500d by day, 1,000d after dark, 2,000d for motorbikes – always get a ticket).

Cyclos are a peaceful way to get around the city. They can be hired by the hour (approximately US$2 per hour) or to reach a specific destination. Some drivers speak English. Each tends to have his own patch which is jealously guarded. Expect to pay more outside the major hotels – it is worth walking around the corner. *Cyclos* found waiting in tourist spots will often offer additional services such as money changing and 'girls'. Some visitors complain of *cyclo* drivers in Saigon having an annoying habit of forgetting the agreed price (though Hanoi is worse). *Cyclos* are being banned from more and more streets in the centre of Saigon which may involve a longer and more expensive journey: this is the excuse trotted out every time (particularly if extra money is demanded) and it is invariably (although not always) true.

Motorcycle taxis (*Honda* or *xe ôm*) are the quickest way to get around town and cheaper than *cyclos*; agree a price and hop on the back. *Xe ôm* drivers can be recognized by their baseball caps, clapped out Honda Cubs and tendency to chain smoke, they hang around on most street corners.

Taxis Saigon has quite a large fleet of meter taxis. There are more than 14 taxi companies fighting bitterly for trade on the streets of Saigon. Competition has brought down prices so they are now reasonably inexpensive and for two or more are cheaper than

Local
Saigon is 72 km from My Tho, 147 from Vinh Long, 113 from Vung Tau, 165 from Can Tho, 299 from Dalat, 338 from Ha Tien, 445 from Nha Trang, 965 from Danang, 1,071 from Hué, 1,710 from Hanoi

Saigon

Train fares from Saigon

Train S2

		6 berth compartment		
To	Soft seat	Top bunk	Middle bunk	Bottom bunk
Nha Trang	118,000	135	160	175
Danang	278,000	318	357	411
Hué	307	352	415	454
Vinh	452	518	611	670
Hanoi	494	567	667	732

Train LH2

	Seat		6 berth compartment		
To	Hard	Soft	Top bunk	Middle bunk	Bottom bunk
Hué	223,000	248,000	266	314	355
Danang	202	224	241	284	321
Nha Trang	86	95	109	120	136

Train SN2

	Seat		6 berth compartment		
To	Hard	Soft	Top bunk	Middle bunk	Bottom bunk
Nha Trang	86	95	109	120	136

Trains S4, S6…S18

	Seat			6 berth compartment		
To	Hard	Soft	A/c	Top bunk	Middle bunk	Bottom bunk
Nha Trang	86	95	102	102	120	136
Danang	202	224	241	241	284	321
Hué	223	258	266	266	314	355
Vinh	329	365	392	392	462	523
Hanoi	359	399	428	428	504	572

cyclos or *xe ôm*. All taxis are metered, ensure the meter is set after you get in. The standard of vehicle and service vary widely and some companies are more expensive than others. All taxis are numbered, in the event of forgotten luggage or other problems ring the company and quote the number of your taxi. *Airport* (white or blue), T8446666; *Mai Linh Taxi* (green and white), T8222666; *Festival* (grey), T8454545; *Saigon Tourist* (red), T8222206; *Vinataxi* (yellow), T8111111; *Mai Linh Deluxe* (white), T8262626.

Long distance **Air** Tan Son Nhat Airport is 30 mins northwest of the city. Taxis to the city centre cost US$5-7. Airport facilities include a branch of the *Vietcombank* and *First Vinabank*, for changing money and a post office.

Bus There are 2 main bus stations (see the maps for locations). Buses north to **Dalat**, **Hué**, **Danang** and all significant points on the road to Hanoi leave from the **Mien Dong terminal**, north of the city centre on Xo Viet Nghe Tinh St. Buses south to the **Mekong Delta**, **Ca Mau**, **Rach Gia**, **Ha Tien**, **Long Xuyen**, **My Tho**, **An Long**, **Can Tho**, **Long Xuyen** and elsewhere leave from the **Mien Tay terminal**, some distance southwest of town on Hung Vuong Blvd. There is also a bus station in Cholon which serves destinations such as **Long An**, **My Thuan**, **Ben Luc** and **My Tho**. A fleet of

4 berth compartment				
181				
426				
471				
694				
758				

4 berth compartment				
390				
352				
149				

4 berth compartment		*4 berth compartment a/c*		
149		*166*		

6 berth compartment a/c			*4 berth compartment*	*4 berth compartment a/c*
Top bunk	*Middle bunk*	*Bottom bunk*		
113	*132*	*150*	*149*	*166*
265	*312*	*353*	*352*	*391*
293	*345*	*391*	*390*	*433*
432	*507*	*575*	*574*	*637*
471	*554*	*629*	*627*	*696*

a/c buses connects central Saigon with the bus terminals, 3,000d. Buses depart from the bus station opposite Ben Thanh Market. Minibuses for **Vung Tau** depart from Ham Nghi St – hop in quickly as they are not meant to pick up passengers in town.

Train The station (*Nha ga*) is 2 km from the centre of the city at the end of Nguyen Thong St. Much improved facilities for the traveller include a/c waiting room, post office and bank (no travellers' cheques). Regular daily connections with **Hanoi** and all points north. Express trains take between 36 and 40 hours to reach Hanoi; hard and soft berths are available. Sleepers should be booked in advance. (See Essentials for more information on rail travel.)

Hydrofoil *Vina Express*, T8253888. Operates 4 hydrofoils per day to **Vung Tau** (US$10 one-way).

Air (See list page 32). **Road** To **Phnom Penh**. *Sinh Café* (see Tours and tour operators, page 308) run a minibus to **Moc Bai**, on the border, US$5, depart 0800, bus or *xe ôm* from there to Phnom Penh. **International connections**

Streetwise

Cyclists and motorbike drivers in Saigon might like to be aware of the laws they could unwittingly breach and the level of fine they might thereby incur.

Bicycle infringements	*Fine (Dong)*
not moving in the right hand lane	*10,000*
three riders cycling shoulder by shoulder	*20,000*
clinging to automobiles or motorbikes, carrying cumbersome things or 'worming' in the street	*50,000*
illegal racing and fleeing after causing accidents	*500,000*
protesting the police officer's decision	*confiscation of bike plus 1,000,000*
organizing illegal races	*2,000,000*

Motorbike infringements	
not moving in the right hand lane	*50,000*
speeding	*100,000*
riding an unlicensed vehicle	*200,000*
riding when drunk	*500,000*
running away after accidents	*up to 2,000,000*
illegal racing	*5,000,000*
illegal racing and protesting the decisions of police officials	*50,000,000*

Directory

Airline offices *Air France*, 130 Dong Khoi St, T8290981, F8220537. *Aeroflot*, 4H Le Loi St, T8293489, F8290076. *Asiana Airlines*, 34 Le Duan St, T8294570, F8222663. *British Airways*, 114A Nguyen Hue St, T8292262, F8256578. *Cathay Pacific*, 58 Dong Khoi St, T8223203 (airport, T8441895), F8258276. *China Airlines*, 132-134 Dong Khoi St, T8251388, F8251390. *China Southern Airlines*, 21-23 Nguyen Thi Minh Khai St, T8296800, F8298417. *Emirates Airlines*, 114A Nguyen Hue St, T8256575, F8256578. *Eva Air*, 32-34 Ngo Duc Ke St, T8224488, F8239712. *JAL*, 115 Nguyen Hue St, T8219098, F8219097. *KLM*, 2A-4A Ton Duc Thang St, T8231990, F8231989. *Korean Air*, 34 Le Duan St, T8242879, F8242877. *Lauda Air*, 9-11 Dong Khoi St, T8297117, F8236857. *Lufthansa*, Continental Hotel,132 Dong Khoi St, T8298549, F8298537. *Malaysian*, 132-134 Dong Khoi St, T8292529, F8242884. *Pacific Airlines*, 177 Vo Thi Sau St, Q3, T9325979, F9325980 (airport, T8442705). *Qantas*, 114A Nguyen Hue St, T8238844, F8256578. *Siem Reap Airways International*, 132-134 Dong Khoi St, T8239288, F8239287. *Singapore Airlines*, 29 Le Duan St, T8231588, F8231554. *Thai Airways*, 65 Nguyen Du St, T8223365, F8223465. *United Airlines*, 58 Dong Khoi St, T8234755, F8230030. *Vietnam Airlines*, 116 Nguyen Hue Blvd, T8320320, F8230273.

Banks It is easy to change money in Saigon. Remember to take your passport if cashing TCs. Money exchange on Le Loi St, corner of Dong Khoi St, central, quick and easy. *ANZ Bank*, 11 Me Linh Square,T8232218. 2% commission charged on cashing TCs into US$ or VND, ATM cashpoint. *HSBC, Hong Kong and Shanghai Bank*, 235 Dong Khoi St, T8292288. Provides all financial services, 2% commission on TCs, ATM cashpoint. *Vietcombank*, 8 Nguyen Hue Blvd (opposite the *Rex Hotel*). 1.1% commission on cashing TCs in US$, 0.6% into VND. Also at 29 Ben Chuong Duong St, T8297245. *Vietnam Export-Import Bank*, 7 Le Thi Hong Gam St, T8251140. *VID Public Bank*, 15A Ben Chuong Duong, T8223583. 1% commission on cashing TCs into US$, 0% into VND.

BFCE, 11 Me Linh Square, T8222824. *Sacom Bank*, 278 Nam Ky Khoi Nghia, Q3 St, T9320420. 1% commission on TCs cashed in dong. 2% on TCs cashed in US$.

Communications

Internet: as there are now so many internet cafes in all parts of town (and virtually every hotel and guesthouse listed here offers internet and email services) it is impossible and unnecessary to list them. Suffice it to say that De Tham, Thai Van Lung and Le Thanh Ton streets on which many hotels and restaurants are located have many internet cafes. Prices in Saigon are very cheap, internet cafes charge in the order of 4,000d per hr (ie US$1 will buy you nearly 4 hrs), but don't expect high-speed connections, and hotels will charge more. **General Post Office:** 2 Cong Xa Paris (facing the cathedral). Open daily 0630-1930. Telex, telegram and international telephone services available. *Vinaphone* and *Mobiphone*, the 2 local mobile phone providers, both have offices around the building for the sale of sim cards.

Embassies & consulates

Australia, Landmark Building, 5B Ton Duc Thang St, T8296035, F8296031. *Belgium*, 115 Nguyen Hue St, T/F8219354. *Cambodia*, 41 Phung Khac Khoan St, T8292751, F8292744. *Canada*, The Metropolitan, 235 Dong Khoi St, T8245025, F8294528. *China*, 39 Nguyen Thi Minh Khai St, T8292457, F8295009. *Cuba*, 45 Phung Khac Khoan St, T8297350, F8295293. *Denmark*, 115 Nguyen Hue St, T8219372, F8219371. *France*, 27 Nguyen Thi Minh Khai St, T8297235, F8291675. *Germany*, 126 Nguyen Dinh Chieu St, Q3, T8291967, F8231919. *Hungary*, 22 Phung Khac Khoan St, T8290130, F8292410. *India*, 49 Tran Quoc Thao St, Q3, T9300273, F9307495. *Indonesia*, 18 Phung Khac Khoan St, T8223799, F8299493. *Italy*, 4 Dong Khoi St, T8298721, F8298723. *Japan*, 13-17 Nguyen Hue Blvd, T8225314, F8225316. *Laos*, 93 Pasteur St, T8297667, F8299272. *Malaysia*, 2 Ngo Duc Ke St, T8299023, F8299027. *Netherlands*, 29 Le Duan St, T8235932, F8235934. *New Zealand*, 41 Nguyen Thi Minh Khai St, Q3, T8226907, F8226905. *Norway*, 21-23 Nguyen Thi Minh Khai St, T8296870, F8272696. *Panama*, 7A Le Thanh Ton St, T8250334, F8236447. *Philippines*, 29 Le Duan St, T8233157, F8233158. *Poland*, 2-2A Tran Cao Van St, T8245244, F8290114. *Russia*, 40 Ba Huyen Thanh Quan St, T9303936, F9303937. *Singapore*, 65 Le Loi St, T8225174, F8214766. *South Korea*, 107 Nguyen Du St, T8225757, F8225750. *Sweden*, 8A/11D1 Thai Van Lung St, T8236865, F8236817. *Switzerland*, 2 Ngo Duc Ke St, T8258780, F8258760. *Thailand*, 77 Tran Quoc Thao St, Q3, T9327637, F9326002. *Ukraine*, 213 Nguyen Van Thu St, T8222490, F8250559. *United Kingdom*, 25 Le Duan St, T8298433, F8221971. *USA*, Le Duan St, T8234642, F8229434.

Laundry

There are several places that will do your laundry around Pham Ngu Lao St.

Medical services

Dental treatment: *Koseikai Dental Office*, Saigon Tower, 29 Le Duan St, T8235918. Japanese facilities, open on Sun. Reasonable rates. *St Paul's Hospital*, 280 Dien Bien Phu St, Q3, T8225052. *Starlight*, 10C Thai Van Lung St, T8222433. A good French-trained Vietnamese lady dentist operates from here. **Hospitals:** *Cho Ray Hospital*, 201 Nguyen Chi Thanh Blvd, Q5, T8554137. *Colombia-Gia Dinh International Clinic*, 1 No Trang Long St, Q Binh Thanh, T8030678, F8030677. American-run emergency clinic with medivac and General Practice services. *Emergency Centre*, 125 Le Loi Blvd, T8292071. 24-hr, usually some English or French-speaking doctors. *Ho Chi Minh City Family Medical Practice*, Diamond Plaza, 34 Le Duan St, T8227848. Well-equipped practice, emergency and evacuation service Australian and European doctors. *International Medical Centre*, 1 Han Thuyen St (opposite the cathedral), T8272366 and at 520 Nguyen Tri Phuong St, Q10, T8654025 – has (English-speaking) French doctors. Reasonably priced. *International SOS*, 65 Nguyen Du St, T8298520, F8298551. Comprehensive 24-hr medical and dental service and medical evacuation, US$45 for consultation with local doctor, US$65 with overseas doctor, check insurance policy before going. *St Paul's Eye Hospital*, 280 Dien Bien Phu St, T8357644.

Saigon

Places of worship

Church services: Holy Communion held 6 times on Sun and 3 times on weekdays and Sat at *Notre Dame Cathedral* at the north end of Dong Khoi St. All services in Vietnamese except 0900 Sun when held in English. Protestant worship held at *Saigon Prince Hotel* on Sun.

Useful addresses

Chamber of Commerce and Industry, 171 Vo Thi Sau St, Q3, T9327301. **Foreign Affairs Service**, 6 Alexandre de Rhodes St, T8223055. **Immigration Office**, 254 Nguyen Trai St, T8322300. Change visa to specify overland exit via Moc Bai if travelling to Cambodia or for overland travel to Laos or China. Also for visa extensions.

The Mekong Delta and the South

7

318	**The Mekong Delta**	**326**	**Can Tho**
318	**Ins and outs**	330	Soc Trang
318	Getting around	331	Long Xuyen
318	Best time to visit	333	Cao Lanh
318	Background	**334**	**Chau Doc**
319	My Tho	337	From Chau Doc to Ha Tien
321	Essentials	337	Rach Gia
322	Ben Tre	339	Rach Gia to Ha Tien
323	Vinh Long	340	Ha Tien
324	Sa Dec	**343**	**Phu Quoc Island**
325	Tra Vinh		

The Mekong Delta and the South

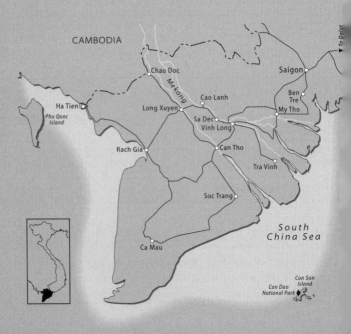

At its verdant best the Mekong Delta is a riot of greens. Pale green rice seedlings deepen in shade as they sprout ever taller. Palm trees and orchards make up an unbroken horizon of green. As the morning sun climbs; all greens pass through a spectrum of hues not to be seen elsewhere. And in the horizontal rays of the setting sun all colours bloom briefly in ravishing intensity.

But at its muddy worst the paddyfields ooze with slime and sticky clay. Grey sky, hostile clouds and incessant rain make daily life a misery while the murky rising waters, the source of all the natural wealth of the Delta, sweep hundreds each year to a wretched death.

Formal sights are thin on the ground in the Mekong Delta and travel can be slow, involving ferry crossings and boat rides. But herein lies the first contradiction of the Delta, for the journey is often more fun than the destination. Boat trips along canals, down rivers and around islands hold more appeal than many of the towns. Driving past paddy fields or cycling through orchards is often more enchanting than the official tourist stops.

The Mekong Delta

Ins and outs

Getting around

See Transport, page 322, for further details The road is relatively good from Saigon to Can Tho, Long Xuyen and Chau Doc; but beyond these towns roads are narrow and pot-holed and travel is generally slow although is improving. Ferry crossings slow travel down still further and if travelling by bus expect long delays waiting in queues (private cars push straight to the front). Completion of the huge My Thuan suspension bridge, a major Australian aid project, just outside Vinh Long has eliminated one ferry journey and made the journey quicker and smoother.

Best time to visit

The months Dec-May are when the Mekong Delta is at its best. During the monsoon from Jun-Nov the weather is poor, with constant background drizzle interrupted by bursts of torrential rain. In Oct flooding may interrupt movement particularly in the remoter areas and around Chau Doc and Dong Thap Province.

Background

The region has had a restless history. Conflict between Cambodians and Vietnamese for ownership of the wide plains resulted in ultimate Viet supremacy although important Khmer relics remain. But it was during the French and American wars that the Mekong Delta produced many of the most fervent fighters for independence.

The Mekong Delta, or Cuu Long (Nine Dragons), is Vietnam's rice bowl, and before the partition of the country in 1954, rice was traded from the south where there was a rice surplus, to the north where there was a rice deficit, as well as internationally. Even prior to the creation of French Cochin China in the 19th century, rice was being transported from here to Hué, the imperial capital. The delta covers 67,000 sq km, of which about half is cultivated. Rice yields are in fact generally lower than in the north, but the huge area under cultivation and the larger size of farms means that both individual households and the region produce a surplus for export. In the Mekong Delta there is nearly three times as much rice land per person as there is in the north. It is this which accounts for the relative wealth of the region.

The Mekong Delta was not opened up to agriculture on an extensive scale until the late 19th and early 20th centuries. Initially it seems that this was a spontaneous process: peasants, responding to the market incentives introduced by the French, slowly began to push the frontier of cultivation southwards into this wilderness area. The process gathered pace when the French colonial government began to construct canals and drainage projects to open more land to wet rice agriculture. By the 1930s the population of the delta had reached 4.5 million with 2,200,000 ha of land under rice cultivation. The Mekong Delta, along with the Irrawaddy (Burma) and Chao Phraya (Thailand) became one of the great rice exporting areas of Southeast Asia, shipping over 1.2 million tonnes annually.

Hydrology of the Mekong Delta

The Mekong River enters Vietnam in two branches known traditionally as the Mekong (to the north) and the Bassac but now called the Tien and the Hau respectively. Over the 200 km journey to the sea they divide to form nine mouths, the so-called Nine Dragons or Cuu Long.

In response to the rains of the Southwest monsoon river levels begin to rise in June, usually reaching a peak in October and falling to normal in December. This seasonal pattern is ideal for growing rice, around which the whole way of life of the delta has evolved.

The Mekong has a unique natural flood regulator in the form of Cambodia's great lake, the Tonlé Sap. As river levels rise the water backs up into the vast lake which more than doubles in size preventing more serious flooding in the Mekong Delta. Nevertheless, the Tien and Hau still burst their banks and water inundates the huge Plain of Reeds (Dong Thap Muoi) and the Rach Gia Depression, home to thousands of water birds.

The annual flood has always been regarded as a blessing bringing, as it does, fertile silt and flushing out salinity and acidity from the soil. During the 1990s, however, frequent serious flooding have made this annual event less benign and an increasingly serious problem.

From 1705 onwards Vietnamese emperors began building canals to improve navigation in the delta. This task was taken up enthusiastically by the French in order to open up new areas of the delta to rice cultivation and export. Interestingly it is thought the canals built prior to 1975 had little effect on flooding.

Since 1975 a number of new canals have been built in Cambodia and Vietnam and old ones deepened. The purpose of some of these predominantly west-east canals is to carry irrigation water to drier parts. Their effect has been to speed up the flow of water across the delta from about 17 days to five. Peak flows across the border from Cambodia have tripled in 30 years, partly as a result of deforestation and urbanisation upriver.

In addition, the road network of the delta has been developed and roads raised above the normal high-water levels. This has the effect of trapping floodwater, preventing it from reaching the Gulf of Thailand or South China Sea and prolonging floods. Many canals have gates to prevent the inundation of sea water; the gates also hinder the outflow of floodwaters.

Information taken from a paper by Quang M Nguyen, 2000.

The Mekong Delta & the South

Given their proximity to prosperous Saigon the inhabitants of the Mekong Delta might have expected some of the benefits of development to trickle their way: in this they have largely been disappointed. Many of the Delta provinces have hardline Communist People's Committees which have staunchly resisted social and economic change, so foreign investment has gone to the more welcoming provinces of Dong Nai and Ho Chi Minh City. The iron grip of the state companies on the tourist industry has resulted in dingy hotels that look upon customers as an irritant rather than a source of business. The contrast with private hotels that eagerly scour the bus stations looking for custom could not be more marked. Despite its potential, tourism in the Mekong Delta remains woefully underdeveloped although the opening of the border with Cambodia at Chau Doc has attracted a number of new visitors.

My Tho

My Tho is an important riverside market town, 5 km off the main highway to Vinh Long and points south, and is the capital of Tien Giang Province. It is 71

Phone code: 073
Colour map 4, grid B3

km southwest of Saigon on the banks of the Tien River, a distributary of the mighty Mekong and about 40 km from the South China Sea. The drive from Saigon is dispiriting, nose-to-tail traffic and virtually uninterrupted ribbon development testify to the population pressure in so much of this land. The town has had a turbulent history: it was Khmer until the 17th century, when the advancing Vietnamese took control of the surrounding area. In the 18th century Thai forces annexed the territory, before being driven out in 1784. Finally, the French gained control in 1862.

Not far from My Tho is the hamlet of **Ap Bac**, the site of the Communists' first major military victory against the ARVN. The battle demonstrated that without direct US involvement the Communists could never be defeated. John Paul Vann was harsh in his criticism of the tactics and motivation of the South Vietnamese Army who failed to dislodge a weak VC position. As he observed from the air, almost speechless with rage, he realized how feeble his Vietnamese ally was; an opinion that few senior US officers heeded – to their cost (see *Bright Shining Lie* by Neil Sheehan).

Sights On the corner of Nguyen Trai Street and Hung Vuong Street, and a five minutes walk from the central market, is **My Tho church** painted with a yellow wash with a newer, white campanile. The **central market** covers a large area from Le Loi Street, down to the river. The river is the most enjoyable spot to watch My Tho life go by. **Vinh Trang Pagoda** is at 60 Nguyen Trung Truc Street. The temple is on the right, through a painted bamboo archway. The entrance to the

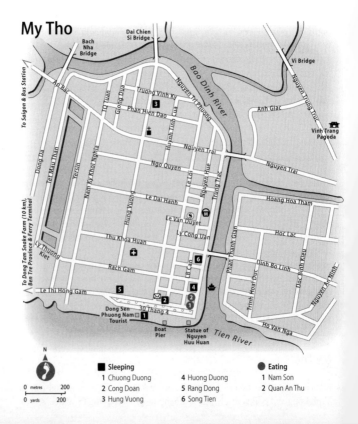

My Tho

Sleeping
1 Chuong Duong
2 Cong Doan
3 Hung Vuong
4 Huong Duong
5 Rang Dong
6 Song Tien

Eating
1 Nam Son
2 Quan An Thu

temple is through an ornate porcelain-encrusted gate. The pagoda was built in 1849, and displays a mixture of architectural styles – Chinese, Vietnamese and colonial. The façade is almost fairytale in inspiration. The temple also has a small collection of animals that would be far happier elsewhere.

There has been a flurry of municipal activity in the past couple of years not much of it beneficial. All the bustling cafés along Trung Trac Street by the side of the small Bao Dinh river have been swept away and in their place is a broad, scorched pavement devoid of any shade. A huge commercial centre has been built on Le Loi Street but its stifling heat, lack of ventilation and high rents have deterred business. ■ *Mon-Sun 0900-1200, 1400-1700. Getting there: it is a long walk; best by bicycle or cyclo.*

There are four islands in the Tien River between My Tho and Ben Tre: **Excursions** Dragon, Tortoise, Phoenix and Unicorn. These can be visited as part of a tour or by renting a boat from one of the eager boatmen along the river bank.

Immediately opposite My Tho is **Tan Long Island**, or Dragon Island. It is pleasant to wander along its narrow paths. Tan Long is noted for its longan production but there are many other fruits to sample as well as honey and rice whisky.

The Island of the Coconut Monk, also known as Con Phung, or Phoenix Island, is about 3 km from My Tho. The 'Coconut Monk' established a retreat on this island shortly after the end of the Second World War where he developed a new 'religion', a fusion of Buddhism and Christianity. He is said to have meditated for three years on a stone slab, eating nothing but coconuts (why, is not clear) – hence the name. Persecuted by both the South Vietnamese government and by the Communists, the monastery has fallen into disuse. ■ *Getting to all the islands: either on a tour from the many tour operators along 30 Thang 4 St (prices vary according to the number of people but expect to pay around US$20-25 to charter a boat for a few hours) or by ferry from the terminal in Le Thi Hong Gam St.*

About 10 km from town; at Dong Tam, a **snake farm** raises serpents for their medicinal qualities – not to remove their venom for use in serum. The belief is that their flesh and gall have strong healing powers. In addition to the snakes, a bear, crocodiles and others are tormented by their Vietnamese visitors. A restaurant serves snake specialities. ■ *Daily 0700-1800, 15,000d. Getting there: take Highway 1 towards Vinh Long, at Dong Tam follow signs to Trai Ran or take the road past the Ben Tre ferry, turn right up a mud lane where you see the sign.*

Essentials

B *Chuong Duong*, 10 30 Thang 4 St, T870875, F874250. A spanking new and huge **Sleeping** hotel occupying a prime riverside location in front of the erstwhile hydrofoil ferry. It is ■ *on map* hard to imagine the place ever being full. The staff are eager to please. *Price codes:* **C** *Hung Vuong*, 40 Hung Vuong St, T876868. A private hotel on the far side of town *see inside front cover* from the river. It has 12 rooms all with a/c and hot water. Seems to be well enough *Phone code: 073* run. **C** *Rang Dong*, 25 30 Thang 4 St, T874400. Private mini hotel, near river, a/c and hot water. **C-D** *Song Tien* (used to be the *Grand*), 101 Trung Trac St, T872009. A/c and fan rooms, lack of customers have forced the authorities to cut prices. Bargain hard. **D-E** *Huong Duong*, 33 Trung Trac St, T872011. A/c and fan rooms. Good river views from upper floors. **E** *Cong Doan*, on the corner of Le Loi and 30 Thang 4 streets. Clean hotel with fan rooms, good views. Recommended.

The Mekong Delta & the South

Eating

on map, page 320

A speciality of the area is *hu tieu my tho* – a spicy soup of vermicilli, sliced pork, dried shrimps and fresh herbs. Sadly most of the good cheap restaurants have been cleared away from Trung Trac St but some remain: it's still the best place to look. **Cay Bo De**, 32 Nam Ky Khoi Nghia St. Good, cheap vegetarian dishes including a delicious veggie *hu tieu*. **Nam Son**, 17 Trung Truc St. Concentrates on *hu tieu*, *mi* and other noodles. **Quan An Thu**, 15 Trung Truc St. Specializes in *bánh xèo*, savoury pancakes filled with beansprouts, mushrooms and prawns, delicious. At night noodle stalls spring up on the pavement of Le Loi St by the junction with Le Dai Han St in front of the failing commercial centre.

Tour operators

Dong Sen Phuong Nam Tourist, 10 30 Thang 4 St, T883133. Offer 2- and 3-hr and 1-day boat tours, eager to help. *Tien Giang Tourism*, 8 30 Thang 4 St, T873184, F873578.

Transport

72 km from Saigon, 70 from Vinh Long, 103 from Can Tho, 179 from Chau Doc, 182 from Rach Gia

Local As in all Mekong Delta towns local travel is often by boat – to visit the orchards, islands and remoter places. On land there are the usual *xe ôms* and the *xe lôi*, the local equivalent of the *cyclo* consisting of a trailer towed by a bicycle or increasingly, these days, a motorbike. **Road Bus**: the bus station (Ben Xe My Tho) is 3-4 km from town on Ap Bac St towards Saigon with regular connections every half hour from 0430 to Saigon's Mien Tay station (2 hrs, 9,000d); Vinh Long (2½ hrs, 13,000d); and Cao Lanh (2½ hrs, 10,500d). Buses to Can Tho and Vinh Long depart at 0430, 0630 and 0830, and to Chau Doc at 0430. **Boat** In a major blow to the development of tourism in the Mekong Delta the hydrofoil has been suspended. Ferry to Chau Doc leaves from the Ben Tre ferry terminal at 1300, 30,000d plus 10,000d for hammock, 24 hrs.

Directory

Banks 5 Le Van Duyet St. **Communications** **Post office:** 59 30 Thang 4 St. Also has facilities for international telephone calls.

Ben Tre

Phone code: 075
Colour map 4,
grid B3

Ben Tre has its fans, but as it is essentially a cul-de-sac, it's not a place you pass through en-route to somewhere else. Consequently, it doesn't attract a lot of foreign, or for that matter, Vietnamese visitors. The province is essentially a huge island of mud at one of the nine mouths of the Mekong. It depends heavily on farming, fishing and coconuts although there are some light industries engaged in processing the local farm output and refining sugar. During the wars of resistance against the French and Americans Ben Tre earned itself a reputation as a staunch Viet Minh/Viet Cong stronghold. Ben Tre is not geared to tourism so do not expect tours or facilities, but for the truly independent traveller there is plenty of interest to be seen in the day-to-day way of life. There are plans to recreate a guerrilla base in one village but quite how compelling an attraction that will prove remains to be seen.

Sleeping

C-D *Dong Khoi*, 16 Hai Ba Trung St, T822632, F822440. Some a/c with fridge, bathroom and hot water, restaurant. **C-D** *People's Committee Guesthouse*, 143 Hung Vuong St, T826134. All a/c, some hot water. **C-D** *Trade Union Guesthouse*, 36 Hai Ba Trung St, T825082. Some a/c, all have bathroom but only some have hot water. **C-E** *Party Committee Guesthouse*, 5 Cach Mang Thang Tam St, T822339, F826205. Some a/c, hot water, most have bathroom attached, as well as some very basic rooms.

Eating

Most of the hotels have restaurants, there is a floating restaurant on the river, but the best option is local noodle and rice stands.

Transport

Ben Tre is 70 km from My Tho, 32 km from Can Tho, and 147 km from Saigon via the My Thuan toll bridge, which charges 7,000d for a car.

Vinh Long

Phone code: 070
Colour map 4, grid B3

Vinh Long is a rather ramshackle, but nonetheless clean, riverside town on the banks of the Co Chien River and is the capital of Vinh Long Province. It was one of the focal points in the spread of Christianity in the Mekong Delta, and there is a **cathedral** and **Catholic seminary** in town. The richly stocked and well-ordered **Cho Vinh Long**, the central market, is on Hung Dao Vuong Street, near the local bus station. Vinh Long makes a reasonable stopping-off point on the road to Long Xuyen, Rach Gia and Ha Tien. There is a **Cao Dai church** not far from the second bridge leading into town from Saigon and My Tho, visible on the right-hand side. The lack of sights and stifling effect of the province's state-run tourist monopoly encourage most travellers to press on to Can Tho.

The **river trips** taking in the islands and orchards around Vinh Long are as charming as any in the Delta, but getting there can be expensive. Officially, *Cuu Long Tourist* has a monopoly on excursions by foreigners and charges US$30 for two for a four-hour trip, although there have been reports of bargaining them down. Local boatmen are prepared to risk a fine and take tourists for one-tenth of that amount. Binh Hoa Phuoc Island makes a pleasant side trip and visitors can stay at (**C**) *Mr Giao's House*, with an attractive orchard and bonsai garden, but as it is part of *Cuu Long*'s package deal it is expensive for the individual traveller. There is a **floating market** at Cai Be, about 10 km from Vinh Long. This is not quite so spectacular as the floating markets around Can Tho (see page 328) but nevertheless makes for a diverting morning's trip.

Excursions

    An Binh Island is just a 10-minute ferry ride from Phan Boi Chau Street; and it represents a great example of delta landscape. The island can be explored either by boat, paddling down narrow canals, or by following the dirt tracks and crossing monkey bridges on foot. Monkey bridges are those single bamboo poles with, if you are lucky, a flimsy handrail – which is there for psychological reassurance rather than for stopping you from falling off. But don't worry, the water is warm and usually shallow and the mud soft. On the island is the ancient Tien Chau Pagoda and a *nuoc mam* (fish sauce factory). Try and find a local boatman to bring you here.

The Mekong Delta & the South

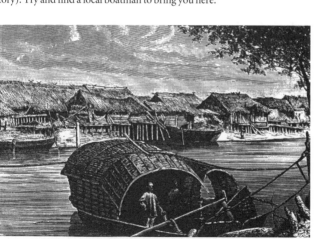

Vinh Long at the end of the 19th century
Source: *The French in Indochina*, first published in 1884

The Khmer Temples at Tra Vinh (see page 326) can be visited on a day trip from Vinh Long. ■ *Getting there: by bus or by motorbike or, for the fabulously wealthy, a trip with* Cuu Long Tourist.

Sleeping
Phone code: 070

B *Cuu Long (B)*, 1 1 Thang 5 St (ie No 1 1st May St), T823656, F823357. A/c, set back from the river, slightly better maintained and more comfortable rooms than its namesake. 34 rooms, price includes breakfast. **B-C** *Cuu Long (A)*, 1 1 Thang 5 St, T822494, F823848. Has the same address but is further up 1 Thang 5 St, right on the river. 16 rather shabby rooms, now with hot water. **B-D** *An Binh*, 3 Hoang Thai Hieu St (opposite post office), T824077, F823190. A/c, fan rooms, dark, unwelcoming, only the more expensive rooms have hot water, restaurant. **D-E** *Nam Phuong*, 11 Le Loi St, T822226. Better rooms have a/c and hot water, cheaper rooms are fan and cold water only, clean and cheap.

Eating

It is remarkably difficult to find anything to eat in Vinh Long apart from the bountiful fruit in the market. There are a few restaurants along 1 Thang 5 St, just beyond *Cuu Long (A) Hotel*. *Lan Que*, 2 2 Thang 9 St, T823262. Away from the hotels but worth finding, friendly, good food, open till 2200. *Nem Nuong*, 12 1 Thang 5 St. Sells grilled meat with noodles. *Phuong Thuy Restaurant*, 1 1 Thang 5 St. A 'stilt' restaurant on the river.

Tour operators

Cuu Long Tourist, 1 Thang 5 St, T823616, F823357, cuulongtourist1@ hcm.vnn.vn English-speaking and eager to please but unfortunately a suffocating influence on tourism in the town and province. Offers a range of 1-, 2- and 3-day tours as well as shorter excursions.

Transport

With the opening of the My Thuan Bridge the journey time to Vinh Long from Saigon and My Tho has been shortened significantly. **Bus** the inter-provincial bus station is at 1A Dinh Tien Hoang St, 4-5 km from the centre of town. From here to town take a *xe lôi*, bicycle or motorbike cart, but pay no more than 10,000d and insist on being taken to the centre. Regular connections, along a reasonable road, with Saigon's Mien Tay station (3½ hrs). Links with Can Tho, My Tho, Long Xuyen, Rach Gia, Sa Dec and other Mekong Delta destinations.

Directory

Banks *Nong Nghiep Bank (Agricultural Bank)*, 28 Hung Dao Vuong St. **Communications** **Post office**: 14 Hoang Thai Hieu St (behind local bus station).

Sa Dec

Phone code: 067
Colour map 4, grid B2

Sa Dec was formerly the capital of Dong Thap Province, a privilege that was snatched by Cao Lanh in 1984 but a responsibility that Sa Dec is better off without. It is a small and friendly town about 20 km west of Vinh Long (see page 323). Its biggest claim to fame is that it was the birthplace of French novelist Margueritte Duras, and the town's three main avenues – Nguyen Hue, Tran Hung Dao and Hung Vuong – together with some attractive colonial villas betray the French influence on this relatively young town.

Sights

Sa Dec's bustling riverside **market** on Nguyen Hue Street is worth a visit. Many of the scenes from the film adaption of Duras' novel *The Lover* were filmed in front of the shop terraces and merchants' houses here. Sit in one of the many riverside cafés to watch the world float by – which presumably, as a young woman, is what Duras did.

Duras' childhood home is across the river and can be reached by a small sampan from in front of the covered market (10,000d round trip). Hers is the first of two villas near the wharf, still rather grand and used by the ward

People's Committee with a small school in the front garden, which would perhaps be of consolation to Duras' mother who was herself the local teacher.

Phuoc Hung Pagoda, at 75/5 Hung Vuong Street, is a splendid Chinese-style pagoda constructed in 1838 when Sa Dec was a humble one-road village. Surrounded by ornamental gardens, lotus ponds and cypress trees, the main temple to the right is decorated with fabulous animals assembled from pieces of porcelain rice bowls. Inside are some marvellous wooden statues of Buddhist figures made in 1838 by the venerable sculptor Cam. There are also some superbly preserved gilded-wooden beams and two antique prayer tocsins. The smaller one was made in 1888 and its resounding mellow tone changes with the weather. The West Hall contains a valuable copy of the 101 volume Great Buddhist Canon. There are also some very interesting and ancient old photos of dead devotees and of pagoda life in the past. In the courtyard take care not to squash the old turtles that plod about amid the greenery.

Excursions

Tu Ton Rose Garden is a few kilometres west of Sa Dec and can be reached either on foot or by *Honda ôm* to Tan Qui Don village. This 6,000 ha nursery borders the river and is home to more than 40 varieties of rose and 540 other types of plant, from medicinal herbs to exotic orchids. For once the local tourist company's breathless prose turns out to be correct.

Sleeping
Phone code: 067

C-D *Sa Dec*, 108/5A Hung Vuong St, T/F861430. More expensive rooms come equipped with a/c, hot water and a fridge, cheaper ones make do with a fan and cold-water showers. Somewhat rundown but kept clean. **D** *Bong Hong*, 5/74 Quoc Lo 80, T861301. A short distance before the bus station on Highway 80 leading into town. Some good value a/c rooms.

Eating

Cay Sung, 2/4 Hung Vuong St, and the next door *Thuy*, 2/3 Hung Vuong St. Both serve good Vietnamese rice dishes for around US$1.

Transport

Bus the bus station is about 500 m southeast of town on the main road just before the bridge. Buses to Vinh Long and Long Xuyen leave from here. The town is 143 km from Saigon and 102 km from Chau Doc, and 20 km from Vinh Long along Highway 80 past dozens of brick kilns.

Directory

Banks *Nong Nghiep Bank*, 77 Ly Thuong Kiet St, off Tran Hung Dao St. **Communications** Post office: on the corner of Hung Vuong St and Nguyen Chinh Sach St. **Tourist office** The local branch of *Dong Thap Tourist Co* is just in front of the *Sa Dec Hotel*, T861432, F861430. Its literature is geared towards local people wanting to see the rest of Vietnam.

Tra Vinh

Phone code: 074
Colour map 4, grid C3

Tra Vinh is the capital of the province of the same name and has a large Khmer population – 300,000 people or 30% of the province's population is Khmer, and at the last count there were 140 Khmer temples. The large Khmer population is a bit of an enigma, for while Khmer people can be found across the Mekong Delta the concentration is highest in this, the most distant Mekong Province from Cambodia. For whatever reason, Tra Vinh established itself as a centre of population some 500 years ago; then, as Vietnamese settlers began fanning across the delta displacing the Khmer, the population of this area remained firmly rooted creating a little pocket of Cambodian ethnicity and culture far from home.

The Mekong Delta & the South

Sights The town itself is an attractive one, with almost every street lined with huge trees, some well over 100 ft tall. The market is on the central square between Dien Bien Phu Street – the town's main thoroughfare – and the Tra Vinh River, which is a relatively small branch of the Mekong compared with most Delta towns. A walk through the market and along the river bank makes a pleasant late afternoon or early evening stroll. Otherwise there is not a lot to do in Tra Vinh, although it's a nice enough place to spend some time. The **Ong Met Pagoda** on Dien Bien Phu Street north of the town centre dates back to the mid-16th century. It is a gilded Chinese-style temple where the monks will be only too happy to ply you with tea and practice their English, although the building itself is fairly unremarkable.

Excursions The two best reasons to come to Tra Vinh are to see the storks and the Khmer temples. Fortunately, these can be combined at two nearby pagodas. **Hang Pagoda** is about 5 km south of town, while **Giong Long** is 43 km southeast. Neither is particularly special architecturally, but the sight of the hundreds of storks that rest in their grounds and wheel around their pointed roofs at dawn and dusk is truly spectacular. ■ *Getting there: go by motorbike.*

Sleeping
Phone code: 074

B-D *Cuu Long*, 999 Nguyen Thi Minh Khai St, T862615, F866027. About 2 km out of town, most rooms have a/c and hot water, they try to please. **B-D** *Thanh Tra*, 1 Pham Thai Buong St, T853621, F853769. Again mostly a/c and hot water, satellite TV, spotless and comfortable. **D-F** *Huong Tra*, 67 Ly Thuong Kiet, T853182. Some a/c, hot water, somewhat grubby bathrooms, primitive but cheap. **D-F** *Phuong Hoang*, 1 Le Thanh Ton St, T858270. Some a/c, hot water, not particularly clean but cheap. **D-F** *Thanh Binh*, 1 Bis Le Thanh Ton St, T858170, F858906. Some a/c, hot water, karaoke.

Eating *Thanh Tra Hotel*, 1 Pham Thai Buong St. Better than your average hotel diner. *Tuy Huong*, 8 Dien Bien Phu St. Opposite the market, good, simple Vietnamese dishes.

Transport **Road Bus**: the bus station is on Nguyen Dan St, about 500 m south of town. Regular connections with Vinh Long.

Directory **Banks** *Nong Nghiep, Agribank*, 70-72 Le Loi St, on the corner of Le Loi St and Nam Ky Khoi Nghia St. Does not change TCs. **Communications** Post office: 3 Phan Dinh Phung St, on the corner of Phan Dinh Phung St and Le Thanh Ton St. **Tourist information** *Tra Vinh Tourist Co* in *Cuu Long Hotel*.

Can Tho

Phone code: 071
Colour map 4, grid B2
Population: 200,000

Can Tho is a large and rapidly growing commercial town situated in the heart of the Mekong Delta. Lying chiefly on the west bank of the Can Tho River it is the capital of Can Tho Province, the largest city in the Delta, and the region's principal transport hub, with roads and canals running to most other important towns. It is also the most welcoming and agreeable of the Delta towns. A small settlement was established at Can Tho at the end of the 18th century, although the town did not prosper until the French took control of the Delta a century later and rice production for export began to take off. Despite the city's rapid recent growth there are still strong vestiges of French influence apparent in the broad boulevards flanked by flame trees, as well as many elegant buildings. Can Tho was also an important US base.

Paul Theroux in The Great Railway Bazaar *wrote:*

> "Can Tho was once the home of thousands of GIs. With the brothels and bars closed, it had the abandoned look of an unused fairground after a busy summer. In a matter of time, very few years, there will be little evidence that the Americans were ever there. There are poisoned rice fields between the straggling fingers of the Mekong Delta and there are hundreds of blond and fuzzy-haired children, but in a generation even these unusual features will change."

Quite the most remarkable feature of Can Tho, however, is its buzz. It is not content to be one of those slothful, dusty towns of the delta but is an exciting, dynamic, restless city whose citizens work hard and enjoy their newfound wealth. Can Tho has just opened its first bowling alley and it has a couple of internet cafés. Pinpricks maybe, but testimony to the intentions of this town and indicative of the fact that the local authorities are open to change. Inevitably this new economic growth has caused human dislocation and social tensions and already a small army of beggar boys has appeared on the streets.

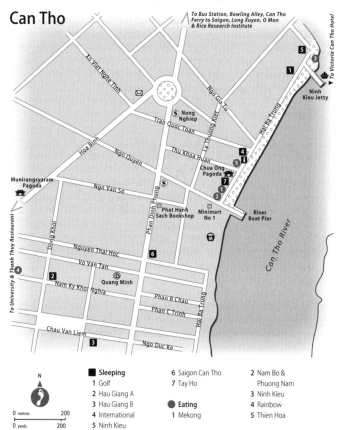

Can Tho

To Bus Station, Bowling Alley, Can Tho Ferry to Saigon, Long Xuyen, O Mon & Rice Research Institute

To Victoria Can Tho Hotel

Ninh Kieu Jetty

Xo Viet Nghe Tinh

Ngo Gia Tu

Hai Ba Trung

Nong Nghiep

Tran Quoc Toan

Hoa Binh

Ngo Quyen

Thu Khoa Huan

Chua Ong Pagoda

Munirangsyaram Pagoda

Ngo Van So

Phan Dinh Phung

Phat Hanh Sach Bookshop

Minimart No 1

River Boat Pier

To University & Thanh Thuy Restaurant

Dong Khoi

Nguyen Thai Hoc

Vo Van Tan

Nam Ky Khoi Nghia

Quang Minh

Phan B Chau

Phan C Trinh

Hai Ba Trung

Chau Van Liem

Ngo Duc Ke

Can Tho River

N

0 metres 200
0 yards 200

■ **Sleeping**
1 Golf
2 Hau Giang A
3 Hau Giang B
4 International
5 Ninh Kieu

6 Saigon Can Tho
7 Tay Ho

● **Eating**
1 Mekong

2 Nam Bo & Phuong Nam
3 Ninh Kieu
4 Rainbow
5 Thien Hoa

The Mekong Delta & the South

Ins and outs

See Transport, page 330, for further details

Getting there For the time being flights to Can Tho are suspended: it is not known if they will resume. There is no hydrofoil but there is a fast boat connection operated by the *Victoria Can Tho Hotel*. Therefore virtually all visitors arrive by road by public bus, tour group minibus or hire car. Now that the My Thuan Bridge is open (near Vinh Long) there is only one ferry crossing between Saigon and Can Tho so journey times have fallen.

Getting around Quite a lot of Can Tho can be explored on foot. Those wishing to do so can engage a *xe lôi* or motorbike taxi. Certain of the sites, the floating markets, for instance are best visited by boat.

Background

Can Tho has its own university, founded in 1966, and also a famous **rice research institute**, located at O Mon 25 km away on Highway 91. Like the International Rice Research Institute (IRRI), its more famous counterpart at Los Banos in the Philippines (and to which it is attached), one of the Can Tho institute's key functions is developing rice hybrids that will flourish in the varied conditions of the delta. Near the coast, rice has to be tolerant of salt and tidal flooding. In Dong Thap Province near Cambodia floating rice grows stalks of 4-5 m in order to keep its head above the annual flood. The task of the agronomists is to produce varities which flourish in these diverse environments and at the same time produce decent yields.

Sights

Hai Ba Trung Street alongside the river is the heart of the town where at dusk families stroll in the park in their Sunday best. Opposite the park, at number 34, is **Chua Ong Pagoda**, dating from 1894 and built by Chinese from Guangzhou. Unusually for a Chinese temple it is not free standing but part of a terrace of buildings. The right-hand side of the pagoda is dedicated to the Goddess of Fortune, while the left-hand side belongs to General Ma Tien, who, to judge from his unsmiling statue, is fierce and warlike and not to be trifled with. The layout is a combination of typical pagoda – with a small open courtyard for the incense smoke to escape – and typical meeting house, complete with its language school, of the overseas Chinese in Southeast Asia. A regulation, much flouted one suspects, states that politics may not be discussed, in particular anything nasty about socialism.

There is a bustling **market** on Hai Ba Trung Street which runs along the bank of the river. The **Munirangsyaram Pagoda** at 36 Hoa Binh Boulevard (southwest from the post office) was built just after the Vietnam War and is a Khmer Hinayana Buddhist sanctuary. The **Vang Pagoda** is on Hoa Binh Street.

Excursions

Boat trips to the **floating markets** at **Phung Hiep**, 33 km away (a nine-hour round trip by sampan or take a bus to Phung Hiep and rent a boat there) and **Phong Dien**, 15 km down the Can Tho River. Bustling affairs, the vendors attach a sample of their wares to a bamboo pole to attract customers. Housewives paddle their sampans from boat to boat and barter, haggle and gossip in the usual way. Phung Hiep also boasts a snake market (on land) and yards making traditional fishing boats and rice barges. The daily markets are busiest at around 0600-0900. **Orchards** and **gardens** abound, small sampans are best as they can negotiate the narrowest canals to take the visitor into the heart of the area, a veritable Garden of Eden. Take at least a five-hour trip in order to see the landscape at a leisurely pace. Highly recommended. Women with sampans to rent will approach travellers in Hai Ba Trung Street near the market waving a book of testimonials from previous satisfied customers. Expect to pay about 20,000d per hour for two people or 30,000d per hour for four people. **Binh Thuy Temple**, which is 6 km along the road to Long Xuyen, dates from the mid-19th century; festivals are held here in the middle of the fourth and twelfth lunar months.

Essentials

A lot of hotel-building has taken place in Can Tho recently, a reflection of the growing economy of this dynamic province.

Sleeping
■ *on map, page 327*
Phone code: 071
Price codes:
see inside front cover

L *Golf Hotel*, 4 Hai Ba Trung St. Not finished at the time of writing but looks as if it will be Can Tho's largest hotel, indeed probably its largest building, and a rather overwhelming feature on Can Tho's waterfront. **LL-A** *Victoria Can Tho*, T810111, F829259, victoriact-res@hcm.vnn.vn New 92-room riverside hotel set in acres of lovely, well-tended garden on its own little peninsula. It is *Victoria Hotel* 'French colonial' style at its best with breezy open reception area and an emphasis on comfort and plenty of genuine period features. It has a pool, tennis court and restaurant. Complimentary shuttle to the Ninh Kieu jetty on Hai Ba Trung St in town. Organizes tours of the surrounding area at slightly above market rates but of greater interest is the *Victoria Hotel* speedboat connection with Saigon, US$59 (5 hours) and Chau Doc, US$39 (3 hrs). **A-B** *Saigon Can Tho*, 55 Phan Dinh Phung St, T825831, F823288, sgcthotel@ hcm.vnn.vn A/c, comfortable, new and central business hotel in the perfectly competent hands of *Saigontourist*.

B *International (Quoc Te)*, 12 Hai Ba Trung St, T822079, F821039. A/c, overlooks the river, good if rather soulless restaurant, massage – if the heavy make-up of the staff is not too off-putting, and dancing on the top floor. **B** *Ninh Kieu*, 2 Hai Ba Trung St, T821171, F821104. Lovely position on the river and good restaurant, a popular venue, in the wedding season for Can Tho's classier wedding receptions. Shabby stair carpets but all a/c and rooms kept clean, breakfast included. **C-D** *Hau Giang A*, 34 Nam Ky Khoi Nghia St, T821851, F821806. A/c and fan rooms, restaurant, breakfast included, quite a well kept and comfortable middle-of-the-range hotel. **D** *Tay Ho*, 36 Hai Ba Trung St, T823392. Central, some hot water, fairly good value. **D-E** *Hau Giang B*, 27 Chau Van Liem St, T821950, F821806. A/c, fan rooms all with hot water, used by backpacker tour groups from Saigon, good value but a little cramped.

Hai Ba Trung St by the river offers a good range of excellent and very well-priced little restaurants, and the riverside setting is an attractive one.

Eating
● *on map, page 327*

Mekong, 38 Hai Ba Trung St. Serves good Vietnamese fare. *Nam Bo*, 50 Hai Ba Trung St, T823908. Excellent little place serving tasty Vietnamese and French dishes in an attractive French house on the corner of the street; try to get a table on the balcony. Small café downstairs with *Walls* ice cream. Recommended. *Ninh Kieu*, 2 Hai Ba Trung St. On the river, good seafood and some Western dishes. *Phuong Nam*, 48 Hai Ba Trung St, T812077. Similar to the next door *Nam Bo*, good food, less stylish, a popular travellers' haunt. *Rainbow*, 54 Nam Ky Khoi Nghia St. Mixed Western and Chinese menu, good fare at the pricier end of the Can Tho spectrum, still represents value for money.

The Mekong Delta & the South

Thanh Thuy, 149 30 Thang 4, T840207. A popular goat hotpot restaurant run by a French Canadian and his Vietnamese wife. Goat, in Vietnam, particularly the poor billy goat's stewed testicles or testicle rice wine, is popular with men who believe that a good helping will boost their sexual potency. Any mention of goat normally results in giggles all round.*Thien Hoa*, 26 Hai Ba Trung St. Used by tour groups but remains good, friendly owner speaks no English.

Entertainment **Bowling** Tran Phu St. This new 24-lane bowling alley is already proving a popular attraction for a fun night out. **Dancing** *International Hotel*, 12 Hai Ba Trung St; and at the new bowling complex on Tran Phu St near the ferry.

Shopping *Minimart No 1*, 1 Ngo Quyen St. By the market for alcohol and other useful items. **Bookshop** *Phat Hanh Sach*, 29 Phan Dinh St, also sells local maps.

Tour operators *Can Tho Tourist* is at 20 Hai Ba Trung St, T821852, F822719. It's quite expensive and organizes tours in powerful boats – not the best way to see the delta.

Transport **Local** *Xe ôm*, *xe lôi* and sampan. Cars can be hired from the larger hotels. **Taxi** Mai Linh Taxi, T822266. **Road** **Bus**: the bus station is about 2 km northwest of town along Nguyen Trai St, at the intersection with Hung Vuong St. Regular connections from Saigon's Mien Tay terminal, 4-5 hrs, 24,500d, and other towns in the Mekong Delta (Rach Gia, 5 hrs, 13,500d; Chau Doc, 4 hrs, 13,500d; Long Xuyen, 8,000d). There is no real timetable, buses depart every 3-4 hrs from 0400 when full. The Can Tho ferry is 24 hrs and highly efficient, not much waiting. **Boat** **Hydrofoil**: alas, the quickest and most comfortable way of getting into the Mekong Delta is no more. See the entry for *Victoria Can Tho* hotel under Sleeping, for speedboat details to Saigon and Chau Doc.

32 km from Vinh Long,
64 from Long Xuyen,
103 from My Tho,
115 from Rach Gia,
120 from Chau Doc,
165 from Saigon,
206 from Ha Tien

Directory **Banks** Are to be found all the way along Phan Dinh Phung St. *Nong Nghiep Bank*, 3 Phan Dinh Phung St. **Communications** Internet: there are several to be found on Vo Van Tan St, including *Quang Minh* at No 55. Alternatively the big hotels (as listed above) have email facilities but charges tend to be high as connections are made through Saigon. **Post office**: on Hoa Binh.

Soc Trang

Phone code: 079
Colour map 4, grid C3

Soc Trang is a large, sprawling and scruffy town which sits astride a narrow branch of the Mekong and is dominated by a huge telecommunications mast. The town is home to a large Khmer community, as is witnessed by the darker skins of many of its inhabitants. Indeed, most of its attraction lies in this connection and for those running to a leisurely timetable it might warrant a visit, which can be done as a day trip from Can Tho.

On the 10th day of the 10th lunar month (around late November/early December) the town dusts itself down and generates a carnival atmosphere for the lively *Ghe Nho Festival*. People come from miles around to watch Khmer boats racing on the river, with hundreds of young men paddling furiously. The event is an echo of the Phnom Penh boat festival which celebrates the turning of the waters when water in the Tonlé Sap branch of the Mekong reverses its flow and backs up into the Tonlé Sap Lake.

Sights At the top end of town on Nguyen Thi Minh Khai Street is the **Kleang Pagoda**, a temple built in traditional Cambodian style, perched on a two-level terrace. Vivid colours adorn the windows and doors while inside sits a fine golden Sakyamuni statue which would look better without its tacky electric halo. Opposite the pagoda is the **Khmer Museum** in which musical instruments, traditional clothing and agricultural tools form the rather uninspired display. ■ *Mon-Fri 0730 -1100, 1330-1700, free.*

About 3 km out of town is the **Matoc Pagoda** or (Maha Tup as it is properly called in Khmer). Follow Le Hong Phong Street and fork right after the fire station. The main pagoda is on the right and is decorated with superb, brightly coloured murals; it has been recently restored with donations from the Vietnamese and Khmer diaspora. Buddhists have worshipped on this holy site for over 400 years, but the pagoda's current incarnation is relatively modern. The chief attraction of the place, Megachiropteraphobes excepted, is the fruit bat. Thousands of these enormous mammals roost in the trees behind the pagoda and at dusk are an impressive sight as they fly off en masse to find food, literally blackening the sky. Also behind the pagoda are the monks' living quarters and the tombs of two five-toed pigs, which have special significance for this community. Look carefully at the picture on the grave! Some living examples can be seen in the pens, lovingly cared for by the monks.

Excursions

B-D *Khanh Hung*, 15 Tran Hung Dao St, T821026, F820099. A/c and fan rooms, hot water, satellite TV, some very nice rooms, friendly. Recommended. **C** *Phong Lan*, 124 Dong khoi St, T821619, F823817. A/c, hot water, some rooms have a balcony overlooking the river. **C-D** *Cong Doan*, 4 Tran Van Sac, T825614. Some a/c, no hot water, walls stained with damp but nevertheless clean though spartan. **D-E** *Dong Tien*. 2 Ha Ngoc Chau St, T828515.

Sleeping
Phone code: 079

Soc Trang has no outstanding eateries, but several restaurants on Hai Ba Trung St do simple and cheap rice dishes. *Khanh Hung Hotel* offers a range of good food. *Phong Lan Hotel* has some Western dishes on a largely Vietnamese menu.

Eating

Road Soc Trang is normally reached on Highway 1 from Can Tho but it's also possible to get here from Tra Vinh by a single ferry crossing (there are several per hour.) **Bus**: the bus station is north of the river at 101C Nguyen Chi Thanh St. Buses to Ca Mau, Can Tho, Rach Gia and Saigon.

Transport
64 km from Can Tho, 126 from My Tho

Banks *Vietcombank*, 27 Hai Ba Trung St. *Nong Nghiep Bank*, 4 Tran Hung Dao St. **Communications Post office**: 2 Tran Hung Dao St and 30 Thang 4 St.

Directory

Long Xuyen

Sprawling for miles along the west bank of the Bassac or Hau River is Long Xuyen, capital of An Giang Province. Driving along the dazzling new dual carriageways into town one anticipates something rather splendid but Long Xuyen disappoints for there is nothing of any interest. It is rather surprising that such a large town can so spectacularly fail to produce anything of note. The town is not mired in poverty but agreeably well off: possibly its comfortable sufficiencies have instilled torpor in its citizens. In fact Long Xuyen would be a strong contender for Vietnam's least memorable town were it not for the glorious countryside around it.

Rice fields predominate and small villages huddle under the shade of fruit trees. The architecture is traditional and modest in scale: houses retain their pitched tile roofs and incorporate plenty of wood. The region remains isolated, for the time being, from the demands of the 21st century so life proceeds at the pace its people have been familiar with for a hundred years. The roads

Phone code: 076
Colour map 4, grid B2
Population: 100,000

are narrow, traffic is light and for visitors with time to spare a tour by bicycle or on motorbike is easily the best way to see the area.

Sights   The large **Catholic Cathedral** on Hung Vuong Street is visible from out of town – two clasped hands form the spire. It was completed shortly before reunification in 1975. A short walk away at 8 Le Minh Nguyen Street is the **Quan Thanh Pagoda**. It contains lively murals on the entrance wall and the figure of General Quan Cong and his two mandarin companions General Chau Xuong and Mandarin Quan Binh at the altar. Also on Le Minh Nguyen Street, close to the intersection with Huynh Thi Huong Street, is the **Dinh Than My Phuoc Pagoda**. Note the roof and the murals on the wooden walls near the altar.

    An Giang Museum is at 7 Thoai Ngoc Hau Street. It fails to rise far above the 'dull' rating so keep it for a rainy day. On display are war relics and Ton Duc Thang's personal effects (such as the leg irons he wore in prison) and some Oc Eo artefacts. ■ *Tue, Thu, Sat and Sun, 15,000d*. Ton Duc Thang was born on nearby Ong Ho island. He later worked in the Bason Shipyard where he incited agitation against the French for which he served a term on Con Dao Island. In 1946 he went to Hanoi and became friends with Ho Chi Minh. Upon the latter's death in 1969 Ton Duc Thang became president of North Vietnam, and in 1975 president of the United Vietnam. On the outskirts of town on Tran Hung Dao Street travelling towards Chau Doc (just after the second bridge, about 500 m), the **Cao Dai church** is worth visiting if you are unable to see the Cao Dai temple at Tay Ninh (see page 289).

Excursions   **Ong Ho Island** is a pleasant trip up the Hau River for fans of Bac Ton (Uncle Ton). Take a boat from the river front.

Sleeping   **C-D** *Cuu Long (Mekong)*, 21 Nguyen Van Cung, T843280, F843176. A/c, hot water, res-
Phone code: 076   taurant, large rooms, clean. **C-D** *Long Xuyen*, 17 Nguyen Van Cung St, T841659, F842483. A/c, hot water, restaurant. **C-D** *Thai Binh 2*, 4 Nguyen Hue St, T841859, F846451. Some a/c, hot water, average. **D** *An Giang*, 40 Hai Ba Trung St, T841297, F846716. All 12 rooms have a/c, hot water, clean and good value. **D** *Thai Binh*, 12 Nguyen Hue. Under renovation. **D-E** *Xuan Phuong*, 68 Nguyen Trai St, T841041. A/c, clean. **E** *Phat Thanh*, 2 Ly Tu Trong St, T841708. A/c and fan rooms. Pretty grubby.

Transport   The most direct route to Long Xuyen from Saigon is to cross the My Thuan Bridge near Vinh Long and take the well signed road via Sa Dec. Alternatively, it's a pleasant drive on Highway 91 from Can Tho via O Mon. It is also possible to get here from Cao Lanh by taking two small ferries (which can carry just one car), frequent service. For those who know the way this is possibly the quickest and certainly the most scenic route back to Saigon. **Road** **Bus**: the station is 1½ km east of town at 414 Tran Hung Dao St. Mini-buses stop on Hung Vuong St, not far from the cathedral. There are regular connec-tions with Saigon's Mien Tay station, 6-7 hrs, Chau Doc, 1½ hrs, Can Tho, Vinh Long and other destinations in the delta. There are a number of private minibus companies in town offering a faster and more comfortable service than the regular buses.

Directory   **Banks** *Vietcombank*, 1 Hung Vuong St (at the junction of Hung Vuong and Nguyen Thi Minh Khai St). *Nong Nghiep Bank*, 51B Ton Duc Thang St. **Communications** **Post office**: 106 Tran Hung Dao St (quite a way over the Hoang Dieu Bridge) and more cen-trally on Ngo Gia Tu St. **Tourist information** *An Giang Tourist Office*, at 17 Nguyen Van Cung St, T841036.

Cao Lanh

Cao Lanh is capital of Dong Thap Province and hard either to like or dislike. *Phone code: 067*
Following its promotion to the big boys' administrative league, Cao Lanh has *Colour map 4, grid B2*
seen a fierce architectural contest as each local government department vies to
impress upon the population just how important it is. So the glass frontage of
Education eclipses Health but the three floors of Planning were easily
trumped by Police's five. Meanwhile, the poor taxpayer can only gasp at the
bureaucrats' brazen profligacy and bumptious pomposity.

To the northeast along Nguyen Hue Street is the **war memorial**, containing **Sights**
the graves of Vietnamese who fell in the war with the US, while 30 Thang 4 St
leads to the **tomb of Ho Chi Minh's father**, Nguyen Sinh Sac, which looks
more like a theme park than a tomb. The vast **Plain of Reeds** (Dong Thap
Muoi) is a swamp that extends for miles north towards Cambodia, particularly in the late season monsoon (September-November). It is an important
wildlife habitat (see below) but in the wet season, when the water levels rise,
getting about on dry land can be a real problem. Extraordinarily, the Vietnamese have not adapted the stilt house solution used by the Khmer, and
every year get flooded out. In the rural districts houses are built on the highest
land available and in a good year the floor will be just inches above the lapping
water. At these times all transport is by boat. When the sky is grey the scene is
desolate and the isolation of the plain can truly feel like the end of the Earth has
been reached. The excursions are the only real reason to visit Cao Lanh, particularly if you are a bird lover or a Ho Chi Minh biographer

Tam Nong Bird Sanctuary (Chim Tram) is an 8,000-ha reserve 45 km north- **Excursions**
west of Cao Lanh. It contains 182 species of bird at various times of year, but
most spectacular is the red-headed crane, rarest of the world's 15 crane species. Between August and November these spectacular creatures migrate
across the nearby Cambodian border to avoid the floods (cranes feed on
land), but at any other time, and particularly at dawn and dusk, they are a
magnificent sight. Floating rice is grown in the area around the Bird Sanctuary
and although the acreage planted diminishes each year this is another of
nature's truly prodigious feats. The leaves float on the surface while the roots
are anchored in mud as much as 4-5 m below; but as so much energy goes into
growing the stalk little is left over for the ears of rice, so yields are low.
■ *Getting there: tours arranged by Dong Thap Tourist Co (see page 334).*
   My An Bird Garden lies 44 km northeast of Cao Lanh near Thap Muoi
town. Here humans and birds live in close proximity to each other, the main
species being the storks and ibises. Again, dawn and dusk are the best times to
visit as the sky is darkened by tens of thousands of birds flying off to feed or
coming home to roost. This can be combined with a boat trip to **Xeo Quyt
Base**, about 20 km northwest of Cao Lanh. There was so little vegetation cover
here that fast-growing eucalyptus trees were planted; but even these took
three years to provide sufficient cover to conceal humans. As the waterlogged
ground prevented tunnelling waterproof chambers sealed with plastic and
resin were sunk into the mud. Stocked with rice, water and candles Communist cadres co-ordinated their resistance strategy from here for almost 15
years. Despite frequent land and air raids the US forces never succeeded in
finding or damaging the base.
   Tower Mound (Go Thap) is the best place from which to get a view of the
immensity and beauty of the surrounding Plain of Reeds. There was a

watchtower here although no one seems sure if it was 10-storeys high or the last in a chain of 10 towers. There are earthworks from which General Duong and Admiral Kieu conducted their resistance against the French between 1861 and 1866.

Sleeping
Phone code: 067

C *Xuan Mai*, 2 Le Quy Don St, T852852, F856776. Clean and spacious new hotel, all a/c, fridge and bath. **C-D** *Hoa Binh*, east of town on Highway 30 towards My Tho, T/F851218. All a/c, some nice rooms. **C-D** *Song Tra*, 175 Nguyen Hue St, T852624, F852623. Currently Cao Lanh's best hotel, a/c, comfortable. **D** *Thien Loi*, 32 Doc Binh Kieu St, T851370. Some a/c, quiet and cheap. **D-E** *Cao Lanh*, 72 Nguyen Hue St, T851061. Some a/c rooms, the cheapest of which are good value. Don't expect too many smiles, however.

Eating

Song Tra, *Xuan Mai* and *My Tra* hotels all have restaurants. **A** *Dong*, 64 Nguyen Hue St. Tasty food and clean. *Tiem Com 44*, 44 Nguyen Hue St. Simple Vietnamese food, fried rice for 10,000d for example.

Transport

Road **Bus**: the bus station is located at the southeast end of Ly Thuong Kiet St. Connections with all delta towns and with Saigon.

Directory

Banks *Nong Nghiep Bank*, Doc Binh Kieu St. *Vietcombank*, 48 30 Thang 4 St. **Communications** Post office: 101 Nguyen Hue St on the corner of Nguyen Hue and Ly Thuong Kiet St. **Tourist information** The *Dong Thap Tourist Co* is at 2 Doc Binh Kieu St, T855638, F855637, dothatour@hcm.vnn.vn Unusually friendly and helpful and good value for a province tourist company, they organize boat trips to all the local sites (US$20-30).

Chau Doc

Phone code: 076
Colour map 4, grid B2
Population: 96,000

Chau Doc is an attractive bustling riverside town (formerly called Chau Phu) in An Giang Province on the west bank of the Hau or Bassac River and bordering Cambodia. The town is an important trading and marketing centre for the surrounding agricultural communities.

Ins and outs

Getting there
See Transport, page 337, for further details

Chau Doc is an increasingly important border crossing into Cambodia. There are connections by boat with Phnom Penh as well as by road. It is also possible (but expensive) to get to Chau Doc by boat from Can Tho and Saigon. There is a boat connection with Ha Tien via the Vinh Te canal which runs along the Cambodian border. There is no longer a hydrofoil connection but it is possible the service will be resumed. Road connections with Can Tho, Vinh Long and Saigon are good.

Getting around

Chau Doc itself is easily small enough to explore on foot. By means of a sampan crossing some nearby Cham villages can be reached and explored on foot. Nui Sam, the nearby sacred mountain, can be reached by motorbike or bus.

Background

Until the mid-18th century Chau Doc was part of Cambodia: it was given to the Nguyen lord, Nguyen Phuc Khoat, after he had helped to put down an insurrection in the area. The area still supports a large Khmer population, as well as the largest Cham settlement in the Delta. Cambodia's influence can be seen in the tendency for women to wear the *kramar*, Cambodia's famous chequered scarf, instead of the *non lá* conical hat, and in the people's darker skin, indicating Khmer blood. Chau Doc district (it was a separate province for a while) is the seat of the Hoa Hao religion which claims about one to 1½ million adherents and was founded in the village of Hoa Hao in 1939 (see page 419).

The Chau Doc **border crossing into Cambodia** has been open to Vietnamese for a number of years but its opening to foreigners in 2001 has given tourism in this little town a welcome boost. Although the hydrofoil has been suspended there is still a boat connection from Chau Doc to Phnom Penh which makes a welcome alternative to the uncomfortable 10-hour bus ride via Moc Bai.

Sights

A large **market** sprawls from the river-front down and along Le Cong Thanh Doc, Phu Thu, Bach Dang and Chi Lang streets. It sells fresh produce and black-market goods smuggled across from Cambodia. Near the market and the river, at the intersection of Gia Long St and Nguyen Van Thoai St, is the **Chau Phu Pagoda**. Built in 1926, it is dedicated to Thai Ngoc Hau, a former local mandarin. The pagoda is rather dilapidated, but has some fine carved pillars.

Excursions

Nui Sam, or Sam Mountain, lies about 5 km southwest of town and is one reason to visit Chau Doc. This mountain was designated a 'Famed Beauty Spot' in 1980 by the Ministry of Culture. Rising from the flood plain, Nui Sam is a favourite spot for Vietnamese tourists who throng here, especially at festival time. The mountain, really a barren rock-strewn hill, can be seen at the end of the continuation of Nguyen Van Thoai Street. It is literally honeycombed with tombs, sanctuaries and temples. Most visitors come only to see Tay An Pagoda, Lady Xu Temple, and the tomb of Thoai Ngoc Hau. But it is possible to walk or drive right up the hill for good views of the surrounding countryside: from the summit it is easy to appreciate that this is some of the most fertile land in Vietnam. At the top is a military base formerly occupied by American soldiers and now by Vietnamese watching their Cambodian flank.

Nui Sam/ Sam Mountain

The Mekong Delta & the South

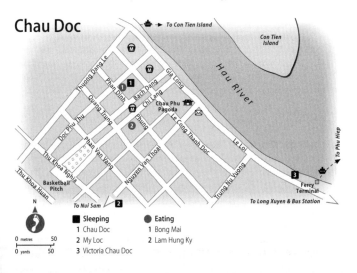

Chau Doc

To Con Tien Island

Con Tien Island

Hau River

Thuong Dang Le
Phan Dinh
Bach Dang
Gia Long
Chi Lang
Quang Trung
Doc Phu Thu
Phu
Chau Phu Pagoda
Le Cong Thanh Doc
Le Loi
Phan Van Vang
Nguyen Van Thoai
Thu Khoa Nghia
Trung Nu Vuong
Thu Khoa Huan
Basketball Pitch
To Phu Hiep
Ferry Terminal
To Nui Sam
To Long Xuyen & Bus Station

N

0 metres   50
0 yards   50

■ **Sleeping**
1 Chau Doc
2 My Loc
3 Victoria Chau Doc

● **Eating**
1 Bong Mai
2 Lam Hung Ky

The **Tay An Pagoda** is at the foot of the hill, facing the road. Built originally in 1847, it has been extended twice and now represents an eclectic mixture of styles – Chinese, Islamic, perhaps even Italian. The pagoda contains a bewildering display of over 200 statues. A short distance on from the pagoda, past shops and stalls, is the **Chua Xu**. This temple was originally constructed in the late 19th century, and then rebuilt in 1972. It is rather a featureless building, though highly revered by the Vietnamese and honours the holy Lady Xu whose statue is enshrined in the new multi-roofed pagoda. The 23rd to the 25th of the fourth lunar month is the period when the holy Lady is commemorated, during which time, if the blurb of *An Giang Tourist* is to be believed (and it's not), two million Vietnamese flock to see her being washed and reclothed. Hyperbole aside, Lady Xu is a major pilgrimage for traders and business from Saigon and the south, all hoping that sales will thereby soar and profits leap. On the other side of the road is the tomb of **Thoai Ngoc Hau** (1761-1829); an enormous head of the man graces the entranceway. Thoai is a local hero having played a role in the resistance against the French but more for his engineering feats in canal building and draining swamps. He is also known as Nguyen Van Thoai and this name is given to one of Chau Doc's streets. The real reason to come here is to watch the pilgrims, rather than study the temples and tombs – which are rather poor – and to climb the hill. ■ *Getting there: either by bus (there is a stop at the foot of the mountain) or, more peacefully, by* xe lôi.

Temples on the mountain Hang Pagoda is a 200-year-old temple situated half way up Nui Sam and is worth visiting for several reasons. In the first level of the temple are some vivid cartoon drawings of the tortures of hell. The second level is built at the mouth of a cave which last century was home to a woman named Thich Gieu Thien. Her likeness and tomb can be seen in the first pagoda. Fed up with her lazy and abusive husband she left her home in Cholon and came to live in this cave, as an ascetic supposedly waited on by two snakes.

Cham Villages There are a number of Cham villages around Chau Doc. One such village is **Phu Hiep**. Phu Hiep is on the opposite bank of the Han River. There are several mosques in the village as the Cham in this part of Vietnam are Muslim. ■ *Getting there: Take a sampan from the ferry terminal near the* Victoria Chau Doc Hotel.

Sleeping **Nui Sam** Almost every café near Sam Mountain has a room for rent and good value can be had by shopping around and bargaining hard. Two at the foot are: **D-E** *Guesthouse 27*, T861006. Some a/c, big rooms. On the mountain itself is **D-E** *Tango*, T861775. Some a/c, with restaurant. **E** *Guesthouse 333*, T861048. Some a/c, friendly and clean.

Essentials

Sleeping
Phone code: 076 **L-A** *Victoria Chau Doc*, 32 Le Loi St, T865010, F865020, victoriachaudoc@hcm.vnn.vn The old building was entirely renovated by this excellent if slightly idiosyncratic French hotel group to produce a lovely hotel right on the river. It is comfortable, equipped with a pool and all mod cons. The *Victoria Group* runs a speedboat from Saigon to Can Tho and from Can Tho to Chau Doc and onwards to Phnom Penh. Not cheap but a good way to travel. See Can Tho for prices, page 329 . **C-D** *My Loc*, 51 Nguyen Van Thoai St, T866455. Some a/c, friendly, more expensive rooms get breakfast included, quiet area. **D** *Tai Ngan*, 11 Nguyen Huu Canh St, T869120, F866435. Near the market, neat and clean. Extra charges for a/c and hot water. **D** *Thanh Tra*, 77 Thu Khoa Nghia St, T866788, F866845.

Some a/c, nice and quiet. **D-E** *Thuan Loi*, 18 Tran Hung Dao St, T866134, F865380. A/c and good river views, clean and friendly, restaurant. **E** *Chau Doc*, 17 Doc Phu Thu St, T866484. Grubby, popular and central. **E** *Hotel 777*, 47 Doc Phu Thu, T866409. Same owners as *Chau Doc Hotel*. Reports say they are no longer welcoming of foreigners.

Try the *Bong Mai* restaurant at the corner of Phan Dinh Phung and Doc Phu Thu streets (next to the *Chau Doc Hotel*), 17 Doc Phu Thu St. Vietnamese and Western dishes in an old colonial mansion, cheap and cheerful. *Lam Hung Ky*, 71 Chi Lang St. Excellent freshly prepared and cooked food. There is a wide range of good food stalls in the market area. **Eating**

Road Bus: the station is southeast of town on the south side of Le Loi St, around 1-2 km from the town centre, past the church. Minibuses stop in town on Quang Trung St. Regular connections with Saigon's Mien Tay station (6-7 hrs), including two ferry crossings. Buses to Long Xuyen (1½ hrs), Can Tho, and other destinations in the delta. **Boat Ferry**: there are daily ferries along the Vinh Te canal to Ha Tien, journey time 10 hrs, 70,000d, a fascinating way to see village life (take plenty of water and food). The 90 km-long canal is a considerable feat of engineering, begun in 1819 and finished in 1824, its purpose was twofold: navigation and defence from the Cambodians. So impressed was Emperor Minh Mang in the achievement of its builder, Nguyen Van Thoai (or Thoai Ngoc Hau), that he named the canal after Thoai's wife, Chau Thi Vinh Te. **Transport**
96 km from Ha Tien,
117 from Can Tho,
179 from My Tho

Banks *Nong Nghiep Bank*, 51B Ton Duc Thang St. *Vietcombank*, 1 Hung Vuong St. **Communications** Post office: 2 Le Loi St. **Directory**

From Chau Doc to Ha Tien

Ha Tien can be reached either by boat or by road. (For travel by boat, see Transport above). The road is in a pitiful state but can be traversed by four-wheel drive, Minsk or bicycle. Nevertheless, it is well worth attempting as it means the south coast can be reached without trailing back the 38 km to Long Xuyen. Also, the scenery as the road skirts the Cambodian border is beautiful and the local way of life little changed in hundreds of years. The road passes Ba Chuc ossuary where the bones of 1,000 Vietnamese killed in 1978 by the Khmer Rouge are displayed in a glass-sided memorial. The nearby Tan Buu Memorial contains grisly photographs of the carnage.

Rach Gia

Unfortunately, Rach Gia is a rather unpleasant little town, but there are a number of pagodas to visit. It is an important deep-water port on the Gulf of Thailand. Already an entry point for goods, both smuggled and legal, from Thailand, it has grown in significance as trade with neighbouring countries has grown grow in significance The centre of the town is in fact an island at the mouth of the **Cai Lon River**. *Phone code: 077*
Colour map 4, grid B2
Population: 125,000

Rach Gia is the capital of Kien Giang Province. The wealth of the province is based on rice and seafood. *Nuoc mam*, a renowned fish sauce, is produced here.

Rach Gia's pagodas include the **Phat Lon Pagoda**, which is on the mainland north of town just off Quang Trung Street, and the **Nguyen Trung Truc Temple** which is not far away at 18 Nguyen Cong Tru Street. The latter is dedicated to the 19th-century Vietnamese resistance leader of the same name. Nguyen Trung Truc was active in Cochin China during the 1860s, and led the raid that resulted in the attack on the French warship *Esperance*. As the French **Sights**

The Mekong Delta & the South

closed in, he retreated to the island of Phu Quoc. From here, the French only managed to dislodge him after threatening to kill his mother. He gave himself up and was executed at the market place in Rach Gia on 27 October 1868.

Tam Bao Temple dates from the 18th century but was rebuilt in 1917. During the First Indochina War it was used to conceal Viet Minh nationalists who published a newspaper from here. There is a small **museum** at 21 Nguyen Van Troi Street in the heart of town and a **market** in the northeast quarter of the island. The wharf area is interesting and the bustling fish market displays the wealth of the seas here. Some attractive colonial architecture survives.

As the straight blue lines on any good map will show, several highly impressive canals converge on Rach Gia. Nguyen Van Thoai, builder of the Chau Doc to Ha Tien canal (see page 337), built the straight-as-an-arrow Long Xuyen to Rach Gia canal in 1822. Highway 80, along which most visitors drive to Rach Gia, runs alongside the canal. It was formely named the Thoai canal in honour of its builder but maps today simply call it the Cai San canal. The O Mon canal was built by the French in 1896 and in 1955 the Rach Soi – Kien Luong canal was built to transport clinker from Kien Luong plant to the Thu Duc cement works on the outskirts of Saigon.

Excursions **Oc-eo** is an ancient city about 10 km inland from Rach Gia. It is of great interest and significance to archaeologists, but there is not a great deal for the

Rach Gia

Highway 80 to Ha Tien

Rach Gia-Ha Tien Canal

Rach Gia-Long Xuyen Canal

Kinh Xang Moi

To Phu Quoc

Highway 80 to Bus Station, Airport & Rach Soi

N

0 metres 100
0 yards 100

■ **Sleeping**
1 Thang 5
2 Binh Minh

3 Palace
4 Thanh Binh
5 To Chau

● **Eating**
1 Hoa Bien

visitor to see bar a pile of stones on which sits a small bamboo shrine. The site is overseen by an elderly custodian who lives adjacent to it. This port city of the ancient kingdom of Funan (see page 353) was at its height between the first and sixth centuries AD. Excavations have shown that buildings were constructed on piles and the city was inter-linked by a complex network of irrigation and transport canals. Like many of the ancient empires of the region, Oc-eo built its wealth on controlling trade between the East (China) and the West (India and the Mediterranean). Vessels from Malaya, Indonesia and Persia docked here. No sculpture has yet been found, but a gold medallion with the profile of the Roman emperor Antonius Pius (AD 152) has been unearthed. ■ *Getting there: the site is near the village of Tan Hoi, and is only accessible by boat. Hire a small boat (the approach canal is very shallow and narrow) from the river front beyond the Vinh Tan Van Market, northeast along Bach Dang Street. The trip takes several hours; expect to pay about US$12.*

(All listed below are on the island.) **C-D** *Palace*, 243 Tran Phu St, T/F863049. A/c, fan rooms. **C-D** *1 Thang 5 (1 May Hotel)*, 137 Nguyen Hung Son St, T862103, F862111. Reasonable, Vietnamese restaurant also. **D** *To Chau*, 41 Le Loi St (aka Ho Chi Minh St) , T863718. A/c, hot water and restaurant. **E** *Binh Minh*, 48 Pham Hong Thai St, T862154. Not a very welcoming place. **E-F** *Thanh Binh*, 11 Ly Tu Trong St, T863053. Shared toilet, fan rooms only but clean, motorbikes for rent.

Sleeping
■ *on map*
Phone code: 077
Price codes:
see inside front cover

Hoa Bien, end of Nguyen Hung Son St, by the sea. Cool breeze, good service. *Thien Nga*, 4A Le Loi St. Kindly helpful owner, good freshly prepared food. **Rach Soi** *Khanh Ngoc*, near Sua Dua Bridge. Specializes in game including venison and hedgehog.

Eating

Air Connections with Phu Quoc Island, 30 mins, and Saigon (via Phu Quoc), 2 hrs, twice a week, US$100 round trip. The airport is at Rach Soi about 10 km east of Rach Gia. **Road** **Bus**: the station is south of town on Nguyen Trung Truc St. Regular connections with Saigon's Mien Tay terminal (8 hrs). Also connections with Can Tho and Long Xuyen. Express buses to Long Xuyen, Sa Dec and Saigon and the local bus to Ha Tien leave from an office at 33 30 Thang 4 St. **Boat** Daily connections to Phu Quoc, departing from the ferry terminal on Nguyen Cong Tru St, T851092, west of the island, 0900, journey time approximately 5 hrs, 66,000d.

Transport
92 km from Ha Tien,
115 from Can Tho,
182 from My Tho,
250 from Saigon

Airline offices *Vietnam Airlines*, 180 Nguyen Trung Truc St, T861848. **Banks** *Nong Nghiep Bank*, 1 Ham Nghi St. *Vietcombank*, 2 Mac Cu St, adjacent to the post office. **Communications** Post office: Tu Duc St (on the mainland, north of the canal). **Tourist information** *Kien Giang Tourism*, is at 12 Ly Tu Trong St (on the island), T862081.

Directory

Rach Gia to Ha Tien

Highway 80 from Rach Gia to Ha Tien follows the Rach Gia-Ha Tien canal virtually the entire way. The road begins well enough with a decent surface and coconut palms and emerald paddies to charm the eye. But it soon degenerates into a pot-holed, dusty track. Add clouds of dust from the Kien Luong cement works and the need for a hotel with running water becomes urgent. Ba Hon village, near the cement works, is the turning for Hon Chong. Towards Ha Tien the road nears the sea where, rooted in the inter-tidal zone, are miles of mangrove forest, most newly replanted. The palms of *Nypa frucitans*, and the distinctively stilt-rooted *Rhizophora apiculata* predominate. The former is extensively used for thatch while the latter produces excellent charcoal.

The Mekong Delta & the South

Ha Tien

Phone code: 077
Colour map 4, grid B1

The town is located west of a lagoon called Dong Ho (East Lake) which is bridged by a floating pontoon (toll charges apply for vehicles and pedestrians). The bridge was built by US Army engineers who would, no doubt, be pleased by the longevity of their construction.

Ha Tien's history is strongly coloured by its proximity to Cambodia, to which the area belonged until the 18th century. The numerical and agricultural superiority of the Vietnamese allowed them to gradually displace the Khmer occupants and eventually military might, under Mac Cuu, prevailed. But it is not an argument the Khmer are prepared to walk away from, as their incursions into the area in the late 1970s showed, and bitter resentments remain on both sides of the border.

Sights Despite its colourful history, modern Ha Tien does not contain a great deal of interest to the visitor and apart from a handful of buildings there is little of architectural merit. The most interesting historical sights and landscapes can be viewed in about a day.

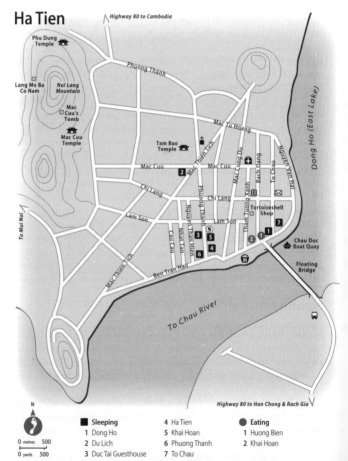

Ha Tien

Highway 80 to Cambodia

Phu Dung Temple

Phuong Thanh

Lang Mo Ba Co Nam

Nui Lang Mountain

Mac Cuu's Tomb

Mac Cuu Temple

Mac Tu Hoang

Tam Bao Temple

Dong Ho (East Lake)

Mac Cuu

Mac Thien Tich

Mac Cuu

Bach Dang

Nguyen Van Hai

Chi Lang

Phuong Thanh

Chi Lang

Tortoiseshell Shop

Lam Son

Nguyen Than Hien

Lam Son

Thanh Thuong Xanh

Cau Cau

Nhat Tao

Chau Doc Boat Quay

Mac Thien Tich

Ben Tran Hau

Floating Bridge

To Chau River

To Mui Nai

Highway 80 to Hon Chong & Rach Gia

N

0 metres 500
0 yards 500

■ Sleeping
1 Dong Ho
2 Du Lich
3 Duc Tai Guesthouse
4 Ha Tien
5 Khai Hoan
6 Phuong Thanh
7 To Chau

● Eating
1 Huong Bien
2 Khai Hoan

There are a number of pagodas in town. The **Tam Bao Temple** at 328 Phuong Thanh Street was founded in the 18th century, as too was **Chua Phu Dung** (Phu Dung Pagoda) which can be found not far away, a short distance along a path to the northwest just off Phuong Thanh Street. A lengthy story is attached to this temple, the 'Cotton Rose Hibiscus Pagoda'. In 1730 newly widowed Nguyen Nghi fled invaders from Laos and landed in Ha Tien with his son and 10-year-old daughter, Phu Cu (the ancient form of Phu Dung with the same floral meaning). Nguyen Nghi was soon appointed Professor of Literature and Poetry to Duke Mac Cuu's son, Mac Tu (see Den Mac Cuu below) and privately tutored his own little daughter, who had taken to dressing as a boy in order to be able to attend school. After Duke Mac Cuu's untimely death in 1735 his son was granted the name Mac Thien Tich and the title Great Admiral Commander-in-Chief, Plenipotentiary Minister of Ha Tien Province. Later he inaugurated a poetry club at which young Phu Cu, still in the guise of a boy, declaimed exquisitely, setting passions ablaze. Surreptitious investigations put the Great Admiral's mind at rest: 'he' was in fact a girl. A long poetic romance and royal wedding followed.

After years of happy marriage the angelic Phu Cu one day begged her husband to let her break with their poetic love of the past and become a nun. The Great Admiral realized he could not but comply. He built the Phu Cu, Cotton Rose Hibiscus Pagoda, wherein his beloved wife spent the rest of her life in prayer and contemplation. The towering pagoda was built so high that it served as a constant reminder and could, in due course, be seen from his own tomb.

Den Mac Cuu, the temple dedicated to the worship of the Mac Cuu and his clan was built in 1898-1902. Mac Cuu was provincial governor under the waning Khmer rule and in 1708 established a Vietnamese protectorate. The temple lies a short way from the town and sits at the foot of **Nui Lang**, or Tomb Mountain. To the left of the altar house is a map showing the location of the tombs of members of the clan. Mac Cuu's own tomb lies a short distance up the hill along a path leading from the right of the temple, from where there are good views of the sea.

Around the back of Nui Lang (a short drive, or longish trek) is **Lang Mo Ba Co Nam** (tomb of Great Aunt Number Five), an honorary title given to the three-year-old daughter of Mac Cuu who was buried alive. It has become an important shrine to Vietnamese seeking her divine intercession in time of family crisis and is more-visited than Mac Cuu's tomb.

Mui Nai lies in a 'tourist park' about 5 km west of town. There are some nicely wooded hills and a muddy beach from where Phu Quoc Island and Cambodia can be seen. The beach gets very crowded and litter-strewn during public holidays. It offers the opportunity of rock scrambling for the nimble footed but is disappointing compared with the sandy beach at Hon Chong. **Thach Dong Pagoda**, 3 km from Ha Tien, and a short hike up from the road, is dedicated to the goddess Quan Am; at the bottom of the mountain is *Bia Cam Thu* (Monument of Hate – the Vietnamese don't mince their words) a memorial to the 130 Vietnamese slain by the Khmer Rouge in March 1978. The temple is inside a limestone hill which consists of a series of caves and clefts in the rock. There are good views of the surrounding, remarkably flat, country. ■ *5,000d, cameras 5,000d.* About 2 km beyond Thach Dong Pagoda is the **Cambodian border**: do not let the fact that it is permeable to locals and contraband of all sorts encourage you to follow; this is not an authorized crossing point for foreigners.

Excursions

The Mekong Delta & the South

Hon Chong is a popular and well-known beach area about 30 km east of Ha Tien. Unlike Ha Tien, Hon Chong has clean white sand and miles of unspoilt beach – much nicer than Ha Tien but not a patch on Phu Quoc. Apart from the beach its main claim to fame is the holy grotto and the interesting limestone formations **Hon Phu Tu**, Father and Son rocks, which lie 100 m or so offshore (it costs 5,000d for a boat ride there). Follow the path through **Chua Hang (Hang Pagoda)** to the beach. The temple with its Buddha of 100 hands loses much of its religious significance and atmosphere at holiday times (notably Tet) when noisy throngs of trippers file through on their way to the beach. Boats accommodating more than 10 people can be hired from some of the cafés for about US$70 per day, smaller boats should be much less. A number of elementary guesthouses including **E** *Hon Trem*, T854331, and **E** *Huong Bien*, T853466. No fan, hot, cramped, very basic, but an excellent restaurant with good food. ■ *Getting there: by car, turn south off Highway 80 at Ba Hon village, 11 km down an appallingly uncomfortable and slow track. Or by bus to Ba Hon, 45 mins*, xe ôm *to Hon Chong, 10,000d, 1½ hrs, very dusty.*

Phu Quoc Island lies 45 km west of Ha Tien. For details, see page 343 .

Sleeping
■ *on map*
Phone code: 077
Price codes:
see inside front cover

D *Khai Hoan*, 239 Phuong Thanh St, T852254. A/c and hot water, probably the pick of the bunch. **D-E** *Dong Ho*, 2 Tran Hau St, T/F852141. Some a/c and even hot water now available, otherwise basic and noisy. **D-E** *Du Lich*, Mac Thien Tich St. Large fan rooms. **E** *Duc Tai Guesthouse*, Phuong Thanh St. Basic and cheap. **E** *Ha Tien*, corner of Ben Tran Hau and Phuong Thanh streets. A real treat for nature lovers: *listen* to the dogs singing in the courtyard, *feel* the pain that the bedbugs inflict, *witness* plagues of mosquitoes unseen since biblical times, *hear* the cockroaches scuttle home from the party under your bed and *enjoy* the sound of rats copulating in the corner. With cold water on a good day and fans. **E** *Phuong Thanh*, Phuong Thanh St. Old, fan only, may not accept westerners. **E** *To Chau*, To Chau St, T852148. Fan only, run down.

Eating
● *on map*

There are numerous food stalls along the river and Ben Tran Hau. *Huong Bien*, Ben Tran Hau. Not bad, but may run out of food. *Khai Hoan*, Ben Tran Hau. Looks scruffy from the outside but the food is good.

Shopping

Ha Tien is known for its tortoiseshell products: carved fans, boxes, combs and other items made from the shells of specially bred tortoises, 999 Tham Tuong Xanh St.

Transport
92 km from Rach Gia,
96 from Chau Doc
(by canal), 206 from
Can Tho, 272 from My
Tho, 338 from Saigon

Road Bus: the bus station is on the southeast edge of town, south of the pontoon bridge that crosses the To Chau River. There are buses from Saigon's Mien Tay station, 10 hrs, and regular connections with Rach Gia, 4 hrs, and Can Tho. **Boat** The ferry wharf is just to the northeast of the pontoon bridge. Ferries to Chau Doc (7-10 hrs, 70,000d) depart at 0600: take food and water. See under Phu Quoc Island, page 343, for ferry details.

Directory   **Banks** *Nong Nghiep Bank*, Tran Hau St. **Communications** Post office: 3 To Chau St.

Phu Quoc Island

Phu Quoc is Vietnam's largest island, lying off the southwest coast of Vietnam. The island remains largely undeveloped with beautiful sandy beaches along much of its coastline and forested hills inland. Most of the beaches benefit from crystal clear waters making it perfect for swimming and a place well worth visiting for those with some time to spend in southern Vietnam. The island's remoteness and lack of infrastructure have meant that it is only recently that tourism has started to be developed, and although new resorts are planned the pace of development is slow owing to the lack of power and water supplies to much of the island.

Phu Quoc's northernmost tip lies just outside Cambodian territorial waters and, like other parts of present day Vietnam in this area, it has been fought over, claimed and reclaimed by Thai, Khmer and Viet. At the moment some of the island is reserved for military use and hence access to one of the most beautiful beaches (Kem Beach) is restricted, but, despite this there remains plenty to explore.

Phone code: 077
Colour map 4, grid B1

Ins and outs

You can get to Phu Quoc by boat or plane but almost all visitors choose to fly from Saigon rather than take the long and uncomfortable boat trip from Rach Gia (5 hrs, daily) or Ha Tien (4 hrs, every 2 days). Flights from Saigon leave daily providing a quick (45 mins) and inexpensive (US$100 round trip) route to the island. A high-speed boat service is due to be in operation from the end of 2002 so this may become a sensible alternative should it materialize.

Getting there
See Transport, page 345, for further details

Phu Quoc Island

While some of the island's roads are surfaced many are still dirt tracks and so the best way to get around is by motorbike (see Transport, page 345). There are plenty of motorbike taxis and motorbikes are easily available and cheap to hire. The only problem that visitors are likely to encounter is the limited signposting which can make some places pretty hard to find without some form of local assistance. Most hotels will provide a free pick-up service from the airport if accommodation is booked in advance.

Getting around

Background

Historically, the island is renowned for its small part in the triumph of the Nguyen Dynasty. In 1765 Pigneau de Behaine was sent here as a young seminarist to train Roman Catholic missionaries; by chance he was on the island when Nguyen Anh (son of emperor-to-be Gia Long) arrived, fleeing the Tay Son. Pigneau's role in the rise of the Nguyen Dynasty is described more fully on page 186.

The Mekong Delta & the South

Another link between the island and wider Vietnamese history is that it was here, in 1919, that the civil servant Ngo Van Chieu communed with the spirit world and made contact with the Supreme Being, leading to the establishment of the Cao Dai religion (see page 419).

Excursions

Most of the resorts are very happy to arrange tours and they are a good source of up-to-date information. Alternatively, *Phu Quoc Discovery Tour*, T846587, arranges most types of tours with English-speaking guides for slightly more cost.

The beautiful white sands of **Sao Beach** are well worth visiting by motorbike but finding the beach can be difficult as it is not well signposted (note that Kem Beach is at present reserved for military use).

The inland streams and waterfalls (**Da Ban** and **Chanh** streams) are not very dramatic in the dry season but still provide a relaxing place to swim and walk in the forests. Either hire motorbikes or arrange a tour through your hotel to get there.

Boat trips around the **An Thoi islands** or up to the north of the island are easy to arrange through resorts and offer opportunities for swimming, snorkelling and fishing. It is also possible to stop off to visit an interesting fishing village at **Thom Island**. A boat trip (for up to eight people) normally costs around US$55-65 for a day, but try to get lunch and transport to the port included in the price. The boats leave from An Thoi town and passports have to be shown before boarding the boat.

Other sights include the fish sauce factory (for which the island is famous), the Old Prison and the Pearl Museum, though these are of questionable interest as there is not always much to see.

Essentials

Sleeping
Phone code: 077

During peak periods such as Christmas and Tet it is advisable to book accommodation well in advance, otherwise accommodation is easily obtained on arrival at the airport. Representatives from different resorts meet most flights providing free transfers and touting for business. Most of the resorts lie along the west coast to the south of Duong Dong and are within a few kilometres of the airport.

B-C *Saigon Phu Quoc Resort*, 1 Trang Hung Dao St, Duong Dong Town, T846999, F847163, sgphuquocresort@hcm.vnn.vn Well-finished a/c bungalows set on a hillside garden overlooking the sea. The resort has good facilities including a decent swimming pool, internet access and a reasonably priced restaurant serving international food. **C** *Tropicana Resort*, Duong Dong, T847127, F847128, tropicana_vn@yahoo.com The resort has high-quality wooden bungalows set in a tropical garden next to the beach. There are a range of prices according to facilities required. The resort has one of the best restaurants, a well-stocked bar and internet access.

D-E *Huong Bien Hotel*, Duong Dong Town, T846113, F847065. The hotel is located on the fringes of the town at the end of the beach. The rooms all have a/c, TV and bathrooms at a reasonable price but the hotel has a slightly sterile feel to it and is not on the best part of the beach. **D-E** *Kim Hoa Resort*, Duong Dong, T847039, F848261, kskimhoa@saigonnet.vn Typical wooden bungalows with facilities varying according to price.

E *Thousand Stars Resort*, Duong Dong, T848203, F848556. A new resort occupying one of the best spots on the beach. It consists of pleasant bungalows with bathrooms and optional a/c. Prices may go up when a swimming pool is built but at the moment it represents good value for money. Recommended. **F** *Kim Linh Hotel*, Duong To village, T846611, F846144, quochoapq@yahoo.com Basic fan rooms in an uninspiring environment at low prices.

Ong Lang Beach E *Phu Quoc Resort/Thang Loi*, Ong Lang Beach, T848341, F846144. Wooden bungalows, no a/c, set in a remote coconut plantation north of Duong Dong. The resort only has electricity in the evenings but has a good bar and restaurant with friendly German owners.

An Thoi Town F *Truong Ngoc Guesthouse*, An Thoi, T844232. Basic rooms with communal facilities – not recommended unless you are forced to stay in An Thoi.

The food on Phu Quoc is generally very good, especially the fish and seafood. On the street in Duong Dong try the delicious *gio cuong* (fresh spring rolls) but do be aware that some of the market stalls appear to cook using water taken straight from the river.

    Most of the resorts mentioned have beachfront restaurants but the *Tropicana* and the nameless restaurant to the south of it are some of the best with quite reasonable prices too. For international food the *Saigon Phu Quoc* resort probably has the widest choice but their food is not especially exciting. For the more adventurous it is worth asking one of the locals about other of the more difficult to find restaurants inland.

Eating

Phu Quoc Tourist Company, Tran Hung Dao St, Duong Dong, T846050, F847065.

Tour operator

Ferry The ferry to and from Ha Tien takes 4 hrs, 43,000d, T851092. See also Getting there page 343, for details. Motorbikes can be rented from most resorts for about US$5-6 per day though do check that the bike is in good working order before setting off as most bikes are cheap Chinese imports and not the Hondas that they claim to be. Cars and bicycles can also be rented from resorts such as the *Tropicana* and *Saigon Phu Quoc*.

Transport

Banks *Nong Nghiep Bank*, Duong Dong, also cashes Tcs. *Phu Quoc Bank* in Duong Dong, cashes TCs. It is best to bring enough money with you to Phu Quoc. Some resorts will exchange travellers cheques as will the banks in Duong Dong but rates are worse than on the mainland.) **Communications Internet**: access tends to be a bit pricey – telephone connections are to Saigon – presently available at the *Tropicana* and *Saigon Phu Quoc* Resorts (at a cost of over 2,000d per min) and more cheaply at *Hi Tech Support*, Huong Vuong Street, Duong Dong Town (800d per min). **Post office**: in Dong Duong town, also for international telephone calls.

Directory

The Mekong Delta & the South

Background

349 History
349 Vietnam prehistory
349 Pre-colonial history
352 Le Dynasty and the emergence
of Vietnam
353 History of non-Viet Civilizations
353 Funan (AD 100-600)
354 Champa (AD 200-1720)
356 The colonial period
358 Resistance to the French:
the prelude to revolution

359 The Vietnam Wars
359 The First Indochina War
(1945-54)
362 The Second Indochina War
(1954-75)
363 The escalation of the armed
conflict (1959-63)
364 The American war in Vietnam
369 1964-68: who was winning?
370 The Tet Offensive, 1968:
the beginning of the end
371 The Paris Agreement (1972)
372 The Final Phase, 1973-75
373 Legacy of the Vietnam War
375 After the war

378 Modern Vietnam
378 Politics
382 Economic reform versus social
degredation
383 International relations
384 Rapprochement with the
United States
385 The future of communism in
Vietnam

386 Economy
386 Partition and socialist
reconstruction 1955-75
386 Reunification and a stab at
socialist reconstruction
(1975-79)

387 The roots of economic reform
(1979-86)
389 Doi moi: the reform economy
(1986-present)
391 Economic challenges

395 Culture
395 People
395 Highland people: the
Montagnards of Vietnam
402 The Hoa: ethnic Chinese
402 The Viet Kieu: Overseas
Vietnamese
403 Art and architecture
406 The Vietnamese Pagoda
409 Crafts

410 Language

411 Literature

414 Drama

415 Religion
415 Mahayana Buddhism
417 Confucianism
417 Taoism
418 Christianity
419 Islam and Hinduism
419 Cao Daism
419 Hoa Hao

420 Land and environment
420 The regions of Vietnam
422 Climate
422 Flora and fauna

426 Books
427 Books on Vietnam
430 Films

History

Vietnam prehistory

The earliest record of humans in Vietnam is from an archaeological site on Do Mountain, in the northern Thanh Hoa Province. The remains discovered here have been dated to the Lower Palaeolithic (early Stone Age). So far, all early human remains have been unearthed in North Vietnam, invariably in association with limestone cliff dwellings. Unusually, tools are made of basalt rather than flint, the more common material found at similar sites in other parts of the world.

Archaeological excavations have shown that between 5,000 and 3,000 BC, two important Mesolithic cultures occupied North Vietnam: these are referred to as the **Hoa Binh** and **Bac Son** cultures after the principal excavation sites in Tonkin. Refined stone implements and distinctive hand axes with polished edges (known as Bacsonian axes) are characteristic of the two cultures. These early inhabitants of Vietnam were probably small and dark-skinned, probably of Melanesian or Austronesian stock.

There are 2,000 years of recorded Vietnamese history and another 2,000 years of legend. The Vietnamese people trace their origins back to 15 tribal groups known as the **Lac Viet** who settled in what is now North Vietnam at the beginning of the Bronze Age. Here they established an agrarian kingdom known as Van-lang which seems to have vanished during the third century BC.

A problem with early **French archaeological studies** in Vietnam was that most of the scholars were either Sinologists or Indologists. In consequence, they looked to Vietnam as a receptacle of Chinese or Indian cultural influences, and spent little time uncovering those aspects of culture, art and life that were indigenous in origin and inspiration. The French archaeologist Bezacier for example, expressed the generally held view that 'Vietnamese' history only began in the seventh century AD. Such sites as Hoa Binh, Dong Son and Oc-eo, which pre-date the seventh century, were regarded as essentially Chinese or Indonesian, their only 'Vietnameseness' being their geographical location. This perspective was more often than not based on faulty and slapdash scholarship, and reflected the prevailing view that Southeast Asian art was basically derivative.

Pre-colonial history

The beginning of Vietnamese recorded history coincides with the start of **Chinese cultural hegemony** over the north, in the second century BC. The Chinese dominated Vietnam for over 1,000 years until the 10th century AD, and the cultural legacy is still very much in evidence, making Vietnam distinctive in Southeast Asia. Even after the 10th century, and despite breaking away from Chinese political domination, Vietnam was still overshadowed and greatly influenced by its illustrious neighbour to the north. Nonetheless, the fact that Vietnam could shrug off 1,000 years of Chinese subjugation and emerge with a distinct cultural heritage and language says a lot for Vietnam's strength of national identity. Indeed, it might be argued, as William Duiker, an expert on Ho Chi Minh, does, that the Vietnamese nation "has been formed in the crucible of its historic resistance to Chinese conquest and assimilation".

The Ly Dynasty (1009-1225) was the first independent Vietnamese dynasty. Its capital, Thang Long, was at the site of present day Hanoi and the dynasty based its system of government and social relations closely upon the Chinese Confucianist model (see page 417). The Vietnamese owe a considerable debt to the Chinese (government, philosophy and arts) but they have always been determined to maintain their

Ly Dynasty

Background

independence. Vietnamese Confucianist scholars were unsparing in their criticism of Chinese imperialism. Continuous Chinese invasions, all ultimately futile, served to cement an enmity between the two countries, which is still in evidence today – despite their having normalized diplomatic relations in October 1991.

The first Ly emperor, and one of Vietnam's great kings, was Ly Cong Uan who was born in AD 974. He is usually known by his posthumous title, **Ly Thai To** and reigned for 19 years from 1009-28. Ly Cong Uan was raised and educated by monks and acceded to the throne when, as the commander of the palace guard in Hoa Lu (the capital of Vietnam before Thang Long or Hanoi) and with the support of his great patron, the monk Van Hanh, he managed to gain the support of the Buddhist establishment and many local lords. During his reign, he enjoyed a reputation not just as a great soldier, but also as a devout man who paid attention to the interests and well-being of his people. He also seemed, if the contemporary records are to be believed, to have been remarkably

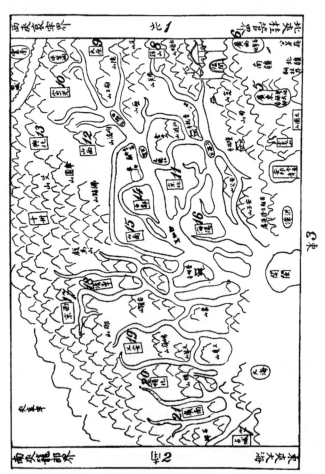

Map of Vietnam under the Lê Dynasty, taken from a manuscript dated 1490 and entitled Geography of Hong Duc. *The orientation given is North (1), South (2), East (3), West (4); one can distinguish in the north, Kouang-tong (5), Kouang-si (6) and in the south, Champa (7). Between these two limits Vietnamese provinces are shown: from north to south and east to west: Lang Son (8), Thái Nguyên (9), Tuyên Quang (10), King Bác (11), Son Tây (12), Hung Hoá (13), Trung Dô (14), Son Nam (15), Hai Durong (16), Tây Kinh (17), Thanh Hoá (18), Nghè An (19), Thuân Hoá (20), Quáng Nam (21).*

sensitive to those he ruled. He tried to re-establish the harmony between ruler and ruled which had suffered during the previous years, and he even sent his son to live outside the walls of the palace so that he could gain a taste of ordinary life and an understanding of ordinary people. As he approached death he is said to have increasingly retired from everyday life, preparing himself for the everlasting.

Ly Cong Uan was succeeded by his son, Ly Phat Ma who is better known as **Ly Thai Tong** (reigned 1028-54). Ly Phat Ma had been prepared for kingship since birth and he proved to be an excellent ruler during his long 26-year reign. It is hard to generalize about this period in Vietnamese history because Ly Phat Ma adapted his pattern of rule no less than six times during his reign. Early on he challenged the establishment, contending for example that good governance was not merely a consequence of following best practice (which the logic of bureaucratic Confucianism would maintain) but depended upon good kingship – in other words, depended upon the qualities of the man at the helm. Later he was more of an establishment figure, holding much greater store by the institutions of kingship. Perhaps his greatest military success was the mounting of a campaign to defeat the Cham in 1044 from which he returned with shiploads of plunder. His greatest artistic legacy was the construction of the One Pillar Pagoda or Chua Mot Cot in Hanoi (see page 75).

Ly Phat Ma was succeeded by his son, Ly Nhat Ton, posthumously known as **Ly Thanh Tong** (reigned 1054-72). History is not as kind about Ly Thanh Tong as it is about his two forebears. Nonetheless he did challenge the might of the Chinese along Vietnam's northern borders – largely successfully – and like his father also mounted a campaign against Champa (see page 354), in 1069. Indeed his expedition against the Cham mirrored his father's in most respects and, like his father, he won. (But unlike his father, he did not execute the Cham king.) Records indicate that he spent a great deal of time trying to father a son and worked his way through numerous concubines and a great deal of incense in the process. At last, after much labour (on his part, and probably on the mother's too, although the texts do not say as much), a son was born to a concubine of common blood in 1066 and named Ly Can Duc.

Ly Can Duc was proclaimed emperor in 1072 when he was only six years old and, surprisingly, remained king until he died in 1127. During the early years of his reign the kingdom faced a succession of crises, largely due to the fact that his young age meant that there was no paramount leader. His death marks the end of the Ly Dynasty for he left no heir, and the crown passed to the maternal clan of his nephew. There followed a period of instability and it was not until 1225 that a new dynasty – the Tran Dynasty – managed to subdue the various competing cliques and bring a semblance of order to the country.

Scholars do not know a great deal about the four generations of kings of the Tran Dynasty. It seems that they established the habit of marrying within the clan, and each king took queens who were either their cousins or, in one case, a half-sister. Such a long period of intermarriage, one imagines, would have had some far-reaching mental consequences, although ironically the collapse of the dynasty seems to have been brought about after one foolish king decided to marry outside the Tran clan. The great achievement of the Tran Dynasty was to resist the expansionist tendencies of the Mongol forces who conquered China in the 1250s and then set their sights on Vietnam. In 1284 a huge Mongol-Yuan force, consisting of no fewer than four armies, massed on the border to crush the Vietnamese. Fortunately the Tran were blessed with a group of brave and resourceful princes, the most notable of whom was Tran Quoc Tuan better known – and now immortalized in street names in just about every Vietnamese town – as **Tran Hung Dao**. Although the invading forces captured Thang Long (Hanoi) they never managed to defeat the Vietnamese in a decisive battle and in the end the forces of the Tran Dynasty were victorious.

Tran Dynasty

Background

Le Dynasty and the emergence of Vietnam

Le Loi   During its struggle with the Cham, nascent Dai Viet had to contend with the weight of Ming Chinese oppression from the north, often in concert with their Cham allies. Despite 1,000 years of Chinese domination and centuries of internal dynastic squabbles the Viet retained a strong sense of national identity and were quick to respond to charismatic leadership. As so often in Vietnam's history one man was able to harness nationalistic sentiment and mould the country's discontent into a powerful fighting force: in 1426 it was Le Loi. Together with the brilliant tactician **Nguyen Trai** (see box, page 353), Le Loi led a campaign to remove the Chinese from Vietnamese soil. Combining surprise, guerrilla tactics and Nguyen Trai's innovative and famous propaganda, designed to convince defending Ming of the futility of their position, the Viet won a resounding victory which led to the enlightened and artistically distinguished Le period. Le Loi's legendary victory lives on in popular form and is celebrated in the tale of the restored sword in water puppet performances across the country. Following his victory against the Ming he claimed the throne in 1428 and reigned until his death five years later.

Le Thanh Ton   With Le Loi's death the Le Dynasty worked its way through a succession of young kings who seemed to hold the throne barely long enough to warm the cushions before they were murdered. It was not until 1460 that a king of substance was to accede: Le Thanh Ton (reigned 1460-97). His reign was a period of great scholarship and artistic accomplishment. He established the system of rule that was to guide successive Vietnamese emperors for 500 years. He also mounted a series of military campaigns, some as far as Laos to the west.

Le expansion   The expansion of the Vietnamese state, under the Le, south from its heartland in the Tonkin Delta, followed the decline of the Cham Kingdom at the end of the 15th century. By the early 18th century the Cham were extinct as an identifiable political and military force and the Vietnamese advanced still further south into the Khmer-controlled territories of the Mekong Delta. This geographical over-extension and the sheer logistical impracticability of ruling from distant Hanoi, disseminating edicts and collecting taxes, led to the disintegration of the – ever tenuous – imperial rule. The old adage 'The edicts of the emperor stop at the village gate' was particularly apt more than 1,000 km from the capital. Noble families, locally dominant, challenged the emperor's authority and the Le Dynasty gradually dissolved into internecine strife and regional fiefdoms, namely Trinh in the north and Nguyen in the south, a pattern that was to reassert itself some 300 years later. But although on paper the Vietnamese – now consisting of two dynastic houses, Trinh and Nguyen – appeared powerful, the people were mired in poverty. There were numerous peasant rebellions in this period, of which the most serious was the **Tay Son rebellion** of 1771 (see page 223). One of the three Tay Son brothers, Nguyen Hue, proclaimed himself **Emperor Quang Trung** in 1788, only to die four years later.

The death of Quang Trung paved the way for the establishment of the **Nguyen Dynasty** – the last Vietnamese dynasty – in 1802 when Emperor Gia Long ascended to the throne in Hué. Despite the fact that this period heralded the arrival of the French – leading to their eventual domination of Vietnam – it is regarded as a golden period in Vietnamese history. During the Nguyen Dynasty, Vietnam was unified as a single state and Hué emerged as the heart of the kingdom.

Nguyen Trai

"Our country, Dai Viet, has long been
A land of ancient culture,
With its own rivers and mountains,
   ways and customs,
Different from those of the North"
(Opening lines of 'Proclamation of victory
over the invaders')

   Nguyen Trai, mandarin, poet and
nationalist rose to prominence as an
adviser to Le Loi during the 10-year
campaign to eject the Ming from Dai Viet.

   His famous counsel "better to win
hearts than citadels" (which mirrors
similar advice during a war over five
centuries later) was heeded by Le Loi who
aroused patriotic fervour in his

compatriots to achieve victory on the
battlefield. It was on Nguyen Trai's
suggestion that 100,000 defeated Ming
troops were given food and boats to
make their way home. After the war,
Nguyen Trai accepted and later resigned
a court post. He was a prolific composer
of verse, which is considered some of the
finest in the national annals. On an
overnight visit to Nguyen Trai, Emperor Le
Thai Tong (Le Loi's son and heir) died
unexpectedly. Scheming courtiers were
able to fix the blame on Nguyen Trai who
in 1442, along with three generations of
his family, were executed, a punishment
known as tru di tam tôc.

History of the non-Viet Civilizations

Any history of Vietnam must include the non-Vietnamese peoples and civilizations. The central and southern parts of Vietnam have only relatively recently been dominated by the Viets. Prior to that, these lands were in the hands of people of Indian or Khmer origins.

Funan (AD 100-600)

According to Chinese sources, Funan was a Hindu kingdom founded in the first century AD with its capital, Vyadhapura, close to the Mekong River near the border with Cambodia. A local legend records that Kaundinya, a great Indian Brahmin, acting on a dream, sailed to the coast of Vietnam carrying with him a bow and arrow. When he arrived, Kaundinya shot the arrow and where it landed he established the capital of Funan. Following this act, Kaundinya married the princess Soma, daughter of the local King of the Nagas (giant water serpents). The legend symbolizes the union between Indian and local cultural traditions – the naga representing indigenous fertility rites and customs, and the arrow, the potency of the Hindu religion.

Funan built its wealth and power on its **strategic location** on the sea route between China and the islands to the south. Maritime technology at the time forced seafarers travelling between China and island Southeast Asia and India to stop and wait for the winds to change before they could continue on their way. This sometimes meant a stay of up to five months. The large port city of Oc-eo (see page 338) offered a safe harbour for merchant vessels and the revenues generated enabled the kings of the empire to expand rice cultivation, dominate a host of surrounding vassal states as far away as the Malay coast and South Burma, and build a series of impressive temples, cities and irrigation works. Although the Chinese chronicler K'ang T'ai records that the Funanese were barbarians – "ugly, black, and frizzy-haired" – it is clear from Chinese court annals that they were artistically and technologically accomplished. It is recorded for example that one Chinese emperor was so impressed by the skill of some visiting musicians in AD 263 that he ordered the establishment of an institute of Funanese music.

Oc-eo

Vietnamese dynasties

Dynasty	Dates	Capital (province)
Hong Bang (legendary)	2876-258 BC	Phong Chau (Son Tay)
Thuc	257-208 BC	Loa Thanh (Vinh Phu)
Trieu	207-111 BC	Phien Ngung (S China)
under Chinese domination 111 BC-AD 23		
Trung Sisters	AD 40-43	Me Linh (Son Tay)
under Chinese domination AD 25- 589		
Early Ly	544-602	various (Hanoi)
under Chinese domination AD 622-938		
Ngo	939-965	Co Loa (Vinh Phuc)
Dinh	968-980	Hoa Lu (Ninh Binh)
Early Le	980-1009	Hoa Lu (Ninh Binh)
Ly	1010-1225	Thang Long (Hanoi)
Tran	1225-1400	Thang Long (Hanoi)
Ho	1400-1407	Dong Do (Hanoi)
Post Tran	1407-1413	
under Chinese domination AD 1414-1427		
Le	1427-1788	Thang Long (Hanoi)
Mac	1527-1592	
Northern Trinh	1539-1787	Hanoi
Southern Nguyen	1558-1778	Hué
Quang Trung	1787-1792	
Nguyen of Tay Son	1788-1802	Saigon
Nguyen	1802-1945	Hué

From the 16th-18th centuries there were up to four centres of power in Vietnam. For a list of Nguyen Emperors see page 178.

Funan reached the peak of its powers in the fourth century and went into decline during the fifth century AD when improving maritime technology made Oc-eo redundant as a haven for sailing vessels. No longer did merchants hug the coastline; ships were now large enough, and navigation skills sophisticated enough, to make the journey from South China to the Malacca Strait without landfall. By the mid-sixth century, Funan, having suffered from a drawn-out leadership crisis, was severely weakened. Neighbouring competing powers took advantage of this crisis, absorbing previously Funan-controlled lands. Irrigation works fell into disrepair as state control weakened, and peasants left the fields to seek more productive lands elsewhere. Funan, having lost both the economic wealth and the religious legitimacy on which its power had been based, was ultimately conquered by the Cham.

What is interesting about Funan is the degree to which it provided a model for future states in Southeast Asia. Funan's wealth was built on its links with the sea, and with its ability to exploit maritime trade. The later rulers of Champa, Langkasuka (Malaya), Srivijaya (Sumatra), and Malacca (Malaya) repeated this formula.

Champa (AD 200–1720)

In South Vietnam, where the dynastic lords achieved hegemony only in the 18th century, the kingdom of Champa – or Lin-yi as the Chinese called it – was the most significant power. The kingdom evolved in the second century AD and was focused on the narrow ribbon of lowland that runs north-south down the Annamite coast, with its various capitals near the present-day city of Danang. Chinese sources record that in AD 192 a local official, Kiu-lien, rejected Chinese authority and established an independent kingdom. From then on, Champa's history was one of conflict with its neighbour: when Imperial China was powerful, Champa was subservient and sent ambassadors and tributes in homage to the Chinese court; when it was weak, the rulers of Champa extended their own influence and ignored the Chinese.

The difficulty for scholars is to decide whether Champa had a single identity or whether it consisted of numerous mini-powers with no dominant centre. The accepted wisdom at the moment is that Champa was more diffuse than previously thought, and that only rarely during its history is it possible to talk of Champa in singular terms. The endless shifting of the capital of Champa is taken to reflect the shifting centres of power that characterized this 'kingdom'.

Like Funan, Champa built its power on its position on the **maritime trading route** through Southeast Asia. During the fourth century, as Champa expanded into previously Funan-controlled lands, they came under the influence of the Indian cultural traditions of the Funanese. These were enthusiastically embraced by Champa's rulers who tacked the suffix '-varman' onto their names (for example Bhadravarman) and adopted the Hindu-Buddhist cosmology. Though a powerful trading kingdom, Champa was geographically poorly endowed. The coastal strip between the Annamite highlands to the west, and the sea to the east, is narrow and the potential for extensive rice cultivation limited. This may explain why the Champa Empire was never more than a moderate power: it was unable to produce the agricultural surplus necessary to support an extensive court and army, and therefore could not compete with either the Khmers to the south nor with the Viets to the north. But the Cham were able to carve out a niche for themselves between the two, and to many art historians, their art and architecture represent the finest that Vietnam has ever produced (see pages 208 and 403). Remains litter the central Vietnamese coast from Quang Tri in the north, to Ham Tan 800 km to the south.

For over 1,000 years the Cham resisted the Chinese and the Vietnamese. But by the time Marco Polo wrote of the Cham, their power and prestige were much reduced: "The people are idolators and pay a yearly tribute to the Great Kaan which consists of elephants and nothing but elephants. ... In the year of Christ 1285 ... the King had, between sons and daughters, 326 children. There are a very great number of elephants in that country, and they have lignaloes (eagle wood) in great abundance. They have also extensive forests of the wood called Bonús, which is jet black, of which chessmen and pencases are made. But there is nought more to tell, so let us proceed." After 1285, when invading Mongol hoardes were repelled by the valiant Viets, Champa and Dai Viet enjoyed an uneasy peace maintained by the liberal flow of royal princesses south across the Col des Nuages (Hai Van Pass) in exchange for territory. During the peaceful reign of Che A-nan a Franciscan priest, Odoric of Pordenone, reported of Champa "'tis a very fine country, having a great store of victuals and of all good things". Of particular interest, he refers to the practice of suti, writing "When a man dies in this country, they burn his wife with him, for they say that she should live with him in the other world also". Clearly, some of the ancient Indian traditions continued.

Champa saw a late flowering under King Binasuos who led numerous successful campaigns against the Viet, culminating in the sack of Hanoi in 1371. Subsequently, the treachery of a low-ranking officer led to Binasuos' death in 1390 and the military eclipse of the Cham by the Vietnamese. The demographic and economic superiority of the Viet coupled with their gradual drift south contributed most to the waning of the Cham Kingdom, but finally, in 1471 the Cham suffered a terrible defeat at the hands of the Vietnamese. 60,000 of their soldiers were killed and another 36,000 captured and carried into captivity, including the King and 50 members of the royal family. The kingdom shrank to a small territory in the vicinity of Nha Trang which

Background

A Spanish account of Champa circa 1595

This account of Champa is taken from an anonymous manuscript compiled in Manila about 1590-95, possibly as part of the documentation assembled by Don Luis Perez das Marinas in justification of his scheme for the conquest of Indochina.

"It is a land fertile in foodstuffs and cows and oxen and very healthy in itself. It is not thickly populated and the people are swarthy and heathens. In this kingdom there is no money nor silver with which to sell anything; and in order to buy what they need, they exchange foodstuffs for cotton blankets and other things which they make for the purpose of buying and selling with each other. Nobody is allowed to go shod, save only the king, and nobody can be married with more than two wives.

Food and drink

These people do not eat anything properly cooked, but only in raw or putrid condition; and in order to digest these foods, they are great drinkers of very strong spirits, which they drink little by little and very frequently, thinking it no disgrace to fall down from drinking too much.

Seasons

They divide the year into six festivals, during the first of which the vast majority of his vassals pay tribute to the king. The king goes to a field, and there they assemble all these tributes, out of which they make alms to the souls of the dead and perform great obsequies and funeral rites in their memory.

The second festival also lasts two months and they spend the whole of this time singing to the exclusion of everything else, except when they are actually eating their meals. During these festivals the women, of whatsoever condition they be, have liberty to do what they like for the space of three days, during which they are not asked to account for their behaviour.

During the third festival they go to the seaside, where they stay fishing for another two months. They make merry catching enough fish to last them for the year, pickling it in their jars, with just a little salt, and they eat it putrid in this manner. And they thrive very strong and lusty on this food.

When the king returns to the city, they display lights by night and day, putting on plays and races in public, in which the king participates. This celebration is the fourth of their festivals.

The fifth is when the king goes hunting elephants, of which there are many in this land, taking with him the nobility and their female elephants; and the females go into the place where the wild elephants are, which follow the former into a little space which they have stockaded off for this purpose, and there they keep them for some days until they are tamed.

The last festival which they celebrate is a tiger-hunt. The tigers come to eat the buffaloes which are tied to a tree in

---

survived until 1720 when surviving members of the royal family and many subjects fled to Cambodia to escape from the advancing Vietnamese.

The colonial period

One of the key motivating factors that encouraged the **French** to undermine the authority of the Vietnamese emperors was their treatment of Roman Catholics. Jesuits had been in the country from as early as the 17th century – one of them, Alexandre-de-Rhodes, converted the Vietnamese writing system from Chinese characters to romanized script (see page 410) – but persecution of Roman Catholics began only in the 1830s. Emperor Minh Mang issued an imperial edict outlawing the dissemination of Christianity as a heterodox creed in 1825. The first European priest to be executed was François Isidore Gagelin who was strangled by six soldiers as he knelt on a scaffold in Hué in 1833. Three days later, having been told that Christians

certain places. They place sentinels over them, so that when the tigers approach, the king is informed. And as soon as this news arrives the king gets ready with a great number of Indians and nets, and they do with the tigers what they do with the elephants, surrounding them at once and killing them there and then. It is the custom with these Indians that at the time when they are occupied with this hunt, the king and his wife send out 100 or more Indians along the roads, with express order that they should not return without filling two gold basins which they give them, full of human gall, which must be from people of their own nation and not foreigners; and these emissaries do as they are told, not sparing anyone they meet, whether of high or low degree. As soon as they can catch a person on the road, they tie him at once to a tree, and there they cut out the gall ... When all this is over the king and his wife bathe and wash with this human gall; and they say that in this way they cleanse themselves of their sins and their faults.

Justice

The justice of this people is peculiar, for they have no fixed criminal code, but only their personal opinions, and when the case is a serious one, they investigate it with two witnesses. Their oaths are made with fire and boiling oil, and those condemned to death are executed with extreme barbarity. Some are sentenced to be trampled to death by elephants; others are flogged to death; others are tortured for two or three days, during which time bits and pieces are cut out of their bodies with pincers until they die. And for very trifling and common offences, they cut off their feet, hands, arms and ears.

Death

They have another custom invented by the Devil himself, which is that when any leading personage dies, they cremate the body, after it has been kept for eight or 10 days until they have made the necessary preparations in accordance with the quality of the deceased, when they burn it in the field. When such a person dies, they sieze all the household servants and keep them until the same day on which they burn the body of their master, and then they throw them alive into the flames, so that they can serve them therewith in the other ... Another custom which they have, which is a very harsh one for women, is that when the husband dies, they burn the wife with him. They say that this law was made to prevent wives from giving poisonous herbs to their husbands, for there are very great witchcrafts and knaveries in these lands. They say that if the wife realizes that her husband will not live any longer than her, she will take good care of his life and ease, and will not dare to kill him with poison.

Background

believe they will come to life again, Minh Mang had the body exhumed to confirm the man's death. In 1840 Minh Mang actually read the Old Testament in Chinese translation, declaring it to be 'absurd'.

Yet, Christianity continued to spread as Buddhism declined, and there was a continual stream of priests willing to risk their lives proselytizing. In addition, the economy was in disarray and natural disasters common. Poor Vietnamese saw Christianity as a way to break the shackles of their feudal existence. Fearing a peasants' revolt, the Emperor ordered the execution of 25 European priests, 300 Vietnamese priests, and 30,000 Vietnamese Catholics between 1848 and 1860. Provoked by these killings, the French attacked and took Saigon in 1859. In 1862 **Emperor Tu Duc** signed a treaty ceding the three southern provinces to the French, thereby creating the colony of Cochin China. This treaty of 1862 effectively paved the way for the eventual seizure by the French of the whole kingdom. The French, through weight of arms, also forced the Emperor to end the persecution of

Christians in his kingdom. In retrospect, although many Christians did die cruelly, the degree of persecution was not on the scale of similar episodes elsewhere: Minh Mang's successors Thieu Tri (1841-47) and Tu Duc (1847-83), though both *fervently* anti-Christian, appreciated French military strength and the fact that they were searching for pretexts to intervene.

The French conquest of the north was motivated by a desire to control trade and the route to what were presumed to be the vast riches of China. In 1883 and 1884, the French forced the Emperor to sign treaties making Vietnam a French protectorate. In August 1883 for example, just after Tu Duc's death, a French fleet appeared off Hué to force concessions. François Harmand, a native affairs official on board one of the ships, threatened the Vietnamese by stating: "Imagine all that is terrible and it will still be less than reality ... the word 'Vietnam' will be erased from history." The emperor called on China for assistance and demanded that provinces resist French rule; but the imperial bidding proved ineffective, and in 1885 the **Treaty of Tientsin** recognized the French protectorates of Tonkin (North Vietnam) and Annam (Central Vietnam), to add to that of Cochin China (South Vietnam).

Resistance to the French: the prelude to revolution

Like other European powers in Southeast Asia, the French managed to achieve military victory with ease, but they failed to stifle Vietnamese nationalism. After 1900, as Chinese translations of the works of Rousseau, Voltaire and social Darwinists such as Herbert Spence began to find their way into the hands of the Vietnamese intelligentsia, so resistance grew. Foremost among these early nationalists were Phan Boi Chau (1867-1940) and Phan Chau Trinh (1871-1926) who wrote tracts calling for the expulsion of the French. But these men and others such as Prince Cuong De (1882-1951) were traditional nationalists, their beliefs rooted in Confucianism rather than revolutionary Marxism. Their efforts and perspectives were essentially in the tradition of the nationalists who had resisted Chinese domination over previous centuries.

Quoc Dan Dang (VNQDD), founded at the end of 1927, was the first nationalist party, while the first significant Communist group was the **Indochina Communist Party (ICP)** established by Ho Chi Minh in 1930 (see profile, page 360). Both the VNQDD and the ICP organized resistance to the French and there were numerous

French colonial troops and a wealthy Vietnamese mandarin flee from a victorious band of nationalist peasant rebels in this 1930s cartoon. The victors are shouting "Wipe out the gang of imperialists, mandarins, capitalists and big landlords!"
Source: Archives Nationales de France

strikes and uprisings, particularly during the harsh years of the Great Depression. The Japanese 'occupation' from August 1940 (Vichy France permitted the Japanese full access to military facilities in exchange for allowing continued French administrative control) saw the creation of the **Viet Minh** to fight for the liberation of Vietnam from Japanese and French control.

The Vietnam Wars

The First Indochina War (1945-54)

The Vietnam War started in September 1945 in the south of the country, and in 1946 in the north. These years marked the onset of fighting **between the Viet Minh and the French** and the period is usually referred to as the First Indochina War. The Communists, who had organized against the Japanese, proclaimed the creation of the Democratic Republic of Vietnam (DRV) on 2 September 1945 when Ho Chi Minh read out the Vietnamese **Declaration of Independence** in Hanoi's Ba Dinh Square. Ironically, this document was modelled closely on the American Declaration of Independence. Indeed, the US was favourably disposed towards the Viet Minh and Ho. Operatives of the OSS (the wartime precursor to the CIA) met Ho and supported his efforts during the War, and afterwards Roosevelt's inclination was to prevent France claiming their colony back. Only Winston Churchill's persuasion changed his mind.

The French, although they had always insisted that Vietnam be returned to French rule, were in no position to force the issue. Instead, in the south, it was British troops (mainly Gurkhas) who helped the small force of French against the Viet Minh. Incredibly, the British also ordered the Japanese, who had only just capitulated, to help fight the Vietnamese. When 35,000 French reinforcements arrived, the issue in the south – at least superficially – was all but settled, with Ca Mau at the southern extremity of the country falling on 21 October. From that point, the war in the south became an underground battle of attrition, with the north providing support to their southern comrades.

In the north, the Viet Minh had to deal with 180,000 rampaging Nationalist Chinese troops, while preparing for the imminent arrival of a French force. Unable to confront both at the same time, and deciding that the French were probably the lesser of two evils, Ho Chi Minh decided to negotiate. He is said to have observed in private, that it was preferable to 'sniff French shit for a while than eat China's all our lives'. To make the DRV government more acceptable to the French, Ho proceeded cautiously, only nationalizing a few strategic industries, bringing moderates into the government, and actually dissolving the Indochinese Communist Party (at least on paper) in November 1945. But in the same month Ho also said: "The French colonialists should know that the Vietnamese people do not wish to spill blood, that it loves peace. But if it must sacrifice millions of combatants, lead a resistance for long years to defend the independence of the country, and preserve its children from slavery, it will do so. It is certain the resistance will win."

In February 1946, the French and Chinese signed a treaty leading to the withdrawal of Chinese forces, and shortly afterwards Ho concluded a treaty with French President de Gaulle's special emissary to Vietnam, Jean Sainteny in which Vietnam was recognized as a 'free' (the Vietnamese word *doc lap* being translated as free, but not yet independent) state within the French Union and the Indochinese Federation.

It is interesting to note that in negotiating with the French, Ho was going against the wishes of most of his supporters who argued for confrontation. But Ho, ever a pragmatist, believed at this stage that the Viet Minh were ill-trained and poorly

Background

Chinese withdrawal

Ho Chi Minh: 'He who enlightens'

Ho Chi Minh, one of a number of pseudonyms Ho adopted during his life, was born Nguyen Sinh Cung, or possibly Nguyen Van Thanh (Ho did not keep a diary during much of his life, so parts of his life are still a mystery), in Nghe An Province near Vinh on the 19 May 1890, and came from a poor scholar-gentry family. In the village, the family was aristocratic; beyond it they were little more than peasants. His father, though not a revolutionary, was a dissenter and rather than go to Hué to serve the French, he chose to work as a village school teacher. Ho must have been influenced by his father's implacable animosity towards the French, although Ho's early years are obscure. He went to Quoc Hoc College in Hué, and then worked for a while as a teacher in Phan Thiet, a fishing village in South Annam.

In 1911, under the name Nguyen Tat Thanh, he travelled to Saigon and left the country as a messboy on the French ship Amiral Latouche-Tréville. He is said to have used the name 'Ba' so that he would not shame his family by accepting such lowly work. This marked the beginning of three years of travel during which he visited France, England, America (where the skyscrapers of Manhattan both amazed and appalled him) and North Africa. Seeing the colonialists on their own turf and reading such revolutionary literature

as the French Communist Party newspaper L'Humanité, he was converted to communism. In Paris he mixed with leftists, wrote pamphlets and attended meetings of the French Socialist Party. He also took odd jobs: for a while he worked at the Carlton Hotel in London and became an assistant pastry chef under the legendary French chef Georges Escoffier.

An even more unlikely story emerges from Gavin Young's book A Wavering Grace. *In the book he recounts an interview he conducted with Mae West in 1968 shortly after he had returned from reporting the Tet offensive. On hearing of Vietnam, Mae West innocently said that she "used to know someone very, very important there ... His name was Ho ... Ho ... Ho something". At the time she was staying at the Carlton while starring in a London show,* Sex. *She confided to Young: "There was this waiter, cook, I don't know what he was. I know he had the slinkiest eyes though. We met in the corridor. We – well ...". Young writes that "Her voice trailed off in a husky sigh ..."*

Gradually Ho became an ever-more-committed communist, contributing articles to radical newspapers and working his way into the web of communist and leftist groups. At the same time he remained, curiously, a French cultural chauvinist, complaining

armed and he appreciated the need for time to consolidate their position. The episode that is usually highlighted as the flashpoint that led to the resumption of hostilities was the French government's decision to open a customs house in Haiphong at the end of 1946. The Viet Minh forces resisted and the rest, as they say, is history. It seems that during the course of 1946 Ho changed his view of the best path to independence. Initially he asked: "Why should we sacrifice 50 or 100,000 men when we can achieve independence within five years through negotiation?", but he later came to the conclusion that it was necessary to fight for independence. The customs house episode might, therefore, be viewed as merely an excuse. The French claimed that 5,000 Vietnamese were killed in the ensuing bombardment, as against five Frenchmen; the Vietnamese put the toll at 20,000.

In a pattern that was to become characteristic of the entire 25-year conflict, while the French controlled the cities, the Viet Minh were dominant in the countryside. By the end of 1949, with the success of the Chinese Revolution and the establishment of the Democratic People's Republic of Korea (North Korea) in 1948, the United States began to offer support to the French in an attempt to stem the 'Red Tide' that

for example about the intrusion of English words like 'le manager' and 'le challenger' (referring to boxing contests) into the French language. He even urged the French Prime Minister to ban foreign words from the French press. In 1923 he left France for Moscow and was trained as a communist activist – effectively a spy. From there, Ho travelled to Canton where he was instrumental in forming the Vietnamese Communist movement. This culminated in the creation of the Indo-China Communist Party in 1930. His movements during these years are scantily documented: he became a Buddhist monk in Siam (Thailand), was arrested in Hong Kong for subversive activities and received a six month sentence, travelled to China several times, and in 1940 even returned to Vietnam for a short period – his first visit for nearly 30 years. Despite his absence from the country, the French had already recognized the threat that he posed and sentenced him to death in absentia in 1930. He did not adopt the pseudonym by which he is now best known – Ho Chi Minh – until the early 1940s.

Ho was a consummate politician and, despite his revolutionary fervour, a great realist. He was also a charming man, and during his stay in France between June and October 1946, he made a great number of friends. Robert Shaplen in his book The Lost Revolution (1965) talks of his "wit, his oriental courtesy, his savoir-faire ... above all his seeming sincerity and simplicity". He talked with farmers and fishermen, and debated with priests; he impressed people wherever he travelled. He died in Hanoi at his house within the former governor's residence in 1969 (see page 75).

Since the demise of communism in the former Soviet Union, the Vietnamese leadership have been concerned that secrets about Ho's life might be gleaned from old comintern files in Moscow by nosy journalists. To thwart such an eventuality, they have, reportedly, sent a senior historian to scour the archives. To date, Ho's image remains largely untarnished – making him an exception amongst the tawdry league of former communist leaders. But a Moscow-based reporter has unearthed evidence implying Ho was married, challenging the official hagiography that paints Ho as a celibate who committed his entire life to the revolution. It takes a brave Vietnamese to challenge established 'fact'. In 1991, when the popular Vietnamese Youth or Tuoi Tre newspaper dared to suggest that Ho had married Tang Tuyet Minh in China in 1926, the editor was summarily dismissed from her post.

Background

seemed to be sweeping across Asia. At this early stage, the odds appeared stacked against the Viet Minh, but Ho was confident that time was on their side. As he remarked to Sainteny "If we have to fight, we will fight. You can kill 10 of my men for every one I kill of yours but even at those odds, I will win and you will lose". It also became increasingly clear that the French were not committed to negotiating a route to independence. A secret French report prepared in 1948 was obtained and then published by the Viet Minh in which the High Commissioner, Monsieur Bollaert wrote: "It is my impression that we must make a concession to Viet-Nam of the term, independence; but I am convinced that this word need never be interpreted in any light other than that of a religious verbalism."

The decisive battle of the First Indochina War was at Dien Bien Phu in the hills of the northwest, close to the border with Laos. At the end of 1953 the French, with American support, parachuted 16,000 men into the area in an attempt to protect Laos from Viet Minh incursions and to tempt them into open battle. The French in fact found themselves trapped, surrounded by Viet Minh and overlooked by artillery. There was some

Dien Bien Phu (1954)

Ho Chi Minh Pseudonyms

Born 1890:	Nguyen Sinh Cung or
	Nguyen Van Thanh (Vinh)
1910:	Van Ba (South Vietnam)
1911:	Nguyen Tat Thanh (Saigon)
1913:	Nguyen Tat Thanh (London)
1914:	Nguyen Ai Quoc (Paris)
1924:	Linh (Moscow)
1924:	Ly Thuy (Moscow)
1925:	Wang (Canton)
1927:	Duong (Paris)
1928:	Nguyen Lai, Nam Son,
	Thau Chin (Siam)
1942:	Ho Chi Minh

suggestion that the United States might become involved, and even use tactical nuclear weapons, but this was not to be. In May 1954 the French surrendered – the most humiliating of French colonial defeats – effectively marking the end of the French presence in Indochina. In July 1954, in Geneva, the French and Vietnamese agreed to divide the country along the 17th parallel, so creating two states (for a fuller account of the battle see page 112) – the Communists occupying the north and the non-Communists occupying the south. The border was kept open for 300 days and over that period about 900,000 – mostly Roman Catholic – Vietnamese travelled south. At the same time nearly 90,000 Viet Minh troops along with 43,000 civilians, went north, although many Viet Minh remained in the south to continue the fight there.

The Second Indochina War (1954-75)

The Vietnam War, but particularly the American part of that war, is probably the most minutely studied, reported, analysed and recorded in history. Yet, as with all wars, there are still large grey areas and continuing disagreement over important episodes. Most crucially, there is the question of whether the US might have won had their forces been given a free hand and were not forced, as some would have it, to fight with one hand tied behind their backs. This remains the view among many members of the US military.

Ngo Dinh Diem At the time of the partition of Vietnam along the 17th parallel, the government in the south was chaotic and the Communists could be fairly confident that in a short time their sympathizers would be victorious. This situation was to change with the rise of Ngo Dinh Diem. Born in Hué in 1901 to a Roman Catholic Confucian family, Diem wished to become a priest. He graduated at the top of his class from the French School of Administration and at the age of 32 was appointed to the post of Minister of the Interior at the court of Emperor Bao Dai. Here, according to the political scientist William Turley "he worked with uncommon industry and integrity" only to resign in exasperation at court intrigues and French interference. He withdrew from political activity during the First Indochina War and in 1946 Ho Chi Minh offered him a post in the DRV government – an offer he declined. Turley describes him as a man who was, in many respects, a creature of the past:

> "For Diem, the mandarin, political leadership meant rule by example, precept, and paternalism. His Catholic upbringing reinforced rather than replaced the Confucian tendency to base authority on doctrine, morality and hierarchy. Utterly alien to him were the concepts of power-sharing, and popular participation. He was in fact the heir to a dying tradition, member of an élite that had been superbly prepared by birth, training, and experience to lead a Vietnam that no longer existed."

In July 1954 Diem returned from his self-imposed exile at the Maryknoll Seminary in New Jersey to become Premier of South Vietnam. It is usually alleged that the US

Background

administration was behind his rise to power, although this has yet to be proved. He held two rigged elections (in October 1955, 450,000 registered voters cast 605,025 votes) which gave some legitimacy to his administration in American eyes. He proceeded to suppress all opposition in the country. His brutal brother, Ngo Dinh Nhu, was appointed to head the security forces and terrorized much of Vietnamese society.

During the period of Diem's premiership, opposition to his rule, particularly in the countryside, increased. This was because the military's campaign against the Viet Minh targeted – both directly and indirectly – many innocent peasants. At the same time, the nepotism and corruption that was endemic within the administration also turned many people into Viet Minh sympathizers. That said, Diem's campaign was successful in undermining the strength of the Communist Party in the south. While there were perhaps 50,000-60,000 Party members in 1954, this figure had declined through widespread arrests and intimidation to only 5,000 by 1959.

The erosion of the Party in the south gradually led, from 1959, to the north changing its strategy towards one of more overt military confrontation. The same year also saw the establishment of Group 559 which was charged with the task of setting up what was to become the Ho Chi Minh Trail, along which supplies and troops were moved from the north to the south (see page 194). But, even at this stage, the Party's forces in the south were kept from open confrontation and many of its leaders were hoping for victory without having to resort to open warfare. There was no call for a 'People's War' and armed resistance was left largely to guerrillas belonging to the Cao Dai (see page 419) and Hoa Hao (Buddhist millenarian) sects. The establishment of the National Liberation Front of Vietnam in 1960 was an important political and organizational development towards creating a credible alternative to Diem – although it did not hold its first congress until 1962.

The escalation of the armed conflict (1959-63)

The armed conflict began to intensify from the beginning of 1961 when all the armed forces under the Communists' control were unified under the banner of the People's Liberation Armed Forces (PLAF). By this time the Americans were already using the term Viet Cong (or VC) to refer to Communist troops. They reasoned that the victory at Dien Bien Phu had conferred almost heroic status on the name Viet Minh. American psychological warfare specialists therefore invented the term Viet Cong, an abbreviation of *Viet-nam Cong-san* (or Vietnamese Communists), and persuaded the media in Saigon to begin substituting it for Viet Minh from 1956.

Viet Cong

Background

The election of **John F Kennedy** to the White House in January 1961 coincided with the Communists' decision to widen the war in the south. In the same year Kennedy dispatched 400 special forces troops and 100 special military advisers to Vietnam – in flagrant contravention of the Geneva Agreement. With the cold war getting colder, and Soviet Premier Nikita Khrushchev confirming his support for wars of 'national liberation', Kennedy could not back down and by the end of 1962 there were 11,000 US personnel in South Vietnam. At the same time the NLF had around 23,000 troops at its disposal. Kennedy was still saying that "In the final analysis, it's their war and they're the ones who have to win or lose it". But just months after the Bay of Pigs débâcle in Cuba, Washington set out on the path that was ultimately to lead to America's first large-scale military defeat.

The bungling and incompetence of the forces of the south, the interference which US advisers and troops had to face, the misreading of the situation by US military commanders, and the skill – both military and political – of the Communists, are most vividly recounted in Neil Sheehan's massive book, *A Bright Shining Lie* (see page 429). The conflict quickly escalated from 1959. The north infiltrated about 44,000 men and women into the south between then and 1964, while the number recruited in the south was between 60,000 and 100,000. In August 1959, the first consignment of arms was carried down the **Ho Chi Minh Trail** into South Vietnam. Meanwhile, Kennedy began supporting, arming and training the Army of the Republic of Vietnam (ARVN). The US however, shied away from any large-scale, direct confrontation between its forces and the Viet Cong.

An important element in Diem's military strategy at this time was the establishment of '**strategic hamlets**', better known simply as 'hamleting'. This strategy was modelled on British anti-guerrilla warfare during Malaya's Communist insurgency, and aimed to deny the Communists any bases of support in the countryside while at the same time making it more difficult for Communists to infiltrate the villages and 'propagandize' there. The villages which were ringed by barbed-wire were labelled 'concentration camps' by the Communists, and the often brutal, forced relocation that peasants had to endure probably turned even more of them into Communist sympathizers. Of the 7,000-8,000 villages sealed in this way, only a fifth could ever have been considered watertight.

In January 1963 at Ap Bac, not far from the town of My Tho, the Communists scored their first significant victory in the south. Facing 2,000 well armed ARVN troops, a force of just 300-400 PLAF inflicted heavy casualties and downed five helicopters. After this defeat, many American advisers drew the conclusion that if the Communists were to be defeated, it could not be left to the ARVN alone – US troops would have to become directly involved. As John Vann, a key American military adviser, remarked after the débâcle when lambasting South Vietnamese officers: "A miserable fucking performance, just like it always is." In mid-1963 a Buddhist monk from Hué committed suicide by dousing his body with petrol and setting it alight. This was the first of a number of self-immolations, suggesting that even in the early days the Diem régime was not only losing the military war but also the 'hearts and minds' war (see page 282). He responded with characteristic heavy-handedness by ransacking suspect pagodas. On 1 December 1963, Diem and his brother-in-law Nhu were both assassinated during an army coup.

The American war in Vietnam

America's decision to enter the war has been the subject of considerable disagreement. Until recently, the received wisdom was that the US administration had already taken the decision, and manufactured events to justify their later actions. However, the recent publication of numerous State Department, Presidential, CIA, Defence Department and National Security Council files – all dating from 1964 – has shed new light on events leading up to American intervention (these files are contained in the United States Government Printing Office's 1,108 page-long *Vietnam 1964*).

In Roger Warner's *Back Fire* (1995) which deals largely with the CIA's secret war in Laos he recounts a story of a war game commissioned by the Pentagon and played by the Rand Corporation in 1962. They were asked to play a week-long game simulating a 10-year conflict in Vietnam. At the end of the week, having committed 500,000 men, the US forces were bogged down, there was student unrest, and the American population had lost confidence in their leaders and in the conduct of the war. When the game was played a year later but, on the insistence of the US Airforce, with much heavier aerial bombing, the conclusions were much the same. If only, if only …

By all accounts, **Lyndon Johnson** was a reluctant warrior. In the 1964 presidential campaign he repeatedly said "We don't want our American boys to do the fighting for Asian boys". This was not just for public consumption. The files show that LBJ always doubted the wisdom of intervention. But he also believed that John F Kennedy had made a solemn pledge to help the South Vietnamese people – a pledge that he was morally obliged to keep. In most respects, LBJ was completely in agreement with Congress, together with sections of the American public, who were disquietened by events in South Vietnam. The Buddhist monk's self-immolation, broadcast on prime-time news, did not help matters.

It has usually been argued that the executive manufactured the '**Gulf of Tonkin Incident**' to force Congress and the public to approve an escalation of America's role in the conflict. It was reported that two American destroyers, the *USS Maddox* and *USS C Turner Joy*, were attacked without provocation in

Vietnam War

NORTH VIETNAM

CHINA

Dien Bien Phu

Haiphong

HANOI

LAOS

Sam Neua

Luang Prabang

Phonsavanh

Plain of Jars

Gulf of Tonkin

VIENTIANE

Mekong

Ho Chi Minh Trail

Demilitarized Zone (22-7-54)

Khe Sanh

Quang Tri

Hamburger Hill

Hué

THAILAND

Danang

My Lai

Kontum

Pleiku

Ia Drang Valley

Qui Nhon

CAMBODIA

SOUTH VIETNAM

Mekong

Ho Chi Minh Trail

Dalat

Cam Ranh Bay

PHNOM PENH

Tay Ninh

Cu Chi

Bien Hoa

Vung Tao

SAIGON

Sihanoukville

Can Tho

Ap Bac

South China Sea

Gulf of Thailand

Ca Mau

N

0 km 100

0 miles 100

Background

A War glossary

Agent Orange	herbicide used to defoliate forests
APC	armoured personnel carrier
ARVN	Army of the Republic of Vietnam; the army of the South
Body Count	the number of dead on a field of battle
BUFF	nick-name for the B-52 bomber; stands for Big Ugly Fat Fellow or, more usually, Big Ugly Fat F*****
COIN	counter-insurgency
DMZ	demilitarized zone; the border between North and South Vietnam at the 17th parallel
Dust-off	medical evacuation helicopter
DZ	parachute drop zone
FAC	forward air controller, airborne spotter who directed bombers onto the target
Fire base	defence fortification for artillery to support Infantry from
Fragging	to kill or attempt to kill with a fragmentation grenade; better known as the killing of US officers and NCOs by their own men. In 1970 one study reported 209 fraggings
Gook	slang, derogatory term for all Vietnamese
Grunt	slang for a US infantryman; the word comes from the 'grunt' emitted when shouldering a heavy pack
Huey	most commonly used helicopter, UH1
LZ	helicopter landing zone
Napalm	jellified fuel, the name derives from two of its constituents, naphthenic and palmitic acids. To be burnt by napalm after an attack was terrible and one of the most famous photo images of the war (taken by Nick Ut) showed a naked local girl (Kim Phuc) running along a road at Trang Bang, northwest of Saigon after being burnt; the girl survived the attack by South Vietnamese aircraft and now lives in Canada
NLF	National Liberation Front
NVA	North Vietnamese Army
PAVN	People's Army of Vietnam
Phoenix	counter-insurgency programme established by the US after the Tet Offensive of 1968 (see page 371)
PLAF	People's Liberation Armed Forces; the army of the Communist North
POW/MIA	prisoner of war/missing in action
Pungi stakes	sharpened bamboo stakes concealed in VC pits: accounted for 2% of US combat wounds
Purple Heart	medal awarded to US troops wounded in action
R&R	Rest & Recreation; leave
ROE	rules of engagement
Rome Plow	20 tonne bulldozer designed to clear forest. Equipped with a curved blade and sharp protruding spike it could split the largest trees
Tunnel Rats	US army volunteers who fought VC in the Cu Chi tunnels
VC, Charlie	Viet Cong (see page 363); US term for Vietnamese Communist; often shortened to Charlie from the phonetic alphabet, Victor Charlie
Viet Minh	Communist troops – later changed to Viet Cong (see above and page 363)
WP, Willy Pete	White phosphorous rocket used to mark a target

Background

international waters on the 2 August 1964 by North Vietnamese patrol craft. The US responded by bombing shore installations while presenting the Gulf of Tonkin Resolution to an outraged Congress for approval. Only two Congressmen voted against the resolution and President Johnson's poll rating jumped from 42% to 72%. In reality, the *USS Maddox* had been involved in electronic intelligence-gathering while supporting clandestine raids by South Vietnamese mercenaries – well inside North Vietnamese territorial waters. This deception only became apparent in 1971 when the *Pentagon papers*, documenting the circumstances behind the incident, were leaked to the *New York Times* (the Pentagon papers were commissioned by Defense Secretary McNamara in June 1967 and written by 36 Indochina experts).

The War in figures

Vietnamese:

Killed (soldiers of the North)	1,100,000
Killed (soldiers of the South)	250,000
Vietnamese civilians	2,000,000

Americans:

Served	3,300,000
Killed	57,605
Captured	766 (651 returned)
Wounded	303,700
MIA	4,993 (121 returned, 4,872 declared dead)

Australians:

Killed	423
Wounded	2,398

At height of the war:

Bombs dropped	1.2 million tonnes/year
Cost of bombs	US$14 bn/year
Area defoliated	2.2 million ha (1962-71)
US air attacks	400,000/year
Refugees	585,000/year
Civilian casualties	130,000/month

But these events are not sufficient to argue that the incident was manufactured to allow LBJ to start an undeclared war against North Vietnam. On 4 August, Secretary of State Dean Rusk told the American representative at the United Nations that: "In no sense is this destroyer a pretext to make a big thing out of a little thing". Even as late as the end of 1964, the President was unconvinced by arguments that the US should become more deeply involved. On 31 August, McGeorge Bundy wrote in a memorandum to Johnson: "A still more drastic possibility which no one is discussing is the use of substantial US armed forces in operation against the Viet Cong. I myself believe that before we let this country go we should have a hard look at this grim alternative, and I do not at all think that it is a repetition of Korea."

But events overtook President Johnson, and by 1965 the US was firmly embarked on the road to defeat. In March 1965, he ordered the beginning of the air war against the north perhaps acting on Air Force General Curtis Le May's observation that "we are swatting flies when we should be going after the manure pile". **Operation Rolling Thunder**, the most intense bombing campaign any country had yet experienced, began in March 1965 and ran through to October 1968. In 3½ years, twice the tonnage of bombs was dropped on Vietnam (and Laos) as during the entire Second World War. During its peak in 1967, 12,000 sorties were being flown each month – a total of 108,000 were flown throughout 1967. North Vietnam claimed that 4,000 out of its 5,788 villages were hit. Most terrifying were the B-52s which dropped their bombs from such altitude (17,000 m) that the attack could not even be heard until the bombs hit their targets. Each aircraft carried 20 tonnes of bombs. By the end of the American war in 1973, 14 million tonnes of all types of munitions had been used in Indochina, an explosive force representing 700 times that of the atomic bomb dropped on Hiroshima. As General Curtis Le May explained on 25 November 1965 – "We should bomb them back into the Stone Age". In the same month that Rolling Thunder commenced, marines landed at Danang to defend its airbase, and by June 1965 there were 74,000 US troops in Vietnam. Despite President Johnson's reluctance to commit the US to the conflict, events forced his hand. He realized that the

The Anzacs in Vietnam

In April 1964, President Johnson called for "more flags" to help defend South Vietnam. Among the countries that responded to his call were Australia and New Zealand. Australia had military advisers in Vietnam from 1962, but in April 1965 sent the 1st Battalion Royal Australian Regiment. Until 1972, there were about 7,000 Australian combat troops in Vietnam, based in the coastal province of Phuoc Tuy, not far from Saigon. There, operating as a self-contained unit in a Viet Cong-controlled zone, and with the support of two batteries of 105 mm artillery (one New Zealand), the Australians fought one of the most effective campaigns of the entire war. As **Chief of Staff, US Army**, **General Westmoreland said**: "Aggressiveness, quick reaction, good use of firepower, and old-fashioned Australian courage have produced outstanding results."

Of the battles fought by the Australians in Phuoc Tuy, one of the most significant was **Long Tan**, on 18 August 1966. Although caught out by the advance of 4,000 Viet Cong, the Australians successfully responded to inflict heavy casualties: 17 dead against about 250 VC.

Following this they managed to expand control over large areas of the province, and then win the support of the local people. Unlike the Americans who adopted a policy of 'search and destroy', the Australians were more intent on 'hearts and minds' (COIN – counter insurgency). Through various health, education and other civic action programmes, the Australians gained the confidence of many villagers, making it much harder for the VC to infiltrate rural areas of Phuoc Tuy.

This policy of gaining the support of the local population was complemented by the highly effective use of small **Special Air Service** (SAS) teams – who worked closely with the US Special Forces. Many of these men were transferred after fighting in the jungles of Borneo during the Konfrontasi between Malaysia and Indonesia. They came well trained in the art of jungle warfare and ended the war with the highest kill ratio of any similar unit: at least 500 VC dead, against none of their own to hostile fire. The Australians left Phuoc Tuy in late 1971 – having lost 423 men. The ARVN were unable to fill the vacuum, and the Viet Cong quickly regained control of the area.

undisciplined South Vietnamese could not prevent a Communist victory. Adhering to the domino theory, and with his own and the US's reputation at stake, he had no choice. As Johnson is said to have remarked to his press secretary Bill Moyers: "I feel like a hitchhiker caught in a hail storm on a Texas highway. I can't win. I can't hide. And I can't make it stop."

Dispersal of the North's industry In response to the bombing campaign, industry in the north was decentralized and dispersed to rural areas. Each province was envisaged as a self-sufficient production unit. The economic effect of this strategy was felt at the time in a considerable loss of productivity; a cost judged to be worth paying to protect the north's industrial base. In order to protect the population in the north, they too were relocated to the countryside. By the end of 1967 Hanoi's population was a mere 250,000 essential citizens – about a quarter of the pre-war figure. The same was true of other urban centres. What the primary US objective was in mounting the air war remains unclear. In part, it was designed to destroy the north's industrial base and its ability to wage war; partly to dampen the people's will to fight; partly to sow seeds of discontent; partly to force the leadership in the north to the negotiating table; partly, perhaps, to punish those in the north for supporting their government. By October 1968 the US realized the bombing was having little effect and they called a halt. The legacy of Operation Rolling Thunder, though, would live on. Turley wrote:

"... the bombing had destroyed virtually all industrial, transportation and communications facilities built since 1954, blotted out 10 to 15 years' potential economic growth, flattened three major cities and 12 of 29 province capitals, and
triggered a decline in per capita agricultural output".

But, it was not just the bombing campaign which was undermining the north's industrial and agricultural base. Socialist policies in the countryside were labelling small land
owners as 'landlords' – in effect traitors to the revolutionary cause – thus alienating
many farmers. In the cities, industrial policies were no less short sighted. Though Ho's
policies in the battlefield were driven by hard-headed pragmatism, in the field of economic development they were informed – tragically – by revolutionary fervour.

William Westmoreland, the general appointed to command the American
effort, aimed to use the United States' superior firepower and mobility to 'search and
destroy' PAVN forces. North Vietnamese bases in the south were to be identified
using modern technology, jungle hide-outs revealed by dumping chemical defoliants, and then attacked with shells, bombs, and by helicopter-borne troops. In
'free-fire zones' the army and airforce were permitted to use whatever level of firepower they felt necessary to dislodge the enemy. 'Body counts' became the measure
of success and collateral damage – or civilian casualties – was a cost that just had to
be borne. As one field commander famously explained: 'We had to destroy the town
to save it'. By 1968 the US had more than 500,000 troops in Vietnam, while **South
Korean**, **Australian**, **New Zealand**, **Filipino** and **Thai** forces contributed another
90,000. The ARVN officially had 1.5 million men under arms (100,000 or more of
these were 'flower' or phantom soldiers, the pay for whom was pocketed by officers
in an increasingly corrupt ARVN). Ranged against this vastly superior force were perhaps 400,000 PAVN and National Liberation Front forces.

1964-68: who was winning?

The leadership in the north tried to allay serious anxieties about their ability to defeat
the American-backed south by emphasizing human over physical and material
resources. **Desertions** from the ARVN were very high – there were 113,000 from the
army in 1965 alone (200,000 in 1975) – and the PAVN did record a number of significant victories. The Communists also had to deal with large numbers of desertions –
28,000 men in 1969. By 1967 world opinion, and even American public opinion,
appeared to be swinging against the war. Within the US, **anti-war demonstrations**
and 'teach-ins' were spreading, officials were losing confidence in the ability of the
US to win the war, and the president's approval rating was sinking fast. As the US
Secretary of Defense, Robert McNamara is quoted as saying in the *Pentagon Papers*:

"... the picture of the world's greatest superpower killing or seriously injuring 1,000
noncombatants a week, while trying to pound a tiny, backward nation into submission on an issue whose merits are hotly disputed, is not a pretty one".

But although the Communists may have been winning the psychological and public
opinion wars, they were increasingly hard-pressed to maintain this advantage on the
ground. Continual American strikes against their bases, and the social and economic
dislocations in the countryside, were making it more difficult for the Communists to
recruit supporters. At the same time, the fight against a vastly better equipped
enemy was also taking its toll in sheer exhaustion. Despite what is now widely
regarded as a generally misguided US military strategy in Vietnam, there were notable US successes (for example the Phoenix Programme, see page 371). American GIs
were always sceptical about the 'pacification' programmes which aimed to win the

Background

'hearts and minds' war. GIs were fond of saying, 'If you've got them by the balls, their hearts and minds will follow'. At times, the US military and politicians appeared to view the average Vietnamese as inferior to the average American. This latent racism was reflected in General Westmoreland's remark that Vietnamese "don't think about death the way we do" and in the use by most US servicemen of the derogatory name "gook" to refer to Vietnamese.

At the same time as the Americans were trying to win 'hearts and minds', the Vietnamese were also busy indoctrinating their men and women, and the population in the 'occupied' south. In Bao Ninh's moving *The Sorrow of War* (1994), the main character, Kien, who fights with a scout unit describes the indoctrination that accompanied the soldiers from their barracks to the field: "Politics continuously. Politics in the morning, politics in the afternoon, politics again in the evening. 'We won, the enemy lost. The enemy will surely lose. The north had a good harvest, a bumper harvest. The people will rise up and welcome you. Those who don't just lack awareness. The world is divided into three camps.' More politics."

By 1967, the war had entered a period of military (though not political) stalemate. As Robert McNamara writes in his book *In retrospect: the tragedy and lessons of Vietnam*, it was at this stage that he came to believe that Vietnam was "a problem with no solution". In retrospect, he argues that the US should have withdrawn in late 1963, and certainly by late 1967. Massive quantities of US arms and money were preventing the Communists from making much headway in urban areas, while American and ARVN forces were ineffective in the countryside – although incessant bombing and ground assaults wreaked massive destruction. A black market of epic proportions developed in Saigon, as millions of dollars of assistance went astray. American journalist Stanley Karnow once remarked to a US official that "we could probably buy off the Vietcong at US$500 a head". The official replied that they had already calculated the costs, but came to "US$2,500 a head".

The Tet Offensive, 1968: the beginning of the end

By mid-1967, the Communist leadership in the north felt it was time for a further escalation of the war in the south, to regain the initiative. They began to lay the groundwork for what was to become known as the Tet (or New Year) Offensive – perhaps the single most important series of battles during the American War in Vietnam. During the early morning of 1 February 1968, shortly after noisy celebrations had welcomed in the New Year, 84,000 Communist troops – almost all Viet Cong – simultaneously attacked targets in 105 urban centres. Utterly surprising the US and South Vietnamese, the Tet Offensive had begun.

Preparations for the offensive had been laid over many months. Arms, ammunition and guerrillas were smuggled and infiltrated into urban areas, and detailed planning was undertaken. Central to the strategy was a 'sideshow' at Khe Sanh. By mounting an attack on the marine outpost at **Khe Sanh** (see page 193), the Communists successfully convinced the American and Vietnamese commanders that another Dien Bien Phu was underway. General Westmoreland moved 50,000 US troops away from the cities and suburbs to prevent any such humiliating repetition of the French defeat. But, Khe Sanh was just a diversion; a feint designed to draw attention away from the cities. In this the Communists were successful; for days after the Tet offensive, Westmoreland and the South Vietnamese President Thieu thought Khe Sanh to be the real objective and the attacks in the cities the decoy.

The most interesting aspect of the Tet Offensive was that although it was a strategic victory for the Communists, it was also a considerable tactical defeat. They may have occupied the US embassy in Saigon for a few hours but, except in Hué (see page 179), Communist forces were quickly repulsed by US and ARVN troops. The government in the south did not collapse, nor did the ARVN. Cripplingly high casualties were inflicted on the Communists – cadres at all echelons were killed – morale was undermined and it became clear that the cities would not rise up spontaneously to support the Communists. Tet, in effect, put paid to the VC as an effective fighting force. The fight now had to be increasingly taken up by the North Vietnamese Army (NVA). Walt Rostow wrote in 1995 that "Tet was an utter military and political defeat for the Communists in Vietnam", but adding "yet a political disaster in the United States". But this was not to matter; Westmoreland's request for more troops was turned down, and US public support for the war slumped still further as they heard reported that the US embassy itself had been 'over-run'. Those who for years had been claiming it was only a matter of time before the Communists were defeated appeared to be contradicted by the scale and intensity of the offensive. Even President Johnson was stunned by the VC's successes for he too had believed the US propaganda. As it turned out the VC incursion was by a 20-man unit from Sapper Battalion C-10 – who were all killed in the action. Their mission was not to take the embassy but to 'make a psychological gesture'. In that regard at least, the mission must have exceeded the leadership's wildest expectations.

The Phoenix Programme, established in the wake of the Tet Offensive, aimed to destroy the Communists' political infrastructure in the Mekong Delta. Named after the Vietnamese mythical bird the Phung Hoang, which could fly anywhere, the programme sent CIA-recruited and trained Counter Terror Teams – in effect assassination units – into the countryside. The teams were ordered to try and capture Communist cadres; invariably they fired first and asked questions later. By 1971, it was estimated that the programme had led to the capture of 28,000 members of the VCI (Viet Cong Infrastructure), the death of 20,000, and the defection of a further 17,000. By the early 1970s the countryside in the Mekong Delta was more peaceful than it had been for years; towns which were previously strongholds of the Viet Cong had reverted to the control of the local authorities. Critics have questioned what proportion of those killed, captured and sometimes tortured were Communist cadres, but even Communist documents admit that it seriously undermined their support network in the area. In these terms, the Phoenix Programme was a great success.

The Tet Offensive concentrated American minds. The costs of the war by that time **The costs** had been vast. The US budget deficit had risen to 3% of Gross National Product by 1968, inflation was accelerating, and thousands of young men had been killed for a cause which, to many, was becoming less clear by the month. Before the end of the year President Johnson had ended the bombing campaign. Negotiations began in Paris in 1969 to try and secure an honourable settlement for the US. Although the last American combat troops were not to leave until March 1973, the Tet Offensive marked the beginning of the end. It was from that date that the Johnson administration began to search seriously for a way out of the conflict. The illegal bombing of Cambodia in 1969, and the resumption of the bombing of the north in 1972 (the most intensive of the entire conflict), were only flurries of action on the way to an inevitable US withdrawal.

The Paris Agreement (1972)

US Secretary of State **Henry Kissinger** records the afternoon of 8 October 1972, a Sunday, as the moment when he realized that the Communists were willing to agree a peace treaty. There was a great deal to discuss, particularly whether the treaty would offer the prospect of peaceful reunification, or the continued existence of two states – a Communist north, and non-Communist south. Both sides tried to force the issue: the US mounted further attacks and at the same time strengthened and

Background

expanded the ARVN. They also tried to play the 'Madman Nixon' card, arguing that **President Richard Nixon** was such a vehement anti-Communist that he might well resort to the ultimate deterrent, the nuclear bomb. It is true that the PAVN was losing men through desertion and had failed to recover its losses in the Tet Offensive. Bao Ninh in his book *The Sorrow of War about Kinh, a scout with the PAVN*, wrote:

> "The life of the B3 Infantrymen after the Paris Agreement was a series of long suffering days, followed by months of retreating and months of counter-attacking, withdrawal, then counter-attack. Victory after victory, withdrawal after withdrawal. The path of war seemed endless, desperate, and leading nowhere."

But the Communist leadership knew well that the Americans were committed to withdrawal – the only question was when, so they felt that time was on their side.

By 1972, US troops in the south had declined to 95,000, the bulk of whom were support troops. The north gambled on a massive attack to defeat the ARVN and moved 200,000 men towards the demilitarized zone that marked the border between north and south. On 30 March the PAVN crossed into the south and quickly overran large sections of Quang Tri province. Simultaneous attacks were mounted in the west highlands, at Tay Ninh and in the Mekong Delta. For a while it looked as if the south would fall altogether. The US responded by mounting a succession of intense bombing raids which eventually forced the PAVN to retreat. The spring offensive may have failed, but like Tet, it was strategically important, for it demonstrated that without US support the ARVN was unlikely to be able to withstand a Communist attack.

Both sides, by late 1972, were ready to compromise. Against the wishes of South Vietnam's President Nguyen Van Thieu, the US signed a treaty on 27 January 1973, the ceasefire going into effect on the same day. Before the signing, Nixon ordered the bombing of the north – the so-called Christmas Campaign. It lasted 11 days from 18 December (Christmas Day was a holiday) and was the most intensive of the war. With the ceasefire and President Thieu, however shaky, both in place, the US was finally able to back out of its nightmare and the last combat troops left in March 1973. As J William Fulbright, a highly influential member of the Senate and a strong critic of the US role in Vietnam, observed: "We [the US] have the power to do any damn fool thing we want, and we always seem to do it."

The Final Phase, 1973-75

The Paris Accord settled nothing – it simply provided a means by which the Americans could withdraw from Vietnam. It was never going to resolve the deep-seated differences between the two régimes and with only a brief lull, the war continued, this time without US troops. Thieu's government was probably in terminal decline even before the peace treaty was signed. Though ARVN forces were at their largest ever and, on paper, considerably stronger than the PAVN, many men were weakly committed to the cause of the south. Corruption was endemic, business was in recession, and political dissent was on the increase. The North's Central Committee formally decided to abandon the Paris Accord in October 1973; by the beginning of 1975 they were ready for the final offensive. It took only until April for the Communists to achieve total victory. ARVN troops deserted in their thousands, and the only serious resistance was offered at Xuan Loc, less than 100 km from Saigon. President Thieu resigned on 27 April. ARVN generals, along with their men, were attempting to flee as the PAVN advanced on Saigon. The end was quick: at 1045 on 30 April a T-54 tank (number 843) crashed its way through the gates of the Presidential Palace, symbolizing the end of the Second Indochina War. For the US, the aftermath of the war would lead to years of soul searching; for Vietnam, to stagnation and isolation.

Background

George Ball, a senior State Department figure reflected afterwards that the war was "probably the greatest single error made by America in its history".

Legacy of the Vietnam War

The Vietnam War (or 'American War' to the Vietnamese) is such an enduring feature of the West's experience of the country that most visitors are constantly on the look-out for legacies of the conflict. There is no shortage of physically deformed and crippled Vietnamese. Many men were badly injured during the war, but large numbers also received their injuries while serving in Cambodia (1979-89). It is tempting to associate deformed children with the enduring effects of the pesticide Agent Orange (1.7 million tonnes had been used by 1973), although this has yet to be proven 'scientifically' – American studies claim that there is no significant difference in congenital malformation. Certainly, local doctors admit that children and babies in the south are smaller today than they were before 1975. But this is more likely to be due to malnutrition than defoliants.

Bomb damage is most obvious from the air: well over five million tonnes of bombs were dropped on the country (north and south) and there are said to be 20 million bomb-craters – the sort of statistic people like to recount, but no one can legitimately verify. Many craters have yet to be filled in and paddy fields are still pockmarked. Some farmers have used these holes in the ground to farm fish and to use as small reservoirs to irrigate vegetable plots; they may also be partially to blame for the dramatic increase in the incidence of malaria. War scrap was one of the country's most valuable exports and PSS (perforated steel sheeting) and other remnants can be seen piled high by roadsides – although even Vietnam is running out of accessible scrap. The cities in the north are surprisingly devoid of obvious signs of the bombing campaigns – Hanoi remains remarkably intact. Hué however, formerly Vietnam's greatest historical treasure, is a tragic sight. The Citadel and Forbidden Palace were extensively damaged during the Tet offensive in 1968 although much has now been rebuilt (see page 181). In response to the American bombing campaign, the North Vietnamese leadership ordered the dispersal of industrial activities to the countryside. Though effective in protecting some of the north's limited industrial base, this strategy created an inefficient pattern of production – a factor which even today hinders the north's efforts at promoting growth.

Bomb damage

Even harder to measure is the effect of the war on the Vietnamese psyche. Bao Ninh in *The Sorrow of War* writes of a driver with the PAVN who, talking with Kien, the book's main character, observes: "I'm simply a soldier like you who'll now have to live with broken dreams and with pain. But, my friend, our era is finished. After this hard-won victory fighters like you, Kien, will never be normal again. You won't even speak with your normal voice, in the normal way again." Later in the book, Kien muses about the opportunities that the war has extinguished. Although the book is a fictional story, the underlying tale is one of truth:

Psychological effect of the war

> "Still, even in the midst of my reminiscences I can't avoid admitting there seems little left for me to hope for. From my life before soldiering there remains sadly little. ... Those who survived continue to live. But that will has gone, that burning will which was once Vietnam's salvation. Where is the reward of enlightenment due to us for attaining our sacred war goals? Our history-making efforts for the next generations have been to no avail."

The Vietnamese Communist Party leadership still seem to be preoccupied by the conflict, and school children are routinely shown War Remnants museums, War

Patriot games: Vietnamese street names

Like other countries that have experienced a revolution, the Vietnamese authorities have spent considerable time expunging street names that honour men and women who lack the necessary revolutionary credentials. Most obviously, Saigon had its name changed to Ho Chi Minh City following reunification. Most towns have the same street names, and most are in memory of former patriots:

Dien Bien Phu   *Site of the Communists' famous victory against the French in 1954 (see page 112).*

Duy Tan   *11th Nguyen emperor (1907-16) until exiled to Réunion by the French for his opposition to colonial rule. Killed in an aircrash in Africa in 1945, his remains were interred in Hué in 1987.*

Hai Ba Trung   *The renowned Trung sisters who led a rebellion against Chinese overlords in AD 40 (see page 81).*

Ham Nghi   *The young emperor who joined the resistance against the French in 1885 at the age of 13 and thus gave it legitimacy.*

Hoang Van Thu   *Leader of the Vietnamese Communist Party, executed by the French in 1944.*

Le Duan   *Secretary-General of Lao Dong from 1959.*

Le Lai   *Brother-in-arms of Emperor Le Loi. Le Lai saved Viet forces by dressing in the Emperor's clothes and drawing away surrounding Chinese troops.*

Le Loi (Le Thai To)   *Leader of a revolt which, in 1426, resulted in the liberation of Vietnam from Ming Chinese overlords. Born into a wealthy family he had a life-long concern for the poor. Founder of the Le Dynasty, he ruled 1426-33.*

Le Thanh Ton(g)   *A successor to Le Loi, ruled 1460-98, poet king, and cartographer he established an efficient administration on strict Confucian lines and an enlightened legal code; literature and the arts flourished.*

Ly Thuong Kiet   *Military commander who led campaigns against the Chinese and Chams during the 11th century, and gained a reputation as a brilliant strategist. He died at the age of 70 in 1105.*

museums and Ho Chi Minh memorials. But despite the continuing propaganda offensive, people harbour surprisingly little animosity towards America or the West. Indeed, of all Westerners, it is often Americans who are most warmly welcomed, particularly in the south. During the Gulf conflict of 1991 young Vietnamese were rooting for the Americans and their allies, not for Saddam Hussein. But it must be remembered that about 60% of Vietnam's population has been born since the US left in 1973, so have no memory of the American occupation.

The deeper source of antagonism is the continuing divide between the north and south. It was to be expected that the forces of the north would exact their revenge on their foes in the south – and many were relieved that the predicted bloodbath did not materialize. But few would have thought that this revenge would be so long-lasting. The 250,000 southern dead are not mourned or honoured, or even acknowledged. Former soldiers are denied jobs, and the government does not seem to accept any need for national reconciliation.

This is the multiple legacy of the War on Vietnam and the Vietnamese. The legacy on the US and Americans is more widely appreciated. The key question which still occupies the minds of many, though, is, was it worth it? Economic historian Walt Rostow, ex-Singaporean prime minister Lee Kuan Yew and others would probably answer 'yes'. If the US had not intervened, communism would have spread farther in Southeast Asia; more dominoes, in their view, would have fallen. In 1973, when US withdrawal was agreed, Lee Kuan Yew observed that the countries of Southeast Asia

Nguyen Du (1765-1820) *Ambassador to Peking, courtier and Vietnam's most famous poet, wrote The Tale of Kieu (see page 412).*

Nguyen Hue *Tay Son brother who routed the Chinese at the Battle of Dong Da. Later became Emperor Quang Trung (see below and page 223).*

Nguyen Thai Hoc *Leader of the Vietnam Quoc Dan Dang Party (VNQDD) (see page) and the leader of the Yen Bai uprisings; captured by the French and guillotined on 17 June 1930 at the age of 28.*

Nguyen Trai *Emperor Le Loi's advisor and a skilled poet, he advised Le Loi to concentrate on political and moral struggle: "Better to conquer hearts than citadels."*

Nguyen Van Troi *Viet Cong hero who in 1963 tried, unsuccessfully, to assassinate Robert McNamara by blowing up a bridge in Saigon. He was executed.*

Phan Boi Chau *A committed anti-colonialist from the age of 19, he travelled to China and Japan to organize resistance to the French. Captured in Shanghai in 1925 he was extradited to Hanoi and sentenced to life imprisonment. Public pressure led to his amnesty in the same year and he spent the rest of his life in Hué where he died in 1940.*

Quang Trung *Leader of the Tay Son peasant rebellion of 1771; defeated both the Siamese (Thais) and the Chinese (see page 223).*

Ton Duc Thang *Became President of the Socialist Republic of Vietnam; he took part in a mutiny aboard a French ship along with other Vietnamese shipmates in the Black Sea in support of the Russian Revolution.*

Tran Hung Dao *13th-century hero who fought and defeated the Yuan Chinese (see page 159). Regarded as one of Vietnam's great military leaders and strategists, also a man of letters writing the classic Binh Thu Yeu Luoc in 1284.*

Tran Nguyen Han *A 15th-century general who fought heroically against the Ming Chinese occupiers.*

Tran Phu *The first Secretary General of the Communist Party of Indo-China, killed by the French in 1931 at the age of 27.*

30 Thang 4 Street *Commemorates the fall of Saigon to the Communists on 30 April 1975.*

Background

were much more resilient and resistant to communism than they had been, say, at the time of the Tet offensive in 1968. The US presence in Vietnam allowed them to reach this state of affairs. Yet Robert McNamara in his book *In Retrospect: the tragedy and lessons of Vietnam*, and one of the architects of US policy, wrote:

> "Although we sought to do the right thing – and believed we were doing the right thing – in my judgment, hindsight proves us wrong. We both overestimated the effects of South Vietnam's loss on the security of the West and failed to adhere to the fundamental principle that, in the final analysis, if the South Vietnamese were to be saved, they had to win the war themselves."

After the war

The Socialist Republic of Vietnam (SRV) was born from the ashes of the Vietnam War on 2 July 1976 when former North and South Vietnam were reunified. Hanoi was proclaimed as the capital of the new country. But few Vietnamese would have guessed that their emergent country would be cast by the US in the mould of a pariah state for almost 18 years. First President George Bush, and then his successor Bill Clinton, eased the US trade embargo bit by bit in a dance of appeasement and procrastination, as they tried to comfort American business clamouring for a slice of the Vietnamese pie, while also trying to stay on the right side of the vociferous lobby

A nation at sea: the boat people

One of the most potent images of Vietnam during the 1970s and 80s was of foundering, overloaded vessels carrying 'boat people' to Hong Kong, Thailand, Malaysia and the Philippines. Beginning in 1976, but becoming a torrent from the late 1970s, these boat people initially fled political persecution. Later, most were 'economic' migrants in search of a better life. Now, the tragedy of the boat people is almost at an end and fast becoming a footnote in history as the last refugees are sent 'home' or onward to what they hope will be a better life.

Escaping the country was not easy. Many prospective boat people were caught by the authorities (often after having already paid the estimated US$500-US$3,000 to secure a place on a boat), and sent to prison or to a re-education camp. Of those who embarked, it has been estimated that at least a third died at sea – from drowning or dehydration, and at the hands of pirates. The boats were usually small and poorly maintained, hardly seaworthy for a voyage across the South China Sea. Captains rarely had charts (some did not even have an experienced sailor on board), and most had never ventured further afield than the coastal waters with which they were familiar.

By 1977, the exodus was so great that some freighters began to stop heaving-to to pick up refugees – a habit which, until then, had been sacrosanct among sailors. Malaysia instructed their coastal patrol vessels to force boats back out to sea – and in the first six months of 1979 they did just that to 267 vessels carrying an estimated 40,000 refugees. One boat drifted for days off Malaysia, with the passengers drinking their own urine, until they were picked up – but not before two children had died of dehydration. The Singapore and Malaysian governments adopted a policy of allowing boats to replenish their supplies, but not to land – forcing some vessels to sail all the way to Australia before they were assured of a welcome (over 8,000 km). Cannibalism is also reported to have taken place; one boy who had only just survived being killed himself told a journalist: "After the body [of a boy] had been discovered, the boatmaster pulled it up out of the hold. Then he cut up the body. Everyone was issued a piece of meat about two fingers wide."

As numbers rose, so did the incidence of piracy – an age-old problem in the South China Sea. Pirates, mostly Thai, realizing that the boats often carried families with all their possessions (usefully converted into portable gold) began to target the refugee boats. Some commentators have estimated that by the late 1970s, 30% of boats were being boarded, and the United Nations High Commissioner for Refugees (UNHCR) in 1981 reported that 81% of women had been raped. Sometimes the boats were boarded and plundered, the women raped, all the passengers murdered, and the boats sunk. Despite all these risks, Vietnamese continued to leave in huge numbers: by 1980 there were 350,000 awaiting resettlement in refugee camps in the countries of Southeast Asia and Hong Kong.

Most of these 'illegals' left from the south of Vietnam; identified with the previous régime, they were systematically persecuted – particularly if they also

in the US demanding more action on the MIA issue. Appropriately, the embargo, which was first imposed on the former North in May 1964, and then nationwide in 1975, was finally lifted a few days before the celebrations of Tet, Vietnamese New Year, on 4 February 1994.

On the morning of the 30 April 1975, just before 1100, a T-54 tank crashed through the gates of the Presidential Palace in Saigon, symbolically marking the end of the Vietnam War. Twenty years later, the same tank – number 843 – became a symbol of the past as parades and celebrations, and a good deal of soul searching,

happened to be ethnic Chinese or Hoa (the Chinese 'invasion' of 1979 did not help matters). But as conditions worsened in the north, large numbers also began to sail from Ha Long Bay and Haiphong. Soon the process became semi-official, as local and regional authorities realized that fortunes could be made providing boats and escorts. Large freighters began to carry refugees – the Hai Hong (1,600 tonnes) which finally docked in Malaysia was carrying 2,500 passengers who claimed they had left with the cognizance of the authorities.

The peak period of the crisis spanned the years from 1976-1979, with 270,882 leaving the country in 1979 alone. The flow of refugees slowed during 1980 and 1981 to about 50,000, and until 1988 averaged about 10,000 each year. But in the late 1980s the numbers picked up once again – with most sailing for Hong Kong and leaving from the north. It seems that whereas the majority of those sailing in the first phase (1976-1981) were political refugees, the second phase of the exodus was driven by economic pressures. Daily wage rates in Vietnam at that time were only 3,000 dong (US$0.25) – so it is easy to see the attraction of leaving for healthier economic climes. With more than 40,000 refugees in camps in Hong Kong, the Hong Kong authorities began to forcibly repatriate (euphemistically termed 'orderly return') those screened as economic migrants at the end of 1989 when 51 were flown to Hanoi. Such was the international outcry as critics highlighted fears of persecution, that the programme was suspended. In May 1992, an agreement was reached between the British and

Vietnamese governments to repatriate the 55,700 boat people living in camps in Hong Kong and the orderly return programme was quietly restarted. As part of their deal with China, the British government agreed to empty the camps before the hand-over date in 1997 (a target they failed to meet).

Ironically, the evidence is that those repatriated are doing very well – better than those who never left the shores of Vietnam – and there is no convincing evidence of systematic persecution, despite the fears of such groups as Amnesty International. With the European Community and the UN offering assistance to returnees, they have set up businesses, enrolled on training courses and become embroiled in Vietnam's thrust for economic growth.

At the beginning of 1996 there were around 37,000 boat people still living in camps in Hong Kong (mostly), Indonesia, Thailand, the Philippines and Japan. The difficulty is that those who are left are the least attractive to receiving countries. As Jahanshah Assadi of the UNHCR put it at the end of 1994, "Our Nobel Prize winners left a long time ago for the West", adding "What we have now is the bottom of the barrel." Even Vietnam is not enamoured with the idea of receiving ex-citizens who clearly do not wish to be citizens again. For the refugees themselves, they have been wasted years. As the UNHCR's Jean-Noel Wetterwald said in 1996: "Leaving Vietnam was the project of their lives." Now they're going back with nothing to show for the years and the tears.

Background

marked the anniversary of the end of the War. To many Vietnamese, in retrospect, 1975 was more a beginning than an end: it was the beginning of a collective struggle to come to terms with the War, to build a nation, to reinvigorate the economy, and to excise the ghosts of the past. Two decades after the armies of the South laid down their arms and the last US servicemen and officials frantically fled by helicopter to carriers waiting in the South China Sea, the Vietnamese government is still trying, as they put it, to get people to recognize that 'Vietnam is a country, not a war'. A further 20 years from now, it may seem that only in 1995 did the War truly end.

Getting our children out of Vietnam: a personal story

It was 1 April 1975. I was watching the news on television. The North Vietnamese had captured Qui Nhon. From my 26-months experience in the war zone of Vietnam, I knew immediately that South Vietnam was going to fall and we, myself and my Vietnamese wife, had to decide now to go to Vietnam to get our children out or possibly never see them again.

We had not heard from them in over a year and did not know if they were still with their grandmother in Luong Phuoc (a village 90 miles northeast of Saigon), whether their village had already been overrun, or if they were already dead. It had been a longer time since we had heard from our son, and believed that he had been killed.

The North Vietnamese had previously moved south and captured Hué and Danang, only to be pushed back. But now they had captured Qui Nhon. They had outflanked the South Vietnamese Army and would now push south to Saigon. The country was lost.

We decided right then to go. In six days, we had our passports, shots and visas and were on our way to Saigon. We had been trying to get our girls out of Vietnam for over three years. But, government red tape prevented us. Before going, everyone thought that we would not come back alive. So we taped our 'last wills' to the kitchen cabinets in our home in Milford Center, Ohio.

We took as much money as possible – we took out a personal loan for as much as we could from the Farmers and Merchants Bank, emptied our savings and checking accounts, and borrowed whatever we could. On 2 April, we got our shots. On 3 April, we left our 10-month-old daughter, Thao, with my parents in Columbus, Ohio, and went to Washington DC, to get my passport and our visas. Then we flew to San Francisco and on to the Philippines. However, we experienced more delays. First, the flight to Saigon was delayed because the President's Palace in Saigon was being bombed. Then, during the delay, my passport was stolen. We went to the American Embassy in Manila and applied for an 'Emergency Passport'. Realizing that Vietnam was about to fall to the North Vietnamese, the Emergency Passport was issued.

Finally, on 10 April 1975, we arrived in Saigon. We got a room in the Embassy Hotel and started to make inquiries about the status of the war. The police in Saigon told us that Luong Phuoc had been evacuated and the villagers were in Vung Tau, a former resort area turned into a refugee camp. Kim Chi went to Vung Tau to find our girls. They were not there and none of the villagers from Luong Phuoc was there. The police had told us the village had been evacuated so they would not have to go to Luong Phuoc to get the girls.

Modern Vietnam

Politics

The Vietnamese Communist Party (VCP) was established in Hong Kong in 1930 by Ho Chi Minh, and arguably has been more successful than any other such party in Asia in mobilizing and then maintaining support. While others have fallen, the VCP has managed to stay firmly in control and in 1998 had a total of 2.3 million members. In 1986, at the sixth party congress, the VCP launched its economic reform programme known as *doi moi* – a momentous step in ideological terms (see page 389). However, although the programme has done much to free up the economy, the party has ensured that it retains ultimate political power. Marxism-Leninism

We had to find someone to go for us. We could not go. I, being an American, and Kim Chi now being too westernized, would both be killed by the Vietcong or stopped by the South Vietnamese Army. We found our cousin, Ty, in Saigon who agreed to go to Luong Phuoc and search for the girls.

Our search for the girls was the main topic of interest at the Embassy Hotel, *as none of the other Americans or Vietnamese staying there expected us to ever find them. We had received word that Luong Phuoc was already cut off from Saigon. Ty had to go by boat in order to bypass the Vietcong and arrived at Luong Phuoc to find Kim Chi's mother and the children. They left everything behind. Even then, they were stopped by the South Vietnamese Army and held for over an hour. The village came under attack by the North Vietnamese and Kim Chi's grandmother pushed the girls to the bottom of the boat and lay on top of them, yelling to the boatman to head for the sea. Under fire, they reached the safety of the ocean and headed south.*

They reached Vung Tau and the following morning took a bus to Saigon. While waiting for the girls to arrive in Saigon, Kim Chi and I had been processing the papers required for their immigration to the United States. However, on 20 April all that changed. The word had come down that all Vietnamese would be given 'refugee' status if they accompanied an

American out of Saigon. You could take anyone you wanted – just as long as you claimed they were a relative. (It really did not matter if they were or not. If an American thought that a Vietnamese should be given refugee status, that was all that mattered.)

We arrived by bus at the Tan San Nhut Airport while the outskirts of the city were being bombed by the North Vietnamese. After several hours, we boarded the Air Force C-141 Transport and flew to the Philippines where we slept on the gymnasium floor of the military base. We were there only four days before President Marcos kicked out all the refugees and we had to go to Guam where we were kept in a 'tent city' constructed by the US Navy. Since we did have most of our papers completed for the girls, Mai and Phuong (12 and 7 years old), we were evacuated on 27 April 1975. We arrived in San Francisco on 28 April 1975 – the day that Saigon fell to the North Vietnamese.

Nearly 15 years later, in 1989, Kim Chi returned to Vietnam to visit her mother. In 1995 she bought property near Luong Phuoc where we hope to eventually build a business.

(The above is the personal experience of Ken Thompson and his wife Kim Chi. Ken flew in Vietnam and Laos as a Forward Air Controller (FAC). In Laos he was designated Raven 58.)

Background

and Ho Chi Minh thought are still taught to Vietnamese school children and even so-called 'reformers' in the leadership are not permitted to diverge from the party line. In this sense, while economic reforms have made considerable progress (but see below) – particularly in the south – there is a very definite sense that the limits of political reform have been reached, at least for the time being.

The last years of the 20th century and the opening ones of the new Millennium have seen a number of arrests and trials of dissidents charged with what might appear to be fairly innocuous crimes (see the section 'The future of communism in Vietnam' page 385) and, although the economic reform enacted since the mid-1980s are still in place, there is limited support within the party for any moves towards greater political pluralism. As the *Far Eastern Economic Review* argued after the 1996 Party Congress, for Vietnamese Communists the collapse of the Soviet Union and the Communist states of Eastern Europe did not reflect a failure of ideas, just a failure of management. Political science is scarcely taught in Vietnam's

Provinces

Background

Provinces
1 Hanoi
2 Hà Tay
3 Hai Phong

4 Thái Bình
5 Nam Ha
6 Ninh Binh
7 Ho Chi Minh City

8 Ba Ria-Vung Tau
9 Dong Tháp
10 Vinh Long
11 Tien Giang

universities reflecting a widespread belief in the hierarchy that there are no (better) alternatives to the present political system.

Looking at the process of political succession in Vietnam and the impression is not one of a country led by young men and women with innovative ideas. Each year commentators consider the possibility of an infusion of new blood and reformist ideas but the Party Congress normally delivers more of the same: dyed-in-the-wool party followers who are more likely to maintain the status quo than challenge it along with just one or two reformers. The Asian economic crisis and the fall of Indonesia's Suharto have, if anything, further retarded the pace of change. To conservative party members the Asian crisis, and the political instability that it caused, were taken as warnings of what can happen if you reform too far and too fast. The latest change of faces in the leadership occurred during the Ninth Party Congress in April 2001. The key change was the appointment of 60-year-old Nong Duc Manh as party general secretary, replacing the unpopular conservative Le Kha Phieu.

But most of the key members of the Politburo kept their positions, including Tran Duc Luong, a conservative technocrat, and Phan Van Khai, the most important so-styled 'reformist'. On his appointment as general secretary Manh – who commentators are hoping will be a little more modern in his outlook than his predecessor – pledged to continue the modernization drive, reform the party, and counter corruption. Nothing new there.

For many Westerners there is something strange about a leadership calling for economic reform and liberalization while, at the same time, refusing any degree of political pluralism. How long the VCP can maintain this charade, along with China, while other Communist governments have long since fallen (with the hardly edifying exceptions of Cuba and North Korea) , is a key question. Despite the reforms, the leadership is still divided over the road ahead. It is common to hear and read of 'conservatives' and 'reformists' or 'pragmatists'. The labels themselves probably mean little – indeed they simplify what is a complex debate between people with multiple stances by reducing the question to a binary one of yes/no, black/white, conservative/reformist. But the fact that debate is continuing, sometimes openly, suggests that there is ongoing disagreement over the necessity for political reform, and the degree of economic reform that should be encouraged.

The crux is, how long will the population of Vietnam continue to accept a standard of living among the lowest in the world? One economist, referring to the momentum that is built into the process of economic reform, tartly observed in 1996 that "Life is stronger than dogma". This will become even more pertinent as *doi moi* brings wealth to a few, but leaves most people living in poverty. This has preoccupied Vietnam's leaders in recent years. In January 1992, the reformist Premier Vo Van Kiet who retired in 1997 said in an interview in the party daily *Nhan Dan* that the "confrontation between luxury and misery, between cities and country" could cause problems and talked of the need to "establish a new order of sharing". As former Party General Secretary Do Muoi put it, with great understatement at the Special Party Conference held at the beginning of 1994, there are "complicated factors" with which the leadership will have to contend. To enable them to get their message to a wider audience, the Communist Party of Vietnam have launched their own website, www.cpv.org.vn It is, in many respects, a perfect reflection of the Party itself: thorough, loyally supported (over two million 'hits') and very, very slow.

The political tensions that are bubbling just beneath the surface of Vietnamese society broke the surface in 1997 when it became clear that there had been **serious disturbances** in the poor coastal northern province of Thai Binh, 80 km southeast of Hanoi. In May, 3,000 local farmers began to stage demonstrations in the provincial capital, complaining of corruption and excessive taxation. There were reports of rioting and some deaths – strenuously denied, at least at first, by officials. However a

Background

lengthy report appeared in the army newspaper *Quan Doi Nhan Dan* in September detailing moral decline and corruption in the Party in the province. For people in Thai Binh, and many others living in rural areas, the reforms of the 1980s and 1990s have brought little benefit. People living in Saigon may tout mobile phones and drive cars and motorbikes, but in much of the rest of the country average incomes are around US$50. The Party's greatest fear is that ordinary people might lose confidence in the leadership and in the system. The fact that many of those who demonstrated in Thai Binh were, apparently, war veterans didn't help either. Nor can the leadership have failed to remember that Thai Binh was at the centre of peasant disturbances against the French. A few months later riots broke out in prosperous and staunchly Roman Catholic Dong Nai, just north of Saigon. The catalyst to these disturbances was the seizure of church land by a corrupt Chairman of the People's Committee. The mob razed the Chairman's house and stoned the fire brigade. Clearly, pent up frustrations were seething beneath the surface for Highway 1 had to be closed for several days while the unrest continued. While the Dong Nai troubles went wholly unreported in Vietnam, a Voice of Vietnam broadcast admitted to them and went on to catalogue a list of previous civil disturbances, none of which was known to the outside world; it appears the purpose was to advise Western journalists that this was just another little local difficulty and not the beginning of the end of Communist rule. But reports of disturbances continue to filter out of Vietnam. At the beginning of 2001 thousands of ethnic minorities rioted in the central highland provinces of Gia Lai and Dac Lac and the army had to be called in to reimpose order. Foreign journalists, significantly, were banned from travelling to the trouble spots.

At around the same time that peasants were demonstrating in Thai Binh, some 12,000 km away the last link with Vietnam's imperial past was extinguished with the **death of Bao Dai** in Paris at the age of 83, the 13th and last emperor of the Nguyen dynasty. Bao Dai, 'Keeper of Greatness', ascended to the throne in Hué in 1925 and abdicated in 1945 after Ho Chi Minh had declared the creation of the Republic of Vietnam. He served for a short time as a special advisor in Ho's government and then fled to Hong Kong before returning under French protection in 1949 to become ruler of the State of Vietnam. Bao Dai was deposed in 1954 following the defeat of the French at Dien Bien Phu, and lived the last four decades of his life in exile in France. There, he gained a name for himself as a bon viveur, gambling with passion and living in a 20 room chateau near Cannes surrounded by fast cars and a retinue of servants. Bao Dai was, it is said, more French than Vietnamese. He dressed in Western clothes, was more comfortable speaking French than Vietnamese, preferred French cuisine to that of his homeland – and converted from Buddhism to Roman Catholicism.

Economic reform versus social degradation

Another theme that has become popular among Party leaders is the fear of social degradation and malaise. In 1996 former general-secretary Do Muoi warned that Saigon had become a 'fertile ground for hostile forces', and talked of 'cultural pollution', 'political destabilization' and 'economic sabotage'. The two succeeding general secretaries, Le Kha Phieu and Nong Duc Manh, have also used speeches to the party faithful to hammer home the point that combating corruption in the party is essential. The Party also refers, as if it is a poisonous cloud, to the 'intrusion of noxious cultures', another reference to the social changes presumed to have been brought about by Vietnam's opening-up process.

For the majority of the Communist leadership, the developments to which Do Muoi referred are intimately associated with the economic reform process and the inflow of foreign investment, foreign goods, foreign ideas, and foreigners. In other words, Westernization. 'Social evils' has become a stock phrase and older people talk with worry and disgust about the growing number of young troublemakers on the streets of the country's larger cities. The government has begun to try and root out what it regards as these malignant influences.

But not everyone sees the problem as lying only – or even mostly – with the market system; some point the finger of blame at the Party itself. Over recent years there has been a spate of anti-corruption drives. At the beginning of 1997, six people were sentenced to death for corruption after a trial in Ho Chi Minh City. Shortly afterwards, the Party adopted new ethical guidelines to stem the spread of corruption in the party, the military, and in government and administration. The crack-down on corruption in the Party continued into 1998 and 1999. 'Thousands' have been expelled from the party and many more disciplined or imprisoned. In April 1999, 74 government officials in Ho Chi Minh were found guilty of smuggling and the two ring leaders executed. A month later another group of more than 70 businessmen and civil servants were accused of fraud in Hanoi and six of these sentenced to death (two later commuted to life imprisonment). Reflecting the view of some in the leadership that things were spiralling out of control, General Secretary La Kha Phieu attacked the 'degradation' in the party during a speech in 1999 marking the birthday of Ho Chi Minh. The fear, of course, is that if the people see the Party as just as corrupt as everyone else it will lose its legitimacy – so painfully won over the years of confrontation against France, the US and China – to lead the country. In April 2001 when Le Kha Phieu stepped down from his post as general secretary he warned that public anger over corruption could threaten the very survival of the Vietnamese Communist Party.

International relations

In terms of international relations, Vietnam's relationship with the countries of the **Association of Southeast Asian Nations (ASEAN)** have warmed markedly since the dark days of the early and mid-1980s and in mid-1995 Vietnam became the association's seventh – and first Communist – member. The delicious irony of Vietnam joining ASEAN was that it was becoming part of an organization established to counteract the threat of Communist Vietnam itself – although everyone was too polite to point this out. No longer is there a deep schism between the capitalist and Communist countries of the region, either in terms of ideology or management. The main potential flashpoint concerns Vietnam's long-term historical enemy – China. The enmity and suspicion which underlies the relationship between the world's last two real Communist powers stretches back over 2,000 years. Indeed, one of the great attractions to Vietnam of joining ASEAN has been the bulwark that it creates against a potentially aggressive China.

China and Vietnam, along with Malaysia, Taiwan, Brunei and the Philippines all claim part (or all) of the South China Sea's **Spratly Islands**. These tiny islands, many no more than coral atolls, would have caused scarcely an international relations ripple, were it not for the fact that they are thought to sit above huge oil reserves. He who claims the islands, so to speak, lays claim to this undersea wealth. Over the last decade China has been using its developing blue water navy to project its power southwards. This has led to skirmishes between Vietnamese and Chinese forces, and to diplomatic confrontation between China and just about all the other claimants. Although the parties are committed to settling the dispute without resort to force, most experts see the Spratly Islands as the key potential 'flashpoint' in Southeast Asia – and one in which Vietnam is seen to be a central player. The **Paracel Islands** further north are similarly disputed by Vietnam and China. As Far Eastern Economic Review correspondent Margot Cohen wrote in a piece on the army draft at the beginning of 2002:

"Haunted by a long history of war, Vietnam is insecure in peace, wary of its giant neighbour, China. Ironically, even dodgers argue that the draft is necessary. 'Psychologically, we are still a country at war,' says one [draft dodger], a 26-year-old, overseas-educated Hanoi man. 'If we let go of the draft, and then we're attacked, it could take too long for us to get our act together.'"

Rapprochement with the United States

One of the keys to a lasting economic recovery (see below) was a normalization of relations with the US. From 1975 until early 1994 the US made it largely illegal for any American or American company to have business relations with Vietnam. The US, with the support of Japan and other Western nations, also black-balled attempts by Vietnam to gain membership to the IMF, World Bank and Asian Development Bank, thus cutting off access to the largest source of cheap credit. In the past, it has been the former Soviet Union and the countries of the Eastern Bloc which have filled the gap, providing billions of dollars of aid (US$6 bn during the period 1986-1990), training and technical expertise. But in 1990 the Soviet Union halved its assistance to Vietnam, making it imperative that the government look to improving relations with the West and particularly the US.

In April 1991 the US opened an official office in Hanoi (to assist in the search for MIAs), the first such move since the end of the war, and in December 1992 allowed US companies to sign contracts to be implemented after the US trade embargo had been lifted. In 1992, both Australia and Japan lifted their embargoes on aid to Vietnam, and the US also eased restrictions on humanitarian assistance. Support for a **full normalization of relations** was provided by French President Mitterand during his visit in February 1993 – the first by a Western leader since the end of the war. He said that the US veto on IMF and World Bank assistance had "no reason for being there", and applauded Vietnam's economic reforms. He also pointed out to his hosts that respect for human rights was now a universal obligation – which did not go down quite so well. Nonetheless he saw his visit as marking the end of one chapter, and the beginning of another.

This inexorable process towards normalization continued with the full lifting of the trade embargo on 4 February 1994 when President Bill Clinton announced the normalization of trade relations. Finally, on 11 July 1995 Bill Clinton announced the full normalization of relations between the two countries, and a month later Secretary of State Warren Christopher opened the new American embassy in Hanoi. On 9 May 1997 Douglas 'Pete' Peterson, the first 'post-war' American ambassador to Vietnam – and a former POW who spent six years of the war in the infamous 'Hanoi Hilton' – took up his post in the capital.

The progress towards normalization was so slow because many Americans still harbour painful memories of the war. With large numbers of ordinary people continuing to believe that servicemen shot down and captured during the war and listed as **Missing in Action** (MIAs) were still languishing in jungle gaols, presidents Bush and Clinton had to tread exceedingly carefully. In a sense, it was recognized long ago that the embargo no longer served American interests; it was just that the public were not yet ready to forgive and forget.

Even though the embargo is now a thing of the past, there are still the families of over 2,000 American servicemen listed as Missing in Action who continue to hope that the remains of their loved ones might, some day, make their way back to the United States. (The fact there are still an estimated 300,000 Vietnamese MIAs is, of course, of scant interest to the American media.) It was this, among other legacies of the war, which made progress towards a full normalization of diplomatic and commercial relations such a drawn-out business. It was only at the beginning of 1995 that Washington opened a 'liaison' office in Hanoi, and even then, in a very un-American show of modesty, there was no US flag flying from the building. As one American diplomat explained to a journalist from *The Economist* at the time, "Washington would very much like this to be an invisible office". This diplomacy-at-a-snail's-pace frustrated many American businessmen who were clamouring for fanfare and celebration, not the slightly embarrassed shuffling of diplomats.

The normalization of trade relations between the two countries was agreed in a meeting between Vietnamese and US officials in July 1999 and marked the culmination of three years' discussions. But conservatives in the politburo prevented the agreement being signed into law worried, apparently, about the social and economic side-effects of such reform. This did not happen until 28 November 2001 when Vietnam's National Assembly finally ratified the treaty. It is expected to lead to a substantial increase in bilateral trade.

The future of communism in Vietnam

In his book *Vietnam at the Crossroads*, BBC World Service commentator Michael Williams asks the question: "Does communism have a future in Vietnam?". He answers that "the short answer must be no, if one means by communism the classical Leninist doctrines and central planning". Instead some bastard form of communism has been in the process of evolving. As Williams adds, "Even party leaders no longer appear able to distinguish between communism and capitalism ...".

There is certainly **political opposition** and disenchantment in Vietnam. At present this is unfocused and dispersed. Poor people in the countryside, especially in the north, resent the economic gains in the cities, particularly those of the south (see the paragraph, page 381, on peasant demonstrations in Thai Binh). But this rump of latent discontent has little in common with those intellectual and middle class Vietnamese itching for more political freedoms; or those motivated entrepreneurs pressing for accelerated economic reforms; or those Buddhist monks and Christians demanding freedom of expression and respect for human rights; or the various groups of 'freedom' fighters operating (sporadically) from bases in Cambodia. Unless and until this loose broth of opposition groups coalesces, it is hard to see a coherent opposition movement evolving.

Nonetheless, each year a small number of brave, foolhardy or committed individuals challenge the authorities. Most are then arrested, tried, and imprisoned for various loosely defined crimes. There is always the possibility that cataclysmic, and unpredictable, political change will occur. As one veteran, but anonymous, Central Committee member said in an interview at the end of 1991: "If the CPSU [Communist Party of the Soviet Union], which had been in power for 74 years, can fall to pieces in 72 hours, we have at least to raise that possibility in Vietnam." Major General Tran Cong Man highlighted these fears when he remarked that:

> "the collapse of the Soviet Union was a devastating blow for [Vietnam] ... [It] was our support, ideologically and psychologically, also militarily and economically. It was our unique model. Now we find it was a false model".

The tensions between reform and control are constantly evident in small and large ways. A **press law** which came into effect in mid-1993 prohibits the publication of works "hostile to the socialist homeland, divulging state or [Communist] party secrets, falsifying history or denying the gains of the revolution". Ly Quy Chung, a newspaper editor in Saigon, described the Vietnamese responding to the economic reforms "like animals being let out of their cage". But, he added, alluding to the tight control the VCP maintains over political debate, "Now we are free to graze around, but only inside the fences". The Party's attempts to control debate and the flow of information has extended to the internet. In 1997 a National Internet Control Board was established and all internet and email usage is strictly monitored. The authorities attempt to fire-wall topics relating to Vietnam in a hopeless attempt to censor incoming information.

Economy

Partition and socialist reconstruction 1955-75

When the French left North Vietnam in 1954 they abandoned a country with scarcely any industry. The north remained predominantly an agrarian society, and just 1.5% of 'material output' (the Socialist equivalent of Gross Domestic Product) was accounted for by modern industries. These employed a few thousand workers out of a population of about 13 million. The French added to the pitiful state of the industrial sector by dismantling many of the (mostly textile) factories that did exist, shipping the machinery back to France.

With **independence**, the government in the north embraced a socialist strategy of reconstruction and development. In the countryside, agricultural production was collectivized. Adopting Maoist policies, land reform proceeded apace. Revolutionary cadres were trained to spot 'greedy, cruel and imperialist landlords', farmers of above average wealth who might themselves have owned tiny plots. Leaders of land reform brigades applied Chinese-inspired rules through people's tribunals and summary justice. An estimated 10,000 people died; Ho Chi Minh was opposed to the worst excesses and, although he failed to curb the zealots, land reform in Vietnam was a much less bloody affair than it was in China. In industry, likewise, the means of production were nationalized, co-operatives were formed, and planning was directed from the centre. Although evidence is hard to come by, it seems that even as early as the mid-1960s both the agricultural and industrial sectors were experiencing shortages of key inputs and were suffering from poor planning and mismanagement. The various sectors of the economy were inadequately linked, and the need for consumer goods was largely met by imports from China. But it was just at this time that the US bombing campaign 'Rolling Thunder' began in earnest (see page 367), and this served to obscure these economic difficulties. It was not until the late 1970s that the desperate need to introduce reforms became apparent. The bombing campaign also led to massive destruction and caused the government in the north to decentralize activity to the countryside in order to protect what little industry there was from the American attacks.

Reunification and a stab at socialist reconstruction (1975-79)

With the reunification of Vietnam in 1975, it seems that most leaders in the north thought that the re-integration of the two economies, as well as their re-invigoration, would be a fairly straightforward affair. As one of the Party leadership tellingly said during the Sixth Plenum at the end of 1979: "In the euphoria of victory which came so unexpectedly, we ... somewhat lost sight of realities; everything seemed possible to achieve, and quickly." This is understandable when it is considered that the north had just defeated the most powerful nation on earth. But the war disguised two economies that were both chronically inefficient and poorly managed, albeit for different reasons and in different ways. The tragedy was that just as this fact was becoming clear, the Vietnamese government embarked on another military adventure – this time the invasion and subsequent occupation of Cambodia in

December 1978. Shortly afterwards, Hanoi had to deploy troops again to counter the Chinese 'invasion' in 1979. As a result, the authorities never had the opportunity of diverting resources from the military to the civilian sectors.

Conditions in the south were no better than in the north. The US had been supporting levels of consumption far above those which domestic production could match, the shortfall being met through massive injections of aid. Following the Communists' victory, this support was ended – overnight. The Americans left behind an economy and society deeply scarred by the war: three million unemployed, 500,000 prostitutes, 100,000 drug addicts, 400,000 amputees and 800,000 orphans. Nor did many in the south welcome their 'liberation'. The programme of socialist transition which began after 1975 was strongly resisted by large sections of the population, and never achieved its aims. As resistance grew, so the government became more repressive, thus leading to the exodus of hundreds of thousands of 'boat people' (see page 376). Even as late as 1978, with the economy close to crisis, sections of the leadership were still maintaining that the problems were due to poor implementation, not to the fact that the policies were fundamentally flawed. The key problem was the characteristic of 'bureaucratic centralism': if a factory wished to transport umbrellas from Tay Ninh to Saigon, less than 100 km, it was required to go through 17 agencies, obtain 15 seals, sign five contracts, and pay numerous taxes.

Top investors – 2001

Country	US$ mn
Holland	577.8
Taiwan	438.8
France	407.1
Singapore	270.5
Japan	158.8
USA	110.8
Korea	99.2
Hong Kong	70.6
China	59.7
British Virgin Islands	57.4

It may seem strange that Holland which hitherto has made only modest investments in Vietnam should suddenly top the list of international investors. The explanation is that BP's major investment in the Nam Con Son project (see box, Nam Con Son, page 394) was channelled through Holland. Other British investments are often made via the British Virgin Islands and Hong Kong meaning that overall the UK is now about the major foreign investor in Vietnam.

Background

The roots of economic reform (1979-86)

In a bid to re-invigorate the economy, the Vietnamese government – like others throughout the Communist and former Communist world – has been introducing economic reforms. These date back to 1979 when a process of administrative decentralization was set in train. Farmers signed contracts with their collectives to deliver produce in return for access to land and inputs like fertilizers and pesticides, thereby returning many aspects of decision making to the farm level. Surplus production could be sold privately. Factories were made self-accounting, and workers' pay was linked to productivity. The reforms of 1979 also accepted a greater role for the private sector in marketing, agriculture and small-scale industry.

Unfortunately these reforms were generally unsuccessful in stimulating Vietnam's moribund economy. Agriculture performed reasonably, but industry continued to decline. Cadres at the regional and local levels often ignored directives from the centre, and critical inputs needed to fuel growth were usually unavailable. Both national income and per capita incomes continued to shrink. The reform process is referred to as *doi moi* or 'renovation', the Vietnamese equivalent of Soviet *perestroika*. Implementation of *doi moi* has not been easy. In Neil Sheehan's book *Two Cities: Hanoi and*

Vietnam: selected economic reforms, 1979-2001

1975, April: end of the Vietnam War

1978, December: Vietnamese forces invade Cambodia.

1979, September: Resolution No 6 issued by the Sixth Plenum of the VCP calls for reforms in industry and agriculture, including a loosening of State control.

1981, April: Directive 100/CT (Contract 100), introduces the first stage of agricultural decollectivization.

1986, December: Doi moi – 'new change' or 'renovation' – officially endorsed at the Sixth Party Congress.

1987, December: liberal foreign investment law promulgated to attract foreign investment.

1988, April: Resolution No 10, makes individual households the basis of agricultural production. Banking reforms introduced separating the roles of the Central Bank and commercial banks. Exchange rate unified.

1989, January: fiscal policy tightened and positive real interest rates introduced. Subsidies to state-operated industries sharply reduced. **March**: price reforms introduced; price subsidies are gradually abolished for most goods.

1992 'Equitization programme' introduced in which a handful of small state-owned enterprises are sold off to employees and others. **June and August**: vague reference in revised Land Law to mortgaging and renting of land.

1993, June: granting of long-term use of agricultural land to peasant families. **July**: new Land Law passed. Households and individuals are allocated land according to household size and given the right to exchange, transfer, lease, inherit and mortgage land use rights.

1994, new bankruptcy law passed making it possible for banks to seize the assets of state-owned enterprises. **February**: normalization of trade relations with the US. **May**: new labour legislation

enacted giving workers the right to strike.

1995, April: National Assembly considers new law partially or fully ending the state monopoly in selected sectors.

1996, Third Amendment to Foreign Investment Law.

1998, February: new foreign investment decree introduced to increase foreign direct investment.

1997, Slow progress on privatization of state-owned enterprises (by late 1997 only 14 small firms, out of a stock of 6,000, had been 'equitized')

1998, announcement of an experimental stock exchange in Ho Chi Minh City. **February**: new investment decree is introduced to ease export and licensing rules.

1999, Central bank announces it will allow the controlled depreciation of the non-convertible dong to bring it in line with market rates. **March**: reduced business costs for foreign investors announced. **June**: government publishes details of its annual budget for the first time. Two foreign insurance companies awarded licenses to operate in Vietnam. **July**: Vietnam and US agree to normalize trade relations. **December**: Prime Minister indicates state monopolies would be dismantled to stimulate the economy.

2000, May: National Assembly approves amendments to Foreign Investment Law designed to further encourage investment. **July**: Vietnam's first stock exchange opens for trading in Ho Chi Minh City. A long-delayed trade agreement is signed with the US.

2001, November: National Assembly ratifies bilateral trade agreement with US

Sources: Rigg, Jonathan (1997) Southeast Asia: the human landscape of modernization and development, London: Routledge; and Keesing's Record of World Events.

Saigon he asked one manager of a state enterprise: "What was worse ... fighting the French in Interzone Five ... or directing a state factory during doi moi?" The answer: "It was easier in Interzone Five."

Tourism in Vietnam

The Vietnamese government nominated 1990 'Visit Vietnam Year'. Although it did not have the razzmatazz of the Visit Thailand (1989), Malaysia (1990) or Indonesia (1991) years, the authorities saw that tourism would become a significant foreign exchange earner in the future.

In 1989, 60,000 tourists visited the country, of whom a quarter were overseas Vietnamese and a further 10% were from former Eastern Bloc countries. In 1990 the figure was 187,000, of whom 40,000 were overseas Vietnamese, and in 1993, 670,000 tourists visited the country.

Despite the high hopes and euphoria of the early 1990s, tourism in Vietnam suffered some serious reverses. The relative paucity of interesting sights (compared with Cambodia or Thailand) has resulted in a low rate of return visits particularly in the higher cost package market.

There were complaints about the high cost of Vietnam. The problem centred around the dual charging structures for internal air and train tickets with foreigners paying two to three times more than Vietnamese. Fortunately the government has taken steps to dismantle the dual charging scheme; foreigners now pay the same as locals on the railways while on Vietnam Airlines the gap has narrowed but despite pledges to eliminate it altogether no one is holding their breath.

In 2000 VNAT, Vietnamese National Administration of Tourism, launched a new drive 'Vietnam: Destination for the New Millennium' to improve their fortunes and indeed tourist arrivals have picked up, reaching 2,300,000 in 2000. Nevertheless, the events of 11 September notwithstanding, tourist arrivals are showing signs of sustained growth and the target of 3.5 to 4 million by 2005 is not unreasonable.

Some commentators have argued that the economic reforms of 1979 demonstrated that the Vietnamese government was forward-looking and prescient. However there is also considerable evidence to show that the pressure for reform was coming as much from the bottom, as from the top. Farm households and agricultural co-operatives, it seems, were engaged in what became known as 'fence-breaking', by-passing the state planning system. The Communist Party, to some degree, was forced to follow where peasants had already gone. This raises the questions of how far Vietnam's 'command' economy was truly commanding. Benedict Kerkvliet, for example, argues that "Even at the height of state economic planning and control, there were social, economic, and political activities in Vietnam that the state did not authorize. ... 'Pluralism' ... has been around in Vietnam for some time". Peasants in Vietnam devoted enormous efforts in time and energy to the cultivation of their small private plots and tried to bypass the collective system through what became known as *khóan chui* or 'sneaky contracts'.

Doi moi: the reform economy (1986-present)

Recognizing that the limited reforms of 1979 were failing to have the desired effect, the VCP leadership embraced a further raft of changes following the **Sixth Congress in 1986**. At the time, the Party daily, *Nhan Dan* wrote that never had "morale been so eroded, confidence been so low or justice been so abused". Subsidies on consumer goods were reduced and wages increased partially to compensate. There was also limited monetary reform, although prices were still centrally controlled. In late 1987 the central planning system was reformed. The net effect of these changes was to fuel inflation which remained high from 1986-88 – in 1988 it was running at well over 100%.

Again, appreciating that the reforms were not having the desired effect, and with the advice of the IMF, a third series of changes were introduced in 1988 and 1989.

Reduction of Poverty in Vietnam

The General Statistics Office of Vietnam carried out a thorough investigation into the nature and extent of poverty in Vietnam between 1993 and 1998. Much of the research was carried out by NGOs such as Action Aid, Oxfam UK and Save The Children UK. The survey was funded by UNDP and SIDA (Sweden) with technical support from the World Bank. The report, Attacking Poverty, was published in 2000.

"Most people in Tra Vinh Province are better off than they were 10 years ago. They have higher incomes, more savings, better nutrition and health, more government services and more of their children are attending school (and staying there longer). Even when remarking upon their personal problems, most respondents strongly confirmed these trends.... In addition, most people in Tra Vinh expect life to continue to get better." Tra Vinh PPA, Oxfam GB (1999).

The most important finding was how the proportion of people below the poverty line dropped dramatically, indeed there are few, if any, examples of such rapid decline in poverty in recent times. From 58% of households below the poverty line in 1992/93 the figure had fallen to 37% in 1997/98. Social indicators such as access to education and health care also improved sharply. School enrolment rates for boys and girls rose and evidence of malnutrition among children under five years of age declined sharply from 51% to 34%. Bicycle ownership rose from 67% to 76%.

Needless to say the pattern of economic growth and reduction of poverty has not been even. This is a major concern for the government and international agencies who are anxious to avoid major economic imbalances and the social tensions these create. While agriculture grew by a healthy 4.5% pa over the five years under study the industrial sector grew by a massive 13%. And of all new jobs created more than half were in the service sector. Rural Vietnam improved but nowhere near as fast as urban Vietnam. Not surprisingly therefore many young people living in the countryside wish to move to towns.

The challenge for the government is to maintain economic growth while ensuring the benefits of that growth extend to all in society.

The market mechanism was to be fully employed to determine wages, output and prices for the great majority of goods. The domestic currency, the dong, was further devalued to bring it into line with the black market rate and foreign investment actively encouraged.

But, with each series of reform measures disquiet in some sections of the Party grows. For example, in 1993 government salary differentials were widened to better reflect responsibilities. Whereas under the old system the differential between the highest and lowest paid workers was only 3.5 to one, the gap under the new system is 13 to one. This may make good sense to World Bank economists, but it is hard to swallow for a Party and leadership who have been raised on ideals of equality.

Until the Asian crisis was heralded with the collapse of the Thai baht at the beginning of July 1997, the Vietnamese economy had done well to ride some pretty serious **external shocks**. With the collapse of communism in Eastern Europe, around 200,000 migrant workers returned to the country and had to be reintegrated. The decline in aid and assistance from the former Soviet Union (which was only partially compensated by aid from Russia) and the corresponding precipitous decline in trade from US$1.8 bn (admittedly at the then unrealistic rouble exchange rate) in 1990 to US$85 mn in 1991, illustrates the extent to which Vietnam had to re-orientate its economy in the face of global political and economic change. No longer able to rely on the Soviet Union to bail it out (although even before then the Vietnamese would

Waste not, want not

lament that the Soviets were 'Americans without dollars'), the Vietnamese government took the drastic step of banning the import of all luxury consumer goods in October 1991 in an attempt to save valuable foreign exchange.

Japan – not the Soviet Union – is now Vietnam's largest trading partner, and foreign interest and investment has grown considerably since the country began to open up to foreigners in the mid-1980s. However, while on paper it may be possible to give Vietnam a favourable report, there are numerous problems still to be overcome. This is reflected in the fact that few people expect the Vietnam-US trade agreement finally approved at the end of 2001, which gives Vietnam considerable trade advantages over competitor countries, will actually lead to much of a boost in exports. Partly this is because the US economy is weak, but at least as important is the fact the Vietnam is not well placed to exploit this trade advantage. As commentator Margot Cohen said in an economic survey at the beginning of 2002, "Vietnam is still very near the bottom of global competitiveness charts". Growth in 2001 was a respectable but hardly remarkable 4.8% and forecasts for 2002 are in the range of 5-6%. This is barely sufficient to generate the jobs necessary to absorb the country's growing number of young people entering the workforce.

Economic challenges

Let's start with the good news: Vietnam's economy is resilient, the population is comparatively well-educated, it has good access to world markets and, as former Singapore Prime Minister Lee Kuan Yew put it, Vietnam also has that "vital intangible" necessary for Newly Industrializing Country-style rapid economic growth. Between 1992 and 1998 Vietnam was one of the 10 fastest growing economies in the world with an average growth of 8.4% per annum.

Up until 1997 it was taken for granted that Vietnam would achieve Asian-style rates of economic growth – apparently for the simple reason that it occupies a piece of Asian geographical space. Not only did the Asian crisis put talk of Tiger economies on the back burner, but even before the crisis there were voices of caution. The gloss of the immediate post-*doi moi* years has dulled, and people now accept that reforms will need to be both deeper and wider.

For a start, many of the reforms apparently in place are not being implemented in the expected manner. Take the process of privatization introduced in 1993. By 1998, out of 5,800 state-owned enterprises only 29 had been partially sold off. Foreign investors, who initially piled into the country thinking there was money to be made, are now shying away, daunted by the red tape, infuriated by the bureaucratic inertia, and fed up with the corruption. In 2000 a new Enterprise Law was enacted to kick start reform by streamlining the approval system. At one level this was a clear

Vietnam exports by value

(US$ mn 2000)
Total Exports   9,365

Of which:
Textiles and garments, 1,450
Petroleum, 1,232
Footwear, 1,032
Rice, 1,024
Marine Products, 858
Coffee*, 594
Rubber, 127
Cashew Nut, 117
Handicraft and fine arts, 111

Coal, 102
Black pepper, 64
Vegetable and fruits, 53
Tea, 51

* Despite being the world's second largest exporter of coffee it ranks as only Vietnam's sixth biggest export by value. The reason is largely due to the collapse of the coffee price (at its lowest level in nearly three decades) caused in large part by Vietnam's rapid increase in production.

improvement on what had gone before. After all, 84 types of licenses necessary to set up some private businesses were scrapped; but another 300 remain. If this is streamlining… Kazi Martin the World Bank's head economist in Vietnam diplomatically stated that he sees "a new-found willingness to unshackle the private sector" but many foreign investors are not so impressed. A related problem is that while there are technocrats who are skilled and knowledgeable about the demands of building a market economy, the Party leadership have very little understanding of what it takes – and it is the Party which ultimately calls the shots. In 1996 the Party Congress reaffirmed the state sector's 'leading role' in building the economy, granting just a supporting role to the private sector. Perhaps this explains the fact that while every official seems to accept the importance of reform – as one senior government economist put it in 2000, "If not, we will die" – few appear willing to put this into concrete action.

But Vietnam's problems do not begin and end with the reform programme. There are also many more rather more familiar challenges.

The population is growing rapidly in a country where there are 900 people for every square kilometre of agricultural land. As the World Bank has pointed out, this means "the country will have to develop on the basis of **human resources** rather than natural resources". But the human resources themselves need substantial 'upgrading': malnutrition is still widespread and, despite rapid progress in the elimination of poverty, poverty in the countryside over large areas of the north and interior uplands remains the norm rather than the exception (see box, Reduction of Poverty in Vietnam, page 390). Education and health facilities also require massive investment, not to mention the physical infrastructure including roads and power. **Strikes** are also becoming more common. Officially, there were over 200 between 1990 and 1996, although most believe that the true figure is considerably higher.

In addition, and despite the much publicized reforms, there is still an extremely large, inefficient and unprofitable **state sector**. As in China, what to do about this part of the economy is proving the most intractable of the government's challenges. In 1996 there were still over 6,000 state-owned enterprises employing 1.5 million workers – admittedly down from 12,000 and some 2.5 million workers in 1990. But the 6,000 that have been closed down or sold off have been the smaller and/or more profitable firms – the big enterprises remain in place, sapping scarce funds. It has been estimated that just a third of these 6,000 enterprises are profitable. By 2000 more state-owned enterprises had been sold but government investment in those remaining actually increased, reaching 9-10% of GDP. Managers and workers in

Looking back on 20 Years of Peace

The 20th anniversary of the end of the Vietnam War fell on 30 April 1995. The celebrations in Saigon raised the issue of whether political reunification had served merely to disguise a continuing sharp divide between the North and the South. Many southerners resent the fact that their graves go unmarked, their losses of 225,000 unacknowledged, and their former lives demeaned. Many find jobs hard to come by, and veterans – unlike those from the army of the former North – receive no pensions.

At the end of the war, 200,000 former southern politicians, soldiers and functionaries were sent to re-education camps – many never returned. One senior northerner remarked to Nayan Chanda, who was himself in Saigon during the final days of the war, that "After 20 years there is no sign of reconciliation ... Our press is still celebrating victory over the Saigon army. Mothers of northern heroes have been decorated and given rewards but mothers of Saigon troops have only humiliation." Despite the attempt to play down the victory for American consumption – who need to be placated for their dollars – in Vietnam the chasm

between the two regions remains.

Nor is it clear, to some at least, from what it was that the former South was liberated. James Webb, a Marine in Vietnam, author of Fields of Fire, *and an apologist for the American presence in the country, wrote on the occasion of the 20th anniversary that "Oddly, Vietnam seems to be emerging into what might have occurred if the war had indeed ended in a negotiated stalemate: an authoritarian, Western-oriented, market economy." These sentiments are echoed by Gabriel Kolko, an anti-war activist and a man with very different views from those of Webb, and with a very different agenda. He wrote, also on the anniversary of the end of the war:*

"The irony of Vietnam today is that those who gave and suffered the most, and were promised the greatest benefits, have gained the least. The Communists are abandoning them to the inherently precarious future of a market economy which increasingly resembles the system the US supported during the war. For the majority of Vietnam's peasants, veterans, and genuine idealists, the war was a monumental tragedy – and a vain sacrifice."

Background

state-owned enterprises are often resistant to changes, fearing the consequences of market 'discipline'. Workers expect to have a 'job for life', irrespective of profitability. The social consequences of the government forcing a change in this assumption are too great to contemplate, so instead state enterprises are being allowed to engage in joint ventures with foreign companies in the forlorn hope that either the problem will simply go away, or become less significant as other parts of the economy grow. The failure – or the unwillingness – of the government to dismantle the state sector is a particular bugbear of the World Bank which in most other respects awards the Vietnamese high marks.

The numbers of **unemployed** are also being boosted by the reduction in the size of the army – which celebrated its 50th anniversary in 1995. By late 1997 the country's standing army had been cut by two-thirds from its strength in 1989, to 500,000. Preparation for civvy life for the hundreds of thousands demobilized seems perfunctory to say the least. As one former soldier, now a *cyclo* driver, recounted to a journalist from *The Economist*, "When I joined, I was told they would help me find a job later. But when I left, all they gave me was a set of clothes, a piece of cloth and a paper that said that I had fulfilled my requirements."

Foreign investors also worry about the lack of legal, banking and accounting systems, and are put off by the archaic physical infrastructure when compared to such other Southeast Asian countries as the Philippines and Indonesia. The fact that, for example, nearly three-quarters of law students were sent to the former Soviet Union

Nam Con Son Gasfield

Years of tense and often frustrating negotiations were concluded in February 2001 when British Petroleum was awarded the contract for the construction of a 399-km pipeline and development of the Nam Con Son gasfield. BP's investment will amount to US$1.3 bn which dwarfs all previous investments in Vietnam. The gas reserves are located in waters 360 km off the coast of Vung Tau.

The awarding of the contract marked a change in government attitudes and indicated an acceptance, if grudging, that the Vietnamese cannot dictate terms but must negotiate if foreign investment is to be used to develop national resources. Gas from the 58 billion cu m reserves will fuel three power stations and a fertiliser plant. More abundant and cheaper electricity and a petrochemicals industry will provide a major boost for industry in the Vung Tau, Bien Hoa and Ho Chi Minh City areas. At its peak in 2006 the project will be generating 40% of Vietnam's electricity. Possibly of greater importance will be the perception among major international investors that Vietnam is now a place to do business and that if BP is staking so much of its own money perhaps they should do so too.

and Eastern Europe for their training, explains the lack of expertise in some crucial areas. At the end of 1994, Le Dang Doanh of Hanoi's Central Institute of Economic Management plainly stated that many of the new laws introduced since the late 1980s to deal with the economic reforms 'are words, not really laws'. Commercial law, for instance, barely exists in Vietnam, and some foreign companies are unwilling to throw money into a country which is, in legal terms, the equivalent of a black hole.

The country's **export base** is also still comparatively narrow: oil, coal, rice, marine products and garments are the country's key exports. In addition, the economic growth of the 1990s has brought its own problems – in the same way that has occurred in China. **Inequalities**, both spatial and personal, are widening as some areas and people benefit, while others do not. Growth in agriculture is down to 3-4%, while industry is expanding at an annual rate of 12%. So, while the economies of Hanoi and Saigon have been growing at an annual rate of about 20%, the countryside is stagnating. Over recent years rural incomes have fallen as rice prices and other agricultural commodities have remained depressed. (The fact that Vietnam is the world's second-largest rice exporter doesn't count for anything if the farmgate price of rice has fallen from 2,000 dong per kilo to less than 1,400 dong.) Nationally, the World Bank estimates that 51% of the population live in poverty; in the cities the figure is 27%. This is drawing people in from the countryside, creating urban problems of both a social (for instance, unemployed people living in poor conditions and a lack of educational facilities) and economic (such as strains on the physical infrastructure) nature. These inequalities are likely to widen further in the short to medium term with the on-going process of reform.

As with industry, the leadership are reluctant to allow rural people to run their own businesses and lives, continually interfering and fine-tuning and without addressing the key shortages which are of credit, training, skills and management. As Bui Quang Toan, senior researcher at the National Institute of Agricultural Planning and Projection, explained to a journalist from the Far Eastern Economic Review: "Cooperatives should be free of politics, free of administrative control…the government must give up the idea that they can use cooperatives as a tool to manage the people."

Widening inequalities are also raising political challenges. Local and provincial governments in wealthy areas are beginning to resent financing poorer parts of the country, and are showing a greater inclination to 'go it alone', ignoring directives from Hanoi. This feeds back to foreign investors who find that they have to deal with different sets of regulations in different parts of the country.

Background

Culture

People

Vietnam is home to a total of 54 ethnic groups including the Vietnamese themselves. The ethnic minorities vary in size from the Tày, with a population of about 1.3 million, to the O-du who number only 100 individuals. Life has been hard for many of the minorities who have had to fight not only the French and Vietnamese but often each other in order to retain their territory and cultural identity. Traditions and customs have been eroded by outside influences such as Roman Catholicism and communism although some of the less alien ideas have been successfully accommodated. Centuries of Viet population growth and decades of warfare have taken a heavy toll on minorities and their territories; increasingly, population pressure from the minority groups themselves poses a threat to their way of life.

Highland people: the Montagnards of Vietnam

The highland areas of Vietnam are among the most linguistically and culturally diverse in the world. In total, the highland peoples number 6-8 million. As elsewhere in Southeast Asia, a broad distinction can be drawn in Vietnam between the peoples of the lowlands and valleys, and the peoples of the uplands. The former tend to be settled, cultivate wet rice, and are fairly tightly integrated into the wider Vietnamese state: in most instances they are Viet. The latter are often migratory, they cultivate upland crops often using systems of shifting cultivation (see page 424), and are comparatively isolated from the state. The generic term for these diverse peoples of the highlands is Montagnard (from the French, 'Mountain People'), in Vietnamese *nguoi thuong* ('highland citizen') or, rather less politely, *moi* ('savage' or 'slave'). As far as the highland peoples themselves are concerned, they identify with their village and 'tribal' group, not as part of a wider 'highland citizens' grouping.

The French attitude towards the Montagnards was often inconsistent. The authorities wanted to control them and sometimes succumbed to the pressure from French commercial interests to conscript them into the labour force, particularly on the plantations. But some officials were positively protective, one, Monsieur Sebatier refused missionaries access to the territory under his control, destroyed bridges to prevent access, and had three tribal wives. He recommended total withdrawal from their lands in order to protect their cultural integrity. In *A Dragon Apparent*, Norman Lewis provides a wonderful account of the Montagnards and their way of life, and perceptively examines the relationship between them and the French.

Relations between the minorities and the Viet have not always been as good as they are officially portrayed. Recognizing and exploiting this mutual distrust and animosity, both the French and American armies recruited from among the minorities. In 1961 US Special Forces began organizing Montagnards into defence groups to prevent Communist infiltration into the Central Highlands from the north. Since 1975 relations between minorities and Viet have improved but there is still hostility, particularly in areas of heavy logging. Official publications paint a touching picture portraying the relationship between Viet and minority peoples: thus we read "successive generations of Vietnamese, belonging to 54 ethnic groups, members of the great national community of Vietnam, have always stood side by side with one another, sharing weal and woe, shedding sweat and blood to defend and build up their homeland ...". The government is keen to stress its role in eradicating poverty and introducing a settled rather than a nomadic existence among the minorities but ignores the consequences, namely the narrowing, blunting and elimination of

Visiting the minorities: house rules

Etiquette and customs vary between the minorities. However, the following are general rules of good behaviour that should be adhered to whenever possible.

1. Dress modestly without great displays of flesh.

2. Ask permission before photographing anyone (old people, pregnant women and mothers with babies often object to having their photograph taken).

3. Only enter a house if invited.

4. Do not touch or photograph village shrines.

5. Do not smoke opium.

6. Avoid sitting or stepping on door sills.

7. Avoid excessive displays of wealth and be sensitive when giving gifts (for children, pens are better than sweets).

8. Avoid introducing Western medicines.

9. Do not sit with the soles of your feet pointing at other people (ie sit cross-legged).

10. If offered a cup of rice wine it is polite to down the first cup in one (what the Vietnamese call tram phan tram – 100%).

cultural differences. In recent years the government has come to regard the minorities as useful 'tourist fodder' – with a splash of colour, primitive villages and ethnic dances, they provide a taste of the 'mystical East' which much of the country otherwise lacks.

Potentially tourism is a more serious and insidious threat to the minorities' way of life than any they have yet had to face. A great deal has been written about cultural erosion by tourism and any visitor to a minority village should be aware of the extent to which he or she contributes to this process. Traditional means of livelihood are quickly abandoned when a higher living standard for less effort can be obtained from the tourist dollar. Long-standing societal and kinship ties are weakened by the intrusion of outsiders. Young people may question their society's values and traditions which may seem archaic, anachronistic and risible by comparison with those of the modern, sophisticated tourist. And dress and music lose all cultural significance and symbolism if they are allowed to become mere tourist attractions.

Nevertheless, this is an unavoidable consequence of Vietnam's decision to admit tourists to the highland areas. Perhaps fortunately, however, for the time being at least, many of the minorities are pretty inaccessible to the average traveller. Visitors can minimize their impact by acting in a sensitive way (it is, for example, perfectly obvious when someone does not want their photograph taken). (See box, page 396, for general advice on visiting minority villages.) But the minority areas of Vietnam are fascinating places and the immense variety of colours and styles of dress add greatly to the visitor's enjoyment.

Ba-na (Bahnar) A Mon-Khmer-speaking minority group concentrated in the central highland provinces of Gia Lai-Kon Tum and numbering about 150,000. Locally powerful from the 15th-18th centuries, they were virtually annihilated by neighbouring groups during the 19th century. Roman Catholic missionaries influenced the Ba-na greatly and they came to identify closely with the French. Some conversions to Roman Catholicism were made but Christianity, where it remains, is usually just an adjunct to Ba-na animism. Ba-na houses are built on stilts and in each village is a communal house, or *rông*, which is the focus of social life. When a baby reaches his first full month he has his ears pierced in a village ceremony equivalent to the Vietnamese *day thang* (see box, Rite of passage, page 397); only then is a child considered a full member of the community. Their society gives men and women relatively equal status. Male and female heirs inherit wealth, and marriage can be arranged by the families of either husband or wife. Ba-na practise both settled and shifting cultivation.

Rite of passage: from baby to infant

In a poor country like Vietnam staying alive for long enough to see one's own first birthday has not always been easy. Fortunately, infant mortality levels have fallen dramatically (from 156/1,000 in 1960 to 33/1,000 in 1996) but remain high by Western standards. Perhaps not surprisingly therefore, Vietnamese families celebrate two important milestones in the early lives of their children.

Day thang, or full month, is celebrated exactly one month after birth. Traditionally, the mother remained in bed with her heavily-swaddled baby for the first month keeping him or her away from sun, rain and demon spirits. At one month the child is beyond the hazardous neo-natal stage and the mother would leave her bed and go out of the house to introduce her baby
to the village. Today, the parents hold a small party for friends and neighbours.

Thoi noi is celebrated at the end of the first year; it marks the time the baby stops sleeping in the cot and, having reached a full year, it is also a thanksgiving that the child has reached the end of the most dangerous year of life. At the party the baby is presented with a tray on which are various items such as a pen, a mirror, scissors, some soil and food; whichever the baby takes first indicates its character and likely job: scissors for a tailor, pen for a teacher, soil for a farmer and so on. Babies are normally weaned at about this time: some Vietnamese mothers use remarkably unsubtle but effective means for turning the baby from the breast, smearing the nipple with charcoal dust or Tiger Balm!

Primarily found on the Lam Dong Plateau in Lam Dong Province (Dalat) with a population of about 100,000. Extended family groups live in longhouses or *buon*, sometimes up to 30 m long. Unusually, society is matrilineal and newly-married men live with their wives' families. The children take their mother's name; if the wife dies young her smaller sister will take her place. Women wear tight-fitting blouses and skirts. Traditional shifting cultivation is giving way to settled agriculture.

Co-ho (also Kohor, with small local groups the Xre, Chil & Nop)

The Dao live in northern Vietnam in the provinces bordering China particularly Lao Cai and Ha Giang. They number, perhaps, half a million in all and include several sub-groupings notably the Dao Quan Chet (Tight Trouser Dao), the Dao Tien (Money Dao) and the Dao Ao Dai (Long Dress Dao). As these names suggest, Dao people wear highly distinctive clothing although sometimes only on their wedding day. The **Dao Tiên** or Money Dao of Hoa Binh and Son La provinces are unique among the Dao in that the women wear black skirts and leggings rather than trousers. A black jacket with red embroidered collar and cuffs, decorated at the back with coins (hence the name) together with a black red-tassled turban and silver jewellery are also worn. By contrast men look rather plain in black jacket and trousers. Head gear tends to be elaborate and includes a range of shapes (from square to conical), fabrics (waxed hair to dried pumpkin fibres) and colours.

Dao (also Mán)

The women of many branches of Dao shave off their eyebrows and shave back their hair to the top of their head before putting on the turban – a hairless face and high forehead are traditionally regarded as attributes of feminine beauty.

Dao wedding customs are as complex as Dao clothing and vary with each group. Apart from parental consent, intending marriage partners must have compatible birthdays, and the groom has to provide the bride's family with gifts worthy of their daughter. If he is unable to do this a temporary marriage can take place but the outstanding presents must be produced and a permanent wedding celebrated before *their* daughter can marry.

The Dao live chiefly by farming: those in higher altitudes are swidden cultivators growing maize, cassava and rye. In the middle zone, shifting methods are again used

Background

to produce rice and maize, and on the valley floors sedentary farmers grow irrigated rice and rear livestock.

Spiritually the Dao have also opted for diversity: they worship *Ban Vuong*, their mythical progenitor as well as their more immediate and real ancestors. The Dao also find room for elements of Taoism, and in some cases Buddhism and Confucianism, in their elaborate metaphysical lives. Never enter a Dao house unless invited, if tree branches are suspended above the gate to a village, guests are not welcome – reasons might include a post-natal but pre-naming period, sickness, death or special ceremony. Since the Dao worship the kitchen god, guests should not sit or stand immediately in front of the stove.

E-de
(also Rhade) Primarily concentrated in the Central Highlands province of Dac Lac and numbering nearly 200,000, they came into early contact with the French and are regarded as one of the more 'progressive' groups, adapting to modern life with relative ease. Traditionally the E-de live in longhouses on stilts; accommodated under one roof is the matrilineal extended family or commune. The commune falls under the authority of an elderly, respected woman known as the *khoa sang* who is responsible for communal property, especially the gongs and jars, which feature in important festivals. In E-de society it is the girl's family that selects a husband, who then comes to live with her (ie society is matrilocal). As part of the wedding festivities the two families solemnly agree that if one of the partners should break the wedding vow they will forfeit a minimum of one buffalo, a maximum of a set of gongs. Wealth and property are inherited solely by daughters. Shifting cultivation is the traditional subsistence system, although this has given way in most areas to settled wet rice agriculture. Spiritually the E-de are polytheist: they number animism (recognizing the spirits of rice, soil, fire and water especially) and Christianity among their beliefs.

Gia rai
(also Zrai) Primarily found in Gia Lai and Kon Tum provinces (especially near Play Ku) and numbering 260,000, they are the largest group in the Central Highlands. They are settled cultivators and live in houses on stilts in villages called *ploi* or *bon*. The Gia-rai are animist and recognize the spiritual dimension of nature; ever since the seventh century they have had a flesh and blood King of Fire and King of Water whose spirit is invoked in rain ceremonies.

Hmông
(also Mèo,
Mieu, Miao) Widely spread across the highland areas of the country, but particularly near the Chinese border down to the 18th parallel. The Hmông number about 750,000 (over 1% of Vietnam's population) and live at higher altitudes than all other hill people – above 1,500 m. Comparatively recent migrants to Vietnam, the Hmông began to settle in the country during the 19th century, after moving south from China. The Hmông language in its various dialects remained oral until the 1930s when a French priest attempted to romanize it with a view to translating the Bible. A more sucessful attempt to create a written Hmông language was made in 1961 but has since fallen into disuse. Nevertheless – or perhaps because of this failure – the Hmông still preserve an extraordinarily rich oral tradition of legends, stories and histories. Hmông people are renowned for their beautiful folk songs. Each branch of the Hmông people preserves its own corpus of love songs, work songs and festival songs which are sung unaccompanied or with the accompaniment of the *khène*, a small bamboo pipe organ, a two stringed violin, flutes, drums, gongs and jew's harps. Numerous Hmông dances also exist to celebrate various dates in the social calendar and to propitiate animist spirits.

They have played an important role in resisting both the French and the Vietnamese. Living at such high altitudes they tend to be one of the most isolated of all the hill people. Their way of life does not normally bring them into contact with the outside world which suits them well – the Hmông traders at Sapa are an exception (see page 121). High in the hills, flooding is not a problem so their houses are built on the ground, not raised up on stilts. Hmông villages are now increasingly found along the river valleys and roads as the government resettlement schemes aim to introduce them to a more sedentary form of agriculture. The Hmông practice slash and burn cultivation growing maize and dry rice. Traditionally opium has been a valuable cash crop. Although fields are often cleared on very steep and rocky slopes, the land is not terraced. There are a number of different groups among the Hmông including the White, Black, Red and Flower Hmông which are distinguishable by the colour of the women's clothes. Black Hmông wear almost entirely black clothing with remarkable pointed black turbans. White Hmông women wear white skirts and the Red Hmông tie their heads in a red scarf while the Flower Hmông wrap their hair (with hair extensions) around their head like a broad-brimmed hat. However, such numerous regional variations occur that even experts on ethnic minority cultures sometimes have problems trying to identify which branch of Hmông they have encountered. Serious social problems have occurred among the Hmông owing to opium addiction; with over 30% of the male population of some Hmông villages addicted, the drug has rendered many incapable of work causing misery and malnutrition for their families, and with the drug finding its way on to the streets of Vietnam's cities, the authorities have resolved to clamp down hard on opium production and in 1995 destroyed 4,500 ha of opium fields. This has had tragic consequences when the Hmông have tried to protect their livelihoods. In 1993 12 Hmông villagers in Son La Province killed a local party official in protest at opium clearances, then burnt themselves to death.

Numbering almost one million the Muòng are the fourth largest ethnic minority in Vietnam. They live in the area between northern Thanh Hoa Province and Yen Bai but predominantly in Hoa Binh Province. It is thought that the Muòng are descended from the same stock as the Viets: their languages are similar, and there are also close similarities in culture and religion. But whereas the Vietnamese came under strong Chinese cultural influence from the early centuries of the Christian era, the Muòng did not. The Muòng belong to the Viet-Muòng language group, their language is closest to Vietnamese of all the ethnic minority languages. It once had its own script but all the original literary works have been lost and today there is no trace. Muòng practise wet and dry rice cultivation where possible, supplementing their income with cash crops such as manioc, tobacco and cotton. Weaving is still practised, items produced including pillowcases and blankets. Culturally the Muòng are akin to the Thái and live in stilt houses in small villages called *quel*; groupings of from three to 30 quel form a unit called a *muong*. Muòng society is feudal in nature with each *muong* coming under the protection of a noble family (*lang*). The common people are not deemed worthy of family names so are all called Bui. Each year the members of a *muong* are required to labour for one day in fields belonging to the *lang*.

Muòng (also Mol)

Marriages are arranged: girls, in particular, have no choice of spouse. Muòng cultural life is rich, literature has been translated into Vietnamese and their legends, poems and songs are considered particularly fine.

Concentrated in Cao Bang and Lang Son provinces, adjacent to the Chinese border, the Nung number approximately one million. They are strongly influenced by the Chinese and most are Buddhist, but like both Vietnamese and Chinese the Nung practise ancestor worship too. In Nung houses a Buddhist altar is placed above the ancestor altar and, in deference to Buddhist teaching, they refrain from eating most types of meat. The Nung are settled agriculturalists and, where conditions permit, produce wet rice; all houses have their own garden in which fruit and vegetables are grown.

Nung

Background

Tày
(also Tho) The Tày are the most populous ethnic minority in Vietnam; they number about 1.3 million and are found in the provinces of northwest Vietnam stretching from Quang Ninh east to Lao Cai. Tày society was traditionally feudal with powerful lords able to extract from the free and semi-free serfs' obligations such as *droit de seigneur*. Today Tày society is male dominated with important decisions being taken by men and eldest sons inheriting the bulk of the family's wealth.

Economically the Tày survive by farming and are highly regarded as wet rice cultivationists, they are also noted for the production of fruits (pears, peaches, apricots and tangerines), herbs and spices. Diet is supplemented by animal and fish rearing and cash is raised by the production of handicrafts. The Tày live in houses on stilts, located in the river valleys. Tày architecture is quite similar in design to that of the Black Thái, but important differences may be identified, most notably the larger size of the Tày house, the deeper overhang of the thatched or (amongst more affluent Tày communities) tiled roof and the extent of the railed balcony which often encircles the entire house.

Like the Thái, Tày ancestors migrated south from southern China contemporaneously with those of the Thái and they follow the three main religions of Buddhism, Confucianism and Taoism in addition to ancestor worship and animist beliefs. Whilst Tày people have lived in close proximity to the Viet majority over a period of many centuries, their own language continues to be their primary means of communication. They hail from the Austro-Asian language family and specifically the Thai-Kadai language group. Tày literature has a long and distinguished history and much has been translated into Vietnamese. During the French colonial period missionaries romanized Tày script.

Thái
(also Táy
& T'ai) Numbering over one million this is the second largest ethnic minority in Vietnam and ethnically distinct from the Thais of modern-day Thailand. There are two main sub-groups, the Black (Thái Den), who are settled mainly in Son La, Lai Chan, Lao Cai and Yen Bai provinces, and the White Thái (Thái Don), who are found predominantly in Hoa Binh, Son La, Thanh Hoa and Vinh Phu provinces, as well as many others, including the Red Thái (Thái Do). The use of these colour-based classifications has usually been linked to the colour of their clothes, particularly the colour of women's shirts. However there has been some confusion over the origins of the terms and there is every reason to believe that it has nothing to do with the colour of their attire, and is possibly linked to the distribution of the sub-groups near the Red and Black rivers. The confusion of names becomes even more perplexing when the Vietnamese names for the sub-groups of Thái people are translated into Thái. Some scholars have taken Thái Den (Black Thái) to be Thái Daeng – *daeng* being the Thái word for red, thereby muddling up the two groups. With the notable exception of the White Thái communities of Hoa Binh traditional costume for the women of both the Black and White Thái generally features a coloured blouse with a row of silver buttons down the front, a long black skirt, a coloured waist sash and a black head-scarf embroidered with intricate, predominantly red and yellow designs.

The traditional costume of the White Thái women of Hoa Binh comprises a long black skirt with fitted waistband embroidered with either a dragon or chicken motif together with a plain pastel coloured blouse and gold and maroon sash.

Being so numerous the Thái cover a large part of northwest Vietnam, in particular the valleys of the Red River and the Da and the Ma rivers, spilling over into Laos and Thailand. They arrived in Vietnam between the fourth and 11th centuries from southern China and linguistically they are part of the wider Thái-Kadai linguistic grouping. Residents of Lac village in Mai Chau claim to have communicated with visitors from Thailand by means of this shared heritage.

The Thái tend to occupy lowland areas and they compete directly with the Kinh (ethnic Vietnamese) for good quality, irrigable farmland. They are masters of wet rice cultivation producing high yields and often two harvests each year. Their irrigation works are ingenious and incorporate numerous labour-saving devices including river-powered water wheels that can raise water several metres. Thái villages (*ban*) consist of 40-50 houses on stilts; they are architecturally attractive, shaded by fruit trees and surrounded by verdant paddy fields. Being, as they so often are, located by rivers one of the highlights of a Thái village is its suspension footbridge. The Thái are excellent custodians of the land and their landscapes and villages are invariably most scenic.

Owing to their geographical proximity and agricultural similarities with the Kinh it is not surprising to see cultural assimilation – sometimes via marriage – and most Thái speak Vietnamese. Equally it is interesting to note the extent to which the Thái retain a distinctive cultural identity, visibly most noticeable in their dress.

When a Thái woman marries, her parents-in-law give her a hair extension (*can song*) and a silver hair pin (*khat pom*) which she is expected to wear (even in bed) for the duration of the marriage. There are two wedding ceremonies, the first at the bride's house where the couple live for one to three years, followed by a second when they move to the husband's house.

Xo-dang

Concentrated in Gia Lai and Kon Tum provinces and numbering about 100,000, the Xo-dang live in extended family longhouses and society is patriarchal. The Xo-dang practise both shifting agriculture and the cultivation of wet rice. A highly war-like people, they almost wiped out the Ba-na in the 19th century. Xo-dang thought nothing of kidnapping neighbouring tribesmen to sacrifice to the spirits; indeed the practice of kidnapping was subsequently put to commercial use and formed the basis of a slave trade with Siam (Thailand). Xo-dang villages, or *ploi*, are usually well defended (presumably for fear of reprisal) and are surrounded by thorn hedges supplemented with spears and stakes. Complex rules designed to prevent in-breeding limit the number of available marriage partners which sometimes results in late marriages.

Other Groups
(with populations of over 50,000)

Hre – Quang Ngai and Binh Dinh provinces, 94,000. *Mnong* – Dac Lac and Lam Dong provinces, 65,000. *Xtieng* – Song Be province 50,000.

Kinh (also Viet)

The 1989 census revealed that 87% of Vietnam's population were ethnic Vietnamese. But with a well-run family planning campaign beginning to take effect in urban areas and higher fertility rates among the ethnic minorities it is likely that this figure will fall. The history of the Kinh is marked by a steady southwards progression from the Red River basin to the southern plains and Mekong Delta. Today the Kinh are concentrated into the two great river deltas, the coastal plains and the main cities. Only in the central and northern highland regions are they outnumbered by ethnic minorities. Kinh social cohesion and mastery of intensive wet rice cultivation has led to their numerical, and subsequently political and economic dominance of the country. Ethnic Vietnamese are also found in Cambodia where some have been settled for generations; recent Khmer Rouge attacks on Vietnamese villages have, however, caused many to flee to Vietnam.

Cham

With the over-running of Champa in 1471 (see page 354) Cham cultural and ethnic identity was diluted by the more numerous ethnic Vietnamese. The Cham were dispossessed of the more productive lands and found themselves in increasingly marginal territory. Economically eclipsed and strangers in their own land, Cham artistic creativity atrophied, their sculptural and architectural skills, once the glory of Vietnam, faded and decayed like so many Cham temples and towers. It is estimated that there are, today, 99,000 Cham people in Vietnam chiefly in central and southern Vietnam in the coastal provinces extending south from Quy Nhon. Small communities are to be found in Ho Chi Minh City and in the Mekong Delta around Chau Doc. They are artistically the poor relations of their forebears but skills in weaving and music live on.

The Cham of the south are typically engaged in fishing, weaving and other small scale commercial activities; urban Cham are poor and live in slum neighbourhoods. Further north the Cham are wet or dry rice farmers according to local topography; they are noted for their skill in wet rice farming and small scale hydraulic engineering.

In southern Vietnam the majority of Cham are Muslim, a comparatively newly acquired religion although familiar from earlier centuries when many became acquainted with Islamic tenets through traders from India and the Indonesian isles. In central Vietnam most Cham are Brahminist and the cult of the linga remains an important feature of spiritual life. In these provinces, away from the influence of Islam, vestiges of matriliny remain.

The Hoa: ethnic Chinese

There are nearly one million **ethnic Chinese** or Hoa in Vietnam, 80% living in the south of the country. Before reunification in 1975 there were even more: persecution by the authorities and the lack of economic opportunities since the process of socialist transformation was initiated, encouraged hundreds of thousands to leave. There are now large Vietnamese communities abroad, particularly in Australia, on the west coast of the US, and France. It has been estimated that the total Viet-kieu population numbers some two million.

With the reforms of the 1980s, the authorities' view of the Chinese has changed – they now appreciate the crucial role they played, and could continue to play, in the economy. Before 1975, the *Hoa* controlled 80% of industry in the south and 50% of banking and finance. Today, ethnic Chinese in Vietnam can own and operate businesses and are once again allowed to join the Communist Party (although only 1,000 out of two million are members), the army, and to enter university. The dark days of the mid to late 1970s seem to be over.

The Viet Kieu: Overseas Vietnamese

Since 1988, **Overseas Vietnamese** or Viet Kieu (most of whom are of Chinese extraction) have been allowed back to visit their relatives, in some cases helping to spread stories of untold wealth in the US, Australia and elsewhere. The largest community of overseas Vietnamese live in the US, about 1.4 million. The next largest populations are resident in France (250,000) and Australia (160,000), with much smaller numbers in a host of other countries. In 1990, 40,000 returned to visit; in 1995, 265,000 returned 'home'.

Many Viet Kieu are former boat people, while others left the country as part of the UN-administered Orderly Departure Programme which began in earnest in the late 1980s. The Viet Kieu have often shown, in their adopted homes, enormous perseverance and grit. Take the small Texan shrimping town of Palacios. Today there are around 300 Americans of Vietnamese extraction, mostly Roman Catholics, living in and around Palacios. When the first settlers arrived in 1976 escaping from the defeated South, most had nothing. Many faced bigotry from racist elements in the local community who feared competition from 'foreigners'. But they worked and saved and by the early 1980s some families had managed to buy shrimping boats for themselves. Another 10 years on and the most successful boats were owned and operated by Vietnamese. By that time, many of their children had been born and raised in the local community, they had gone through local schools (often winning the top scholastic prizes) and few questioned their credentials to be counted as Americans. As *The Economist* put it, locals 'say the Vietnamese remind them of traditional American virtues: family, community, God, a Herculean work effort, and a passionate hatred of communism' (1 August 1998).

Having discovered some measure of prosperity in the West, the Vietnamese government is anxious to welcome them back – or rather, welcome their money. So far, however, flows of investment for productive purposes have been rather disappointing and largely concentrated in the service sector – particularly hotels and restaurants. Far more is thought to have been invested in land and property as, since 2000, overseas Vietnamese have been able to purchase property in their own name. Part of the problem is that many Viet Kieu were escaping from persecution in Vietnam and of all people continue to harbour doubts about a government which is, in essence, the same as the one they fled. On the government's side, they worry that the Viet Kieu may be a destabilizing influence, perhaps even a Fifth Column intent on undermining the supremacy of the Communist Party. Again the leadership have cause for concern as the most vocal opponents of the US policy of rapprochement have been Viet Kieu. They have also been the main source of funds for (the admittedly ineffectual) groups trying to overthrow the government. Nor are the Overseas Vietnamese quite as rich as their ostentatious displays of wealth on the streets of Saigon and Hanoi would indicate. They do not have the economic muscle of the Overseas Chinese, for example, and in most cases have only been out of the country for less than 20 years, many having lost everything in their attempt to escape. Many young Viet Kieu have, however, equipped themselves with qualifications and skills while overseas and can find lucrative employment back in Vietnam.

Art and architecture

The first flourishing of Vietnamese art occurred with the emergence of the Dongson culture (named after a small town near Thanh Hoa where early excavations were focused) on the coast of Annam and Tonkin between 500 and 200 BC. The inspiration for the magnificent bronzes produced by the artists of Dongson originated from China: the decorative motifs have clear affinities with earlier Chinese bronzes. At the same time, the exceptional skill of production and decoration argues that these pieces represent among the first, and finest, of Southeast Asian works of art. This is most clearly evident in the huge and glorious **bronze drums** which can be seen in museums in both Hanoi and Saigon (see box, page 404).

Dongson culture

If there was ever a 'golden' period in Vietnamese art and architecture, it was that of the former central Vietnamese **kingdom of Champa**, centred on the Annamite coast, which flowered in the 10th and 11th centuries. Tragically however, many of the 250 sites recorded in historical records have been pillaged or damaged and only 20 have survived the intervening centuries in a reasonable state of repair. Most famous are the sites of My Son and Dong Duong, south of Danang. Many of the finest works have been spirited out of the country to private collections and foreign museums; others destroyed by bombing and artillery fire during the Vietnam War. Nonetheless, the world's finest collection – with some breathtakingly beautiful work – is to be found in Danang's Cham Museum (see page 204).

Cham art

The earliest Cham art belongs to the Mi Son E1 period (early eighth century). It shows stylistic similarities with Indian Sanchi and Gupta works, although even at this early stage in its development Cham art incorporated distinctive indigenous elements, most clearly seen in the naturalistic interpretation of human form. By the Dong Duong period (late ninth century), the Cham had developed a unique style of their own. Archaeologists recognize six periods of Cham art:

Background

Brilliance in Bronze: rain drums of Dongson

Of the artefacts associated with the Dongson culture, none is more technologically or artistically impressive than the huge bronze kettle drums that have been unearthed. Vietnamese archaeologists, understandably, have been keen to stress the 'Vietnamese-ness' of these objects, rejecting many of the suggestions made by Western scholars that they are of Chinese or Indian inspiration. As Professor Pham Huy Thong of the Academy of Sciences writes, Western studies are "marked by insufficient source material, prejudices and mere deductions", and that their "achievements [in understanding the drums] remain insignificant". He supports the view that these magnificent objects were products of the forebears of the Viet people. The jury on the issue remains out.

The squat, waisted, bronze Dongson drums show their makers to have been master casters of the first order. They can measure over 1 m in height and width and consist of a decorated tympanum, a convex upper section, waisted middle, and expanding lower section. Decoration is both geometric and naturalistic, most notably on the finely incised drum head. An area of continuing debate concerns the function of the drums. They have usually been found associated with human remains and other precious objects, leading archaeologists to argue that they symbolized power and prestige, and were treasured objects in the community. Also known as 'rain drums', they are sometimes surmounted with bronze figures of frogs (or toads). It is thought that the drums were used as magical instruments to summon rain – frogs being associated with rain. Other decorative motifs include dancers (again, possibly part of rain-making rites) and boats with feather-crowned passengers (perhaps taking the deceased to the Kingdom of the Dead). Other Dongson drums have been found as far east as the island of Alor in Nusa Tenggara, Indonesia, indicating trade links between northern Vietnam and the archipelago.

As if to emphasize the nationalist symbolism of the drum, an image of an ornate tympanum is used as an icon by Vietnamese television, and Vietnam Airlines prints the motif on their tickets.

My Son E1	early eighth century
Hoa Lai	early ninth century
Dong Duong	late ninth century
Late Tra Kieu	late 10th century
Thap Mam	12th-13th century
Po Klaung Garai	13th-16th century

The Cham Kingdom was ethnically and linguistically distinct, but was overrun by the Vietnamese in the 15th century. It might be argued, then, that their monuments and sculptures have little to do with 'Vietnam' *per se*, but with a preceding dynasty.

More characteristic of Vietnamese art and architecture are **the pagodas and palaces at Hué** (see page 177) and in and around Hanoi (page 68). But even this art and architecture is not really 'Vietnamese', as it is highly derivative, drawing heavily on Chinese prototypes. Certainly there are some features which are peculiarly Vietnamese, but unlike the other countries of mainland Southeast Asia, the Vietnamese artistic tradition is far less distinct. Vietnamese artistic endeavour was directed more towards literature than the plastic arts. In his art history of Indochina, French art historian Bernard Groslier – better known for his work on Angkor – writes, rather condescendingly:

Hué architecture

'From 1428 to 1769 Vietnamese art is bogged down in formulas. Despite the absorption of Champa, no foreign influence, save that of China, affected them. However, execution and technique greatly improved, so that some of the works take an honourable place among Chinese provincial products' (1962: 227).

The beginnings of contemporary or modern Vietnamese art can be traced back to the creation of the **École de Beaux Arts Indochine** in Hanoi in 1925. By this time there was an emerging Westernized intelligentsia in Vietnam who had been schooled in French ways and taught to identify, at least in part, with French culture. Much of the early painting produced by students taught at the École de Beaux Arts Indochine was romantic, portraying an idyllic picture of Vietnamese life and landscape. It was also weak. However by the 1930s a Vietnamese nationalist tone began to be expressed both in terms of subject matter and technique. For example, paintings on silk and lacquer became popular around this time.

Contemporary Vietnamese art

Background

In 1945, with the Declaration of Independence, the École de Beaux Arts Indochine closed, and art for art's sake came to an end. From this point, artists were strongly encouraged to join in the revolutionary project and, for example, paint posters of heroic workers, stoic peasants and brave soldiers. Painting landscapes or bucolic pictures of rural life was no longer on the agenda.

In 1950 a new **School of Fine Art** was established in Viet Bac with the sole remit of training revolutionary artists. Central control of art and artists became even more stringent after 1954 when many artists were sent away to re-education camps. Established artists like Bui Xuan Phai, for example, were no longer permitted either to exhibit or to teach so lacking were they in revolutionary credentials.

In 1957 a new premier art school was created in the capital – the **Hanoi School of Fine Arts**. Students here were schooled in the methods and meanings of socialist-realism and western art became, by definition, capitalist and decadent. But while the State saw to it that artists kept to the revolutionary line, fine art in North Vietnam never became so harsh and uncompromising as in China or the Soviet Union; there was always a romantic streak. In addition, the first director of the Hanoi School of Fine Arts, Nguyen Do Cung, encouraged his students to search for inspiration in traditional Vietnamese arts and crafts, in simple village designs, and in archaeological artefacts. Old woodblock prints, for example, strongly influenced the artists of this period.

Modern Vietnamese art

Contemporary art in Vietnam, as elsewhere in Southeast Asia, has recently benefited from an upsurge in interest from young Asian collectors with plenty of money and a preference for arts oriental to arts occidental. Exhibitions in Hong Kong, New York, Paris and London have helped bring contemporary Vietnamese art to a wider public. Galleries have opened in all the major cities of Vietnam and although much of the work displayed is purely commercial, artists now have an opportunity to exhibit pictures which until recently were considered subversive. Vietnam has three art colleges, in Saigon, Hué and the School of Fine Arts in Hanoi, which was founded by the French in 1925.

Although most Vietnamese painting is still conservative in subject, idiom and medium, some painters of the younger generation, including Dao Hai Phong, Tran Trong Vu and Truong Tan, are experimenting with more abstract ideas and, in the more liberal artistic clime of the new millennium, their work is more expressive and less clichéd than that of 10 or 20 years ago. Even established artists such as Ly Quy Chung, Tran Luu Hau and Mai Long are taking advantage of their newly found artistic freedom to produce exciting experimental work; Trinh Cung and Tran Trong Vu are noted for their abstract paintings and Nguyen Thanh Binh's famous but faceless schoolgirls in ao dais hang in drawing rooms across Asia and Europe. The popularity of this theme has been seized upon by many lesser artists. Among the most respected artists of the older generation are Professor Nguyen Thu, Colonel Quang Tho and Diep Minh Chau, whose work draws heavily on traditional Vietnamese themes, particularly rural landscapes, but also episodes from recent history: the battle of Dien Bien Phu, life under American occupation and pencil sketches of Ho Chi Minh. Such traditional art forms as watercolour paintings on silk and lacquerwork are still popular.

For further information visit www.thavibu.com/vietnam

With *doi moi* – economic reform – has come a greater degree of artistic freedom. Nguyen Van Linh, the late secretary-general of the Vietnamese Communist Party, talked of 'untying the strings', to give artists greater freedom of individual expression. Today there are numerous art galleries in Hanoi and Saigon and while artists still paint within limits set by the Communist Party, these limits have been considerably loosened. The first exhibition of abstract art in Vietnam was held in 1992.

The Vietnamese Pagoda

The pagoda or *chua* is a Buddhist temple, and shows clear affinities with its Chinese equivalent (see page 415 for a background to Vietnamese Buddhism). A Vietnamese pagoda is not a many-tiered tower – it is usually a single-storeyed structure. But some pagodas do have a tower (*thap*) which in most cases was erected as a memorial to the founder of the pagoda. Most will have a sacred pond (often with sacred turtles), bell tower, and yard. The main building – the pagoda itself – usually consists of a number of rooms. At the front are three main doors which are opened only for special festivals. Behind these doors are the front hall, outer hall and the inner or main altar hall, the former being at the lowest level, the altar hall at the highest. There will be Buddha statues, sometimes three, past, present and future. At the back of the pagoda are living quarters for monks and nuns, as well as gardens and other secular structures. Monks and nuns never serve in the same pagoda. While a temple may be dedicated to a hero, a mythical character or holy animal a pagoda is an exclusively Buddhist place of worship.

Avalokitesvara or Ti-Ts'ang Wang: the compassionate male Boddhisattva, usually depicted in an attitude of meditation with his attributes, a water flask and lotus. The figure is sometimes represented with four arms, in which case his attributes are a rosary and book, as well as the lotus and water flask. He is merciful and offers help and solace to those suffering the torments of hell.

Bodhisattvas: enlightened beings or future Buddhas who have renounced nirvana to remain on earth. They are in theory countless, although just a handful are usually represented, most easily recognizable to the devotee. Bodhisattvas are usually depicted as princes with rich robes and a crown or head-dress.

Buddha (Sakyamuni): the Buddha, or the historic Buddha; usually depicted seated on a throne or thrones (often a lotus) in one of the mudras or 'attitudes' of the Buddha, and clothed in the simple dress of an ascetic. Among the Buddha's features are elongated ear lobes, the *urna* or third 'eye' in the centre of the forehead, and tightly curled hair.

Buddha of the Past (Amitabha): central to the Pure Land faith. Adherents chant the Amitabha sutra, and on their death are transported to the Western Paradise where they are guided to nirvana. The Amitabha Buddha is merciful and wise. Recent interpretations can sometimes be identified by a very long right arm – so carved so that the Buddha can embrace all of humanity, and bring salvation to everyone.

Ch'eng-huang Yeh (City God): each town will have its own deity who controls the behaviour of the population. He also keeps the records of the dead, and sends out his henchmen to collect people when their due date has arrived. He is therefore greatly feared. More generally, he controls the demons and therefore has some power over natural disasters like flood and pestilence.

Dragon (long/rong): not the evil destructive creature of Western mythology but divine and beneficial. Often associated with the emperor.

Fertility Goddesses: there are lots of these, of which the most famous is Quan Am. Other popular fertility goddesses can usually be identified by the children that they hold in their laps. Sometimes they are surrounded by attendants who hold infants, or are shown breast-feeding, teaching or playing with them.

Judges or Magistrates: these 10 men run the Ten Courts of the Afterworld and are usually arranged in two rows of five (often on either side of the hall). Their mission is

Vietnamese pagoda

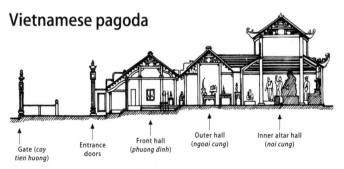

Gate (*cay tien huong*)

Entrance doors

Front hall (*phuong dinh*)

Outer hall (*ngoai cung*)

Inner altar hall (*noi cung*)

Adapted from Bezacier, Louis (1959) *Relevés des monuments anciens du Nord Viet-nam*, Ecole Française D'Extrême-Orient, Paris

to sentence the dead according to their role and life on earth. Each Judge is responsible for a different sin – murder, unfilial acts, arson, and so on – and having judged an individual passes them on to the next Judge. But just like the real world, sinners can have their sentences lightened by handing over money (Hell Money), so corruption works even here! Having passed through the hands of 10 Judges, the poor soul then arrives at the feet of **Mother Meng**. She gives the extirpated sinner the Soup of Oblivion, whereupon he or she forgets everything and is in a suitable state to be re-born in the real world.

Ong Tao: ascends to heaven at the end of the old year to inform God of the family's conduct during the previous 12 months. He is, therefore, fêted and petitioned for days before.

Patron deities: this includes a large number of deities that look after the interests of particular groups of people – fishermen (see Thien Hau), actors, policemen, farmers, and so on.

Quan Am: Chinese Goddess of Mercy (Kuan-yin), often all-white, and usually depicted holding her adopted son in one arm and standing on a lotus leaf (the symbol of purity). Quan Am's husband is occasionally depicted as a parakeet (see page 76). Quan Am is sometimes represented as a man, and as a Bodhisattva – Avalokitesvara – the two are fused in a single representation.

Quan Cong and companions: usually red-faced and green-cloaked and accompanied by his two trusty companions, General Chau Xuong and the Mandarin Quan Binh, and sometimes also with his horse and groom.

Swastika: running either left to right or vice versa, it is often complicated by various additions. The motif symbolizes the 'heart of the Buddha', 'long life' and 'ten thousand'. In Buddhist and Cao Dai temples, swastikas run in opposite directions. Cao Dai believers argue that 'their' direction is in harmony with the movement of the universe.

Thien Hau Thanh Mau (also Ma Tsu): goddess of the sea and protector of sailors. She first appeared, so to speak, in Fukien province in China during the 11th century. Folklore has it that she was the daughter of a fisherman named Lin and that she died while a virgin. She appears to fishermen in times of extreme peril and saves their lives. Thien Hau Thanh Mau is usually represented seated, with a flattened crown. But the real giveaway are her two companions, who go by the great names of **Thousand-mile Eye** and **Follow the Wind Ear**. These are both tamed demons who the goddess uses to provide long range weather forecasts to fishermen. Thousand-mile Eye is red-skinned and peers towards the horizon, hand shading his eyes; Follow the Wind Ear is green-skinned and is usually depicted cupping his hand to his ear as he listens for minor climatic changes. The three of them are usually seen, unsurprisingly, in coastal towns.

T'u-ti Kung or Fu-te Cheng-shen (Earth God): the Lord of the Earth is effectively a petty official and not to be greatly feared as he merely does the work of much more powerful gods. He keeps track of birth, deaths and marriages – as headmen do in real life. He is usually represented as an old man.

Yin-yang symbol: the Taoist symbol, a circle divided by an 'S' line, splitting the circle into dark and light halves and symbolizing the dualism of the world (see page 417).

Crafts

The art of making lacquerware is said to have been introduced into Vietnam after Emperor Le Thanh Ton (1443-59) sent an emissary to the Chinese court to investigate the process. Lacquer is a resin from the son tree (*Rhus succedanea or R vernicifera*) which is then applied in numerous coats (usually 11) to wood (traditionally teak), leather, metal or porcelain. Prior to lacquering, the article must be sanded and coated with a fixative. The final coat is highly polished with coal powder. The piece may then be decorated with an incised design, painted, or inset with mother-of-pearl. If mother-of-pearl is to be used, appropriately shaped pieces of lacquer are chiselled out and the mother-of-pearl inset. This method is similar to that used in China, but different from Thailand and Burma. The designs in the north show Japanese influences, apparently because Japanese artists were employed as teachers at the École des Beaux Arts in Hanoi in the 1930s.

Lacquerware (*son mai*)
True Vietnamese influence is best seen in crafts

This cone-shaped hat is one of the most common and evocative sights in Vietnam's countryside. Worn by women (and occasionally men), it is usually woven from latania leaves. The poem hats of Hué are the best known examples (see page 198).

Non Lá conical hat

The garment that exhibits more conspicuously what it was intended to hide. National women's costume of Vietnam, literally, but prosaically, 'long dress'. *Ao dai* consists of a long flowing tunic of diaphanous fabric worn over a pair of loose-fitting white pants; the front and rear sections of the tunic are split from the waist down. The modern design was created by a literary group called the *Tu Luc Van Doan* in 1932, based on ancient court costumes and Chinese dresses such as the chong san. In traditional society, decoration and complexity of design indicated the status of the wearer (for example gold brocade and dragons were for the sole use of the emperor; purple for higher-ranked mandarins). The ao dai's popularity has spread worldwide and the annual *Miss Ao Dai* pageant at Long Beach attracts entrants from all over the US. Today *ao dai* is uniform for hotel receptionists and many office workers, particularly in Saigon but less so in cooler Hanoi. French designer Elian Lille: "The first thing most people see when they come to Vietnam is the young students wearing a white ao dai, with their long hair clipped back and sitting very straight on their bicycles. It is exquisite."

Ao dai

Background

Buffalo teeth

Prickles

Jaw bone of the cricket

Kapok

Spines

Toucan's beak

Rice pounder patterns

Bird's feathers

Vietnam War textile patterns

Montagnard textile patterns
(after Dournes, Boulbert, Huard and Maurice and France Asie.)

Montagnard There are over 50 different hill peoples, so their crafts are highly diverse. Textiles,
crafts jewellery and basketwork are the most widely available. The finely worked clothing
of the Mùòng (with Dongson-derived motifs) and indigo-dyed cloth of the Ba-na are
two examples of Montagnard crafts.

Language

The Vietnamese language has a reputation for being fiendishly difficult to master. Its
origins are still the subject of dispute – at one time thought to be a Sino-Tibetan language (because it is tonal), it is now believed to be Austro-Asiatic and related to
Mon-Khmer. Sometime after the ninth century, when Vietnam was under Chinese
domination, Chinese ideograms were adapted for use with the Vietnamese language. This script – *chu nho* ('scholars script') was used in all official correspondence
and in literature right through to the early part of the 20th century. Whether this
replaced an earlier writing system is not known. As early Vietnamese nationalists
tried to break away from Chinese cultural hegemony in the late 13th century, they
devised their own script, based on Chinese ideograms but adapted to meet Vietnamese language needs. This became known as *chu nom* or 'vulgar script'. So, while
Chinese words formed the learned vocabulary of the intelligentsia – largely inaccessible to the man on the street or in the paddy field – non-Chinese words made up a
parallel popular vocabulary.

Finally, in the 17th century, European missionaries under the tutelage of Father
Alexandre-de-Rhodes, created a system of romanized writing – *quoc ngu* or 'national
language'. It is said that Rhodes initially thought Vietnamese sounded like the 'twit-
tering of birds' (a view interestingly echoed by Graham Greene in *The Quiet American*: "To take an Annamite to bed with you is like taking a bird: they twitter and sing
on your pillow") but had mastered the language in six months. The first quoc ngu
dictionary (Vietnamese-Portuguese-Latin), *Dictionarium Annamiticum Lusitanum et
Latinum*, was published in 1651. Quoc ngu uses marks – so-called diacritical marks –
to indicate tonal differences. Initially it was ignored by the educated unless they
were Catholic, and it was not until the early 20th century that its use became a mark
of modernity among a broad spectrum of Vietnamese. Even then, engravings in the
mausolea and palaces of the royal family continued to use Chinese characters. It
seems that the move from chu nom to quoc ngu, despite the fact that it was
imposed by an occupying country, occurred as people realized how much easier it
was to master. The first quoc ngu newspaper, *Gia Dinh Bao* (Gia Dinh Gazette), was
published in 1865 and quoc ngu was adopted as the national script in 1920.

'Standard Vietnamese' is based on the language spoken by an educated person
living in the vicinity of Hanoi. This has become, so to speak, Vietnam's equivalent of
BBC English. There are also important regional dialects in the centre and south of the
country, and these differ from Standard Vietnamese in terms of tone and vocabulary,
but use the same system of grammar.

For some useful Vietnamese words and phrases, see page 433 and the food and
drink and shopping boxes on pages 438 and 439 respectively.

Literature

In ancient Vietnam, texts were reproduced laboriously, by scribes, on paper made from the bark of the mulberry tree (*giay ban*). Examples exist in Saigon, Paris, Hanoi and Hué. Printing technology was introduced in the late 13th century, but unfortunately, because of the hot and humid climate no early examples exist.

Vietnam has a rich folk literature of **fables**, **legends**, **proverbs** and **songs**, most of which were transmitted by word of mouth. In the 17th and 18th centuries, satirical poems and, importantly, verse novels (*truyen*) appeared. These were memorized and recited by itinerant story-tellers as they travelled from village to village.

Like much Vietnamese art, Vietnamese literature also owes a debt to China. Chinese characters and literary styles were duplicated and although a tradition of *nom* literature did evolve (nom being a hybrid script developed in the 13th century), Vietnamese efforts remained largely derivative. One exception was the scholarly **Nguyen Trai** (see box, page 353) who bridged the gap; he excelled in classical Chinese chu nho as well as producing some of the earliest surviving, and very fine, poetry and prose in the new chu nom script. An important distinction is between the literature of the intelligentsia (essentially Chinese) and that of the people (more individualistic). These latter nom works, dating from the 15th century onwards, were simpler and concerned with immediate problems and grievances. They can be viewed as the most Vietnamese of literary works and include *Chinh Phu Ngam* (Lament of a Soldier's Wife), an anti-war poem by Phan Huy Ich (1750-1822). The greatest Vietnamese literature was produced during the social and political upheavals of the 19th century – *Truyen Kieu* (The Tale of Kieu) written by Nguyen Du (1765-1820) is a classic of the period. This 3,254-line story is regarded by most Vietnamese as their cultural statement *par excellence* (see box, page 412 for a taster). Nguyen Du was one of the most skilled and learned mandarins of his time, and was posted to China as Vietnam's Ambassador to the Middle Kingdom. On his return, Nguyen Du wrote the *Truyen Kieu* (or *Kim Van Kieu*), a celebration of Vietnamese culture, in the lines of which can be traced the essence of Vietnamese-ness.

French influence, and the spread of the Romanized Vietnamese script, led to the end of the Chinese literary tradition by the 1930s and its replacement by a far starker, freer, Western-derived style. Poetry of this period is known as *Tho Moi* (New Poetry). The Communist period has seen restrictions on literary freedom, and in recent years there have been numerous cases of authors and poets, together with journalists, being imprisoned owing to the critical nature of their work. Much of Vietnam's literature is allegorical (which the people readily understand); this reflects a centuries old intolerance of criticism by the mandarinate and royal family. Although the Communist party might be expected to approve of anti-royal sentiment in literature it seldom does, fearing that the Party itself is the true object of the writer's scorn.

Background

A Vietnamese account of the 'American' War

Most visitors to Vietnam, if they were not involved in the war themselves, gain their views from literature and films made by Westerners, for Westerners. It is rare for people to have access to Vietnamese literary perspectives on the war, partly because most that do exist are untranslated and because, in comparison to the torrent of especially American accounts, there have been comparatively few written by Vietnamese. One of these few is Bao Ninh's moving and poetic *The Sorrow of War* which was first published in Vietnamese in 1991 under the title *Thân Phân Cua Tinh Yêu*. In Vietnam it was a huge success, no doubt prompting its translation into English by Frank Palmos. The English edition was published in 1994 and it is now available in paperback, see Books, page 426. This is not a romantic vision of war; nor a macho account relishing the fight; nor once revelling in victory. It is a deeply sad and

Kieu: oriental Juliet or prototype Miss Saigon?

The Tale of Kieu is a story of pure love corrupted by greed and power. It also offers a fascinating glimpse into the Vietnamese mind and Vietnamese sexual mores. Kieu is in love with the young scholar Kim and early on in the story she displays her physical and moral qualities:

> "A fragrant rose, she sparkled in full bloom,
> bemused his eyes, and kindled his desire.
> When waves of lust had seemed to sweep him off,
> his wooing turned to wanton liberties.
> She said: 'Treat not our love as just a game –
> please stay away from me and let me speak.
> What is a mere peach blossom that one should
> fence off the garden, thwart the bluebird's quest?
> But you've named me your bride – to serve her man,
> she must place chastity above all else.'"

But the overriding theme of the story is the ill-treatment of an innocent girl by a duplicitous and wicked world unopposed by Heaven. Unmoved by Kieu's sale into prostitution the fates actively oppose her wishes by keeping her alive when she attempts to kill herself.

Any respite in her tale of woe proves short-lived and joy turns quickly to pain. The story illustrates the hopelessness of women in a Confucianist, male-dominated world: Kieu likens herself to a raindrop with no control over where she will land. Early on in the story when Kim is away attending to family matters Kieu has to choose between Kim, to whom she has pledged herself, and her family. Such is the strength of family ties that she offers herself to be sold in marriage to raise money for her kith and kin:

> "By what means could she save her flesh and blood?
> When evil strikes you bow to circumstance.
> As you must weigh and choose between your love
> and filial duty, which will turn the scale?
> She put aside all vows of love and troth –
> a child first pays the debts of birth and care."

Kieu gets married off to an elderly 'scholar' called Ma who is in fact a brothel keeper; but so as not to arouse Kieu's suspicion before removing her from her family he deflowers her. Kieu is now commercially less valuable but Ma believes he can remedy this:

> "One smile of hers is worth pure gold – it's true.
> When she gets there, to pluck the maiden bud,
> princes and gentlefolk will push and shove.
> She'll bring at least three hundred liang, about
> what I have paid – net profit after that.
> A morsel dangles at my mouth – what God
> serves up I crave, yet money hate to lose.
> A heavenly peach within a mortal's grasp:
> I'll bend the branch, pick it, and quench my thirst.
> How many flower-fanciers on Earth
> can really tell one flower from the next?
> Juice from pomegranite skin and cockscomb blood
> will heal it up and lend the virgin look.
> In dim half-light some yokel will be fooled:
> she'll fetch that much, and not one penny less."

Kieu's sorrows deepen; she becomes a concubine of a married brothel patron, Thuc. After a year of happiness together with Thuc his spurned wife, Hoan, decides to spoil the fun. Kieu ends up as a slave serving Thuc and Hoan. She laments her fate knowing full well the reason for it:

> "I've had an ample share of life's foul dust,
> and now this swamp of mud proves twice as vile.
> Will fortune never let its victims go
> but in its snares and toils hold fast a rose?
> I sinned in some past life and have to pay:
> I'll pay as flowers must fade and jade must break."

She later commits her only earthly crime stealing a golden bell and silver gong from the shrine she is charged with keeping, and flees to seek sanctuary in a Buddhist temple. But when her crime comes to light she is sent to live with the Bac family which, again on the pretext of marriage, sells her to another brothel. This time she meets a free-spirited warlord Tu Hai:

> "A towering hero, he outfought all foes
> with club or fist and knew all arts of war.
> Between the earth and heaven he lived free...."

who rescues her from the brothel. They become soul- and bed-mates until, after six months, Tu Hai's wanderlust and urge to fight take him away from her. He returns a year later victorious in battle. At this stage the story reaches a happy (and false) ending; Tu Hai sends his Captains out to round up all those who have crossed Kieu's path.

> "Awesome is Heaven's law of recompense –
> one haul and all were caught, brought back to camp.
> Under a tent erected in the midst,
> Lord Tu and his fair lady took their seats.
> No sooner had the drumroll died away
> than guards checked names, led captives to the gate.
> 'Whether they have used you well or ill,' he said,
> 'pronounce yourself upon their just deserts.'"

Those who have shown Kieu kindness are rewarded while those who have harmed her are tortured horribly. The only exception is Hoan who, cruel though she was, Kieu releases (after torture, of course) in a show of mercy following Hoan's plea "I have a woman's mind, a petty soul, and jealousy's a trait all humans share" – Kieu had, after all, been living with Hoan's husband for a year.

All is well for five years until another warlord, Lord Ho, flatters Kieu encouraging her to persuade Tu to put down his sword and make peace with the emperor. Guileless Kieu does so and "Lord Tu lets flags hang loose, watch-drums go dead. He slackened all defence – imperial spies / observed his camp and learned of its true state." All is lost: Tu is killed, Kieu has betrayed her hero and she is married off to a tribal chief. She throws herself into a river but yet again fails to die. Eventually Kieu, is reunited with Kim and her family:

> "She glanced and saw her folks – they all were here:
> Father looked quite strong, and Mother spry;
> both sister Van and brother Quan grown up;
> and over there was Kim her love of yore."

Background

Kieu and Kim hold a wedding feast and share a house but not a bed; Kim has sons by Van, Kieu's sister, and they all settle down to an untroubled life overseen by a more benevolent Heaven.

Huynh Sang Thong's translation (see recommended reading) is considered the finest and is accompanied by excellent notes which explain the Vietnamese phrasing of the original and which set the story in context. Translation and commentary will bring Truyen Kieu to a wider and, one hopes, appreciative audience and help shed some light on what many Vietnamese regard as their most important cultural statement.

melancholic book. Perhaps this is because Bao Ninh is recounting his story from the position of one who was there. He served with the Glorious 27th Youth Brigade, joining-up in 1969 at the age of 17. Of the 500 who went to war with the Glorious 27th, he was one of just 10 to survive the conflict. For those who want an alternative perspective, the book is highly recommended.

Drama

Classical Vietnamese theatre, known as *hat boi* (hat = to sing; boi = gesture, pose), shows close links with the classical theatre of China. Emperor Tu Duc had a troupe of 150 female artists and employed stars from China via a series of extravagant productions. Since the partition of the country in 1954, there has developed what might be termed 'revolutionary realist' theatre and classical Vietnamese theatre is today almost defunct. However, the most original theatrical art form in Vietnam is *mua roi nuoc* or **water puppet theatre**. This seems to have originated in Northern Vietnam during the early years of this millennium when it was associated with the harvest festival (at one time scholars thought water puppet theatre originated in China before being adopted in Vietnam). An inscription in Nam Ha province mentions a show put on in honour of King Ly Nhan Ton in 1121. By the time the French began to colonize Vietnam at the end of the 19th century it had spread to all of the major towns of the country.

As the name suggests, this form of theatre uses the surface of the water as the stage. Puppeteers, concealed behind a bamboo screen symbolizing an ancient village communal house, manipulate the characters while standing in a metre of water. The puppets – some over half a metre tall – are carved from water resistant *sung* wood which is also very lightweight and then painted in bright colours. Most need one puppeteer to manipulate them, but some require three or four. Plays are based on historical and religious themes: the origins of the Viet nation, legends, village life, and acts of heroism. Some include the use of fireworks – especially during battle scenes – while all performances are accompanied by folk opera singers and traditional instruments. Performances usually begin with the clown, Teu, taking the stage and he acts as a linking character between the various scenes.

The most famous and active troupe is based in Hanoi (see page 95), although in total there are about a dozen groups. Since the 1980s Vietnamese writers have turned their attention from revolutionary heroes to commentary on political and social issues of the day. Consequently, many plays have failed to see the light of day and those that have, have often been badly mauled by the censoring committee's scissors; references to corrupt officials and policemen seldom make the transition from page to stage.

Religion

Vietnam supports adherents of all the major world religions, as well as followers of religions that are peculiarly Vietnamese: Theravada and Mahayana Buddhism, Protestant and Roman Catholic Christianity, Taoism, Confucianism, Islam, Cao Daism, Hoa Hao and Hinduism. In addition, spirit and ancestor worship (*To Tien*) are also practised. Confucianism, although not a formal religion, is probably the most pervasive doctrine of all. Nominal Christians and Buddhists will still pay attention to the moral and philosophic principles of Confucianism and it continues to play a central role in Vietnamese life.

Following the Communist victory in 1975, the authorities moved quickly to curtail the influence of the various religions. Schools, hospitals and other institutions run by religious organizations were taken over by the state and many clergy either imprisoned and/or sent to re-education camps. The religious hierarchies were institutionalized, and proselytizing severely curtailed.

During the late 1980s and into the early 1990s some analysts identified an easing of the government's previously highly restrictive policies towards religious organizations. At the beginning of 1993, former General Secretary of the Vietnamese Communist Party, Do Muoi, even went so far as to make a pair of official visits to a Buddhist monastery and a Roman Catholic church. However it is clear the Communist hierarchy is highly suspicious of priests and monks. They are well aware of the prominent role they played in South Vietnamese political dissension and are quick to crack down on any religious leader or organization that becomes involved in politics.

There is no question that more people today are attending Buddhist pagodas, Christian churches and Cao Dai temples. However, whether this rise in attendance at temples and churches actually means some sort of religious re-birth is questionable. Dang Nghiem Van, head of Hanoi's Institute of Religious Studies, interviewed in 1996, poured scorn on the notion that young people are finding religion. They "are not religious", he said, "just superstitious. This isn't religion. It's decadence".

Mahayana Buddhism

Although there are both Theravada (also known as Hinayana) and Mahayana Buddhists in Vietnam, the latter are by far the more numerous. Buddhism was introduced into Vietnam in the second century AD: Indian pilgrims came by boat and brought the teachings of Theravada Buddhism, while Chinese monks came by land and introduced Mahayana Buddhism. In particular, the Chinese monk Mau Tu is credited with being the first person to introduce Mahayana Buddhism in AD 194/195.

Initially, Buddhism was very much the religion of the élite, and did not impinge upon the common Vietnamese man or woman. It was not until the reign of Emperor Ly Anh Tong (1138-75) that Buddhism was promoted as the State Religion – nearly 1,000 years after Mau Tu had arrived from China to spread the teachings of the Buddha. By that time it had begun to filter down to the village level, but as it did so it became increasingly syncretic: Buddhism became enmeshed with Confucianism, Taoism, spirituality, mysticism and animism. In the 15th century it also began to lose its position to Confucianism as the dominant religion of the court.

There has been a resurgence of Buddhism since the 1920s. It was the self-immolation of Buddhist monks in the 1960s which provided a focus of discontent against the government in the south (see page 282), and since the Communist victory in 1975, monks have remained an important focus of dissent – hence the persecution of Buddhists during the early years following reunification. Mahayana Buddhists are concentrated in the centre and north of the country, and the dominant sect is the Thien (Zen)

Background

In Siddhartha's footsteps: a short history of Buddhism

Buddhism was founded by Siddhartha Gautama, a prince of the Sakya tribe of Nepal, who probably lived between 563 and 483 BC. He achieved enlightenment and the word buddha means 'fully enlightened one', or 'one who has woken up'. Siddhartha Gautama is known by a number of titles. In the west, he is usually referred to as The Buddha, ie the historic Buddha (but not just Buddha); more common in Southeast Asia is the title Sakyamuni, or Sage of the Sakyas (referring to his tribal origins).

Over the centuries, the life of the Buddha has become part legend, and the Jataka tales which recount his various lives are colourful and convoluted. But, central to any Buddhist's belief is that he was born under a sal tree, that he achieved enlightenment under a bodhi tree in the Bodh Gaya Gardens, that he preached the First Sermon at Sarnath, and that he died at Kusinagara (all in India or Nepal).

The Buddha was born at Lumbini (in present-day Nepal), as Queen Maya was on her way to her parents' home. She had had a very auspicious dream before the child's birth of being impregnated by an elephant, whereupon a sage prophesied that Siddhartha would become either a great king or a great spiritual leader. His father, being keen that the first option of the prophesy be fulfilled, brought him up in all the princely skills – at which Siddhartha excelled – and ensured that he only saw beautiful things, not the harsher elements of life.

Despite his father's efforts Siddhartha saw four things while travelling between palaces – a helpless old man, a very sick man, a corpse being carried by lamenting relatives, and an ascetic, calm and serene as he begged for food. The young prince renounced his princely origins and left home to study under a series of spiritual teachers. He finally discovered the path to enlightenment at the Bodh Gaya Gardens in India. He then proclaimed his thoughts to a small group of disciples at Sarnath, near Benares, and continued to preach

and attract followers until he died at the age of 81 at Kusinagara.

In the First Sermon at the deer park in Sarnath, the Buddha preached the Four Truths, which are still considered the root of Buddhist belief and practical experience: suffering exists; there is a cause of suffering; suffering can be ended; and to end suffering it is necessary to follow the 'Noble Eightfold Path' – namely, right speech, livelihood, action, effort, mindfulness, concentration, opinion and intention.

Soon after the Buddha began preaching, a monastic order – the Sangha – was established. As the monkhood evolved in India, it also began to fragment into different sects. An important change was the belief that the Buddha was transcendent: he had never been born, nor had he died; he had always existed and his life on earth had been mere illusion. The emergence of these new concepts helped to turn what up until then was an ethical code of conduct, into a religion. It eventually led to the appearance of a new Buddhist movement, Mahayana Buddhism which split from the more traditional Theravada 'sect'.

Despite the division of Buddhism into two sects, the central tenets of the religion are common to both. Specifically, the principles pertaining to the Four Noble Truths, the Noble Eightfold Path, the Dependent Origination, the Law of Karma, and nirvana. In addition, the principles of non-violence and tolerance are also embraced by both sects. In essence, the differences between the two are of emphasis and interpretation. Theravada Buddhism is strictly based on the original Pali Canon, while the Mahayana tradition stems from later Sanskrit texts. Mahayana Buddhism also allows a broader and more varied interpretation of the doctrine. Other important differences are that while the Thervada tradition is more 'intellectual' and self-obsessed, with an emphasis upon the attaining of wisdom and insight for oneself, Mahayana Buddhism stresses devotion and compassion towards others.

meditation sect. Of the relatively small numbers of Theravada Buddhists, the majority are of Cambodian stock and are concentrated in the Mekong Delta. In Vietnam, Buddhism is intertwined with Confucianism and Taoism. See also box, page 416.

Confucianism

Although Confucianism is not strictly a religion, the teachings of the Chinese sage and philosopher Confucius (551-479 BC) form the basis on which Vietnamese life and government were based for much of the historic period. Even today, Confucianist perspectives are, possibly, more strongly in evidence than Communist ones. Confucianism was introduced from China during the Bac Thuoc Period (111 BC-AD 938) when the Chinese dominated the country. The 'religion' enshrined the concept of imperial rule by the mandate of heaven, effectively constraining social and political change.

In essence, Confucianism stresses the importance of family and lineage, and the worship of ancestors. Men and women in positions of authority were required to provide role models for the 'ignorant', while the state, epitomized in the emperor, was likewise required to set an example and to provide conditions of stability and fairness for his people. Crucially, children had to observe filial piety. This set of norms, which were drawn from the experience of the human encounter at the practical level, were enshrined in the Forty-seven Rules for Teaching and Changing first issued in 1663. A key element of Confucianist thought is the Three Bonds (*tam cuong*) – the loyalty of ministers to the emperor, the obedience of children to their parents, and the submission of wives to their husbands. Added to these are mutual reciprocity among friends, and benevolence towards strangers. Not surprisingly the Communists are antipathetic to such a hierarchical view of society although ironically Confucianism which inculcates respect for the elderly and authority unwittingly lends support to a politburo occupied by old men. In an essay entitled 'Confucianism and Marxism', Vietnamese scholar Nguyen Khac Vien explains why Marxism proved an acceptable doctrine to those accustomed to Confucian values: "Marxism was not baffling to Confucians in that it concentrated man's thoughts on political and social problems. By defining man as the total of his social relationships, Marxism hardly came as a shock to the Confucian scholar who had always considered the highest aim of man to be the fulfilment of his social obligations ... Bourgeois individualism, which puts personal interests ahead of those of society and petty bourgeois anarchism, which allows no social discipline whatsoever, are alien to both Confucianism and Marxism."

Taoism

Taoism was introduced from China into Vietnam at about the same time as Confucianism. It is based on the works of the Chinese philosophers Lao Tzu (circa sixth-fifth centuries BC) and Chuang Tzu (fourth century BC). Although not strictly a formal religion, it has had a significant influence on Buddhism (as it is practised in Vietnam) and on Confucianism. In reality, Taoism and Confucianism are two sides of the same coin: the Taoist side is poetry and spirituality; the Confucianist side, social ethics and the order of the world. Together they form a unity. Like Confucianism, it is not possible to give a figure to the number of adherents of Taoism in Vietnam: it functions in conjunction with Confucianism and Buddhism, and also often with Christianity, Cao Daism and Hoa Hao.

Of all the world's religions, Taoism is perhaps the hardest to pin down. It has no formal code, no teachings, and no creed. It is a cosmic religion. Even the word Tao is usually left untranslated – or merely translated as "The Way". The inscrutability of it all is summed up in the writings of the Chinese poet Po Chu-i:

> "Those who speak know nothing,
> Those who know keep silence."
> These words, as I am told,
> Were spoken by Lao Tzu.
> But if we are to believe that Lao Tzu
> Was himself one who knew,
> How comes it that he wrote a book
> Of five thousand words?

Or to quote Chuang Tzu, and even more inscrutably: "Tao is beyond material existence ... it may be transmitted, but it cannot be received [posessed]. It may be attained, but cannot be seen. It exists prior to Heaven and Earth, and, indeed, for all eternity ... it is above the Zenith, but is not high; it is beneath the Nadir, but it is not low. It is prior to Heaven and Earth, but it is not ancient. It is older than the most ancient, but it is not old."

Central to Taoist belief is a world view based upon *yin* and *yang*, two primordial forces on which the creation and functioning of the world are based. The yin-yang is not specifically Taoist or Confucianist, but predates both and is associated with the first recorded Chinese ruler, Fu-hsi (2852-2738 BC). The well-known *yin-yang* symbol symbolizes the balance and equality between the great dualistic forces in the universe: dark and light, negative and positive, male and female. JC Cooper explains in *Taoism: the Way of the Mystic* the symbolism of the black and white dots: "There is a point, or embryo, of black in the white and white in the black. This ... is essential to the symbolism since there is no being which does not contain within itself the germ of its opposite. There is no male wholly without feminine characteristics and no female without its masculine attributes." Thus the dualism of the *yin-yang* is not absolute, but permeable.

To maintain balance and harmony in life it is necessary that a proper balance be maintained between *yin* (female) and *yang* (male). This is believed to be true both at the scale of the world and the nation, and also for an individual – for the human body is the world in microcosm. The root cause of illness is imbalance between the forces of *yin* and *yang*. Even foods have characters: 'hot' foods are *yang*, 'cold', *yin*. Implicit in this is the belief that there is a natural law underpinning all of life, a law upon which harmony ultimately rests. Taoism attempts to maintain this balance, and thereby harmony. In this way, Taoism is a force promoting inertia, maintaining the status quo. Traditional relationships between fathers and sons, between siblings, within villages, and between the rulers and the ruled, are all rationalized in terms of maintaining balance and harmony. Forces for change – like communism and democracy – are resisted on the basis that they upset this balance.

Christianity

Christianity was first introduced into Vietnam in the 16th century by Roman Catholic missionaries from Portugal, Spain and France. The first Bishop of Vietnam was appointed in 1659, and by 1685 there were estimated to be 800,000 Roman Catholics in the country. For several centuries Christianity was discouraged, and at times, outlawed. Many Christians were executed and one of the reasons that the French gave for annexing the country in the late 19th century was religious persecution (see page 356). Today, 8-10% of the population are thought to be Catholic, some six million people; less than 1% are Protestant. This Christian population is served by around 2,000 priests.

Following reunification in 1975, many Catholics in the former south were sent to re-education camps. They were perceived to be both staunchly pro-American and anti-Communist, and it was not until 1988 that many were returned to normal life. Today, Catholics are still viewed with suspicion by the state and priests felt to be drifting from purely religious concerns into any criticism of the state are detained. Indicative of this 'fear' of Christianity are the vacancies in the diocese of Hung Hoa which has been vacant since 1992, Haiphong and Bui chu, both of which have been vacant since 1999. The ancient Bishop of Hanoi is unable to resign as the government will not allow the Vatican to replace him with someone younger.

More generally, the authorities have been slow to permit Vietnamese men to become ordained, and they have limited the production and flow of religious literature.

Islam and Hinduism

The only centres of Islam and Hinduism are among the Cham of the central coastal plain and Chau Doc, a province in the Mekong Delta. The Cham were converted to Islam by Muslim traders. There are several mosques in Saigon and Cholon – some of them built by Indians from Kerala.

Cao Daism

Cao Dai took root in southern Vietnam during the 1920s after Ngo Van Chieu, a civil servant, was visited by 'Cao Dai' or the 'Supreme Being' and was given the tenets of a new religion. Ngo received this spiritual visitation in 1919 on Phu Quoc Island. The Cao Dai later told Ngo in a seance that he was to be symbolized by a giant eye. The religion quickly gained the support of a large following of dispossessed peasants. It was both a religion and a nationalist movement. In terms of the former, it claimed to be a synthesis of Buddhism, Christianity, Taoism, Confucianism and Islam. Cao Dai 'saints' include Joan of Arc, the French writer Victor Hugo, Sir Winston Churchill, Sun Yat Sen, Moses and Brahma.

Debates over doctrine are mediated through the spirits who are contacted on a regular basis through a strange wooden contraption called a *corbeille-à-bec* or planchette. The five Cao Dai commandments are: do not kill any living creature; do not covet; do not practise high living; do not be tempted; and do not slander by word. But, as well as being a religion, the movement also claimed that it would restore traditional Vietnamese attitudes, and was anti-colonial and modestly subversive. Opportunist to a fault, Cao Dai followers sought the aid of the Japanese against the French, the Americans against the Viet Minh, and the Viet Minh against the south. Following reunification in 1975, all Cao Dai lands were confiscated and their leadership emasculated. The centre of Cao Daism remains the Mekong Delta where – and despite the efforts of the Communists – there are thought to be perhaps two million adherents and perhaps 1,000 Cao Dai temples. The Cao Dai Great Temple is in the town of Tay Ninh, 100 km from Saigon (see page 289).

Hoa Hao

Hoa Hao is another Vietnamese religion which emerged in the Mekong Delta. It was founded by Huynh Phu So in 1939, a resident of Hoa Hao village in the province of Chau Doc. Effectively a schism of Buddhism, the sect discourages temple-building and worship, maintaining that simplicity of worship is the key to better contact with God. There are thought to be perhaps one to 1.5 million adherents of Hoa Hao, predominantly in the Chau Doc area.

Background

Land and environment

The regions of Vietnam

The name Vietnam is derived from that adopted in 1802 by Emperor Gia Long: Nam Viet. This means, literally, the Viet (the largest ethnic group) of the south (Nam), and substituted for the country's previous name, Annam. The country is 'S' shaped, covers a land area of 329,600 sq km and has a coastline of 3,000 km. The most important economic zones, containing the main concentrations of population, are focused on two large deltaic areas. In the north, there are the ancient rice fields and settlements of the Red River, and in the south, the fertile alluvial plain of the Mekong. In between, the country narrows to less than 50 km wide, with only a thin ribbon of fertile lowland suited to intensive agriculture. Much of the interior, away from the coastal belt and the deltas, is mountainous. Here minority hilltribes (Montagnards), along with some lowland Vietnamese resettled in so-called New Economic Zones since 1975, eke out a living on thin and unproductive soils. The rugged terrain means that only a quarter of the land is actually cultivated. Of the remainder, somewhere between about 20% and 25% is forested and some of this is heavily degraded.

Northern highlands Vietnam consists of five major geographical zones. In the far north are the northern highlands which ring the Red River Delta and form a natural barrier with China. The rugged mountains on the west border of this region – the Hoang Lien Son – exceed 3,000 m in places. The tributaries of the Red River have cut deep, steep-sided gorges through the Hoang Lien Son, which are navigable by small boats. The eastern portion of this region, bordering the Gulf of Tonkin, is far less imposing; the mountain peaks of the west have diminished into foothills, allowing easy access to China. It was across these hills that the Chinese mounted their successive invasions of Vietnam, the last of which occurred as recently as 1979.

Red River Delta The second region lies in the embrace of the hills of the north. This, the Red River Delta, can legitimately claim to be the cultural and historical heart of the Viet nation. Hanoi lies at its core and it was here that the first truly independent Vietnamese polity was established in AD 939 by Ngo Quyen. The delta covers almost 15,000 sq km and extends 240 km inland from the coast. Rice has been grown on the alluvial soils of the Red River for thousands of years. Yet despite the intricate web of canals, dykes and embankments, the Vietnamese have never been able to completely tame the river, and the delta is the victim of frequent and sometimes devastating floods. The area is very low-lying, rarely more than 3 m above sea level, and often less than 1 m. The high water mark is nearly 8 m above the level of the land in some places. During the monsoon season, the tributaries of the Red River quickly become torrents rushing through the narrow gorges of the Hoang Lien Son, before emptying into the main channel which then bursts its banks. Although the region supports one of the highest agricultural population densities in the world, the inhabitants have frequently had to endure famines – most recently in 1989.

South of the Red River Delta South of the Red River Delta region lie the central lowlands and the mountains of the Annamite Chain. The **Annam Highlands**, now known as the **Truong Son Mountain Range**, form an important cultural divide between the Indianized nations of the west and the Sinicized cultures of the east. Its northern rugged extremity is in Thanh Hoa Province. From here the Truong Son stretches over 1,200 km south, to peter out 80 km north of Saigon. The highest peak is Ngoc Linh Mountain in Kon Tum Province at 2,598 m. The Central Highlands form an upland plateau on which the hill resorts of **Buon Ma Thuot** and **Dalat** are situated. On the plateau, plantation agriculture and hill farms are interspersed with stands of bamboo and tropical forests. Once rich in wildlife, the plateau was a popular hunting ground during the colonial period.

The Mekong: mother river of Southeast Asia

The Mekong River is one of the 12 great rivers of the world. It stretches 4,500 km from its source on the Tibet Plateau in China to its mouth (or mouths) in the Mekong Delta of Vietnam. (On 11 April 1995 a Franco-British expedition announced that they had discovered the source of the Mekong – 5,000 m high, at the head of the Rup-Sa Pass, and miles from anywhere.) Each year, the river empties 475 billion cu m of water into the South China Sea. Along its course it flows through Burma, Laos, Thailand, Cambodia and Vietnam – all of the countries that constitute mainland Southeast Asia – as well as China. In both a symbolic and a physical sense then, it links the region. Bringing fertile silt to the land along its banks, but particularly to the Mekong Delta, the river contributes to Southeast Asia's agricultural wealth. In former times, a tributary of the Mekong which drains the Tonlé Sap (the Great Lake of Cambodia), provided the rice surplus on which the fabulous Angkor empire was founded. The Tonlé Sap acts like a great regulator, storing water in time of flood and then releasing it when levels recede.

The first European to explore the Mekong River was the French naval officer Francis Garnier. His Mekong Expedition (1866-68), followed the great river upstream from its delta in Cochin China (southern Vietnam). Of the 9,960 km that the expedition covered, 5,060 km were 'discovered' for the first time. The

motivation for the trip was to find a southern route into the Heavenly Kingdom – China. But they failed. The river is navigable only as far as the Lao-Cambodian border where the Khone rapids make it impassable. Nonetheless, the report of the expedition is one of the finest of its genre.

Today the Mekong itself is perceived as a source of potential economic wealth – not just as a path to riches. The Mekong Secretariat was established in 1957 to harness the waters of the river for hydropower and irrigation. The Secretariat devised a grandiose plan incorporating a succession of seven huge dams which would store 142 billion cu m of water, irrigate 4.3 million ha of riceland, and generate 24,200MW of power. But the Vietnam War intervened to disrupt construction. Only Laos' Nam Ngum Dam on a tributary of the Mekong was ever built – and even though this generates just 150MW of power, electricity exports to Thailand are one of Laos' largest export earners. Now that the countries of mainland Southeast Asia are on friendly terms once more, the Secretariat and its scheme have been given a new lease of life. But in the intervening years, fears about the environmental consequences of big dams have raised new questions. The Mekong Secretariat has moderated its plans and is now looking at less ambitious, and less contentious, ways to harness the Mekong River.

Background

To the east, the Annamite Chain falls off steeply, leaving only a narrow and fragmented band of lowland suitable for settlement – the central coastal strip. In places the mountains advance all the way to the coast, plunging into the sea as dramatic rockfaces and making north-south communication difficult. At no point does the region extend more than 64 km inland, and in total it covers only 6,750 sq km. The soils are often rocky or saline, and irrigation is seldom possible. Nonetheless, the inhabitants have a history of sophisticated rice culture and it was here that the Champa Kingdom was established in the early centuries of the Christian era. These coastal lowlands have also formed a conduit along which people have historically moved. Even today, the main road and rail routes between the north and south cut through the coastal lowlands.
Central coastal strip

Finally, there is the Mekong Delta. Unlike the Red River Delta this region is not so prone to flooding, and consequently rice production is more stable. The reason why flooding is less severe lies in the regulating effect of the Great Lake of Cambodia, the
Mekong Delta

Tonlõ Sap. During the rainy season, when the water flowing into the Mekong becomes too great for even this mighty river to absorb, rather than overflowing its banks, the water backs up into the Tonlõ Sap, which quadruples in area. The Mekong Delta covers 67,000 sq km and is drained by five branches of the Mekong, which divides as it flows towards the sea. The vast delta is one of the great rice bowls of Asia producing nearly half of the country's rice, and over the years has been cut into a patchwork by the canals that have been dug to expand irrigation and rice cultivation. Largely forested until the late 19th century, the French supported the settlement of the area by Vietnamese peasants, recognizing that it could become enormously productive. The deposition of silt by the rivers that cut through the delta, means that the shoreline is continually advancing – by up to 80 m each year in some places. To the north of the delta lies **Saigon** or **Ho Chi Minh City**.

The three regions The French sub-divided Vietnam into three regions, administering each separately: *Tonkin* or **Bac Ky** (the north region), *Annam* or **Trung Ky** (the central region) and *Cochin China* or **Nam Ky** (the south region). Although these administrative divisions have been abolished, the Vietnamese still recognize their country as consisting of three regions, distinct in terms of geography, history and culture. Their new names are **Bac Bo** (north), **Trung Bo** (centre) and **Nam Bo** (south).

Climate

Vietnam stretches over 1,800 km from north to south and the weather patterns in the two principal cities, Hanoi in the north and Saigon in the south, are very different (for best time to visit, see page 20). Average temperatures tend to rise the further south one ventures, while the seasonal variation in temperature decreases. The exceptions to this general rule of thumb are in the interior highland areas where the altitude means it is considerably colder.

North Vietnam The seasons in the north are similar to those of South China. The winter stretches from November to April, with temperatures averaging 16°C, and little rainfall. The summer begins in May and lasts until October. During these months it can be very hot indeed, with an average temperature of 30°C, along with heavy rainfall and the occasional violent typhoon.

Central Vietnam Central Vietnam experiences a transitional climate, half way between that in the south and in the north. Hué has a reputation for particularly poor weather: it is often overcast, and an umbrella is needed whatever the month – even during the short 'dry' season between February and April. The annual rainfall in Hué is 3,250 mm (see page 178 for best time to visit).

South Vietnam Temperatures in the south are fairly constant through the year (25°C-30°C) and the seasons are determined by the rains. The dry season runs from November to April (when there is virtually no rain whatsoever) and the wet season from May to October. The hottest period is during March and April, before the rains have broken. Typhoons are quite common in coastal areas between July and November.

Highland Areas In the hill resorts of Dalat (1,500 m), Buon Ma Thuot and Sapa nights are cool throughout the year, and in the 'winter' months between October to March it can be distinctly chilly with temperatures falling to 4°C. Even in the hottest months of March and April the temperature rarely exceeds 26°C.

Flora and fauna

Together with overseas conservation agencies such as the Worldwide Fund for Nature, Vietnamese scientists have, in recent years, been enumerating and protecting their fauna and flora. The establishment of nature reserves began in 1962 with the gazetting of the Cuc Phuong National Park. Today there are a total of 87 reserves covering 3.3% of Vietnam's land area. However, some of them are too small to sustain sufficiently large breeding populations of endangered species and many parks are quite heavily populated. For instance 80,000 people live, farm and hunt within the 22,000 ha Bach Ma National Park. Vietnamese scientists with support from outside agencies, in particular WWF have begun the important task of cataloguing and protecting Vietnam's wildlife. There have been some pleasant surprises.

The **Javan rhinoceros** is one of the rarest large mammals in the world and until recently was thought only to survive in the Ujung Kulon National Park in West Java, Indonesia. However in November 1988 it was reported that a Stieng tribesman had shot a female Javan rhino near the Dong Nai River around 130 km northeast of Saigon. When he tried to sell the horn and hide he was arrested and this set in train a search to discover if there were any more of the animals in the area. Researchers discovered that Viet Cong soldiers operating in the area during the war saw – and killed – a number of animals. One former revolutionary, Tran Ngoc Khanh, reported that he once saw a herd of 20 animals and that between 1952 and 1976 some 17 animals were shot by the soldiers. With the Viet Cong shooting the beasts whenever they chanced upon them, and the Americans 'spraying' tonnes of defoliant on the area, it is a wonder than any survived through to the end of the war. However, a study by George Schaller and three Vietnamese colleagues in 1989 found tracks, also near the Dong Nai River, and estimated that a population of 10-15 animals probably still survived in a 750 sq km area of bamboo and dipterocarp forest close to and including the Nam Cat Tien National Park.

This remarkable find was followed by, if anything, an even more astonishing discovery: of two completely new species of mammal. In 1992 British scientist Dr John MacKinnon discovered the skeleton of an animal now known as the **Vu Quang ox** (*Pseudoryx nghetinhensis*) but known to locals as *sao la*. The Vu Quang ox was the first new large mammal species to be found in 50 years; scientists were amazed that a large mammal could exist on this crowded planet without their knowledge. In June 1994 the first live specimen (a young calf) was captured and shortly afterwards a second *sao la* was caught and taken to the Forestry Institute in Hanoi. Sadly, both died in captivity but in early 1995 a third was brought in alive. The animals look anything but ox-like, and have the appearance, grace and manner of a small deer. The government responded to the discovery by extending the Vu Quang Nature Reserve and banning hunting of *sao la*. Local hilltribes, who have long regarded *sao la* as a tasty and not uncommon beast, have therefore lost a valued source of food and no longer have a vested interest in the animal's survival. *Sao la* must rue the day they were 'discovered'. In 1993 a new species of deer which has been named the **giant muntjac** was also found in the Vu Quang Nature Reserve. The scientists have yet to see the beast alive but villagers prize its meat and are reported to trap it in quite large numbers.

Large rare mammals are confined to isolated pockets where the government does its best to protect them from hunters. On Cat Ba Island, the national park is home to the world's last wild troops of white-headed langur. In North Vietnam tigers have been hunted close to extinction and further south territorial battles rage between elephants and farmers. Rampaging elephants sometimes cause loss of life and are in turn decimated by enraged villagers.

Among the **larger mammals**, there are small numbers of tiger, leopard, clouded leopard, Indian elephant, Malayan sun bear, Himalayan black bear, sambar deer, gibbon and gaur (wild buffalo). These are rarely seen, except in zoos, although many of the minorities in the Central Highlands capture and train elephants for domestic use. There are frequent news reports of farmers maiming or killing elephants after their crops have been trampled or their huts flattened. The larger reptiles include two species of crocodile, the estuarine (*Crocodilus porosus*) and Siamese (*Crocodilus*

Fields in the forest – shifting cultivation

Shifting cultivation, also known as slash-and-burn agriculture or swiddening, as well as by a variety of local terms, is one of the characteristic farming systems of Southeast Asia. It is a low-intensity form of agriculture, in which land is cleared from the forest through burning, cultivated for a few years, and then left to regenerate over 10-30 years. It takes many forms, but an important distinction can be made between shifting field systems where fields are rotated but the settlement remains permanently sited, and migratory systems where the shifting cultivators shift both field (swidden) and settlement. The land is usually only rudimentarily cleared, tree stumps being left in the ground, and seeds sown in holes made by punching the soil with a dibble stick. In Vietnam shifting cultivation is confined to the upland areas and practised by tribal minorities thus adding an ethnic and political dimension to the shifting versus sedentary farming debate.

For many years, shifting cultivators were regarded as 'primitives' who followed an essentially primitive form of agriculture and their methods were contrasted unfavourably with 'advanced' settled rice farmers. There are still many government officials in Vietnam and in the wider Southeast Asian region who continue to adhere to this mistaken belief, and further argue that shifting cultivators are the principal cause of forest loss and soil erosion. They are, therefore, painted as the villains in the region's environmental crisis, neatly sidestepping the considerably more detrimental impact that commercial logging has had on Southeast Asia's forest resources.

Shifting cultivators have an intimate knowledge of the land, plants and animals on which they depend. One study of a Dayak tribe, the Kantu' of Kalimantan (Borneo), discovered that households were cultivating an average of 17 rice varieties and 21 other food crops each year in a highly complex system. Even more remarkably, Harold Conklin's classic 1957 study of the Hanunóo of the Philippines – a study which is a benchmark for such work even today – found that the Hanunóo identified 40 types and subtypes of rocks and minerals when classifying different soils. The shifting agricultural systems are usually also highly productive in labour terms, allowing far more leisure time than farmers using permanent field systems.

But shifting cultivation contains the seeds of its own extinction. Extensive, and geared to low population densities and abundant land, it is coming under pressure in a region where land is becoming an increasingly scarce resource, where patterns of life are dictated by an urban-based élite, and where populations are pressing on the means of subsistence.

siamensis). The former grows to a length of 5 m and has been reported to have killed and eaten humans. Among the larger snakes are the reticulated python (*Python reticulatus*) and the smaller Indian python (*Python molurus*), both non-venomous constrictors. Venomous snakes include two species of cobra (the king cobra and common cobra), two species of krait, and six species of pit viper.

Given the difficulty of getting to Vietnam's more remote areas, the country is hardly a haven for amateur naturalists. Professional photographers and naturalists have been escorted to the country's wild areas, but this is not an option for the average visitor. Getting there requires time and contacts. A wander around the markets of Vietnam reveals the variety and number of animals that end up in the cooking pot: deer, bear, snakes, monkeys, turtles etc. The Chinese penchant for exotic foods (such gastronomic wonders as tigers' testicles and bear's foot) has also become a predilection of the Vietnamese, and most animals are fair game.

The cycle of wet rice cultivation

There are an estimated 120,000 rice varieties. Rice seed – either selected from the previous harvest or, more commonly, purchased from a dealer or agricultural extension office – is soaked overnight before being sown into a carefully prepared nursery bed. Today farmers are likely to plant one of the Modern Varieties or MVs bred for their high yields.

The nursery bed into which the seeds are broadcast (scattered) is often a farmer's best land, with the most stable water supply. After a month the seedlings are uprooted and taken out to the paddy fields. The fields will also have been ploughed, puddled and harrowed, turning the heavy clay soil into a saturated slime. Traditionally, buffalo and cattle would have performed the task and although today rotavators, and even tractors are sometimes used the sight of men and boys ploughing with a buffalo is an unmistakable feature of the Vietnamese landscape. The seedlings are transplanted into the mud in clumps. Before transplanting the tops of the seedlings are twisted off (this helps to increase yield) and then they are pushed in to the soil in neat rows. The work is back-breaking and it is not unusual to find labourers – both men and women – receiving a premium – either a bonus on top of the usual daily wage or a free meal at midday, to which marijuana is sometimes added to ease the pain.

After transplanting, it is essential that the water supply is carefully controlled. The key to high yields is a constant flow of water, regulated to take account of the growth of the rice plant. In 'rain-fed'

systems where the farmer relies on rainfall to water the crop, he has to hope that it will be neither too much nor too little. Elaborate ceremonies are performed to appease the rice spirits and to ensure bountiful rainfall.

In areas where rice is grown in irrigated conditions, farmers need not concern themselves with the day-to-day pattern of rainfall, and in such areas two or even three crops can be grown each year. But such systems need to be carefully managed, and it is usual for one man (very rarely, woman) to be in charge of irrigation. He decides when water should be released, organizes labour to repair dykes and dams and to clear channels, and decides which fields should receive the water first.

Traditionally, while waiting for the rice to mature, a farmer would do little except weed the crop from time to time. He and his family might move out of the village and live in a field hut to keep a close eye on the maturing rice. (A good harvest, after all, is a matter of life and death.) Today, farmers also apply chemical fertilizers and pesticides to protect the crop and ensure maximum yield. After 90-130 days, the crop should be ready for harvesting.

Harvesting also demands intensive labour. Traditionally, farmers in a village would secure their harvesters through systems of reciprocal labour exchange. Today, wage labouring is more common. After harvesting, the rice is threshed, sometimes out in the field, and then brought back to the village to be stored in a rice barn, or sold. It is only at the end of the harvest, with the rice safely stored in the barn, that the festivals begin.

Background

Birds

Birds have, in general, suffered rather less than mammals from over-hunting and the effects of the war. There have been some casualties however: the eastern sarus crane of the Mekong Delta – a symbol of fidelity, longevity and good luck – disappeared entirely during the war. However, in 1985 a farmer reported seeing a single bird, and by 1990 there were over 500 pairs breeding on the now pacified former battlefields. A sarus crane reserve has been established in Dong Thap Province. Among the more unusual birds are the snake bird (named after its habit of swimming with its body submerged and only its snake-like neck and head above the surface), the argus pheasant, which the Japanese believe to be the mythical phoenix, the little bastard quail of which the male hatches and rears the young, three species of vulture, the osprey (sea eagle), and two species of hornbill (the pied and great Indian). Vietnam also has colonies of the endangered white-winged wood duck, one of the symbols of the world conservation movement. The Vietnamese, or Vo Quy, pheasant which was thought to be extinct was recently rediscovered in the wild and two males are now held in captivity in Hanoi zoo.

Books

Books on the region

Dingwall, Alastair, *Traveller's literary companion: South-east Asia* (In Print: Brighton, 1994). Experts on Southeast Asian language and literature select extracts from novels and other books by western and regional writers. The extracts are annoyingly brief, but it gives a good overview of what is available.

Dumarçay, Jacques, *The palaces of South-East Asia: architecture and customs* (OUP: Singapore, 1991). A broad summary of palace art and architecture in both mainland and island Southeast Asia.

Fenton, James, *All the wrong places: adrift in the politics of Asia* (Penguin: London, 1988). British journalist James Fenton skilfully and entertainingly recounts his experiences in Vietnam, Cambodia, the Philippines andorea.

Fraser-Lu, Sylvia, *Handwoven textiles of South-East Asia* (OUP: Singapore, 1988). Well illustrated, large-format book with informative text.

Higham, Charles, *The archaeology of mainland Southeast Asia from 10,000 BC to the fall of Angkor* (Cambridge University Press: Cambridge, 1989). Best summary of changing views of the archaeology of the mainland.

Keyes, Charles F, *The golden peninsula: culture and adaptation in mainland Southeast Asia* (Macmillan: New York, 1977). Academic, yet readable summary of the threads of continuity and change in Southeast Asia's culture. The volume has been recently republished by Hawaii University Press, but not updated or revised.

King, Ben F and **Dickinson, EC**, *A field guide to the birds of South-East Asia* (Collins: London, 1975). Best regional guide to the birds of the region.

Osborne, Milton, *Southeast Asia: an introductory history* (Allen & Unwin: Sydney, 1979). Good introductory history, clearly written, published in a portable paperback edition. A new revised edition is not on the shelves.

Rawson, Philip, *The art of Southeast Asia* (Thames & Hudson: London, 1967). Portable general art history of Myanmar, Cambodia, Vietnam, Thailand, Laos, Java and Bali; by necessity, rather superficial, but a good place to start.

Reid, Anthony, *Southeast Asia in the age of commerce 1450-1680: the lands below the winds* (Yale University Press: New Haven, 1988). Perhaps the best history of everyday life in Southeast Asia, looking at such themes as physical well-being, material culture and social organization.

Reid, Anthony, *Southeast Asia in the age of commerce 1450-1680: expansion and crisis* (Yale University Press: New Haven, 1993). Volume 2 in this excellent history of the region.

Rigg, Jonathan, *Southeast Asia: a region in transition* (Unwin Hyman: London, 1991). A thematic geography of the ASEAN region, providing an insight into some of the major issues affecting the region today.

Rigg, Jonathan, *Southeast Asia: the human landscape of modernization and development* (London: Routledge, 1997). A book which covers both the market and former command economies (ie Myanmar, Vietnam, Laos and Cambodia) of the region. It focuses on how people in the region have responded to the challenges of modernization.

SarDesai, DR, *Southeast Asia: past and present* (Macmillan: London, 1989). Skilful but at times frustratingly thin history of the region from the first century to the withdrawal of US forces from Vietnam.

Savage, Victor R, *Western impressions of nature and landscape in Southeast Asia* (Singapore University Press: Singapore, 1984). Based on a geography PhD thesis, the book is a mine of quotations and observations from western travellers.

Steinberg, DJ et al, *In search of Southeast Asia: a modern history* (University of Hawaii Press: Honolulu, 1987). The best standard history of the region; it skilfully examines and assesses general processes of change and their impacts from the arrival of the Europeans in the region.

Tarling, Nicholas, *Cambridge History of Southeast Asia* (Cambridge: Cambridge University Press, 1992 (edit). Two volume edited study, long and expensive with contributions from most of the leading historians of the region. A thematic and regional approach is taken, not a country one, although the history is fairly conventional.

Waterson, Roxana, *The living house: an anthropology of architecture in South-East Asia* (OUP: Singapore, 1990). An academic but extensively-illustrated book on Southeast Asian architecture and how it links with lives and livelihoods. Fascinating material for those interested in such things.

Books on Vietnam

Hejzlar, J, *The art of Vietnam* (Hamlyn: London, 1973). The text is rather heavy going, but has numerous photographs.

Art & archaeology

Le Brusq, Arnauld and **de Selva, Léonard**, *Vietnam, A Travers L'Architecture Coloniale* (Patimoines et Medias, 1999). Also available in German but not in English. A meticulously researched and fascinating guide to Vietnam's colonial architecture chronicling the evolution of the colonial cities and describing the history of many of Vietnam's public buildings erected during French rule. Superbly illustrated with contemporary colour photographs and archive pictures and plans.

Parmentier, Henri with **Mus, Paul** and **Aymonier, Etienne**, *Cham Sculpture in the Tourane Museum: Religious ceremonies and superstitions of Champa*, (White Lotus, 2001). Reprint of a classic 1922 text by Parmentier who was responsible for assembling the Cham sculptures and after whom the museum in Danang was originally named.

Fenn, Charles, *Ho Chi Minh: a biographical introduction* (Studio Vista: London, 1973)

Biography & autobiography

Greene, Graham, *Ways of escape*. (1980). Autobiographical.

Ho Chi Minh (nd) *Prison diary* (Hanoi: Foreign Languages Publishing House). A collection of poems by Ho Chi Minh while he was incarcerated in China in 1942. They are autobiographical, recording his prison experiences and his yearning for home.

Page, Tim, *Derailed in Uncle Ho's victory garden* (Touchstone Books, 1995), war photojournalist Tim Page makes a return visit to Vietnam, amusing in places.

Tin, Bui, *Following Ho Chi Minh* (Hurst: London, 1995). Autobiographical account of a North Vietnamese Colonel's disillusionment with the Communist regime following Ho Chi Minh's death. Western readers may find it rather self-congratulatory in tone but nevertheless an interesting read.

Crawford, Ann Caddell (nd) *Customs and culture of Vietnam* (Charles Tuttle: Rutland, Vermont).

Culture

Hickey, Gerald, *Village in Vietnam* (Yale University Press: New Haven, 1964); classic village study, only available second-hand.

Background

| Economics, politics & development | **Beresford, Melanie**, *Vietnam: politics, economics and society* (Pinter: London, 1988). Academic account of social, economic and political developments to mid-1980s; too early to include much discussion of economic reform programme. |

Beresford, Melanie, *Vietnam: politics, economics and society* (Pinter: London, 1988). Academic account of social, economic and political developments to mid-1980s; too early to include much discussion of economic reform programme.

Kemf, Elizabeth, *Month of pure light: the regreening of Vietnam* (The Women's Press: London, 1990) Account of the attempts to overcome the after-effects of US defoliation and regreen the Vietnamese countryside; more light travelogue than objective book.

Nugent, Nicholas, *Vietnam: the second revolution* (London: In Print, 1996) A good summary of the main changes in Vietnam's economy and society. Also covers the more recent changes dating from the early 1990s.

Popkin, Samuel L, *The rational peasant: the political economy of rural society in Vietnam* (Berkeley: University of California Press, 1979). This book was written in response to James Scott's *The moral economy of the peasant*. Popkin contests the view that traditional Southeast Asia (here, Vietnam) was a moral economy where village solidarity and community spirit were dominant.

Scott, James C, *The moral economy of the peasant: rebellion and subsistence in Southeast Asia* (New Haven: Yale University Press, 1976). The classic historical study of the 'moral' economy of the peasant. Available as a portable paperback.

Templer, Robert, *Shadows and wind: a view of life in modern Vietnam* (London: Little Brown, 1998). Templer was an Agence France Presse correspondent and this is his account of modern Vietnam and where it is headed. It is a downbeat picture of the country, one where bureacratic inertia and political heavy handedness constrain progress.

Turner, Robert F, *Vietnamese Communism: its origins and development* (Hoover Institution Press: Stanford, 1975). Academic study of the rise of communism in Vietnam.

Williams, Michael C, *Vietnam at the crossroads* (Pinter: London, 1992). Most recent survey of political and economic reforms by a senior BBC World Service commentator; lucid and informed.

Young, Marilyn, *The Vietnam Wars 1945-1990* (Harper Collins: New York, 1990) Good account of the origins, development and aftermath of the Vietnam wars.

History

Elliott, Mai , *Sacred willow: four generations in the life of a Vietnamese family* (Oxford: OUP, 1999). Recounts the history of Vietnam through the life of the Duong family from the 19th century to the tragedy of Boat People. A story of Vietnam through Vietnamese eyes.

Osborne, Roger, *The Deprat Affair: Ambition, Revenge and Deceit in French Indochina* (Jonathan Cape, 1999). An account of the extraordinary pickle into which Jacques Deprat, a brilliant young geologist, got himself. Whether he was guilty of professional deceit or not the book gives a useful insight into colonial society and mores in the first two decades of the 20th century.

Taylor, Keith Weller, *The birth of Vietnam* (University of California Press: Berkeley, 1983) Academic history of early Vietnam from the third century BC to 10th century.

Wintle, Justin, *The Vietnam Wars* (Weidenfeld and Nicholson: London, 1991). Not just about *the* War, but about all of Vietnam's interminable conflicts.

Novels

Duras, Marguerite, *The Lover* (London: Flamingo, 1984). Now a film starring Jane March; this is the story of the illicit relationship between an expat French girl and a Chinese from Cholon set in the 1930s.

Greene, Graham, *The Quiet American* (Heinemann: London, 1954). What is remarkable about this novel is the way that it predicts America's experience in Vietnam. The two key figures are Alden Pyle, an idealistic young American, and Thomas Fowler, a hard-bitten and cynical British journalist. It is set in and around Saigon as the war between the French and the Viet Minh intensifies.

Grey, Anthony, *Saigon* (Pan: London, 1983). Entertaining novel.

Garstin, Crosbie, *The Voyage from London to Indochina* (Heinemann, 1928). Hilarious, rather irreverent account of a journey through Vietnam.

Lewis, Norman, *A dragon apparent: travels in Cambodia, Laos and Vietnam*. (1951) One of the finest of all travel books.

Stewart, Lucretia, *Tiger balm: travels in Laos, Cambodia and Vietnam* (London: Chatto & Windus, 1998).

Theroux, Paul, *The great railway bazaar* (Penguin: London, 1977). Theroux describes a graphic account of one American's attempt to travel by rail between Saigon and Hué.

Vu Tu Lap and **Taillard, Christian**, *An Atlas of Vietnam* (Reclus – La Documentation Française, 1994). Summary of the population and economy of Vietnam in maps.

Cawthorne, Nigel, *The bamboo cage* (Leo Cooper, 1992). The story of MIAs and POWs.

Doyle, Jeff with **Grey, Jeffrey** and **Pierce, Peter**, *Australia's Vietnam War*, (A&M University Press, 2002). Australia's role in the Vietnam War is little known and this book examines Australia's motives for joining and contribution to America's war effort.

Fall, Bernard B, *Hell in a very small place: the Siege of Dien Bien Phu* (Pall Mall Press, 1967).

Fitzgerald, Francis, *Fire in the lake* (Vintage Books: New York, 1972). Pulitzer prize winner; a well-researched and readable account of the US involvement.

Harrison, James P, *The endless war: fifty years of struggle in Vietnam* (Free Press: New York, 1982).

Herr, Michael, *Dispatches* (Knopf: New York, 1977). An acclaimed 'account' of the war written by a correspondent who experienced the conflict first hand. It is the story of the war told through the eyes and words of the narrator – a journalist.

Kaiser, David, *American Tragedy: Kennedy, Johnson and the origins of the Vietnam War*, (Harvard University Press, 1999). This account is based on newly-opened archives and provides a penetrating insight into America's involvement in Vietnam.

Karnow, Stanley, *Vietnam: a history* (Viking Press: New York, 1983 and 1991). A comprehensive and readable history; second edition published in 1991; the best there is.

Kissinger, Henry, *The White House Years* (Little, Brown, 1979). Part one of the memoirs of America's best known diplomat. This covers the first Nixon term and ends with the Paris Peace Accord of 1973. Also, *Years of Upheaval* (Little, Brown, 1982). This covers the turbulent months from his visit to Hanoi in February 1973 to Nixon's resignation in August 1974. And, *Years of Renewal* (Simon and Schuster, 1999). The third and concluding volume of the memoirs covers the end of the Vietnam war and collapse of the South.

Lunn, Hugh, *Vietnam: a reporter's war* (University of Queensland Press: St Lucia, Australia, 1985). Account of Australian reporter Hugh Lunn's year in Vietnam with Reuters between 1967 and 1968, including an account of the Tet Offensive.

McNamara, Robert S and **Mark, Brian Van de**, *In retrospect: the tragedy and lessons of Vietnam* (Times/Random House: New York, 1995). McNamara was Secretary for Defense from 1961 to 1968 and this is his cathartic account of the war. Informed from the inside, he concludes that the war was a big mistake.

Mangold, Tom and **Penycate, John**, *The tunnels of Cu Chi* (1985). Compelling account of the building of the tunnels and the VC who fought in them.

Mason, Robert, *Chickenhawk* (Penguin: Harmondsworth, 1984). Autobiography of a helicopter pilot, excellent.

Ninh, Bao, *The sorrow of war* (Secker & Warburg, London, 1993). Wartime novel by a North Vietnamese soldier, wonderful account of emotions during and after the war.

Roth, Philip, *The Human Stain* (Jonathan Cape, 2000). Not, ostensibly, about the Vietnam war at all but it has an excellent account of American war vets coming to terms with their traumas and the country that shuns them.

Sheehan, Neil, *A Bright Shining Lie* (Jonathan Cape: London, 1989). A meticulously researched 850-page account of the Vietnam War, based around the life of John Paul Vann; recommended.

Sheehan, Neil, *Two cities: Hanoi and Saigon* (in US *After the war was over*) (Jonathan Cape: London, 1992). A short but fascinating book which tries to link the past with the present in a part autobiography, part travelogue, part contemporary commentary.

SIPRI, *Ecological consequences of the Second Indochina War* (Almqvist & Wiksell: Stockholm, 1976). Academic study of environmental side-effects of war.

Swain, Jon, *River of Time* (Heinemann, 1996). A gripping account of this war correspondent's time throughout the Vietnam War. He expounds the interesting hypothesis that the reason the American generals were willing to sacrifice so many men was that they saw the war in Vietnam as a rehearsal for a future war in Europe against the Red Army.

Turley, William S, *The Second Indochina War: a short political and military history 1954-75* (Westview: Boulder, 1986). A clear, well-balanced academic account of the war.

Young, Gavin, *A wavering grace: a Vietnamese family in war and peace* (London: Viking, 1997). This is Young's account of the war in Vietnam – he was a reporter in the country – told through the lives of a Vietnamese family. Moving and atmospheric.

Vietnamese literature in English **Nguyen Du,** *The tale of Kieu* (also known as *Truyen Kieu*) (Yale University Press: New Haven, 1983), *tr.* Huynh Sanh Thong. Early 19th century Vietnamese classic and, for many, the masterpiece of Vietnamese poetry. It is also published locally in Vietnam (in English) by the Foreign Languages Publishing House. It tells the story of a beautiful girl and her doomed love affair with a soldier.

Films

The better-known films on Vietnam are American as US filmakers attempt to explain or come to terms with their country's disastrous involvement in Vietnam. Francis Ford Coppola's *Apocalypse Now* won two Oscars in 1979. Coppola substitutes Vietnam for the Africa of Joseph Conrad's *Heart of Darkness*: it remains the best known and most outstanding of all Vietnam films. *The Deer Hunter*, which stars Robert de Niro won five Oscars in 1978. It charts the horrors into which three tough steelworkers were plunged in Vietnam. Stanley Kubrick's *Full Metal Jacket*, 1987, followed GIs from Boot Camp to the Tet Offensive and was acclaimed as a 'riveting condemnation of the Vietnam war'. The set for the devastation of the Tet Offensive in Hué was the disused gas works at Becton in East London. "We had a wrecking ball there for two months, with the art director telling the operator which hole to knock in which building... We brought in palm trees from Spain and a hundred thousand plastic tropical plants from Hong Kong.." said Kubrick.

Good Morning Vietnam is the Robin Williams classic with Williams as an irreverent DJ working for the armed services radio. The comedy of the film is hilarious without trivialising the seriousness of the situation. Oliver Stone's trilogy of Vietnam films *Platoon*, *Born on the Fourth of July* and *Heaven and Earth*, is quite a contrast. The first two deal with the war from the perspective of the American soldier: *Platoon* actually in Vietnam and *Born on the Fourth of July* on adjusting to life after the war. *Heaven and Earth* looks at the wars from the 1960s onwards from the perspective of a Vietnamese woman, Le Ly Hayslip, and the aftermath of war.

Three French films have nicely captured the atmosphere of Vietnam at peace although with a frisson of tension never too far away: *Indochine* starring Catherine Deneuve won acclaim for its beautiful sets and scenery. *The Lover* with Jane March adapted from Marguerite Duras' book. The little known but delightful *Scent of green papaya*, by Tran Anh Hung is an account of family relationships and the secret love of the family's young servant. Set in Saigon in the 1950s, it was filmed entirely in a Paris studio. Tran Anh Hung's next film was the terrifying *Cyclo* revealing the violent life in the underworld of Saigon. In 2001 a new version of Graham Greene's *The Quiet American* was shot in Vietnam and Australia, starring Michael Caine as Fowler and Brendan Fraser as the naïve American.

Footnotes

9

Footnotes

433 Useful words and phrases

435 Glossary

437 Food glossary

439 Shopping glossary

440 Index

444 Shorts

446 Map index

448 Advert index

Vowel sounds

a	as in rather
aê	as in cut
aå	as in hum
e	as in egg
eâ	as in say
I	as in bin
y	as in be
o	as in saw
oå	as in so
ô	as in blur
u	as in rule
ö	as in put

Consonant sounds

ch	as in child
-ch	as in eke (end position)
d	as in zip
ñ	as in dad
g	as in gad
gi	as in zip
kh	as in king
ng	as in singer
nh	as in onion
ph	like an "f"
r	like a "z" in the North
	"r" in the South
th	as in ten
tr	as in train
x	like an "s"

Introduction:

hello or goodbye
xin chaøo
I'm glad to see you
Raát haân haïnh ñöôïc gaëp oâng/baø
How are you?
OÅng/baø khoûe khoâng?
I'm fine, thanks.
Caûm ôn, toâi khoûe.
What's your name ?
OÅng/baø teân laø gì ?
My name is …
Toâi teân laø …
How old are you ?
OÅng/baø bao nhieâu tuoåi ?
Are you married ?
Anh/chò laäp gia ñình chöa ?
Do you have children ?
OÅng/baø coù con khoâng ?
This is my wife/husband.
Ñaây laø nhaøtoâi.
daughter   *con gaùi*
son   *con trai*
What is your job ?
OÅng/baø laøm ngheà gì ?

I'm a…   *Toâi laø…*

businessman	*thöông gia*
doctor	*baùc só*
nurse	*y taù*
teacher	*giaùo vieân*
student	*hoïc sinh*
engineer	*kyõ sö*
journalist	*nhaø baùo*
lawyer	*luaät sö*
secretary	*thö kyù*
clerk	*vieân chöùc vaên*
	phoøng
worker	*coâng nhaân*
farmer	*noâng daân*
scientist	*khoa hoïc gia*
tourist	*khaùch du lòch*

Which country are you from ?
OÅng/baø laø ngöôøi nöôùc naøo ?

I am English	*Toâi laø ngöôøi Anh*
American	*Myõ*
Australian	*Uùc*
Austrian	*AÙo*
Chinese	*Trung Quoác*
Danish	*Ñan Maïch*
Dutch	*Haø Lan*
French	*Phaùp*
German	*Ñöùc*
Indian	*Aán Ñoä*
Italian	*Yù*
Japanese	*Nhaät*
Korean	*Haøn Quoác*
Norwegian	*Na Uy*
Russian	*Nga*
Swedish	*Thuïy Ñieån*
Swiss	*Thuïy Só*

Numbers

1	*moät*
2	*hai*
3	*ba*
4	*boán*
5	*naêm*
6	*saùu*
7	*baûy*
8	*taùm*
9	*chín*
10	*möôøi/ moät chuïc*
11	*möôøi moät*
12	*möôøi hai*
15	*möôøi laêm…ect*
20	*hai möôi*
21	*hai möôi moát*
22	*hai möôi hai…ect*
30	*ba möôi…ect*
100	*moät traêm*
101	*moät traêm leû moät*
	or *moät traêm moät*

200	*hai traêm…ect*
1,000	*moät nghìn /moät ngaøn*
10,000	*möôøi nghìn/möôøi ngaøn*
100,000	*moät traêm nghìn*
1,000,000	*moät trieäu*

Date and time

morning	*buoåi saùng*
noon	*tröa*
afternoon	*buoåi chieàu*
evening	*buoåi toái*
night	*ban ñeâm*
day time	*ban ngaøy*
today	*hoâm nay*
yesterday	*hoâm qua*
tomorrow	*ngaøy mai*
Sunday	*chuû nhaät*
Monday	*thöù hai*
Tuesday	*thöù ba*
Wednesday	*thöù tö*
Thursday	*thöù naêm*
Friday	*thöù saùu*
Saturday	*thöù baûy*
month	*thaùng*
January	*tháng gieâng*
Febuary	*thaùng hai*
March	*thaùng ba*
April	*thaùng tö*
May	*thaùng naêm*
June	*thaùng saùu*
July	*thaùng baûy*
August	*thaùng taùm*
September	*thaùng chín*
October	*thaùng möôøi*
November	*thaùng möôøi moät*
December	*thaùng möôøi hai*
spring	*muøa xuaân*
summer	*muøa haï/heø*
autumn	*muøa thu*
winter	*muøa ñoâng*

Directions

Where is the …?
  ôû ñaâu…?

airport	*phi tröôøng*
bus station	*beán xe*
church	*nhaø thôø*
ferry station	*beán phaø*
market	*chôï*
museum	*vieän baûo taøng*
hospital	*beänh vieän*
pagoda	*chuøa*
phamarcy	*hieäu thuoác taây*
police station	*traïm caûnh saùt*
post office	*böu ñieän*

railway station	*ga xe löûa*
school	*tröôøng hoïc*
university	*tröôøng ñaïi hoïc*

Could you show me the way to…?
  OÂng/bao coù theå chæ toâi ñöôøng tôùi…?

Is it far ?	*Coù xa khoâng ?*
Is it near ?	*Coù gaàn khoâng ?*
go straight	*ñi thaúng*
turn left	*queïo/reõ traùi*
turn right	*queïo/reõ phaûi*
crossroads	*ngaõ tö*
T-junction	*ngaõ ba*
roundabout	*buøng binh*

Taking a trip

I want a ticket to …
  Toâi muoán moät veù ñi …

How much is a ticket?
  Bao nhieâu tieàn moät veù?

return-ticket	*veù khöù hoài*
one-way ticket	*veù moät chieàu*

I want to go to …
  Toâi muoán ñi ñeán …

Is there a bus to Hanoi ?
  Coù chuyeán xe buyùt ñi Haø Noäi khoâng ?

Does this bus go to Sapa?
  Xe naøy coù ñi ñeán Sapa khoáng ?

train	*xe löûa/ taøu hoûa*
car	*xe hôi/oâtoâ*
flight	*chuyeán bay*
boat	*thuyeàn*
ship	*taøu*
ferry	*phaø*

When is the next train?
  Chuyeán xe löûa keá tieáp vaøo luùc naøo ?

How long does the trip take ?
  Haønh trình maát bao laâu ?

I want the next train to Hué
  Toâi muoán moät chuyeán taøu sôùm nhaát ñi Hueá

I want to go by express train
  Toâi muoán moät chuyeán taøu toác haønh

What time does the train arrive ?
  Xe löûa ñeán luùc maáy giôø ?

What time will the train depart ?
  Xe löûa seõ khôûi haønh luùc maây giò ?

The train is late
  Chuyeán xe löûa bò treã

The train has been cancelled
  Chuyeán xe löûa bò huûy

See *Language* section page 26.

Glossary

Ao dai long flowing silken tunic worn over trousers by Vietnamese school girls and women

Amulet protective medallion

Ben Xe bus station

Bia hoi freshly brewed beer, 3%, so not too strong, cheap and thirst quenching. Normally drunk squatting on small plastic stools

Bia ôm dimly-lit bars with young female hostesses to entertain clients

Binh dân (popular) street restaurants

Bodhi the tree under which the Buddha achieved enlightenment (*Ficus religiosa*)

Bodhisattva a future Buddha. In Mahayana Buddhism, someone who has attained enlightenment, but who postpones nirvana to help others reach it.

Brahma the Creator, one of the gods of the Hindu trinity, usually represented with four faces, and often mounted on a hamsa

Cao Dai composite religion of south Vietnam (see page 419)

Champa rival empire of the Khmers, of Hindu culture, based in present day Vietnam (see page 354)

Cho market

Chua pagoda, a place of Buddhist worship (see page 406)

Cyclo bicycle trishaw

Dau Ong Ba Ancestor worship

Den Non Buddhist temple

Deva a Hindu-derived male god

Dharma the Buddhist law

Dinh palace or temple for the worship of non Buddhist god, relic or historical figure

Dipterocarp family of trees (*Dipterocarpaceae*) characteristic of Southeast Asia's forests

Doi moi 'renovation', Vietnamese perestroika

Duong street

Funan the oldest Indianized state of Indochina and precursor to Chenla

Ganesh elephant-headed son of Siva

Geomancy the art of divination by lines and figures. Geomancers were responsible for the site and orientation of a palace, tomb or other auspicious building.

Gopura crowned or covered gate, entrance to a religious area

Hamsa sacred goose, Brahma's mount; in Buddhism it represents the flight of the doctrine

Hinayana 'Lesser Vehicle', major Buddhist sect in Southeast Asia, usually termed Theravada Buddhism (see page 415)

Hoi Quan Chinese assembly house or clan house

Honda ôm motorcycle taxi (*ôm* means 'to cuddle')

Hot toc hair cut

Ikat tie-dyeing method of patterning cloth

Jataka(s) the birth stories of the Buddha; they normally number 547, although an additional three were added in Burma for reasons of symmetry in mural painting and sculpture; the last ten are the most important

Lambro or **xe lam** small three-wheeled motorized van

Laterite bright red tropical soil/stone commonly used in construction of Cham monuments

Li xi Lucky money given to children in red envelopes at *Tet*

Linga phallic symbol and one of the forms of Siva. Embedded in a pedastal (yoni) shaped to allow drainage of lustral water poured over it, the linga typically has a succession of cross sections: from square at the base through octagonal to round. These symbolise, in order, the trinity of Brahma, Vishnu and Siva

Lintel a load-bearing stone spanning a doorway; often heavily carved

Mahayana 'Greater Vehicle', major Buddhist sect (see page 415)

Mandarin Royal civil servant, emissary of the king

Meru sacred or cosmic mountain at the centre of the world in Hindu-Buddhist cosmology; home of the gods

Montagnard 'hill people', from the French (see page 395)

Moon cakes Cakes eaten at the mid-Autumn Festival (Moon Festival) made of green bean paste with egg yolk, some with pumpkin seeds or melon seeds in pastry

Naga benevolent mythical water serpent, enemy of Garuda

Nha ga Train station

Nirvana release from the cycle of suffering in Buddhist belief; 'enlightenment'

Non lá Conical straw hat; **non lá bai tho** version of the conical hat made in Hué which has a poem woven in

Ong Tao God of the kitchen. He ascends to heaven a week before the end of the old year to report to Ong Troi on the behaviour of the family

Ong Troi or **Thuong De** God of Heaven in traditional Vietnamese mythology

paddy/padi unhulled rice or an irrigated field in which rice is grown

Pagoda a Mahayana Buddhist temple

Pali the sacred language of Theravada Buddhism

Parvati consort of Siva

Quan Am Chinese goddess of mercy (see page 76)

Rama incarnation of Vishnu, hero of the Indian epic, the *Ramayana*

Rattan Forest creeper that is woven into baskets or furniture. Sometimes mistaken for bamboo

Rong the Bahnar rong house is instantly recognizable by its tall thatched roof. The height of the roof is meant to indicate the significance of the building and make it visible to all. It is a focal point of the village for meetings of the village elders, weddings and other communal events

Sakyamuni the historic Buddha

Sampan a small wooden boat, traditionally made of three planks of wood

Singha mythical guardian lion

Siva the Destroyer, one of the three gods of the Hindu trinity; the sacred linga was worshipped as a symbol of Siva

Stela/e inscribed stone panel/s

Stucco plaster, often heavily moulded

Stupa dome-like Buddhist monument. Originally a topknot of hair, the building symbolises variously the upper part of the head, a tree's stem and a tower reaching up to heaven

Taoism Chinese religion (see page 417)

Tavatimsa heaven of the 33 gods at the summit of Mount Meru

Tay ba lo (insult) Western backpacker living on a tight budget. Unwashed and badly dressed.

Tet Vietnamese (Chinese) New Year (see page 54)

Tet Trung Thu Mid Autumn Festival, lantern festival or mooncake festival

Theravada 'Way of the Elders'; major Buddhist sect also known as Hinayana Buddhism ('Lesser Vehicle') (see page 415)

Uy ban nhan dan People's Committee (ie local government)

Vahana 'vehicle', a mythical beast, upon which a deva or god rides

Viet Cong Vietnamese Communist troops who fought the Americans (see page 363)

Viet Minh Vietnamese Communist troops who fought the French (see page 359)

Vishnu the Protector, one of the gods of the Hindu trinity, generally with four arms holding a disc, conch shell, ball and club

Xe ôm motorbike taxi

Eating: useful words and phrases

Can I have the menu, please? *Xin cho toâi xem thöïc ñôn?*
I'm a vegetarian *Toâi aên chay*
No chilli, please *Xin ñöøng cho ôùt*
MSG *boät ngoït/ mì chính (N)*
chilli *ôùt*
I'd like some rice *Toâi muoán moät ít côm*
spring rolls *chaû gioø*
noodles *mì; huû tieáu; buùn*
bread *baùnh mì*
fish sauce *nöôùc naém*
soya sauce *nöôùc töông*
meat *thịt*
pork *thịt heo*
beef *thịt boø*
chicken *thịt gaø*
duck *thịt vòt*
goat *thịt deâ*
fish *caù*
crab *cua*
eel *löôn*
lobster *toâm huøm*
shrimp *toâm*
squid *möïc*
egg *tröùng*
vegetable *rau caûi*
tofu *ñaäu huõ*
spinach *rau moáng*
bamboo shoot *maêng*
bean sprouts *giaù*
beans *ñaäu*
cauliflower *boâng caûi*
green pepper *ôùt Naø Laït*
corn *baép/ ngoâ*
tomato *caø chua*
carrot *caø roát*
cucumber *döa leo*
lettuce *rau saø laùch*
onion *haønh taây*
potato *khoai taây*
mushroom *naám*
soup *canh/xuùp*
boiled *luoäc*

steamed *haáp*
fried *chieân/ raùn*
roasted *quay*
grilled *nöôùng*
fruits *traùi caây*
avocado *traùi/quaû bô*
banana *traùi/quaû chuoái*
grapefruit *traùi/quaû böôûi*
lemon *traùi/quaû chanh*
longan *traùi/quaû nhaõn*
lychee *traùi/qua vaûi*
mandarin *traùi/quaû quyùt*
orange *traùi/quaû cam*
papaya *traùi/quaû ñu ñuû*
peach *traùi/quaû ñaøo*
pineapple *traùi/quaû thôm/döùa*
plum *traùi/quaû maän/roi*
rambutan *traùi/quaû choâm choâm*
watermelon *traùi/quaû döa haáu*
Do you have traditional food?
Coù moùn aên truyeàn thoáng khoâng?
Do you have any special dishes?
Moùn naøo laø ñaëc saûn cuûa quaùn?
It's delicious *Raát ngon*
I'm thirsty *Toâi khaùt nöôùc*
Cold water please *Cho toâi xin moät coác nöôùc laïnh*
no sugar *khoâng ñöôøng*
no ice *khoâng ñaù*
black coffee *caø pheâ ñen*
iced coffee *caø pheâ ñaù*
iced coffee with milk *Caø pheâ söõa ñaù*
tea *traø/cheø (N)*
a bottle of beer *Moät chai bia*
a can of beer *Moät lon bia*
a bottle of mineral water *Moät chai nöôùc suoái*
Is the water safe to drink? *Nöôùc uoáng coù saïch khoâng?*
lemon juice *nöôùc chanh*
orange juice *cam vaét*
coconut *nöôùc döøa*
pineapple shake *sinh toá thôm*
rice wine *röôïu ñeá*

Meat *Thịt*
Sliced grilled beef *Bò tung xẻo*
Beef dipped in vinegar *Bò nhúng dấm*
Grilled beef wrapped in leaf/pork fat
    Bò nướng lá lốt/mỡ chài
Diced beef with french fries *Bò lúc lắc*
Stewed beef *Bò kho*
Roasted young pork *Heo sữa quay*
Fresh spring rolls *Gỏi cuốn*
Grilled pork noodles *Bún thịt nướng*
Trang Bang fresh spring rolls *Bánh tráng Trảng Bàng*
Pickled pork *Dưa đầu heo*
Pork/shrimp spring rolls *Chả giò thịt/ tom*
Chinese sausage *Lạp xưởng*

Chicken *Gà*
Chicken wings fried in fish sauce
    Cánh gà chiên nước mắm
Chicken salad *Gỏi gà/Gà xé phay*
Boneless chicken feet salad *Chân gà rút xương*
Roasted chicken *Gà quay*
Grilled chicken *Gà nướng*
Chicken rice soup *Cháo gà*
Chicken curry *Cà ri gà*

Fish *Cá*
Grilled trout wrapped in banana leaf
    Cá lóc nướng lá chuối
Grilled trout wrapped in clay *Cá lóc nướng đất sét*
Trout grilled in straw *Cá lóc nướng trui*
Deep fried fish *Cá tai tượng chiên xù*
Fish sour soup *Canh chua cá*
Steamed fish *Cá hấp*
Fish hot pot *Lẩu cá*
Fried catfish with ginger sauce *Cá trê chiên chấm mắm gừng*
Deep fried anchovy *Cá cơm chiên dòn*

Duck *Vịt*
Roasted duck *Vịt quay*
Dry duck *Vịt lạp*
Duck rice soup *Cháo vịt*
Duck with bamboo shoot noodles
    Bún măng vịt

Frog *Ếch*
Frog fried in butter *Ếch chiên bơ*
Deep fried frog *Ếch lăn bột*

Crab *Cua*
Tamarind crab *Cua rang me*
Salted crab *Cua rang muối*
Crab steamed with ginger *Cua hấp gừng*
Crab steamed in beer *Cua hấp bia*

Shellfish *Sò*
Raw oyster *Hào sống*
Grilled/steamed shellfish *Sò nướng/hấp*
Shellfish rice soup *Cháo sò huyết*
Mussel rice *Cơm hến*
Mussel rice soup *Cháo hến*
Mussel salad with star fruit *Gỏi hến xào khế*
Grilled clam *Nghêu nướng*

Shrimps *Tôm*
Grilled lobster *Tôm càng nướng*
Grilled prawn *Tôm nướng*
Tiger prawns steamed in coconut
    Tôm sú hấp nước dừa
Shrimps steamed in beer *Tôm hấp bia*
Lotus stem and shrimp salad
    Gỏi tôm ngó sen
Seafood hotpot *Lẩu hải sản*

Squid *Mực*
Dried squid mixed with grapefruit
    Khô mực trộn bưởi
Stirred fried squid *Mực xào*
Deep fried squid *Mực tươi lăn bột chiên*

Snails *Ốc*
Snails steamed with ginger *Ốc hấp gừng*
Pork stuffed snails *Ốc nhồi*
Snails with coconut milk *Ốc len xào dừa*

Vegetable *Rau*
Morning glory fried with garlic *Rau muống xào tỏi*
Spinach fried with garlic *Cải bó xôi xào tỏi*
Pickled vegetable *Dưa chua*
Fried cauliflower *Bông cải xào*
Fried pumpkin flower *Bông bí xào*
Vegetable soup *Canh rau*
Papaya salad *Gỏi đu đủ*
Banana flower salad *Gỏi bắp chuối*

Soup *Xúp*

Crab soup *Xúp cua*

Fish soup *Xú bong bóng cá*

Rice soup with salted duck eggs
   Cháo trắng hột vịt muối

Crab & asparagus soup *Xúp măng cua*

Noodles *Mì*

Crispy fried noodles *Mì xào giòn*

Chinese duck noodles *Mì vịt tiềm*

Won Ton soup *Hoành thánh*

Quang Nam noodles *Mì Quảng*

Soup with flat white noodles *Phở*

Pork noodles *Hủ tíu*

Vermicelli *Miến*

Fat round rice noodles *Bánh canh*

Huế beef noodles *Bún bò Huế*

Other dishes *Các Món Khác*

Huế sizzling cake *Bánh khoái*

Sizzling cake *Bánh xèo*

Cantonese fried rice *Cơm chiên*
   Dương Châu

Rice in clay pot *Cơm niêu*

Grilled pork rolls *Nem nướng*

Pickled pork wrapped in leaf
   Nem chua

Words and phrases for shopping

I'd like to buy some clothes	*Tôi muốn mua một ít quần áo*
shoes	*giày*
sandals	*dép*
socks	*vớ*
hat	*nón*
rucksack	*ba lô*
bag	*giỏ xách*
pottery	*đồ gốm*
handicaft	*đồ thủ công*
paintings	*tranh*
How much is it?	*Giá bao nhiêu?*
It's too expensive	*Mắc quá*
Can you lower the price?	*Có bớt không?*
Oh, it's still very expensive	*Ồ, vẫn còn mắc lắm*
Is 10,000 dong OK?	*10,000 đồng, được không?*
Can I have a look?	*Tôi có thể xem được không?*
Sorry, I don't like it	*Rất tiếc, tôi không thích*
Do you have another one?	*Ông/bà có cái khác không?*
I will take this one	*Tôi sẽ mua cái này*
They don't/ It doesn't fit me	*Nó không vừa với tôi*
It's too small	*Nó nhỏ quá*
Do you have one in a bigger size?	*Ông/ bà có cỡ lớn hơn không?*
smaller/bigger	*nhỏ hơn/lớn hơn*
longer/shorter	*dài hơn/ngắn hơn*
tighter/looser	*chật hơn/ rộng hơn*

Index

A

AIDS 303
air
 airports 33
 getting around 38
 getting there 31
 airport tax 33
Alexandre-de-Rhodes 356, 410
An Binh Island 323
Annam Highlands 420
anti-war demonstrations 369
Ao dai 409
Ap Bac 320
art and architecture 403
Army of the Republic of Vietnam
 (ARVN) 364
art 403

B

Ba Be National Park 137
Ba Chuc 337
Bac Can 136
Bac Ha 130
Bac My An Beach 206
Bac Quang 131
Bac Son 145
Bach Ma National Park &
 Hill Station 199
Bai Chay 161
 directory 165
 eating 164
 sleeping 163
 transport 164
Ban Co 109
Ban Don village 232
Ba-na 396
Bana Hill Station 208
Bao Loc 259
bars 54
Ben Tre 322
Bich Dong 168
bicycle & motorbike
 getting around 44
bicycles 44
Bien Ho 225
Bien Hoa 291
Binh Chau 268
Black Lady Mountain 290
Bo Cung Pass 142
Boat People 376
books on Vietnam 427
border
 with Cambodia 335, 341
 with China 128, 143
border with Laos 177
Buddhism 415, 416
Buon Juin 231
Buon Ma Thuot 230

Buon Tur 232
bus
 getting around 42
business hours 34

C

Ca Na 244
Cam Ranh Bay 242
Can Gio 290
Can Tho 326
Cao Bang 138
 sights and excursions 139
 sleeping and eating 141
Cao Dai Great Temple 289
Cao Dai Temple 205
Cao Daism 419
Cao Lanh 333
Cao-Bac-Lang 136
car hire
 getting around 44
cash machines 31
Cat Ba Island 154
Cat Ba National Park 156
Cat Cat village 125
Cau Da 237
Cham 401
Cham Ponagar Temple complex 236
Champa 354
Chau Doc border crossing into
 Cambodia 335
Chau Doc 334
China Beach 205
Chinese domination of Vietnam 349
Cho Con 205
Cholon, Saigon 284
Christianity 418
Chu Pao Pass 227
Chua village 175
climate
 See also under individual regions
 when to go 20
clothing 33
Co Loa Citadel 81
Coc Bo Cave 141
Cochin China 357
Co-ho 397
Con Dao 268
Con Dao National Park 269
Confucianism 417
Cost of living 31
Cost of travelling 31
crafts 409
credit cards 31
Cu Chi tunnels 288
Cua Dai Beach 217
Cua Lo 175
Cuc Dua village 108
Cuc Phuong National Park 169
currency 30

customs 30
Cyclo
 getting around 45

D

Dalat 249
 directory 258
 eating 257
 sights 250
 sleeping 255
 transport 258
Dambri Falls 259
Danang 202
 directory 212
 eating 211
 sights 204
 sleeping 210
Dao 105, 397
Demilitarized Zone (DMZ) 193
Democratic Republic of Vietnam
 (DRV) 359
Diem 364
Diem, Ngo Dinh 362
Dien Bien Phu 111, 361
 sights 114
 sleeping and eating 115
disabled travel 27
Do Son 152
doi moi 381, 387, 389
Domestic Airline fares 43
dong 30
Dong Duong 210
Dong Ha 176
Dong Hoi 176
Dong Van 135
Dong Van-Meo Vac Region 133
Dongson culture 403
drama 414
drink 50
drugs 34
Duras, Margueritte 324
duty free 30

E

eating
 etiquette 34
 markets 52
economy 386
E-de 398
Ede villages 232
email 47
emergency telephone numbers 34
Emperor Tu Duc 357
entertainment and nightlife 54
ethnic Chinese 402
etiquette
 visiting minorities 396

F

fauna 422
fax services 49
films about Vietnam 430
Finding out more 26
First Indochina War (1945-54) 359
flora 422
French surrender in Vietnam 362
Frontier Campaign of 1947-50 142
Funan 353

G

Garnier, Francis 421
gay and lesbian travel 27
Getting around 38
Gia rai 398
Glossary 435
Gulf of Tonkin Incident 365

H

Ha Giang 132
Ha Tien 340
Hai Van Pass 201
Haiphong 146
  directory 151
  sights 147
  sleeping and eating 150
Halong Bay 158
Halong City 161
Hanoi 63
  Army Museum 79
  36 Streets 69
  Ba Dinh Square 76
  bars 94
  cafés 94
  directory 99
  eating 90
  entertainment 94
  Festivals 95
  Fine Arts Museum 79
  Hanoi Hilton 74
  history 64
  History Museum 72
  Ho Chi Minh Museum 76
  Ho Chi Minh's Mausoleum 75
  Hoan Kiem Lake 68
  Museum of the Vietnamese
    Revolution 72
  Old City (36 Streets) 69
  One Pillar Pagoda 75
  Opera House 72
  Outer Hanoi 79
  Saint Joseph's Cathedral 73
  shopping 95
  sights 68
  sleeping 86
  sports 95
  tour operators 96
  transport 97
  travel cafés 94
  Van Mieu Pagoda (Temple of
    Literature) 76

Vietnam Museum of Ethnology 80
Health 56
Henry Kissinger 371
Hien Luong Bridge 194
Highland Areas 422
Highland people, see
  Montagnards 395
Hinduism 419
history
  ancient 349
  colonial 356
  post-war 375
  pre-colonial 349
  resistance to the French 358
  See also under individual regions
    and towns
Hmông 398
Ho Chi Minh 66, 71, 82, 113, 175,
  284, 358, 360, 378, 386
Ho Chi Minh City (see Saigon)
Ho Chi Minh Trail 194, 363, 364
Ho Chi Minh's Mausoleum 75
Ho Coc 268
Hoa 402
Hoa Binh 104
Hoa Hao 419
Hoa Lu 167
Hoan Kiem Lake, Hanoi 68
Hoi An 212
  directory 220
  sleeping and eating 217
hoi quan 213
holidays 54
  when to go 20
Hon Chong Headland 238
Hon Chong 342
Hon Gai 162
  directory 165
  eating 164
  sleeping 163
Hon Mot 238
Hon Mun 238
Hon Rom 246
Hon Tam 238
Hué 177
  best time to visit 178
  directory 199
  eating 196
  Imperial City 180
  sights 180
  sleeping 194
  transport 198
Hué architecture 405
Hung Kings' Temples 81
Huong Giang 177

I

Imperial City, Hué 180
Indochina Communist Party
  (ICP) 358, 359, 360
International Rice Research
  Institute 328
internet 47
Islam 419
Island of the Coconut Monk 321

J

jackfruit 50
Japanese 'occupation' of
  Vietnam 359
Japanese Covered Bridge 213
Jarai villages 226
Johnson, Lyndon 364

K

Kennedy, John F 363
Keo Pagoda 85
Khe Sanh 194, 370
  Battle of 193
Kieu, Tale of 412
Kinh 401
Kon D'Re 229
Kon Kotu 229
Kontum 227
Kontum K'Nam 229

L

La Nga Lake 259
Lac, White Thái village 107
lacquerware 409
Lai Chau 116
Lak Lake 231
Lake of Sighs 254
Lang Co 200
Lang Si 134
Lang Son 143
language 26, 410
Lao Bao 177
Lao Cai 128
Laos, border crossing 177
Lat communities 255
Le Dynasty 352
Le Loi 352
Le Thanh Ton 352
literature 411
local customs and laws 33
Long Hai 267
Long Xuyen 331
Lung Phay Pass 141
Ly Dynasty 349

M

M'nong villages 231
Ma Phi Leng Pass 136
Mahayana Buddhism 415
Mai Chau 106
Mán, see Dao 397
mango 50
mangosteen 50
maps 47
Marble Mountains 206
Marco Polo 355
markets 52
media 49
Mekong Delta 318
  geography 421

Mekong River 421
Meo Vac 136
Mieu Island 238
Minh Danh 268
Mol, see Muòng 399
money 30
　cash 31
　credit cards 31
　currency 30
　travellers cheques 31
Montagnards 395
motorbikes 44
Motorcycle taxi
　getting around 44
Mount Fan Si Pan 123
Mui Ne 246
Muòng 105, 399
My Khe 205
My Lai 222
　massacre 221, 222
My Son 208
My Tho 292, 319

Nam Cat Tien National Park 259
Nam Con Son Gasfield 394
Nam Dinh 165
Nam O 202
National Liberation Front of
　Vietnam (NLF) 363
newspapers 49
Ngang Pass 175
Ngo Dinh Diem 362
Ngoan Muc Pass 248
Nguyen Dynasty 352
Nha Trang 234
　directory 242
　sights 236
　sleeping and eating 239
Ninh Binh 166
Ninh Chu Beach 243
Nixon, President Richard 372
noise 36
Non Nuoc Beach 207
normalization 384
Nui Ba Den 290
Nung 399

O

Oc-eo 353, 358
open bus ticket
　getting around 44
Operation Rolling Thunder 367

P

Pac Bo 140
pagodas 406
papaya 50
Paris Accord 372
people 395
People's Liberation Armed Forces
　(PLAF) 363
Perfume Pagoda 85

Phan Rang 243
Phan Thiet 245
Phat Diem 169
Phi Hay White Hmông village 118
Phoenix Programme 371
Phong Nha Cave 176
Phong Tho 120
Phu Quoc Island 343
Plain of Reeds
　(Dong Thap Muoi) 333
Play Ku 225
Play To Ngia 228
Plei Fun 226
Pleiku (see Play Ku)
Plei Mrong 226
Plei Mun 226
Po Klong Garai 243
Po Ro Me 243
police 36
politics 378
Pomelo 50
post 48
Prohibitions 34
Pu Ka village 116

Q

Quan Ba 134
Quang Ngai 222
Quoc Dan Dang (VNQDD), first
　Vietnamese nationalist party 358
Quy Nhon 223

R

Rach Gia 337
Rambutan 50
Red River Delta 420
religion 34, 415
　Christianity 418
　Confucianism 417
　Mahayana Buddhism 415
　Taoism 417
responsible tourism 35
restaurants 52
Rhade, see E-de 398
rice cultivation 425
road
　getting around 42
　getting there 32
　traffic 37

S

Sa Dec 324
Sa Phin 134
safety 35
Saigon (Ho Chi Minh City) 271
　Archbishop's Palace 280
　bars 302
　Ben Thanh Market 283
　Binh Tay Market 286
　Botanical Gardens and zoo 281
　cafés 304
　Central 278
　Chinatown (Cholon) 284

Cholon (Chinatown) 284
　directory 312
　eating 297
　entertainment 304
　excursions 288
　Fine Art Museum 283
　General Post Office 280
　Giac Lam Pagoda 286
　Giac Vien Pagoda 286
　Historical Museum 281
　history 274
　Ho Chi Minh Museum (Dragon
　House Wharf) 284
　Mariamman Hindu Temple 283
　Museum of Ho Chi Minh
　Campaign 280
　Nghia An Assembly Hall 285
　Notre Dame Cathedral 280
　Old Market 284
　Opera House 279
　Outer Saigon 287
　Pham Ngu Lao 295
　Phung Son Pagoda 286
　Phuoc Hai Tu (Emperor of Jade
　Pagoda) 287
　Quan Am Pagoda 286
　Reunification Hall 282
　Revolutionary Museum 283
　Rex Hotel 278
　shopping 304
　sights 278
　sleeping 292
　sport 306
　Tam Son Assembly Hall 285
　Thien Hau Pagoda 285
　Tomb and Temple of Marshal Le
　Van Duyet 287
　Ton Duc Thang Museum 284
　tour operators 308
　Tran Hung Dao Temple 287
　transport 309
　Vinh Nghiem Pagoda 287
　War Remnants Museum 281
　War Surplus Market 284
　Xa Loi Pagoda 281
salak 50
Salangane islands 238
Sam Mountain 335
Sam Son 174
Sapa 121
　eating 127
　sights 122
　sleeping 125
sea
　getting around 47
　getting there 32
Sen 175
shopping 53
Sin Chai village 125
Sin Ho 119
sleeping
　hotel classification 38
　where to stay 37
Soc Trang 330
Socialist Republic of Vietnam
　(SRV) 375
Son La 107

Footnotes

Son My
  massacre 221, 222
Son My (My Lai) 222
Special Air Service (SAS) 368
Sport and special interest travel 55
strategic hamlets 364
student travellers 27

T

T'ai, see Thai 400
T20 Beach 205
Ta Phin Red Dao village 123
Tam Coc 168
Tam Dao 83
Tam Duong 120
Tam Nong Bird Sanctuary 333
tamarind 50
Tan Long Island 321
Tan Son Nhat Airport 310
Taoism 417
taxi
  getting around 46
Tày 400
Tay Ninh 289
Tay Phuong National Park 85
Tay Son rebellion 352
Táy, see Thái 400
telephone services 49
Tet 21
Tet Offensive 370
Thái 400
Thang Long 65
Thanh Hoa 174
Thap Doi Cham towers 223
Thay Pagoda 85
the 17th parallel, creation of 362
Thien Hau Pagoda 285
Tho, see Tày 400
Thuan An Beach 191
Thuan Chau 110
Thuy Duong 268
time 34
tipping 34
tourist information 33
tours and tour operators 21
Tra Vinh 325
Trai Mat village 254
Trai, Nguyen 353
train
  getting around 46
  getting there 32
Tran Dynasty 351
transport
  bicycles and motorbikes 44
  buses 42
  getting there 31
  taxis 46
  trains 46
travel advisories 36
travellers' cheques 31
Treaty of Tientsin 358
Truong Son Mountain Range 420
Tuan Giao 110
Tuan Tu 243

V

Van Mieu Pagoda 76
VC, see Viet Cong 363
Viet Cong 363
Viet Kieu 402
Viet Minh 359
Viet, see Kinh 401
Vietnam War 362
Vietnam Wars 359
Vietnamese Communist Party 378
Vinh 174
Vinh Long 323
Vinh Tuy 131
visas 29
Voluntary work 28
Vung Tau 260

W

water puppet theatre 414
weights and measures 34
Westmoreland, General
  William 368, 369, 370
what to take 30
women travellers 27
working in Vietnam 28

X

Xo-dang 401
Xom Mo 105
Xuan Huong Lake 250
Xuan Thieu Beach 202

Y

Yen Minh 134
Yen Tu Mountains 162
yin and yang 418
Yok Don National Park 232

Z

Zrai, see Gia rai 398

Shorts

376   A nation at sea: the boat people
356   A Spanish account of Champa circa 1595
366   A War glossary
303   AIDS in Vietnam
193   battle at Khe Sanh (1968), The
112   Battle of Dien Bien Phu, The
159   Battles of Bach Dang River (AD 938 and AD 1288), The
 67   Beautiful Hanoi needs a miracle, says British MP
 52   Bird's nest soup
 91   Bites but no bark in a Vietnamese restaurant
143   border crossing, The
125   Bridge of confusion
404   Brilliance in Bronze: rain drums of Dongson
282   Buddhist martyrs: self-immolation as protest
201   By train from Hué to Danang
278   Crossing the road
186   death and burial of Emperor Gia Long (1820), The
 50   Distinctive fruits
 45   Every man and his pig
 77   examination of 1875, The
424   Fields in the forest – shifting cultivation
192   funeral of a King, The
378   Getting our children out of Vietnam: a personal story
266   Going to the dogs
 66   Hanoi's names: (AD 200-present)
362   Ho Chi Minh Pseudonyms
360   Ho Chi Minh: 'He who enlightens'
307   Horse races
319   Hydrology of the Mekong Delta
416   In Siddhartha's footsteps: a short history of Buddhism
412   Kieu: oriental Juliet or prototype Miss Saigon?
393   Looking back on 20 Years of Peace
406   Modern Vietnamese art
222   My Lai – 30 years on
394   Nam Con Son Gasfield
178   Nguyen Dynasty Emperors (1802-1945)
353   Nguyen Trai
128   No man's land
132   Off-road in the Northeast
374   Patriot games: Vietnamese street names
105   People of the north
305   Raid
291   Rebirth of a forest
390   Reduction of Poverty in Vietnam
397   Rite of passage: from baby to infant
 98   Road to nowhere
221   Son My (My Lai) Massacre, The
 76   story of Quan Am, The

312   Streetwise
263   Superior God of the Southern Sea
 73   Syndicated loans keep the sharks away
223   Tay Son Rebellion (1771-88), The
 97   Tearaways terrorize townsfolk
368   The Anzacs in Vietnam
425   The cycle of wet rice cultivation
421   The Mekong: mother river of Southeast Asia
367   The War in figures
387   Top investors 2001
389   Tourism in Vietnam
 81   Trung sisters, The
191   Tu Duc's lament
 44   Vietnam Airlines booking offices
392   Vietnam exports by value
388   Vietnam: selected economic reforms, 1979-2001
 48   Vietnamese addresses
354   Vietnamese dynasties
396   Visiting the minorities: house rules
269   Vo Thi Sau
391   Waste not, want not
237   Yersin, Alexandre

Map index

232 Around Buon Ma Thuot
206 Around Danang
 84 Around Hanoi
184 Around Hué
288 Around Saigon
124 Around Sapa
130 Bac Ha
230 Buon Ma Thuot
327 Can Tho
154 Cat Ba Island & Halong Bay
156 Cat Ba Town
335 Chau Doc
285 Cholon
250 Dalat
256 Dalat centre
203 Danang
114 Dien Bien Phu
113 Dien Bien Phu battle site
152 Do Son
340 Ha Tien
148 Haiphong
162 Halong City
 70 Hanoi
167 Hoa Lu and the Temple of Dinh Tien Hoang
 87 Hoan Kiem
214 Hoi An
179 Hué
195 Hué detail
181 Hué Imperial City
228 Kontum
116 Lai Chau
129 Lao Cai & Border Crossing to China
246 Mui Ne
320 My Tho
235 Nha Trang
296 Pham Ngu Lao Area - Saigon
243 Phan Rang
245 Phan Thiet
343 Phu Quoc Island
226 Play Ku
338 Rach Gia
276 Saigon
279 Saigon centre
293 Saigon Centre Detail
126 Sapa
108 Son La
 82 The Hung Kings' Temples
185 Tomb of Emperor Gia Long

187 Tomb of Emperor Minh Mang
189 Tomb of Tu Duc
380 Vietnam - Provinces
 39 Vietnam Airlines domestic routes
365 Vietnam War
261 Vung Tau
264 Vung Tau centre

Footnotes

Advert index

Tear out card
Travel bag Adventures, UK

Colour
455   Asian Trails, Thailand
454   Asiatica Travel, Vietnam
456   Audley Travel, UK
451   Bangkok Airways, Thailand
454   Buffalo Tours, Vietnam
453   Green Bamboo Travel, Vietnam
456   Hoi An Hotel & Hoi An Beach Resort, Vietnam
453   Travelbag Adventures, UK
452   Windsor Vietnam Group, Vietnam

308   ATLAS Tours & Voyages, Vietnam
25   Hasia, Land of Dragons, Vietnam
160   Huong Hai Junk Halong, Vietnam
23   Myths & Mountains, USA
23   Nine Dragons Travel & Tours, USA
92   Press Club, Hanoi
21   Silks Steps Ltd, UK
21   Tennyson Travel Ltd, UK
22   Travelbag Adventures, UK
308   Vyta Tours, Vietnam

Footprint travel list

Footprint publish travel guides to over 120 countries worldwide. Each guide is packed with practical, concise and colourful information for everybody from first-time travellers to travel aficionados . The list is growing fast and current titles are noted below. For further information check out the website **www.footprintbooks.com**

Andalucía Handbook
Argentina Handbook
Bali & the Eastern Isles Hbk
Bangkok & the Beaches Hbk
Barcelona Handbook
Bolivia Handbook
Brazil Handbook
Cambodia Handbook
Caribbean Islands Handbook
Central America & Mexico Hbk
Chile Handbook
Colombia Handbook
Costa Rica Handbook
Cuba Handbook
Cusco & the Sacred Valley Hbk
Dominican Republic Handbook
Dublin Handbook
East Africa Handbook
Ecuador & Galápagos Handbook
Edinburgh Handbook
Egypt Handbook
Goa Handbook
Guatemala Handbook
India Handbook
Indian Himalaya Handbook
Indonesia Handbook
Ireland Handbook
Israel Handbook
Jordan Handbook
Laos Handbook
Libya Handbook
London Handbook
Malaysia Handbook
Marrakech & the High Atlas Hbk
Myanmar Handbook
Mexico Handbook
Morocco Handbook

Namibia Handbook
Nepal Handbook
New Zealand Handbook
Nicaragua Handbook
Pakistan Handbook
Peru Handbook
Rajasthan & Gujarat Handbook
Rio de Janeiro Handbook
Scotland Handbook
Scotland Highlands & Islands Hbk
Singapore Handbook
South Africa Handbook
South American Handbook
South India Handbook
Sri Lanka Handbook
Sumatra Handbook
Syria & Lebanon Handbook
Thailand Handbook
Tibet Handbook
Tunisia Handbook
Turkey Handbook
Venezuela Handbook
Vietnam Handbook

Also available from Footprint
Traveller's Handbook
Traveller's Healthbook
Traveller's Internet Guide

Available at all good bookshops

Footprint feedback

We try as hard as we can to make each Footprint Handbook as up-to-date and accurate as possible but, of course, things always change. Many people email or write to us with corrections, new information, or simply comments. If you want to let us know about your experiences and adventures – be they good, bad or ugly – then don't delay; we're dying to hear from you. And please try to include all the relevant details and juicy bits. Your help will be greatly appreciated, especially by other travellers. In return we will send you details about our special guidebook offer.

email Footprint at:
vie3_online@footprintbooks.com

or write to:
Elizabeth Taylor
Footprint Handbooks
6 Riverside Court
Lower Bristol Road
Bath   BA2 3DZ
UK

'UNESCO World Heritage Sites :
Sukhothai (Thailand), Luang Prabang (Laos),
Hue' (Vietnam) and Angkor (Cambodia)

Join Bangkok Airways on an innovative heritage tour of **4** historic kingdoms. From the City of Angels, Bangkok, fly to the first capital of Thailand, Sukhothai. Then explore Luang Prabang, the ancient capital of Laos. Next stop Hué, the former capital of Vietnam, and from there on to Siem Reap in Cambodia, home of the legendary Angkor Wat, before returning to Bangkok. Five great experiences in one great tour* of the Mekong region. Exclusively with Bangkok Airways.

*Tour starting in July 2002

For more information of the tour, please contact

DIETHELM TRAVEL	Tel : + 66 2 255 9150-70	E-mail : dto@dto.co.th
INDOCHINA SERVICES	Tel : + 66 2 255 4001-7	E-mail : info@is-intl.com
MEKONGLAND	Tel : + 66 2 256 7176-9	E-mail : mekongld@mekongland.com
PINK ROSE HOILDAYS	Tel : + 66 2 255 8966	E-mail : info@pinkroseholidays.com

FRANKFURT OFFICE Tel : (49 69) 133 77 565/566 Fax : (49 69) 133 77 567 E-mail : bkkair.fra@t-online.de
BANGKOK HEAD OFFICE Tel : +66 2 229 3434/3456 Fax : +66 2 229 3450/3454 E-mail : pg@bangkokair.co.th
www.bangkokair.com

WINDSOR VIETNAM GROUP

 Amigo Char Grill Restaurant
The only real steak house in
Vietnam offering Prime Rib

55 Nguyen Hue, Dist. 1, HCMC
Tel:(848) 8290437

 Gartenstadt Restaurant
The oldest European restaurant
in HCMC serving the best Draught
German Beer and Homemade
German Sausages

34 Dong Khoi, Dist. 1, HCMC
Tel:(848) 8223623

 Harbour View Restaurant
The only river-front restaurant in
Saigon Chinese, Thai, Vietnamese
cuisines with an emphasis on seafood

2A Ton Duc Thang,Dist.1, HCMC
Tel:(848) 8299137 / 8299139

 Seasons Szechuan Restaurant
Spicy Chinese cuisine

193 Tran Hung Dao,Dist.1,HCMC
Tel:(848) 8369890

 Café Central
The first New York deli style
restaurant in Vietnam Plus Café
Central Lounge with live music
every night

115 Nguyen Hue, Dist.1, HCMC
Tel:(848) 8219303

 Windsor Saigon Hotel
Located in the heart of HCMC
extremely large and comfortable
rooms with first class service

193 Tran Hung Dao,Dist.1,HCMC
Tel:(848)8367848 Fax:8367889

Gourmet Royale

Coffees, Teas, Bagels, Sandwiches,
Pastries
235 Dong Khoi, Dist. 1, HCMC
Tel:(848) 8245017

French Vietnamese cuisine
193 Tran Hung Dao,Dist.1,HCMC
Tel:(848) 8367848

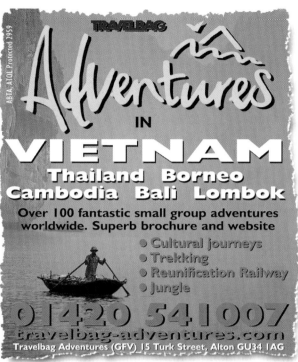

454

Trails of Asia

Journey through lost kingdoms and
Hidden history of Southeast Asia
and let Asian Trails be your guide!

T R A I L S
Blazing new paths in travel

Choose Asian Trails, the specialists in Southeast Asia.
We will organise your holiday, hotels, flights and tours to the region's
most facinating and undiscovered tourist desinations.
Contact us for our brochure or log into
www.asiantrails.net or www.asiantrails.com

CAMBODIA: No. 33, Street 240, P.O. Box 621, Phnom Penh
Tel: (855 23) 216 555, Fax: (855 23) 216 591, E-mail: asiantrails@bigpond.com.kh

INDONESIA: JI. By Pass Ngurah Rai No. CL. 46, Sanur, Denpasar 80228, Bali
Tel: (62 361) 285 771, Fax: (62 361) 281 514-5, E-mail: willem@asiantrailsbai.com

LAO P.D.R.: Unit No. 5, Baan Sokpaluang, Muang Sisatanak, P.O. Box 8430, Vientiane
Tel: (856 21) 351 789, Fax: (856 21) 351 789, E-mail: atrailsv@laotel.com

MALASIA: Wisma UOA II, Suite No. 9-11, 9/F, JI. Pinang, 50450 Kuala Lumpur
Tel: (60 3) 2710 1215, Fax: (60 3) 2710 1216, E-mail: res@asiantrails.com.my

MYANMAR: 471 Pyay Road, Kamyut Township, Yangon
Tel: (95 1) 502229, 500657, 727422, 705982, Fax: (95 1) 524978, E-mail: res@asiantrails.com.mm

THAILAND: 15th Floor, Mercury Tower, 540 Ploenchit Road, Bangkok 10330
Tel: (662) 658 6080-9, Fax: (66 2) 658 6099, E-mail: res@asiantrails.org

VIETNAM: Unit 721 7/F Saigon Trade Center, 37 Ton Duc Thang St., D. 1, Ho Chi Minh City
Tel: (84 8) 9 10 28 71-3, Fax: (84 8) 9 10 28 74, E-mail: asiantrails@hcm.vnn.vn

456

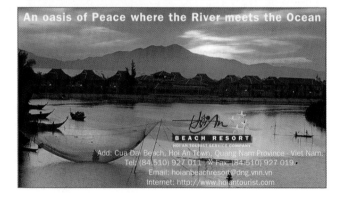

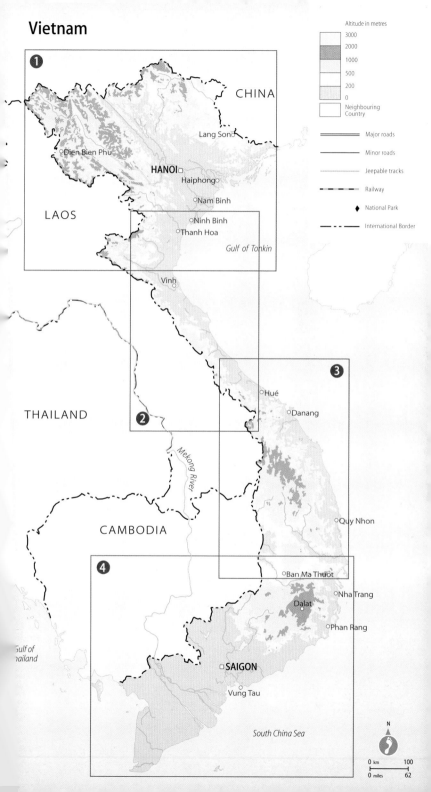

Map 1

Qua

Ha Gia

Bac Quang

Vinh Tuy

Thac
Lac

Th

Yen D

phu Si Lung
(3,076m)

Phong Tho

Bac Ha

Lao Cai

Muong Te

Sin Ho

Tam Duong

Mt Fan Si Pan
(3,143m)

Sapa

Hoang Lien Son Mountain Range

Con Voi Mountain Range

Red River

Lai Chau

Da River

Phu Luong
(2,985m)

Tuan Giao

Ban Co

Dien Bien Phu

Mt Co Pia
(1,817m)

Thuan Chau

Son La

Na San

Song Da Lake

Ma

LAOS

Map 2

N

0   km   20

0   miles   20

Truong Son Mountain Range

Ca River

A

B

C

①   ②   ③

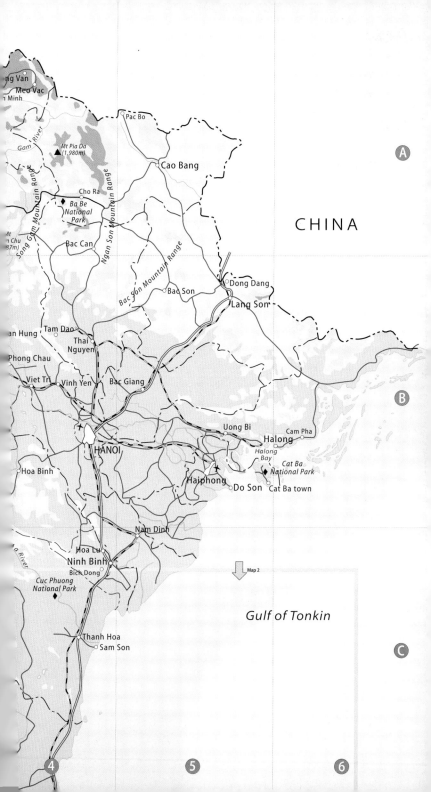

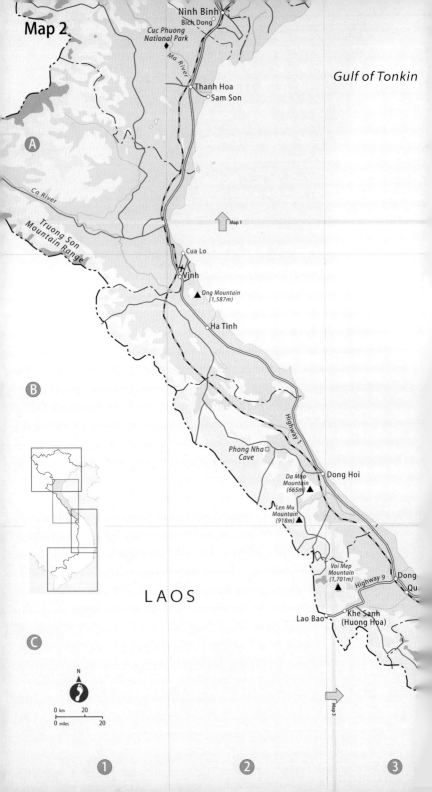

Map 4

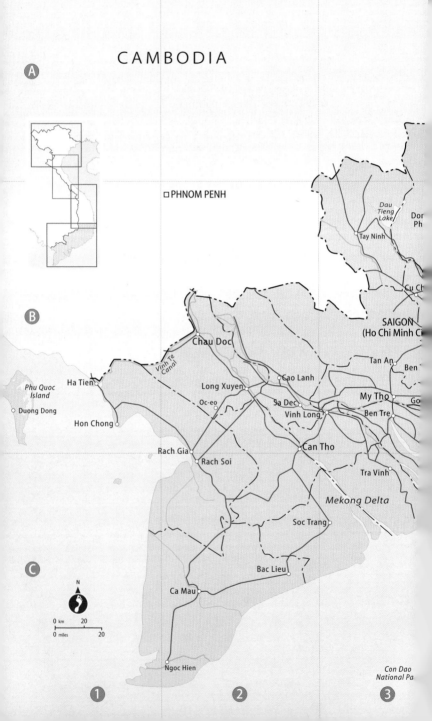

CAMBODIA

□ PHNOM PENH

Dau Tieng Lake

Tay Ninh

Dor Ph

Cu Ch

SAIGON (Ho Chi Minh C

Chau Doc

Vinh Te Canal

Tan An

Ben

Ha Tien

Long Xuyen

Cao Lanh

Phu Quoc Island

Oc-eo

Sa Dec

My Tho

Go

Duong Dong

Vinh Long

Ben Tre

Hon Chong

Can Tho

Rach Gia

Rach Soi

Tra Vinh

Mekong Delta

Soc Trang

Bac Lieu

Ca Mau

Ngoc Hien

Con Dao National Pa

N

0 km 20
0 miles 20

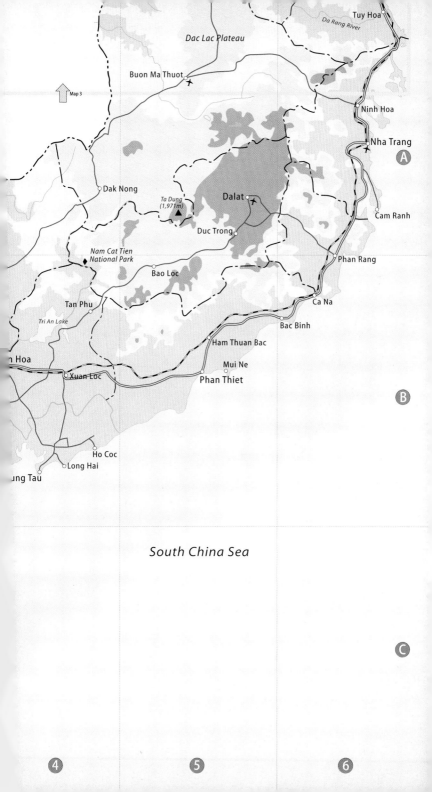

www.footprintbooks.com
A new place to visit

Acknowledgements

With thanks to Joshua Eliot for researching and writing the original Vietnam section of what was then the *Thailand, Indochina and Burma Handbook*. His continuing contributions to the book are much appreciated.

Special thanks to Chau for her dedication and hard work in updating so much of the Central Highlands, Nha Trang and the North, and for all her work on the maps. Thank you to Bao Anh for her meticulous checking of telephone numbers and fine detail. Thanks too to Steph and Nick Cox for their updating of Con Dao; Andrew Bartlett, London, for his work on Phu Quoc; Richard Craik for his help on birdlife and Stephen Griffin, England, for his useful comments on Nha Trang.

About the author

John Colet first visited Vietnam in 1988 and moved to the country in 1995 to help run a charity. He has travelled Vietnam's length and breadth many times, partly conducting research for the earlier editions of this Handbook and partly for the sheer pleasure of life in rural and coastal Vietnam. His greatest delight is the cultural diversity of the hill-tribes and Vietnamese food. Besides writing the Footprint Vietnam and Cambodia handbooks, he has written numerous articles on Vietnam and Southeast Asia.